BESTSELLING Annual Bible Commentary

KJV SEPTEMBER–AUGUST 2025–2026

KING JAMES VERSION

Editors
Taylor Z. Stamps
Bethany R. Tippin

Contributing Editors
Jason Hitchcock
Ronald L. Nickelson
Jessica J. Schroeder

Volume 73

Standard®
PUBLISHING
part of the David C Cook family

In This Volume

KJV Standard Lesson Commentary® is published annually by Standard Publishing, an imprint of David C Cook, DavidCCook.org. 4050 Lee Vance Drive, Colorado Springs, CO 80918, U.S.A. Standard Lesson Quarterly® Curriculum and David C Cook and its related logo are registered trademarks of David C Cook. Regular Print Edition ISBN 978-0-830-78758-6. Deluxe Edition ISBN 978-0-830-78760-9. Large Print Edition ISBN 978-0-830-78761-6. Printed in the United States of America. Scripture taken from the *King James Version*. Lessons and/or Readings are based on the *Uniform Series International Sunday School Lessons International Bible Lessons for Christian Teaching*

Index of Printed Texts

The printed texts for 2025–2026 are arranged here in the order in which they appear in the Bible.

Cumulative Index

A cumulative index for Scripture passages used in Standard Lesson Commentary *for September 2022–August 2026 is provided below.*

Judah, from Isaiah to Exile

Special Features

Lessons

Unit 1: Isaiah and the Renewal of the Temple

Unit 2: Jeremiah and the Promise of Renewal

Unit 3: Ezekiel and the Exile of Judah

Quarterly Quiz

Use these questions as a pretest or as a review. The answers are on page iv of This Quarter in the Word.

Lesson 1

1. Isaiah's throne-room vision occurred in the year that King Uzziah died. T/F. *Isaiah 6:1*

2. How many additional years did the Lord promise Hezekiah? (1; 15; 20) *Isaiah 38:5*

Lesson 2

1. It was decided that Hezekiah's Passover would occur in the _________ month. *2 Chronicles 30:2*

2. Hezekiah's Passover celebration resulted in "great _____ in Jerusalem." *2 Chronicles 30:26*

Lesson 3

1. Who gave "the book of the law" to Shaphan? (Ahikam, Hilkiah, Asaiah) *2 Chronicles 34:15*

2. Which prophetess did Hilkiah speak with concerning the book of the law? (Huldah, Deborah, Noadiah) *2 Chronicles 34:22*

Lesson 4

1. The servant was "wounded for our _________." *Isaiah 53:5*

2. The Lord has laid on the servant the iniquity of us all. T/F. *Isaiah 53:6*

Lesson 5

1. Jeremiah considered himself too old to speak. T/F. *Jeremiah 1:6*

2. Jeremiah prophesied that "this house" (the temple) would become like what other location? (Sheol, Shechem, Shiloh) *Jeremiah 26:9*

Lesson 6

1. The Lord warned that lying words repeat this phrase: "The _______ of the Lord." *Jeremiah 7:4*

2. The Lord asked, "Is this house, . . . become a den of _________ in your eyes?" *Jeremiah 7:11*

Lesson 7

1. Who commanded the Rechabites to never drink wine? (Joshua, Jonadab, Jehu) *Jeremiah 35:6*

2. The Rechabites lived in tents, just as they were commanded. T/F. *Jeremiah 35:10*

Lesson 8

1. In which did the Lord say He would "write" the law? (hearts, souls, minds) *Jeremiah 31:33*

2. Which two "came by Jesus Christ"? (choose two: law, grace, covenant, truth) *John 1:17*

Lesson 9

1. How many men did the king command Ebedmelech to take to rescue Jeremiah? (13; 30; 300) *Jeremiah 38:10*

2. Immediately after his rescue, Jeremiah left "the court of the prison." T/F. *Jeremiah 38:13*

Lesson 10

1. Nebuchadnezzar's siege against Jerusalem began in the _______ year of Zedekiah's reign. *2 Kings 25:1*

2. Who set fire to the temple, palace, and houses in Jerusalem? (Nebuchadnezzar, Zedekiah, Nebuzaradan) *2 Kings 25:8–9*

Lesson 11

1. The Lord called Ezekiel by what title? (Son of Judah, Son of man, Son of Jacob) *Ezekiel 3:10*

2. Ezekiel would be a "signal" to the people of Judah. T/F. *Ezekiel 24:27*

Lesson 12

1. The Lord made Ezekiel a "_________ unto the house of Israel." *Ezekiel 33:7*

2. The Lord God takes no pleasure in the death of the wicked. T/F. *Ezekiel 33:11*

Lesson 13

1. The man went eastward and measured a total of 4,000 ________. *Ezekiel 47:3–5*

2. Ezekiel saw "very many ________" on both sides of the river. *Ezekiel 47:7*

Quarter at a Glance

by Editorial Staff

This quarter invites us to discover and appreciate how God, through prophets and other leaders, gave help and guidance to the people of Judah. As we study these people, we will see God's hand at work in their lives, just as He is at work in our lives and all human affairs.

Isaiah and the Renewal of the Temple

The first unit presents us with the prophetic ministry of Isaiah. These lessons recount the theological reasons for the decline of Judah, seen mainly through Isaiah and two faithful kings of Judah. Lesson 1 introduces the call of that prophet and the substance of his witness to a king of Judah (Isaiah 6:1–8; 38:1–5; see lesson 1).

While most kings of Israel and Judah earn bad grades from the writers of Kings and Chronicles, two seventh-century kings of Judah are revealed as seeking the Lord and reforming worship. King Hezekiah celebrates Passover according to what was written in the Law of Moses (2 Chronicles 30:1–9, 26–27; see lesson 2), while King Josiah is a "by-the-book strategist" who sought proper obedience to the Lord (34:15–22, 26–27; see lesson 3).

The destruction of the temple, according to Scripture, was the result of social injustice, moral decay, and covenantal disobedience. Isaiah finds a spark of hope in the devastation—the prophetic suffering of the people has a redemptive purpose, testifying to God's judgment and restoration. Near the end of the Babylonian exile, the prophet envisages a humiliated and afflicted servant who carries the sins of many (Isaiah 52:13–53:12; see lesson 4).

Jeremiah and the Promise of Renewal

The second unit explores the prophetic career of Jeremiah, a prophet who lived during the worst of the Babylonian assault on Judah and Jerusalem. The Lord called Jeremiah to preach a harsh message to the people of Judah, one they wouldn't heed (Jeremiah 26:8–9, 12–15; see lesson 5).

Through the prophet, the Lord warned the people: "Amend your ways and your doings" (Jeremiah 7:3; see lesson 6). The people had repeatedly forsaken the covenant; therefore, Jeremiah warns that judgment is coming. As Jerusalem teeters on the brink of extinction, Jeremiah is given a word of hope: after punishment, God will bring the people back home. On that day, the law of God will no longer be written in stone but in the human heart (31:33; see lesson 8).

Ezekiel and the Exile of Judah

The final lessons recount Ezekiel's prophetic messages to the people in exile. The account of 2 Kings 24:18–25:9, detailing the last days of Judah, is hard to read, as it is full of violence and desperation (lesson 10). Into that environment, the prophet-priest Ezekiel, in Babylon among the exiles, reports the devastation in Jerusalem (Ezekiel 24:20–21; see lesson 11). His prophecies are replete with visions, signs, and symbolic actions, testifying to the utter ruin of the homeland and promises of renewal.

> *Ezekiel serves as a "watchman" to the people, keeping the promise of a return from exile alive.*

When Ezekiel's wife dies, he obediently follows God's command not to mourn as a sign to the people that no one will weep when Jerusalem falls (Ezekiel 24:15–16). Ezekiel serves as a "watchman" to the people, keeping the promise of a return from exile alive (33:7–16a; see lesson 12).

Ezekiel's message reaches its hopeful climax in his vision of a renewed temple with water flowing from it (Ezekiel 47:1–12; see lesson 13). Ezekiel died in captivity, his life a living symbol that God's Word is forever active, present, and powerful. His ministry helped transform the people into the remnant who find a renewed orientation for hope in the promises of God.

Get the Setting

by Ryan D. Donell

The Role of a Prophet

Who were the prophets? Prophets are God's mouthpieces delivering a divine perspective on history, politics, and the behavior of God's people (Deuteronomy 18:18; Jeremiah 1:9; etc.). While prophecies could contain unforeseen horizons, such as Jesus' messianic first and second advents, they were nevertheless primarily concerned with the present crisis of their audience and the immanent consequences of responding to or neglecting God's messages (Matthew 13:17; 1 Peter 1:10–12).

Prophets and prophecy were already present in cultures outside of Israel in the Iron Age throughout the ancient Near East and identified as "seers" and "prophets." However, the unique embodiment of God's oracles to Israel was represented by the prophets' indictments, judgment, instruction, support, and explanations in the aftermath of events. Understanding their role in God's purposes will provide a crucial background for many of the lessons this quarter.

Jeremiah's Example

We turn now to consider one vignette in the ministry of the prophets of ancient Israel, following the fall of Samaria in 722 BC. Jeremiah was a prophet to the southern kingdom of Judah. His experiences convey a glimpse of God's heart that wept over Jerusalem. Even as a young prophet, he pleaded with a rebellious generation to repent.

The prophets were the poet-preachers of inconvenient truths. Grief poignantly marked the life of Jeremiah and won him the title "the weeping prophet." Jeremiah's anguish joined God's lament against Judah's repeated rejection of His words and ways (Jeremiah 13:17; 9:1, 10). Jeremiah was sent to prophesy against kings in his own community: Josiah, Jehoiakim, and Zedekiah. After Jehoiakim's deportation in 598 BC, instead of endorsing Zedekiah's false hopes, Jeremiah dares to tell the king to submit to Babylon and the assured invasion (38:1–4). If Judah surrenders to Babylon, they will survive. However, this requires them to renounce the propaganda that God's people will never suffer defeat. Unable—or refusing—to believe that God would use a prophet to predict the siege of Jerusalem, Judah's officials accuse Jeremiah of not seeking "the welfare of this people" (38:4). Jeremiah is thrown into a deep cistern and left in the mire to die (38:6). Even when he is finally lifted out, he does not soften God's challenges to Zedekiah, no matter how harsh. Despite the hard words Jeremiah delivers, Zedekiah fails to yield. He refuses to heed the word of the Lord, and as a result Jerusalem is laid waste with a second wave of exiles being deported in 586 BC.

Application for Today

God's messages through the prophets prefigured the bodily disclosure of God's Word, Jesus Christ (John 1:1–18; Hebrews 1:1–3). While the majority of us will not be called upon to serve in the same kind of prophetic role as Jeremiah and other Old Testament prophets were, we do have a part to play in bringing God's word to His people today. According to Old Testament scholar Walter Brueggemann, the church today must embody three prophetic tasks. First, we are to announce the reality of things, speaking forth the truth. Second, we are to grieve over sin both within God's people and without. Third, we must offer the hope of restoration. In recovering and living into this prophetic role, we may reclaim this promise given by Jesus in His Sermon on the Mount: "Blessed are ye, when men shall revile you, and persecute you, and shall say all manner of evil against you falsely, for my sake. Rejoice, and be exceeding glad: for great is your reward in heaven: for so persecuted they the prophets which were before you" (Matthew 5:11–12).

Mon, Nov. 17	**Love Others Despite Suffering**	1 Peter 4:1–11
Tue, Nov. 18	**Rejoice to Share Christ's Sufferings**	1 Peter 4:12–19
Wed, Nov. 19	**Answering for Sin**	Ezekiel 18:1–9
Thu, Nov. 20	**I Confess My Iniquity**	Psalm 38:1–2, 10–22
Fri, Nov. 21	**Restore One Another in Gentleness**	Galatians 6:1–10
Sat, Nov. 22	**See to Your Own Sins First**	Matthew 7:1–6
Sun, Nov. 23	**Let the Wicked Repent**	Ezekiel 33:7–16a
Mon, Nov. 24	**God Breathes New Life**	Ezekiel 37:1–7
Tue, Nov. 25	**A Resurrection of Hope**	Ezekiel 37:8–14
Wed, Nov. 26	**The Thirsty Will Be Refreshed**	Isaiah 55:1–9
Thu, Nov. 27	**Rivers of Living Water**	John 7:2–10, 37–39
Fri, Nov. 28	**Hope for God's New Creation**	Revelation 21:1–7
Sat, Nov. 29	**The Tree of Life**	Revelation 22:1–5
Sun, Nov. 30	**The River of Life**	Ezekiel 47:1–9, 12

Answers to the Quarterly Quiz on page 2

Lesson 1—1. True. 2. 15. **Lesson 2**—1. second. 2. joy. **Lesson 3**—1. Hilkiah. 2. Huldah. **Lesson 4**—1. transgressions. 2. True. **Lesson 5**—1. False. 2. Shiloh. **Lesson 6**—1. temple. 2. robbers. **Lesson 7**—1. Jonadab. 2. True. **Lesson 8**—1. hearts. 2. grace, truth. **Lesson 9**—1. 30. 2. False. **Lesson 10**—1. ninth. 2. Nebuzaradan. **Lesson 11**—1. Son of man. 2. False. **Lesson 12**—1. watchman. 2. True. **Lesson 13**—1. cubits. 2. trees.

This Quarter in the Word

Mon, Sep. 1	**God Sends a Messenger**	Mark 1:1–8
Tue, Sep. 2	**God Defends the Chosen People**	Isaiah 7:1–7
Wed, Sep. 3	**God Warns of Coming Disaster**	Isaiah 20:1–6
Thu, Sep. 4	**God Fulfills Promises**	Matthew 11:1–6
Fri, Sep. 5	**God Works through a Messenger**	Matthew 11:7–15
Sat, Sep. 6	**God Is Gracious and Merciful**	Psalm 145:1–12
Sun, Sep. 7	**God Strengthens the Called**	Isaiah 6:1–8; 38:1–5
Mon, Sep. 8	**An Everlasting Kingdom**	Psalm 145:13–21
Tue, Sep. 9	**A Call to Bear Good Fruit**	Matthew 3:4–12
Wed, Sep. 10	**A Summons to Repent**	Acts 3:12–20
Thu, Sep. 11	**A Ministry of Care and Comfort**	James 5:12–18
Fri, Sep. 12	**A Feast of Remembrance**	Exodus 12:3–14
Sat, Sep. 13	**A Dwelling for God's Name**	Deuteronomy 12:5–12
Sun, Sep. 14	**An Act of Repentance and Renewal**	2 Chronicles 30:1–9, 26–27
Mon, Sep. 15	**The Command to Love**	Matthew 22:36–40
Tue, Sep. 16	**Righteous in God's Sight**	Romans 2:9–16
Wed, Sep. 17	**Promised Restoration**	Deuteronomy 30:1–10
Thu, Sep. 18	**Choose Life**	Deuteronomy 30:11–21
Fri, Sep. 19	**A Greater Message**	Hebrews 1:13–2:4
Sat, Sep. 20	**Hidden Treasure**	Matthew 13:44–52
Sun, Sep. 21	**Sorrow Leads to Joy**	2 Chronicles 34:15–22, 26–27

Mon, Sep. 22	**The Humble Servant**	Philippians 2:5–10
Tue, Sep. 23	**The Faithful Servant**	Isaiah 42:1–7
Wed, Sep. 24	**The Resurrected Servant**	Acts 2:25–31
Thu, Sep. 25	**A Light for the World**	Acts 13:44–49
Fri, Sep. 26	**A Doorkeeper in God's House**	Psalm 84
Sat, Sep. 27	**God's Servant Obeys**	Isaiah 50:4–9
Sun, Sep. 28	**The Suffering Servant**	Isaiah 53:1–7
Mon, Sep. 29	**Passion for God's Laws**	2 Chronicles 34:1–7
Tue, Sep. 30	**The Piercing Word of God**	Hebrews 4:12–16
Wed, Oct. 1	**Return to the Father**	Jeremiah 3:12–19
Thu, Oct. 2	**Cleanse Yourselves and Be Saved**	Jeremiah 4:5–14
Fri, Oct. 3	**God's Discipline Proves God's Love**	Hebrews 12:3–17
Sat, Oct. 4	**God Is a Consuming Fire**	Hebrews 12:18–29
Sun, Oct. 5	**A Defiant Prophet**	Jeremiah 1:6–10; 26:8–9, 12–15
Mon, Oct. 6	**Endure to the End**	Mark 13:1–13
Tue, Oct. 7	**God Will Protect God's People**	Mark 13:14–27
Wed, Oct. 8	**To Obey Is Better than Sacrifice**	1 Samuel 15:20–26
Thu, Oct. 9	**Keep Christ's Commandments**	John 14:12–17
Fri, Oct. 10	**An Indestructible Temple**	John 2:12–22
Sat, Oct. 11	**The Sacrifice That Pleases God**	Psalm 51:15–19
Sun, Oct. 12	**Amend Your Ways!**	Jeremiah 7:1–11, 21–23
Mon, Oct. 13	**The Dangers of Strong Drink**	Proverbs 23:29–35
Tue, Oct. 14	**Keep Earthly Pleasures in Perspective**	Ecclesiastes 9:4–10
Wed, Oct. 15	**Be Filled with the Spirit**	Ephesians 5:11–19
Thu, Oct. 16	**The Nazirite Vow**	Numbers 6:1–8
Fri, Oct. 17	**Called to Holiness**	1 Thessalonians 4:1–7
Sat, Oct. 18	**Keep Awake!**	1 Thessalonians 5:1–10
Sun, Oct. 19	**A Vow of Holiness**	Jeremiah 35:5–11

Mon, Oct. 20	**A New Salvation**	Joel 2:28–32
Tue, Oct. 21	**A New Heart**	Ezekiel 36:25–35
Wed, Oct. 22	**The Law's Essence**	Deuteronomy 10:12–21
Thu, Oct. 23	**A New Covenant**	2 Corinthians 3:1–6
Fri, Oct. 24	**A New Spirit**	2 Corinthians 3:7–11
Sat, Oct. 25	**A New Freedom**	2 Corinthians 3:12–17
Sun, Oct. 26	**A New Relationship with God**	Jeremiah 31:27–34
Mon, Oct. 27	**Speak as the Spirit Leads**	Matthew 10:16–27
Tue, Oct. 28	**Do Not Fear Mortal Powers**	Matthew 10:28–42
Wed, Oct. 29	**Wait Patiently for the Lord**	Psalm 37:1–13
Thu, Oct. 30	**God Never Forsakes the Righteous**	Psalm 37:25–28, 35–40
Fri, Oct. 31	**Overcome Evil with Good**	Romans 12:12–21
Sat, Nov. 1	**Speak Even When the Message Stings**	Jeremiah 38:1–6
Sun, Nov. 2	**An Advocate Pleads for Justice**	Jeremiah 38:7–13
Mon, Nov. 3	**The Master Is Coming Soon**	Luke 12:42–48
Tue, Nov. 4	**The Purifying Fire of Change**	Luke 12:49–53
Wed, Nov. 5	**The Lord's Purifying Purpose**	Lamentations 2:17–22
Thu, Nov. 6	**Hope in the Lord**	Lamentations 3:21–36
Fri, Nov. 7	**Faith Tested by Fire**	1 Peter 1:1–12
Sat, Nov. 8	**Prepare for Action**	1 Peter 1:13–25
Sun, Nov. 9	**God's Judgment Is Sure**	2 Kings 24:18–25:9
Mon, Nov. 10	**With Righteousness Comes Suffering**	1 Peter 3:8–17
Tue, Nov. 11	**Christ Exalted through Suffering**	1 Peter 3:18–22
Wed, Nov. 12	**God Rescues Us from Our Afflictions**	Psalm 34:6–19
Thu, Nov. 13	**Comfort for the Brokenhearted**	Matthew 5:3–12
Fri, Nov. 14	**Speak if People Listen or Not**	Ezekiel 3:4–11
Sat, Nov. 15	**Steadfastness amid Persecution**	2 Thessalonians 1:1–4
Sun, Nov. 16	**Unspeakable Grief**	Ezekiel 24:15–27

Lesson Cycle Chart

International Sunday School Lesson Cycle, September 2022–August 2026

Year	Fall Quarter (Sep, Oct, Nov)	Winter Quarter (Dec, Jan, Feb)	Spring Quarter (Mar, Apr, May)	Summer Quarter (Jun, Jul, Aug)
2022–2023	**God's Exceptional Choice** Genesis, Exodus, Deuteronomy, Judges, 1 Samuel, Ephesians	**From Darkness to Light** 2 Chronicles, Isaiah, Joel, Luke, 1 Corinthians, 2 Timothy, James, 1 Peter	**Jesus Calls Us** Matthew, Mark, Luke, John, Acts	**The Righteous Reign of God** Prophets, Matthew, Romans, 1 Corinthians, Galatians
2023–2024	**God's Law Is Love** Luke, John, Acts, Romans, 1 Corinthians, Galatians, Colossians	**Faith That Pleases God** Ruth, 1 Samuel, 2 Chronicles, Proverbs, Prophets, Matthew, Luke, Romans, Hebrews	**Examining Our Faith** Matthew, Mark, Luke, Acts, Romans, 2 Corinthians, 1 Peter, Jude	**Hope in the Lord** Psalms, Lamentations, Acts, Epistles
2024–2025	**Worship in the Covenant Community** Genesis, Exodus, 2 Samuel, 1 & 2 Kings, 2 Chronicles, Psalms, Isaiah, John	**A King Forever and Ever** Ruth, 2 Samuel, Psalms, Matthew, Luke	**Costly Sacrifices** Exodus, Leviticus, Numbers, Deuteronomy, 1 & 2 Chronicles, Ezra, Matthew, Hebrews, 1 John, Revelation	**Sacred Altars and Holy Offerings** Genesis, Gospels, Romans, 1 Corinthians, Ephesians, Hebrews, 1 Peter
2025–2026	**Judah, From Isaiah to Exile** 2 Kings, 2 Chronicles, Isaiah, Jeremiah, Ezekiel	**Enduring Beliefs of the Church** Exodus, Psalms, Gospels, Acts, Epistles, Revelation	**Social Teachings of the Church** Genesis, Exodus, Deuteronomy, Nehemiah, Psalms, Prophets, Gospels, Acts, Epistles	**Faithful Witnesses** Judges, 1 Samuel, Amos, Gospels, Acts, 2 Timothy, Philemon

Prep with Internet Resources

Teacher Tips by Tanae Murdic

Many teachers desire additional resources to guide them in their study and preparation for teaching adults. You can move beyond physical resource limitations if you have access to the internet. Use of various websites can expand your access to resources exponentially, bringing numerous options to your fingertips with just a few clicks. Please note that the listing of websites in this article is neither exhaustive nor is it necessarily an endorsement of everything to be found on these sites. Standard Lesson serves a broad audience, and some sites may have been created by those who hold different doctrinal convictions from ours or your own. As in all things, use discernment.

Resources for Nearly Any Lesson

No concordance handy? No worries! Just visit www.biblegateway.com. You can search for keywords and topics on this site. It also contains a wide range of Bible translations that can be displayed in parallel columns for side-by-side comparison. Another Bible site is www.blueletterbible.org, which offers several Bible translations alongside commentaries and other study tools.

For matters of history and setting, you may want to visit www.bible-history.com. The Bible History home page displays a long list of categories on the left side of the screen, which may aid your preparation. This site also includes several church history resources. Another helpful resource is the "Resource Pages for Biblical Studies" found at www.torreys.org/bible. Here you can find pages that examine texts and translations, electronic publications, and materials relating to the social aspects of the Mediterranean world.

Like Bible Gateway, the Bible Study Tools site (www.biblestudytools.com) is a great resource with many aids. It houses several Bible translations as well as Bible commentaries, encyclopedias, dictionaries, a parallel Bible, and an interlinear Bible. In the search window, you can search within specified categories, such as Bible, topic, Bible study, references, Bible stories, and even pastors. The "References" tab holds a wealth of resources, including the works of Josephus. Josephus's works are a wonderful resource for a typically reliable, though not inspired, history of the Jews from the first century.

For archaeological evidence and background for Bible lessons, visit www.biblehistory.net. This site has several tabs ("volumes") that contain links to various articles that may prove useful in lesson preparation. Clicking on a link will open a page that you can save to your computer as a PDF file, which you can use as a handout or simply read in preparation for the lesson. For example, the information found at www.biblehistory.net/joshua.html provides some interesting details about a letter that archaeologists discovered, which was sent from Jerusalem to Egypt asking for help against the "Habiru" (possibly referring to the "Hebrews").

Regarding Old Testament studies, some Jewish resources can be helpful. One such site is www.jewishencyclopedia.com, which provides the entire text of the 1906 print edition of the Jewish Encyclopedia online. Topics can be found instantly by typing a word in the search window.

Finding Information on General Sites

General search engines can also provide help. But use these with care. As with any media consumption, consider the reputability of your source. Since just about anyone can post anything to the internet, the presence of information there does not necessarily mean it is accurate. Use discretion when deciding which sources to use and cite in your study preparation.

Isaiah's Call and Ministry

Devotional Reading: Isaiah 2:1–5
Background Scripture: Isaiah 6:1–13; 7:1–7; 20:1–6; 38:1–22

Isaiah 6:1–8

1 In the year that king Uzziah died I saw
also the Lord sitting upon a throne, high and
lifted up, and his train filled the temple.
2 Above it stood the seraphims: each one
had six wings; with twain he covered his face,
and with twain he covered his feet, and with
twain he did fly.
3 And one cried unto another, and said,
Holy, holy, holy, is the LORD of hosts: The
whole earth is full of his glory.
4 And the posts of the door moved at the
voice of him that cried, and the house was filled
with smoke.
5 Then said I, Woe is me! for I am undone;
because I am a man of unclean lips, and I dwell
in the midst of a people of unclean lips: for mine
eyes have seen the King, the LORD of hosts.
6 Then flew one of the seraphims unto me,
having a live coal in his hand, which he had
taken with the tongs from off the altar:
7 And he laid it upon my mouth, and said,
Lo, this hath touched thy lips; and thine iniq-
uity is taken away, and thy sin purged.
8 Also I heard the voice of the Lord, saying,
Whom shall I send, and who will go for us?
Then said I, Here am I; send me.

Isaiah 38:1–5

1 In those days was Hezekiah sick unto
death. And Isaiah the prophet the son of Amoz
came unto him, and said unto him, Thus saith
the LORD, Set thine house in order: for thou
shalt die, and not live.
2 Then Hezekiah turned his face toward the
wall, and prayed unto the LORD,
3 And said, Remember now, O LORD, I
beseech thee, how I have walked before thee in
truth and with a perfect heart, and have done
that which is good in thy sight. And Hezekiah
wept sore.
4 Then came the word of the LORD to Isa-
iah, saying,
5 Go, and say to Hezekiah, Thus saith the
LORD, the God of David thy father, I have
heard thy prayer, I have seen thy tears: behold,
I will add unto thy days fifteen years.

Key Text

Also I heard the voice of the Lord, saying, Whom shall I send, and who will go for us? Then said I, Here am I; send me. —**Isaiah 6:8**

Judah, from Isaiah to the Exile

Unit 1: Isaiah and the Renewal of the Temple

Lessons 1–4

Lesson Aims

After participating in this lesson, each learner will be able to:

1. Summarize what Isaiah saw and his reaction to it.

2. Compare and contrast Isaiah's reaction to God's call with that of Jeremiah in reaction to his own call (lesson 5).

3. Express how to distinguish an authentic call of God from a mere felt need.

Lesson Outline

Introduction

- A. It's Your Call (and His)
- B. Lesson Context

I. Commissioned by God (Isaiah 6:1–8)

- A. What Isaiah Saw (vv. 1–2)
- B. What Isaiah Heard (v. 3)
- C. What Isaiah Sensed (v. 4)
- D. What Isaiah Said (v. 5)
  - *Majesty Approached*
- E. What Isaiah Received (vv. 6–8)
  - *Discerning God's Call*

II. Communication with a King (Isaiah 38:1–5)

- A. Message of Death (v. 1)
- B. Tears of Bitterness (vv. 2–3)
- C. Extension of Life (vv. 4–5)

Conclusion

- A. Here Am I. Send Me!
- B. Prayer
- C. Thought to Remember

Introduction

A. It's Your Call (and His)

At age 11, I first sensed God calling me to vocational ministry. During a revival meeting, an evangelist approached me and said, "Young man, I'm setting you aside for the ministry." At that time, the encounter did not impact me, but I reconsidered the evangelist's words years later.

Throughout my teenage years, I continued to sense that call to ministry. Trusted friends repeatedly encouraged me. People in my congregation confirmed the call and encouraged me to begin training for ministry. Backed by the encouragement and confirmation from my congregation, I enrolled in a Bible college to follow the Lord's call.

There seem to be two types of calls from God. The first type is what we might designate as a "general" call. These are the thoughts, actions, and attitudes that God expects of every believer. The expectations of this call are found in the pages of Scripture.

The second type is what we might designate as a "specific" call: a sensed call of God to a particular or specialized ministry. There is disagreement regarding whether every believer receives this kind of call. Today's lesson examines the details of a call unmistakably from God.

B. Lesson Context

Isaiah began his prophetic ministry about 200 years after the nation of Israel divided. In 931 BC, the united monarchy of Israel split into two parts: Israel (the northern kingdom) and Judah (the southern kingdom). Isaiah's ministry focused on the southern kingdom of Judah, as reflected by the Judean kings listed in Isaiah 1:1.

Surprisingly, the Lord's call on Isaiah doesn't occur until Isaiah 6. This is at variance from the usual pattern of recording a prophet's call at or very near a book's beginning (examples: Jeremiah 1:4–19; Ezekiel 1:1–3:15). Perhaps the writer wanted to establish the context of the call, which the first five chapters of Isaiah accomplish.

The people of Judah had become a "sinful nation," being openly rebellious against the Lord (Isaiah 1:1–5). A sense of self-sufficiency accompanied a facade of economic prosperity, military security, and religious arrogance (2:7–8). The Lord depicts His people as a vineyard that produced unacceptable fruit (5:1–7). In their doing of injustice, they had redefined the terms *good* and *evil* (5:20).

Such was the era that Isaiah found himself in when his call came about.

I. Commissioned by God

(Isaiah 6:1–8)

A. What Isaiah Saw (vv. 1–2)

1a. In the year that king Uzziah died.

Uzziah (also known as "Azariah" in 2 Kings 15:1–7) reigned as *king* of Judah for 52 years (2 Chronicles 26:3). We don't know the exact years of his reign, but one estimate gives the range of 792–740 BC.

For much of his reign, Uzziah did "right in the sight of the Lord" and, as a result, God allowed him to experience blessing (2 Chronicles 26:4–5). However, pride led to his downfall when he entered the temple to burn incense (26:16–21).

1b. I saw also the Lord sitting upon a throne, high and lifted up, and his train filled the temple.

At least two possibilities exist regarding the setting of *the temple*. One possibility is that the setting is the earthly temple of Solomon in Jerusalem. Another option is that Isaiah sees the heavenly temple. Given the actions of Uzziah in the Jerusalem temple (see above), some commentators suggest this setting allows Isaiah to realize that the presence of the Lord has not departed from the temple (contrast Ezekiel 11:22–23). Still, others suggest that the vision's grandeur indicates the heavenly temple (compare Revelation 11:19). Regardless, the significance is that Isaiah sees the location where the enthroned Lord rules.

That Isaiah *saw . . . the Lord* is echoed in John 12:41. This fact does not contradict Exodus 33:20 or John 1:18. What Isaiah sees is called a *theophany*, which is a manifestation of God, not God in His actual essence (compare Genesis 28:13–15; Exodus 24:9–11; 1 Kings 22:19).

The Lord's position *sitting upon a throne* reveals Him as the living heavenly King. Although the earthly King Uzziah has died, the Lord still reigns! The throne's elevated location, *high and lifted up*, reflects the exalted nature of His being (compare Isaiah 57:15; Revelation 4:2).

The expansive nature of the *train* of His garment is echoed in Revelation 1:13. Special garments marked the identity of significant figures, like priests or kings (compare Exodus 28:33–34; 39:24–26, where the word is translated "hem"). However, the garment Isaiah sees is unlike any garment worn by a human. The size of this garment *filled the temple*, leaving Isaiah incapable of giving further description.

2. Above it stood the seraphims: each one had six wings; with twain he covered his face, and with twain he covered his feet, and with twain he did fly.

The word *seraphims* is a transliteration (not a translation) of a Hebrew word. That's where a word in one language is brought over into another language simply by swapping the letters of the word in the original language into the letters that sound the same in the receptor language.

The transliteration of this word occurs only here and in Isaiah 6:6, below. This Hebrew word elsewhere refers to serpents (Numbers 21:6, 8; Deuteronomy 8:15; Isaiah 14:29; 30:6). The root of this word may come from a Hebrew word meaning "fiery" or "burning." One possibility is that the seraphims appear as flaming, winged creatures.

What Do You Think?

What does the covering of the seraphims reveal to us about postures of worship and prayer?

Digging Deeper

How do physical, mental, and emotional postures affect your acts of worship?

B. What Isaiah Heard (v. 3)

3a. And one cried unto another, and said, Holy, holy, holy, is the LORD of hosts.

The proclamation of the seraphims *Holy, holy, holy, is the Lord of hosts* is similar to that of the four "beasts" in Revelation 4:8. The repetition of the word *holy* stresses its significance: the Lord's holiness is unparalleled!

The Hebrew adjective translated "holy" appears in 34 verses in Isaiah; clearly, it's a vital concept to the writer, implying "separation" or "distinctiveness." The Lord's holiness means that He is separate from His creation in that He is morally perfect (Deuteronomy 32:4; 1 Samuel 2:2; Psalm 18:30; Habakkuk 1:12–13; etc.).

The designation *Lord of hosts* or "Lord God of hosts" appears 274 times in the Old Testament, with about 75 percent of those occurring in the prophetic books of Isaiah, Jeremiah, Haggai, Zechariah, and Malachi. As the timeline of history advances, God's power is increasingly stressed since the title reflects the Lord's power as king and commander of the heavenly armies (see 1 Samuel 4:4; Psalm 24:10; Isaiah 1:24; etc.).

3b. The whole earth is full of his glory.

No human-made structure can confine the glory of God (1 Kings 8:27). Since *the whole earth* belongs to God as its creator, it cannot but help to reflect His *glory* (Numbers 14:21; Psalm 72:19).

> **What Do You Think?**
> How do you describe the relationship between God's holiness and the holiness of His people (1 Peter 1:15–16)?
> **Digging Deeper**
> How can you help others worship God for His holiness?

C. What Isaiah Sensed (v. 4)

4. And the posts of the door moved at the voice of him that cried, and the house was filled with smoke.

The seraph's *voice* has an impressive impact, causing *the posts of the door* to move. Although the text does not indicate the location of this door, it is likely at the entrance of the envisioned temple (see Isaiah 6:1b, above).

The presence of *smoke* in Scripture is sometimes associated with the presence of God (example: Exodus 19:18). That presence can be in a negative sense of divine judgment (example: Isaiah 9:18–19). Or it can be in a positive sense of divine guidance or care (example: Isaiah 4:5). Smoke also serves to conceal the viewer from seeing aspects of the divine directly, thus preventing death (Leviticus 16:13). The smoke in the context of the verse at hand brings to mind the cloud that "filled the house of the Lord" in Solomon's time (1 Kings 8:10).

D. What Isaiah Said (v. 5)

5. Then said I, Woe is me! for I am undone; because I am a man of unclean lips, and I dwell in the midst of a people of unclean lips: for mine eyes have seen the King, the LORD of hosts.

Isaiah pronounces *woe* more than 20 times in his book. All but two of those are voiced against those who conduct themselves in ways that oppose God. In the remaining two uses, the prophet pronounces "woe" against himself (here and in Isaiah 24:16).

The expression *Woe is me!* reveals Isaiah's feeling of unworthiness to experience the sights and sounds before him. He knows his unholiness prevents him from being in the presence of a holy God, *the Lord of hosts*, even in a vision. The prophet confesses that his sin makes him unclean. He also admits to living among *a people of unclean lips*, but this admission is not to shift the blame to excuse his own sinful condition. In acknowledging his own unholiness, he is taking personal responsibility for it.

> **What Do You Think?**
> In what ways can our corporate worship include times of confession?
> **Digging Deeper**
> What biblical examples of corporate confession can you name?

Majesty Approached

My first visit to Colorado was not what I expected. I was attending a conference near the base of Pikes Peak, one of the tallest mountains in the state. I looked forward to a few days of crisp air, blazing sunshine, and exhilarating mountain views.

When my friend and I arrived, a dense fog hung over the landscape like a blanket. We arrived at our hotel and parked our rental car without catching a glimpse of Pikes Peak. But the following morning, the sky was clear, and the sun was dazzling. As we drove toward the conference center, Pikes Peak dominated our view. Of course, the mountain had been there the night before, but the fog had concealed it. What the fog had concealed was now revealed!

The sight of a towering mountain has a way of humbling me, reminding me of the majesty of its Creator. Isaiah felt unworthy to view the majesty of the holy and enthroned Lord. How do you combine that same realization with Hebrews 4:16 in approaching His throne in prayer? —N. H.

E. What Isaiah Received (vv. 6–8)

6. Then flew one of the seraphims unto me, having a live coal in his hand, which he had taken with the tongs from off the altar.

In response to Isaiah's admission in the previous verse, *one of the seraphims* goes into action on the man's behalf. *The altar* from which the seraph takes *a live coal* refers possibly to the altar in the temple Solomon built (1 Kings 9:25). But an altar in a temple of the heavenly environs cannot be ruled out because an altar is present there as well (Revelation 6:9; 14:18; 16:7). Isaiah undoubtedly watches with great apprehension as the scene unfolds. Having just confessed his own sinful unworthiness, is he about to be punished?

7. And he laid it upon my mouth, and said, Lo, this hath touched thy lips; and thine iniquity is taken away, and thy sin purged.

We can only imagine the emotions that surge through Isaiah as he witnesses the seraph approaching with a burning coal. Three of Isaiah's five senses have informed his experience thus far. By sight he has beheld the Lord (Isaiah 6:1); by hearing he has perceived the declaration of the seraphims (6:3); by sight and (assumed) smell he is aware of smoke (6:4). Now the fourth sense, touch, comes into play. We do not know if Isaiah feels any sting or pain from the red-hot coal that touches his lips. If so, it must be temporary, as the words *thine iniquity is taken away, and thy sin purged* speak not of judgment but of forgiveness.

At least four Hebrew words can be translated "(burning) coal," so we should be rigorous in

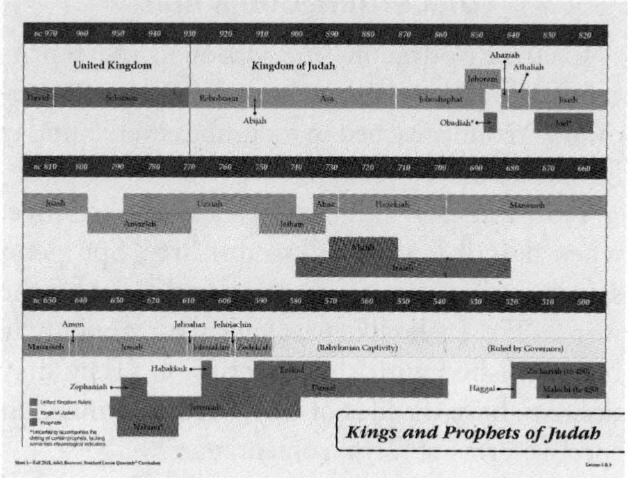

Visual for Lessons 1 & 9. *Display this visual as you discuss the prophets and kings of this quarter's lessons.*

allowing context to determine meaning and significance. The act of touching this coal to Isaiah's *mouth* symbolizes his purification from *sin*. We also notice that although Isaiah's unholiness is corrected through the cleansing action taken by one of the seraphims, the prophet's own confession of unholiness comes first.

8a. Also I heard the voice of the Lord, saying, Whom shall I send, and who will go for us?

First, the seraphims spoke (Isaiah 6:3, above). Then Isaiah spoke (6:5). Then one seraph spoke (6:7). Now, *the Lord* Himself speaks by asking two questions. The first question deals with "sender action," and the second deals with "servant action." These are important questions because the Lord expects those who trust in Him to be His hands and feet at times (Romans 10:15). Sadly, that does not always happen (example: Ezekiel 22:30).

The first-person plural pronoun *us* is similar to the language used in account of creation and in response to the building of the Tower of Babel (Genesis 1:26; 11:7). The plural pronoun may refer to the Lord and the seraphim who make up His heavenly counsel (compare 1 Kings 22:19). Other commentators suggest that the plural pronoun may refer to the three persons of the Trinity: God the Father, God the Son, and God the Holy Spirit.

Isaiah, however, is probably not mulling over such matters at this point; all he hears is the call for someone to *go* on the Lord's behalf. And he wastes no time in responding.

Discerning God's Call

Charles Spurgeon, the famous nineteenth-century preacher, had no formal theological education. Yet he preached to thousands every Sunday for more than 40 years!

How did God call him to such a task? Once, when describing his call to ministry, Spurgeon said it was "an intense, all-absorbing desire for the work." Those who like neat logical categories may be unsatisfied with that description. They may desire to have the idea of God's calls examined in specific terms of form, content, etc.

Perhaps we may discern a more practical approach in the New Testament, where God's calls seem to come about as character and spiritual giftedness are observed. The first-century church chose "seven men of honest report, full of the Holy Ghost and wisdom" to serve in a specific capacity (Acts 6:3–5). Can we not conclude that they answered God's call to do so? Barnabas seems initially to have simply grown into his leadership role, having been recognized by others as a "son of consolation" who led by example and spoke up on behalf of others (4:36–37; 9:27). These traits were evident before he was set apart for missionary travels by a specific directive of the Holy Spirit (13:2).

Martin Luther was on target when he described his call as "God's voice heard by faith." When our aptitudes, spiritual gifts, circumstances, and opportunities come together, let us make sure we are not overlooking God's call. —C. R. B.

8b. Then said I, Here am I; send me.

Isaiah's once unclean lips are ready to serve on the Lord's behalf. He is willing to go wherever the Lord would *send* him. His willingness to be sent contrasts with the hesitancy of prophets such as Moses (Exodus 3:11) and Jeremiah (Jeremiah 1:6).

How to Say It

Amoz	*Ay*-mahz.
Habakkuk	Huh-*back*-kuk.
Hezekiah	Hez-ih-*kye*-uh.
theophany	the-*ah*-fuh-nee.
seraphims	*sair*-uh-fimz.
Uzziah	Uh-*zye*-uh.

What Do You Think?

What prevents believers from saying, "Here am I. Send me!" to God?

Digging Deeper

What steps can believers take to remove these barriers?

II. Communication with a King

(Isaiah 38:1–5)

The events of Isaiah 38:1–5 occur sometime before the deliverance of Jerusalem from Assyrian invasion, described in Isaiah 36–37. This is based on Isaiah 38:6, which describes the rescue as a future promise. By this time, Isaiah's lengthy prophetic ministry was several decades old. The parallel accounts to Isaiah 38:1–6 are found in 2 Kings 20:1–6 and 2 Chronicles 32:24–26.

A. Message of Death (v. 1)

1a. In those days was Hezekiah sick unto death.

Hezekiah reigned as king of Judah from 715 to 686 BC. The king's diagnosis is untold. Part of his suffering includes a skin ailment, causing Isaiah to direct him to use "a lump of figs" as "a plaister upon the boil" (Isaiah 38:21).

1b. And Isaiah the prophet the son of Amoz came unto him, and said unto him, Thus saith the Lord, Set thine house in order: for thou shalt die, and not live.

We do not know whether the ailing king sent for *Isaiah the prophet* or whether the Lord directed Isaiah to appear before the king. Either way, Isaiah's earlier proclamation, "Here I am; send me" (Isaiah 6:8b, above), is consistent with his role as God's messenger.

The descriptor of the prophet being the *son of Amoz* appears thirteen times in the Old Testament, seven of which appear in the book of Isaiah (here and in Isaiah 1:1; 2:1; 13:1; 20:2; 37:2, 21). Scripture gives no other details regarding Isaiah's father.

The message Isaiah brings is not of his own but from *the Lord*. Two phrases repeat the same mortal warning: Hezekiah *shalt die* and *not live*. Isaiah gives no promise of healing. Instead, he directs the king to *set* his affairs *in order*.

> **What Do You Think?**
> How would you support someone who has received news of a terminal diagnosis?
>
> **Digging Deeper**
> In such a case, how do you discern whether or not to show your support by speaking up or remaining silent?

B. Tears of Bitterness (vv. 2–3)

2. Then Hezekiah turned his face toward the wall, and prayed unto the LORD.

The prophet's somber message devastates *Hezekiah*. Perhaps the king is lying on his bed when he receives Isaiah's word. Turning *his face toward the wall* may be an attempt to hide his reaction from others present or to focus on his prayer—or both.

3. And said, Remember now, O LORD, I beseech thee, how I have walked before thee in truth and with a perfect heart, and have done that which is good in thy sight. And Hezekiah wept sore.

Hezekiah has reason to claim that he had *done that which is good*. As king of Judah, he has renovated the temple, overseen its purification, and restored worship practices there (2 Chronicles 29). He has removed artifacts of pagan worship throughout Judah (2 Kings 18:4). The phrase *wept sore* is a two-word summary of the anguish he expresses in Isaiah 38:9–14.

C. Extension of Life (vv. 4–5)

4. Then came the word of the LORD to Isaiah, saying.

The parallel account in 2 Kings 20:4 adds more detail. It describes how Isaiah departs after giving the message but has not gone far when *the Lord* directs him to give another *word* to the king.

5a. Go, and say to Hezekiah, Thus saith the LORD, the God of David thy father.

The declaration *thus saith the Lord* indicates that the prophet's message is not his own. Instead, Isaiah brings it from the Lord (compare Exodus 4:22; 2 Samuel 7:5; Jeremiah 2:2). The appeal to *David thy father* highlights Hezekiah's position as David's descendant (1 Chronicles 3:10–13).

5b. I have heard thy prayer, I have seen thy tears: behold, I will add unto thy days fifteen years.

This message announces a reversal. The biblical record reveals that, at first, Hezekiah became prideful (2 Chronicles 32:24–25). But subsequent repentance paved the way for notable accomplishments (32:26–33).

Conclusion

A. Here Am I. Send Me!

Not everyone will experience the same call to vocational ministry as I described at the outset. However, God calls everyone to serve Him. Regardless of where God calls us to serve, we should answer with our version of "Here am I; send me!"

When we respond humbly and willingly, God will use us to represent Him to others. Some of us may serve God through vocational ministry. Others will serve Him via their witness through their "9-to-5" jobs, relationships with family and friends, financial support of mission work, etc. When we follow God's call, regardless of where it takes us, we are in a place of service to Him.

B. Prayer

Heavenly Father, help us be attentive to how You have called us to go into the world and represent You. Give us the courage to speak of You to a world that desperately needs to know You and Your message of salvation. In Jesus' name, we pray, Amen.

C. Thought to Remember

Respond to God's call!

Visuals FOR THESE LESSONS

The visual pictured in each lesson (example: page 13) is a small reproduction of a large, full-color poster included in the *Adult Resources* packet for the Fall Quarter. Order No. 9780784739136 from your supplier.

Involvement Learning

Enhance your lesson with KJV Bible Student *(from your curriculum supplier) and the reproducible activity page (at www.standardlesson.com or in the back of the* KJV Standard Lesson Commentary Deluxe Edition*).*

Into the Lesson

Begin class time by offering the following imaginary scenarios:

1. You are lost in a dark cave without a companion, weapon, or light. You hear a rumbling noise deep in the cave. The sound grows louder and seems to approach you. What would you do next?
2. You open your mailbox and discover an envelope containing a cashier's check written for $10,000. The check is made out to you, but there is no personal information regarding the source of the check. What would you do next?

Alternative. Ask participants to describe when they experienced an extraordinary or surprising occurrence. How did they respond?

After either activity, lead into the Bible study by saying, "When we experience something extraordinary, our response may have a lasting and powerful effect. In today's study, consider how Isaiah responded to the extraordinary call of God."

Into the Word

Ask a volunteer to read aloud Isaiah 6:1–8. Divide participants into four groups: **Sight Group**, **Smell Group**, **Sound Group,** and **Touch Group**. Distribute a sheet of paper and a pen to each group. Ask them to write down words or phrases from the text related to their assigned sense. Then, encourage groups to use their "sanctified imagination" to add further details to the narrative regarding their assigned sense.

Alternative. Distribute copies of the "Four Senses" exercise from the activity page, which you can download. Have learners work with a partner to complete as indicated.

Option 1. Distribute copies of the "Problem and Solution" activity from the activity page. Have participants complete it in groups of three before discussing conclusions in whole-class discussion.

Option 2. Divide the class into two groups: **Isaiah Group** and **Jeremiah Group**. Have each group read Isaiah 6:1–8 and Jeremiah 1:4–19. Distribute handouts (you create) to each group with questions for in-group discussion.

Isaiah Group. 1–Describe how Isaiah reacted to God's call. 2–How did God respond to Isaiah? 3–Compare Isaiah's call with the call of Jeremiah.

Jeremiah Group. 1–Describe how Jeremiah reacted to God's call. 2–How did God respond to Jeremiah? 3–Compare Jeremiah's call with the call of Isaiah.

After five minutes of discussion, reconvene the groups to share their findings.

Divide the class into small groups. Have groups study Isaiah 38:1–5 and decide whether each statement below is true or false. Distribute a handout (you create) with the statements:

1. Isaiah spoke a word to King Manasseh.
2. The king rejected Isaiah's word and refused to turn to God in prayer.
3. The king requested that the Lord remember the good works of the king's ancestors.
4. Isaiah wept when he saw the response of the king.
5. The Lord promised to add five years to the life of the king.

If the statement is false, they should rewrite it to make it true. (Note: every statement is false.) Give groups several minutes, then review as a whole class.

Into Life

Lead into the activity by saying, "Think of a time when you believed you had received a message or call from God. How did you know it was from God? How did you respond?" Ask participants to share responses with a partner. After three minutes, ask pairs to brainstorm ways to discern an authentic call of God from a mere felt need. Ask volunteers to share responses and write them on the board.

Distribute index cards and pens to participants. Read aloud Isaiah 6:8 as participants write down the phrase "Here am I; send me." Challenge participants to post the cards in a visible place as a daily reminder to pray for obedience to God's call.

Hezekiah's Passover

Devotional Reading: Psalm 1
Background Scripture: 2 Chronicles 30:1–27

2 Chronicles 30:1–9, 26–27

1 And Hezekiah sent to all Israel and Judah, and wrote letters also to Ephraim and Manasseh, that they should come to the house of the LORD at Jerusalem, to keep the passover unto the LORD God of Israel.

2 For the king had taken counsel, and his princes, and all the congregation in Jerusalem, to keep the passover in the second month.

3 For they could not keep it at that time, because the priests had not sanctified themselves sufficiently, neither had the people gathered themselves together to Jerusalem.

4 And the thing pleased the king and all the congregation.

5 So they established a decree to make proclamation throughout all Israel, from Beersheba even to Dan, that they should come to keep the passover unto the LORD God of Israel at Jerusalem: for they had not done it of a long time in such sort as it was written.

6 So the posts went with the letters from the king and his princes throughout all Israel and Judah, and according to the commandment of the king, saying, Ye children of Israel, turn again unto the LORD God of Abraham, Isaac, and Israel, and he will return to the remnant of you, that are escaped out of the hand of the kings of Assyria.

7 And be not ye like your fathers, and like your brethren, which trespassed against the LORD God of their fathers, who therefore gave them up to desolation, as ye see.

8 Now be ye not stiffnecked, as your fathers were, but yield yourselves unto the LORD, and enter into his sanctuary, which he hath sanctified for ever: and serve the LORD your God, that the fierceness of his wrath may turn away from you.

9 For if ye turn again unto the LORD, your brethren and your children shall find compassion before them that lead them captive, so that they shall come again into this land: for the LORD your God is gracious and merciful, and will not turn away his face from you, if ye return unto him.

---

26 So there was great joy in Jerusalem: for since the time of Solomon the son of David king of Israel there was not the like in Jerusalem.

27 Then the priests the Levites arose and blessed the people: and their voice was heard, and their prayer came up to his holy dwelling place, even unto heaven.

Key Text

So there was great joy in Jerusalem: for since the time of Solomon the son of David king of Israel there was not the like in Jerusalem. **—2 Chronicles 30:26**

Judah, from Isaiah to the Exile

Unit 1: Isaiah and the Renewal of the Temple

Lessons 1–4

Lesson Aims

After participating in this lesson, each learner will be able to:

1. Identify qualities of Hezekiah's leadership.
2. Compare and contrast Hezekiah's Passover celebration with that of Josiah in 2 Chronicles 35.
3. Suggest leadership traits that are desirable for Christians today.

Lesson Outline

Introduction
- A. Renewing Relationships
- B. Lesson Context: Hezekiah and Judah
- C. Lesson Context: 1 and 2 Chronicles

I. Renewing Passover (2 Chronicles 30:1–5)
- A. Israel and Judah (v. 1)
- B. Problem and Solution (vv. 2–3)
- C. Approval and Publicity (vv. 4–5)
  - *The Power of Celebration*

II. Returning to God (2 Chronicles 30:6–9)
- A. What to Do (v. 6)
- B. What Not to Do (vv. 7–8)
- C. Why to Do It (v. 9)
  - *Reason for Obedience*

III. Result of Celebration (2 Chronicles 30:26–27)
- A. Joyous People (v. 26)
- B. Blessed People (v. 27)

Conclusion
- A. The Hope of Unity
- B. Prayer
- C. Thought to Remember

Introduction

A. Renewing Relationships

Families, friends, and communities sometimes grow apart and become estranged. Sometimes, separation occurs due to external circumstances, such as one person moving away from the other; other times, the division results from conflict in the relationship.

When passive tensions or outright hostilities exist, meals with family during the holidays sour. High-school reunions fail to reunite old friends. There is no hope for any possibility of restarting past traditions, celebrating common values, or renewing relationships.

Following years of separation between the northern kingdom of Israel and the southern kingdom of Judah, an opportunity arose for the two to reunite. Would unified celebration and worship overcome years of hostility?

B. Lesson Context: Hezekiah and Judah

The division of the united monarchy of Israel into the kingdoms of Israel and Judah occurred in 931 BC during the reign of Solomon's son, Rehoboam. Instead of peaceful coexistence, the two kingdoms were hostile toward each other (1 Kings 15:16, 32; 2 Chronicles 13:1–20).

Nearly 200 years later, Ahaz ascended to the throne in Judah (reigned 735–715 BC). Evil and unfaithfulness marked his reign (2 Chronicles 28:1–4). A few years before Ahaz began his reign, Assyrian forces under Tiglathpileser III (reigned 745–727 BC) had started to pressure the northern kingdom of Israel. The pressure was relieved temporarily by paying tribute (2 Kings 15:19–20). The Assyrian king, also known as "Pul," deported members of the tribes of Reuben, Gad, and Manasseh in the process (1 Chronicles 5:6, 26).

The pressure returned after King Ahaz of Judah offered Tiglathpileser tribute in exchange for military help against Syria and the northern kingdom of Israel (2 Kings 16:7–9; 2 Chronicles 28:16–21). One thing led to another, and two eventual results were (1) the exile of the 10 northern tribes of Israel in 722 BC (2 Kings 17:5–6) and (2) the providential (but temporary) deliverance of the city of Jerusalem in 701 BC, during the reign of Hezekiah (2 Kings 18:17–19:36; Isaiah 37).

When Ahaz's son Hezekiah took the throne (reigned approximately 715–685 BC), the temple was in physical disrepair and spiritual defilement. As a result, Hezekiah initiated a restoration project to purify the temple so that the people might again faithfully worship the Lord (2 Chronicles 29:3). After the project concluded in only 16 days (29:17), the king held a rededication ceremony, which included rightly ordered worship (29:20–36).

C. Lesson Context: 1 and 2 Chronicles

The books of 1 and 2 Chronicles (treated as one book in Hebrew texts) were among the last Old Testament books to be written. Authorship is uncertain. Because of this uncertainty, scholars often refer to the writer simply as "the Chronicler."

We may wonder why the Chronicles are even needed, given that most of their material is already recorded in the books of 2 Samuel and 1–2 Kings. A clue lies in the title of the Chronicles as it appears in the Septuagint, the ancient Greek version of the Old Testament. The title of Chronicles there translates to something like "Things Omitted." For example, compare the account of King Amaziah in 2 Kings 14:1–22 with its counterpart in 2 Chronicles 25:1–28; the latter is longer by some 40 percent. This is even more the case with today's text regarding Hezekiah's Passover—it is completely lacking in the book of 2 Kings.

I. Renewing Passover

(2 Chronicles 30:1–5)

A. Israel and Judah (v. 1)

1a. And Hezekiah sent to all Israel and Judah, and wrote letters also to Ephraim and Manasseh.

The division between *Israel and Judah,* now 200 years along, works against any chances for unified worship in Jerusalem. But given Israel's oppression at the hands of the Assyrians, *Hezekiah* perceives an opportunity to reunite the people in worship. He is eager to return the purified and consecrated temple to its intended service for all Israelites.

Hezekiah invites *all* of Israel and Judah, mentioning two tribes of Israel by name. The significance of *Ephraim* is that the designation is often synonymous with the entire kingdom of Israel (examples: Jeremiah 7:15; Hosea 5:1–3). The tribe of *Manasseh* is the largest of the 12 tribes in terms of geographic size. Its land allotment is specified in Joshua 17:7–11.

1b. That they should come to the house of the LORD at Jerusalem, to keep the passover unto the LORD God of Israel.

The house of the Lord at Jerusalem (the temple) and its predecessor, the tabernacle, was to be the focus of Israelite worship. However, following the division of the kingdom, King Jeroboam I established pagan worship practices for the northern kingdom of Israel. These practices were intended to keep his people from going to worship at the temple (1 Kings 12:25–33). His practices directly disobeyed God; the result would be the exile of the northern tribes (2 Kings 17:1–20). Over a dozen evil kings followed Jeroboam I on the throne of the northern kingdom of Israel. We wonder how much hope Hezekiah has in attracting Israelites in the northern territory *to keep the passover.*

Passover commemorates God's deliverance of His people from Egypt (Exodus 12:1–14, 21–30). The Law of Moses prescribes this yearly observance "at the place which the Lord thy God shall choose to place his name in" (Deuteronomy 16:1–6; compare 12:1–7). A well-attended Passover would be the climax of Hezekiah's restoration project (see Lesson Context).

How to Say It

Ahaz	*Ay*-haz.
Assyrians	Uh-*sear*-e-unz.
Beersheba	Beer-*she*-buh.
Hezekiah	Hez-ih-*kye*-uh.
Ephraim	*Ee*-fray-im.
Jeroboam	Jair-uh-*boe*-um.
Josiah	Jo-*sigh*-uh.
Levites	*Lee*-vites.
Manasseh	Muh-*nass*-uh.
Rehoboam	Ree-huh-*boe*-um.
Tiglathpileser	*Tig*-lath-pih-*lee*-zer.

> **What Do You Think?**
> How can believers celebrate God's work of deliverance and salvation?
> **Digging Deeper**
> What steps can your class take to include such a celebration in your congregation's yearly calendar?

B. Problem and Solution (vv. 2–3)

2. For the king had taken counsel, and his princes, and all the congregation in Jerusalem, to keep the passover in the second month.

The Law of Moses dictates that observance of *the passover* should begin at twilight on the fourteenth day of the first month of the Israelite year (Leviticus 23:5). The Lord allows observance *in the second month* under certain conditions (Numbers 9:9–13).

3. For they could not keep it at that time, because the priests had not sanctified themselves sufficiently, neither had the people gathered themselves together to Jerusalem.

The scope of the Passover observance Hezekiah envisions requires much planning and lead time. These realities reveal two obstacles that prevent the celebration from occurring on the fourteenth day of the first month (*at that time*).

The first hindrance, a shortage of sanctified *priests*, echoes the same shortage mentioned in 2 Chronicles 29:34. This is one of six places where the Chronicler mentions the issue of self-sanctification (1 Chronicles 15:12; 2 Chronicles 5:11; 29:5; 30:3, 17). What this involves for priests is outlined in Leviticus 21:1–22:16.

The second hindrance is reflected in that not everyone had *gathered themselves together* in time to observe. Some time is needed to communicate the invitation and for those accepting it to arrive in *Jerusalem*. The logistics of this is the subject of 2 Chronicles 30:4–5a, below.

C. Approval and Publicity (vv. 4–5)

4–5a. And the thing pleased the king and all the congregation. So they established a decree to make proclamation throughout all Israel, from Beersheba even to Dan, that they should come to keep the passover unto the LORD God of Israel at Jerusalem.

Some form of the phrase *from Beersheba even to Dan* occurs nine times in the Old Testament to reflect the entirety of the kingdom of Israel before the division of 931 BC (here and Judges 20:1; 1 Samuel 3:20; 2 Samuel 3:10; 17:11; 24:2, 15; 1 Kings 4:25; 1 Chronicles 21:2). Beersheba is about 45 miles to the south-southwest of Jerusalem, and Dan is more than 150 miles to the north. A walking pace of 3 miles per hour would require 100 hours of walking round trip to get the *proclamation* to Dan and its people. The round trip would likely require the better part of two weeks, depending on various factors.

5b. For they had not done it of a long time in such sort as it was written.

A long time, approximately 200 years, had elapsed since the united monarchy ended. The phrase *such sort as it was written* probably refers to the instructions in Deuteronomy 16:1–8.

> **What Do You Think?**
> How might your congregation work with a congregation in another part of town to plan a revival or worship celebration?
> **Digging Deeper**
> When was the last time that you participated in such an event?

The Power of Celebration

I've hosted an annual Super Bowl party for friends and family for several years. While I don't care much for the game, I like hosting the party. I value the celebration, food, laughter, conversation, and community resulting from the gathering. Friends become "rivals" for the day as they cheer for their preferred team. New acquaintances become like old friends after spending several hours cheering together. The party brings us together and allows us to enjoy one another's company. And that is something I can get excited about.

Hezekiah invited people from Israel and Judah to celebrate Passover and thereby reorient their spiritual focus. The gathering would remind the people of their shared spiritual heritage. Through the celebration, the people could put aside differences and attend to what they had in common as the people of God.

When did you last celebrate togetherness despite differences? How could you celebrate your shared spiritual heritage with the entire body of Christ that is the church? —N. H.

II. Returning to God
(2 Chronicles 30:6–9)

A. What to Do (v. 6)

6a. So the posts went with the letters from the king and his princes throughout all Israel and Judah, and according to the commandment of the king, saying.

The Hebrew word translated *posts* is actually a participle in the original language. The verb form of this word communicates the idea of running (example: 2 Chronicles 23:12). We can hardly imagine the messengers literally running the 150 miles between Jerusalem and Dan without stopping. Hence, the idea is more along the lines of "without delay."

The fact that they are sent *throughout all Israel and Judah* necessitates that they take multiple copies of the invitation—hence the plural word *letters.* The messengers' strategy is to take the invitation "from city to city" (2 Chronicles 30:10, not in today's text). The content of the letters comes next.

6b. Ye children of Israel, turn again unto the Lord God of Abraham, Isaac, and Israel, and he will return to the remnant of you, that are escaped out of the hand of the kings of Assyria.

We recall that *Israel* was the name of the patriarch whose original name was Jacob (Genesis 32:28; 35:10). In the era after the division of the monarchy, the designation *children of Israel* usually refers only to those of the 10 northern tribes (examples: 2 Chronicles 13:16, 18; 31:1). And so it seems to be here.

The decree's message is simple: *turn again* to *the Lord God of Abraham, Isaac, and Israel.* The people had turned from the Lord through their idolatry. They had rejected the God of their ancestors—the only God there is.

As a result of this sin, the Lord would allow foreign invasion. *Kings of Assyria* took people captive (2 Kings 15:29; 1 Chronicles 5:26). Inhabitants of Israel who were left behind in the land or had escaped captivity were designated as *the remnant.*

Visual for Lesson 2. *Point to this visual as you ask learners to silently reflect on ways that believers can delight in God's ways.*

B. What Not to Do (vv. 7–8)

7. And be not ye like your fathers, and like your brethren, which trespassed against the Lord God of their fathers, who therefore gave them up to desolation, as ye see.

The problem noted in the invitation parallels Hezekiah's previous warning to the priests and Levites (2 Chronicles 29:4–6). Centuries before Hezekiah's day, the Lord warned the people through Moses of the devastation that would come about should the people reject the Lord (Deuteronomy 4:15–28; etc.). The Lord's words came true. Because of the sin of the Israelites, they were conquered by the Assyrians. The remnant Israelites could *see* for themselves the *desolation* that had occurred as a result of the invasion.

What Do You Think?

How will you live so future generations can see you as an example of faithful living and obedience to God?

Digging Deeper

During the upcoming week, how will you encourage younger believers in their faithfulness to God?

8a. Now be ye not stiffnecked, as your fathers were.

To be *stiffnecked* is to be stubborn. The Old Testament refers to the Israelite people numerous times; several of those connect being stiffnecked across generations (2 Kings 17:14; Nehemiah 9:16; Jeremiah 7:26). This problem persists into the New Testament era (Acts 7:51).

8b. But yield yourselves unto the LORD, and enter into his sanctuary, which he hath sanctified for ever: and serve the LORD your God, that the fierceness of his wrath may turn away from you.

The invitation features three imperatives for returning to the Lord: *yield, enter,* and *serve.* The three words being translated are found together in only one other place in the Old Testament: Exodus 13:5. There, the order and the actors are somewhat different.

Exodus 13:5:	*give*	*bring*	*keep*
	↓	↓	↓
2 Chronicles 30:8:	yield	enter	serve

In Exodus 13:5, it is the Lord Himself who performs the first two actions. It's almost as if the text is saying, "The Lord took the first actions, and did His parts long ago; now it's your turn." The contexts of the two texts are the same in that both deal with the Passover celebration.

For God to exercise *the fierceness of his wrath* is not inevitable—not yet, anyway. There's still an opportunity for change so that God's anger *may turn away from* those receiving the invitation. This is the second time that Hezekiah gives awareness of divine anger; the first time is in 2 Chronicles 29:10 (compare 2 Chronicles 28:11, 13).

C. Why to Do It (v. 9)

9. For if ye turn again unto the LORD, your brethren and your children shall find compassion before them that lead them captive, so that they shall come again into this land: for the LORD your God is gracious and merciful, and will not turn away his face from you, if ye return unto him.

Sound familiar? It should, since what we see here is a relentless theme in the Old Testament. One commentator observes that the message of the Old Testament prophets can be boiled down to three words: *Repent or die!* Some passages in regard to (re) turning to God are Deuteronomy 30:2–5; Isaiah 1:16; 55:7; Jeremiah 25:5; and Ezekiel 33:11.

The Lord's willingness to renew relationship with His people comes from His *gracious and merciful* character. Moses identified these attributes of the Lord's character after seeing the Lord on Mount Sinai (Exodus 34:6). The worship of Israel also proclaimed these attributes (Psalms 103:8; 111:4; 145:8; etc.). The Lord extends grace and mercy to those who seek Him.

Reason for Obedience

A few years ago, we brought home a traumatized, 90-pound rescue dog named Sam. We don't know what he experienced before we got him, but previous owners seemed to have hurt him. He would need extensive training, and the first step was earning his trust.

Our training started with simple commands like "sit" and "stay." When Sam obeyed, we gave him high-value rewards, like chicken and bacon. He became increasingly comfortable with us and began trusting us more. Eventually, he would follow our commands without the need for treats. Obedience itself had become his reward. He seemed to know that we were for his good, so he was comforted by our guidance and eager to receive it.

Watching Sam, I can't help but think how I relate to God, my trusted leader. I hasten to add that we should reject any analogy of "God is to us as we are to dogs."

God expects our obedience because He is our Creator, Ruler, and Redeemer, not because He bestows high-value earthly "treats." Is that why you obey? —N. H.

III. Result of Celebration

(2 Chronicles 30:26–27)

Although the king's invitation was sent throughout Israel and Judah, it was not always received positively. Some people "humbled themselves, and came to Jerusalem" (2 Chronicles 30:11); others responded with laughter and mockery (30:10). All of Judah, some from Israel, and foreigners in Judah celebrated Passover and the Feast of Unleavened Bread together in Jerusalem (30:13–25).

A. Joyous People (v. 26)

26. So there was great joy in Jerusalem: for since the time of Solomon the son of David king of Israel there was not the like in Jerusalem.

The time of Solomon is some 200 years in the past at this point. So, the *great joy in Jerusalem* is not due to any personal recall of previous Passover celebrations. Rather, the people seem to realize that they've received anew something they've been missing (see 2 Chronicles 7:8–10).

Several decades after King Hezekiah, his great-grandson Josiah became king of Judah (reigned 640–609 BC). Like his great-grandfather, Josiah "did that which was right in the sight of the Lord" (2 Chronicles 34:2). After destroying items of pagan worship (34:3–7), Josiah would oversee efforts to restore the temple. That included reinstituting Passover celebration (35:1). Comparing the animal sacrifices of 2 Chronicles 30:24 with those of 35:7–9, we surmise that Josiah's Passover drew almost twice the number of people to Jerusalem as did Hezekiah's. The Chronicler describes Josiah's Passover similarly to Hezekiah's: "There was no passover like to that kept in Israel from the days of Samuel the prophet; neither did all the kings of Israel keep such a passover as Josiah kept" (35:18).

> **What Do You Think?**
> How will you worship God with "great joy" in the upcoming week?
>
> **Digging Deeper**
> What is a new worship practice you can participate in during the upcoming week?

B. Blessed People (v. 27)

27. Then the priests the Levites arose and blessed the people: and their voice was heard, and their prayer came up to his holy dwelling place, even unto heaven.

References to *the priests* and *Levites* remind us that all priests are Levites (that is, descended from the tribe of Levi), but not all Levites are priests (Numbers 3; etc.). Bestowing a blessing on *the people* was one of the tasks given to the Levites by the Law of Moses (Deuteronomy 10:8; 21:5). Perhaps this blessing was modeled after the priestly blessing given by the first priest, Aaron (Numbers 6:23–27). The content of the *prayer* of the priests and Levites may reflect the same sentiment as King Solomon's prayer at the dedication of the temple (2 Chronicles 6:21, 24–31, 34).

Conclusion

A. The Hope of Unity

Christians are not immune to division. Unfortunately, a brief look at social media, not to mention centuries of history itself, reveals hostilities and disputes among believers. However, when faced with these attitudes, we can look to the example of Hezekiah. His leadership in the face of sin and other dysfunction can be an example for us in the twenty-first century AD.

First, we must always turn to the Lord and repent; this requires realizing that the most important thing is to be with Him. Second, we should unite with other believers and come before God in worship as a repentant people. When these happen, blessings result.

> **What Do You Think?**
> What behaviors or ideologies prevent you from a life of repentance and unity?
>
> **Digging Deeper**
> What steps will you take to eliminate these barriers?

B. Prayer

Lord God, we want to be united as Your people. Remind us to turn to You in worship. Show us how we can gather with other believers to serve You and offer our praise to You. Help us be attentive to the unifying work of the Holy Spirit in our lives. Fill us with Your love so that we can enjoy unity with other believers. In Jesus' name we pray, Amen.

C. Thought to Remember

Worship and serve as the unified people of God.

Involvement Learning

Enhance your lesson with KJV Bible Student *(from your curriculum supplier) and the reproducible activity page (at www.standardlesson.com or in the back of the* KJV Standard Lesson Commentary Deluxe Edition*).*

Into the Lesson

Distribute an index card and a pen to each participant. Ask them to write down a meaningful family tradition that is no longer observed or celebrated. Then, ask them to flip the card over and write an idea or ideas to revive this tradition or make it applicable for a modern-day context.

After one minute, invite volunteers to share their responses with the group. Be prepared to start the discussion with an example from your own experience. Ask, "Why is it important to remember traditions that have faded away?"

Alternative. Distribute copies of the "Passover Puzzle" exercise from the activity page, which you can download. Have learners work in pairs to complete as indicated before discussing conclusions as a whole class.

Lead into the Bible study by saying, "King Hezekiah worked to bring people back to God by celebrating the Passover. Let's see how his leadership can help develop leadership traits for today."

Into the Word

Ask a volunteer to read aloud 2 Chronicles 30:1–5. Divide the class into two groups: the **Covenant Keepers Group** and the **Unity Seekers Group**. Distribute a pen and sheet of paper to each group. Ask the groups to discuss the following questions: 1–What was the purpose of Hezekiah's invitation to observe Passover? 2–How did Hezekiah's actions reflect a move toward religious and national unity? 3–In what ways was this Passover different from those celebrated before? After three minutes, ask a volunteer from the **Covenant Keepers Group** to share the group's responses.

Alternative. Distribute copies of the "Restore the Unity" activity from the activity page. Have participants complete it individually in a minute or less before reviewing responses with a partner.

Invite another volunteer to read 2 Chronicles 30:6–9 aloud before directing both groups to discuss the following questions: 1–What does the call to return to the Lord (2 Chronicles 30:6b) imply about the spiritual state of Israel and Judah? 2–How does the invitation extend beyond a simple call to worship? 3–What can we learn from the reactions of the people and leaders to Hezekiah's call? After a few minutes, have a volunteer from the **Unity Seekers Group** share the group's responses.

Option. Instruct participants to research King Hezekiah's life. Divide them into six groups and assign each group one of the following texts:

2 Kings 18:1–16 | *2 Kings 18:17–37*
2 Kings 19:1–19 | *2 Kings 19:20–37*
2 Kings 20:1–11 | *2 Kings 20:12–21*

Have groups answer the following questions: 1–What significant act does Hezekiah undertake in this text? 2–What leadership trait does Hezekiah demonstrate? After five minutes, ask a volunteer from each group to summarize the group's responses.

Next, have the groups silently read 2 Chronicles 35:1–19. Challenge the groups to contrast Hezekiah's Passover celebration with Josiah's celebration. Ask volunteers to list leadership traits evident in Hezekiah. Write responses on the board.

Into Life

Ask the class to think about essential leadership qualities for Christians today. Direct them to use the list of leadership traits from the previous activity. Invite participants to call out a leadership quality they think is essential and write that trait on the board.

Distribute an index card and pen to each participant. Invite them to pick one trait from the board that they feel gifted in to use to serve the church. Ask them to write that on the index card. Challenge participants to pray and think about how God can lead them to use that trait in their lives.

September 21
Lesson 3 (KJV)

Hilkiah's Discovery

Devotional Reading: Romans 7:7–12
Background Scripture: 2 Chronicles 33:1–33

2 Chronicles 34:15–22, 26–27

15 And Hilkiah answered and said to Shaphan the scribe, I have found the book of the law in the house of the LORD. And Hilkiah delivered the book to Shaphan.

16 And Shaphan carried the book to the king, and brought the king word back again, saying, All that was committed to thy servants, they do it.

17 And they have gathered together the money that was found in the house of the LORD, and have delivered it into the hand of the overseers, and to the hand of the workmen.

18 Then Shaphan the scribe told the king, saying, Hilkiah the priest hath given me a book. And Shaphan read it before the king.

19 And it came to pass, when the king had heard the words of the law, that he rent his clothes.

20 And the king commanded Hilkiah, and Ahikam the son of Shaphan, and Abdon the son of Micah, and Shaphan the scribe, and Asaiah a servant of the king's, saying,

21 Go, inquire of the LORD for me, and for them that are left in Israel and in Judah, concerning the words of the book that is found: for great is the wrath of the LORD that is poured out upon us, because our fathers have not kept the word of the LORD, to do after all that is written in this book.

22 And Hilkiah, and they that the king had appointed, went to Huldah the prophetess, the wife of Shallum the son of Tikvath, the son of Hasrah, keeper of the wardrobe; (now she dwelt in Jerusalem in the college:) and they spake to her to that effect.

---

26 And as for the king of Judah, who sent you to inquire of the LORD, so shall ye say unto him, Thus saith the LORD God of Israel concerning the words which thou hast heard;

27 Because thine heart was tender, and thou didst humble thyself before God, when thou heardest his words against this place, and against the inhabitants thereof, and humbledst thyself before me, and didst rend thy clothes, and weep before me; I have even heard thee also, saith the LORD.

Key Text

Hilkiah answered and said to Shaphan the scribe, I have found the book of the law in the house of the LORD. And Hilkiah delivered the book to Shaphan. **—2 Chronicles 34:15**

Judah, from Isaiah to the Exile

Unit 1: Isaiah and the Renewal of the Temple

Lessons 1–4

Lesson Aims

After participating in this lesson, each learner will be able to:

1. Identify what Hilkiah found.

2. Contrast King Josiah's reaction to hearing Scripture read to that of his son King Jehoiakim in Jeremiah 36:20–26.

3. Make a plan to value the public and private reading of Scripture in an effort to keep God's Word from being neglected.

Lesson Outline

Introduction

A. The Dead Sea Scrolls

B. Lesson Context

I. Discovering a Book (2 Chronicles 34:15–21)

A. Reporting and Reading (vv. 15–18)

Sugar Cookies

B. Reacting and Requesting (vv. 19–21)

Lost in the Temple Today

II. Consulting a Prophet (2 Chronicles 34:22, 26–27)

A. Identity and Location (v. 22)

B. Response and Reason (vv. 26–27)

Conclusion

A. Listening to God

B. Prayer

C. Thought to Remember

Introduction

A. The Dead Sea Scrolls

The world of archeology was turned upside down in 1947 after shepherds made a startling discovery in a cave near the Dead Sea: seven ancient scrolls encased in jars. Over the next 10 years, hundreds more scrolls were found in the surrounding area, most dating from the third century BC to the first century AD. The collection, called the Dead Sea Scrolls, became one of the most significant archeological finds of the twentieth century.

These scrolls shed significant light on life during the time between the testaments, the practices and beliefs of the people who lived in that region, and the reliability of the Old Testament texts. These scrolls had been "lost" for centuries, waiting to be discovered. Since their unearthing, our knowledge of the time period that Jesus walked on earth has significantly expanded.

Today's lesson details an account of a significant archeological discovery made in the temple complex in the seventh century BC. The response of Judah's king to this finding would have significant ramifications for him and the kingdom.

B. Lesson Context

This lesson continues exploring the kings and prophets of the kingdom of Judah. As such, the context of lesson 2 also applies to this lesson.

Following the reign of Hezekiah in Judah (715–685 BC), the Jerusalem temple fell into disrepair and neglect. Much of this occurred during the reign of Judah's longest-reigning king, Manasseh (696–642 BC). His reign was marked by sin and evil. He reestablished idolatrous practices (2 Kings 21:3), shed innocent blood (21:16; 24:4), and "did that which was evil in the sight of the Lord" (21:2). His sinful acts culminated in his desecration of the Jerusalem temple (21:7), the same temple that Hezekiah had purified (see lesson 2). Scripture lists Manasseh's sinful actions as a reason Judah faced disaster, destruction, and exile (21:10–15).

Manasseh was succeeded as king by his son, Amon. He was also an evil king: he worshiped idols and "humbled not himself before the Lord" (2 Chronicles 33:22–23). Two years into his reign, he was assassinated. His eight-year-old son, Josiah, replaced him on the throne of Judah (34:1).

Josiah's reign (640–609 BC) differed from those of his father and grandfather. At age 16, he began to "seek after" God (2 Chronicles 34:3a). Four years later, he made efforts to cleanse both Judah and Jerusalem of idolatry (34:3b–7). Then, at age 26, in the eighteenth year of his reign, he took steps to repair the temple in Jerusalem (34:8). This act was significant because previous kings had allowed the temple complex to fall into ruin (34:11). In the years preceding the project, little faithful worship had occurred in the temple, except during a brief season (33:14–17). The temple's restoration was the climactic reform of Josiah's reign. Yet, it yielded an unexpected finding, as today's lesson will show.

The parallel account of 2 Chronicles 34:15–22, 26–27 (today's lesson) can be found in 2 Kings 22:8–14, 18–19.

I. Discovering a Book

(2 Chronicles 34:15–21)

A. Reporting and Reading (vv. 15–18)

15. And Hilkiah answered and said to Shaphan the scribe, I have found the book of the law in the house of the Lord. And Hilkiah delivered the book to Shaphan.

Scripture mentions at least seven individuals named Hilkiah (1 Chronicles 26:11; 2 Kings 18:18; etc.). This particular *Hilkiah* is the high priest during the reign of Josiah (2 Kings 22:8). He is also the great-grandfather of Ezra (Ezra 7:1).

Shaphan is part of the group responsible for overseeing the repairs to the temple (2 Chronicles 34:8). His work as a secretary or *scribe* likely focuses on protecting and maintaining royal documents.

The temple renovation project (see Lesson Context) likely unearthed many items that had been buried, including money (2 Chronicles 34:17, below). Hilkiah, however, discovers something more significant *in the house of the Lord*: "a book of the law of the Lord given by Moses" (34:14).

Visual for Lesson 3. *Display this visual as you ask the discussion questions associated with 2 Chronicles 34:15.*

Because modern bookbinding techniques had not yet been invented, this "book" may have been rolled in the form of a scroll (compare Jeremiah 36:2; Ezekiel 2:9).

The consensus among commentators is that the book was a form of Deuteronomy. The title *Deuteronomy* means "the second [giving of the] law"—a reference to the Law of Moses. There are several reasons why this book could have been a copy of Deuteronomy.

First, the phrase "the book of the covenant" in 2 Chronicles 34:30 can fit Deuteronomy, since that book is in the form of a covenant renewal treaty. However, that same phrase is used in Exodus 24:7, most likely to describe the material in Exodus 20–23.

Second, the emphasis in Deuteronomy 12 on worship in one place is consistent with Josiah's reforms. Third, the purging of the land of pagan cultic places is found in Deuteronomy 12. This depiction could have made an impression on Josiah since that is precisely what he had been doing even before the book of the law was found. Fourth, the reference to curses in 2 Chronicles 34:24 could point to the extended curses spelled out in Deuteronomy 27:9–26; 28:15–68. Fifth, the celebration of Passover in 2 Chronicles 35 is similar to the commands of Deuteronomy 16:1–8.

A final argument in support of Deuteronomy is its emphasis that keeping the land depends on obedience to the covenant. Reading Deuteronomy

29 alone would be enough to cause Josiah to tear his clothes in anguish in this regard (see 2 Chronicles 34:19, below).

The text gives no reason why this document was lost in the first place. It is possible that most, if not all, copies were lost or hidden during the idolatrous reigns of Manasseh and Amon. Some commentators speculate that this book was deposited in a secure location during the repairs to the temple that occurred during Hezekiah's reign (2 Chronicles 29). Over time, those who served in the temple may have forgotten about the book.

What Do You Think?

What *personal* practices and habits help prevent God's Word from becoming neglected?

Digging Deeper

What *corporate* practices and habits also help in this regard?

16. And Shaphan carried the book to the king, and brought the king word back again, saying, All that was committed to thy servants, they do it.

The parallel account states that *Shaphan* read the book after receiving it from Hilkiah (2 Kings 22:8). In addition to bringing *the book to the king*, Shaphan reports on the status of the work on the temple. Such extensive renovation required the service of carpenters, stone masons, and other laborers (see 2 Chronicles 34:10–11).

17. And they have gathered together the money that was found in the house of the Lord, and have delivered it into the hand of the overseers, and to the hand of the workmen.

The text does not state the source of this *money* or where it was discovered *in the house of the Lord*. Regardless of its source, the money is distributed to *the overseers* and *the workmen* of the temple restoration project.

18. Then Shaphan the scribe told the king, saying, Hilkiah the priest hath given me a book. And Shaphan read it before the king.

Before revealing the contents of the *book*, its chain of custody needed to be established. *Shaphan*, whose role as a *scribe* involves handling documents, is given the book by *Hilkiah the priest*, who discovered it. Shaphan then reads it aloud in the presence of *the king* (and presumably others in his court).

The book of Deuteronomy contains a directive for the public reading of "this law" before all Israel (Deuteronomy 31:9–13). Deuteronomy also stipulates that the king is to read a copy of the law "all the days of his life" (17:19; compare Joshua 1:8). As Shaphan reads the book, all those present—including the king—hear the law, which probably had not been read publicly for many decades.

Sugar Cookies

My grandmother's sugar cookies have been part of my family's Christmas celebration for as long as I can remember. Her memory lives on whenever we pull out her recipe card and make the same cookie dough. My grandmother's handwriting swirls across the card with peaks and dips like ocean waves.

I didn't want to lose the treasure of this tradition. Last year, I gifted my mom a glass cutting board with the recipe etched onto its surface. I didn't just want to remember the recipe; I wanted to preserve my grandmother's legacy. The cutting board serves as a lasting reminder of my family's history gathered around her table, eating her sugar cookies.

We preserve the things we treasure. That's why it's so tragic that the people in Judah lost the book

How to Say It

Abdon	*Ab*-dahn.
Ahikam	Uh-*high*-kum.
Deuteronomy	Due-ter-*ahn*-uh-me.
Hezekiah	Hez-ih-*kye*-uh.
Hilkiah	Hill-*kye*-uh.
Huldah	*Hul*-duh.
Jehoiakim	Jeh-*hoy*-uh-kim.
Manasseh	Muh-*nass*-uh.
Nahum	*Nay*-hum.
Noadiah	*No*-uh-**die**-uh.
Rehoboam	Ree-huh-*boe*-um.
Shallum	*Shall*-um.
Tikvath	*Tick*-vath.

of the law. This book reminded the people of their past: how the Lord had made them His covenant people. In this way, the book of the law is significant and worth treasuring; it was the way the people remembered their history.

What steps can you take to ensure that God's Word doesn't become "lost" to you? —N. H.

B. Reacting and Requesting (vv. 19–21)

19. And it came to pass, when the king had heard the words of the law, that he rent his clothes.

The word of the Lord demands a response. Some reject it, while others submit to it. Josiah dramatically responds as *he rent* (tore) *his clothes*. The act of tearing one's clothing signals remorse, humility, and repentance (examples: 2 Samuel 1:11–12; Isaiah 36:22–37:1; Acts 14:13–15; contrast Leviticus 10:6; 21:10).

After hearing *the words of the law*, Josiah is horrified. Although he has worked to remove idolatry from Judah (see Lesson Context), he knows that Judah is far from being completely obedient to the law. Some outward reform had occurred, but Josiah recognizes the need for something else (see 2 Chronicles 34:21b, below).

> **What Do You Think?**
> When was a time that God's Word evoked strong feelings in you?
> **Digging Deeper**
> How did those feelings lead you to action regarding obedience to the Word of God?

20. And the king commanded Hilkiah, and Ahikam the son of Shaphan, and Abdon the son of Micah, and Shaphan the scribe, and Asaiah a servant of the king's, saying.

The group *the king commanded* consists of select members of the king's court. We know very little about these individuals. *Ahikam the son of Shaphan* protected the prophet Jeremiah (Jeremiah 26:24). In the parallel account of this narrative, *Abdon the son of Micah* is named "Achbor the son of Michaiah" (2 Kings 22:12). This narrative contains the only mention in Scripture of *Asaiah a servant of the king's*.

21a. Go, inquire of the LORD for me, and for them that are left in Israel and in Judah, concerning the words of the book that is found.

Josiah directs this group to seek a better understanding of *the Lord* in order to discern the significance and meaning of *the words of the book* of the law. The king's directive is not just for his own knowledge, but also for the good of others. The findings would affect all inhabitants of the divided kingdoms: the remnant *left in Israel* (reference absent from 2 Kings 22:13) and the residents of *Judah*.

> **What Do You Think?**
> What further training or expertise do you need to deepen your study of God's Word?
> **Digging Deeper**
> Who from your community will you invite to join you in studying God's Word?

Lost in the Temple Today

My father set a good example for us. He read the Bible often, taught Sunday school from this commentary, and was otherwise very involved with fellow Christians in general and church ministry in particular. He had been church treasurer, took communion to shut-ins, and helped with interior renovations of our church building. The list goes on.

Then something changed. He stopped going to church. He would leave the room rather than discuss Christianity. He stopped reading his Bible—I heard him say once that "It's all just speculation."

In effect, the Word of God became "lost" to my father. His Bible was still just right there on the shelf within easy reach, but it might as well have been gathering dust in someone else's basement hundreds of miles away.

As we read today's text, we may wonder how a lengthy scroll of a Bible book can get "lost" within the very confines of the temple itself! But it still happens. Given that our bodies are the temple of God today (1 Corinthians 6:19; 2 Corinthians 6:16; etc.), think how easily it is for God's Word to get "lost" in there as the issues and things of earthly life take priority. What guardrails can you erect so that you aren't one of the "stony places" that Jesus spoke about in Matthew 13:5, 20–21?

—R. L. N.

21b. For great is the wrath of the LORD that is poured out upon us, because our fathers have not kept the word of the LORD, to do after all that is written in this book.

Josiah recognizes that the burden Israel and Judah continued to experience was due to disobedience to the Lord. The Law of Moses clearly specifies the results of *the wrath of the Lord* that is to befall the people because of their rebellious idolatry (Leviticus 26:14–45; Deuteronomy 28:15–68; 29:18–28; etc.).

What Do You Think?

What is your comfort level in discussing God's anger?

Digging Deeper

How do you resolve that God is love (1 John 4:8, 16) but that He also demonstrates wrath (Psalm 7:11; Romans 1:18–19; Ephesians 5:6; etc.)?

II. Consulting a Prophet

(2 Chronicles 34:22, 26–27)

A. Identity and Location (v. 22)

22. And Hilkiah, and they that the king had appointed, went to Huldah the prophetess, the wife of Shallum the son of Tikvath, the son of Hasrah, keeper of the wardrobe; (now she dwelt in Jerusalem in the college:) and they spake to her to that effect.

Several prophets serve in Judah during Josiah's reign, namely Jeremiah, Zephaniah, and Nahum. The king's entourage visits none of those, however, but rather seeks out *Huldah the prophetess.* Other female prophets mentioned by name in the Bible are Miriam (Exodus 15:20), Deborah (Judges 4:4), Noadiah (Nehemiah 6:14), and Anna (Luke 2:36).

The role of Huldah's husband, *Shallum,* as *keeper of the wardrobe* is not given. But perhaps he cares for the priestly garments in the temple. (A similar role is described in 2 Kings 10:22.) The *college* where they live is likely the second district in the northern (newer) part of *Jerusalem.* This quarter is near the temple complex, thus allowing Shallum easy access to the temple. Given the probability that both Huldah and her husband are somehow connected to the temple, she is the ideal person to inquire about the book of the law.

B. Response and Reason (vv. 26–27)

26. And as for the king of Judah, who sent you to inquire of the LORD, so shall ye say unto him, Thus saith the LORD God of Israel concerning the words which thou hast heard.

The first part of Huldah's prophetic response is in 2 Chronicles 34:23–24, not part of today's lesson text. It describes the disaster and curses that are to come on Judah because the people have worshiped pagan gods and rebelled against the Lord (34:25; see 33:2–9). The kingdom of Judah would experience conquest and exile from the land, as promised by the Law of Moses (Deuteronomy 28:15, 36).

The second part of Huldah's response is in the verse now before us. Whereas she had previously identified King Josiah simply as "the man that sent you to me" (2 Chronicles 34:23), she now identifies him specifically as *the king of Judah.* This casts the spotlight on Josiah personally. See the next verse.

27a. Because thine heart was tender, and thou didst humble thyself before God, when thou heardest his words against this place, and against the inhabitants thereof, and humbledst thyself before me, and didst rend thy clothes, and weep before me.

Huldah's response acknowledges Josiah's humble and contrite response to receiving the book of the law. First, the state of his *heart* has been demonstrated by his mourning of Judah's sin and his desiring to follow God's will. When Josiah heard the words of the book read, he submitted, grieved, and repented. Most of Judah's kings were prideful and rejected the Lord. A few, however, demonstrated humility before the Lord: Rehoboam (2 Chronicles 12:12), Hezekiah (32:26), and even Manasseh (33:12–13). Even today, God favors those who are humble (James 4:6 and 1 Peter 5:5–6, both quoting Proverbs 3:34).

In the years to follow, Josiah's son Jehoiakim would ascend to the throne of Judah (609–598 BC). He would lack the humility of his father. Jehoiakim's officials would gain possession of a scroll that contains "all the words" the Lord had given to the prophet Jeremiah regarding Israel, Judah, and all the nations (Jeremiah 36:2, 21). When Jehoiakim would hear the words, he would cut the scroll to pieces and throw them into the fire (36:22–23). Rather than repent and mourn the words of the Lord, Jehoiakim and his officials would not express fear or would not tear their garments (36:24).

King Josiah listened to the word of the Lord, humbled himself, and obeyed. King Jehoiakim, however, did the opposite: he exalted himself and rejected the Lord's warnings. Josiah honored the prophetess Huldah, but Jehoiakim had the prophet Jeremiah arrested (Jeremiah 36:26). Josiah was spared the horrors of exile. Jehoiakim, however, was not; because of his disregard for the word of the Lord, he was carried into exile in Babylon (2 Chronicles 36:5–7).

What Do You Think?

What steps will you take to cultivate a tender heart and humble attitude before the Lord?

Digging Deeper

What barriers prevent you from cultivating these things? How will you deal with such obstacles?

27b. I have even heard thee also, saith the Lord.

Josiah's actions and attitudes do not go unnoticed. Through the prophecy of Huldah, the Lord gave Josiah a promise of hope: "I will gather thee to thy fathers, and thou shalt be gathered to thy grave in peace, neither shall thine eyes see all the evil that I will bring upon this place, and upon the inhabitants of the same" (2 Chronicles 34:28). The prophecy revealed that Josiah would not experience the pending disaster of exile. However, this did not mean he lived a long and peaceful life. Approximately 13 years later, Josiah died following a questionable decision to engage the Egyptians in battle (2 Chronicles 35:20–25).

Even so, we do not lose track of the fact that Josiah was spared the horrors of exile because of his humility and desire to obey the word of the Lord. His was a posture of humility. As such, the Lord responded with mercy and grace.

Conclusion

A. Listening to God

Josiah received the book of the law, heard its words, and humbly sought the Lord. His example gives us a model for responding to God's Word today. Josiah received God's words *attentively* and *submissively.*

To listen attentively assumes a posture of receptivity. We set aside our defensive tendencies, desires to deflect, and self-justifications. When we listen attentively to God's Word, we set aside our expectations. Instead, we patiently receive God's Word and let its power transform us.

After listening attentively, we submit to God's Word and let it lead us into obedience. We hear God's Word and commit to follow it. We are God's children, obedient to His Word.

We can only receive God's Word if our spiritual "ears" are prepared to "hear." This reception occurs when we have a heart willing to repent of our sins, submit to God's word, and seek Him above all else. Only then can we listen attentively to God's words.

How do you receive God's Word? Are you like Josiah and listen to it attentively and submissively? The one who is Creator, Ruler, and Redeemer has revealed Himself through Scripture. How can we not be interested to what He has to say?

B. Prayer

Lord God, we seek You night and day as we listen to Your voice and meditate on Your Word. Give us soft hearts so we might obey Your Word and submit to Your guidance for our lives. In Jesus' name we pray. Amen.

C. Thought to Remember

Be a Josiah, not a Jehoiakim.

Involvement Learning

Enhance your lesson with KJV Bible Student *(from your curriculum supplier) and the reproducible activity page (at www.standardlesson.com or in the back of the* KJV Standard Lesson Commentary Deluxe Edition*).*

Into the Lesson

Before class, look up the definition of *reform* and write it on the board. Lead a discussion by asking the following questions: 1–List examples of reform. 2–In what ways do you agree or disagree with the definition on the board? 3–In what ways does reform involve returning to core values or principles that have been neglected or forgotten?

Alternative. Distribute copies of the "Historical Reforms" exercise from the activity page, which you can download. Have learners complete it individually in a minute or less before discussing answers and conclusions with a partner.

Lead into the Bible study by saying, "The concept of reformation is not just a modern-day idea; we see it in the narratives of Scripture. Today, we will explore an important reform led by King Josiah. His reform teaches us the value of not neglecting God's Word."

Into the Word

Divide the class into three groups: **Heart Changers Group**, **Temple Restorers Group**, and **Covenant Renewal Group**. To each group, distribute copies (you prepare) of the text of 2 Chronicles 34:15–22, 26–27, highlighters of two different colors, and handouts of the questions below for in-group discussions.

Heart Changers Group. Read 2 Chronicles 34:15–18. 1–Highlight in one color the key actions mentioned in these verses. 2–Highlight in a different color the individuals mentioned in these verses. 3–Draw a box around the key acts of reform in these verses. 4–How do these acts of reform demonstrate a change of heart toward God's law?

Temple Restorers Group. Read 2 Chronicles 34:19–21. 1–Highlight in one color the key actions mentioned in these verses. 2–Highlight in a different color the individuals mentioned in these verses. 3–How do Josiah's efforts to restore the temple reveal a restoration of faith?

Covenant Renewal Group. Read 2 Chronicles 34:22, 26–27. 1–Highlight in one color the key actions mentioned in these verses. 2–Highlight in a different color the individuals mentioned in these verses. 3–Draw a box around words or phrases that describe the key features of the covenant renewal ceremony. 4–What was the significance of this ceremony for the people?

Gather the groups together to present their findings in a whole-group discussion. Make notes on the board of key findings.

Write this question on the board:

How is God's Word "lost" today?

Invite learners to brainstorm responses to this question. Write down responses on the board. After five minutes of discussion, ask, "What steps can we take to restore God's Word to its proper place in our lives?" Allow the learners a few moments to write their ideas in response. Then, facilitate a discussion based on what they have shared.

Into Life

Say, "God speaks to us through His Word. Today's lesson serves as a call to reflect on our personal and collective commitment to Scripture, both in our private lives and within the body of Christ."

Distribute an index card and pen to each learner. Direct participants to work with a partner to make a plan to value the public and private reading of Scripture in an effort to keep God's Word from being neglected. Encourage pairs to write down the plan's steps on their index cards and how they will follow these steps in the upcoming week.

Option. Distribute the "Reviving Our Roots" activity from the activity page. Direct participants to complete the activity as a take-home. Encourage completion by stating that you will ask volunteers to share about the writing experience at the start of the next class.

The Servant's Suffering

Devotional Reading: Matthew 12:14–21
Background Scripture: Isaiah 52:13–53:12

Isaiah 53:1–7

1 Who hath believed our report? and to whom is the arm of the LORD revealed?

2 For he shall grow up before him as a tender plant, and as a root out of a dry ground: he hath no form nor comeliness; and when we shall see him, there is no beauty that we should desire him.

3 He is despised and rejected of men; a man of sorrows, and acquainted with grief: and we hid as it were our faces from him; he was despised, and we esteemed him not.

4 Surely he hath borne our griefs, and carried our sorrows: yet we did esteem him stricken, smitten of God, and afflicted.

5 But he was wounded for our transgressions, he was bruised for our iniquities: the chastisement of our peace was upon him; and with his stripes we are healed.

6 All we like sheep have gone astray; we have turned every one to his own way; and the LORD hath laid on him the iniquity of us all.

7 He was oppressed, and he was afflicted, yet he opened not his mouth: he is brought as a lamb to the slaughter, and as a sheep before her shearers is dumb, so he openeth not his mouth.

Key Text

All we like sheep have gone astray; we have turned every one to his own way; and the LORD hath laid on him the iniquity of us all. —**Isaiah 53:6**

Judah, from Isaiah
to the Exile

Unit 1: Isaiah and the Renewal of the Temple

Lessons 1–4

Lesson Aims

After participating in this lesson, each learner will be able to:

1. Identify the suffering servant.
2. Relate the servant's suffering to the concept of substitutionary atonement.
3. Write a prayer of gratitude for what the servant's suffering accomplished.

Lesson Outline

Introduction

A. Three Discouraging Words

The following scenario has happened to most of us, likely more than once. We're watching an hour-long television program that features high drama and lots of action. We can't wait for every commercial break to end. As the conclusion approaches, we're on the edge of our seats, waiting for the exciting finish. Then, three words appear on the screen: "To be continued." We'll have to wait for another episode to learn how the plot ends!

Scripture tells us that Old Testament prophets, like Isaiah, desired to know what their prophecies meant or how they would be fulfilled. But they were told that it was not theirs to experience the fulfillment of their words, only to proclaim them faithfully (1 Peter 1:10–12). The Lord, in His own timing and His own way, would see to it that their words would be proven true and their ministries would be vindicated. He alone would determine when the words "to be continued" would no longer be necessary or relevant—though in many cases, the waiting period would be much longer than one week!

B. Lesson Context

When we cross from chapter 39 to chapter 40 in the book of Isaiah, we enter what is commonly called "the book of comfort." The chapters therein include some of the most significant prophecies of Jesus and the impact of His life and ministry. This section begins with a word of "comfort" to God's people and assures Jerusalem that "her iniquity is pardoned" and that she has "received of the Lord's hand double for all her sins" (Isaiah 40:1–2). This likely describes how the captivity of the people in Babylon, predicted in Isaiah 39, was to end.

There was, however, another more serious and oppressive captivity affecting God's people: the captivity of sin. This captivity was the primary cause for the heartbreak of exile experienced by both the northern kingdom of Israel (to Assyria in 722 BC) and the southern kingdom of Judah (to Babylon in 586 BC).

The solution to this spiritual bondage was described by Isaiah in terms of a "servant" raised

Visual for Lesson 4. *Display this visual and ask, "In what ways did Jesus Christ fulfill the prophecies in Isaiah 53:1–7?"*

up by the Lord to provide the needed deliverance. This is highlighted in what is often called Isaiah's "servant passages" or "servant songs" since they are written in the style of Hebrew poetry. Four passages from Isaiah are usually included among the servant passages: 42:1–9; 49:1–7; 50:4–9; and 52:13–53:12. In some cases, the length of a given passage may be subject to some variation among Bible commentators. Some commentators include Isaiah 61:1–4 as part of the servant passages. Those verses do not use the word *servant*; however, the passage was read by Jesus in Luke 4:16–21 and declared by Jesus to be fulfilled in Him.

Isaiah 53:1–7 (today's text) is found within what is perhaps the most powerful of the servant passages listed above. That passage of Isaiah 52:13–53:12 is quoted seven times in the New Testament (Matthew 8:17; Luke 22:37; John 12:38; Acts 8:32–33; Romans 10:16; 15:21; 1 Peter 2:22) and alluded to there in more than two dozen other places.

Some Bible commentators describe Isaiah as using what is called the "prophetic past tense." This means that even though Isaiah was looking centuries into the future in foretelling these events concerning Jesus, Isaiah spoke as though they had already happened. This is a way of highlighting the certainty of the prediction.

I. Servant's Appearance

(Isaiah 53:1–3)

A. Reported and Revealed (v. 1)

1. Who hath believed our report? and to whom is the arm of the LORD revealed?

The chapter opens with two rhetorical questions. The first question indicates that the *report* from God's people would be challenging to believe. Isaiah wonders whether this message will be met with acceptance.

The phrase *the arm of the Lord* is anthropomorphic language—attributing human characteristics to God in order to aid our understanding of who God is and what God does. Even though God is a Spirit (John 4:24), Scripture speaks of Him as having physical characteristics (example: Psalm 34:15–16). Writers of Scripture often refer to the Lord's "arm" to express His power, might, and eternity (Deuteronomy 4:34; 5:15; 33:27; Psalm 77:15; Isaiah 52:10; etc.).

This verse is quoted twice in the New Testament. The gospel of John quotes this verse to express amazement regarding the people's rejection of Jesus despite seeing the mighty acts of God revealed through Jesus' miracles (John 12:37–38). The apostle Paul quotes part of this verse to convey his disappointment regarding Jewish unbelief of the gospel (Romans 10:16). The thread running through these passages is that people disbelieve the servant of the Lord.

What Do You Think?

What are common barriers that prevent people from believing and accepting the message of Christ?

Digging Deeper

How can you help people address those barriers while trusting in the Holy Spirit's power to soften hearts?

B. Humble and Unattractive (v. 2)

2a. For he shall grow up before him as a tender plant, and as a root out of a dry ground.

Disbelief regarding the servant might be due, in part, to his humble and unattractive origin and disposition. The phrase *he shall grow up before him* shows a relationship with distinction between God the Father and His servant.

The text uses two botanical metaphors to express the servant's humble origin. *A tender plant* is delicate, ready to break under adverse conditions; *a root out of a dry ground* is in danger of dying without proper water (contrast Psalm 1:3). These two metaphors highlight the perceived weakness of the servant and his questionable origin in the eyes of the world (compare Isaiah 11:1).

This description may bring to mind Nathanael's comment when he hears that Jesus came from the town of Nazareth: "Can there any good thing come out of Nazareth?" (John 1:46). The Pharisees will be skeptical along this line as well (7:41–52).

2b. He hath no form nor comeliness; and when we shall see him, there is no beauty that we should desire him.

Having identified the servant's humble origin, the text turns to describe his appearance and presentation. To arrive with *no form nor comeliness* predicts that the servant's physical appearance will not be the reason that anyone is drawn to him (compare Isaiah 52:14).

When we see the line *there is no beauty that we should desire him,* we remind ourselves that we are reading a form of Hebrew poetry that contains literary parallelism. Therefore, we have one thought in this half-verse, not two: nothing about the servant's appearance will cause people to notice him, unlike the appearances of some of Israel's kings (1 Samuel 9:2; 16:12).

How to Say It

Assyria	Uh-*sear*-ee-uh.
Babylon	*Bab*-uh-lon.
chastisement	*chas*-tize-munt or chas-*tize*-munt.
Corinthians	Ko-*rin*-thee-unz (*th* as in *thin*).
Ezekiel	Ee-*zeek*-ee-ul or Ee-*zeek*-yul.
Hezekiah	Hez-ih-*kye*-uh.
iniquities	in-*ik*-wu-teez.
Isaiah	Eye-*zay*-uh.
Leviticus	Leh-*vit*-ih-kus.
Nathanael	Nuh-*than*-yull (th as in thin).
Nazareth	*Naz*-uh-reth.

C. Despised and Rejected (v. 3)

3. He is despised and rejected of men; a man of sorrows, and acquainted with grief: and we hid as it were our faces from him; he was despised, and we esteemed him not.

Despite outward appearances, the servant will indeed draw attention—negative attention. The treatment predicted will be far from welcoming. Two parallel thoughts also occur in this verse: to be *despised* and to be *rejected.* As history bears out, this happens not only by individuals but also by nations (Isaiah 49:7).

During His earthly ministry, Jesus faced rejection by the world and His own people: "He was in the world, and the world was made by him, and the world knew him not. He came unto his own, and his own received him not" (John 1:10–11; compare Mark 6:1–5). Crowds gathered to hear His teachings and witness His miracles. But after He was arrested and crucified, most turned their backs on Him—even His own disciples.

The servant is to experience inner turmoil as described in the next parallel: to be *a man of sorrows* is to be *acquainted with grief.* This pictures the floods of emotional pain (example: Luke 19:41).

What Do You Think?

What are some ways we do not esteem Christ as we should?

Digging Deeper

How do the directives in John 14:15 and 1 John 4:20 help us correct this problem?

II. Servant's Suffering

(Isaiah 53:4–7)

A. Stricken by God (v. 4)

4a. Surely he hath borne our griefs, and carried our sorrows.

We continue to see parallel ideas, with the phrase *borne our griefs* equivalent to the phrase *carried our sorrows.* The description of the servant's great personal pain now includes an explanation for the suffering: he bears the weight of our griefs and sorrows. Matthew 8:17 quotes this verse following a description of Jesus' healing ministry. It is clear that Matthew interprets the fulfillment of Isaiah's prophecy in the healing work of Jesus. Thus, we see a connection between our sufferings and the servant's.

> **What Do You Think?**
> What griefs and sorrows do you need to turn over to Christ today?
> **Digging Deeper**
> In what ways can you carry the griefs of other believers so that you love others just as Christ has loved us (John 13:34)?

4b. Yet we did esteem him stricken, smitten of God, and afflicted.

In an inexcusable interpretation of the servant's life and ministry, the people the servant comes to rescue end up being the very ones to pronounce him *stricken, smitten of God.* People believe that his punishment is deserved. They know that God never acts unjustly, so they naturally reason that the servant must have done something to deserve the punishment (Mark 14:64).

Witnesses to Jesus' crucifixion interpret that event as a test of the servant's identity as they cry, "If he be the King of Israel, let him now come down from the cross, and we will believe him. He trusted in God; let him deliver him now, if he will have him: for he said, I am the Son of God" (Matthew 27:42b–43; compare Psalm 22:8). This implies that if God did not deliver the servant, then the servant deserved whatever pain and suffering the crucifixion inflicted on him.

The servant is indeed *smitten of God,* but not in the sense that the onlookers to the crucifixion suppose. The crucifixion of Jesus fulfills God's "determinate counsel and foreknowledge" (Acts 2:23; compare Luke 22:22; Acts 3:18; 4:27–28). Our next verse explains this further.

B. Punished for Us (vv. 5–6)

5a. But he was wounded for our transgressions, he was bruised for our iniquities.

The prophet turns to the physical punishment the servant experienced. This is also expressed through parallel thoughts: *wounded* is equivalent to *bruised*, and *our transgressions* is equivalent to *our iniquities*. The critics of the servant are right in seeing God's punishment at work in the crucifixion. However, they miss the point that in the crucifixion, the servant receives and accepts the punishment for humanity's sins.

5b. The chastisement of our peace was upon him; and with his stripes we are healed.

We now move to the result of the servant's suffering. Through it we can experience *peace* with God and be *healed* from our sins. Such peace and reconciliation are available because of the servant's sacrifice (Romans 3:24–26; 4:25; 2 Corinthians 5:18–19; Hebrews 9:28; 10:10).

This transfer of punishment is known as the doctrine of substitutionary atonement. Christ acted as a substitute on our behalf for the result of our spiritual healing. Being the sinless Son of God (2 Corinthians 5:21; 1 Peter 2:22, quoting Isaiah 53:9), only Jesus could pay such a price. The New Testament connects being healed by the servant's *stripes* most directly in 1 Peter 2:24. Thus, the prophet Isaiah emphasizes—hundreds of years in advance—Jesus' triumph over sin and its impact on humanity.

> **What Do You Think?**
> What is the significance of the New Testament connecting Christ's work with our being "healed"?
> **Digging Deeper**
> What other phrases does the New Testament use to describe Christ's work on the cross?

A Great Reversal

A few years ago, a dear friend invited me to help with a retreat for ministry leaders in India. Growing up as a missionary kid, my friend has a passion for supporting people doing ministry in challenging situations. She regularly takes teams of people overseas to pray for, listen to, and support local ministry workers. Having visited India before, I looked forward to visiting friends, ready to serve God and local ministry leaders.

Toward the end of the retreat, I fell ill, bedridden

in my room. I reported my illness to my friend, and she asked others to pray for me. But they didn't only pray; they put their prayers into action. Soon, two local leaders knocked on my door. I didn't want to open it. I was a mess. *What if I got them sick? Wasn't I supposed to be serving them?*

I felt vulnerable and embarrassed, but I opened the door. The two visitors had ordered me some soup and had called a doctor. After I stumbled back to bed, one of the visitors sat beside me, wiping my fevered forehead with a cold rag while we waited.

I vividly remember how this person was willing to "enter" into my suffering for my care! How very Jesus-like she was! When was the last time you served Jesus in this way? See John 13:1–17.

—N. H.

6. All we like sheep have gone astray; we have turned every one to his own way; and the Lord hath laid on him the iniquity of us all.

People are compared to *sheep* in numerous places in the Bible (examples: 2 Samuel 24:17; Psalms 78:52; 95:7; Ezekiel 34:11–12; Matthew 9:36; John 10:1–16). The comparisons are not flattering. Sheep tend to go *astray,* and people inevitably do the same when they go their *own way* and live independently of God's guidance. Of course, the specific ways people describe their sinfulness change from culture to culture, but the fundamental problem has remained the same since Eden: we prefer our own way to God's.

Despite such rebellion, the Lord placed on the servant *the iniquity of us all.* Notice how the word *all* appears at both the beginning and the end of this verse. Everyone is guilty of sin; the sacrifice (substitutionary atonement) of Jesus, however, is provided for all by the Lord's grace and mercy. The fact that the Lord has laid on Jesus the iniquity of us all brings to mind the symbolic action carried out by Israel's high priest on the Day of Atonement. Once yearly, the high priest laid his hands on the scapegoat and placed upon it the sins of the nation (Leviticus 16:20–22); this symbolized and foreshadowed what Jesus was to do once, for all time.

We may also consider the prophet Ezekiel, who was commanded to "bear" the iniquity of the people through a series of symbolic actions (Ezekiel 4:4–6; 5:1–4; etc.). What Jesus carried out at the cross was not another symbolic act. He took upon Himself the complete punishment for human sin. In Paul's words, God "made him to be sin for us" (2 Corinthians 5:21). God did so "that he might be just, and the justifier of him which believeth in Jesus" (Romans 3:26).

Jesus Died for *Me*

About 18 years ago, I had a dream that changed my life. In the dream, I'm sitting on a grassy hill with Jesus; the shadow of the cross is in the distance. The air is cool and pleasant, and we are seated face-to-face. I'm fully aware that He is about to walk down that hill and give His life on the cross. And yet, He's amazingly calm. He lovingly looks at me and says, "It's time," as He stands and walks toward the cross. There is no mistake that He's about to do this for me, for my sin and shame.

For a moment, it was as if I was the only person in the world. And the reality of His love was landing squarely on me. I was filled with sorrow over the cost of my sin and amazement at His willingness to pay that price.

That dream changed my view of the cross from being an abstract doctrinal idea to something deeply personal. Of course, Jesus died for all and not just for me. And, of course, we are not to claim dreams or anything else as adding to the Scripture (Hebrews 1:1–2; Revelation 22:18; etc.). But if I focus solely on the fact that Jesus died for all, I can forget how personal His love is for me. In what ways could your faith grow by seeing the cross more personally?

—N. H.

C. Silent by Choice (v. 7)

7. He was oppressed, and he was afflicted, Yet he opened not his mouth: he is brought as a lamb to the slaughter, and as a sheep before her shearers is dumb, so he openeth not his mouth.

Two more parallels now present themselves. The first is easy to see, with *oppressed* being another way to say *afflicted,* as Isaiah returns to a description of the servant. Once again, the prophet focuses on the servant's suffering.

The second parallel is actually a parallel within

a parallel. The writer combines these in the shape of an *X*. It looks like this:

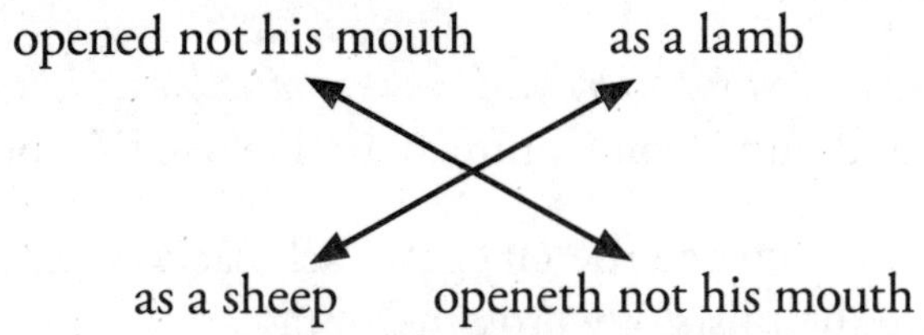

The servant does not cry out in anger or vow to exact revenge upon those who afflict him, as the diagram reveals (compare Mark 14:60–61; 15:3–5; Acts 8:32). The servant being likened to a *lamb* may bring to mind the times Jesus is depicted as a lamb in the New Testament (John 1:29, 35–36; Revelation 21:22–23; 22:1, 3). But that isn't what's in view here. The idea, instead, is that of a sacrificial lamb (Exodus 12:3–6; 1 Corinthians 5:7).

The silence of Jesus during His persecution contrasts with how often He spoke during His ministry. He used words to command storms to cease, to cast out demons, to heal a wide range of diseases, and even to raise the dead. And ironically, His words silenced His enemies (Luke 14:2–6; 20:20–26). But when it came to speaking up for His own well-being, He said nothing. Jesus' silence in the face of bitter opposition embodied His determination to fulfill His Father's redemptive purpose. His was a "silent might." No doubt there are times when we, in silence, should reflect on how powerfully Jesus' silence still speaks.

> **What Do You Think?**
> In what ways does Jesus' powerful silence still speak to you today?
>
> **Digging Deeper**
> In what ways is Jesus' silence a model for your actions?

Conclusion

A. Three Encouraging Words

The Introduction called attention to the words *to be continued* as three discouraging words. In the sense of salvation history, the *to be continued* of the Old Testament has been superseded by the *it is fulfilled* of the New Testament (Matthew 26:54–56; Luke 24:44; etc.).

As we consider Isaiah's ministry to King Hezekiah (as seen in lesson 1) and compare it with the content in Isaiah 53, we see the twofold nature of a prophet's ministry. One may be called *forthtelling*, in which the prophet proclaimed God's message to those of his own surroundings. The other may be labeled as *foretelling*, in which the prophet looked forward in time to declare God's plan for the future. This plan, which included the ministry of the suffering servant, impacted not only the original audience but also the entire world. In each role, God's prophet was "moved by the Holy Ghost" (2 Peter 1:21).

It is instructive at this point to call attention to a New Testament passage cited in lesson 1: John 12:41. In that passage, the apostle John describes Isaiah as one who "saw [Jesus'] glory, and spake of him." In that lesson, the focus was on the glory that Isaiah saw by means of his vision of the Lord "high and lifted up" in His heavenly temple (Isaiah 6:1). In Isaiah 53, Isaiah also foresaw Jesus' glory, but in a completely different way. This was the glory seen when Jesus was high and lifted up on the cross (John 12:32–33).

This is the glory of both God's love and His holiness (Romans 3:21–26), demonstrated in an act that was looked upon with disdain and disgust by the people of Jesus' day. It was, as the apostle Paul put it, one of "the foolish things of the world" that God used to "confound" the wise and the mighty (1 Corinthians 1:27).

Some commentators have proposed that the cross reveals glory to God in the *lowest*. That is the glory of Jesus that Isaiah saw in our passage today. And as a result of the servant's suffering, death, and resurrection, we worship Him in the highest (Ephesians 1:18–23).

B. Prayer

Father, after reading today's passage, saying "thank You" hardly seems adequate. And it isn't. We ask for Your help in offering ourselves in grateful service as ambassadors for Jesus, wherever we are and whenever You choose. In Jesus' name, Amen.

C. Thought to Remember

Jesus is the servant we serve.

Involvement Learning

Enhance your lesson with KJV Bible Student *(from your curriculum supplier) and the reproducible activity page (at www.standardlesson.com or in the back of the* KJV Standard Lesson Commentary Deluxe Edition*).*

Into the Lesson

Using the prompt, "We all know someone who," describe a person in your congregation without using that person's name. Describe the person by listing positive actions or behaviors, descriptors about appearance, or details of a time when this person impacted your life. Allow time for participants to guess who you are talking about.

Option. Direct learners to get in pairs and play this game, choosing other classmates or well-known figures to describe. Remind pairs to choose positive descriptors when describing this individual!

Lead into Bible study by saying, "How would you describe Jesus to someone who had never heard of Him or met Him? In today's lesson, consider how the prophet Isaiah paints a word picture of the servant and how this word picture describes the person and work of Jesus."

Into the Word

Ask a volunteer to read aloud Isaiah 53:1–3. Divide the class into two groups: **Reared Group** and **Rejected Group**. Distribute handouts (you create) with the following prompts for discussion.

Reared Group: 1–How does Isaiah 53:1–3 describe the upbringing of the servant? 2–How are Matthew 13:54–58; Mark 6:3–4; Luke 2:39–40, 51–52; and John 1:10–14 related to Isaiah 53:1–3? 3–How did people receive and respond to Jesus?

Rejected Group: 1–How does Isaiah 53:1–3 describe the rejection the servant would face? 2–How are Matthew 23:37; 27:21–23; John 11:32–37; and Acts 2:22–23 related to Isaiah 53:1–3? 3–How did people receive and respond to Jesus?

After five minutes, ask a volunteer from each group to review their group's responses. Then ask a volunteer to read aloud Isaiah 53:4–5. Ask the **Reared Group** to read Matthew 27:22–50 and the **Rejected Group** to read John 19:1–37. Direct groups to look for words and phrases that show the fulfillment of Isaiah's prophecy. After 10 minutes, reconvene the class and ask each group to share their lists of words and phrases.

Alternative. Distribute copies of the "Fulfillment of Prophecy" exercise from the activity page, which you can download. Have participants work in pairs to complete as indicated.

After calling time for either activity, explain the concept of *substitutionary atonement.* Use the lesson commentary, if needed, to aid your explanation. Invite learners to consider and discuss how they have been impacted by the sacrifice of the servant who is Christ Jesus.

Ask a volunteer to read aloud Isaiah 53:6–7. Say, "In this section, Isaiah compares people to sheep and the servant to a lamb." Rename the two groups from the previous activity the **Sheep Group** and the **Lamb Group**. Distribute posterboard and markers to each group. Use the following instructions to direct each group

Sheep Group. Use Isaiah 53:6; John 10:1–16, 26–30 to create a poster identifying the qualities of the "sheep."

Lamb Group. Use Isaiah 53:7; John 1:36; 1 Corinthians 5:7; 1 Peter 1:18–19; and Revelation 5:12 to create a poster identifying the qualities of the "lamb." Display the posters and compare the posters through whole-class discussion.

Into Life

Invite learners to re-read Isaiah 52:1–7 and choose one significant attribute of the servant. Distribute an index card and pen to each participant so they can write a prayer of gratitude for that attribute and what the servant's suffering accomplished.

Alternative. Distribute copies of the "What He Has Done" activity from the activity page. Have learners complete the first part in a minute or less. Then direct them to finish the rest of the activity at home. At the beginning of the next meeting, provide an opportunity for participants to share reflections.

October 5
Lesson 5 (KJV)

Jeremiah's Call and Arrest

Devotional Reading: Jeremiah 1:11–19
Background Scripture: Jeremiah 1:1–10; 6:10–11; 8:18; 9:2; 26:1–24

Jeremiah 1:6–10

6 Then said I, Ah, Lord GOD! behold, I cannot speak: for I am a child.

7 But the LORD said unto me, Say not, I am a child: for thou shalt go to all that I shall send thee, and whatsoever I command thee thou shalt speak.

8 Be not afraid of their faces: for I am with thee to deliver thee, saith the LORD.

9 Then the LORD put forth his hand, and touched my mouth. And the LORD said unto me, Behold, I have put my words in thy mouth.

10 See, I have this day set thee over the nations and over the kingdoms, to root out, and to pull down, and to destroy, and to throw down, to build, and to plant.

Jeremiah 26:8–9, 12–15

8 Now it came to pass, when Jeremiah had made an end of speaking all that the LORD had commanded him to speak unto all the people, that the priests and the prophets and all the people took him, saying, Thou shalt surely die.

9 Why hast thou prophesied in the name of the LORD, saying, This house shall be like Shiloh, and this city shall be desolate without an inhabitant? And all the people were gathered against Jeremiah in the house of the LORD.

---

12 Then spake Jeremiah unto all the princes and to all the people, saying, The LORD sent me to prophesy against this house and against this city all the words that ye have heard.

13 Therefore now amend your ways and your doings, and obey the voice of the LORD your God; and the LORD will repent him of the evil that he hath pronounced against you.

14 As for me, behold, I am in your hand: do with me as seemeth good and meet unto you.

15 But know ye for certain, that if ye put me to death, ye shall surely bring innocent blood upon yourselves, and upon this city, and upon the inhabitants thereof: for of a truth the LORD hath sent me unto you to speak all these words in your ears.

Key Text

The LORD said unto me, Say not, I am a child: for thou shalt go to all that I shall send thee, and whatsoever I command thee thou shalt speak.? —**Jeremiah 1:7**

Judah, from Isaiah to the Exile

Unit 2: Jeremiah and the Promise of Renewal

Lessons 5–9

Lesson Aims

After participating in this lesson, each learner will be able to:

1. Summarize the context of Jeremiah's call.
2. Compare and contrast Jeremiah's reaction to God's call with that of Isaiah in reaction to his own call (Lesson 1).
3. Develop a plan to encourage congregational ministry free from age discrimination.

Lesson Outline

Introduction
- A. Plucking and Planting
- B. Lesson Context

I. Appointed to Prophesy (Jeremiah 1:6–10)
- A. Jeremiah's Objection (v. 6)
- B. The Lord's Response (vv. 7–8)
  - *Confounding the Wise*
- C. Jeremiah's Commission (vv. 9–10)
  - *En Pointe*

II. Condemned to Death (Jeremiah 26:8–9)
- A. Unwelcome Message (v. 8)
- B. Unruly Crowd (v. 9)

III. Determined to Speak (Jeremiah 26:12–15)
- A. Assured Promise (vv. 12–13)
- B. Dire Warning (vv. 14–15)

Conclusion
- A. Each Christian's Call
- B. Prayer
- C. Thought to Remember

Introduction

A. Plucking and Planting

Although I want my lawn to be a healthy mix of grasses, unwelcome visitors also grow there: weeds. A particularly irksome offender is nutsedge, which initially masquerades as grass. Untreated, it can take over large sections of a lawn. While spraying with weed killers has some effect, new plants seem to return in a few days. By midsummer, the only way I have found to control nutsedge is to get on my knees and pluck out every single plant by the roots.

In the same lawn, I annually overseed sections where the grass is thin. This adds new growth and increases the lawn's thickness and health. Often, I overseed an area damaged by nutsedge and my clumsy extractions of this weed.

So the same turf area may see "plucking" and "planting" as uprooting and renewing. Such imagery is used in the book of Jeremiah to describe the Lord's control over the rise and fall of nations. Nations are "plucked" (face disaster) or "planted" (allowed to prosper) according to the Lord's plans. This lesson looks at God's purposes in the history of nations and the role of His prophets (like Jeremiah) in announcing and interpreting these events.

B. Lesson Context

Jeremiah's prophetic ministry began in 627 BC, about 70 years after Isaiah. He was a priest at Anathoth (Jeremiah 1:1), therefore from the tribe of Levi and an educated person. About this time, the last great Assyrian king died, ending the dominance of this cruel nation over the people of Israel. But other foreign menaces came to dominate Judah: first Egypt, then Babylon. This climaxed in 586 BC when the armies of Babylonian king Nebuchadnezzar captured Jerusalem and destroyed both the city walls and the temple (see 2 Kings 25:1, 8–11).

Jeremiah's career spanned the reigns of the last five kings of Judah before this catastrophe. Jeremiah is known as the "Mournful Prophet." His name contributes to the English term "jeremiad," a bitter railing against opponents. He is credited as the author of the book that bears his name as well as the book of Lamentations.

I. Appointed to Prophesy

(Jeremiah 1:6–10)

A. Jeremiah's Objection (v. 6)

6. Then said I, Ah, Lord God! behold, I cannot speak: for I am a child.

The book of Jeremiah begins with God calling to him to be a "prophet unto the nations" (Jeremiah 1:5). We may compare this to other callings such as those of Moses (Exodus 3:5–10), Isaiah (Isaiah 6:1–13), Samuel (1 Samuel 3:10–21), Ezekiel (Ezekiel 2:3–8), and Amos (Amos 7:14–15).

It is common for a person the Lord is calling on to express various inadequacies. Moses claimed to be "slow of speech" (Exodus 4:10). Isaiah protested he was a "man of unclean lips" (Isaiah 6:5). Amos noted he was a farmer, not a trained prophet (Amos 7:14). Jeremiah asserts he is but a *child* and therefore cannot be expected to *speak* like a prophet. We do not know how old Jeremiah was, but given that he was already serving as a priest suggests he was not a young child. He may not have been a seasoned orator, but he was hardly a small boy. The phrase *I am a child* can also be translated "I am a young man." Regardless of his exact age, Jeremiah appears to use his age as a reason for not being up to the task.

In Jeremiah's response, we also see a curious capitalization of "God" in the title *Lord God*. If translated in strict alignment with other occurrences of these two Hebrew terms, *adonai Yahweh* would be rendered "Lord Lord." To avoid redundancy while maintaining the dual nature of this title, translators capitalize all letters of "God" to stand in for the word typically rendered "Lord."

What Do You Think?

When is a time that you doubted you were capable of something you felt God asking you to do?

Digging Deeper

How can we move through feelings of inadequacy to respond to God more readily in obedience and faith?

B. The Lord's Response (vv. 7–8)

7. But the Lord said unto me, Say not, I am a child: for thou shalt go to all that I shall send thee, and whatsoever I command thee thou shalt speak.

The Lord will have none of Jeremiah's objections. Jeremiah would *go* where the Lord would *send* him and would speak *whatsoever* the Lord might *command*. God was not expecting Jeremiah to venture out as an unequipped spokesman with no support. The Lord would direct his ministry and supply content for his messages.

We have come to associate prophecy with predictions of the future and prophets with those who reveal future events. This, however, is not the whole of what Jeremiah is called to do when he speaks. He is the Lord's spokesman, who goes and speaks as the Lord directs him. This message may include revealing God's plans for the future (Jeremiah 31:31–34, etc.). It may also be a denunciation of sin and a call to repentance for those of the prophet's day (8:4–7; 18:5–11, etc.).

The messages of prophets such as Jeremiah often include warnings of God's potential acts of punishment while promising blessings for those who listen, repent, and obey. Prediction of future events was something the people could evaluate and thereby judge the veracity of any prophet (see Deuteronomy 18:21–22). In Jeremiah's situation, he denounced false prophets for promising "peace" to the people because it was a message the public wanted to hear. Jeremiah knew this was a false prediction, that foreign invasion was on the horizon (Jeremiah 6:13–15, etc.).

Confounding the Wise

As a mom of four, I referee a lot of disagreements. One day, I overheard my two youngest having an argument. My son Garrett had offered his younger sister Morgan what seemed like a good solution, but for some reason she wouldn't agree. After listening to both sides, it still seemed that Garrett's solution was reasonable.

Turning to Morgan to ask her why she wouldn't agree to it, she thought for a moment. She looked up with sad eyes and lamented, "I know it makes sense, but it's like my body won't agree. It just can't catch up to what he is saying." I was stunned by how deep and rich her words were. I realized that instead of pushing her to move toward a solution, she just needed a little time. After being allowed that time, she and Garrett went on to enjoy their game.

The necessary wisdom to handle this tiff came from a 7-year-old. It's not always the most educated, lofty, and powerful voices that teach us. God often communicates His truth by means of humble, unlikely sources. When was the last time you encountered truth in an unlikely place? How did you receive it? —N. H.

8. Be not afraid of their faces: for I am with thee to deliver thee, saith the LORD.

Jeremiah likely considers that he will face opposition to his message and new vocation. This can include stiff animosity from those he is to address with words from the Lord. To be *afraid of their faces* implies anxiety over face-to-face encounters. Jeremiah will not be posting to social media, let alone sending a letter. He will be in the physical presence of people who reject his message in threatening ways.

C. Jeremiah's Commission (vv. 9–10)

9. Then the LORD put forth his hand, and touched my mouth. And the LORD said unto me, Behold, I have put my words in thy mouth.

Because the prophet is to be God's spokesman, Jeremiah's mouth will become a symbol for his task. Here we are reminded of the prophet Isaiah. When Isaiah received his great vision of the Lord on His heavenly throne, he felt completely out of place in God's presence and protested that he was a man of "unclean lips" (Isaiah 6:5). When an angel took a burning coal from the altar in heaven and touched it to Isaiah's mouth, he was spiritually cleansed and empowered. When God asked for a volunteer to speak to the people, Isaiah responded, "Here am I; send me" (6:8; see lesson 1).

The call of Jeremiah has similarities. Jeremiah's sense of inadequacy for his call also brings a touch to his *mouth,* this time by the Lord's *hand.* This is not to cure a speech impediment or to repair damaged vocal cords. Rather, Jeremiah is told that the Lord has *put* His *words in* the prophet's *mouth.* Jeremiah will never need to worry about a situation in which he thinks, "I don't know what to say." God gives him a task and will surely give him a message.

What Do You Think?

When was fear a barrier to obeying God's direction in your life?

Digging Deeper

What steps can you take to grow your faith and combat fear?

En Pointe

One day, feeling overwhelmed by ministry responsibilities, I reached out to a mentor for advice. She responded with an interesting fact about ballet dancers. "If they move to pointe shoes too soon," she said, "they risk breaking their ankles."

I felt the truth of her words immediately. I had taken on too much, effectively "moving to pointe" too soon. The weight of it all was about to break me. I thanked her for her wise words and considered where I could make some ankle-saving adjustments. A couple of years later, this advice came to mind again when my daughter came home from dance class, announcing that her teacher had invited her to move to pointe shoes. We celebrated with gusto, reveling in this achievement. I couldn't help but reflect on how, for me, the idea of pointe shoes had represented weightiness and struggle. For my daughter, they were a thrill and a joy.

What was the difference? It all depended on the teacher making the call. When the teacher makes

How to Say It

adonai (Hebrew)	ad-owe-*nye*.
Anathoth	*An*-uh-thoth.
Jehoiakim	Jeh-*hoy*-uh-kim.
Jeremiah	Jair-uh-*my*-uh.
Nebuchadnezzar	*Neb*-yuh-kud-*nez*-er.
Shiloh	*Shy*-low.

the call, we can trust that we are well-equipped to do the work He has given us. Consider making a list of the things you feel called to do. Do you feel equipped? Why or why not? —N. H.

10. See, I have this day set thee over the nations and over the kingdoms, to root out, and to pull down, and to destroy, and to throw down, to build, and to plant.

Jeremiah's call is not to be squandered on denouncing the petty sins of his community. God's plans for Jeremiah are much bigger, international in scope. We should understand this carefully, though. Jeremiah is not appointed and empowered to be a kingmaker or judge over *nations* in any way apart from God's control and plan. His role as God's spokesman is weighty, delivering the verdicts and judgments of the "King of nations" (Jeremiah 10:7).

One of the many figurative ways the book of Jeremiah illustrates this plucking and planting is the work of a potter in Jeremiah 18. The Lord is pictured as the ultimate maker of clay pots, a metaphor for nations. Jeremiah equates the divine potter's actions in shaping a pot with plucking up, pulling down, and destroying (Jeremiah 18:7).

In this verse, the actions of building and planting are also included. The founding and blessing of nations are in God's hands, as are their punishment and destruction. Even a nation that has been planted and built up by the Lord is subject to being uprooted and destroyed if it persists in disobedience (Jeremiah 18:9–10).

The act of uprooting is further described using three terms with political overtones. First, *nations* will be pulled down, which has the connotation of being overthrown. Once-powerful nations will be conquered by other nations and placed in a servile position. Second, nations will be destroyed. This is the next step beyond conquering. It means the nation ceases to exist like the northern kingdom of Israel, utterly dismantled by the Assyrians in the eighth century BC.

Third, nations will be thrown down. This can refer to the actual razing of buildings, even the complete decimation of a city. It is the opposite of the next act of the Lord Jeremiah mentions, *to build*, which indicates construction. For a nation, this could be the infrastructure of buildings and fortifications that come with national longevity. We may marvel at the grand buildings of the ancient Egyptians or Mayans and the legacies they leave of defunct empires. But the Lord may leave little trace of the nations He destroys, thus allowing for reconstruction by another people.

What Do You Think?

How might God use a person's ministry to bring both warning and blessing to others?

Digging Deeper

What are some things such a person would need to be cautious about?

II. Condemned to Death

(Jeremiah 26:8–9)

A. Unwelcome Message (v. 8)

8. Now it came to pass, when Jeremiah had made an end of speaking all that the Lord had commanded him to speak unto all the people, that the priests and the prophets and all the people took him, saying, Thou shalt surely die.

Our lesson moves to the central section of the book of Jeremiah to give us a glimpse of how the opening verses of his call to be a prophet in chapter 1 were actualized in the events of his ministry. In chapter 26, Jeremiah goes to Jerusalem to speak God's words during the reign of King Jehoiakim (Jeremiah 26:1). This is often called the "Temple Sermon" and may be the same incident related in chapter 7 (see Lesson 6). The material in Jeremiah is not always related in chronological order. In that regard, this later account—from a slightly different perspective—may help us understand what happened in chapter 7. The thrust of Jeremiah's message in chapter 7 is that the people's expectation of future peace (7:20, 34) and their pride in the protection of the temple (7:4) are mistaken.

Jehoiakim probably became king in 609 BC, so this would be roughly 20 years after Jeremiah began his prophetic ministry. The Lord's message through Jeremiah was that the people must keep the law and turn from their evil ways (Jeremiah

26:3–4). If not, the Lord would curse them and make Jerusalem like "Shiloh," a deserted site that lived only in memory (26:6; see also 7:12–15).

When Jeremiah finishes delivering God's words, the reaction of *the priests, and the prophets, and all the people* is to threaten his life. They are deeply offended, having no desire to repent or return to the Law of Moses. When they say, "*Thou shalt surely die,*" we can understand this to mean, "We are going to kill you" (compare Jeremiah 26:11). Rather than obey the Lord's word given through Jeremiah, their first impulse is to seek his death.

B. Unruly Crowd (v. 9)

9. Why hast thou prophesied in the name of the LORD, saying, This house shall be like Shiloh, and this city shall be desolate without an inhabitant? And all the people were gathered against Jeremiah in the house of the LORD.

This response shows us that the people have understood Jeremiah clearly. He has promised that the temple would be *like Shiloh,* a former site of the temple's predecessor, the tabernacle (Joshua 18:1). Shiloh was abandoned after the army of Israel was defeated by the Philistines around 1050 BC. In this battle, the ark of the covenant was captured (1 Samuel 4:4, 10–11), a national disaster for Israel.

Initially, Jeremiah's words find no listeners who take them to heart. There is no repentance, only hostility to the messenger. Even though Jeremiah claims to speak *in the name of the Lord,* his message is rejected by *all the people.* Instead, they continue to believe the temple's false prophets, who have assured them of future peace and prosperity (for example, Jeremiah 23:16).

> **What Do You Think?**
> When have you witnessed someone ridiculed or threatened for doing what was right?
>
> **Digging Deeper**
> How might you learn from the example of such people to live confidently and boldly in your own life?

III. Determined to Speak
(Jeremiah 26:12–15)

A. Assured Promise (vv. 12–13)

12. Then spake Jeremiah unto all the princes and to all the people, saying, The LORD sent me to prophesy against this house and against this city all the words that ye have heard.

Jeremiah's courage is on display here. Although he surely expects he will be executed, he takes a last opportunity to speak the word of the Lord. He reminds his audience that his message is not his own concoction but the prophecy *the Lord sent* him to deliver against *this house* (the temple) *and against this city* (Jerusalem). He is not pronouncing judgment based on his own standards; he is voicing the judgments of the Lord.

13. Therefore now amend your ways and your doings, and obey the voice of the LORD your God; and the LORD will repent him of the evil that he hath pronounced against you.

Jeremiah's summary advice is simple: *amend your ways* (repent) and *obey* the Lord's *voice* (follow the Law of Moses). Jeremiah promises that if the people repent (change their ways), the Lord will *repent* of *the evil* He has planned. We refer to this as conditional or contingent prophecy. The Lord reveals, through a prophet, the future that awaits if the people do not repent. This disastrous course lies in store for the people if nothing changes in their attitudes and actions.

B. Dire Warning (vv. 14–15)

14. As for me, behold, I am in your hand: do with me as seemeth good and meet unto you.

Having reiterated his message without compromise, Jeremiah submits himself to the *hand* of his enemies. He has been faithful to his call, and now he accepts the potential consequences. Implicit here is Jeremiah's faith in the Lord. Without such faith, he would not be able to confidently hand himself over to his enemies. This does not mean that Jeremiah knows it will go well for him. Rather, despite not knowing the outcome, he has faith in the one who called him. This was the right path for him to take, regardless of how it would end.

What Do You Think?

How have you had to entrust yourself to God's care for your well-being and safety?

Digging Deeper

What is an example of a way God might ask you to take a risk for the sake of Christ's kingdom?

15. But know ye for certain, that if ye put me to death, ye shall surely bring innocent blood upon yourselves, and upon this city, and upon the inhabitants thereof: for of a truth the LORD hath sent me unto you to speak all these words in your ears.

While he offers no resistance to his would-be executioners, Jeremiah issues a warning to them. He is *innocent,* so his death would be murder and bring *blood* upon his critics, Jerusalem, and all its citizens. His only "crime" would be the speaking of *truth* given by the *Lord* who *sent* him. We should remember that the shedding of *innocent blood* is one of the greatest crimes of which Jeremiah accuses the leaders of Israel (see Jeremiah 7:6; 22:3).

Jeremiah's pleas find a sympathetic response in some of the "princes" or elders of the land (Jeremiah 26:16). They intervene, and Jeremiah's life is spared (26:24), but there is no sign the people heed his warnings and repent. The destruction of Jerusalem promised by the Lord is still on track for fulfillment.

Conclusion

A. Each Christian's Call

Jeremiah knew from an early age that obeying the Lord's call would be difficult, even dangerous. His messages of future destruction would be unpopular among the ruling elite of Jerusalem, and they would sway the people against him. Yet he faithfully delivered these hard words, even at the risk of his own life.

Today, you may not be called to deliver God's words to elites in places of societal power. Your roles may be confined to your church, family, school, or workplace. Nevertheless, speaking truth may be just as challenging as it was for Jeremiah. As with Jeremiah, this may come upon you at a young age. Ministries of truth and service are not just for mature believers.

What inhibits you from assuming a more active ministry for the Lord? Do you think you are too young? Too inexperienced? Do you think you are too old? Do you think you don't know the Bible well enough? Do you think you are too busy? Are you slowed by fear of rejection?

Jeremiah likely felt many of these things. He could have lived a respectful life as a priest enjoying the quiet stability of a small village. The Lord had other plans for him. He was called to be God's spokesman of judgment to the elites of his land, even the great nations of his world. Although he did not seek or relish this responsibility, he faithfully carried it out. May we follow the example of brave Jeremiah in the calls to ministry that the Lord extends to every Christian.

B. Prayer

Lord, You know us intimately. May we yield our hearts to this loving relationship and find ways to serve You and Your people. May we never be fearful but always faithful. We pray in the name of the innocent one who was faithful unto death, Jesus our Lord. Amen.

C. Thought to Remember

Walk in obedient faith, not fear.

Visual for Lesson 5. *Display this visual and ask participants to reflect on Jeremiah's situation and the Lord's words of comfort to him.*

Involvement Learning

Enhance your lesson with KJV Bible Student *(from your curriculum supplier) and the reproducible activity page (at www.standardlesson.com or in the back of the* KJV Standard Lesson Commentary Deluxe Edition*).*

Into the Lesson

Begin by writing this question on the board:

What would you do if you were not afraid of failing?

Distribute an index card to each participant and ask them to write down answers to these questions: 1–What aspirations do you have? 2–How does fear of failure prevent you from achieving those aspirations?

After one minute, ask for volunteers to share their answers with the class. (Many learners may not be comfortable with sharing. Be prepared to share your own answers.) Express gratitude for the volunteers and acknowledge the diversity of ideas.

Lead into the Bible study by saying, "In the Bible, there are many stories where people first told God they couldn't do what He asked because they were afraid. They made excuses. But God didn't change His mind about choosing them. Today, we will talk about someone like that: the prophet Jeremiah. Let's discover the reasons for his fear and the excuse he gave."

Into the Word

Divide the class into the **Prophet's Call Group** and the **Prophet's Challenge Group**. Distribute handouts (you create) of the following questions for in-group discussion.

Prophet's Call Group. Read Jeremiah 1:6–10. 1–What was Jeremiah's initial reaction to God's call? 2–How does God respond to Jeremiah's hesitation? 3–What promises does God make to Jeremiah to assure him?

Prophet's Challenge Group. Read Jeremiah 26:8–9, 12–15. 1–What was the response of the officials and people when Jeremiah spoke at the temple? 2–How did Jeremiah defend his actions and message? 3–What can we learn from Jeremiah's response to opposition and danger?

Direct each group to present their findings to the class. Facilitate a discussion on Jeremiah's initial apprehensions and how those fears and hesitations were transformed.

Option. Ask a volunteer to read Isaiah 6:1–8. In a whole-class discussion, compare Jeremiah's reaction to God's call with Isaiah's response to God's call.

Distribute highlighters and copies of the Scripture text of Jeremiah 26:8–9, 12–15. Instruct the **Prophet's Call Group** to highlight every word spoken by Jeremiah and the **Prophet's Challenge Group** to highlight every word spoken by the Lord.

Alternative. Distribute copies of the "Prophet's Words" exercise from the activity page, which you can download. Have learners work in small groups to complete as indicated.

After calling time for either activity, have groups present their findings before the class. Ask, "At what point in the passage do you observe Jeremiah transition from speaking out of fear to speaking with conviction?"

Into Life

Say, "Today's lesson highlights that God can use individuals, regardless of age or natural ability." Invite learners to brainstorm ideas for intergenerational congregational ministry. Record their ideas on the board.

Choose a ministry from the options on the board and have participants work in pairs to create a description of the ministry. Direct pairs to consider how the ministry could include youth in its leadership. After five minutes, reconvene the class and ask volunteers to share their ideas. Encourage learners to pray about their concept over the week and consider proposing it to the church's leadership.

Option. Distribute copies of the "Divine Call" activity from the activity page. Have learners complete it individually in a minute or less before discussing conclusions in small groups.

October 12
Lesson 6 (KJV)

Jeremiah's Message

Devotional Reading: Luke 6:40–46
Background Scripture: Jeremiah 7:1–26

Jeremiah 7:1–11, 21–23

1 The word that came to Jeremiah from the LORD, saying,

2 Stand in the gate of the LORD's house, and proclaim there this word, and say, Hear the word of the LORD, all ye of Judah, that enter in at these gates to worship the LORD.

3 Thus saith the LORD of hosts, the God of Israel, Amend your ways and your doings, and I will cause you to dwell in this place.

4 Trust ye not in lying words, saying, The temple of the LORD, The temple of the LORD, The temple of the LORD, are these.

5 For if ye throughly amend your ways and your doings; if ye throughly execute judgment between a man and his neighbour;

6 If ye oppress not the stranger, the fatherless, and the widow, and shed not innocent blood in this place, neither walk after other gods to your hurt:

7 Then will I cause you to dwell in this place, in the land that I gave to your fathers, for ever and ever.

8 Behold, ye trust in lying words, that cannot profit.

9 Will ye steal, murder, and commit adultery, and swear falsely, and burn incense unto Baal, and walk after other gods whom ye know not;

10 And come and stand before me in this house, which is called by my name, and say, We are delivered to do all these abominations?

11 Is this house, which is called by my name, become a den of robbers in your eyes? Behold, even I have seen it, saith the LORD.

---

21 Thus saith the LORD of hosts, the God of Israel; Put your burnt offerings unto your sacrifices, and eat flesh.

22 For I spake not unto your fathers, nor commanded them in the day that I brought them out of the land of Egypt, concerning burnt offerings or sacrifices:

23 But this thing commanded I them, saying, Obey my voice, and I will be your God, and ye shall be my people: and walk ye in all the ways that I have commanded you, that it may be well unto you.

Key Text

This thing commanded I them, saying, Obey my voice, and I will be your God, and ye shall be my people: and walk ye in all the ways that I have commanded you, that it may be well unto you. —**Jeremiah 7:23**

Judah, from Isaiah
to the Exile

Unit 2: Jeremiah and the Promise of Renewal

Lessons 5–9

Lesson Aims

After participating in this lesson, each learner will be able to:

1. State what the Lord had commanded the people when He brought them out of Egypt.
2. Contrast the Judeans' daily activities with their temple worship practices.
3. Write a note that expresses gratitude to God for His rescue during a time of injustice.

Lesson Outline

Introduction

A. Trusting Lying Words

While doing short-term missions work in a foreign country, I once bought a name-brand wristwatch for a low price. I was told by the seller that his watches were "seconds" from a factory in China that he obtained because they had minor defects. I loved that stylish timekeeper for a couple of years until it quit working. When I took it to a jeweler to have the battery replaced, he told me the watch was a fake. It was so convincing, he did not realize it until he removed its back and saw its cheap innards. Have you ever trusted in lies or deception, buying something you later realized was a fake?

Jeremiah identified the danger of trusting "lying words" as he spoke to the people of Jerusalem 2,600 years ago. The reason for his warning still holds true today, and the consequences in spiritual matters are far more serious than that of a fake watch.

B. Lesson Context

As mentioned in Lesson 5, chapters 7 and 26 in the book of Jeremiah seem to be describing the same event, sometimes called the "Temple Sermon." This is shortly after the death of King Josiah in a battle against the Egyptians in 609 BC (2 Kings 23:29). Various indicators suggest that Jeremiah's message in today's lesson was delivered early in the reign of King Jehoiakim (originally named Eliakim), son of Josiah (Jeremiah 1:3; 26:1). Jehoiakim had been installed by Pharaohnechoh as a vassal ruler who was required to pay a steep tribute to Egypt (2 Kings 23:34–35). Jehoiakim ruled for 11 years but was eventually exiled to Babylon after he rebelled against Nebuchadnezzar (2 Chronicles 36:5–6). Jehoiakim's evil influence is evident in the nearly two dozen mentions of his name in the book of Jeremiah.

By profession, Jeremiah was a priest who lived in the village of Anathoth (Jeremiah 1:1), about three miles northeast of Jerusalem. Regarding his appointment to be a prophet, see last week's lesson. A trip from Anathoth to the temple would have taken him an hour or so. This made it possible for him to come quickly to the temple in his role as a prophet and deliver a message from the Lord.

I. Message Introduced

(Jeremiah 7:1–2)

A. Imperative for the Prophet (vv. 1–2a)

1–2a. The word that came to Jeremiah from the LORD, saying, Stand in the gate of the LORD's house, and proclaim there this word, and say.

The primary task of a prophet is to communicate God's *word* to whomever He directs. And Jeremiah receives direction in this regard numerous times in the book that bears his name.

The gate of the Lord's house, where the message is to be proclaimed, is a strategic choice of location. The content of the message that is to come establishes why this is so.

B. Imperative for the People (v. 2b)

2b. Hear the word of the LORD, all ye of Judah, that enter in at these gates to worship the LORD.

The message is targeted specifically toward those Judeans who *enter in at these gates to worship the Lord.* The sheer size of the territory of Judah, encompassing some 3,400 square miles, means that not all Judeans can make it to Jerusalem on a weekly basis to worship at the temple. So we don't really know how big the prophet's audience is. If it's during a yearly pilgrimage observance, the crowd could be many times larger than the average weekly attendance (Exodus 23:14–17; Deuteronomy 16:16).

II. Change Needed

(Jeremiah 7:3–4)

A. The Right Solution (v. 3)

3. Thus saith the LORD of hosts, the God of Israel, Amend your ways and your doings, and I will cause you to dwell in this place.

Jeremiah identifies the source of his message with the synonymous expressions *the Lord of hosts* and *the God of Israel.* The two are one and the same. This doubled expression is a favorite of Jeremiah's. The two designations occur together more than 30 times in this book, compared to fewer than 10 times in the rest of the Old Testament. The *hosts* in this sense are armies (see Jeremiah 50:25), the armies of heaven. Jeremiah's message is a simple if-then statement, with the words *if* and *then* being unstated although implied at this point; both will be stated plainly a bit later.

The positive action to take is stated with the word *amend.* The evil *ways* to be amended have just been specified in Jeremiah 6. These involve oppression, wickedness, and corruption (6:6–7, 28), among other sins.

B. The Wrong Solution (v. 4)

4. Trust ye not in lying words, saying, The temple of the LORD, The temple of the LORD, The temple of the LORD, are these.

The foundational change is that the people must decide where they will place their *trust.* Will the people choose what they want to hear rather than what they need to hear, or vice versa? *Lying words* characterize the messages of the false prophets (Jeremiah 5:31; 14:14–15; 23:9–32). This problem is central to Jeremiah's message throughout the book.

Apparently, the people have been told by these charlatans that *the temple of the Lord* is inviolable and eternal. Thus they place their trust in a building rather than in the one whom the building is to honor (Jeremiah 7:14). The people seem to reason that if God intended to preserve the temple, then they, too, were protected from harm, regardless of their actions. Yet Jeremiah reminded them that, as far back as the time of King Hezekiah, they had been warned that the destruction of the temple was a possibility (26:18–19).

> **What Do You Think?**
> What attracts people to believing or trusting in lies?
>
> **Digging Deeper**
> How might God's people protect against believing falsehoods?

III. Outcomes Desired

(Jeremiah 7:5–7)

A. Be Just (v. 5)

5. For if ye thoroughly amend your ways and

your doings; if ye thoroughly execute judgment between a man and his neighbour.

Jeremiah goes on to specify the actions (*ways* and *doings*) that must change as trust is redirected. He demands an overhaul of the people's behaviors that have brought the Lord displeasure. Right behaviors logically involve two general categories: things *to do* and things *not to do.* To *thoroughly execute judgment* fits the first category.

B. Cease Oppression (v. 6a)

6a. If ye oppress not the stranger, the fatherless, and the widow, and shed not innocent blood in this place.

Now the prophet turns to the second category, things *not* to do. Interestingly, *oppress not* later becomes the positive action "deliver him that is spoiled out of the hand of the oppressor" (Jeremiah 21:12). God's concern is for *the stranger* (non-Israelite foreigners who live among the residents of Judah), *the fatherless* (orphans), and *the widow* (women who have lost the financial security of having a husband). God's concern for this triad of the most vulnerable people is seen numerous times throughout the Old Testament (Deuteronomy 27:19, etc.). All three categories of people live day-to-day, destitute and susceptible to exploitation. That Jeremiah even needs to mention them indicates the callous attitude his hearers have toward the neediest among them (compare Jeremiah 5:28).

The person who seems to have led the way in the shedding of *innocent blood* is King Manasseh, who reigned over Judah a few decades earlier (2 Kings 21:16; 24:3–4). This refers to what have been called "judicial murders": the execution of innocent people resulting from the perversion of the courts. This is the antithesis of justice. The fact that the courts are being used for killing indicates violation of the ninth commandment, against false testimony (Exodus 20:16) and the sixth commandment, against murder (20:13). An Old Testament example of judicial murder is that of Naboth the Jezreelite (1 Kings 21). The most obvious example of the same in the New Testament is, of course, the crucifixion of Jesus (Matthew 26:59–61; 27:4). Jeremiah himself barely escapes this fate (Jeremiah 26:12–15).

C. Reject Idolatry (v. 6b)

6b. Neither walk after other gods to your hurt.

The worship of *other gods* is warned against and condemned numerous times in the Old Testament and is the first of the Ten Commandments (Exodus 20:3; Deuteronomy 5:7). To engage in such a practice is to worship idols (Isaiah 2:8, 20). The false prophets and evil kings lead the way in this regard (2 Kings 21:1–11; Jeremiah 2:8).

The sins of King Manasseh were so great that they became the primary factor in the Lord's decision to punish Judah (Jeremiah 15:4). Manasseh reached the depth of spiritual depravity by sacrificing his son to a false god (2 Kings 21:6). Thus the sin of shedding innocent blood (considered above) connects with idol worship (compare Psalm 106:38). As Jeremiah warns, the Lord will not overlook such horrendous wickedness. The sin of idol worship is so serious that it is likened to adultery (Jeremiah 3:6–13; Ezekiel 23).

This self-delusion results in self-*hurt* as the people miss out on blessings from the real God. Instead, the people reap a harvest of what they've sown (Proverbs 11:18–19; 22:8; Galatians 6:7–8).

D. Dwell in the Land (v. 7)

7. Then will I cause you to dwell in this place, in the land that I gave to your fathers, for ever and ever.

This verse completes the if-then statement. If the people repent and abandon their oppressive and ungodly behavior, a promise awaits. The Lord will allow them to continue to live in Jerusalem and the surrounding regions of Judah and Ben-

How to Say It

Anathoth	*An*-uh-thoth.
Baal	*Bay*-ul.
Jehoiakim	Jeh-*hoy*-uh-kim.
Jezreelite	*Jez*-ree-el-ite.
Josiah	Jo-*sigh*-uh.
Manasseh	Muh-*nass*-uh.
Nebuchadnezzar	*Neb*-yuh-kud-***nez***-er.
Pharaohnechoh	*Fair*-o-*nee*-kow.

jamin, *the land that* the Lord *gave to* their *fathers.* Reference to this land invites a consideration of the time scale involved: the residents of Judah have been in the promised land for over 800 years! This is more than enough time for the people to have noticed and taken to heart the consequences of disobedience and the promises of obedience. But the people continually misinterpret events.

IV. Hypocrisy Exposed

(Jeremiah 7:8–11, 21–23)

A. Misplaced Trust (v. 8)

8. Behold, ye trust in lying words, that cannot profit.

Jeremiah's message moves to the heart of the people's moral dysfunction. They have completely believed the *lying words* of their evil leaders and false prophets. This especially indicts the false prophets who have gained influence over the people. While lives built on lies may seem rewarding in the short term, God will not allow dishonesty and corruption to thrive in the long run. Those who believe lies *cannot profit* in the end. False prophets fail to yield profits!

Consequences of Blind Trust

Alana, a trusting young woman, met a charming young man online named Michael. They quickly forged a friendship, and soon Alana was falling deeply for him. Michael seemed genuinely interested in her. She became captivated by him.

Michael charmed her with gifts, making all types of promises of a fairy-tale future. She never questioned his stories, although some details seemed inconsistent. Michael claimed he was an only child and that his parents were dead. When asked about his friends, he gave excuses for why Alana couldn't meet them.

One day, Alana got a frantic call from Michael saying he had an emergency and needed to borrow a large sum of money. Assured that he would pay her back, Alana agreed without hesitation. She met Michael and handed over the money.

That was the last day Alana saw Michael. Weeks turned into months; he was nowhere to be found. His cell phone was disconnected. The company that he said he worked for confirmed he was never an employee. It was all a lie. Have you ever been deceived by someone? Were there signs you missed seeing that could have cued you into the lies?

—S. S.

B. Sin and Idolatry (v. 9)

9. Will ye steal, murder, and commit adultery, and swear falsely, and burn incense unto Baal, and walk after other gods whom ye know not.

Jeremiah's indictment includes charges of breaking six of the Ten Commandments (see Exodus 20:1–17; Deuteronomy 5:7–21). These are the prohibitions against theft (eighth commandment), *murder* (sixth), *adultery* (seventh), false witness (ninth), worship of *Baal* as an idol (second), and following *other gods* (first). The charge of idolatry is the most serious, and Baal is one of those "other gods." Jeremiah refers to Baal 12 times in his book, and in two of those cases the designation *Baal* is plural (Jeremiah 2:23; 9:14). Prophesying a century before Jeremiah, the prophet Hosea warned the northern kingdom of divided Israel likewise concerning the Baals (Hosea 2:13, 17; 11:2). They didn't listen either.

> **What Do You Think?**
>
> Why is it so easy to justify sinful behavior?
>
> **Digging Deeper**
>
> Where do you see hypocrisy present in your own life?

C. Deluded Thinking (vv. 10–11)

10. And come and stand before me in this house, which is called by my name, and say, We are delivered to do all these abominations?

It is not hard to imagine that Jeremiah's voice crescendos to a peak with this verse. He directly calls out their hypocrisy. Coming into the temple, "the Lord's house" (Jeremiah 7:2, above), and not experiencing pangs of guilt and remorse shows the depth of their depravity. They stand in the temple court believing they *are delivered* (allowed) to continue *to do all these abominations.*

11. Is this house, which is called by my name, become a den of robbers in your eyes? Behold, even I have seen it, saith the LORD.

Jeremiah's word from the Lord concludes this section by repeating the temple's designation as a *house, which is called by* the Lord's *name.* It is the Lord's "dwelling place" (Psalm 76:2), His "holy mountain" (Joel 3:17), a place where the people of Israel come to encounter their God. But more than that, it is the "Lord's house," a place to which the Lord has allowed His name to be attached. This means God's reputation is at stake. Unfortunately, since it has become *a den of robbers,* then the Lord's name has been dishonored. Tragically, God judges this to be the case, affirming, "*I have seen it.*"

Centuries later, Jesus draws on the imagery of this verse when He cleanses the temple (Matthew 21:13; Mark 11:17; Luke 19:46). At least one issue at that time will be the same as in Jeremiah's day: the corrupt temple leadership takes advantage of the weak for their own gain. Even worse, the temple leaders of Jesus' day plot His death so that they can hold on to their own power (John 11:48).

> **What Do You Think?**
> What are actions you deem inappropriate for doing inside a dedicated place of worship?
> **Digging Deeper**
> Are such actions inappropriate in some places but appropriate elsewhere?

D. Useless Sacrifice (vv. 21–23)

21. Thus saith the LORD of hosts, the God of Israel; Put your burnt offerings unto your sacrifices, and eat flesh.

Jeremiah's repeated use of the extended title *the Lord of hosts, the God of Israel* (see Jeremiah 7:3, above) underlines the serious tone of this section as the prophet introduces sarcasm. In effect, Jeremiah is saying, "Go right on ahead and continue violating the rules about *burnt offerings,* and see how things turn out!"

Burnt offerings were sacrifices in which a whole animal was burned on the altar in the courtyard of the temple, a task that Jeremiah himself had likely undertaken as a priest. Such a sacrifice would be fully consumed by fire (see Exodus 29:18; Leviticus 1, 6:8–13). The phrase *unto your sacrifices* refers to the general (and generally improper) way the original readers are conducting all their sacrifices, burnt offerings being only one part of those.

> **What Do You Think?**
> What are ways Christians might perform the right action but lack the right heart posture?
> **Digging Deeper**
> How can we develop a greater awareness of when we are merely "going through the motions"?

22. For I spake not unto your fathers, nor commanded them in the day that I brought them out of the land of Egypt, concerning burnt offerings or sacrifices.

Some have claimed that this verse nullifies the entire sacrificial system of Israel and its temple as a later addition to the duties of the people of Israel, but this is unlikely. Jeremiah has high respect for the Pentateuch (the first five books of the Old Testament), which include detailed instructions on *burnt offerings or sacrifices.* We must understand the message here in light of the next verse.

23. But this thing commanded I them, saying, Obey my voice, and I will be your God, and ye shall be my people: and walk ye in all the ways that I have commanded you, that it may be well unto you.

Simply put, proper sacrifices result from obeying the *voice* of God. While performing temple rituals may have quieted the consciences of some of the people, they must listen to the Lord's *voice* and walk *in all the ways* that He has commanded, not just some of them or just the ones that are most convenient. Obedience to the law is required. But that by itself isn't enough. God does not delight in insincere sacrifices (see Amos 5:22). Without the correct posture of heart and subsequent action, their sacrifices are useless and meaningless (Hosea 6:6; Matthew 9:13; 12:7).

In Jeremiah's situation, no one seems to listen and repent (Jeremiah 8:6). His numerous enemies include "the kings of Judah, . . . the princes thereof, . . . the priests thereof, and . . . the people of the land" (1:18).

Some readers today may wonder whether Jeremiah holds out hope that some will heed his message, turn from their wickedness, and claim the promise of future blessing. That's a natural question to ask, but the more important idea is that when the fair warning proves to be true, the reality of who is a true prophet of God and who is not will be established (Jeremiah 28:9).

What Do You Think?
How does obeying God's Word affect your relationship with Him?

Digging Deeper
What are ways to foster obedience to God from a place of love, joy, and delight?

Comfort in God's Ways

When life feels full and difficult, I wrongly tend to seek comfort in control. At such times, if something doesn't go my way, I get frustrated. Too often I find myself fighting against the Lord's ways, insisting on my own instead.

However, as much as the allure of control may drive and attract me, eventually I realize that my actions are causing harm. Choosing my own stubbornness wreaks havoc on my closest relationships. Instead of submitting to the way of love and humility, I fume—alone—in my stubborn anger.

Once I finally yield to God's ways, I find true comfort and peace. Taking the Lord's way—heeding how He wants us to live our lives in relationship with Him and with one another—gives life. Along such paths, it will go well with us. When are times you struggle with submitting to God's ways, taking your own paths instead? How can you work toward returning to His ways more readily in the future? —J. J. S.

Conclusion

A. Trusting the Wrong Thing

Like Jeremiah's audience for the "Temple Sermon," Christians have been known to place their trust in things that are temporary. Individual churches rise and fall in every community. Powerful preachers and teachers do not last forever. Glorious structures once full of worshipers may become condominiums or nightclubs. How can we avoid trusting in the earthly and temporary?

Visual for Lesson 6. *Point to this visual and ask participants to suggest ways they can walk in obedience in the upcoming week.*

The false solution held by the original hearers of Jeremiah's sermon was a vacuous mantra, "The temple of the Lord! The temple of the Lord! The temple of the Lord!" They viewed the building itself as a kind of talisman or good-luck charm. They refused to face divine reality even after its destruction (Jeremiah 44:17–18).

The underlying themes of Jeremiah's plea still apply. The Lord wants a relationship based on our willing obedience, not insincere ritual. The Lord wants worship that comes from sincere hearts, not just the trappings of outward devotion. While Jeremiah died 25 centuries ago, his message is timeless. We are wise to heed his call to hear the voice of the Lord and respond with repentance and obedience.

B. Prayer

Father, may we listen to Your voice as found in Scripture and respond with repentance and obedience. We pray in the name of Jesus, who values mercy more than sacrifice. Amen.

C. Thought to Remember

False prophets yield false profits.

Involvement Learning

Enhance your lesson with KJV Bible Student *(from your curriculum supplier) and the reproducible activity page (at www.standardlesson.com or in the back of the* KJV Standard Lesson Commentary Deluxe Edition*).*

Into the Lesson

Ask participants to brainstorm traditions specific to your congregation. Write responses on the board. Ask if anyone knows the history of these traditions and how they began in the congregation. Participants should be allowed to use smartphones to research the history of these traditions if needed.

As time allows, ask when people have tried to change traditions and failed. Include a discussion regarding why the attempt to make changes failed.

Lead into the Bible study by saying, "Change can be difficult. Many people find security in traditions and preferences. In today's lesson, we will see how a refusal to change, despite God's prompting, ultimately led to God's judgment of Judah."

Into the Word

Divide participants into pairs. Ask participants to recount an instance when they only got half the story right. Then ask participants to explain what happened when they learned the "whole story" and their reaction after that realization. Encourage pairs to create a definition of *half-truth*. Reconvene the class and allow each pair to share their definitions.

Have a volunteer read aloud Jeremiah 7:1–11, 21–23. Use the following questions for whole-class discussion of how the people may have been guilty of worshiping with half-truths: 1–What did the Lord command the people when He brought them out of Egypt? 2–In what ways had the people not been obedient to this command? 3–How had the people demonstrated their trust in half-truths: "lying words, that cannot profit" (Jeremiah 7:8)? 4–How would you summarize Jeremiah's message in this passage?

Ask a volunteer to reread Jeremiah 7:23 aloud. Conclude this section by asking the following questions for whole-class discussion: 1–How would you describe the relationship between God and His people? 2–How could the people obey God and walk in His commands?

Option. Distribute copies of the "A Den of Robbers" exercise from the activity page, which you can download. Have learners work in pairs to complete as indicated. After calling time, ask volunteers to share results.

Option 2. Share the "rest of the story" with your participants by saying, "Not long after Jeremiah confronted the people, the Babylonians conquered Jerusalem, destroyed the temple, and placed many residents of Judah into exile. God gave the people opportunities to repent. He warned them that their disobedience would lead to their destruction. They didn't listen."

Into Life

Ask participants to spend one minute in personal self-reflection about a time when God rescued them from a time of oppression or injustice. Invite them to share their examples with the whole class.

Distribute an index card and pen to each participant. Direct participants to write a note of gratitude to God for His rescue during a time of oppression or injustice. Remind your students that God warns and gives numerous opportunities for us to repent and turn back to Him. We shouldn't take that for granted. Such a loving God deserves our love and obedience.

Conclude class time by asking for volunteers to read their prayers out loud as an act of corporate prayer.

Alternative. Distribute copies of the "Expression of Gratitude" exercise from the activity page. Offer the exercise as a take-home activity and encourage completion by reminding learners that they will have time to share results in the next class if they desire.

A Family's Example

Devotional Reading: 2 Corinthians 6:16–7:4
Background Scripture: Jeremiah 35:1–19

Jeremiah 35:5–11

5 And I set before the sons of the house of the Rechabites pots full of wine, and cups, and I said unto them, Drink ye wine.

6 But they said, We will drink no wine: for Jonadab the son of Rechab our father commanded us, saying, Ye shall drink no wine, neither ye, nor your sons for ever:

7 Neither shall ye build house, nor sow seed, nor plant vineyard, nor have any: but all your days ye shall dwell in tents; that ye may live many days in the land where ye be strangers.

8 Thus have we obeyed the voice of Jonadab the son of Rechab our father in all that he hath charged us, to drink no wine all our days, we, our wives, our sons, nor our daughters;

9 Nor to build houses for us to dwell in: neither have we vineyard, nor field, nor seed:

10 But we have dwelt in tents, and have obeyed, and done according to all that Jonadab our father commanded us.

11 But it came to pass, when Nebuchadrezzar king of Babylon came up into the land, that we said, Come, and let us go to Jerusalem for fear of the army of the Chaldeans, and for fear of the army of the Syrians: so we dwell at Jerusalem.

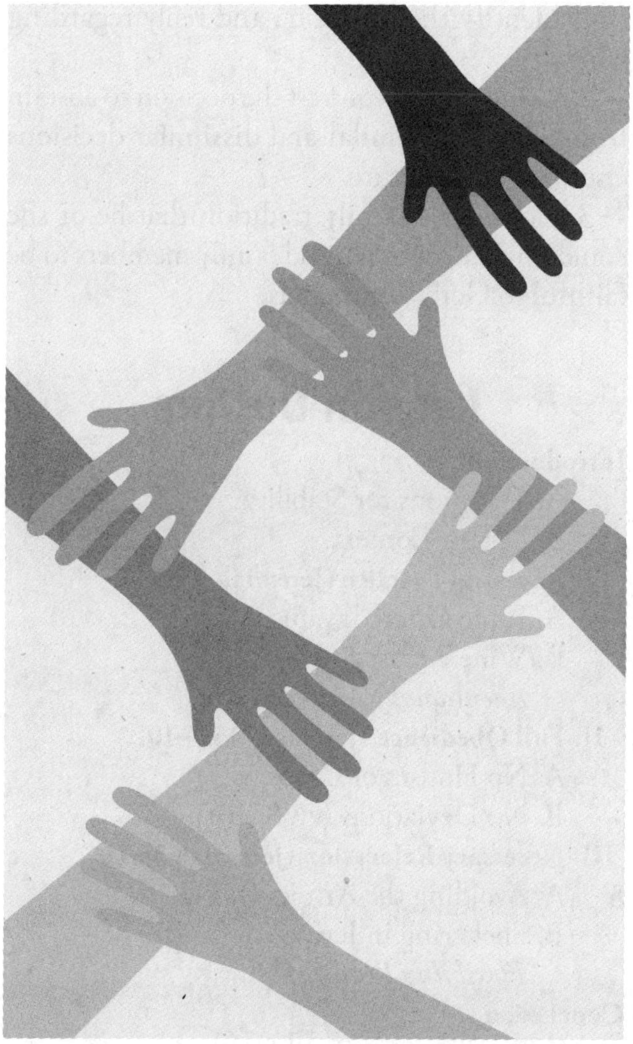

Key Text

For unto this day they drink none, but obey their father's commandment. —**Jeremiah 35:14b**

Visual © Getty Images

Judah, from Isaiah
to the Exile

Unit 2: Jeremiah and the Promise of Renewal

Lessons 5–9

Lesson Aims

After participating in this lesson, each learner will be able to:

1. Identify the invitation and reply regarding wine.

2. Compare and contrast the decision to abstain from wine with similar and dissimilar decisions elsewhere in Scripture.

3. Consider a family tradition that he or she could implement to remind family members to be faithful to God's commands.

Lesson Outline

Introduction
- A. Traditions for Stability
- B. Lesson Context

I. Ancestral Practice (Jeremiah 35:5–6)
- A. Wine Offered (v. 5)
- B. Wine Refused (v. 6)
  - *Intentionally Marked*

II. Full Obedience (Jeremiah 35:7–10)
- A. No Houses or Crops (v. 7)
- B. No Deviations (vv. 8–10)

III. Necessary Relocation (Jeremiah 35:11)
- A. Avoiding the Armies (v. 11a)
- B. Sheltering in Jerusalem (v. 11b)
  - *Flexibility Required*

Conclusion
- A. Traditions for Faithfulness
- B. Prayer
- C. Thought to Remember

Introduction

A. Traditions for Stability

In the musical *Fiddler on the Roof*, viewers are oriented by the first and well-known song, "Tradition." The main character, Tevya, acts as a guide throughout the song, telling how traditions help his Jewish community maintain its sense of balance and cohesiveness. After describing one of the traditions he and his fellow Jews follow, Tevya raises a question: "How did this tradition get started? I'll tell you. I don't know." Then he adds emphatically, "But it's a tradition. And because of our traditions, every one of us knows who he is and what God expects him to do." Later Tevya declares that, without the traditions guiding him and his fellow Jews, "our lives would be as shaky as a fiddler on the roof."

That's an interesting philosophy, and it can be very appealing with regard to family unity. But a given tradition's ultimate value is validated only insofar as it aligns with God's Word (Matthew 15:1–7; compare Luke 14:26). Today's Scripture text from the book of Jeremiah invites us to explore this connection.

B. Lesson Context

Today's lesson is the third in a series of five from the book of Jeremiah. The overall context is the same as those: Jeremiah's 40-year prophetic ministry was to warn the people of Judah of God's judgment to come at the hands of the Babylonians. This was to happen because of the Judeans' sinfulness and rebellion against the Lord.

Our Scripture text for today's lesson records events that took place "in the days of Jehoiakim the son of Josiah king of Judah," which is the period 609–598 BC (Jeremiah 35:1). To understand the significance of this time frame, we should view it against the larger backdrop of three chronological pressure points of Babylonian dominance in Palestine. Those three are the years 605, 597, and 586 BC; they are the years the Judeans were carried into exile in successive stages (2 Kings 24:1, 12; 25:1–21). The reference in Jeremiah 35:11 to a family's relocation to Jerusalem due to Babylonian incursion indicates that the invasion of 605 BC is in view.

Those were indeed turbulent times. In an earthly sense, there were power struggles between the world powers of Assyria and Babylon. Nineveh, the capital of Assyria, fell in 612 BC. Babylon's victory at the epic Battle of Carchemish in 605 BC (Jeremiah 46:2) meant the passing of one oppressor only to be replaced by a new one. Is it any wonder that Jeremiah felt inadequate for his task (1:6)?

The incident in today's text occurred at roughly the halfway point in Jeremiah's 40-year efforts to convince God's people to repent of their wrongdoing and return to the Lord. These efforts included use of some rather striking visual aids as teaching tools, all commanded by God: a soiled linen "girdle" or sash (Jeremiah 13:1–11), a visit to a potter's house (18:1–11), and the wearing of a makeshift yoke to symbolize submission to Babylon (27:1–7). Today's Scripture text records yet another visual aid by which Jeremiah tried to appeal to an increasingly wayward people.

A footnote: Jeremiah 35:3 mentions "Jaazaniah the son of Jeremiah," but he is a different Jeremiah than the prophet (compare Jeremiah 1:1 with 35:3).

I. Ancestral Practice

(Jeremiah 35:5–6)

A. Wine Offered (v. 5)

5. And I set before the sons of the house of the Rechabites pots full of wine, and cups, and I said unto them, Drink ye wine.

The opening verses of Jeremiah 35 establish the time, place, and persons of the teaching illustration that is about to unfold. Jeremiah is meeting with *the sons of the house of the Rechabites* and offering them *wine* to *drink* because of the Lord's command to do so (Jeremiah 35:2). Other than in this chapter of Jeremiah, the Bible reveals little about the Rechabites. A genealogy listing locates them as being from the tribe of Judah (1 Chronicles 2:55), at least at first glance. A closer look, however, reveals that they are descendants of "the Kenites," whose identity, loyalty, and actions are sketched in Numbers 24:21–22; Judges 1:16; 4:11, 17; and 1 Samuel 15:6.

What Do You Think?

Consider a recent time when your deeply held convictions were challenged. What did you do?

Digging Deeper

Looking back on that situation, how would God have been honored or dishonored if you had acted differently?

B. Wine Refused (v. 6)

6. But they said, We will drink no wine: for Jonadab the son of Rechab our father commanded us, saying, Ye shall drink no wine, neither ye, nor your sons for ever.

The Rechabites' response to Jeremiah's offer is immediate and firm: *We will drink no wine.* They base this decision on the instructions of *Jonadab the son of Rechab,* a forefather of some 200 years previous. He was a prominent leader among the Rechabites during the time of King Jehu (reigned 841–814 BC). Jonadab knew the king personally and had been invited on a "ride along" to help the king abolish idol worship in Samaria, part of the northern kingdom of divided Israel (2 Kings 10:15–17). The southern kingdom of Judah was not immune to such influences, as Jeremiah well knew (Jeremiah 11:13; 32:35, etc.).

Jonadab's specific reason for the prohibition is unknown. Wine is depicted in both positive and cautionary ways, depending on the context. In the Old Testament, wine is depicted as a source of refreshment and delight (Psalm 104:15; Zechariah 10:7) and is associated with the blessing of the Lord (Genesis 27:28; Deuteronomy 7:13; 11:14). Wine was used during celebratory occasions (Genesis 14:17–20; Isaiah 25:6), though it certainly was possible to abuse it as illustrated by Noah (Genesis 9:20–23; compare Proverbs 23:29–35; Isaiah 5:11, 22).

Wine was prohibited to those engaged in special service to the Lord (Leviticus 10:8–9) and to those who had taken a Nazarite vow (Numbers 6:1–3). At the same time, wine was included in certain offerings to the Lord (Leviticus 23:13; Numbers 15:5, etc.). Cups of wine are also used to symbolize the wrath and judgment of the Lord (Psalm 75:8; Revelation 14:10; 16:19).

The book of Jeremiah itself illustrates this variety of approaches to wine, using it to describe scenes of both celebration (Jeremiah 31:12) and judgment (25:15). Jeremiah even compared himself to a "drunken man . . . whom wine hath overcome," so disturbed was he at the lies being spread by the false prophets of his day (23:9).

Perhaps Jonadab desired his descendants to participate in the Nazarite vow (or something similar) in order to reflect passionate devotion to the Lord (compare Judges 13:1–7). Possibly such abstinence could serve as a deterrent to taking part in Baal worship or other pagan religious practices. Jeremiah 35:7, next, seems to offer the bigger-picture answer.

What Do You Think?

What are examples of traditions or habits you have inherited from a family member?

Digging Deeper

Which of these traditions or habits do you find fruitful? Which are potentially harmful?

Intentionally Marked

My grandfather loved to be the videographer at family gatherings. I saw a few of his clips when I was a kid, and there was something distinct in all of them: his trademark. We knew the films were his because at some point during filming, he would turn the camera upside down. He was known for his shenanigans, and not just when behind the camera. This quirky tradition marks every film he made.

As my grandfather's films bore his "trademark," my faith is marked by the things I do with consistency. It's often been easy for me to fall into patterns. Continued long enough, these patterns may become traditions. While these patterns can be good, at times—if I'm honest—they can be questionable. Perhaps like me, you adopt the same prayer posture or return to the same requests. Maybe you insist on doing your devotions at the same time each day. Occasionally, I wonder whether I've been as eager to follow God as I've been to follow my routines. When I recognize this, I ask God to help me see things in a new way. As you hold your own routines and traditions before your heavenly Father, what would He say about them? —B. R.

II. Full Obedience

(Jeremiah 35:7–10)

A. No Houses or Crops (v. 7)

7. Neither shall ye build house, nor sow seed, nor plant vineyard, nor have any: but all your days ye shall dwell in tents; that ye may live many days in the land where ye be strangers.

This verse offers some insight as to Jonadab's command to abstain from drinking wine. The restriction seems to be part of a larger pool of prohibitions to improve chances of long life. The picture of living *in tents* is that of a nomadic, easily movable lifestyle as contrasted with a settled, agrarian one. The latter would require planting *seed* for the harvesting of grain and the cultivation of a *vineyard* for making wine (compare and contrast the use of the words *house(s)* and *vineyard(s)* in Deuteronomy 28:30; Isaiah 65:21–22; Jeremiah 32:15; etc.).

To forego all the trappings that accompany a settled life carries with it the possibility of both positive and negative results. The positive is the envisioned longer life, perhaps based on the idea that there won't be a temptation to resist an invading army to protect house and crops. In this sense the people of the tribe would be *strangers* in and to the land. There also would not be a temptation of defilement by mixing seed (Leviticus 19:19; Deuteronomy 22:9). Negatively, one can see a risk of legalism as human prohibitions add to and supersede God's Word (compare Matthew 15:1–9; Mark 7:9–13).

Various factors may have contributed to Jonadab's requirement of a mobile lifestyle. One should keep in mind the challenging times in which he lived in the 800s BC. The worship of Baal was heavily promoted in the northern kingdom of Israel, primarily by King Ahab, who was spurred on by his evil wife, Jezebel (1 Kings 21:25). Jezebel had no scruples whatsoever about seizing the vineyard of Naboth, a godly man whose devotion to the Lord's law prevented him from selling his vineyard to Ahab, who had his heart set on possessing it (1 Kings 21:1–7). The depth of her depravity is evident in the steps she took to have Naboth executed on false charges so Ahab could have his vineyard (21:8–16). Perhaps Jonadab concluded that not owning property such as a vineyard was one way to avoid the malicious intentions of power-mad individuals such as Jezebel and Ahab. The Lord's prophets indicted ruthless men who abused their power and took houses and fields at will from those who had no ability to resist them (Micah 2:1–2, etc.). Perhaps for Jonadab and his fellow Rechabites, the philosophy was, "You can't lose what you don't have."

But there may be a simpler explanation still. Sale of property was highly restrictive in the promised land (Leviticus 25:13–34; Numbers 36). So perhaps Jonadab just decided to go with the flow that a nomadic lifestyle offered in the environment. Additionally, a nomadic lifestyle reflected that of the patriarch Abraham (Hebrews 11:9–10).

> **What Do You Think?**
> What about being a Christian causes you to feel like you "stand out" among others you know?
>
> **Digging Deeper**
> If asked about why your life shows these differences, how would you respond?

B. No Deviations (vv. 8–10)

8–9. Thus have we obeyed the voice of Jonadab the son of Rechab our father in all that he hath charged us, to drink no wine all our days, we, our wives, our sons, nor our daughters; nor to build houses for us to dwell in: neither have we vineyard, nor field, nor seed.

The Rechabites exhibit complete compliance to their ancestor Jonadab's desire. We don't know precisely how the Rechabites survived under such a restrictive lifestyle, but evidently they had up to that point. Perhaps Jonadab, again in deference to Abraham, taught his family to walk by faith and to trust that God would provide their daily needs.

> **What Do You Think?**
> What helps traditions or habits to "catch on" within a family?
>
> **Digging Deeper**
> What traditions or habits would you like to foster in your family or community? How would you help these "catch on"?

10. But we have dwelt in tents, and have obeyed, and done according to all that Jonadab our father commanded us.

More than 200 years have passed since Jonadab's lifetime, and the Rechabites remain faithful in their obedience to his requirements. The promised land had experienced much turmoil since his day, including the conquest of the northern kingdom in 722 BC. Yet the Rechabites find Jonadab's desire still valuable and workable. At some level, this can illustrate what God intends for His covenant people so that faithful obedience to Him can be passed on generation after generation.

III. Necessary Relocation
(Jeremiah 35:11)

A. Avoiding the Armies (v. 11a)

11a. But it came to pass, when Nebuchadrezzar king of Babylon came up into the land, that we said, Come, and let us go to Jerusalem for fear of the army of the Chaldeans, and for fear of the army of the Syrians.

Here we learn why the Rechabites are in Jerusalem and available to receive the invitation to drink wine. The Babylonian king *Nebuchadrezzar* (an alternate spelling of *Nebuchadnezzar*) had begun his invasion of Judah in 605 BC, the fourth year of Jehoiakim's reign (Jeremiah 25:1). Accordingly, the Rechabites' plan of relocation described in this verse may have occurred not long after they learned that Nebuchadnezzar and his troops were on their way. The Babylonians' brutality was probably well-known throughout the territory. This verse refers to them as *the Chaldeans*, which is another name for them.

The Rechabites calculated that it would be safer for them to enter well-fortified Jerusalem rather

Visual for Lesson 7. *As you discuss Jeremiah 35:10, point to this visual and ask participants to share a tradition that could point others to God.*

than risk being overrun by two armies. Jerusalem would in time prove unable to resist the Babylonians; several passages make clear that the Lord was allowing the Babylonians to serve as the instruments of His judgment in attacking Jerusalem (2 Chronicles 36:15–21; Jeremiah 34:1–2, etc.).

During their invasion of Judah, the Babylonians secure the assistance of other peoples. These include those who had once been subject to the Israelites and are eager for revenge. The Syrians had faced more dealings with the now-exiled northern kingdom of Israel since their territory lay just to the northeast of Israel. Conflicts between the Syrians and the northern kingdom became especially frequent during the reign of King Ahab and the ministries of the prophets Elijah and Elisha in the 800s BC (1 Kings 20–21; 2 Kings 6:8–7:20, etc.). But the Syrians had also come under the control of King David during the expansion of his kingdom (see 2 Samuel 8:5–6). We easily imagine that they were more than willing to administer any "payback."

B. Sheltering in Jerusalem (v. 11b)

11b. So we dwell at Jerusalem.

We can see from this turn of events that Jonadab's instructions about living as nomadic "strangers" were not considered inviolable. Should circumstances change and the Rechabites' find themselves threatened by deadly force, they did not see themselves to be betraying Jonadab by shifting to self-preservation mode. This may be seen as a kind of "rigid flexibility" or "flexible rigidity."

The point of this real-life illustration is driven home in the eight verses that follow this one. God, through the prophet Jeremiah, challenges the people of Judah and *Jerusalem* to learn from the Rechabites' example of faithfully following the instructions of their ancestor (Jeremiah 35:12–16). The message is delivered in the form of what is called an *a fortiori* argument. This kind of logical argument takes a "how much more" format, either stated or implied. Here, the idea is, "If the Rechabites can follow their ancestor's instructions faithfully, how much more should you residents of Judah follow the instructions of your heavenly Father?"

These *a fortiori* arguments in the Bible are particularly important in Paul's letter to the Romans for proving the reality of God's grace (Romans 5:9–10, 15, 17; 11:24). If only God's covenant people had followed the Lord's instructions that faithfully! Blessings awaited for doing so. Refusal to obey was inconsistent with logic.

Because they refused to listen to and obey the Lord's voice, judgment was inevitable. The final statement in Jeremiah's message to the people in this chapter conveys the Lord's disappointment: "I have spoken unto them, but they have not heard; and I have called unto them, but they have not answered" (Jeremiah 35:17).

How to Say It

a fortiori	a for-she-*or*-eye.
Ahab	*Ay*-hab.
Assyria	Uh-*sear*-e-uh.
Babylonians	Bab-ih-***low***-nee-unz.
Chaldeans	Kal-***dee***-unz.
Jaazaniah	Jay-ah-zuh-*nye*-uh.
Jonadab	*John*-uh-dab.
Kenite	*Ken*-ite.
Nazarite	*Naz*-uh-rite.
Nebuchadnezzar	*Neb*-yuh-kud-***nez***-er.
Nebuchadrezzar	*Neb*-uh-kad-***rez***-er.
Rechabites	*Reck*-uh-bites.
Samaria	Suh-*mare*-ee-uh.
Syrians	*Sear*-ee-unz.

Also notable is a contrast with King Jehoiakim in the next chapter (Jeremiah 36). That chapter opens by noting the time to be the fourth year of his reign, or about 605 BC (compare Jeremiah 25:1). Here, the Lord yet again tries to get the attention and obedience of both king and people, this time via a written scroll (36:1–3). With the Babylonian invasion underway (36:9), the message on the scroll did cause fear among the people, but not changed behavior (36:16).

In contrast with the Rechabites, King Jehoiakim did not follow the godly example of his father, Josiah (see 2 Kings 23:25). Instead of heeding God's message, Jehoiakim cut the scroll in pieces and burned them (Jeremiah 36:22–23). This demonstrated his utter contempt for God's words. This action contrasted sharply with that of his father, who in anguish tore not the message but his clothes when he realized how far the people had strayed from the Lord's words (2 Kings 22:11). Jehoiakim was demonstrating disrespect not only for his father, but for the Lord as well.

What Do You Think?

When have you had to reconsider a deeply held-to tradition or habit, whether to be consistent or to change course?

Digging Deeper

What sort of circumstances would justify the changing of a long-held tradition or habit?

Flexibility Required

When we have tried-and-true methods that faithfully produce good results, it can be difficult—and sometimes even unnecessary—to question our ways. But occasionally, extenuating circumstances upend "the way we've always done it."

This was certainly the case in education in recent years. During the initial months of the COVID-19 lockdown, remote instruction became the norm for teachers all over the world. Overnight, their tried-and-true methods no longer worked. Activities and methods always used to teach certain concepts were set aside. Faced with unprecedented months of being unable to gather in person, it was clear that something needed to change.

Such necessary adaptations didn't mean that the former ways were bad. Rather, new circumstances demanded a shift. We can struggle to know when to hold fast to our traditions and when we should loosen our grips due to a change in circumstances. The important qualifier is what God is asking from us, not what makes us comfortable. Is there a tradition that you need to bring before God, asking for His wisdom to evaluate? —B. R.

Conclusion

A. Traditions for Faithfulness

Traditions are a double-edged sword. Often the very word *tradition* carries a negative connotation. It can be associated with an old-fashioned, out-of-date practice that people adhere to with little, if any, thought about its significance. We do something a certain way because "that's the way we've always done it." In a positive sense, traditions can help us not repeat mistakes of the past as we walk in faithful obedience to the Lord's commands.

While the Rechabites' traditions are not necessary for us to follow today—nor were they for all people of that time—their example of faithfulness ought to serve as an inspiration. In sharp contrast to the Israelites, who lived in sin and failed to repent of their wicked ways, the Rechabites lived in obedience to the ways set down by their father, Jonadab: ways that did not conflict with God's Word. May we follow their example when it comes to heeding God's Word, walking in faithful obedience to how He has called us to live.

B. Prayer

Father, grant us the courage to examine our traditions and the wisdom to know which to keep, which to modify, and which to abandon. May our traditions always be a way of serving You as You would have us. Use us to encourage the formation of families and communities who honor You. In Jesus' name. Amen.

C. Thought to Remember

Use traditions to foster faithfulness to God.

Involvement Learning

Enhance your lesson with KJV Bible Student *(from your curriculum supplier) and the reproducible activity page (at www.standardlesson.com or in the back of the* KJV Standard Lesson Commentary Deluxe Edition*).*

Into the Lesson

Write the following phrase on the board:

What it means to be in my family.

Distribute an index card and a pen to each learner and instruct them to write a sentence that describes their family's legacy. Collect the cards and select three to read aloud. As time allows, give learners time to talk about what legacy means and how essential legacies and traditions are in society—even when society seems to be quickly changing.

Alternative. Distribute copies of the "Family Traditions" exercise from the activity page, which you can download. Have learners complete it individually in a minute or less before discussing results with a partner.

Lead into the Bible study by saying, "In today's lesson, pay attention to what a family's legacy and traditions indicate about their beliefs and values. Consider why Jeremiah points this family out as a notable example to God's people."

Into the Word

Divide the class into two groups: **Context Group** and **Legacy Group**. Distribute a sheet of paper and pen to each group. Instruct the groups to list the following words as headers on their sheets of paper: *Who, What, When, Where,* and *Why.*

Ask a volunteer to read aloud Jeremiah 35:5–6. Direct the groups to read the following passages and use the question words to compare the passage with Jeremiah 35:5–6.

Context Group: Jeremiah 35:1–4.
Legacy Group: 2 Kings 10:15–28.

After calling time, direct learners to pair up with someone from the other group and share their notes with each other.

Option. Distribute copies of the "Family Tree" activity from the activity page. Have learners work in small groups to complete as indicated.

Ask a volunteer to read aloud Jeremiah 35:7–10. Direct the two groups to list the rules and traditions that Jonadab established for his family and discuss how each listed item indicates a temporary or unsettled lifestyle. Then, ask the groups to compare Jeremiah 35:7–10 with Hebrews 11:13–16.

Bring the groups back together and ask the following question for whole-class discussion: "How might the strict nomadic lifestyle of the Rechabites be an indicator of their faith in God?"

Ask a volunteer to read aloud Jeremiah 35:11. Divide learners into three groups: **Faithful Group**, **Inconsistent Group**, and **Rebellious Group**. Ask the groups to discuss how the Rechabites' decision to dwell in Jerusalem might be seen as faithful, inconsistent, or rebellious to the command given to them by their ancestor. Challenge them to develop two or three points to defend their position and share it with the class. They could include other examples from Scripture where people showed faithfulness to God through abstaining or not abstaining from wine, if that helps their arguments.

Have each group present their argument(s) before the whole class. For whole-class discussion, ask, "Why are the Rechabites used as an example of faithfulness and obedience?"

Into Life

Ask a volunteer to read Jeremiah 35:14b aloud to the whole class. Say, "God held up the Rechabites as an example of faithfulness and steadfast obedience, honoring their ancestor and their family."

Invite learners to brainstorm a family tradition they might establish that could be passed down to future generations. Invite learners to share their ideas with a partner. Ask, "What testimony could this tradition demonstrate to others about your family's faith and commitment to the Lord?"

Challenge learners to work on implementing their traditions during the week.

Changes Promised

Devotional Reading: Psalm 103:17–22
Background Scripture: Jeremiah 31:1–40; John 1:17; Hebrews 8:7–13

Jeremiah 31:29–34

29 In those days they shall say no more, The fathers have eaten a sour grape, and the children's teeth are set on edge.

30 But every one shall die for his own iniquity: every man that eateth the sour grape, his teeth shall be set on edge.

31 Behold, the days come, saith the LORD, that I will make a new covenant with the house of Israel, and with the house of Judah:

32 Not according to the covenant that I made with their fathers in the day that I took them by the hand to bring them out of the land of Egypt; which my covenant they brake, although I was an husband unto them, saith the LORD:

33 But this shall be the covenant that I will make with the house of Israel; After those days, saith the LORD, I will put my law in their inward parts, and write it in their hearts; and will be their God, and they shall be my people.

34 And they shall teach no more every man his neighbour, and every man his brother, saying, Know the LORD: for they shall all know me, from the least of them unto the greatest of them, saith the LORD: for I will forgive their iniquity, And I will remember their sin no more.

John 1:17

17 For the law was given by Moses, but grace and truth came by Jesus Christ.

Key Text

I will put my law in their inward parts, and write it in their hearts; and will be their God, and they shall be my people. **—Jeremiah 31:33b**

Judah, from Isaiah to the Exile

Unit 2: Jeremiah and the Promise of Renewal

Lessons 5–9

Lesson Aims

After participating in this lesson, each learner will be able to:

1. Locate the two places in the New Testament that quote Jeremiah 31:31–34.
2. Harmonize Jeremiah 31:29–30 with Exodus 20:5; 34:7.
3. Notice the Holy Spirit's work of bringing awareness of sin and giving desires to love God faithfully.

Lesson Outline

Introduction
- A. Better than Before
- B. Lesson Context

I. Change in Attitude (Jeremiah 31:29–30)
- A. Old Proverb (v. 29)
- B. New Reality (v. 30)
  - *Shirking Responsibility*

II. Change in Covenant (Jeremiah 31:31–34)
- A. Why It's Needed (vv. 31–32)
- B. How It's Different (vv. 33–34)
  - *Action from the Heart*

III. Change in Mediator (John 1:17)
- A. Law (v. 17a)
- B. Grace and Truth (v. 17b)

Conclusion
- A. Fresh Start
- B. Prayer
- C. Thought to Remember

Introduction

A. Better than Before

Moving into a house with no built-in dishwasher, my father bought a used portable model, the kind that hooked up to the sink faucet with a hose. It was in good shape except for the top, a butcher block deeply scratched and stained. Dad decided to make it like new. It took him many months. Night after night, he would go out to our carport to sand it by hand. He must have sanded a half inch off the top of that butcher block to get past the deepest gouges.

When he was finally satisfied, he began to apply varnish. He would apply a coat, then sand it, and repeat. He must have applied 30 coats of varnish to that wood! When he was finished, it was clean and scratch-free, even better than new. That old butcher block was given a new life.

A vital theme of the Bible is the need and plan for a new covenant, a fresh beginning for God's people. The gouges of sin were deep, and a thorough refresh was in order. Jeremiah was privileged to prophesy the future reality of that new covenant; we are privileged to experience it.

B. Lesson Context

The book of Jeremiah serves more as a collection of episodes rather than a linear chronology of his ministry. As an example, the episode that begins in Jeremiah 32:1 occurs *after* the one that begins in chapter 36. Therefore we should not be surprised when tone and content change abruptly as the book moves from topic to topic. We see such an abrupt change as chapter 30 begins.

The way Jeremiah organized his material has led some to call Jeremiah 30–33 the "Book of Consolation" because its theme gives hope that the Babylonian captivity is not the final word. Today's text takes us into the vital heart of this Book. As we consider our text, we keep in mind how it fits within the larger context: God promised to make the exiles His people once again (Jeremiah 30:22), to return them to their land (32:41), and to establish once and for all time the Davidic dynasty as originally promised (30:9; 33:15–26).

The overall theme of the Book of Consolation

is: "I will cause their captivity to return" (Jeremiah 32:44; see also 30:3, 18; 33:7, 26). The covenant theme of "Ye shall be my people, and I will be your God" is also repeated (30:22; see also 31:1; 32:38). The seemingly incurable wound (30:12, 15) could be healed only by the Lord (30:17). Chapter 31 depicts the coming restoration as a time of great blessing, when mourning would be turned into joy (31:13).

I. Change in Attitude

(Jeremiah 31:29–30)

A. Old Proverb (v. 29)

29. In those days they shall say no more, The fathers have eaten a sour grape, and the children's teeth are set on edge.

Many changes are to characterize the forthcoming restoration (see Lesson Context), including the rejection of how a certain proverbial expression is misused. Those who are already exiled in Babylon are using this proverb to shift the blame and exonerate themselves (see Ezekiel 18:2).

The intent of this proverb's misuse is impossible to miss. Eating a *sour grape* is unpleasant; it causes the mouth to pucker. This puckering effect is transferred from the older generation, who have eaten unwisely, to the following generation, who are seen as innocent victims of their ancestors' actions. Thus we have a metaphor for generational blame-shifting (compare Lamentations 5:7).

The proverbial expression is actually based in the Law of Moses, where God is seen to visit "the iniquity of the fathers upon the children unto the third and fourth generation of them that hate me" (Exodus 20:5; compare Exodus 34:7; Numbers 14:18; Jeremiah 32:18). Today we readily observe the intergenerational consequences of parents who are sent to jail for committing crimes. Children often do suffer as a result of the sins of their fathers (compare Jeremiah 32:18–19). But the fact that the sins of one generation have consequences for another is not the same as saying that God punishes an innocent group for the sins of a guilty group.

Even so, Israelite history does indeed record instances of children dying as a consequence of their parents' sins (see Numbers 16:23–33; Joshua 7:24–25; 2 Samuel 11:1–12:19; 21:1–9). Although there are times when the all-knowing and sovereign God deems this to be fitting, it is rare and certainly not the norm. The problem in today's text is that when exile comes, the people will apply the proverb to disavow any culpability for their situation. Indeed, that was already happening by those who were already in exile; Ezekiel 18:1–20 records the Lord's lengthy refutation.

What Do You Think?

What life consequences have you been tempted to blame on a past generation's or a family member's sin?

Digging Deeper

Where might there be truth in this? Where might this be a faulty assumption?

How to Say It

Babylon	*Bab*-uh-lon.
Deuteronomy	Due-ter-*ahn*-uh-me.
extispicy	*eks*-ti-spi-see.
Hosea	Ho-*zay*-uh.
Jeremiah	Jair-uh-*my*-uh.
Thessalonians	*Thess*-uh-*lo*-nee-unz (*th* as in *thin*).

B. New Reality (v. 30)

30. But every one shall die for his own iniquity: every man that eateth the sour grape, his teeth shall be set on edge.

In Jeremiah's prophetic scenario, the shifting of blame will cease. The old proverb is replaced by a new statement about reality. Each person will be liable and, as a sinner, will *die for his own iniquity.*

In some ways, this is a hopeful promise, for it dispels any idea that the nation is cursed and incapable of thriving in the future. Each generation determines how faithful or sinful it will be based on its own actions. We should be careful to point out that this is actually a "new again" reality because the Law of Moses has consistently prohibited imposing the death penalty on children for parental sin or vice versa per Deuteronomy 24:16. We see that prohibition honored in 2 Kings 14:6 and its parallel in 2 Chronicles 25:4.

> **What Do You Think?**
> Under what circumstances do you struggle most to take responsibility for your own actions?
>
> **Digging Deeper**
> What image or metaphor would you use to describe how it feels to face the consequences of your sin?

Shirking Responsibility

I was a very curious child growing up. One summer when I was about 10 years old, I decided to explore the cabinet under the bathroom sink. My mom had previously given me strict instructions not to touch anything there, but I disobeyed. Exploring a packet of single-edged razor blades, I had barely opened the package before I sliced my finger. Blood gushed everywhere; I panicked. Should I tell my mom the truth, or should I lie?

While cleaning up, I planned out the story I would tell when my mother saw the two bandages on my fingers. I went into the garden, picked some roses, and put them in a vase on her dresser. When she got home, I excitedly told her that I had a surprise. I led her to the room and showed her the roses I had picked. When she saw my fingers, I said the rose thorns had cut me. She looked quite distressed about the cuts but at the same time was overjoyed at the thoughtful act I had done for her.

I never confessed this lie until I was an adult. That memory is still seared in my mind. I deliberately avoided taking responsibility for my disobedience by means of an elaborate narrative. Under what circumstances do you do the same? —S. S.

II. Change in Covenant

(Jeremiah 31:31–34)

A. Why It's Needed (vv. 31–32)

31. Behold, the days come, saith the Lord, that I will make a new covenant with the house of Israel, and with the house of Judah.

The verses that follow this new (or renewed) approach to generational culpability forms the basis for one of the most important texts in the Old Testament for anticipating the new covenant. Jeremiah 31:31–34 is quoted in its entirety in Hebrews 8:8–12 and is the longest single quotation of any Old Testament text by a New Testament author (see also Hebrews 10:16–17). It is a groundbreaking message.

The beneficiaries of the *new covenant* are to be those who broke the old one: *the house of Israel* and *the house of Judah* (Jeremiah 11:10). Correcting the blame-shifting will not be enough. The Lord is moving beyond attempts to guide people back to Him via the old covenant.

But when is this to occur? When will *the days come?* Although Jeremiah speaks of *Israel* and *Judah*, additional context in subsequent verses and later fulfillment establish that this comes with the life, death, resurrection, and ascension of Jesus Christ.

32. Not according to the covenant that I made with their fathers in the day that I took them by the hand to bring them out of the land of Egypt; which my covenant they brake, although I was an husband unto them, saith the Lord.

Here the old *covenant* is portrayed in marriage language. *The Lord* is the *husband*, and the people, collectively, are the wife. This kind of metaphor is frequent in the prophets. Ezekiel symbolically pictures the Lord as finding Israel as an abandoned baby girl, raising her, and then entering a marriage covenant with her (Ezekiel 16:4–8). But this wife becomes a prostitute, a symbol of Israel's worship of other gods, including sacrificing their own children to idols (16:15, 20–21, 36). The book of Hosea is built around the prophet's marriage to a prostitute, whose unfaithfulness is likened to the idolatry of Israel (Hosea 1:2). Jeremiah himself pictures the Lord as married to two unfaithful sisters, Israel and Judah, who both commit spiritual adultery and must be divorced (Jeremiah 3:8).

Jeremiah pictures the very beginning of Israel as a nation like a marriage between the Lord and the people. At that time, the Lord *took them by the hand*. The Lord's rescue of the Israelites from *the land of Egypt* was like the husband leading his new wife from the home of her father to his own home. Such imagery stirs our hearts, suggesting the care and closeness possible within the closest of human relationships.

However, the vows of this symbolic marriage between the Lord and Israel were soon and often violated. It was a *covenant they brake*, resulting in the language of adultery for their breaking of the covenant given through Moses (Exodus 19:5–8; 24:3–8). They violated this covenant before they even entered the promised land! This happened by making and worshiping a golden calf idol on the very day Moses was on the mountain receiving the terms of the covenant (32:1–8). Moses was even forewarned that after the people entered into the promised land, they would continue to break the covenant and worship false gods (Deuteronomy 31:20).

That warning proved sadly true as the Israelites proved themselves incapable of keeping the covenant. The all-too-numerous episodes that follow help us understand why the new covenant was not to be *according to* the one the Lord *made with their fathers*. A new method was necessary.

What Do You Think?

When has someone overlooked a past offense and showed you undeserved grace?

Digging Deeper

What did it feel like to receive that grace? What did it enable in that relationship?

B. How It's Different (vv. 33–34)

33. But this shall be the covenant that I will make with the house of Israel; After those days, saith the LORD, I will put my law in their inward parts, and write it in their hearts; and will be their God, and they shall be my people.

Jeremiah reveals a new approach. The old covenant is written on stone (Exodus 24:12; 31:18; 34:1), and the people of its era were to internalize its laws (Deuteronomy 6:4–9). The new covenant, by contrast, is written on *inward parts* and *hearts*

Visual for Lesson 8. *Display this visual and ask participants to discuss what it means to have God's law "written on their hearts."*

by God Himself (compare Hebrews 10:16). It is through the Holy Spirit, who indwells each and every Christian, that God does so, as indicated by Romans 8:5–11. Obedience will not depend merely on human ability. Rather, God's people will exhibit Spirit-empowered, loving obedience to His ways, which will flow from the inside out.

During Jeremiah's ministry, Israel's collective "heart" is described as uncircumcised (see Jeremiah 9:26; compare 4:4; 9:14; 11:8; 18:12). This imagery depicts self-exclusion from the covenant God made with His people. Reference to this covenant goes back even further than that of the Mosaic covenant, to the covenant with Abraham (Genesis 15, 17). The only way for a covenant with the Lord to succeed was to begin with new hearts (Ezekiel 18:31; 36:26), hearts that are spiritually circumcised (Deuteronomy 10:16; 30:6; Jeremiah 4:4; Romans 2:29).

The expression of God's law being written on their "inward parts" may be a reference to the ancient Near Eastern practice known as *extispicy*. In this practice, diviners would seek revelation from a deity, asking that the truth be written on the entrails of an animal to be sacrificed. While admittedly an odd image to us today, consider how it would be taken by an audience familiar with such a practice. God's revelation—His truth, His law, His ways—would be written on His people's own inward parts.

Note the relationship made possible through this

new covenant. The Lord says, *I . . . will be their God, and they shall be my people.* When initially establishing His covenant with Israel, the Lord told them they would be His special people, a "peculiar treasure," if they "obey my voice . . . and keep my covenant" (Exodus 19:5–6). But as we see countless times throughout the Old Testament—particularly in the prophets—the people could not maintain what it took to be God's very own.

What Do You Think?

How does your life look different when you know something "by heart" instead of needing to look it up?

Digging Deeper

What are thing you do know "by heart"? In what ways do they shape how you live?

Action from the Heart

My mother grew up Roman Catholic, but claims she came to true faith as an adult in a Protestant church setting. There she finally understood God's grace. As a child, I took her story to heart and incidentally inherited a distaste for anything rote or ritualistic. Faith was supposed to be lively, from the heart.

Little did I know that I would one day belong to a church where liturgy is central. The liturgy I participate in week after week is not rote—quite the opposite. Our church family experiences what some might call "rules and rituals" as life-giving and grounding. They are this way for us because we engage them from our hearts. Our concern is not for performance, but for words and actions done in response to God. These are not in order to get something from Him, but because of what He has already done in and for us.

Such words and actions flow naturally and lovingly from hearts enlivened by the Holy Spirit. How might actions in your life of faith be better directed by the Holy Spirit's work in your heart?

—J. J. S.

34. And they shall teach no more every man his neighbour, and every man his brother, saying, Know the LORD: for they shall all know me, from the least of them unto the greatest of them, saith the LORD: for I will forgive their iniquity, and I will remember their sin no more.

This verse predicts a perfect state of affairs: no one is needed to teach about the Lord because everyone already has the knowledge. This seems puzzling since we understand that a teaching function does indeed exist under the new covenant (Matthew 28:19–20; Romans 12:7; etc.).

One interpretation proposes that this verse looks to the time after Jesus' second coming when our presence with God in heaven yields our fullest knowledge of Him. Another interpretation proposes that Jeremiah's prediction contrasts the need for human mediators under the old covenant (priests of the tribe of Levi) with the direct access to God that people have under the new covenant (1 Thessalonians 4:9; Hebrews 4:16; 10:19–22; 1 John 2:27). Either way, the time of the new covenant will be an era when the people of God include more than the peoples of ancient Israel and Judah. Knowledge of God will spread to peoples of all nations and languages (Revelation 7:9).

The paradox and tragedy of Jeremiah's time was that many Judeans did not know the Lord or follow His ways even though they were hereditary members of God's chosen people (Jeremiah 2:17–19, etc.). What will it be like for people with new hearts, those under the new covenant? They will *know the Lord!* The express teaching of God's Word by a select group of priests will no longer be necessary because *they shall all* know the Lord, *from the least* to *the greatest.* While this statement of inclusion initially appears to refer to social class, it also points forward to the eventual inclusion of Gentiles in the new covenant (see Ephesians 3:6).

The people will not only have God's Spirit in their hearts to guide and instruct them; they will also be a forgiven people. The Lord promises to *forgive their iniquity,* to *remember their sin no more.* This is the fresh start that the new covenant promises, beginning anew with a clean slate not encumbered by the sins and failures of the past. This brings back to mind the change indicated in Jeremiah 31:29–30, above. Not only will everyone be responsible for their own actions, but once forgiven, those sins are remembered no more—no more to condemn us or those who come after us.

> **What Do You Think?**
> What does it feel like to consider the fact that the sins you can't forget, God doesn't remember?
> **Digging Deeper**
> How does knowing that you are forgiven affect how you view yourself and interact with others?

III. Change in Mediator

(John 1:17)

A. Law (v. 17a)

17a. For the law was given by Moses.

To understand the contrast introduced here in John 1:17a, we should consider what immediately precedes it. There, the author declares, "of [the Son's] fulness have all we received, and grace for grace" (John 1:16). The translation "grace for grace" could be understood to signify something like "grace on top of grace already received." Or it may carry the idea of the replacement of one kind of grace with another kind. Both ideas carry the significance of "unmerited favor" and set the stage for understanding verse 17.

Moses experienced God's grace (see Exodus 33:12–17). And the law that came through him was by the initiative of the gracious God. Yet the primary characteristic of the Law of Moses is its "commandments," "statutes," and "ordinances." There was nothing inherently wrong with these—quite the opposite! But the passage of time proved humans to be incapable of keeping these 100 percent of the time. So the initial grace of the old covenant received through Moses as mediator needed to be replaced by the grace of a new and superior covenant, the one about which Jeremiah 31:31–34 speaks.

B. Grace and Truth (v. 17b)

17b. But grace and truth came by Jesus Christ.

This superior covenant is mediated by a far superior mediator: *Jesus Christ,* the Word become flesh (John 1:14). Compared to the Law of Moses, His "yoke is easy" and His "burden is light" (Matthew 11:30).

Like our analysis of the word *grace,* to attribute the coming of *truth* to Jesus is not to deny that Moses received truth! The truth Jesus brings is the truth regarding the new covenant.

Conclusion

A. Fresh Start

Many Christians who read their Bibles faithfully struggle with understanding what to do with the commands and regulations they find in the Old Testament. Because we believe in the inspiration and value of the entire Bible, we must take these passages seriously. The prophecy in Jeremiah 31 helps us put other portions of the Old Testament into perspective. The Law of Moses revealed God's will for the people of Israel and in so doing revealed many things about His nature and character. Jeremiah's perspective shows that this initial covenant did not work for Israel. This was not because God failed, but because of the people's disobedience. Eventually, Israel was punished by the destruction of Jerusalem and its temple followed by exile.

The new covenant Jeremiah speaks of is a fresh start for humanity. This new covenant defines its adherents not in terms of obedience to law, but as those who have experienced the grace of being forgiven through Jesus' atonement for our sins.

As new covenant people, we have much we can learn from the old covenant, but we rejoice in the reality of the new covenant. What the prophets searched for diligently, we now experience (1 Peter 1:10–11).

B. Prayer

Lord, we marvel at the new covenant mediated by Your Son, our Savior, Jesus Christ. We thrive because of Your grace and rejoice over Your truth. We thank You for giving us Your Spirit so we may truly know You. It is in Jesus' name we pray. Amen.

C. Thought to Remember

Jesus mediates a new covenant based on grace.

Involvement Learning

Enhance your lesson with KJV Bible Student *(from your curriculum supplier) and the reproducible activity page (at www.standardlesson.com or in the back of the* KJV Standard Lesson Commentary Deluxe Edition*).*

Into the Lesson

Ask volunteers to share an example of a time when they used a manufacturer's warranty to fix or replace a broken item. (Be prepared to give your own example if no one volunteers.) Discuss setbacks that would have resulted without the warranty and how having the warranty helped. Ask, "In what ways was the replacement superior to the original?"

Lead into the Bible study by saying, "In today's lesson, we will study how God offered a new covenant that would redeem His people. As we study, consider why the new covenant is superior to the old covenant."

Into the Word

Say, "The book of Deuteronomy explains how God made a covenant with His people. By the time of the prophet Jeremiah, the people had broken the covenant. The beauty of Jeremiah 31 is that it is God Himself who establishes a new covenant that will ultimately be fulfilled in Christ."

Place participants in small groups and have each group read Jeremiah 31:31–34. Then ask the groups to locate and identify the following in the text: (a) the key verse that summarizes it all and (b) the eternal promise. After three minutes, ask the following questions for whole-class discussion: 1–When and how will this promise be fulfilled? 2–How would the promised new covenant differ from the old one? 3–What is the role of the Holy Spirit in the new covenant? See the lesson commentary for ideas to stimulate and supplement the discussion.

Option. Divide the class into two groups: **High Priestly Group** (Hebrews 8:1–13) and **Sacrifice Group** (Hebrews 10:11–18). Have each group read their assigned Scripture text and compare it with Jeremiah 31:29–34. Distribute a handout (you create) to each group that contains the following questions: 1–What does this passage reveal about the new covenant? 2–How does this passage elaborate upon Jeremiah 31:29–34? After five minutes, reconvene the class and ask volunteers to share their responses.

Invite a volunteer to read John 1:17. Ask the following questions for whole-class discussion: 1–Explain how this verse expands on Jeremiah 31:29–34. 2–What is the significance of Moses in this verse? 3–How is Jesus Christ a superior mediator?

Option 1. Distribute copies of the "God's Covenant Promise" exercise from the activity page, which you can download. Have learners work in pairs to complete as indicated. After calling time, ask volunteers to share their findings.

Option 2. Distribute copies of the "Psalms of Promise" activity from the activity page. Have learners work with a partner to complete as indicated.

Into Life

Lead into the activity by saying, "Today's study taught us that God's people have been promised the presence of God's Spirit, the Holy Spirit. The Lord promises that the Spirit will guide and instruct us."

Write the following phrases as headers on the board:

1. *Bringing Awareness of Sin*
2. *Giving Desires to Love God Faithfully*

Ask participants to work with a partner to brainstorm ways they can notice the Holy Spirit's work in each category listed. Write responses on the board under the correct header.

Ask learners to join you in a closing guided prayer. Lead learners in a prayer of praising God for His grace and salvation. Allow time for silent prayer for confession of sin. Conclude by thanking Jesus for securing our eternal life through this new covenant.

November 2
Lesson 9 (KJV)

Jeremiah's Rescue

Devotional Reading: Romans 13:1–10
Background Scripture: Jeremiah 20:1–6; 37:1–38:28; 43:1–7

Jeremiah 38:7–13

7 Now when Ebedmelech the Ethiopian, one of the eunuchs which was in the king's house, heard that they had put Jeremiah in the dungeon; the king then sitting in the gate of Benjamin;

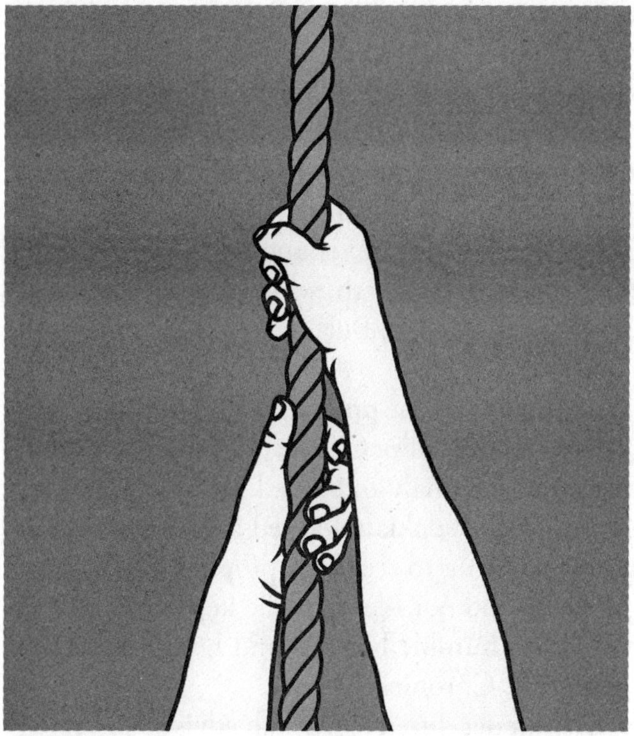

8 Ebedmelech went forth out of the king's house, and spake to the king, saying,

9 My lord the king, these men have done evil in all that they have done to Jeremiah the prophet, whom they have cast into the dungeon; and he is like to die for hunger in the place where he is: for there is no more bread in the city.

10 Then the king commanded Ebedmelech the Ethiopian, saying, Take from hence thirty men with thee, and take up Jeremiah the prophet out of the dungeon, before he die.

11 So Ebedmelech took the men with him, and went into the house of the king under the treasury, and took thence old cast clouts and old rotten rags, and let them down by cords into the dungeon to Jeremiah.

12 And Ebedmelech the Ethiopian said unto Jeremiah, Put now these old cast clouts and rotten rags under thine armholes under the cords. And Jeremiah did so.

13 So they drew up Jeremiah with cords, and took him up out of the dungeon: and Jeremiah remained in the court of the prison.

Key Text

Then the king commanded Ebedmelech the Ethiopian, saying, Take from hence thirty men with thee, and take up Jeremiah the prophet out of the dungeon, before he die. **—Jeremiah 38:10**

Judah, from Isaiah to the Exile

Unit 2: Jeremiah and the Promise of Renewal

Lessons 5–9

Lesson Aims

After participating in this lesson, each learner will be able to:

1. Summarize the historical context of Jeremiah 38.

2. Explain the points of view and motives of the various parties involved.

3. Identify the specific needs of someone who requires spiritual or physical rescue.

Lesson Outline

Introduction

A. Unjustly Imprisoned

B. Lesson Context

I. Jeremiah's Predicament (Jeremiah 38:7–10)

A. Noticed by an Ally (vv. 7–9)

Malnutrition and Dehydration

B. Addressed by the King (v. 10)

II. Jeremiah's Rescue (Jeremiah 38:11–13)

A. Springing to Action (v. 11)

Urgency Required

B. Creative Solution (vv. 12–13)

Conclusion

A. Rescuers

B. Prayer

C. Thought to Remember

Introduction

A. Unjustly Imprisoned

In 1962, Nelson Mandela was arrested and sentenced to five years' imprisonment for working to overthrow the racist regime of his country of South Africa. In 1964, justices handed down a sentence of life imprisonment. For 18 years, Mandela was kept in the notorious Robben Island prison, a former leper colony and mental asylum.

But through all those years, Mandela's voice was not stilled, and international observers continued to monitor his status. He was eventually released in 1990 and, in an abrupt turn in 1994, was elected South Africa's first Black president. Although imprisonment for political reasons is wrong, it can sometimes have an effect that the persecutors do not expect. And so it is with today's text.

B. Lesson Context

Zedekiah was the last king of Judah before the destruction of Jerusalem in 586 BC. In 597 BC, King Nebuchadnezzar of Babylon seized control of Jerusalem. He deported the then-current king—Jehoiachin—to Babylon along with the royal family, court officials, 7,000 elite fighters, and other prominent citizens (2 Kings 24:14–16). Nebuchadnezzar installed Jehoiachin's 21-year-old uncle in his place, changing his name from Mattaniah to Zedekiah, which means "the Lord is righteous" (24:17). But Zedekiah did not honor the Lord.

Zedekiah and the prophet Jeremiah had a complicated relationship. On the one hand, Zedekiah consulted Jeremiah and asked him to pray (Jeremiah 37:3). Zedekiah wanted a "word from the Lord," seeming to trust the prophet (37:17). But Zedekiah did not like what he kept hearing. He refused to humble himself and heed Jeremiah's message (2 Chronicles 36:12).

Even under duress, Jeremiah advised surrender to the Babylonians to save lives (Jeremiah 38:2–3). This led to accusations of being a traitor, resulting in imprisonment (37:11–16). A subsequent audience with the king resulted in more lenient treatment for a time (37:17–21). Yet the enemies of Jeremiah still conspired with King Zedekiah to have the prophet put to death (38:4–6; compare 26:11). Jeremiah has long predicted the doom of Jerusalem, and this isn't the first time he has advocated outright surrender (see 27:11). A previous king in Jerusalem had actually done just that several years prior (2 Kings 24:12).

All in all, Jeremiah is seen as a threat to the vested interests of the leaders of Judah and Jerusalem as he opposes their attitudes and practices again and again. One example is his criticism of their re-enslaving freed slaves (Jeremiah 34:8–22), a violation of the Law of Moses (compare Exodus 21:2–6; Deuteronomy 15:12). It has all led up to this point of being cast into a dungeon to die slowly of dehydration and malnutrition, the harshest punishment yet (Jeremiah 38:1–6).

I. Jeremiah's Predicament

(Jeremiah 38:7–10)

A. Noticed by an Ally (vv. 7–9)

7a. Now when Ebedmelech the Ethiopian, one of the eunuchs which was in the king's house, heard that they had put Jeremiah in the dungeon.

Jeremiah's location *in the dungeon,* where his enemies have left him to die, draws the attention of a certain *Ebedmelech the Ethiopian.* This dungeon is an underground reservoir used to collect water. Many private homes may have had their own such cisterns for collecting water in this period (see 2 Kings 18:31). But given the dire needs of the besieged city, this one has become empty and is evidently deep due to the enemies' need to lower Jeremiah into it by use of "cords" (Jeremiah 38:6). There is no way to escape without outside help. Jeremiah was completely trapped, left to starve to death in a horrible pit where he could not even lie down. We might imagine that they got the idea from Genesis 37:18–23.

If Jeremiah's legs sank even a couple of feet into the clay, any escape would be impossible; Jeremiah was in a hopeless situation. Perhaps Jeremiah's friends might notice his disappearance, but his corpse might not be discovered for months, if ever. Psalm 40:2 offers a similar word picture and praises God for a rescue from a (figurative) "horrible pit" filled with "miry clay." It was probably of little comfort to Jeremiah that such facilities for storing water were ceremonially clean (Leviticus 11:36).

The word *Ebedmelech* means "servant of the king." Thus this may be the man's job description rather than a personal name. His country of origin is also known as the kingdom of Cush, which is south of Egypt. He may be friendly to Jeremiah because of being re-enslaved per discussion of Jeremiah 34:8–22, above (although he is not of the 12 tribes of Israel). Based on the way he acts in the narrative, he appears to be someone of authority, someone the king trusts.

Describing him as *one of the eunuchs* might mean only that he was a royal official (not necessarily someone who has been castrated, although that is possible). The underlying Hebrew word occurs dozens of times in the Old Testament. It is translated "officer" in a variety of contexts (for instance, Genesis 39:1; 1 Samuel 8:15). While the Hebrew term for *official* might also be used in a more technical sense to describe eunuchs, it is not clear whether the kings of Israel and Judah had eunuchs in their service, as did other kings in the ancient Near East (compare 2 Kings 9:32; 20:18). The 45 occurrences of the Hebrew word at issue are translated "eunuch(s)" 38 percent of the time, with translations "chamberlains" at 29 percent, "officer(s)" at 27 percent, and as a proper name at 6 percent in the *King James Version* of the Old Testament.

7b. The king then sitting in the gate of Benjamin.

Ebedmelech knows the king's habits and

How to Say It

Babylonians	Bab-ih-*low*-nee-unz.
Ebedmelech	*Eh*-bed-**meh**-lek.
Ethiopian	E-thee-*o*-pee-un (*th* as in *thin*).
Jehoiachin	Jeh-*hoy*-uh-kin.
Josephus	Jo-*see*-fus.
Malchiah	Mal-*kye*-uh.
Mattaniah	Mat-uh-*nye*-uh.
Nebuchadnezzar	*Neb*-yuh-kud-**nez**-er.
Zedekiah	Zed-uh-*kye*-uh.

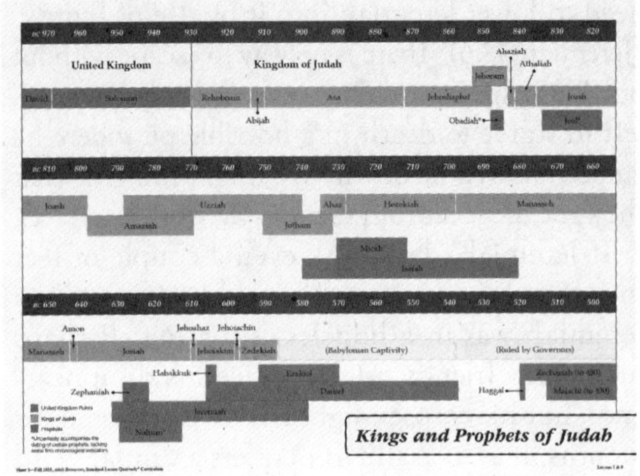

Visual for Lessons 1 & 9. *Display this chart as you help participants familiarize themselves with the timeline of Judah's kings and prophets.*

movements. *The gate of Benjamin* is likely on the northeastern corner of Jerusalem's wall; it is the gate that Jeremiah tried to use in attempting to return to Anathoth (Jeremiah 1:1). Jeremiah had been beaten there (20:1–2), and his arrest at this same gate has led to his current confinement (37:11–17).

A city gate was more than a fortified entry point. Some gates had benches for elders of the community to sit and render judgments (see 2 Samuel 19:8; Jeremiah 26:10). Gates were gathering places for those seeking authoritative rulings on legal matters (2 Samuel 15:2). King Zedekiah was at the gate presumably to administer judgments in his official capacity. Thus his servant knows where to find him. He can go to seek an audience, like the other citizens of Jerusalem.

8. Ebedmelech went forth out of the king's house, and spake to the king, saying.

To travel from *the king's house* to the Benjamin gate is a distance of no more than a quarter of a mile. The royal palace, built by King Solomon some 330 years prior, is probably to the immediate south of the temple. Various details of the original palace complex are found in 1 Kings 7:1–12, but we don't know which of those are still present by Jeremiah's day.

Ebedmelech approaches the man who had given tacit approval to Jeremiah's execution (Jeremiah 38:5). The approach takes place in a public venue, where witnesses will hear an official response. It could be that Ebedmelech suspects that the king is willing to let Jeremiah die, but admitting it publicly is another matter.

The king's servant seems to have no problem gaining an audience with King Zedekiah. Ebedmelech's case concerns a life-and-death matter, a dire need that goes beyond the usual questions of property disputes or inheritance rights (as in Ruth 4).

> **What Do You Think?**
> When was a time you had to choose the right moment to begin an important conversation?
>
> **Digging Deeper**
> What is similar and what is different about the ways that Esther approaches King Ahasuerus in Esther 5:1–8?

9. My lord the king, these men have done evil in all that they have done to Jeremiah the prophet, whom they have cast into the dungeon; and he is like to die for hunger in the place where he is: for there is no more bread in the city.

We speculated earlier on the reason for Ebedmelech's intervention. Now we see more of the immediate context: given that people are beginning to starve due to the siege, no one will be throwing bread down to Jeremiah (if there were anyone doing so to begin with). The fact that the prophet has been treated unjustly and does not deserve to die is summed up in the line *these men have done evil in all that they have done to Jeremiah the prophet.*

This servant of the king trusts in the legitimacy of Jeremiah's message, or at least the earnestness of the prophet's ministry. The servant seems to be persuaded that Jeremiah has spoken the truth. But even if the king were to choose not to listen to Jeremiah, it would be wicked to leave him to die in a pit by an unapproved means of execution enacted without due process.

Ebedmelech's words sound as if he believes the king to be unaware of what Jeremiah's opponents have done to the prophet. Indeed, the king's statement, "Behold, he is in your hand: for the king is not he that can do any thing against you," in

Jeremiah 38:5 almost sounds like an admission of powerlessness or at least intentional ignorance. Ebedmelech may be phrasing his appeal tactfully and diplomatically, without a specific accusation. Even if he blames Zedekiah, the servant does not accuse his *lord the king* in public, with witnesses at the gate who can overhear.

Instead, Ebedmelech chooses not to identify Jeremiah's enemies by name specifically (*these men*). A willingness to "shed innocent blood" was among the gravest charges that Jeremiah had brought against King Zedekiah and his predecessors (2 Kings 24:3–4; Jeremiah 22:3, 17). Jeremiah had warned the kings to pursue "judgment and righteousness" in order to avoid the most destructive consequences. But instead, the nobles turned against the prophet because of his willingness to speak the truth and seek the good of his city. Jeremiah's own futile ministry had become the ultimate demonstration of the cravenness of Judah's ruling powers (Jeremiah 5:20–21).

What Do You Think?

What is an example of a time when you witnessed a person treated unfairly?

Digging Deeper

Consider David's prayers in Psalm 72:1–2, 12–14. How does Jeremiah 38 illustrate the failure of Judah's kings?

Malnutrition and Dehydration

Quick—place your hand over the next paragraph so you don't see the answer to this question: What word fits this definition: "An attempt to explain or justify one's own behavior or attitude with plausible reasons, even if these are not true or appropriate"?

The word being defined above is *rationalize.* We humans are good at doing that, aren't we? Think about nutritional guidelines. On the one hand, there are many such guidelines and standards that we acknowledge as being healthy and reasonable. But on the other hand, our reasons for violating them are often little more than transparent rationalizations.

The same is true in a spiritual sense—perhaps more so. Instead of seeking the bread of life (John 6:48), people rationalize reasons for feeding themselves impure spiritual bread made "with old leaven, . . . the leaven of malice and wickedness" (1 Corinthians 5:8). Instead of seeking the one who provides living water (John 4:10–14; 7:38), people favor "broken cisterns, that can hold no water" (Jeremiah 2:13).

Who in your circle of influence needs living water and the bread of life today? —R. L. N.

B. Addressed by the King (v. 10)

10. Then the king commanded Ebedmelech the Ethiopian, saying, Take from hence thirty men with thee, and take up Jeremiah the prophet out of the dungeon, before he die.

We notice that the king's orders are to stop the damage that is in progress, not to find and punish those responsible. Of course, readers understand why the king does not seek those who are responsible, because he gave them permission in the first place (see Lesson Context)! He was caught in the difficulty of his own making with a failed attempt on Jeremiah's life now exposed to public scrutiny. So the king gives orders to show that he is doing something about the situation. He will be able to claim that he saved Jeremiah's life.

The king is likely surrounded by bodyguards, and they are likely the source of the *thirty men* Ebedmelech is to take *from hence;* this is the suggestion of Josephus, the first-century Jewish historian. Or they may merely be men of the city who have some role in the city's defense. A band of this size will be sufficient to overcome anyone who tries to stop them from freeing the prophet. The wording *before he die* paints a picture of urgency.

What Do You Think?

Have you been tempted to take credit for an idea that wasn't yours? When have you witnessed this in others?

Digging Deeper

Jesus says the "heart" is where evil thoughts begin (Matthew 15:19). Why do we do the right thing for the wrong reasons?

II. Jeremiah's Rescue

(Jeremiah 38:11–13)

A. Springing to Action (v. 11)

11a. So Ebedmelech took the men with him, and went into the house of the king under the treasury.

An earlier place of Jeremiah's confinement was "the court of the prison" (Jeremiah 32:2, 8; 33:1; 37:21). He is now in the same area, but below ground in a reservoir for water. We were previously told that the "dungeon" chosen for Jeremiah's captivity was under the house of Malchiah. This house was part of the "court of the prison," meaning it bordered on an open area given that name (38:6). *Hammelech* can be either a proper name or it can mean "the king." However, even if Malchiah is "son of the king," he is not the son of Zedekiah. He is one of the "princes" who are pressuring the king and seeking Jeremiah's death. Malchiah was the father of Pashur, one of four named individuals who confronted Zedekiah in the first place, demanding Jeremiah be killed (38:1, 4).

Before proceeding to the cistern itself, Ebedmelech and his men go to a room in the king's palace. This is identified as being *under the treasury*, a different room in the palace on a higher level. The reason they go here comes next.

11b. And took thence old cast clouts and old rotten rags, and let them down by cords into the dungeon to Jeremiah.

They find *old cast clouts* as well as *old rotten rags* in the storage area. "Clout" is an old English term that refers to a cloth or leather patch used to repair clothes. What the men were gathering was a bundle of worn-out clothes, patched and ragged.

Archaeologists have found dozens of ancient cisterns around Jerusalem, some 100 feet deep. One, known as the "Great Cistern," is estimated to have the capacity of two million gallons of water, although this cavity seems to have been built after Jeremiah lived. We can easily imagine the relief that Jeremiah experiences: the cover of his prison is removed, he is able to hear friendly voices at the top, and soon a soft bundle is lowered from above.

What Do You Think?

Have you ever struggled to deliver help to someone in need? What made it difficult?

Digging Deeper

What is a practical way that you might fulfill a need without being noticed or credited?

Urgency Required

When I was a sophomore in college, I received a phone call that no one wants to receive: my dad was being rushed to the hospital. My dad was eating a sandwich when he accidentally swallowed part of his dentures. It lodged in his throat and began to obstruct his airway.

Paramedics came immediately and rushed my dad to the hospital. Preparations were underway in the event that surgical removal was required. Swelling in his esophagus was life-threatening. Just before the decision to perform surgery, an emergency room doctor was able to remove the obstruction. My dad could breathe again! His voice took time to return, but he eventually made a full recovery.

Likewise, when the king's servant noticed Jeremiah's need, he didn't linger. He sought an immediate solution and brought the right people to help. If those around us are in need of rescue, we may not have the skills or experience to perform surgery, but we can set everything aside to make ourselves available. For spiritual needs, we can always point our friends and neighbors to the Savior, who is an expert rescuer!

If immediate action is required, are you prepared to respond? —B. R.

B. Creative Solution (vv. 12–13)

12. And Ebedmelech the Ethiopian said unto Jeremiah, Put now these old cast clouts and rotten rags under thine armholes under the cords. And Jeremiah did so.

The purpose behind the collection of old clothes is now revealed. They are to serve as padding for the *cords*. Ropes or cords of antiquity would be rough and could cut into Jeremiah's skin as he is hauled to the surface, possibly ending his life through a nasty infection. Perhaps Jeremiah is bare-chested or was stripped naked before being placed in the cistern. If so, his skin could be made raw as the cords are used to tug and pull him out of the mud. The men have to bring him up slowly and carefully, with the rope rigged around his body under his arms. Fortunately, they are not too late. Jeremiah has not lost consciousness; he is able to do what they tell him and arrange his padded harness.

13. So they drew up Jeremiah with cords, and took him up out of the dungeon: and Jeremiah remained in the court of the prison.

Pulling the prophet *out of the dungeon* is surely a long and nerve-wracking procedure. With his rescue complete, Jeremiah does not attempt to flee the city. He remains where he was previously confined, the *court of the prison*. He may be intentionally remaining in a type of "protective custody" so that he can steer clear of rearrest or assassination from the nobles and false prophets who are after him.

The epilogue to this story is that, later, Jeremiah calls Ebedmelech back to the court of the prison where he is confined. The courageous official is told that he shall escape unharmed from Jerusalem's impending destruction when the Babylonians breach the walls. The Lord's message to this deliverer is that, because of his trust in the Lord, on that day, "I will surely deliver thee" (Jeremiah 39:18). On that day, the rescuer would be rescued.

What Do You Think?

Why do you imagine that Ebedmelech risked so much to save the life of Jeremiah?

Digging Deeper

Compare how God spared Ebedmelech here and Rahab in Joshua 6:22–23. What about God's character is revealed in these two stories?

Conclusion

A. Rescuers

The story of Jeremiah, Zedekiah, the plotting princes, and Ebedmelech teaches several lessons. For Jeremiah, as with many of God's prophets, the task of accurately reporting the word of the Lord was a difficult path to walk. Jesus Himself would later travel to Jerusalem and experience deadly resistance, like the prophets of Israel's past (see Matthew 23:37). Jesus warns those who wish to be His disciples that they too shall face resistance, shall be asked to "take up [a] cross" in order to follow Him (Matthew 16:24). In the example of Zedekiah, we glimpse the consequences of cowardice, of caring only about a public perception instead of seeking truth. God's plans may have disrupted the self-serving actions of Jerusalem's nobles, but a just king should have stepped in to protect Jeremiah and listen to God's message.

Ebedmelech is an example of a courageous rescuer, one who risked the disapproval of his own boss to save the life of God's servant. And God responded to this individual's faithfulness, protecting him in the middle of a war zone. God is faithful to individuals, which is especially clear to those who are in desperate situations (see Joshua 6:22–23; 1 Samuel 23:26–29; Ruth 4:13–17).

Modern "rescuers" may take the form of professionals with high-tech equipment and training. When someone needs physical rescue, we are taught to call these emergency services. But there are many other opportunities for believers to perform small acts of deliverance for one another: giving financial assistance, offering care for children, and sitting with those experiencing tragedy or loss. A faithful rescuer should not give up. Ebedmelech risked his favorable position, perhaps even his life, to confront the king at the gate and direct Jeremiah's deliverance. He did what was right for someone who needed his help, and he did not look away.

B. Prayer

Lord God, give us spiritual sight to see those who are struggling and whom we can help. May we never look away when we see suffering and injustice. We pray in the name of Jesus, our rescuer from the powers of sin and death. Amen.

C. Thought to Remember

God might ask us to take risks to help others.

Involvement Learning

Enhance your lesson with KJV Bible Student *(from your curriculum supplier) and the reproducible activity page (at www.standardlesson.com or in the back of the* KJV Standard Lesson Commentary Deluxe Edition*).*

Into the Lesson

Write the following phrase on the board:

If you can't say anything nice,
don't say anything at all.

Ask volunteers to give examples of when they followed or did not follow that advice. Encourage them to elaborate on the consequences of saying something or remaining silent in their examples. Be prepared to share an example from your life to start the discussion.

Lead into the Bible study by saying, "Today, we will learn how one man stood up to the king and the officials. Because this man chose to speak up, Jeremiah's life was saved. As we study, consider how today's lesson can guide us in helping others who need rescue or intervention."

Into the Word

Before class, choose a volunteer to give a five-minute presentation on the historical and biblical context of today's Scripture text. The volunteer can use the Lesson Context section and other commentaries in preparation. Ensure that the presentation includes an explanation of Jeremiah's proclamation (Jeremiah 38:2–3), the directives of King Zedekiah (38:4–5), and the actions of the officials (38:6).

Divide participants into three groups: **Jeremiah Group**, **Ebedmelech Group**, and **Zedekiah Group**. Direct each group to read Jeremiah 38:7–13 and create a presentation on the group's namesake. Encourage groups to use online resources in their presentation. Ensure that each presentation addresses the following questions: 1–What are the words and actions of your character in today's Scripture? 2–What word(s) best describes your character? 3–What other passages from Scripture, if any, mention your character? 4–In what ways can we learn from the words and actions of your character?

After 15 minutes of in-class preparation, reconvene the groups and direct each group to present their findings for the class. Ask each group to share any conclusions they have about their assigned character.

Option 1. Distribute copies of the "Prophet Puzzle" activity from the activity page, which you can download. Have learners complete it individually in a minute or less before reviewing answers with a partner.

Option 2. Ask a volunteer to read Jeremiah 38:7–13 aloud. Have three volunteers play the roles of Jeremiah, Ebedmelech, and King Zedekiah, each one taking turns telling the story from their perspective. (It's best to recruit these actors in advance.) Allow opportunities for reactions and feedback.

Into Life

Write the following phrases as headers on the board: *Physical Needs / Spiritual Needs*. Lead into the activity by saying, "We too can be bold and stand up for those in spiritual and physical need." Conduct a whole-class brainstorming session by challenging learners to suggest ways your class or congregation can meet the physical needs and spiritual needs of members of the community. Write responses under the appropriate header.

Divide learners into groups of three or four. Ask groups to identify one way they can meet either a physical or spiritual need listed on the board. Challenge groups to create a specific plan to accomplish this in the upcoming weeks. If they plan to address a physical need, is there a related spiritual need they can also address?

Conclude class time with small-group prayer, asking God for wisdom and insight to meet the physical and spiritual needs of others.

Option. Distribute copies of the "Prayer Practice" exercise from the activity page. Have learners work with a partner to complete as indicated. After calling time, ask for several volunteers to share their prayer list.

Jerusalem's Fall

Devotional Reading: Lamentations 1:18–22
Background Scripture: 2 Kings 23:1–25:21

2 Kings 24:18–20

18 Zedekiah was twenty and one years old when he began to reign, and he reigned eleven years in Jerusalem. And his mother's name was Hamutal, the daughter of Jeremiah of Libnah.

19 And he did that which was evil in the sight of the LORD, according to all that Jehoiakim had done.

20 For through the anger of the LORD it came to pass in Jerusalem and Judah, until he had cast them out from his presence, that Zedekiah rebelled against the king of Babylon.

2 Kings 25:1–9

1 And it came to pass in the ninth year of his reign, in the tenth month, in the tenth day of the month, that Nebuchadnezzar king of Babylon came, he, and all his host, against Jerusalem, and pitched against it; and they built forts against it round about.

2 And the city was besieged unto the eleventh year of king Zedekiah.

3 And on the ninth day of the fourth month the famine prevailed in the city, and there was no bread for the people of the land.

4 And the city was broken up, and all the men of war fled by night by the way of the gate between two walls, which is by the king's garden: (now the Chaldees were against the city round about:) and the king went the way toward the plain.

5 And the army of the Chaldees pursued after the king, and overtook him in the plains of Jericho: and all his army were scattered from him.

6 So they took the king, and brought him up to the king of Babylon to Riblah; and they gave judgment upon him.

7 And they slew the sons of Zedekiah before his eyes, and put out the eyes of Zedekiah, and bound him with fetters of brass, and carried him to Babylon.

8 And in the fifth month, on the seventh day of the month, which is the nineteenth year of king Nebuchadnezzar king of Babylon, came Nebuzaradan, captain of the guard, a servant of the king of Babylon, unto Jerusalem:

9 And he burnt the house of the LORD, and the king's house, and all the houses of Jerusalem, and every great man's house burnt he with fire.

Key Text

For through the anger of the LORD it came to pass in Jerusalem and Judah, until he had cast them out from his presence, that Zedekiah rebelled against the king of Babylon. **—2 Kings 24:20**

Judah, from Isaiah
to the Exile

Unit 3: Ezekiel and the Exile of Judah

Lessons 10–13

Lesson Aims

After participating in this lesson, each learner will be able to:

1. Summarize the life and fate of King Zedekiah.

2. Explain the circumstances that led to the exile.

3. State one way he or she will reflect on God's patient mercy in the coming week.

Lesson Outline

Introduction
- A. Foreseen Disaster
- B. Lesson Context

I. Another Evil King (2 Kings 24:18–20a)
- A. Zedekiah's Reign (vv. 18–19)
- B. The Lord's Anger (v. 20a)

II. Another Reckless Rebellion (2 Kings 24:20b–25:5)
- A. Siege Begins (24:20b–25:1)
  - *What's in Your Playbook?*
- B. Siege Ends (vv. 2–3)
- C. Siege Aftermath (vv. 4–5)

III. Another Harsh Result (2 Kings 25:6–9)
- A. Zedekiah Sentenced (vv. 6–7)
  - *Our Blindness*
- B. Jerusalem Burned (vv. 8–9)

Conclusion
- A. Hope Beyond Disaster
- B. Prayer
- C. Thought to Remember

Introduction

A. Foreseen Disaster

Most of our unwelcome experiences are unforeseen. An accident, a negative medical diagnosis, a conflict with a loved one—if we could foresee such events, we would likely take steps to avoid them.

Some things, however, we *can* reasonably foresee or predict. Failure to fix a leak in the roof will result in more and more damage. A poor diet will lead to a variety of illnesses. "I should have known better" is what we say when a foreseeable disaster befalls us. We experience the pain of regret and shame, thinking of what we could have done to avoid it. We may try to shift the blame. But our experiences in that regard are nothing new to the human condition, as today's lesson makes clear.

B. Lesson Context

Today's text takes us to the time frame of 597–586 BC. Many centuries had passed since Moses warned the Israelites of the consequences of breaking God's covenant (Deuteronomy 29:9–28; 30:15–18). The prophets reminded Israel and Judah of the coming judgment (2 Kings 24:2). The exile of the northern kingdom of Israel in 722 BC had proven the prophets' warnings true (17:3–23). Now Judah too would face God's judgment.

The blame for the tragedy in today's text is most directly traced to the nation's line of leadership. Were we to draw a "good and evil" timeline of Judah's 20 rulers since the beginning of the divided monarchy in the tenth century BC (1 Kings 12), we would see startling swings from evil to good and back again to evil. Today's lesson introduces us to the last in that line of 20 kings, a man named Zedekiah.

Zedekiah's father, Josiah, was the last godly king of Judah (2 Kings 22:1–23:28). Josiah had four sons, Zedekiah being the third of those (1 Chronicles 3:15). Zedekiah might never have been king were it not for the untimely death of his father in battle (2 Kings 23:29–30; 2 Chronicles 35:20–24; compare Jeremiah 46:2).

Following Josiah's death, his ungodly son Jehoahaz (also known as Shallum, 1 Chronicles 3:15; Jeremiah 22:11–12) ruled briefly before being deported to Egypt by Pharaoh (2 Kings 23:30–33). Concurrently, Pharaoh installed Eliakim—another son of Josiah—as king, changing his name to Jehoiakim (23:34). When Jehoiakim died 11 years later, he was succeeded by his son Jehoiachin (24:1–6).

By that time the Babylonians were on the march, overtaking Jerusalem a scant three months after Jehoiachin's ascent to the throne. The Babylonians installed one of his relatives, Mattaniah, in his place as king (2 Kings 24:8–17), renaming him Zedekiah. The first three verses of our lesson's text are worded almost identically to that of Jeremiah 52:1–3 and are very similar to 2 Chronicles 36:11–13.

I. Another Evil King

(2 Kings 24:18–20a)

A. Zedekiah's Reign (vv. 18–19)

18. Zedekiah was twenty and one years old when he began to reign, and he reigned eleven years in Jerusalem. And his mother's name was Hamutal, the daughter of Jeremiah of Libnah.

The four kings who reigned over the final days of Judah were all very young by today's standards when ascending to the throne: Jehoahaz (23), Jehoiakim (25), Jehoiachin (18), and Zedekiah

How to Say It

Babylonians	Bab-ih-*low*-nee-unz.
Chaldeans	Kal-*dee*-unz.
Chaldees	Kal-*deez*.
Eliakim	Ee-*lye*-uh-kim.
Hamutal	Ha-mu-*tal*.
Jehoahaz	Jeh-*ho*-uh-haz.
Jehoiachin	Jeh-*hoy*-uh-kin.
Jehoiakim	Jeh-*hoy*-uh-kim.
Josiah	Jo-*sigh*-uh.
Mattaniah	Mat-uh-*nye*-uh.
Nebuchadnezzar	*Neb*-yuh-kud-***nez***-er.
Nebuzaradan	*Neb*-you-***zar***-a-dun.
Pharaoh	*Fair*-o or *Fay*-roe.
Zedekiah	Zed-uh-*kye*-uh.

Visual for Lesson 10. *Display this visual as you discuss the consequences of evil actions unaccompanied by repentance.*

(21). Some modern studies have proposed that the human brain does not fully mature until about age 25. Thus impulse control is often lower until that point of development.

We may be tempted to blame the sins of the kings on the impulsiveness of youth. After all, it was a preference for the advice of "young men" over that of "old men" that had led to the division of Israel's monarchy centuries before (1 Kings 12:1–19). But lest we be too hasty in that regard, we remind ourselves that King Josiah, one of Judah's godliest rulers, was only 8 years old when he became king. He began to seek God by age 16. And in the twelfth year of his reign, at age 20, "he began to purge Judah and Jerusalem" of their idolatry (2 Chronicles 34:1–3).

Hamutal was the mother of Jehoahaz (see Lesson Context) and of *Zedekiah* (2 Kings 23:31). This *Jeremiah of Libnah* is not the same man as the more familiar prophet Jeremiah who was from Anathoth (Jeremiah 1:1; 29:27).

19. And he did that which was evil in the sight of the Lord, according to all that Jehoiakim had done.

The disheartening evaluation of having done *evil* or being wicked *in the sight of the Lord* occurs about 50 times in the Old Testament; the vast majority of those instances occur in 1–2 Kings and 1–2 Chronicles. By contrast, the evaluation of having done "right in the sight of the Lord" occurs less than half as often—King Josiah having been the last to be acknowledged in that manner (2 Kings 22:2; see Lesson Context).

For Zedekiah to conduct himself in evil ways carries a certain sad but pointed irony. His very name means "the Lord is righteous." The irony intensifies as we see that this name was imposed on him by a pagan king (2 Kings 24:17)!

The scope of Zedekiah's sin is revealed in the phrase *according to all that Jehoiakim had done.* Similar copycat behavior is attributed to Jehoiakim himself as well as to Jehoahaz and Jehoiachin (2 Kings 23:37; 23:32; and 24:9, respectively; see also Lesson Context). The expression "according to all that his father(s) had done" repeated in 2 Kings suggests not merely passive tolerance of evil but active promotion of it.

On Zedekiah's reign, personality, fate, and interactions with the prophet Jeremiah, see Jeremiah 21:1–7; 24:8–10; 27:1–12; 32:1–5; 34:21–22; 37:1–39:7 (compare 2 Chronicles 36:11–13).

What Do You Think?

How do you think watching his father Jehoiakim's evil behavior impacted King Zedekiah?

Digging Deeper

How can we break patterns of generational sin in our own lives and families?

B. The Lord's Anger (v. 20a)

20a. For through the anger of the LORD it came to pass in Jerusalem and Judah, until he had cast them out from his presence.

Historians often point to political and military causes for Judah's ruin. When the people of Israel in the north seceded from the united kingdom under Jeroboam (1 Kings 12), Solomon's son Rehoboam was left only the small territories of Judah and Benjamin in the south. This little kingdom sat between two regions of great power: Egypt to the west and Mesopotamia to the east. Great empires sought to subdue Israel on their way to conquering other great kingdoms. Seen through this lens of relative military and political power, the kings of Israel and Judah did their best to navigate these treacherous waters by means of treaties to play one power off against another.

But the biblical authors do not see the falls of the northern and southern kingdoms as inevitable results of rebellion against superior military powers. Instead, they attribute these falls to *the anger of the Lord.* When God defends His people, they need no human allies (compare Isaiah 7:1–12; 30:1–5; 31:1; 36:6). When He withdraws His protection, then comes their defeat.

God's anger is not selfish or petulant, as human anger often is. Rather, God's anger is a reaction to rebellion and idolatry (Deuteronomy 9:7–9; 11:16–17; Judges 3:7–8; 1 Kings 16:33; 22:53; etc.). God's covenant with Israel had conditions for Israel to meet; failure to meet those conditions would result in promised consequences (Deuteronomy 28:15–68). For the residents of Judah, it is their violation of the covenant that results in God's wrath (4:25–27).

II. Another Reckless Rebellion

(2 Kings 24:20b–25:5)

A. Siege Begins (24:20b–25:1)

20b. That Zedekiah rebelled against the king of Babylon.

Now we learn the specific action that triggers Judah's ultimate exile. The book of Jeremiah records straightforward talks between king and prophet (Jeremiah 37:6–10, 17–20; 38:14–26; etc.). Jeremiah warned of the coming exile, but the king chose to be persuaded by influential advisors and false prophets. They claimed that Judah could escape Babylon's control by aligning with Egypt (Jeremiah 28; 37:5; Ezekiel 17:15; contrast Deuteronomy 17:16). Rebellion had already been tried against Babylon a few years earlier, and it had failed (2 Kings 24:1). It would fail again.

What Do You Think?

In what ways do our sins drive a wedge between God and His people?

Digging Deeper

How can we honor God's heart by taking care of the innocent and the vulnerable in our societies?

What's in Your Playbook?

Sally worked for a prestigious firm where she had oversight of a major account. One day she inadvertently gave a client incorrect information. She debated whether to keep silent or go to her boss, Jeff, to explain what she had done. She chose the latter. As she explained the error to him, she burst into tears, aware that she could be fired.

But that's not what happened. At the end of the explanation, Jeff told Sally that they would call the client. He allowed her to take the lead in apologizing for her error. Jeff himself assured the client that he shared the responsibility. He affirmed that the company would accept loss of revenue or termination of business relationship as necessary.

The client was upset but also deeply impressed by Jeff's humility in taking responsibility. In the end, the client decided to stay with the company and pay the correct billing amount. As Sally rose through the ranks of the company, she used that experience as an example of how leaders act humbly.

The Bible makes clear in many passages that humility and pride are opposites, such as in Proverbs 3:34 (quoted in both James 4:6 and 1 Peter 5:5). Pride says we are self-sufficient; humility admits our need. Trusting God's word for needed action was not in King Zedekiah's playbook (2 Chronicles 36:12–13). Is it in yours? —S. S.

25:1. And it came to pass in the ninth year of his reign, in the tenth month, in the tenth day of the month, that Nebuchadnezzar king of Babylon came, he, and all his host, against Jerusalem, and pitched against it; and they built forts against it round about.

The siege of Jerusalem likely began on January 15, 588 BC, as the Babylonian king takes extreme action to squash the rebellion (see also next week's lesson). What is described is the beginning of a siege against a walled city. The Babylonians were skilled at such warfare, and their abundant artwork celebrating successful sieges shows the pride they took in their cruel skill.

The plan of a siege is simple: seal off the city from any outside source of food and water (compare Isaiah 3:1; Ezekiel 4:16), then wait until the defenders give up due to starvation. Deuteronomy 28:53–57 and Jeremiah 19:9 predicted that parents would eat their own children. This gruesome prediction came true (2 Kings 6:24–29). To begin the siege, the Babylonians (Chaldeans) build encircling *forts;* these are siege works and include battering rams (Ezekiel 4:2; 21:22).

B. Siege Ends (vv. 2–3)

2–3. And the city was besieged unto the eleventh year of king Zedekiah. And on the ninth day of the fourth month the famine prevailed in the city, and there was no bread for the people of the land.

A siege of Jerusalem in 701 BC had failed (2 Kings 19:32–36), but this one does not. Jerusalem falls *on the ninth day of the fourth month* of Zedekiah's *eleventh year* of reign, computed to be July 18, 586 BC. Thus the siege takes a bit longer than two and a half years before it succeeds. Sieges gradually weaken the defenders and their defenses. Starvation and dehydration are deadly, and we may wonder how Jerusalem could have held out for more than 30 months!

Various factors contributed to the length of this siege. Previous kings of Judah had built cisterns for holding water supplies and had improved Jerusalem's defenses (2 Chronicles 26:9–10). Furthermore, Jerusalem may have had a source of water within its walls (2 Kings 20:20; Isaiah 22:9–11). But undoubtedly the biggest contributing factor to the siege's length was that it was lifted temporarily in order for the besiegers to deal with a threat from the Egyptian army (Jeremiah 37:5, 11). This respite undoubtedly allowed food and supplies to be restocked. We should also not discount pure human resilience as another factor.

What Do You Think?

During the two-year siege, do you think Zedekiah sought the Lord?

Digging Deeper

How can we learn to see and take advantage of the opportunities God gives us to change?

C. Siege Aftermath (vv. 4–5)

4. And the city was broken up, and all the men of war fled by night by the way of the gate between two walls, which is by the king's garden: (now the Chaldees were against the city round about:) and the king went the way toward the plain.

The text of Jeremiah 52:7–8 repeats the narrative we see here, while Jeremiah 39:2–5 adds detail. The three narratives in general and the phrase *the city was broken up* in particular do not indicate that Zedekiah surrendered the city or otherwise capitulated (contrast 2 Kings 24:10–12). Instead, a violent breaching of a wall or gate is in view.

Earlier, the prophet had warned that only two outcomes were possible: (1) if Zedekiah surrendered to the Babylonians, then he and the city would be spared; but (2) failure to surrender would result in the opposite (Jeremiah 38:17–23). As *the king* and *all the men of war* flee, they belatedly seem to realize that Jeremiah was right, and they know the fate that awaits them should they stay.

A knowledge of Jerusalem's topography helps us understand the escape route the defeated soldiers use. Valleys border Jerusalem to the east, the south, and (to a lesser extent) the west. Such areas are virtually unusable for an attacking army wishing to launch a direct assault against the city. So an attack has to come from the north. And although *the Chaldees were against the city round about,* the main strength of their force is undoubtedly located in that northerly direction. Indeed, the additional information in Jeremiah 39:3 regarding "the middle gate" indicates just that.

Piecing together various texts reveals that the king's escape route was not quite the same as that of his soldiers. Although this text states that the soldiers flee *by night by the way of the gate between two walls, which is by the king's garden,* it does not say that King Zedekiah did likewise. We find the king's escape route prophesied in Ezekiel 12:12: he would exit via a hole dug through the wall.

Presuming that the king would want to stay near his remaining soldiers, this hole is probably close to "the gate . . . by the king's garden." This serves to place the exit points at and near the gate of the fountain, which is at the extreme southeastern end of the city, near what came to be called the Pool of Siloah (Nehemiah 3:15).

Travel during the darkness of *night* was very difficult in a preindustrial era. At the same time, the lack of light pollution from cities allowed the stars and moonlight to better illuminate the landscape. The defenders of Jerusalem thus likely had some light for sneaking through this thinly guarded section of the Babylonian lines. We speculate that the king and his entourage hoped to obscure their identities and so perhaps escape death or exile.

On the location of *the plain,* see the next verse.

> **What Do You Think?**
> Why do you think the army fled at this pivotal moment?
>
> **Digging Deeper**
> How do we receive courage to face difficult situations in our own lives?

5. And the army of the Chaldees pursued after the king, and overtook him in the plains of Jericho: and all his army were scattered from him.

The Chaldees (Babylonians) know what they're doing, and their pursuit of *the king* ends successfully *in the plains of Jericho.* This area is also mentioned in Joshua 4:13; 5:10. More commonly, however, the area is known as "the plains of Moab" "by" or "near Jericho" (Numbers 22:1; 26:3, 63; etc.). It is located in the Jordan River valley to the east of Jerusalem. The capture of Zedekiah in this area means that the king and others have traveled some 15 miles and negotiated an elevation drop of some 3,300 feet only to have their escape attempt foiled. The prophecies of Jeremiah 21:7; 32:4–5; and Ezekiel 12:12–13 are thus fulfilled in this verse and the next two, below.

III. Another Harsh Result

(2 Kings 25:6–9)

A. Zedekiah Sentenced (vv. 6–7)

6. So they took the king, and brought him up to the king of Babylon to Riblah; and they gave judgment upon him.

Riblah is a city that is well known to the residents of Judah: it is the very place where King Jehoahaz had been imprisoned by Pharaoh some two decades prior (2 Kings 23:33). The distance to be covered to get there is nearly 300 miles. Zedekiah has several days to ponder his fate and why he didn't learn from the result of Jehoiachin's rebellion (2 Kings 24:15–16).

7. And they slew the sons of Zedekiah before his eyes, and put out the eyes of Zedekiah, and bound him with fetters of brass, and carried him to Babylon.

The Babylonian king exacts a vicious and gruesome price for Zedekiah's disloyalty. Such punishments were to serve as vivid examples to others contemplating rebellion. Also executed are all those of high standing in Judah (Jeremiah 39:6; 52:10).

Our Blindness

A titan of the computer industry once said that people tend to overestimate where technology will take us in two years and underestimate where it will take us in ten years. I like that observation and find it useful—to a point.

All observations that are based on human wisdom can be wrong (notice the waffling in the phrase "tend to"). We need only to think about the stock markets to see the truth of that: no one is able to pick all the right stocks to invest in all the time, despite various predictive tools at the trader's disposal. Our foresight into the future just isn't what God's is. Neither was Zedekiah's, whose spiritual blindness resulted in physical blindness.

The choice is stark: to determine where we end up in eternity, we can either trust the eyes of our personal experience or trust God's eyes, which see the certainties of the eternal future. Note that it's "either-or," not "both-and." And today is the day to make your choice. —R. L. N.

B. Jerusalem Burned (vv. 8–9)

8. And in the fifth month, on the seventh day of the month, which is the nineteenth year of king Nebuchadnezzar king of Babylon, came Nebuzaradan, captain of the guard, a servant of the king of Babylon, unto Jerusalem.

Our narrator now shifts from naming the year of Zedekiah's reign to naming that of the Babylonian king, *Nebuchadnezzar*. Judah is vanquished. Babylon is utterly in charge. As historians correlate the dates of the kings' reigns, a month or less has passed since Jerusalem fell.

9. And he burnt the house of the Lord, and the king's house, and all the houses of Jerusalem, and every great man's house burnt he with fire.

Having made an example of Zedekiah, the Babylonians now make an example of the entire city of Jerusalem. The prophets had predicted this outcome (Amos 2:4–5; Micah 3:9–12), and the speaker in Psalm 74:3–8 laments it.

What Do You Think?

How do we determine whether punishments are just or unjust?

Digging Deeper

How do we seek God's justice in our own lives and communities?

Conclusion

A. Hope Beyond Disaster

The story of the fall of Jerusalem attests to God's patience and justice. God told His people what would happen if they broke His covenant (Deuteronomy 28:15–29:29). He saved them from their enemies and gave them time to repent (Judges 2:10–23). Because they failed to repent, the covenant curses fell on Judah (2 Kings 24:1–4).

But judgment was not the last word. God also promised to restore His people and bring them into full relationship with Him (Jeremiah 31:31–34). He sent Jesus Christ to keep that promise (Luke 22:20; 2 Corinthians 3:6). And God is still patient with us (2 Peter 3:9).

B. Prayer

God of justice, we acknowledge You are right in all Your ways. Your righteousness shows us our wickedness, and so we come to You in repentance. Empower us to seek, learn, and apply lessons from Bible history. In the name of Jesus we pray. Amen.

C. Thought to Remember

God means what He says!

Involvement Learning

Enhance your lesson with KJV Bible Student *(from your curriculum supplier) and the reproducible activity page (at www.standardlesson.com or in the back of the* KJV Standard Lesson Commentary Deluxe Edition*).*

Into the Lesson

Before students arrive, write the words *Justice* and *Mercy* as headers on the board.

Begin class time by asking learners to brainstorm attributes of justice and mercy. Write responses on the board under the correct header.

Lead into Bible study by saying, "Today's lesson will look at a terrible story describing how a king of Judah was violently removed from his home. We'll consider why this was an act of God's justice and why believers today can also see God's patient mercy."

Into the Word

Before class, ask a volunteer to prepare a five-minute presentation to explain the setting and context for today's lesson. Encourage the volunteer to use the Lesson Context of this lesson and other lessons from this unit. Ask the volunteer to share that presentation at this point in the class time. The presentation should address the following questions: 1–Who was Zedekiah? 2–What was the nature of his relationship with Jeremiah? 3–How did Zedekiah respond to Jeremiah's various warnings regarding the future of Judah and Jerusalem?

Have two participants read the 12 verses of today's lesson aloud, alternating with each verse. Afterward, announce a closed-Bible pop quiz on how much learners remember about those verses. State that you won't collect the quizzes and that everyone will grade their own. Then distribute handouts (you prepare) with the following multiple-choice questions. *Time limit: one minute!*

1–How old was Zedekiah when he began to reign?
a. 11 b. 12 c. 21
2–How long did Zedekiah's reign last?
a. 10 years b. 11 years c. 12 years
3–Which Babylonian king marched against Jerusalem?
a. Nebuchadnezzar b. Nebuzaradan c. Darius
4–Which of the following is said to have occurred on the "ninth day of the fourth month"?
a. plague b. hailstorm c. famine
5–Who was killed in front of Zedekiah?
a. his wife b. his sons c. his daughters
6–Who is said to have burned down the house of the Lord in Jerusalem?
a. Nebuchadnezzar b. Nebuzaradan c. Darius
[*Answers:* 1-c; 2-b; 3-a; 4-c; 5-b; 6-b]

Option. Distribute copies of the "Many Warnings" exercise from the activity page, which you can download. Have learners work together in pairs to complete as indicated. (This exercise will be more time-consuming than it appears at first glance.) After calling time, ask for volunteers to share responses. Ask learners to consider how the warnings describe some of the events of today's text.

Conclude either activity by asking the following questions for whole-class discussion: 1–How do the events in today's Scripture text reveal God's anger? 2–What was God's anger a response to? 3–How does today's text reveal God's patience and justice?

Into Life

Ask the class: "When have you seen God's patient mercy on display, even amid punishment?" Allow time for the class to give examples.

Lead a brainstorming session on how believers can reflect on God's patient mercy today, especially in the face of disobedience. Write their responses on the board.

Distribute an index card and pen to each participant. Invite them to write one way they will reflect on God's mercy throughout the week.

Alternative. Distribute copies of the "Diary of My Devotion" activity from the activity page. Have learners complete the chart as a take-home activity. To encourage completion, say that you will review responses at the beginning of the next class time.

Conclude class time by reading aloud Lamentations 3:22–23. Close with a prayer expressing gratitude to God for His patient mercy.

November 16
Lesson 11 (KJV)

Ezekiel's Sign

Devotional Reading: 2 Corinthians 1:2–6
Background Scripture: Ezekiel 1:1–3; 2:1–3:27; 8:1–4; 11:22–25; 24:15–24; 33:30–33

Ezekiel 3:10–11

10 Moreover he said unto me, Son of man, all my words that I shall speak unto thee receive in thine heart, and hear with thine ears.

11 And go, get thee to them of the captivity, unto the children of thy people, and speak unto them, and tell them, Thus saith the Lord GOD; whether they will hear, or whether they will forbear.

Ezekiel 24:15–24, 27

15 Also the word of the LORD came unto me, saying,

16 Son of man, behold, I take away from thee the desire of thine eyes with a stroke: yet neither shalt thou mourn nor weep, neither shall thy tears run down.

17 Forbear to cry, make no mourning for the dead, bind the tire of thine head upon thee, and put on thy shoes upon thy feet, and cover not thy lips, and eat not the bread of men.

18 So I spake unto the people in the morning: and at even my wife died; and I did in the morning as I was commanded.

19 And the people said unto me, Wilt thou not tell us what these things are to us, that thou doest so?

20 Then I answered them, The word of the LORD came unto me, saying,

21 Speak unto the house of Israel, Thus saith the Lord GOD; Behold, I will profane my sanctuary, the excellency of your strength, the desire of your eyes, and that which your soul pitieth; and your sons and your daughters whom ye have left shall fall by the sword.

22 And ye shall do as I have done: ye shall not cover your lips, nor eat the bread of men.

23 And your tires shall be upon your heads, and your shoes upon your feet: ye shall not mourn nor weep; but ye shall pine away for your iniquities, and mourn one toward another.

24 Thus Ezekiel is unto you a sign: according to all that he hath done shall ye do: and when this cometh, ye shall know that I am the Lord GOD.

---

27 In that day shall thy mouth be opened to him which is escaped, and thou shalt speak, and be no more dumb: and thou shalt be a sign unto them; and they shall know that I am the LORD.

Key Text

Moreover he said unto me, Son of man, all my words that I shall speak unto thee receive in thine heart, and hear with thine ears. **—Jeremiah 3:10**

Judah, from Isaiah

to the Exile

Unit 3: Ezekiel and the Exile of Judah

Lessons 10–13

Lesson Aims

After participating in this lesson, each learner will be able to:

1. Describe the status of the inhabitants of Judah in general and Ezekiel in particular.
2. Explain the role of a prophet as a "visual aid" that God uses to communicate difficult truths.
3. Suggest ways that Christians can become a "visual aid" to proclaim the gospel of Jesus.

Lesson Outline

Introduction
- A. Shaken to Our Senses
- B. Lesson Context: Ezekiel, the Man
- C. Lesson Context: Ezekiel, the Book

I. Two Imperatives (Ezekiel 3:10–11)
- A. Listen Carefully (v. 10)
  - *Believing in What You "Sell"*
- B. Speak Carefully (v. 11)

II. Unusual Reaction (Ezekiel 24:15–18)
- A. God's Command (vv. 15–17)
- B. Ezekiel's Obedience (v. 18)

III. Sobering Prophecy (Ezekiel 24:19–24, 27)
- A. People's Inquiry (v. 19)
- B. Jerusalem's Fate (vv. 20–23)
- C. Ezekiel's Role (vv. 24, 27)
  - *Glowing in the Dark*

Conclusion
- A. Delivering a Hard Word
- B. Prayer
- C. Thought to Remember

Introduction

A. Shaken to Our Senses

John Newton (1725–1807), author of the beloved hymn "Amazing Grace," had a dishonorable past. Infamous among his misdeeds was his involvement in the slave trade. Even prior to this, he lived far from what would be considered a moral life. At age 11, he lost his mother and was sent off to sea to live with his father. There he soon succumbed to sinful behavior and immoral habits.

After several years as a mariner, he encountered a life-threatening storm. Biographies point to this experience as marking the start of his journey to a committed life of faith. The fear and pain of the near-death experience caused him to struggle with who and what he had become. The result was a conversion experience that marked a shift in the direction of his life and his view of God. Newton repented of his role in the slave trade and joined England's abolition movement.

Sometimes it takes pain and suffering to bring an awareness of our sin. At times, God chooses to allow such circumstances to awaken His people and remind us of who He is and who we are not: God.

B. Lesson Context: Ezekiel, the Man

The prophet Ezekiel was a contemporary of the prophet Jeremiah. Both lived at the time of the Babylonian captivity in the mid-sixth century BC. Ezekiel was 30 years old in "the fifth year of king Jehoiachin's captivity," which was the year 592 BC (Ezekiel 1:1–2; compare 2 Kings 24:8–15).

The Babylonian captivity occurred in three stages: the deportations of 605, 597, and 586 BC (2 Kings 24–25; 2 Chronicles 36). Ezekiel's involuntary relocation to Babylon was a part of the second stage of exile in 597 BC. He was among the 10,000 of the elite citizenry taken at that time (2 Kings 24:12–14). Daniel and other Jews who had been deported in the first stage ended up serving "in the king's palace" (Daniel 1:4). While Ezekiel, coming in the second stage, found himself in a completely different setting. He was "among the captives by the river of Chebar" in Babylon (Ezekiel 1:1).

Ezekiel is introduced as "the priest" (Ezekiel

1:3). And that is what he would have remained had it not been for the divine wrath that was to be visited on the southern kingdom of Judah at the time. His call to be a prophet is described in Ezekiel 2, which is not part of today's study.

C. Lesson Context: Ezekiel, the Book

The book of Ezekiel is commonly and most simply outlined in terms of three sections:

I. Judgment on the covenant people (chapters 1–24)
II. Judgment on foreign nations (chapters 25–32)
III. New hope for God's people (chapters 33–48)

Today's study occurs in the first of these three sections.

One important feature of this book is its many references to exact dates. These are found in Ezekiel 1:1–3; 8:1; 20:1; 24:1; 26:1; 29:1, 17; 30:20; 31:1; 32:1, 17; 33:21; 40:1. Most of these dating formulas introduce a communication from God to the prophet. One example relates news of the fall of Jerusalem from a man who had escaped that carnage (Ezekiel 33:21; compare 4:16–17; 5:10–12). Today's study concerns God's communication before that event happens.

I. Two Imperatives
(Ezekiel 3:10–11)

A. Listen Carefully (v. 10)

10a. Moreover he said unto me, Son of man.

This verse and the next offer us just a small part of Ezekiel's commissioning to be a prophet of God. That lengthy commissioning is described in all of chapters 2 and 3! The idea is that the man Ezekiel must be prepared for his new role.

If we are familiar with the phrase *Son of man* as a self-designation of Jesus, we may be surprised to see it used here to refer to Ezekiel. In fact, of the nearly 200 occurrences of this phrase in the Bible, close to half are found in the book of Ezekiel. Its use here may be to stress Ezekiel's mortality. It is in that light that the prophet is to measure himself against God.

10b. All my words that I shall speak unto thee receive in thine heart, and hear with thine ears.

In Ezekiel 2:8–3:3, the prophet-in-training was commanded to eat a message contained on a "roll of a book" (a scroll) and to fill his "belly" and "bowels" with its words. When we place that command alongside the instruction here for Ezekiel to *receive in* his *heart* what he hears with his *ears* that God has to say, the picture is one of complete and total acceptance of the Lord's message (contrast the people's response in Isaiah 6:9–10).

Believing in What You "Sell"

When I see celebrities or social-media influencers endorse various products, I always wonder if they really believe in and use the products themselves. Are those spokespersons true believers, or are they just taking a paid gig?

The Bible has a lot to say about beliefs and practices that spring from both self-centered and God-centered motives (1 Samuel 12:3–4; Acts 8:18–19; 16:16–21; 2 Corinthians 2:17; 4:1–2; etc.). The cure for wrong motives is to be so thoroughly permeated with the Word of God that there is no room for them.

Here's a challenge in that regard: read the Bible cover to cover, word for word every year for at least 10 years. Having done just that myself, I'm always alert to the danger of substituting my word for God's. Will you take the challenge? —R. L. N.

B. Speak Carefully (v. 11)

11. And go, get thee to them of the captivity, unto the children of the people, and speak unto them, and tell them, Thus saith the Lord GOD; whether they will hear, or whether they will forbear.

To this point in the book, the Lord has spoken of the audience Ezekiel will be addressing as "impudent," "stiffhearted," and "hardhearted" (Ezekiel 2:4; 3:7). As such, they are "briers," "thorns," and "scorpions" (2:6). Ezekiel won't have to travel far to address them because he lives right among *them of the captivity* (see Lesson Context: Ezekiel, the Man).

In sharing in the fate of *the children of the people,* it will be natural for Ezekiel to speak with compassion. But Ezekiel's compassion must not be allowed to soften the Lord's message. *Whether they will hear, or . . . forbear* is irrelevant in that regard (compare Ezekiel 2:5, 7). The prophet's duty is to remain faithful to the Lord's message.

His listeners must decide for themselves whether they will do the same.

> **What Do You Think?**
> Why do you think God told Ezekiel to speak His word whether the people listened or not?
> **Digging Deeper**
> When might God call you to speak, whether or not it seems likely people will receive it?

II. Unusual Reaction

(Ezekiel 24:15–18)

A. God's Command (vv. 15–17)

15–16a. Also the word of the LORD came unto me, saying, Son of man, behold, I take away from thee the desire of thine eyes with a stroke.

The prophet has obeyed God without fail in communicating *the word of the Lord* to the people. Much of this communication has involved him using himself in and as illustrations of God's wrath to come against the covenant people (Ezekiel 4:1–13; 5:1–12; etc.). Another illustration is coming: the loss of *the desire of* the prophet's *eyes,* the death of Ezekiel's wife. What this death is designed to illustrate is revealed in Ezekiel 24:21, below.

16b–17. Yet neither shalt thou mourn nor weep, neither shall thy tears run down. Forbear to cry, make no mourning for the dead, bind the tire of thine head upon thee, and put on thy shoes upon thy feet, and cover not thy lips, and eat not the bread of men.

In a series of nine commands, God directs that Ezekiel's outward, visible and audible reaction to his loss is to be strictly countercultural. Mourning the death of another can involve lengthy and demonstrative behavior in various cultures, both ancient and modern (compare Genesis 37:34–35; 50:1–14). The funeral and accompanying days of mourning would involve all friends and family who could attend. Musicians might be hired to sing laments or play instruments (Matthew 9:23–24, etc.). The volume of sound would be quite high (Mark 5:38, etc.).

The phrases *put on thy shoes upon thy feet, and cover not thy lips* indicate a shared expectation regarding proper "mourning attire" (compare 2 Samuel 14:2; Jeremiah 6:26). Similarly, the phrase *eat not the bread of men* points to food that is customary at funeral meals (compare 16:7).

There is a certain overlap in the meanings of these nine prohibitions, and it's tempting to examine each of the nine in minute detail. It's more valuable, however, to focus on the bigger picture: the larger task of prophetic communication must take precedence over all else.

> **What Do You Think?**
> When has God asked you to go through something difficult, such as the loss of a loved one?
> **Digging Deeper**
> Has God used difficult events in your life to speak to someone else?

B. Ezekiel's Obedience (v. 18)

18. So I spake unto the people in the morning: and at even my wife died; and I did in the morning as I was commanded.

Ezekiel obeys God—period. Even so, we can't help but notice that the text is striking for what it does not say and the obvious questions it does not answer. The timeline of *in the morning . . . at even[ing] . . . in the morning* indicates a period of many hours' duration between Ezekiel's receiving God's instruction, the death of the prophet's *wife*, and the man's divinely commanded visible non-reaction to it. What did Ezekiel do during the hours between those three events? Did he tell his wife about her pending death? Did he pray to God that death would not happen? Had his wife been at the point of death anyway due to illness? The text simply does not say.

III. Sobering Prophecy

(Ezekiel 24:19–24, 27)

A. People's Inquiry (v. 19)

19. And the people said unto me, Wilt thou not tell us what these things are to us, that thou doest so?

The people notice Ezekiel's odd behavior. He exhibits none of the typical actions, emotions, or postures of grief. Interested curiosity is a good first step toward understanding something. But as we move from curiosity to investigation to understanding, we must be aware of what we use as a "filter" in reaching conclusions. Another way to say this is that we must acknowledge our presuppositions. Then we must be prepared to change them as the evidence requires.

This challenge repeats itself throughout the book of Ezekiel as God labors to change the mindset of His people. That mindset is one of rebellion against God, a fact stressed about a dozen times in this book (Ezekiel 12:2–3, etc.). God's repeated technique is to catch people's attention through certain actions or inactions of His prophet (compare 12:9; 17:12). If the explanation for those behaviors doesn't match what the people expect to hear (that is, it doesn't line up with their presuppositions), then the explanation is rejected or twisted in some way (compare 20:49).

B. Jerusalem's Fate (vv. 20–23)

20. Then I answered them, The word of the LORD came unto me, saying.

The author's frequent use of the words *I* and *me* leaves no doubt that Ezekiel himself was writing of his personal experiences regarding his interactions with God. As the prophet passes along divine communication, he is fulfilling his role as a watchman (Ezekiel 3:16–27; 33:1–20). The phrase *the word of the Lord* makes clear that what the prophet is about to say does not originate with himself.

The numerous uses of this introductory formula in the Bible usually don't specify exactly how the communication occurred. Those cases where that "how" is specified include communication by dreams or visions (1 Kings 3:5; Daniel 2:19; etc.), through an angel (Judges 6:12, etc.), and from a burning bush (Exodus 3). But the method is not important here. What's important is that the prophecy proves to be true.

21a. Speak unto the house of Israel.

People are more open to learning something new if they themselves open the discussion. That seems to be the technique here as Ezekiel has waited for the people to ask, "Why?" before he gives the answer that begins in this verse.

The response *unto the house of Israel* invites a review of the terminology used to identify God's covenant people of the Old Testament era. Shortly after the death of King Solomon in 930 BC, the united kingdom of Israel's 12 tribes divided into two kingdoms (1 Kings 11:41–12:20). After that happened, the word *Israel* often became associated with only the 10 northernmost tribes (1 Kings 12:21, etc.). Even so, that distinction had also been used before the monarchy divided (2 Samuel 19:41–43, etc.). Concurrently, the designation *Judah* often was shorthand for the 2 southern tribes of Judah and Benjamin (Jeremiah 6:1; compare Ezra 4:1 with Ezra 4:4). The tribe of Benjamin was much smaller than that of Judah (Numbers 1:20–46; 26:1–51; Judges 20–21; 1 Samuel 9:21).

But that distinction in sense and reference was not always airtight after the monarchy divided. In the text before us, for example, the word *Israel* does not seem to include the 10 northern tribes since the audience is those of Judah (and Benjamin) who were in Babylonian exile; the 10 northernmost tribes had been taken into Assyrian exile over 130 years prior (2 Kings 18:9–12). That conclusion harmonizes with the way the writer refers to Israelites in Ezekiel 2:3; 3:7; 6:5; etc. (compare Ezekiel 9:9).

We also should investigate differing ways the covenant people are identified as we consider the first part of the phrase *the house of Israel.* The Hebrew translated *house* describes the people group as a single family. But the Old Testament describes the Israelites in several other ways as well: as "sons of Israel," "people of Israel," etc. In referring to the residents of Judah, Ezekiel prefers

How to Say It

Assyrians	Uh-*sear*-e-unz.
Babylonians	Bab-ih-*low*-nee-unz.
Chaldeans	Kal-*dee*-unz.
Chebar	Kee-*bar.*
Pharaoh	*Fair*-o or *Fay*-roe.

Visual for Lesson 11. *Point to this visual as you conclude the lesson and consider the question in this visual as a class.*

to use some form of the word *Israel* rather than *Judah* by a ratio of nearly 11 to 1.

21b. Thus saith the Lord God: Behold I will profane my sanctuary, the excellency of your strength, the desire of your eyes, and that which your soul pitieth; and your sons and your daughters whom ye have left shall fall by the sword.

This is the answer to the "Why?" question of Ezekiel 24:19, above. The prophet's audience is expected to see that his reaction (or, more precisely, his lack of reaction) to the death of his wife as an analogy:

I. Loss of Ezekiel's wife = loss of temple (*the desire of your eyes*);
II. Ezekiel = the people;
III. Ezekiel's reaction = people's reaction to the destruction and death.

As the Assyrians were God's tool to exile Israel's 10 northern tribes in 722 BC (2 Kings 17:3–6; Isaiah 7:18–25), so also the Babylonians (Chaldeans) would be to the southern kingdom of Judah in 586 BC (Ezekiel 24:1–2; 33:21). The temple is not some kind of good-luck charm that protects evil people (Jeremiah 7:1–4; see also Lesson 6).

Although Ezekiel's audience in Babylon would not personally experience the destruction to be wrought by Nebuchadnezzar, they would share in the horror of that event nonetheless. They would experience the dismay expressed in texts such as Psalms 79, 137, or Lamentations 2. This would be the punishment for their sin of idolatry.

22–23. And ye shall do as I have done: ye shall not cover your lips, nor eat the bread of men. And your tires shall be upon your heads, and your shoes upon your feet: ye shall not mourn nor weep; but ye shall pine away for your iniquities, and mourn one toward another.

The prophet now drives home the analogy. No one can miss the "this will be like that" connections between his reactions (and lack of reactions) to his wife's death and those that will characterize the people when they hear of Jerusalem's fall. As Ezekiel speaks, it is January 15, 588 BC (Ezekiel 24:1); Jerusalem would fall on July 18, 586 BC. Thus Jerusalem has only a bit longer than two and a half years before it will be destroyed.

We may wonder how a city could survive a siege that lasts more than 30 months. The answer is found in Jeremiah 37:11—the siege was lifted temporarily while the Babylonian (Chaldean) army dealt with a threat regarding Pharaoh's army.

What Do You Think?

What do you think it was like for the Israelites, being unable to mourn openly for the loss of their loved ones and their city?

Digging Deeper

What does mourning communicate about the people we have lost?

C. Ezekiel's Role (vv. 24, 27)

24. Thus Ezekiel is unto you a sign: according to all that he hath done shall ye do: and when this cometh, ye shall know that I am the Lord God.

We dare not miss the point here! False prophets and their false prophecies are rampant in this era (Ezekiel 13:1–7; 22:28). Their messages contradict those of the true prophets of God. So, how are the people to know who is a true prophet and who is a false prophet? The obvious answer is to wait and see whose prophecies come true. It is in that sense that the prophet *Ezekiel* will be *a sign* (compare 4:3; 12:6, 11; and 24:27, below).

What Do You Think?

What do you think God wanted the Israelites to realize through the prophecy?

Digging Deeper

In what ways do you struggle to recognize that God is in control and the one that we should go to for help?

Glowing in the Dark

My children have always loved glow sticks—the kind you can find at dollar stores. Glow sticks are meant to be enjoyed in the dark. And for them to work at all, they have to be broken. It can seem counterintuitive to break a brand-new item. But that's what makes glow sticks work. Without breaking them, they cannot glow.

For a person to come to (or return to) God requires a certain "breaking" of one's spirit or attitude (Psalms 34:18; 51:17; Isaiah 57:15; 66:2; etc.). It's only when we're broken that we realize our need for Him (compare Luke 18:9–14). Our glow can serve to light the world best when we're in our darkest hour. The prophet Ezekiel is a prime example still today. In his darkest times, Ezekiel was a shining light for the Lord.

Everyone is broken at some time and in some way. The resulting darkness can be lonely and frightening. But it is at such times that our character can shine brightest. Consider the differing outlooks in Job 2:9 and Matthew 5:14–16. Which will you pick when disaster strikes? —B. R.

27. In that day shall thy mouth be opened to him which is escaped, and thou shalt speak, and be no more dumb: and thou shalt be a sign unto them; and they shall know that I am the Lord.

This verse signals a shift away from God's address to the people (through Ezekiel) and toward the prophet himself. The time frame signified by *in that day* is the time of Jerusalem's predicted fall.

A feature of Ezekiel's being *a sign* is that he was to react to his grief by not reacting to it per Ezekiel 24:16b–17, above. That reaction was to include silence. This verse reverses that, as the prophet's *mouth* is to *be opened* and he is allowed *to speak, and be no more dumb* (compare Ezekiel 3:26–27). The phrase *to him which is escaped* refers to a man in Ezekiel 33:21–22; that passage also lifts the prophet's silence.

What Do You Think?

How do you think the people felt when events occurred just as Ezekiel and other prophets had said?

Digging Deeper

How can we take care to listen to what God has to say to us?

Conclusion

A. Delivering a Hard Word

The prophets often brought words of warning or imminent destruction and pain due to the people's lack of faithfulness to God. We see this time and time again in Scripture. The prophets were also responsible for bringing the word of God to people, whether they listened or not. Both the messages and the messengers were often rejected (Luke 11:47–51). God even predicted that such things would happen (Jeremiah 7:27; Ezekiel 3:7).

It's probably safe to say that few, if any, of us will be asked to do something quite like Ezekiel was required to do. Even so, we all face times when speaking difficult truths to people is uncomfortable. Although the gospel is good news, it is also a stumbling block. As it tells us that we can have forgiveness in Christ, it also tells us we are sinners in need of a Savior. To speak this is our task.

B. Prayer

Heavenly Father, we struggle to pay attention during times of crisis because we do not want to face the need for change in our own lives. Empower us to make the changes we need in order to be better followers of Your Son, Jesus Christ. In His name we pray. Amen.

C. Thought to Remember

Know the message. Live the message.
Be the message.

Involvement Learning

Enhance your lesson with KJV Bible Student *(from your curriculum supplier) and the reproducible activity page (at www.standardlesson.com or in the back of the* KJV Standard Lesson Commentary Deluxe Edition*).*

Into the Lesson

Write this prompt on the board for class members to see as they arrive:

An example that made a difference to me . . .

Distribute a slip of paper and a pen to each class member and ask them to jot down a phrase or a sentence to respond to the prompt. They should not sign their slip. Collect the slips and read them back to the class.

Ask the following questions for whole-class discussion: 1–What do these examples have in common? 2–How would you define a "difference maker"? 3–What would motivate you to be a difference maker?

Lead into Bible study by saying, "Today begins a three-week study on the life of Ezekiel: a prophet who became a 'visual aid' for God's message. In today's study, we'll consider the message of Ezekiel and how we can serve as a 'visual aid' for the gospel."

Into the Word

Before class, recruit a volunteer to present a brief overview of the life and call of Ezekiel. Direct the volunteer to use the Lesson Context and other commentaries. Ask the volunteer to begin the presentation by asking, "What do you know about Ezekiel?" Write answers on the board. Have the volunteer present their overview at this point.

Divide the class into pairs and direct each pair to read Ezekiel 3:10–11; 24:15–24, 27. Distribute pens and copies of the handout (you create) with the following questions: 1–Describe Ezekiel's mission. 2–Describe Ezekiel's context. 3–Where was Ezekiel when he received the call? 4–What is significant or surprising about his call? 5–How did Ezekiel communicate God's warnings? 6–What challenging command did God give to Ezekiel? 7–Why did God give this command?

After no more than 10 minutes, reconvene the class and ask for volunteers to share their responses. After whole-class discussion, direct participants to work with their partners to write a short diary entry for Ezekiel on the day he received this command from God. After five minutes, ask volunteers to share their diary entries.

Alternative. Distribute copies of the "Ezekiel's Challenging Mission" exercise from the activity page, which you can download. Have participants work in pairs to complete as indicated.

After either alternative, have groups present their findings for whole-class discussion. Ask the following question: "How was Ezekiel a 'visual aid' to communicate God's message of promises and judgments?"

Into Life

Write the following words as headers on the board: *Home / Work / Community.* Ask the following for whole-class discussion: "How can we live as a 'visual aid' to proclaim the gospel of Jesus at home, at work, and in our community?" Conduct a whole-class brainstorming session by challenging participants to complete the columns on the board.

Distribute index cards and pens to learners. Have them work in pairs to write down their choices of how they will be "visual aids" to proclaim the gospel of Jesus throughout the week.

Alternative. Mount large sheets of blank butcher paper on your classroom walls. Instead of using index cards, ask pairs to sketch a picture to illustrate how they will be "visual aids" to proclaim the gospel. Let pairs explain their pictures to the whole class. Consider writing a label under each picture to remind class members of the explanations.

Alternative. Distribute copies of the "Worship Only God" activity from the activity page. Have learners complete the first section individually in a minute or less before discussing the rest of the page with a partner. After several minutes, allow pairs to share with the whole class.

November 23
Lesson 12 (KJV)

Ezekiel's Responsibility

Devotional Reading: Jeremiah 17:5–10
Background Scripture: Ezekiel 18:1–32; 33:1–20

Ezekiel 33:7–16a

7 So thou, O son of man, I have set thee a watchman unto the house of Israel; therefore thou shalt hear the word at my mouth, and warn them from me.

8 When I say unto the wicked, O wicked man, thou shalt surely die; if thou dost not speak to warn the wicked from his way, that wicked man shall die in his iniquity; but his blood will I require at thine hand.

9 Nevertheless, if thou warn the wicked of his way to turn from it; if he do not turn from his way, he shall die in his iniquity; but thou hast delivered thy soul.

10 Therefore, O thou son of man, speak unto the house of Israel; Thus ye speak, saying, If our transgressions and our sins be upon us, and we pine away in them, how should we then live?

11 Say unto them, As I live, saith the Lord God, I have no pleasure in the death of the wicked; but that the wicked turn from his way and live: turn ye, turn ye from your evil ways; for why will ye die, O house of Israel?

12 Therefore, thou son of man, say unto the children of thy people, The righteousness of the righteous shall not deliver him in the day of his transgression: as for the wickedness of the wicked, he shall not fall thereby in the day that he turneth from his wickedness; neither shall the righteous be able to live for his righteousness in the day that he sinneth.

13 When I shall say to the righteous, that he shall surely live; if he trust to his own righteousness, and commit iniquity, all his righteousnesses shall not be remembered; but for his iniquity that he hath committed, he shall die for it.

14 Again, when I say unto the wicked, Thou shalt surely die; if he turn from his sin, and do that which is lawful and right;

15 If the wicked restore the pledge, give again that he had robbed, walk in the statutes of life, without committing iniquity; he shall surely live, he shall not die.

16a None of his sins that he hath committed shall be mentioned unto him:

Key Text

So thou, O son of man, I have set thee a watchman unto the house of Israel; therefore thou shalt hear the word at my mouth, and warn them from me. **—Ezekiel 33:7**

Judah, from Isaiah
to the Exile

Unit 3: Ezekiel and the Exile of Judah

Lessons 10–13

Lesson Aims

After participating in this lesson, each learner will be able to:

1. Identify righteous and unrighteous behavior.

2. Compare and contrast Ezekiel's role as a watchman with the New Testament's imperatives in that regard.

3. Make a plan to speak the truth in love and warn others of danger, even when the news is unwelcome.

Lesson Outline

Introduction

A. Learning about Hot Stoves

B. Lesson Context

I. Watchman to the Exiles (Ezekiel 33:7)

A. Commissioned (v. 7a)

B. Commanded (v. 7b)

What to Watch First

II. Warning the Unrighteous (Ezekiel 33:8–9)

A. Guilt and Accountability (v. 8)

None of Your Business?

B. Guilt and Immunity (v. 9)

III. Warning the Israelites (Ezekiel 33:10–16a)

A. Irrelevant Past (vv. 10–12)

B. Reversible Present (vv. 13–16a)

Conclusion

A. Living as a Watchman

B. Prayer

C. Thought to Remember

Introduction

A. Learning about Hot Stoves

Philosophies regarding learning styles go in and out of fashion. Categorizing people as visual learners, auditory learners, or kinesthetic (physical activity) learners has its adherents. Categorizing learning theories as cognitive, behaviorist, constructivist, humanist, and connective holds sway in some quarters. The list goes on and on.

Let's try a simpler approach by proposing that there are two general ways to learn things: by *wisdom* and by *experience.* Wisdom is when you learn from the mistakes of others; experience is when you learn from your own mistakes. Parents readily see these two learning styles in their children. The mother warns that the stove is hot. One child heeds the warning and doesn't touch it (wisdom); the other child puts his hand on the stove anyway, only to withdraw it quickly in pain (experience).

We've all heard the old saying, "Experience is the best teacher." But we easily see the fallacy of this axiom when the alternative is to be taught by wisdom. In today's lesson, the residents of Judah now in Babylonian exile continue to learn the hard way (by experience) the consequences of disobeying God; they are also reminded of the alternative.

B. Lesson Context

References to "the twelfth year" of the Babylonian exile bracket today's lesson text of Ezekiel 33:7–16a (see Ezekiel 32:1, 17; 33:21). That exile happened in three stages, with deportations taking place in the years 605, 597, and 586 BC (2 Kings 24:1–25:21). "The twelfth year" dates from 597 BC (Ezekiel 1:2). Thus our lesson today takes us into the year of the fall of Jerusalem, in 586 BC. The residents of Judah who had been in exile already for 12 years and longer were about to experience another wave of their countrymen joining them in captivity.

Regarding literary context, the text for today's lesson is part of the larger unit of Ezekiel 33:1–20. This unit examines and illustrates Ezekiel's role as a prophet, the messages he is to convey, what mindset to expect from his audience, and how to respond to wrong thinking. Ezekiel 33:1–

20 is something of a condensed version of Ezekiel 18, in which the prophet corrects an exaggerated view of group responsibility that sees its members as children suffering for the sins of their parents.

I. Watchman to the Exiles

(Ezekiel 33:7)

A. Commissioned (v. 7a)

7a. So thou, O son of man, I have set thee a watchman unto the house of Israel.

This half-verse offers three phrases that are familiar by this point in the book of Ezekiel. Regarding the 93 uses of the phrase *son of man* to designate Ezekiel, see commentary on Ezekiel 3:10 in last week's lesson. Regarding the initial designation of the prophet as *a watchman,* see Ezekiel 3:17. Regarding the use of the phrase *the house of Israel,* see commentary on Ezekiel 24:21 in last week's lesson (compare Jeremiah 36:2).

The word *watchman* appears in the *King James Version* a total of 19 times; 5 of those 19 are in the book of Ezekiel. In a physical sense, a watchman is a sentinel whose observation post is at the top of an elevated tower. From there he can relay information regarding the approach of enemy forces (2 Kings 9:17, etc.). He is the ancient version of an electronic early warning system. God calls Ezekiel to be a spiritual watchman over His people.

B. Commanded (v. 7b)

7b. Therefore thou shalt hear the word at my mouth, and warn them from me.

The second half of the verse leaves no doubt regarding Ezekiel's role as watchman: he is to *warn* the people of approaching consequences for sinful behavior. Again, this is nothing new to Ezekiel; the command seen here reinforces the one already given in Ezekiel 3:17.

What to Watch First

A friend's young daughter overheard her father telling the neighbor something that wasn't 100 percent accurate. And with all the boldness of a 6-year-old, she confronted her father about his lie. She reminded him of his own words to her about lying and why it was wrong.

Adults seem to become less bold in that regard as the years pass. When witnessing sin, it's often easier just to remain silent. We don't want to "make waves." We justify our silence by misinterpreting the "judge not" of Matthew 7:1. We fear the various repercussions that can ensue (compare John 7:13; 9:22; 12:42; 19:38; etc.). One repercussion for Ezekiel was to be treated dismissively (Ezekiel 20:49).

We move toward a godly solution by pausing to realize what we should watch first and foremost: ourselves (Luke 17:1–2; Galatians 6:1; 1 Timothy 4:16). Failure to do so results in hypocrisy. And in our continuous self-watch, we make certain we are using God's Word as the standard for the evaluation (2 Timothy 3:16; Hebrews 4:12; contrast 2 Corinthians 10:12). What steps can you take today to watch yourself more faithfully? —S. S.

II. Warning the Unrighteous

(Ezekiel 33:8–9)

A. Guilt and Accountability (v. 8)

8. When I say unto the wicked, O wicked man, thou shalt surely die; if thou dost not speak to warn the wicked from his way, that wicked man shall die in his iniquity; but his blood will I require at thine hand.

A repeated theme in this book is that of personal responsibility for sin (compare Ezekiel 33:14, 20; 18:4). And for the prophet Ezekiel to turn a blind eye toward such sin will result in his bearing some level of responsibility for the resulting deaths (*his blood will I require at thine hand*). In a spiritual sense, we would place such intentional blindness in the category of a "sin of omission"—failing to do something required by God (Numbers 9:13, etc.). In an earthly sense, this might be similar to "negligent homicide," where a person's conduct disregards the life and safety of others (compare 35:22–23). The attitude of the runaway prophet Jonah is informative here.

The Hebrew verb translated *warn* here occurs frequently in the book of Ezekiel compared with the rest of the Old Testament. What may be implied regarding the responsibility of other biblical prophets is stated to Ezekiel clearly and often.

What Do You Think?

Do you think it is fair that Ezekiel will be responsible for the blood of those he does not warn? Why or why not?

Digging Deeper

What are ways we might be called to warn those around us?

None of Your Business?

Imagine this situation: you are standing on the platform of a commuter train station. You look up and see someone standing on the railroad tracks, blissfully unaware that a train is approaching. Would you not instinctively yell at your loudest to warn that person to get off the tracks?

Now change that scene to be spiritual in nature as you imagine that the train is God's wrath as it approaches an unrepentant sinner who isn't aware of the danger. Shouldn't you likewise shout a warning, or would you merely think, *How sad, but that's none of my business?*

Let's push this further. If in either situation you shout the warning, but the endangered person shouts in reply, "Where I'm standing and what I'm doing is none of your business!" What would you do next? —R. L. N.

B. Guilt and Immunity (v. 9)

9. Nevertheless, if thou warn the wicked of his way to turn from it; if he do not turn from his way, he shall die in his iniquity; but thou hast delivered thy soul.

This verse repeats Ezekiel 3:19. The prophet will not bear any responsibility for the death of the unrepentant if Ezekiel has done his job of communicating the divine will. We may wonder why such a prophetic warning is even necessary! Have the covenant people not had the Ten Commandments and the Law of Moses for centuries at this point? Indeed, they have. But things can get "lost in the shuffle" in various ways (2 Kings 22:8–13, etc.). And we humans seem to have a desire to interpret actions and attitudes in sinful ways (Isaiah 5:20, etc.).

III. Warning the Israelites

(Ezekiel 33:10–16a)

A. Irrelevant Past (vv. 10–12)

10a. Therefore, O thou son of man, speak unto the house of Israel.

See commentary on Ezekiel 33:7a, above, regarding these two phrases.

10b. Thus ye speak, saying, If our transgressions and our sins be upon us, and we pine away in them, how should we then live?

God anticipates an if-then response from the people, and He begins to prepare His prophet to answer it. The *if* part indicates that the truth of the people's personal responsibility for their *transgressions* and *sins* is beginning to sink in.

When a person is in a very negative situation, there's typically an attempt to discover why. Often this involves "playing the blame game," as others are seen to be responsible. But, as Ezekiel 18 also tells us, God will have none of this! As the people begin to "get it" in this regard, they will wonder what they can do to reverse the situation. Change will seem hopeless given the fact that they now are low on strength (*pine away*) to change things as they languish in exile. Their experience of pining away was itself part of the covenantal curses (Leviticus 26:39; compare Ezekiel 4:17; 24:23.)

How Ezekiel is to respond to the if-then question is established in the next verse.

What Do You Think?

Why do you think it was hard for the Israelites to turn away from their sins, even when they knew that their sins were killing them?

Digging Deeper

What sins do we find especially hard to turn from as individuals? As a community?

11. Say unto them, As I live, saith the Lord God, I have no pleasure in the death of the wicked; but that the wicked turn from his way and live: turn ye, turn ye from your evil ways; for why will ye die, O house of Israel?

The oath-phrase *as I live* occurs 16 times in

Ezekiel—far more than in any other book of the Bible. With its use, God takes an oath in the only worthy name: His own. Since people swear oaths by something higher than themselves and nothing is higher than God, God swears an oath in His own name (Hebrews 6:13; compare Matthew 5:33–37; 23:16–22). This solemn oath is God's assurance that He is willing and able to reclaim the repentant person's life. But there must be a permanent turning from sin.

The one who created us takes no delight in our suffering, even when it is deserved. As 2 Peter 3:9 puts it, God is "longsuffering to us-ward, not willing that any should perish, but that all should come to repentance" (compare Ezekiel 18:23, 32). Unlike Jonah, who wanted sinners destroyed, Ezekiel agrees with God. The prophet's words aim to help the people change, not merely to condemn. He holds out hope that God's words can again be honored.

This hope extends not just to individuals, but to the people as a whole. The rhetorical question *why will ye die* becomes both an invitation to live and a recognition that change is possible.

12a. Therefore, thou son of man, say unto the children of thy people.

On the designation *son of man*, see the discussion above and of last week. The phrase *children of thy people* is a near-literal translation of the underlying Hebrew; a very literal translation would be "sons of thy people." The phrase is interesting because of its rarity. The exact Hebrew lettering occurs only eight times in the Old Testament, and six of those eight are in Ezekiel—and four of those six are here in chapter 33. (For all eight, see Leviticus 19:18; Ezekiel 3:11; 33:2, 12, 17, 30; 37:18; Daniel 12:1.) The idea seems one of all-inclusiveness; the word of God applies to multiple generations.

How to Say It

Deuteronomy	Due-ter-*ahn*-uh-me.
Ezekiel	Ee-*zeek*-ee-ul or Ee-*zeek*-yul.
Leviticus	Leh-*vit*-ih-kus.
Zacchaeus	Zack-*key*-us.

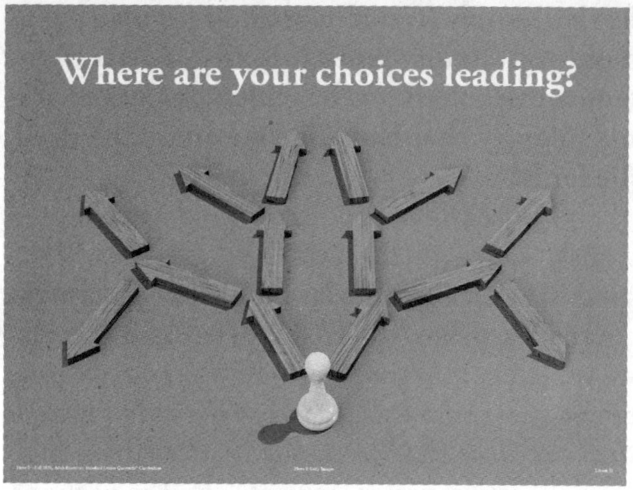

Visual for Lesson 12. *Display this visual as you discuss the commentary associated with Ezekiel 33:13–16a.*

12b. The righteousness of the righteous shall not deliver him in the day of his transgression: as for the wickedness of the wicked, he shall not fall thereby in the day that he turneth from his wickedness.

This verse can be summed up this way: whichever way you turn, the past doesn't count. If a *righteous* person rebels, his past life of *righteousness* won't count. If a *wicked* person repents, her past life of wickedness won't count. The phrase *the righteousness of the righteous* is interesting because of its rarity; it is found only here and in Ezekiel 18:20 in the Old Testament.

For its part, the Hebrew word translated *righteous* is rendered differently in other passages, depending on context. In Ezekiel 45:10, it is translated three times as "just" (as in "fair"). In Proverbs 8:15, it is translated "justice." In all instances, the reference is to something positive.

12c. Neither shall the righteous be able to live for his righteousness in the day that he sinneth.

The prophet's earlier use of this vocabulary in the lengthy chapter of Ezekiel 18 adds a nuanced, realistic view of human affairs. Proper treatment of others and devotion to God can break cycles of injustice and impiety. Those cycles do exist and have real power unless vigorously identified and resisted.

B. Reversible Present (vv. 13–16a)

13. When I shall say to the righteous, that

he shall surely live; if he trust to his own righteousness, and commit iniquity, all his righteousnesses shall not be remembered; but for his iniquity that he hath committed, he shall die for it.

This verse stresses a contrast that has been previously sketched (Ezekiel 18:24; etc.). It will be stressed again centuries later in the era of the new covenant (Hebrews 10:38; 2 Peter 2:20–21). As we see God promising life *to the righteous,* we hasten to stress that the phrases *shall surely live* and *shall die for it* refer primarily to eternal life and eternal condemnation, respectively. The pages of the Bible bear witness to many instances of godly, righteous people who were persecuted to the point of losing their earthly lives as they lived out Matthew 10:28.

Digging deeper into the intent of this verse, we may wonder what kind of sin the phrase *commit iniquity* refers to, and it's easy to draw the wrong conclusions. A righteous person will still sin, but less and less so as spiritual maturity progresses. But people don't actually *become* righteous under either the old or new covenant; the reality of sin prevents that. Rather, God has a plan that allows us to be *counted as if* we were righteous. Romans 4, quoting Genesis 15:6 and Psalm 32:1–2, explains this. For those in Christ, the debt for all our sins—past, present, and future—has been paid by the blood of Christ (Romans 3:21–26; 1 John 1:9). What God speaks through Ezekiel, rather, seems to deal with a decisive change in allegiance by a person, the new allegiance being to wickedness and iniquity (1 John 2:15–17).

> **What Do You Think?**
> What do you think it means that righteous people can "trust" in their righteousness and still "commit iniquity"?
> **Digging Deeper**
> How can we guard against acting as though they were above the law?

14. Again, when I say unto the wicked, Thou shalt surely die; if he turn from his sin, and do that which is lawful and right.

These two verses revisit a topic already discussed; in this case the reference is to Ezekiel 18:27; 33:8, above. A choice of taking the path of *the wicked* is not an irreversible one. For the wicked to switch to the path of the righteous is possible, as it involves both attitude and action. The attitude is to *turn from sin* as the person renounces that path. The action embraces positive behaviors that are consistent with those of a righteous person according to God's expectations.

The words *lawful* and *right* are translations of two common Hebrew words that appear together about 100 times in the Old Testament. Together in the phrase *that which is lawful and right,* they occur only 7 times, all in this book (Ezekiel 18:5, 19, 21, 27; 33:14, 16, 19). In this regard, the two words seem to be used as synonyms or near-synonyms, such as they are used together in poetic passages (Psalms 36:6; 72:1; etc.). The word translated *lawful* is also translated "judgments" in Ezekiel 20:11; there it is teamed up with the word *statutes* to identify the path of life.

> **What Do You Think?**
> If a person may repent and receive mercy, what does this tell us about how God feels about people who do evil things?
> **Digging Deeper**
> How should this change how we feel about or treat such people?

15. If the wicked restore the pledge, give again that he had robbed, walk in the statutes of life, without committing iniquity; he shall surely live, he shall not die.

We can't miss the mirror image of Ezekiel 33:14–15 as these two verses reflect 33:13. This verse deals with some wrongs to be made right as the formerly wicked person walks the new path. *The pledge* refers to collateral or security taken for something that is on loan to someone else.

This issue is addressed in at least a dozen Old Testament passages. Regarding the nature of the collateral, six passages speak of an article of clothing (Exodus 22:26; Deuteronomy 24:17; Job 22:6; Proverbs 20:16; 27:13; Amos 2:8). Three passages identify the collateral or security deposit in terms of a millstone (Deuteronomy 24:6), an ox (Job 24:3), and a child (Job 24:9). Those in Ezekiel 33:15; 18:12, 16 have an uncertain reference.

The observation "the borrower is servant to the lender" (Proverbs 22:7) reflects the fact that the lender has a lot of power over the borrower. This power is subject to abuse (compare 6:1–5; 11:15; 17:18). In an era without banks or other lending institutions, loans were person to person for purposes of survival, not for raising capital to start businesses. This tempted lenders to use failure to repay as an excuse for oppression.

The wicked pay no attention to restrictions in the Law of Moses either as they relate to retaining a pledge or to requirements for restitution (Exodus 22:1–4; Leviticus 6:2–5; Numbers 5:5–8). The phrase *give again that he had robbed* is another indicator of the right behavior of one who changes from the path of death to the path of life. This reminds us of the repentant attitude and promised action of Zacchaeus (Luke 19:8).

What Do You Think?

Repentance in this passage involves giving back what was taken. What might a person do when this is not possible?

Digging Deeper

What is an example of amends you have made when repenting of past sin?

16a. None of his sins that he hath committed shall be mentioned unto him.

God's wrath awaits the unrepentant. But once repentance comes, God holds no grudges (Isaiah 43:25; Ezekiel 18:22), unlike people (compare Leviticus 19:18). Divine forgiveness is not a "one and done" feature of God's love. It is ongoing, and its "talk" must be accompanied by its "walk" for a God-honoring outcome.

Conclusion

A. Living as a Watchman

As members of the new covenant, today we continue to ponder the connection between sin and suffering for those living under the old covenant (compare Job 21:19; Luke 13:1–5; John 9:2). Righteous people do indeed suffer because of realities beyond their control. But today's lesson says that the path of the righteous is the one to travel nonetheless. Walking the path of the wicked results in destruction. Considering God's charge to Ezekiel to be a watchman, how might we live out a watchman role?

At the outset, it is important to understand that Ezekiel received his call to serve as a prophetic watchman by direct revelation from God. Ezekiel filled this role at a particular time in history, to a particular group of people, in ways that were relevant to his time, place, and audience. We are not prophets in the same sense that Ezekiel was. Those who claim today to be commissioned by God to be prophets in the sense of being able to foretell the future may well be proven wrong (Deuteronomy 18:22; Hebrews 1:1–2).

Even so, there are opportunities for us to speak a watchman's words of warning and wisdom to those around us. God doesn't desire that anyone should perish (2 Peter 3:9). He punishes disobedience justly, but He is also gracious, merciful, and patient. He invites sinners to repent and turn from their wicked ways to find life in His Son. We have this good news to proclaim!

Moreover, it is not up to us whether people heed our words. Like Ezekiel, our responsibility is to tell the story of the good news of the gospel (Matthew 28:19–20). Whether that good news is accepted or rejected is not within our control. However, our own faithfulness in proclaiming it is.

B. Prayer

O God our Father, who does not desire anyone to be lost in sin or crushed by despair, speak good news into our broken world so that we may make wrongs right and restore relationships to a state of health. Keep us from the path of eternal death. Grant us strength as we continue on the way of the One who is "the way, the truth, and the life," Your Son, Jesus. It is in His name we pray. Amen.

C. Thought to Remember

Speak and act as a watchman!

Involvement Learning

Enhance your lesson with KJV Bible Student *(from your curriculum supplier) and the reproducible activity page (at www.standardlesson.com or in the back of the* KJV Standard Lesson Commentary Deluxe Edition*).*

Into the Lesson

Display images of various "warning signs." For each image, ask participants to answer the following questions: 1–Why is the sign needed? 2–What would happen if the sign wasn't there? 3–What would happen if a person ignored the sign?

Alternative 1. Divide the class into small groups, ensuring each group includes at least one member with a smartphone. Have groups complete an internet search for pictures of warning signs. Direct groups to choose one image and use it to answer the questions above. After calling time, bring groups together to share their signs and responses.

Lead into the Bible study by saying, "We all know that warnings are valuable and maybe necessary. Today, we'll study one of God's spokesmen who God charged to warn His people. We'll see how the man's actions might be an example for us."

Into the Word

Help students understand the setting for today's study by summarizing material found under the Lesson Context for this lesson and lesson 11. Include information regarding Ezekiel, his ministry, and the historical events occurring during his ministry.

Option. Distribute copies of the "Standing on Our Own" exercise from the activity page, which you can download. Have learners work in small groups to complete as indicated. After five minutes, ask volunteers to share how Ezekiel 18 gives further context to today's lesson.

Ask a volunteer to read Ezekiel 33:7–16a aloud. Divide students into equal groups. Distribute a handout (you create) with the following questions for in-group discussion: 1–What are the if-then statements in Ezekiel 33:7–16a? 2–Which statement(s) describe(s) the consequences of righteous behavior? 3–Which statement(s) describe(s) the consequences of unrighteous behavior? 4–What is the role of the "watchman" in this text?

After calling time, reconvene the class to review their findings. After groups have shared, ask volunteers to read aloud Matthew 18:15–19; Galatians 6:1–5; and Ephesians 4:11–16, 25. Distribute a handout (you create) with the following questions for in-group discussion: 1–How do these texts explain the Christian's role as a "watchman" or "lookout" for sin? 2–How would you define the role of a spiritual "watchman" or "lookout"? 3–What are the challenges believers face in filling this role? After calling time, reconvene the class to review their findings.

Into Life

Ask participants to brainstorm modern-day situations that require a spiritual "watchman" or "lookout." Write responses on slips of paper, one response per slip. Ask for volunteers to role-play these situations. Call the volunteers to the front of the class and allow them to choose one of the slips of paper. After allowing one minute for the volunteers to prepare, call on them to role-play the situation.

After the activity, ask the following questions for whole-class discussion: 1–What are some motivations to have a similar difficult conversation? 2–How do these conversations require speaking truth in love? 3–Why is it essential that these conversations come from an attitude of love rather than hostility?

Distribute a pen and index card to each learner. Challenge participants to identify a situation requiring them to speak the truth in love and warn others of danger, even when the news is unwelcome. Direct learners to write down a plan for doing so. Conclude class with small-group prayer for grace and boldness to act on the identified concerns.

Option. Distribute copies of the "Letter to a Friend" activity from the activity page. Have learners complete it individually in a minute or less before discussing conclusions with a partner.

November 30
Lesson 13 (KJV)

Ezekiel's Vision

Devotional Reading: Revelation 7:9–17
Background Scripture: Ezekiel 47:1–12

Ezekiel 47:1–9, 12

**1 Afterward he brought me again unto the
door of the house; and, behold, waters issued
out from under the threshold of the house
eastward: for the forefront of the house stood
toward the east, and the waters came down
from under from the right side of the house, at
the south side of the altar.
2 Then brought he me out of the way of
the gate northward, and led me about the way
without unto the utter gate by the way that
looketh eastward; and, behold, there ran out
waters on the right side.
3 And when the man that had the line in his
hand went forth eastward, he measured a thou-
sand cubits, and he brought me through the
waters; the waters were to the ancles.
4 Again he measured a thousand, and
brought me through the waters; the waters
were to the knees. Again he measured a thou-
sand, and brought me through; the waters were
to the loins.
5 Afterward he measured a thousand; and
it was a river that I could not pass over: for the
waters were risen, waters to swim in, a river
that could not be passed over.
6 And he said unto me, Son of man, hast
thou seen this? Then he brought me, and
caused me to return to the brink of the river.
7 Now when I had returned, behold, at the
bank of the river were very many trees on the
one side and on the other.
8 Then said he unto me, These waters issue
out toward the east country, and go down into
the desert, and go into the sea: which being
brought forth into the sea, the waters shall be
healed.
9 And it shall come to pass, that every thing
that liveth, which moveth, whithersoever the
rivers shall come, shall live: and there shall be
a very great multitude of fish, because these
waters shall come thither: for they shall be
healed; and every thing shall live whither the
river cometh.**

**12 And by the river upon the bank thereof,
on this side and on that side, shall grow all
trees for meat, whose leaf shall not fade, nei-
ther shall the fruit thereof be consumed: it
shall bring forth new fruit according to his
months, because their waters they issued out
of the sanctuary: and the fruit thereof shall be
for meat, and the leaf thereof for medicine.**

Key Text

By the river upon the bank thereof, on this side and on that side, shall grow all trees for meat, whose leaf shall not fade, neither shall the fruit thereof be consumed: it shall bring forth new fruit according to his months, because their waters they issued out of the sanctuary: and the fruit thereof shall be for meat, and the leaf thereof for medicine. **—Ezekiel 47:12**

Judah, from Isaiah to the Exile

Unit 3: Ezekiel and the Exile of Judah

Lessons 10–13

Lesson Aims

After participating in this lesson, each learner will be able to:

1. List some key features of Ezekiel's vision.
2. Explain the nature of prophecy, whose fulfillment can arrive in unexpected or surprising ways.
3. Identify one image of the vision that he or she finds most encouraging and explain why it gives hope.

Lesson Outline

Introduction
- A. Mirage or Hope?
- B. Lesson Context

I. Guiding (Ezekiel 47:1–2)
- A. East and South (v. 1)
  - *Speaking Compass*
- B. North and East (v. 2)

II. Wading (Ezekiel 47:3–5)
- A. First Thousand Cubits (v. 3)
- B. Second Thousand Cubits (v. 4a)
- C. Third Thousand Cubits (v. 4b)
- D. Fourth Thousand Cubits (v. 5)

III. Learning (Ezekiel 47:6–9, 12)
- A. Numerous Trees (vv. 6–7)
  - *The Blackberry Bush That Could*
- B. Flourishing Fish (vv. 8–9)
- C. Productive Trees (v. 12)

Conclusion
- A. Hope for Abundant Life
- B. Hope for Eternal Life
- C. Prayer
- D. Thought to Remember

Introduction

A. Mirage or Hope?

A character in a movie is alone in a hot and arid place. He is parched with thirst and nearing heat exhaustion from the blazing sun. Suddenly, he sees a glimmering pool near a tree. Water and shade! The character experiences a surge of hope. But hopes are dashed when he eventually realizes that he has been fooled by a shimmering illusion. What seemed to support life turned out to be only a mirage.

The presence of water is a sign of life. This inescapable fact invites powerful comparisons and imagery in the Bible (examples: Jeremiah 2:13; John 7:37–39). Today's lesson offers one of the most powerful of those.

B. Lesson Context

Most of the contextual information in the previous lessons from Ezekiel still applies and need not be repeated here. What's changed about the context is a shift from addressing the Judahites's then-present situation in Babylon to a vision of the future. All of Ezekiel 40–48, about 20 percent of the entire book, relates this vision. Understanding the meaning and significance of the vision is crucial to appreciate this great book fully. The imagery of the "water of life" river and its surroundings has parallels elsewhere in the Bible. Revelation 22, in particular, offers several points for fruitful comparison.

The vision is meant to encourage God's people. The exile had decimated their homeland. Their capital had been razed. Their temple was destroyed. The exiles now lived in a strange land under a foreign power. While the prophets had predicted a return (Jeremiah 29:10–14), many feared they would never see Judah again. Ezekiel's visions offer these exiles reason to hope. The visions concern a new city and a transformed homeland. The glory of this new Jerusalem and Judah will be greater than what was lost.

The vision opens in Ezekiel 40:1 with a record of the date. By comparison with various texts and calendars, that date would likely be around 573 BC. As the reader moves through the text from 40:1,

Ezekiel is seen to receive details concerning a restored city and temple. These prophetic images include particulars regarding the officials to serve in the new temple, allotment of land, and instructions regarding offering procedures for Passover and other special days. Then we arrive at chapter 47.

I. Guiding

(Ezekiel 47:1–2)

A. East and South (v. 1)

1. Afterward he brought me again unto the door of the house; and, behold, waters issued out from under the threshold of the house eastward: for the forefront of the house stood toward the east, and the waters came down from under from the right side of the house, at the south side of the altar.

The pronoun *he* refers to the "man" (perhaps an angel) who has been guiding Ezekiel's visionary tour from the beginning (Ezekiel 40:3). Previously, the man had taken Ezekiel to the temple's "porch" (40:48–49) and "door" (41:1–2). Now they are back again *unto the door of the house* (the temple). Like Solomon's temple before it, Ezekiel envisions this temple facing *toward the east,* the direction from which the sun rises (compare with the prophet's vision of the old temple in Ezekiel 8:16).

On arrival, Ezekiel witnesses a bizarre sight: water flowing *from under the threshold of the house eastward.* We think of a threshold as the small gap between the bottom of a closed door and the floor. That flow of water is to the south side of the altar (south is to Ezekiel's *right side* if he is facing east, watching the water flow away from the door). Apparently the waters are flowing in a southeasterly direction. We will see why shortly.

Speaking Compass

I "speak compass," but my wife doesn't. On our way to work together one day, we encountered a road-blocking hazard as we traveled south. So, I immediately turned east into a neighborhood that was completely unfamiliar to us. Soon, we turned south and I began trying to decide the best street to turn west on.

When we did turn west, we had driven a few blocks when my wife exclaimed, "I have no idea where we are!" No sooner had those words escaped her lips than we found ourselves right where we should be: at the driveway entrance to our workplace.

Not everyone "speaks compass" in a physical, earthly sense, and GPS can make it unimportant to be able to do so. But what about the spiritual sense? The book of Ezekiel uses the four compass directions about 150 times—far more than any other book in the Bible. Here's a challenge for your spiritual growth: look up those 150 times and study them to discern their spiritual purposes.

—R. L. N.

B. North and East (v. 2)

2. Then brought he me out of the way of the gate northward, and led me about the way without unto the utter gate by the way that looketh eastward; and, behold, there ran out waters on the right side.

The guide now leads the prophet outside the envisioned Jerusalem. To get to the outside of the *gate . . . that looketh eastward,* they first head north to exit the city by *the gate* there. They then move clockwise until they reach their destination. We may wonder why they don't just go out the east gate rather than take a long way around. The answer is in Ezekiel 44:1–3: the Lord has closed that gate.

In his new location, the prophet notes consistency in the direction the water flows.

> **What Do You Think?**
> How can water, in its various contexts, illustrate the character or actions of God?
>
> **Digging Deeper**
> How do Psalms 23:1–2; 24:1–2; Isaiah 43:20; 48:18; and John 7:37–39 inform your response?

II. Wading

(Ezekiel 47:3–5)

A. First Thousand Cubits (v. 3)

3. And when the man that had the line in his hand went forth eastward, he measured a

thousand cubits, and he brought me through the waters; the waters were to the ankles.

The man leads Ezekiel *eastward,* the direction toward which the waters flow. The man has a *line in his hand* for measuring. This may be the same "line of flax" mentioned at the beginning of the vision (Ezekiel 40:3).

Walking a distance of *a thousand cubits,* the two find themselves in ankle-deep water. If the cubits mentioned are the standard ones of 18 inches, they have walked about 500 yards, a little short of three-tenths of a mile. If the cubit used is the 21-inch long cubit of Ezekiel 43:13, then the distance is one-third of a mile. Walking at a rate of two miles per hour requires 10 minutes or less to cover the distance.

B. Second Thousand Cubits (v. 4a)

4a. Again he measured a thousand, and brought me through the waters; the waters were to the knees.

The computation of possible distances is the same as in the previous verse. Wading through the water at a rate of one mile per hour means it takes 17 to 20 minutes, depending on the cubit-length used (see above), to reach this segment of the visionary tour.

C. Third Thousand Cubits (v. 4b)

4b. Again he measured a thousand, and brought me through; the waters were to the loins.

By this point, it is surely apparent that the source of the water cannot be Jerusalem's Gihon Spring or any other naturally occurring flow! And this contributes to an issue of what to expect. Some commentators believe that the imagery of Ezekiel 40–48 depicts a literal, physical temple that is yet to be rebuilt. In that case, Ezekiel is foreseeing God's plans to alter the topography (landscape) and hydrology of Jerusalem miraculously.

Other commentators believe, however, that the vision of the restored temple and its changed surroundings are figurative. This position may be supported by how Luke 3:4–6 uses the changed topography of Isaiah 40:4 as a metaphor for the ministry of John the Baptist (compare Matthew 3:3; Mark 1:3; John 1:23). The leveling of the terrain could refer to the change of peoples' hearts, receptivity, etc. Images of a temple in Revelation 11:19; 14:15; 15:5–8; etc. are also interpreted as figurative since Revelation 21:22 says that no temple was seen in the heavenly city of Jerusalem.

Another support for this position is that although numerous dimensions are given for the restored temple (and some of its furnishings and surroundings) in Ezekiel's vision, the height of the temple itself is never specified (contrast Ezekiel 40:5, 12, 42; 43:13).

D. Fourth Thousand Cubits (v. 5)

5. Afterward he measured a thousand; and it was a river that I could not pass over: for the waters were risen, waters to swim in, a river that could not be passed over.

With walking and wading a total distance of 4,000 cubits now, the prophet and his guide have covered a distance of between 1.14 and 1.33 miles in the vision, depending on cubit length (see above). But now the two must turn back because of the river's increasing depth as the flow of water continues unchecked.

III. Learning

(Ezekiel 47:6–9, 12)

A. Numerous Trees (vv. 6–7)

6. And he said unto me, Son of man, hast thou seen this? Then he brought me, and caused me to return to the brink of the river.

On the address *Son of man,* see commentary on Ezekiel 3:10 in lesson 11. The guide's question may be posed as an exclamation of wonder: "Son of man, look at this! Isn't all this something?"

After an unspecified time of experiencing their amazement, Ezekiel and his guide seemingly head back to the point where they had begun wading into *the river.* They are back on dry land.

7. Now when I had returned, behold, at the bank of the river were very many trees on the one side and on the other.

The book of Ezekiel speaks of trees in about 30 verses—more than any other Bible book; about half of those 30 verses are in the prophet's vision of

Ezekiel 40–48. The imagery of *trees* in this verse finds a parallel in the vision of Revelation 22:2, given more than 600 years later. The author of Revelation envisions the trees of Ezekiel's vision as trees of life (Genesis 2:9). Verse 12 will provide the reason for this connection.

Taking the book of Ezekiel as a whole, the prophet's reference is usually to ordinary trees (examples: Ezekiel 15:2, 6). But the prophet also refers to the trees of Eden (31:16, 18). Tree imagery occurs extensively in Jesus' teachings centuries after Ezekiel (examples: Matthew 7:15–20; Luke 13:6–9).

The Babylonians' devastation of the land during the siege of Jerusalem included the cutting of trees for the building of siege ramps (Jeremiah 6:6). The Israelites were constrained in the use of trees for such purposes (Deuteronomy 20:19–20), but the Babylonians knew no such constraint. Since Ezekiel's vision speaks to renewal of the land, that includes renewal of trees, both those that produce fruit and those that don't, as signs of recovery.

What Do You Think?

How can you use tree imagery to illustrate an aspect of Christian faith?

Digging Deeper

Which of Scripture's uses of tree imagery is the most compelling to you? Why?

The Blackberry Bush That Could

My sister-in-law's massive, flourishing garden surprised us. When she was first getting it started, someone gave her a blackberry bush. It was small and seemingly lifeless. Without much planning or research, she planted it off to the side with hardly a thought for its growth. She was far more concerned about her peppers and tomatoes, which grew in abundance.

One day, we went to visit so my husband could see the results of her work. We immediately noticed something striking: the blackberry bush had overtaken nearly an entire corner of her garden! It was thriving to the point of encroaching on the sweet potatoes and green beans. The plant was loaded with sweet, juicy blackberries.

Visual for Lesson 13. *Display this visual as you ask the discussion questions associated with Ezekiel 47:9.*

Ezekiel's vision reminds us that our current circumstances do not determine the future God has or desires for us. Things as they are now are not permanent. New life can come to those experiencing an arid deadness of spirit. New life comes when we connect with the source of living water: Jesus (John 7:37–38). Whether in Old Testament times or New, the need for living water doesn't change. Before you choose your source, read Jeremiah 2:13.

—B. R.

B. Flourishing Fish (vv. 8–9)

8. Then he said unto me, These waters issue out toward the east country, and go down into the desert and the sea: which being brought forth into the sea, the waters shall be healed.

The two-word phrase *east country* is unique in the Old Testament. The Hebrew word translated *country* is quite rare. In two of its four occurrences elsewhere, it designates general areas of non-Israelite habitation (Joshua 13:2; Joel 3:4). In Ezekiel's vision, however, the territory must be Israelite. This is because *the sea,* which is the Dead Sea, is receiving water flowing from Jerusalem. The *desert* that intervenes is Israelite territory.

The city of Jerusalem lies at almost exactly the same latitude as the northernmost tip of the Dead Sea. Therefore, the waters flowing from Jerusalem's temple toward this sea have to flow a bit to the south as well as east in order to go into the sea rather than end up connecting with the Jordan River.

The Dead Sea is several times saltier than the oceans. The vast majority of aquatic creatures cannot survive in an environment such as that of the Dead Sea. In Ezekiel's vision, however, the waters become fresh, allowing life to flourish not only in the water but all around its banks. The sea that symbolizes sterility and death comes to symbolize vibrant life (compare 2 Kings 19–22).

Picking up on the image of water flowing from Jerusalem is Zechariah 14:8. That passage foresees "living" waters flowing not only toward the Dead Sea but also westward into the Mediterranean Sea (compare Joel 3:18; John 7:38; Revelation 22:1–2).

9. And it shall come to pass, that every thing that liveth, which moveth, whithersoever the rivers shall come, shall live: and there shall be a very great multitude of fish, because these waters shall come thither: for they shall be healed; and every thing shall live whither the river cometh.

A consequence of the healing that occurs *whithersoever the rivers shall come* is that marine life is able to exist and flourish where it previously could not, especially in the once "dead" sea. We could say that the "River of Life" has created the "Sea of Life." Fish, which could not have survived in the overly salty waters of the old Dead Sea, are now described as *a very great multitude.* Fresh water will yield abundant life in the formerly brackish water and on the land that is near the water.

> **What Do You Think?**
> In addition to salty water, what other images—biblical and otherwise—strike you as illustrations of one's spiritual deadness before coming to Christ? Why?
>
> **Digging Deeper**
> What images strike you as illustrations of one's spiritual life in Christ?

C. Productive Trees (v. 12)

12. And by the river upon the bank thereof, on this side and on that side, shall grow all trees for meat, whose leaf shall not fade, neither shall the fruit thereof be consumed: it shall bring forth new fruit according to his months, because their waters they issued out of the sanctuary: and the fruit thereof shall be for meat, and the leaf thereof for medicine.

Ezekiel's "tour guide" now returns to describing the trees seen earlier in the vision. Here they are described as *all trees for meat* (or food, which in this case is fruit). That their produce will not *be consumed* speaks to the fact that the fruit will not be susceptible to disease or anything else that would make it inedible. The prediction that each tree *shall bring forth new fruit according to his months* means that these trees will bear fruit every month—quite unlike ordinary trees, with their dormant cycles—because of the effect of the *waters* flowing from *the sanctuary.* The leaves of the trees have life-giving properties, just as the waters do. All this reminds us of the presence of "the tree of life" in the Garden of Eden (Genesis 2:9), only here there are numerous trees of life!

There is much here that is also reflected in Revelation 22:1–2, 14, 19. Like Ezekiel, John points toward a world made Eden-like, fit for the redeemed as their new home. Both use the imagery of a perfect place that is connected with a restored and perfected relationship between God and His faithful people. Revelation 22:1–2 also says that the tree of life will provide fruit for God's people, and its leaves will bring healing.

In a figurative sense, the prophet Ezekiel sometimes sees trees as valuable symbols of the return to wholeness that awaits God's people. An example is the extended vision of renewal in Ezekiel 34:11–31. There, the revival of forests, fields, and pastures accompanies the end of the Babylonian domination

How to Say It

Assyrian	Uh-*sear*-e-un.
Babylonian	Bab-ih-*low*-nee-un.
Deuteronomy	Due-ter-*ahn*-uh-me.
Ezekiel	Ee-*zeek*-ee-ul or Ee-*zeek*-yul.
Jerusalem	Juh-*roo*-suh-lem.
Mediterranean	*Med*-uh-tuh-***ray***-nee-un.
Tabernacles	***Tah***-burr-*nah*-kulz.

of the land of Israel and the return of the people to their homeland. In part, this was because invading Assyrian and Babylonian armies systematically and deliberately felled trees in order to oppress the local populations they attacked (see comments to Ezekiel 47:7, above). The fruitful nature of the trees reflects God's pleasure to provide for the repentant and faithful. The fruit does not run out before the next crop comes along, so abundant is it. Ezekiel attributes this great abundance of the stream flowing *out of the sanctuary*. The temple becomes the symbol of God's great generosity.

> **What Do You Think?**
> How will you be a source of "rivers of living water" (John 7:38) in the upcoming week?
>
> **Digging Deeper**
> How will you be attentive to the Holy Spirit's leading in this regard?

Conclusion

A. Hope for Abundant Life

The most significant word picture in today's passage is that of *water*. The Old Testament uses water imagery to convey the message that God's "water of life" is never stagnant but always available, active, and life-giving (Psalms 1:3; 36:8; 84:5–6; Isaiah 12:3; 41:18; 43:19; 66:12; Jeremiah 31:9). Jesus used the imagery of water on various occasions to depict the abundant life He came to bring. When He attended the Feast of Tabernacles in Jerusalem, He declared, "If any man thirst, let him come unto me, and drink. He that believeth on me, as the scripture hath said, out of his belly shall flow rivers of living water" (John 7:37–38; compare 4:10, 14).

Jesus was not quoting a single, particular Old Testament passage, but the general message derived from several passages, including our text for today. Interestingly, the climax of the Feast of Tabernacles featured the pouring out of water as part of the symbolism. It was in such a setting—perhaps during the pouring-out ceremony itself—that Jesus made His promise of living water.

One observer noted that the water-pouring ceremony at this feast in Jesus' day was interpreted in various Jewish traditions as a symbolic anticipation of the outpouring of the Spirit in fulfillment of various Scriptures, including Ezekiel 47:1–9. The Gospel of John says that Jesus used "living water" to refer to the Spirit (John 7:39). This means that we can now enjoy the benefits of the spiritual refreshment from the Holy Spirit.

B. Hope for Eternal Life

We see Ezekiel's vision reaching its clearest and ultimate expression in Revelation 22. There the apostle John saw a certain river as the source of life. Trees on either side of John's river were fruitful, just like Ezekiel's. And the leaves of the trees that John saw were a source of healing, again just like Ezekiel's. Such parallels indicate how Ezekiel's great vision should be understood. It does not appear that the temple layout shown to that prophet was ever intended to be followed by the exiles who returned or by any other group of God's people. Since the vision portrays something unique and miraculous, we must allow God Himself to declare how its fulfillment is to be understood. That is what the New Testament does for us. It points to a fulfillment initiated by Jesus' first coming and climaxed by His second coming. At Jesus' return, His holy city will become inhabited for eternity by His people. It is a city built by God Himself (Hebrews 11:10).

> **What Do You Think?**
> How does today's text encourage you regarding the hope for eternal life?
>
> **Digging Deeper**
> In what ways will you worship God as a response to that hope?

C. Prayer

O God, we see a world both broken and beautiful. Help us to see Your new world, not only in time and space but also in human souls deeply connected to You, our Creator. Help us find ways to live in that world dawning because of Your Son. Amen.

D. Thought to Remember

Our current situation isn't permanent.

Involvement Learning

Enhance your lesson with KJV Bible Student *(from your curriculum supplier) and the reproducible activity page (at www.standardlesson.com or in the back of the* KJV Standard Lesson Commentary Deluxe Edition*).*

Into the Lesson

Announce a game to identify benefits and problems related to the use of water in its liquid and solid (ice) forms. Allow one minute of silent reflections before you start.

Begin the game by randomly pointing to a learner as you say one of these four phrases: *liquid benefit, liquid problem, solid benefit,* or *solid problem*. That person has five seconds to come up with an answer in that regard. They then get to call on another person while voicing one of the four phrases. Jot responses on the board to make sure they are not repeated.

When learners run out of answers, lead into Bible study by saying, "Although water isn't always beneficial in either form, today's lesson uses an image of water that is of great benefit."

Into the Word

Today's lesson format will be guided instruction through the text. Ask volunteers to read the text aloud, as it is sectioned below. Some discussion starters are suggested, but it will be important to follow each discussion starter with this question: "What impact could this section of text have had on the original audience exiled in Babylon?" Expected and possible responses are in italics. Write responses on the board.

Verses 1–2: Identify the source of the water and to which direction it flows. *(The temple is the immediate source, but learners may note that God must be the ultimate source. The water flows eastward.* ***Original impact:*** *Exiles made aware that the temple is to be renewed in some sense, etc.)*

Verses 3–5: Explain what is happening in the progression of these three verses. *(The flowing water gets deeper and deeper as the distance increases.* ***Original impact:*** *This must be supernatural since there is no river in that area.)*

Verses 6–7: Identify a result of the river flowing. *(Trees begin to be visible.* ***Original impact:*** *The presence of trees implies a reversal of homeland devastation.)*

Verses 8–9: Explain the effect the flowing river has on things in its path. *(The waters of the Dead Sea become fresh, able to sustain a fishing industry.* ***Original impact:*** *Implies more than the homeland merely reverting to its status before the exile; this is a supernatural improvement to the area.)*

Verse 12: Explain the relationship between the river and the trees. *(The river makes it possible for the trees to grow; trees, in turn, provide a continual source of food and medicine.* ***Original impact:*** *Divine healing of both land and people.)*

Conclude this segment by asking learners how today's text reminds them of other sections of Scripture. *(Possible responses are Genesis 2:8–10 and Revelation 21:1–2; 22:1–3.)*

Alternative. Distribute a handout (you create) with the following words as headers across the top: *Verse / Vision / Verbiage / Meaning.* Under the *Verse* heading, add six rows labeled: *verse 1, verse 2, verses 3–5, verse 6, verses 7–9, verse 12.* Ask participants to work in small groups to complete the chart using Ezekiel 47:1–9, 12. After 10 minutes, ask groups to compare responses in whole-class discussion.

Option. Distribute copies of the "A River Runs through Scripture" activity from the activity page, which you can download. Discuss insights after completing in small groups.

Into Life

Review the list created after either activity of Into the Word. Divide learners into pairs and ask them to identify at least one item from the list that encourages them about their future.

Option. Distribute copies of the "Meditations for Others" activity from the activity page. Have learners complete it as a take-home activity. Remind learners that you will ask volunteers to share at the beginning of the next class.

Enduring Beliefs of the Church

Special Features

Lessons

Unit 1: Our God and the Holy Scriptures

Unit 2: Grace and Reconciliation

Unit 3: The Church and Its Teachings

Quarterly Quiz

Use these questions as a pretest or as a review. The answers are on page iv of This Quarter in the Word.

Lesson 1

1. "The law of the LORD is _______." *Psalm 19:7*

2. Paul tells Timothy that Scripture makes one "_______ unto salvation." *2 Timothy 3:15*

Lesson 2

1. The beauty of the "lilies of the field" is more glorious than which Old Testament figure? (Saul, David, Solomon) *Matthew 6:28–29*

2. Jesus taught, "Seek ye first the kingdom of God, and his ___________." *Matthew 6:33*

Lesson 3

1. The shepherd invites his friends and neighbors to rejoice upon finding the lost sheep. T/F. *Luke 15:6*

2. Christ died for us while we were still _______. *Romans 5:8*

Lesson 4

1. The Holy Spirit testifies that we are children of Abraham. T/F. *Romans 8:16*

2. Who intercedes for us when we don't know what to pray for? (the Father, the Son, the Spirit) *Romans 8:26*

Lesson 5

1. Walking in what results in fellowship with other believers? (light, truth, joy) *1 John 1:7*

2. We know that we know God if we keep His _________. *1 John 2:3*

Lesson 6

1. The father responded to his son's return with compassion. T/F. *Luke 15:20*

2. Peter describes the Holy Ghost as what? (blessing, honor, gift) *Acts 2:38*

Lesson 7

1. Abraham claimed that he was "dust and ashes" before the Lord. T/F. *Genesis 18:27*

2. Jesus' parable depicts whom? (choose two: Sadducee, Pharisee, publican, zealot) *Luke 18:10*

Lesson 8

1. Who revealed to Peter that Jesus is the Christ? (the Father, Jonah, Elijah) *Matthew 16:17*

2. Jesus inquires of Peter's love _______ times. *John 21:17*

Lesson 9

1. Jesus uses parables to describe the "_______ of God." *Mark 4:26, 30*

2. In Ephesians 4, Paul mentions "deacons" as one of the offices of the church. T/F. *Ephesians 4:11*

Lesson 10

1. Jesus told His followers to baptize exclusively in the name of the Son. T/F. *Matthew 28:19*

2. Jesus said the cup is the "new _______" in His blood. *1 Corinthians 11:25*

Lesson 11

1. "Remember the sabbath day, to keep it _______." *Exodus 20:8*

2. John heard a "great voice" like a cymbal. T/F. *Revelation 1:10*

Lesson 12

1. Jesus was asked when He would restore the kingdom to Israel. T/F. *Acts 1:6*

2. Who did Paul ask to help finish the Corinthians' gift of grace? (Timothy, Thomas, Titus) *2 Corinthians 8:6*

Lesson 13

1. The commandment that is "first of all" is the command to "love thy neighbour as thyself." T/F. *Mark 12:29–30*

2. According to James, faith is "dead" if not accompanied by what? (grace, works, prayer) *James 2:17*

Quarter at a Glance

by Joshua Seth Houston

The lessons of this quarter invite us to meditate on the fundamental beliefs of the Christian faith. This study will show us that God has revealed His grace and mercy. As a result, God's people are called to live by His standard—a standard that is often countercultural.

Our God and the Holy Scripture

The quarter begins as we study the Trinitarian God—Father, Son, and Holy Spirit—whom we know through Scripture's revelation. Scripture recounts how God's people can know Him and live faithfully through faith in Christ Jesus (2 Timothy 3:14–15; see lesson 1).

Through various word images, Scripture conveys characteristics of God and reveals aspects of our relationship with Him—He is our caring heavenly Father (Matthew 6:24–34; see lesson 2), the shepherd who seeks lost sheep (Luke 15:3–7; see lesson 3), and our advocate or comforter (Romans 8:26–27; see lesson 4).

Grace and Reconciliation

The apostle Paul teaches that humans are in a state of sin (Romans 3:23). The letter of 1 John expands on this fact, reminding us that no one can claim to "have no sin" (1 John 1:8; see lesson 5). However, Jesus Christ, the Son of God, has become our advocate and the "propitiation" for sins (2:1–6). Christ's defeat of sin on the cross introduces us to the gracious gift of new life. We are invited to respond to this gift through repentance, seeking forgiveness for our sins (Acts 2:38–39; see lesson 6).

Our reception of God's gracious gift of salvation leads us to "walk in the light" of new life (1 John 1:7). We walk in this way as we become disciples of Jesus Christ, following Him with obedience, worship, and humility (see lesson 7). The journey of discipleship will not always be easy—the life of the apostle Peter demonstrates the ups and downs of discipleship (see lesson 8)! However, we don't have to go on this journey alone. In Christ, we are reconciled to God and one another, called into the covenant community: the church.

The Church and Its Teachings

The final unit focuses on the church as the one body of Christ, spiritually gifted for ministry and mission (see Ephesians 1:22–23; 4:4–6; see also lesson 9). Each member is essential to the function of the body (Romans 12:4–8; 1 Corinthians 12:12). Together, all parts work to build each other up for the edification and growth of the body that is the church.

> *In Christ, we are reconciled to God and one another, called into the covenant community: the church.*

Christ gave the church two ordinances vital for its mission and witness. Baptism serves as the ritual entry to the life of faith and a way to follow the example of our Savior, who Himself was baptized (Matthew 3:13–17; see lesson 10). The Lord's Supper invites us to a time of self-examination as we remember Christ's sacrifice and anticipate His bodily return (1 Corinthians 11:23–29; see lesson 10). Through these ordinances, the church receives spiritual nourishment and empowerment for its mission: calling people to repentance and proclaiming the reign of Christ "unto the uttermost part of the earth" (Acts 1:8; see lesson 12).

The church's mission flourishes when we obey God and proclaim the gospel and its transforming power. One way we can contribute to this mission is through our generosity and hospitality, reminiscent of the practices of the burgeoning first-century church (see 2 Corinthians 8:3–9; see also lesson 12). When the church remembers and obediently follows its mission, we learn to love God and our neighbors, thus fulfilling the two greatest commands (Mark 12:28–34; see lesson 13).

Get the Setting

by Brenner S. Carlson

On the night He was betrayed, Jesus established an institution we call the Lord's Supper. This meal inaugurates a new covenant and a new community: the assembly of Christ's followers called *church*.

In some ways, this group was like others of its time: its initiates underwent a practice for entry into the community (baptism), met regularly to celebrate special meals (the Lord's Supper), and had expectations for ethical behavior. However, the trajectory of the church has always differed from the prevailing culture.

Early Organization and Practices

Since the earliest days, apostles and leaders have urged the church to live up to its mission and potential. Acts describes the leadership of this fledgling movement and its strategy of mission to the world from the city of Jerusalem (6:1–7; 15:1–41; etc.). Equally, Paul's letters to local church leaders call for the careful structuring of organization and practices so that Christians might present a proper witness (1 Timothy 2:1–3:13, Titus 1:5–9). In the decades to follow, these churches continued to codify their moral instructions and expectations for one another.

One additional witness is the anonymous Christian document called the Didache (which means "teaching"). The short text offers guidance on baptism, fasting, prayer, and the Lord's Supper (Didache 7:1–9:4). It concludes with standards of conduct for church leaders, much like similar sections of the New Testament (Didache 11–13, 15). This extrabiblical text shows the efforts of the early church to organize itself according to the example and ministry of first-century apostles.

Religious and Social Movements

The ancient Mediterranean world had many religious clubs and cults: the Greek "mystery religions" of Demeter and Dionysus, the Egyptian cults of Isis and Osiris, and the Persian cult of Mithras, among others. These movements offered camaraderie between adherents and "communion" with a pagan deity but not necessarily with high expectations of personal morality. Individual behavior was usually not an issue of *morality* but of *legality*: any action was permissible so long as it did not rouse the ire of authorities.

The best example of this is the celebration of Bacchanalia, a festival of drunken revelry in honor of Bacchus, the Roman title for the Greek god Dionysus. The first-century historian Livy depicts the immorality of the celebration and describes the official response. The Roman authorities did not condemn the immorality of the celebration but sought to restrict the revelers to mitigate any social disruption from their antics. It would seem that Roman authorities were suspicious of civil unrest but ignored the immorality of their citizens.

A Community Set Apart

Christianity, by contrast, was never a simple "social club" of shared symbols and beliefs that have no bearing on morality. Although the cultural milieu of the early church emphasized social peace over individual morality, the church—then and now—is called to a higher standard: love of God and love of others (Matthew 22:37–39). God expects the community of Christ to uphold certain behaviors and attitudes, and not mere ritualism—a criticism that Old Testament prophets leveled against Israel and Judah (Psalm 50:7–11, 23; Jeremiah 7:9–15; Hosea 6:6; etc.).

The church consists of people set apart from the world, precisely because the church is the light of the world and witness of Christ's kingdom (Matthew 5:14–16). God expects the church, first and foremost, to love Him and, as a result, to act morally and ethically. While order and charity has always been essential for collective worship (compare Romans 6:3–4; 1 Corinthians 11:17–22; etc.), God's transformation goes deeper to include the human heart.

Mon, Feb. 16	**Blessings to Those Who Give**	Malachi 3:7–12
Tue, Feb. 17	**Giving More than Enough**	Exodus 36:2–7
Wed, Feb. 18	**May God's Ways Be Known**	Psalm 67
Thu, Feb. 19	**Ready with a Voluntary Gift**	2 Corinthians 9:1–6
Fri, Feb. 20	**Bountiful Sowing and Reaping**	2 Corinthians 9:6–15
Sat, Feb. 21	**Go and Make Disciples**	Matthew 28:16–20
Sun, Feb. 22	**Excel in Generous Giving**	2 Corinthians 8:3–9
Mon, Feb. 23	**Work Toward Common Good**	Nehemiah 4:15–23
Tue, Feb. 24	**Welcome One Another in Christ**	Romans 15:1–17
Wed, Feb. 25	**Do Good Whenever You Can**	Proverbs 3:27–32
Thu, Feb. 26	**Fulfill Your Vows**	Ecclesiastes 5:4–7
Fri, Feb. 27	**Bear One Another's Debts**	Philemon 8–21
Sat, Feb. 28	**Provide for Others and Demonstrate Faith**	James 2:14–26
Sun, Mar. 1	**Love God and Love Your Neighbor**	Mark 12:28–34

Answers to the Quarterly Quiz on page 114

Lesson 1—1. perfect. 2. wise. **Lesson 2**—1. Solomon. 2. righteousness. **Lesson 3**—1. True. 2. sinners. **Lesson 4**—1. False. 2. the Son. **Lesson 5**—1. joy. 2. commandments. **Lesson 6**—1. True. 2. gift. **Lesson 7**—1. True. 2. Pharisee, publican. **Lesson 8**—1. the Father. 2. three. **Lesson 9**—1. kingdom. 2. False. **Lesson 10**—1. False. 2. testament. **Lesson 11**—1. holy. 2. False. **Lesson 12**—1. True. 2. Titus. **Lesson 13**—1. False. 2. works.

This Quarter in the Word

Mon, Dec. 1	**God's Word Reclaimed**	2 Kings 22:1–10
Tue, Dec. 2	**God's Word Leads to Repentance**	2 Kings 22:11–20
Wed, Dec. 3	**God's Word Touches Hearts**	Luke 24:25–32
Thu, Dec. 4	**God's Word Interpreted**	Nehemiah 8:1–8
Fri, Dec. 5	**God's Word Testifies of Jesus**	John 5:37–47
Sat, Dec. 6	**God's Word Is Truth**	John 17:14–19
Sun, Dec. 7	**God's Word Is Perfect**	Psalm 19:7–13
Mon, Dec. 8	**The Father's Compassion**	Isaiah 49:13–17
Tue, Dec. 9	**The Father Seeks Authentic Worshippers**	John 4:20–24
Wed, Dec. 10	**The Father Strengthens the Powerless**	Isaiah 40:27–31
Thu, Dec. 11	**The Father Exacts Discipline**	Isaiah 64:1–8
Fri, Dec. 12	**The Father Blesses and Forgives**	Psalm 103:1–18
Sat, Dec. 13	**The Father Gives Perfect Gifts**	James 1:13–18
Sun, Dec. 14	**The Father Cares for Our Needs**	Matthew 6:24–34
Mon, Dec. 15	**Sitting at the Lord's Right Hand**	Psalm 110
Tue, Dec. 16	**Christ Died for the Ungodly**	Romans 5:1–11
Wed, Dec. 17	**Christ Offers Eternal Life**	John 3:14–21
Thu, Dec. 18	**Christ Cares for His Sheep**	John 10:9–16
Fri, Dec. 19	**Welcome the Davidic Heir**	Isaiah 9:3–7
Sat, Dec. 20	**The Messiah Reigns**	Psalm 2
Sun, Dec. 21	**Rejoicing for Repentance**	Luke 15:1–7

Mon, Dec. 22	**The Spirit Has Power**	Zechariah 4:1–7
Tue, Dec. 23	**The Spirit Bestows Gifts**	1 Corinthians 12:1–13
Wed, Dec. 24	**The Spirit Gives Wisdom and Understanding**	Isaiah 11:1–9
Thu, Dec. 25	**The Spirit Works in Jesus' Birth**	Matthew 1:18–25
Fri, Dec. 26	**The Spirit Reveals God's Glory**	Acts 7:51–60
Sat, Dec. 27	**The Spirit Creates and Renews**	Psalm 104:24, 29–35
Sun, Dec. 28	**The Spirit Affirms Our Adoption**	Romans 8:12–17, 26–27
Mon, Dec. 29	**The Man and the Woman Sin**	Genesis 3:1–13
Tue, Dec. 30	**God Pronounces Judgment**	Genesis 3:14–24
Wed, Dec. 31	**God's Wrath Is Revealed**	Romans 1:18–25
Thu, Jan. 1	**Jesus Warns against Defilement**	Mark 7:14–23
Fri, Jan. 2	**A Prayer for God's Mercy**	Psalm 51:1–12
Sat, Jan. 3	**God Demands Right Living**	Micah 6:1–8
Sun, Jan. 4	**Jesus, Our Advocate**	1 John 1:5–2:6
Mon, Jan. 5	**Turn Away from Sin**	Ezekiel 18:20–23, 27–32
Tue, Jan. 6	**Learn to do Righteousness**	Isaiah 1:10–21
Wed, Jan. 7	**Jesus Has Power to Forgive Sins**	Mark 2:1–12
Thu, Jan. 8	**Draw Near to God by Faith**	Hebrews 11:1–10
Fri, Jan. 9	**Repent and Seek God's Face**	2 Chronicles 7:11–22
Sat, Jan. 10	**Repent and Be Baptized**	Acts 2:32–39
Sun, Jan. 11	**The Prodigal Returns**	Luke 15:11–32
Mon, Jan. 12	**Praying for Wisdom**	James 1:2–8
Tue, Jan. 13	**Praying and Seeking God**	Jeremiah 29:10–14
Wed, Jan. 14	**Praying with Thanksgiving**	Philippians 4:4–9
Thu, Jan. 15	**Praying for Protection**	Psalm 61
Fri, Jan. 16	**Praying as Jesus Taught**	Matthew 6:5–15
Sat, Jan. 17	**Praying for Others**	Genesis 18:23–33
Sun, Jan. 18	**Praying for Mercy**	Luke 18:9–14

Mon, Jan. 19	**Grow by Following Jesus**	Matthew 4:18–22
Tue, Jan. 20	**Grow in Love for God**	Deuteronomy 7:7–11
Wed, Jan. 21	**Grow in Spiritual Wisdom**	Colossians 1:3–12
Thu, Jan. 22	**Grow in the Fear of the Lord**	Proverbs 1:2–7
Fri, Jan. 23	**Grow in Discerning Good from Evil**	Proverbs 1:8–12
Sat, Jan. 24	**Keep on Growing**	Philippians 3:10–16
Sun, Jan. 25	**Grow in Grace and Knowledge**	2 Peter 3:14–18
Mon, Jan. 26	**A Community of Testimony and Praise**	Psalm 22:22–28
Tue, Jan. 27	**A Community of Hope-Filled Heirs**	Ephesians 1:15–23
Wed, Jan. 28	**A Community with Divine Authority**	Matthew 16:13–20
Thu, Jan. 29	**A Community Made Strong Together**	Ecclesiastes 4:7–12
Fri, Jan. 30	**A Community United in Worship**	Psalm 150
Sat, Jan. 31	**A Community Silently Growing**	Mark 4:26–32
Sun, Feb. 1	**A Community United**	Ephesians 4:4–16
Mon, Feb. 2	**Saved through the Sea**	Exodus 14:21–31
Tue, Feb. 3	**Baptized into a New Life**	Romans 6:1–14
Wed, Feb. 4	**God Provides Bread**	Exodus 16:13–16, 31
Thu, Feb. 5	**Jesus Is the Bread of Life**	John 6:28–40
Fri, Feb. 6	**A Blessing with Bread and Wine**	Genesis 14:14–20
Sat, Feb. 7	**Beloved Child of God**	Matthew 3:13–17
Sun, Feb. 8	**A Meal of Remembrance**	1 Corinthians 11:23–29
Mon, Feb. 9	**God Rests on the Seventh Day**	Genesis 1:31–2:4a
Tue, Feb. 10	**The Promise of Entering God's Rest**	Hebrews 4:1–11
Wed, Feb. 11	**Delight in the Sabbath**	Isaiah 58:8–14
Thu, Feb. 12	**Jesus Is Lord of the Sabbath**	Matthew 12:1–13
Fri, Feb. 13	**The Day of Resurrection**	Matthew 28:1–10
Sat, Feb. 14	**Keep the Sabbath Day Holy**	Exodus 20:1, 8–11
Sun, Feb. 15	**Living or Dying to the Lord**	Romans 14:1–8

Map Feature

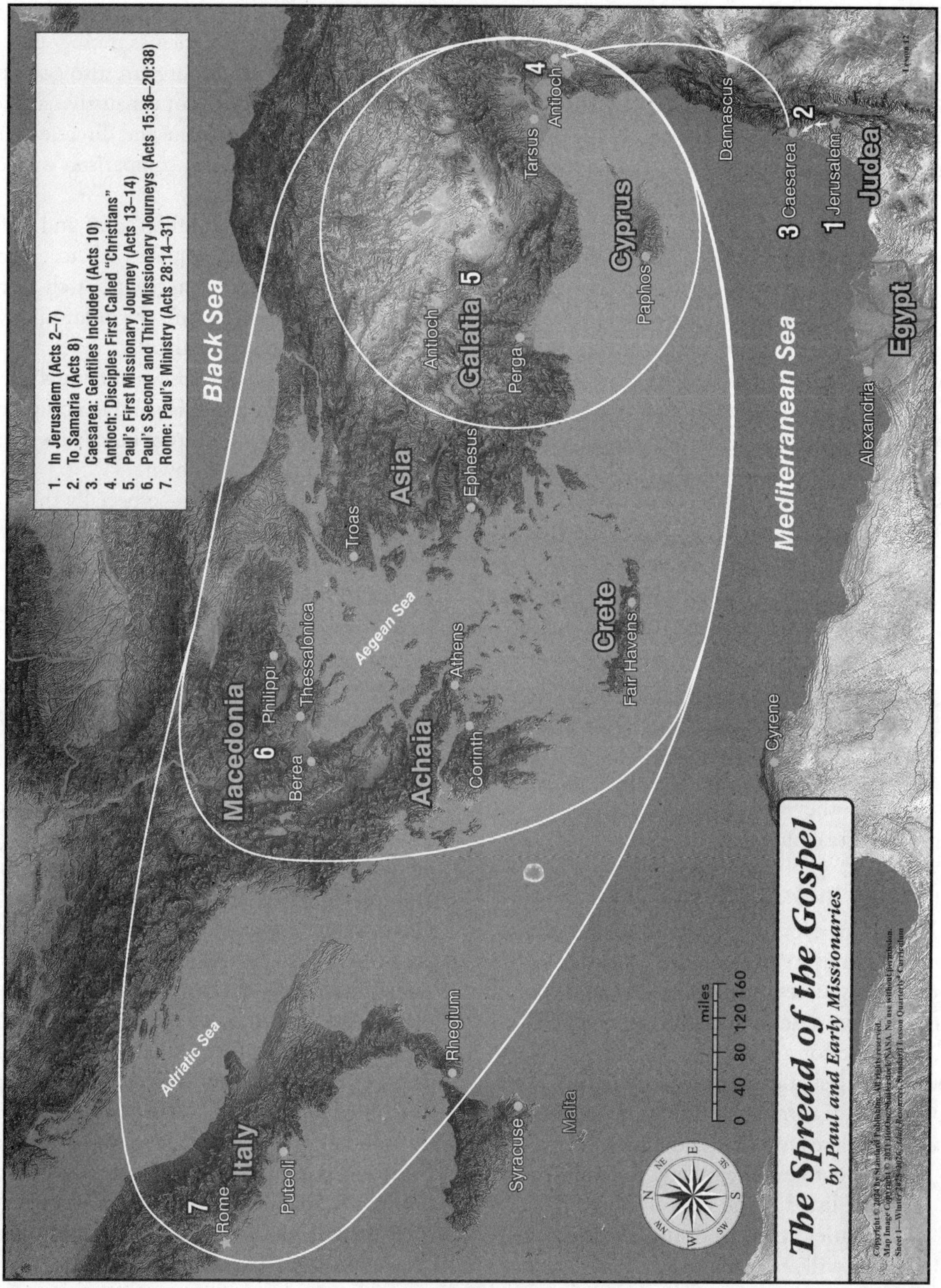
1. In Jerusalem (Acts 2–7)
2. To Samaria (Acts 8)
3. Caesarea: Gentiles Included (Acts 10)
4. Antioch: Disciples First Called "Christians"
5. Paul's First Missionary Journey (Acts 13–14)
6. Paul's Second and Third Missionary Journeys (Acts 15:36–20:38)
7. Rome: Paul's Ministry (Acts 28:14–31)
Black Sea
Aegean Sea
Adriatic Sea
Mediterranean Sea
Macedonia
Achaia
Asia
Galatia
Cyprus
Crete
Italy
Judea
Egypt
Philippi
Thessalonica
Berea
Athens
Corinth
Troas
Ephesus
Antioch
Perga
Paphos
Tarsus
Damascus
Caesarea
Jerusalem
Alexandria
Cyrene
Fair Havens
Rome
Puteoli
Rhegium
Syracuse
Malta
miles
0 40 80 120 160
The Spread of the Gospel
by Paul and Early Missionaries
Copyright © 2024 by Standard Publishing. All rights reserved.

Using Internet Resources

Teacher Tips by Tanae Murdic

In this article, we will expand on part one (found in the Fall 2025 quarter) and explore resources that can aid you in (1) developing lesson plans from *Standard Lesson* and (2) presenting your teachings. We will also discuss criteria to consider when selecting reliable Internet resources.

Lesson Helps from *Standard Lesson*

Visit www.standardlesson.com to find teaching help for *Standard Lesson Commentary* or *Standard Lesson Quarterly*. There you will discover monthly newsletters, weekly teacher tips, "In the World" articles, activity pages, and more. It is a one-stop shop to help you prepare for the week's lesson.

Sites Providing Helps for Presentation

Video clips, audio files, and PowerPoint presentations are frequent additions to Bible study curriculum. You can find these resources online. Here are potential websites to assist you:

- www.bible.org
- www.biblegateway.com
- www.bibleproject.com

As these websites are not tied to any specific lesson or topic, they will provide continuing help to enrich your teaching.

Selecting Internet Resources

Just as not every book on a topic is necessarily useful for every purpose, the same can be true of online resources. Since websites can be posted with far more ease than books can be published, it is possible for anyone to easily broadcast any notion or falsehood via the Internet. That is why it pays to be discerning regarding your sources and resources. Here are a few guidelines:

- Make sure to explore general resources (such as those listed in the section above). Bible dictionaries, maps, and studies of historical context will serve you well.
- Treatments of texts, such as those found at www.blueletterbible.org, are also good places to begin. These are not exhaustive studies, but they provide a tone and direction that can serve as a helpful comparison with other materials you find.
- When you find unfamiliar ideas and theories, see how they square with accepted resources. If they disagree, research further to see whether you find the unfamiliar view critiqued by other sources.
- Information from websites of reputable colleges and seminaries is good to compare with ideas acquired from other sites that are not as familiar or known.
- Discuss your findings—especially those of which you are uncertain—with your minister or another knowledgeable Bible teacher in your congregation.

Even after you've had an opportunity to ascertain the value of the material, it is still vital to be selective. In fact, only after you have evaluated a website's material are you equipped to be selective.

Conclusion

The Internet provides a library at your fingertips. But one additional caution is in order: *There are no shortcuts to good preparation*. Even with the vast information you can receive from the Internet, what it cannot do is prepare for you. You must research, assess the validity of the information, compile (and sometimes scrap) that information, and incorporate what is relevant into your presentation. A website can neither decide on the main thrust you intend for the lesson nor form the outline or choose the teaching methods and illustrations.

In other words, to be an effective teacher, you still must put forth the effort to prepare. But if you use your expanded study possibilities wisely and prepare well, you will enjoy the fruits of your labor as you present effective Bible lessons.

December 7
Lesson 1 (KJV)

God's Word

Devotional Reading: Psalm 119:105–112
Background Scripture: Deuteronomy 6:4–9; Joshua 1:8–9;
2 Kings 22:8–20; Acts 17:10–12

Psalm 19:7–13

**7 The law of the LORD is perfect, convert-
ing the soul: the testimony of the LORD is sure,
making wise the simple.**
**8 The statutes of the LORD are right, rejoic-
ing the heart: the commandment of the LORD
is pure, enlightening the eyes.**
**9 The fear of the LORD is clean, enduring for
ever: the judgments of the LORD are true and
righteous altogether.**
**10 More to be desired are they than gold,
yea, than much fine gold: sweeter also than
honey and the honeycomb.**
**11 Moreover by them is thy servant warned:
and in keeping of them there is great reward.**
**12 Who can understand his errors? cleanse
thou me from secret faults.**
**13 Keep back thy servant also from pre-
sumptuous sins; let them not have dominion
over me: then shall I be upright, and I shall be
innocent from the great transgression.**

2 Timothy 3:14–15

**14 But continue thou in the things which
thou hast learned and hast been assured of,
knowing of whom thou hast learned them;**
**15 And that from a child thou hast known
the holy scriptures, which are able to make thee
wise unto salvation through faith which is in
Christ Jesus.**

Key Text

All scripture is given by inspiration of God, and is profitable for doctrine, for reproof, for correction, for instruction in righteousness: that the man of God may be perfect, throughly furnished unto all good works.

—2 Timothy 3:16–17

Enduring Beliefs
of the Church

Unit 1: Our God and the Holy Scriptures

Lessons 1–4

Lesson Aims

After participating in this lesson, each learner will be able to:

1. Identify the role of Scripture in revealing God and His desires.
2. Explain how the two lesson passages teach believers to value God's Word.
3. Make a plan to look to God's Word for guidance in making wise choices.

Lesson Outline

Introduction
- A. Treasured Possessions
- B. Lesson Context

I. Gifts from God (Psalm 19:7–11)
- A. Life-Giving Instructions (v. 7)
- B. Trustworthy Guidance (v. 8)
- C. Enduring Value (vv. 9–11)

II. Purpose for the Gifts (Psalm 19:12–13; 2 Timothy 3:14–15)
- A. Warning Against Wrongs (Psalm 19:12–13)
  To See Ourselves as Others See Us
- B. Granting Wisdom (2 Timothy 3:14–15)
  A Value of Childhood

Conclusion
- A. Book of Immeasurable Value
- B. Prayer
- C. Thought to Remember

Introduction

A. Treasured Possessions

My mother was a woman of exemplary Christian faith. After she went to be with the Lord, members of our family began going through her belongings. Among the items we found were various Bibles that mom had kept through the years. There were a couple of Bibles in which she kept family records, bookmarks, newspaper clippings, and small pieces of paper filled with Scripture references. More recently, mom had acquired a large study Bible with footnotes and commentary helps. Even those bore the signs of regular use. I was reminded of the saying, "A Bible that's falling apart usually belongs to someone who isn't."

Mom didn't just treasure the Bibles in her home; she memorized Scripture, which kept the wisdom of God on her lips and near her heart. As a result, she found opportunities to apply Scripture in many situations. Through her testimony of faithfulness, the Spirit of God was active.

B. Lesson Context

This lesson pairs two texts—one from the Old Testament and one from the New—that praise God for revealing Himself. Although the canon of Scripture was not complete when either of today's texts were written, the claims of these texts apply to the entirety of God's self-revelation in Scripture. It is not the invention of any human; it is inspired by God and communicated by human witnesses (2 Peter 1:16; compare Hebrews 1:1).

The superscription of Psalm 19 calls it a "Psalm of David," meaning the words could have been written by David, the "sweet psalmist of Israel" (2 Samuel 23:1), or written for him, perhaps as a reminder that Israel's kings should listen carefully to God. The psalm is known as the great "hymn of revelation" within the corpus of the Psalms because it speaks to both "general" and "special" revelation. The first half of Psalm 19 heralds God's revelation as made known from the fact of creation; this is information available to everyone (compare Romans 1:20). The second half of the psalm, which includes the reading for today, turns to praise for God's spoken and written word.

These two sources of divine self-revelation—creation and word—hang together because they find their source in God's desire to communicate with those created in His image.

When we shift to considering the New Testament text for this study, we will be moving forward in time more than 1,000 years from the writing of Psalm 19. Our arrival point will be about AD 67, when the apostle Paul was near the end of his ministry (and his life), and he knew it (2 Timothy 4:6–8). It's easy to sense a tone of urgency in his second letter to his protégé Timothy as the aged apostle stressed anew which was the more important revelation.

I. Gifts from God

(Psalm 19:7–11)

A. Life-Giving Instructions (v. 7)

7. The law of the LORD is perfect, converting the soul: the testimony of the LORD is sure, making wise the simple.

Beginning with this verse, the psalmist shifts from general revelation to special revelation (see the Lesson Context for the distinction). Each of the six lines of Psalm 19:7–9 begins with a noun; these are set in parallel phrases, each expressing something about God's revealed truth. The six nouns are *law* and *testimony* here in verse 7, "statutes" and "commandment" in verse 8, plus "fear" and "judgments" in verse 9.

It's tempting to work through these terms individually to detect minute differences in meaning. But to do so is to risk missing the bigger picture of how the feature of parallelism works in Hebrew poetry. That parallelism is characterized by the use of synonyms to express the same thought. Such parallelism is at work in the first four of the six words noted above: *law*, *testimony*, *statutes*, and *commandment*. Each word has specific characteristics, but all four are synonymous.

Parallelism isn't the only feature we see here. These verses also contain repetition of sentence structure. In verses 7 and 8, we see this pattern four times:

synonym for law + LORD + fact + outcome

Parallelism is much less evident in the outcomes in our text, and that is the psalmist's point: reading and heeding God's instructions have many benefits. The first to be mentioned among the four is the role the instructions have in *converting the soul.* The word *converting* has the sense of "restoreth," as translated in Psalm 23:3.

The nature of *making wise the simple,* the second outcome, is significantly expanded in Psalm 119:98–100, 130. The word *simple,* as used in our daily conversations to describe people, is often a positive evaluation. In that sense, it may refer to someone who is free from vanity. But in the Old Testament, "the simple" are those who are either gullible, lack a moral compass, or are inclined toward evil (Proverbs 1:4; 7:7; 21:11; etc.).

B. Trustworthy Guidance (v. 8)

8. The statutes of the LORD are right, rejoicing the heart: the commandment of the LORD is pure, enlightening the eyes.

The parallelism in sentence structure explained above continues. The purity and correctness of God's stated requirements produce two results (in addition to those of the previous verse): *rejoicing the heart* and *enlightening the eyes.* Descriptors "right," "upright," and "pure" can describe people (Job 11:4; Psalm 24:4; Proverbs 29:10; etc.). God may also be praised as "upright" (Psalms 25:8; 92:15). But in this verse, these qualities even apply to the directives that come from God.

This verse corrects a common misunderstanding—that the teachings of God will stifle human enjoyment or make life dull. Instead, wisdom from God is like a treasure to be uncovered or a reward to be enjoyed (Proverbs 2:1–4; compare Psalm 119:162). In other texts, merriment for the heart—the intent of God's *statutes*—comes from hearing music, enjoying wine, or receiving a kind word (45:8; 104:15; Proverbs 12:25). These are not activities of a dull life!

At the same time, living by God's standards will train the human gaze to focus on what is good in God's sight, thus avoiding "lust of the eyes" (1 John 2:16). Eyes that are trained to see people and situations as *God* sees can glimpse with clarity. That kind of gaze is sound—physically, mentally, emotionally, and spiritually—for God does not leave His people to grope blindly through life with no sense of direction. God's declarations are a trustworthy guide.

C. Enduring Value (vv. 9–11)

9. The fear of the LORD is clean, enduring for ever: the judgments of the LORD are true and righteous altogether.

Fear of the Lord is known as "the beginning of wisdom" (Psalm 111:10; Proverbs 9:10), since all wisdom has its source in God. "Fear," in this case, means a reverent respect for God's authority, which also accepts *the judgments of the Lord.* Fear of God is sometimes coupled with disdain for evil—even the evil that might arise in one's own selfish motives (8:13).

Submission to God's authority means accessing a "fountain of life" (Proverbs 14:27; compare Deuteronomy 30:19–20). God's people can be confident that the Creator knows what is best, for "the fear of the Lord is the beginning of knowledge" (Proverbs 1:7).

The word *clean* is often used for ceremonial purity (Leviticus 10:10; Deuteronomy 12:15). This can also describe God's words, perhaps by analogy to "pure gold" (compare Exodus 25:11–39). To revere God and abide by His words leads to a clean life (Psalm 119:9; compare John 15:3). As the *true and righteous* judge, God is always fair and immune to bribes or partiality (Deuteronomy 10:17).

What Do You Think?

How will you practice "fear of the Lord" this week?

Digging Deeper

In what ways is our "fear of the Lord" connected to our love for Him? How do Deuteronomy 10:12 and 1 John 4:18 inform your response?

10. More to be desired are they than gold, yea, than much fine gold: sweeter also than honey and the honeycomb.

David uses a pair of comparisons to highlight the value of God's Word. *Gold* and *honey* are each pleasing and satisfying in their own way, but neither can provide the spiritual riches and nourishment that God's Word can. Even the highest quality of each of these items (the finest gold; honey from the *honeycomb*) will provide only temporary pleasure (compare Psalm 119:72, 103, 127). Gold cannot refresh the soul; it cannot give lasting joy to the heart.

What Do You Think?

What modern-day comparisons would you use to highlight the value of God's Word?

Digging Deeper

How will you use these comparisons to teach others to study God's Word?

11. Moreover by them is thy servant warned: and in keeping of them there is great reward.

In many Bibles, the words of Jesus are printed in red to call attention to them. What if Bibles were printed in another color whenever words of warning appear? Many verses would bear that color, for numerous warnings can be found within God's Word. Therein lies part of the value of the Scriptures: they are honest in their assessment of the human condition and make very clear the consequences of choosing to reject what God has spoken.

On the other hand, the Scriptures are just as clear concerning the *reward* that comes to those who faithfully keep their message. Both warnings and rewards are seen in passages such as the blessings and curses that Moses set before the Israelites in Deuteronomy 28. The New Testament epistles include an abundance of "great and precious promises" (2 Peter 1:4), but they also contain numerous warnings to Christians. The book of Hebrews provides several examples of both: promises of blessing (Hebrews 4:14–16; 6:9–10; 12:22–24; 13:14) and solemn warnings (2:1–4; 4:12–13; 10:26–31; 12:25).

II. Purpose for the Gifts

(Psalm 19:12–13; 2 Timothy 3:14–15)

A. Warning Against Wrongs (Psalm 19:12–13)

12. Who can understand his errors? cleanse thou me from secret faults.

The psalm takes a sudden turn as David, in the middle of extolling the greatness of the Lord and the virtues of His Word, pauses to reflect on his personal failures to measure up to the high standards revealed therein. Much the same occurs in Psalm 139, where David praises the Lord for His awareness of every detail of David's life (139:1–18) then ends with a prayer for God to examine him and reveal any areas of his life that He finds displeasing (139:23–24). In the previous verse of Psalm 19, David notes the "great reward" awaiting those who have kept the Lord's commandments (19:11, above). Then, looking into his own heart, he wonders, "Have *I* kept them? What if there are *secret* sins I am unaware of?" Given the context, David is likely referring to secret or unknown thoughts, words, and actions that have not been pleasing to God (compare 90:8; 139:23–24). David echoes what the prophet Jeremiah declared about the human heart: it is "deceitful above all things, and desperately wicked: who can know it?" (Jeremiah 17:9).

David's plea for cleansing is similar to his words of repentance in Psalm 51:1–2. God alone can create a clean heart (51:10). Only He can wash our sins so that they are as white as snow (Isaiah 1:18). We should also take note of how Psalm 19 concludes: with David's prayer that both his words and his thoughts will be pleasing before the Lord (Psalm 19:14, not in our printed text).

What Do You Think?

How does confession to another believer lead to revealing and cleansing "secret faults"?

Digging Deeper

Who is another believer to whom you may confess sin and be strengthened in your obedience to God?

To See Ourselves as Others See Us

One of my fellow hospital chaplains had a problem with habitual sin. He was angry at a fellow chaplain, and that anger affected the way he did his job. He struggled to maintain a professional relationship with the other chaplain. The enraged chaplain was tempted to gossip about this other person. When he did so, he felt justified in having a bad attitude toward the chaplain he did not get along with.

When we pointed this out to him in one of our meetings, he was shocked. He had not realized he was doing this, and he immediately apologized to the group and the other chaplain. This blind spot now revealed provided an opportunity for growth.

God's Word can show us our blind spots in uncountable ways. If this doesn't happen—and we all have blind spots—spiritual growth is stunted. When was the last time God's Word revealed one of yours? —L. M. W.

13. Keep back thy servant also from presumptuous sins; let them not have dominion over me: then shall I be upright, and I shall be innocent from the great transgression.

Presumptuous sins is the category of deliberate, intentional sin, committed not in ignorance but in defiance. Whether the sins are "secret" (Psalm 19:12, above) or committed in willful rebellion against the Lord, David wants no part. His prayer brings to mind the example that Jesus set for us in the Lord's Prayer: "Lead us not into temptation, but deliver us from evil" (Matthew 6:13).

However, we note that David did not always follow his own prayer. David is called a man after God's own heart (1 Samuel 13:14; Acts 13:22), yet David and the nation were punished because of his presumptuous, sinful pride (1 Chronicles 21:17). His adultery with Bathsheba and his role in the death of Uriah would have a significant effect on his life and the lives of his descendants (2 Samuel 11–12). Therefore, David well knows that certain types of sin may exert a powerful sway over people. He describes this influence as *dominion*. We are wise to recognize that the devil may have strongholds of sin in our lives (see 2 Corinthians 10:4).

How to Say It

Bathsheba	Bath-*she*-buh.
Eunice	U-*nye*-see or *U*-nis.
Lois	*Lo*-is.
Uriah	Yu-*rye*-uh.

The content of the temptations in our high-tech contemporary world is far different from what David faced, though the issues are the same (such as lust, pride, and hatred). God's Word remains our "sword of the Spirit" (Ephesians 6:17); without it, we leave ourselves vulnerable to "the wiles of the devil" (6:11).

What Do You Think?

How can believers overcome destructive sin habits that "dominate" our lives?

Digging Deeper

To what extent is this possible through personal willpower? through mutual accountability? through the Holy Spirit?

B. Granting Wisdom (2 Timothy 3:14–15)

In this letter, Paul has been very candid with his protégé Timothy about the latter's need for exceptional courage, strength, and spiritual discipline (2 Timothy 1:7; 2:1, 22). Paul warns Timothy of the "perilous times" to come in the "last days" (3:1). This is because of the variety of "perilous people" who will oppose Timothy and his message (3:2–9). That message, however, possesses an authority and a power that stands above the times, no matter how perilous they may be.

14. But continue thou in the things which thou hast learned and hast been assured of, knowing of whom thou hast learned them.

The apostle Paul has placed the spotlight primarily on himself up to this point in the letter. This is seen in his use of the words *me, my,* and *I* about twice as often as he uses the words *thee* and *thou* in 2 Timothy 1:1–3:13.

But the imperative *but continue thou* signals a change in focus. From 3:14 through 4:5, the spotlight shifts to Timothy, Paul's "son in the faith" (1 Timothy 1:2). He is the one being encouraged —even commanded—to embrace and practice fully the things he *hast learned and hast been assured of.*

15. And that from a child thou hast known the holy scriptures, which are able to make thee wise unto salvation through faith which is in Christ Jesus.

The ultimate basis of Timothy's faith and practice is to be *the holy scriptures* since "all scripture is given by inspiration of God, and is profitable for doctrine, for reproof, for correction, for instruction in righteousness: That the man of God may be perfect, throughly furnished unto all good works" (2 Timothy 3:16–17, not in our printed text). Because the New Testament as we know it does not exist at the time Paul writes to Timothy, Paul is affirming the texts we know as the Old Testament to be capable of making one *wise unto salvation through faith in Christ Jesus* (compare Luke 24:27; Acts 8:30–35; Romans 1:2–4).

But lest we be too eager to jump to that ultimate basis, we should take note of a model in that regard: the apostle Paul himself. Paul is the one from whom Timothy "hast learned and hast been assured of," regarding the final phrase of the previous verse. To this point in the letter, Paul has been stressing himself as a pattern to follow (2 Timothy 1:8, 13; 2:2–3). Two other patterns for Timothy to follow are those of his own "grandmother Lois" and "mother Eunice" (1:5), since they were undoubtedly the ones who ensured that Timothy knew the Scriptures from his childhood days.

What Do You Think?

In what ways can you be a spiritual "parent" or "grandparent" to a younger believer?

Digging Deeper

What steps will you take to mentor a younger believer in studying Scripture?

A Value of Childhood

Recently a coworker complained to me that she had made a mistake that another employee then blamed on the woman's youth. The complainer was frustrated because she did not think her youth had contributed to her mistake. As she spoke, the words of 1 Timothy 4:12 came to mind. There, Paul urges Timothy not to let others look down on him because of his youth.

I likely stored this gem away in my heart and memory during my early days of Sunday school and youth group. While I admit that Scripture memorization is not a big part of my adult life, the verses I memorized as a child still come to mind in relevant circumstances.

Our text from 2 Timothy 3:15 reminds us that those Scriptures we have learned in childhood are foundational to who we are today. What role can you play in teaching children Scripture?

—L. M. W.

Conclusion

A. Book of Immeasurable Value

In May 2023, a Hebrew Old Testament described as "one of the most important and singular texts in human history" became the most valuable manuscript ever sold at an auction. The Codex Sassoon, dating from the late ninth or early tenth century AD, sold for $38.1 million at Sotheby's in New York City. It may be the very earliest single volume containing all the books of the Hebrew Bible.

That multimillion-dollar auction value may tempt us to connect it with Psalm 19:9–10, which values God's Word above gold. But no matter how much an ancient or modern Bible sells for, it renders no eternal value to the one possessing it who does not read and heed its contents. Today's lesson texts highlight this timeless truth. There is a value to the Bible that cannot be measured in monetary terms.

But not all agree, and the Bible's timeless value has been called into question by various challenges, attacks, and misunderstandings as the ages of history have progressed. But truth is truth in any era of history. What David acknowledged back in the Iron Age was reaffirmed by Paul in the Classical Age and invites reaffirmation today in the Information Age.

One particular challenge of the Information Age is the sheer volume of information available. Were they alive today, we might wonder if the writer of Ecclesiastes would change the word *books* to *websites* in this observation: "Of making many books there is no end; and much study is a weariness of the flesh" (Ecclesiastes 12:12)! One observer of culture commented that people today don't actually *read* while on the Internet; they are

Visual for Lesson 1. *Allow one minute for silent personal reflection on the statement shown, following the lesson's conclusion.*

merely *scanning for information*. The difference between the two is important. If we slip into the scanning approach, the Bible will become for us no more than a collection of proof texts lacking genre and historical context.

When was the last time you read an entire book of the Bible in one sitting? If it's been a while, try this right now: read the whole letter of 2 Timothy without interruption. This will take no more than nine minutes of reading at a leisurely pace of 200 words per minute. If you "don't have time" to do so, what does this say about your Bible study habits?

B. Prayer

Thank You, heavenly Father, for providing us with the precious treasure of Your Word, the Bible. It is indeed a light for us in this dark world. Thank You for its timeless wisdom and, most of all, for its message of salvation through the living Word, Christ Jesus. In His name we pray. Amen.

C. Thought to Remember

Keep the words of Scripture—
and they will keep you.

Visuals FOR THESE LESSONS

The visual pictured in each lesson (example: page 127) is a small reproduction of a large, full-color poster included in the *Adult Resources* packet for the Winter Quarter. Order No. 9780784739631 from your supplier.

Involvement Learning

Enhance your lesson with KJV Bible Student *(from your curriculum supplier) and the reproducible activity page (at www.standardlesson.com or in the back of the* KJV Standard Lesson Commentary Deluxe Edition*).*

Into the Lesson

Begin class time with an icebreaker game of charades. Divide participants into two teams. On index cards, write keywords or phrases from today's Scripture, such as "God's Word," "wisdom," and "teaching." Instruct each group to choose a team member to act out the words or phrases without talking. The volunteer from the first team selects a card and has a time limit of two minutes for their team to guess the word or phrase. If the team guesses correctly, they earn a point. Repeat this activity with the second team. As time allows, alternate between teams until all cards have been used. The team with the most points at the end of the game wins.

Lead into Bible study by saying, "Our game used keywords from today's text. Today, we will study two passages that give us insight into the role of God's Word, how it affects us each day, and its power in our lives."

Into the Word

Divide the class in half, designating one as the **Psalmist Group** and the other as the **Timothy Group**. Distribute handouts of the questions below for in-group discussion.

Psalmist Group. Read Psalm 19:7–13. 1–What are the descriptions the psalmist uses about God's Word? 2–How does the psalmist explain the effect of God's Word on those who listen to it? 3–What do these verses reveal about God and His desires for His people? 4–How can you apply the wisdom of these verses to your relationship with God? 5–How do these verses challenge your understanding of Scripture? 6–What personal experiences have you experienced, like those listed by the psalmist?

Timothy Group. Read 2 Timothy 3:14–17. 1–What are some of this passage's descriptions of God's Word? 2–What do these verses teach us about the importance of Scripture? 3–What do these verses teach us about the influence of spiritual role models and influences? 4–What do these verses teach us about the wisdom found in God's Word? 5–How do these verses challenge your understanding of Scripture? 6–How can you encourage others to engage more deeply with God's Word?

Option 1. Distribute blank sheets of paper and art supplies. Invite participants to create a representation of a key theme or verse from today's text. This visual could be in the form of a picture, symbol, or even a word cloud. Support students who do not consider themselves "creative" by providing examples or encouraging them to work together.

Option 2. Distribute copies of the "Treasure Hunt" exercise from the activity page, which you can download. Have learners work in small groups to complete as indicated.

If willing, provide time for those who completed Option 1 to share their creations briefly. As a class, discuss how the two lesson passages teach believers to value God's Word.

Into Life

In whole-class discussion, ask volunteers to share how they are equipped by God's Word. If you have willing volunteers, ask them to share how they successfully established the habit of Bible study and memorization. Ask that they give advice to classmates looking to develop a better pattern of Bible study.

Divide participants into pairs. Invite partners to work together to make a plan to study God's Word for guidance and wisdom. If participants need examples, consider asking them to commit to reading a chapter of the Bible each day and to spend time praying after they read. In this example, encourage participants to use a journal to record insights, questions, and personal applications from their reading.

Our Heavenly Father

Devotional Reading: Ephesians 1:3–10
Background Scripture: Exodus 34:4–7; Psalm 103:10–14; Isaiah 40:27–31

Matthew 6:24–34

24 No man can serve two masters: for either he will hate the one, and love the other; or else he will hold to the one, and despise the other. Ye cannot serve God and mammon.

25 Therefore I say unto you, Take no thought for your life, what ye shall eat, or what ye shall drink; nor yet for your body, what ye shall put on. Is not the life more than meat, and the body than raiment?

26 Behold the fowls of the air: for they sow not, neither do they reap, nor gather into barns; yet your heavenly Father feedeth them. Are ye not much better than they?

27 Which of you by taking thought can add one cubit unto his stature?

28 And why take ye thought for raiment? Consider the lilies of the field, how they grow; they toil not, neither do they spin:

29 And yet I say unto you, That even Solomon in all his glory was not arrayed like one of these.

30 Wherefore, if God so clothe the grass of the field, which to day is, and to morrow is cast into the oven, shall he not much more clothe you, O ye of little faith?

31 Therefore take no thought, saying, What shall we eat? or, What shall we drink? or, Wherewithal shall we be clothed?

32 (For after all these things do the Gentiles seek:) for your heavenly Father knoweth that ye have need of all these things.

33 But seek ye first the kingdom of God, and his righteousness; and all these things shall be added unto you.

34 Take therefore no thought for the morrow: for the morrow shall take thought for the things of itself. Sufficient unto the day is the evil thereof.

Key Text

Take therefore no thought for the morrow: for the morrow shall take thought for the things of itself. Sufficient unto the day is the evil thereof —**Matthew 6:34**

Enduring Beliefs
of the Church

Unit 1: Our God and the Holy Scriptures
Lessons 1–4

Lesson Aims

After participating in this lesson, each learner will be able to:

1. Summarize the totality of God's provision for the needs of all creation.
2. Explain how to trust God in order to be free from worries.
3. Make a plan for serving to meet the basic needs of people in the community.

Lesson Outline

Introduction
- A. Pulling Back the Curtain
- B. Lesson Context

I. Serve or Despise the Father? (Matthew 6:24)

II. Worry or Trust the Father? (Matthew 6:25–32)
- A. Anxious for Provision (v. 25)
- B. Examples of Provision (vv. 26–29)
- C. God of Provision (vv. 30–32)
  Mississippi Wildflowers

III. Kingdom Living (Matthew 6:33–34)
- A. Righteousness First (v. 33)
- B. Today, Not Tomorrow (v. 34)
  Living Day by Day

Conclusion
- A. Connecting People to the Father
- B. Prayer
- C. Thought to Remember

Introduction

A. Pulling Back the Curtain

In the classic movie *The Wizard of Oz*, Dorothy and her companions go "off to see the wizard" to get what each so desperately wants. The wizard has a reputation as someone who has the ability to grant their requests.

On first encountering the wizard, they are intimidated by the booming voice of a mysterious, imposing figure. But soon, the curtain is pulled back, revealing that the "wizard" is not an intimidating figure at all!

When thinking about the person and work of Jesus, the opposite often occurs. People at first tend to think much *less* of Jesus than who He really is. That seems as true now as it was in the first century. Jesus "pulled back the curtain" between heaven and earth to reveal the truth about God. Today's lesson reveals one of those truths.

B. Lesson Context

Today's lesson text comes from a section of Jesus' teaching called the "Sermon on the Mount" (Matthew 5–7). In his record of Jesus' life, Matthew sometimes arranges the material in topical rather than chronological order. The Sermon on the Mount is a case in point. It is located early in Matthew's Gospel, but it was actually delivered during the first half of the second year of Jesus' ministry. Some commentators have called this second year of ministry Jesus' "year of popularity" because large crowds gathered wherever He went (Matthew 4:25).

Matthew 6 begins with Jesus' warning about hypocrisy as one serves God in various ways. Then come instructions on prayer, fasting, and priorities. Today's lesson text continues Jesus' teaching on living a life that depends on a loving heavenly Father's gracious provision of all our needs. Luke 12:22–31 and 16:13 are parallel texts.

I. Serve or Despise the Father?

(Matthew 6:24)

24. No man can serve two masters: for either he will hate the one, and love the other; or else

he will hold to the one, and despise the other. Ye cannot serve God and mammon.

Jesus continues His teaching about living as citizens of the kingdom of heaven, a teaching He began in Matthew 6:19. The word *master* in this context implies a singular individual who has overall charge of a group and its mission. Can any group function smoothly with two bosses who are equal in authority? Think about a *maestro* (an Italian word meaning "master") who conducts an orchestra. The orchestra is composed of many individuals and their instruments, but there can be only one maestro. Otherwise, there can be confusion. The same can be said for trying to live one's life under *two masters*. Those who attempt to do so will find themselves constantly torn between who or what receives their attention.

The specific contrast that Jesus depicts is service to *God* versus service to *mammon*. The word *mammon* comes from an Aramaic word that refers to wealth and riches. It is found elsewhere in the New Testament (compare Luke 16:9, 11, 13). Jesus is saying it is impossible for a person to give their total allegiance both to God and wealth. We note that financial wealth can be used to serve God and the church (example: 1 Corinthians 16:1–4). However, these things are secondary to serving God.

In another teaching from Jesus on this topic, it is noteworthy that following His teaching, "the Pharisees also, who were covetous, heard all these things: and they derided him" (Luke 16:14). The temptation to place excessive value on items that constitute mammon is what makes covetousness such a deadly trap. Covetousness is a sin addressed numerous times in the Scriptures (see Exodus 20:17; Joshua 7:21; Acts 20:33; Romans 13:9).

> **What Do You Think?**
> How does our culture encourage people to give allegiance to financial wealth?
> **Digging Deeper**
> What steps can we take to ensure that wealth and its pursuit remain secondary to serving God?

Visual for Lesson 2. *Point to this visual and ask, "In what ways has our heavenly Father provided what we need?"*

II. Worry or Trust the Father?
(Matthew 6:25–32)

A. Anxious for Provision (v. 25)

25. Therefore I say unto you, Take no thought for your life, what ye shall eat, or what ye shall drink; nor yet for your body, what ye shall put on. Is not the life more than meat, and the body than raiment?

By saying *take no thought*, Jesus is not expressing His opposition to careful planning. The apostle Paul engaged in a great deal of planning (examples: Romans 1:13; Acts 20:13–16; 2 Corinthians 9:5). Instead, the phrase is connected to the concept of worry. We should try to provide for ourselves, our families, and others. However, concerns regarding these necessities should not create worry or anxiety—which is sometimes easier said than done.

Readers should be aware that the bigger picture may be missed if one's attention becomes tunnel-vision focused on procuring the necessities of life. The idea is not to be overly concerned (see Philippians 4:6).

It can be challenging in today's culture to hear Jesus' words above the barrage of sounds and allure of sights in advertisements that encourage us to "take much thought" about life's needs. Jesus encouraged us to see the more significant, heaven-oriented picture regarding such matters: there is more to life than food and clothing.

B. Examples of Provision (vv. 26–29)

26. Behold the fowls of the air: for they sow not, neither do they reap, nor gather into barns; yet your heavenly Father feedeth them. Are ye not much better than they?

In a lesser-to-greater argument, Jesus illustrates His point with an image familiar to anyone in His audience: birds. Humans *sow, reap,* and *gather into barns,* but birds do not (compare Psalms 104:27–28; 147:9). Since the *heavenly Father* nonetheless feeds them, will He not also provide for those who are created in His image (Genesis 1:26–27), who labor at sowing, harvesting, and storing?

In declaring God to be heavenly Father, Jesus reinforces Old Testament teaching about God (compare Deuteronomy 1:29–31; 32:6; 2 Samuel 7:12–14; Jeremiah 31:9). This is just one of the numerous times Jesus refers to God this way in the Sermon on the Mount. No matter how much we labor to meet our needs, we should never forget that our heavenly Father is ultimately the one who provides for us (contrast Luke 12:16–21). Ignoring that truth can lead to yet another "two-master" situation, against which Jesus has just warned.

27. Which of you by taking thought can add one cubit unto his stature?

The phrase *taking thought* translates the same Greek word used by Jesus two verses earlier. Of additional interest here is the translation regarding adding *one cubit unto his stature.* The underlying Greek word translated as *stature* refers to physical height, as it is also translated in Luke 12:25; 19:3. But it may also refer to one's "age," as it is translated in John 9:21, 23 and Hebrews 11:11.

How to Say It

Aramaic	*Air*-uh-***may***-ik.
Corinthians	Ko-*rin*-thee-unz (*th* as in *thin*).
Demas	*Dee*-mus.
Gentiles	*Jen*-tiles.
Pontius Pilate	*Pon*-shus or *Pon*-ti-us *Pie*-lut.
Thessalonians	*Thess*-uh-***lo***-nee-unz (*th* as in *thin*).

The idea either way is to ask the rhetorical question: *Why be overly concerned about things beyond your control?*

Worry can consume us as we waste time stewing over matters that we have no power to change. Excessive worry can contribute to a wide range of health issues and actually shorten our lives in the process.

> **What Do You Think?**
> When do we cross the line between making prudent decisions about the future and engaging in undue worry about the future?
>
> **Digging Deeper**
> What questions do you ask to help you discern in this regard?

28–29. And why take ye thought for raiment? Consider the lilies of the field, how they grow; they toil not, neither do they spin: And yet I say unto you, That even Solomon in all his glory was not arrayed like one of these.

Jesus now addresses the issue of clothing (*raiment*). To illustrate the counterproductive nature of worry, He again uses a lesser-to-greater comparison. This one involves a word picture of flowers, specifically *lilies of the field.* God provides what is necessary for them to grow and develop. He is responsible for their beauty.

The *glory* of *Solomon*—referring to the wealth and splendor of his kingdom—was known and admired throughout the world of his day. The queen of Sheba remarked, after having witnessed several examples of that splendor, "The half was not told me" (1 Kings 10:7). Yet nothing produced by human wisdom or creativity can match the simple beauty seen in the flowers God has created and provides for. The God who invests such care regarding flowers is the same heavenly Father who created and cares for us.

C. God of Provision (vv. 30–32)

30. Wherefore, if God so clothe the grass of the field, which to day is, and to morrow is cast into the oven, shall he not much more clothe you, O ye of little faith?

The life expectancy of some vegetation is quite long, redwood trees being an example. But those are an exception. The life expectancy of most plants is relatively short compared to humans. And so it is with *the grass of the field.* That is true in terms of both natural life expectancy and the use of flowers and grass to heat the ovens for baking bread. Once again, Jesus' point is that if God bestows such beauty upon items in nature that are so short-lived, how much more will He care for human beings? Even so, we must do what flowers and grass are incapable of doing: exercise faith that God will provide such care for us (contrast Matthew 8:26; 14:31; 16:8).

Mississippi Wildflowers

I remember the first spring we lived in Mississippi. An unremarkable patch of grass just down the road from our house suddenly began to bloom with the most beautiful wildflowers I had ever seen. They were not part of a garden or a carefully tended landscape. The flowers appeared out of nowhere and took over the plot of land.

I drove by that beautiful scene nearly every day. And every day, I admired their loveliness. Imagine my surprise when, by midsummer, the property owner had simply mowed them all down! What a loss! I briefly considered knocking on the homeowner's door and demanding an explanation.

The truth is, I knew why. Summer in Mississippi is brutally hot. The flowers were already wilting under the extreme heat. They would never have survived the temperatures. But once again, in the spring, the wildflowers returned and flourished for their season.

God cares for the wildflowers and the grass, even though they wilt in the heat. If He cares about something so seemingly insignificant as seasonal flowers, how much more can we trust that He cares for us? When you consider His tender care for nature, in what ways are you encouraged to believe He cares deeply for your needs?

—B. R.

31–32. Therefore take no thought, saying, What shall we eat? or, What shall we drink? or, Wherewithal shall we be clothed? (For after all these things do the Gentiles seek:) for your heavenly Father knoweth that ye have need of all these things.

With His repeat of *take no thought,* Jesus returns to the challenge He issued in the first verse of today's study. In the first century, pagan worshipers often sacrificed to their gods, hoping to appease them and receive blessings. However, for followers of Jesus, the situation is different. Jesus demands nothing besides faith, highlighting the stark contrast between pagan practices and the assurance provided by faith in Him.

A tunnel-vision focus on the necessities of life is characteristic of the *Gentiles.* The underlying Greek word is also translated as "nations" (Matthew 24:9). The term points to non-Jewish peoples. Jesus calls His followers to possess an outlook or mindset different from theirs. The new mindset is based on acknowledging the awareness of the *heavenly Father.* He knows that we need the necessities of life (*all these things*). The question is whether we possess the faith to trust in His provision for us.

That does not imply that God endorses carelessness regarding our earthly responsibilities. Followers of Jesus should be known for their diligence (Hebrews 6:11–12), respected for their honest work (2 Thessalonians 3:7–10), and worthy examples of loving service (Acts 6:1–4).

What Do You Think?

In what ways can we grow in faith to trust in God's provision?

Digging Deeper

How do you balance faith in God and personal responsibility in this regard?

III. Kingdom Living

(Matthew 6:33–34)

A. Righteousness First (v. 33)

33a. But seek ye first the kingdom of God, and his righteousness.

The verse now before us switches the instruction from the negative (what to avoid) to the positive (what to seek as *first* priority). That priority is *the kingdom of God, and his righteousness.* Jesus does not want His followers to be so consumed by the concerns of this world that those concerns influence the priorities they set, the decisions they make, and the time they spend. There is something else worth seeking that is of far greater, more lasting value.

Jesus began the Sermon on the Mount with a reference to this kingdom, calling it the "kingdom of heaven," to which the "poor in spirit" belong (Matthew 5:3). The realms of the "kingdom of God" and "kingdom of heaven" are one and the same (compare Matthew 4:17; Mark 1:15). Jesus taught His followers to pray, "Thy kingdom come" (Matthew 6:10). As His crucifixion drew near, Jesus stood before a puzzled Pontius Pilate and told him, "My kingdom is not of this world" (John 18:36). Jesus did not come to institute a kingdom like the typical kingdoms of history, which use military strength to exercise and expand their control. (That was the kind of kingdom that many in Jesus' day expected the Messiah to establish; compare Acts 1:6). But the power that characterizes God's kingdom is a different kind of power (1 Corinthians 4:20). His kingdom is characterized by "righteousness, and peace, and joy in the Holy Ghost" (Romans 14:17).

The nature of Jesus' kingdom can also be seen in the words that follow "Thy kingdom come" in the Lord's Prayer. They are the words, "Thy will be done in earth, as it is in heaven" (Matthew 6:10). To seek first the kingdom of God is to make His will the most important pursuit and priority in our lives. Jesus' kingdom is not a matter of conquering nations or peoples by force but of individuals submitting to King Jesus and prioritizing His will daily. To seek God's *righteousness* is to seek what He wants in the world in an effort to make the world right—in a way, to bring heaven to earth by being the salt and light that Jesus calls His followers to be (Matthew 5:13–16).

Thus, we could rephrase the question asked in the previous verse as follows: Do the concerns of the *kingdom of God* consume our attention to the extent that they influence the priorities we set, the decisions we make, and the money and time we spend trying to satisfy these concerns? Which kingdom are we seeking: the earthly or the heavenly?

> **What Do You Think?**
> What concerns and actions are indicative of the kingdom of God and the righteousness of God?
>
> **Digging Deeper**
> What steps will you take to prioritize the kingdom of God in the upcoming week?

33b. And all these things shall be added unto you.

The phrase *all these things* refers to the food, drink, and clothing previously discussed. Jesus promises that when we dedicate ourselves to the pursuit of the kingdom of God, the things that consume so much of the world's attention will no longer dominate our thoughts since they will be provided. As Jesus has already clarified, our loving heavenly Father will be the provider.

We note, however, that countless Christians throughout history and from around the world have suffered and died from dehydration, malnourishment, and starvation. This verse is not saying that these things result from a lack of faith. Instead, it is a promise that God is the ultimate provider for His people. One way that He provides for His people in need is through the generosity of others. As believers "seek . . . first the kingdom of God" (Matthew 6:33a, above), they will show generosity to others in need (Mark 10:30; Luke 12:33; compare 2 Corinthians 8:3–5).

We must remember that Jesus' words transcend all times and cultures. They are meant to be a standard for His followers, no matter the time in history in which they are living. Since Jesus' kingdom is "not of this world," His promise still holds true, regardless of the time or place in history, when and where we are living.

B. Today, Not Tomorrow (v. 34)

34. Take therefore no thought for the morrow: for the morrow shall take thought for the things of itself. Sufficient unto the day is the evil thereof.

The degree to which we hoard *for the morrow* may indicate the degree to which we trust God to provide for our daily needs. An excellent example of this problem is found in Exodus 16:4, where the Israelites were instructed to gather enough manna only for the day (except for the sixth day). Most followed the instructions, but some didn't (Exodus 16:20).

Fear of the future can keep us from seeking first the kingdom of God by making us overly earth-centered (compare the case of Demas in 2 Timothy 4:10). We cannot be servants of "two masters"!

Each *day* will likely include some measure of *evil* or tragic, unpleasant circumstances. That's because we continue to live in a world reeling from the curse of sin. Yet, to discipline our thinking and focus our attention on kingdom priorities, we must maintain our intent. Paul's words challenge us: "Set your affection on things above, not on things on the earth" (Colossians 3:2). This is also part of being "transformed by the renewing of your mind" and living all of life as an act of service to God (see Romans 12:1–2).

What Do You Think?

How can we balance focusing on "things above" with the need to pursue justice and righteousness in the world?

Digging Deeper

In what ways do Micah 6:8; Matthew 5:13–16; Acts 20:32–35; and James 1:27 inform your response?

Living Day by Day

Several years ago, my husband and I found ourselves in the midst of a personal financial crisis. We both needed jobs, and we spent nearly every moment searching online job boards and applying for various positions. In the meantime, bills were piling up, and our pantry stockpile was quickly dwindling. Anxiety was overwhelming us.

Before long, my husband stumbled upon an app offering daily work and pay. He started working immediately, and his wages would be deposited into our bank account each day. There was rarely enough for more than the bills or groceries, but God provided just enough each day. During that season, we learned to trust God to give us our "daily bread" and not worry about the future. He was our provision.

Living day-by-day does not come easy. We prefer to live in security, knowing for sure that we will have more than enough to cover our own needs. But life is not always that predictable. Our inability to control may be exposed in the form of a troubling health diagnosis, job loss, or unexpected news. How might the Lord teach you to trust Him for your daily needs? —B. R.

Conclusion

A. Connecting People to the Father

All followers of Jesus can demonstrate the difference that living in the trust of a loving heavenly Father can make. Each of us has a sphere of influence that includes people to whom God seems far away. In some cases, this distance can become magnified during the Christmas season for various reasons. A change in people's understanding of God may not occur overnight through our efforts. Still, with patience and prayer perhaps we can use the illustration in the Lesson Introduction, "pulling back the curtain" and helping people see how much their Father really does love them.

In this season, when we celebrate how God came near in a special way, perhaps in some small way, you can show someone around you, through your simple acts of kindness, that their Father has not forgotten them.

B. Prayer

What a sacred privilege it is to know You as our Father in heaven! May we never take this relationship for granted, and may we help others to see what a blessing it is to know You in that way and the difference it makes in our lives, both now and for eternity. In Jesus' name we pray. Amen.

C. Thought to Remember

No one knows our earthly needs better than our heavenly Father.

Involvement Learning

Enhance your lesson with KJV Bible Student *(from your curriculum supplier) and the reproducible activity page (at www.standardlesson.com or in the back of the* KJV Standard Lesson Commentary Deluxe Edition*).*

Into the Lesson

Divide the class into small groups and distribute a sheet of paper and a pen to each group. Direct groups to write the following words as headers of three columns on the sheet of paper: *Minor, Serious, Unusual.*

Under the appropriate header, ask groups to write down examples of minor, serious, and unusual worries or concerns people may have. After three minutes of group work, reconvene the class and ask volunteers to share examples. Then, ask the following questions for whole-class discussion: 1–How often do we think about our fears? 2–How often do we let our fears consume our thinking? 3–How do we handle our fears?

Alternative. Distribute copies of the "Timeline of a Day" exercise from the activity page, which you can download. Have learners complete it individually in a minute or less before discussing conclusions with a partner.

Lead into the Bible study by saying, "We have all felt fear and worry. Sometimes, these things take up a significant part of our thoughts and concerns. Today's study on Matthew's Gospel will recount a teaching from Jesus regarding our trust in God's provision."

Into the Word

Ask a volunteer to read aloud Matthew 6:24–34. Divide the class into three groups: **Life Group, Provision Group,** and **Kingdom Group.** Distribute handouts of the questions below for in-group discussion.

Life Group. Reread Matthew 6:24–27. 1–Explain Jesus' claim in verse 24. Why is this true? 2–Explain Jesus' mention of "fowls" (v. 26). What is the significance of their mention? 3–How would you summarize Jesus' teachings in these verses?

Provision Group. Reread Matthew 6:28–30. 1–What is Jesus teaching in these verses? 2–What is the significance of God caring about "the grass of the field" (v. 30)? 3–What do these verses teach regarding God's care and provision for our needs?

Kingdom Group. Reread Matthew 6:31–34. 1–What is Jesus teaching in these verses? 2–What does it mean to seek God's kingdom and righteousness? 3–What do you think Jesus meant when He said, "Take therefore no thought for the morrow: for the morrow shall take thought for the things of itself" (v. 34)?

After calling time, bring the groups back together. Ask a volunteer from each group to summarize their group's findings. Conclude by asking the following questions for whole-class discussion: 1–What reasons does Jesus give as to why we don't need to worry? 2–What do these verses teach us about God?

Into Life

Say, "One way we can deal with worry is to notice the needs of others in our community." Ask participants to create a list on the board of difficulties that people in your community may face. Lead a brainstorming session on ways to address those difficulties. To help with brainstorming, ask the following questions: 1–What is already being done to help with these difficulties? 2–How can we partner with those already addressing these difficulties? Write brainstorming responses on the board.

As a class, circle the most viable ways your class can help. Take time to write a plan and timetable for implementing that community plan.

Option. Distribute copies of the "Visualize Trust" exercise from the activity page. Have learners complete the activity as a take-home activity. To ensure completion, state that you will ask volunteers for their responses at the beginning of the next class period.

Conclude class by praying and thanking God for His concern over every detail of your life.

December 21
Lesson 3 (KJV)

Christ the Savior

Devotional Reading: 2 Timothy 2:8–13
Background Scripture: John 3:14–17; 10:9–11, 14–16, 27–28

Luke 15:3–7

3 And he spake this parable unto them, saying,

4 What man of you, having an hundred sheep, if he lose one of them, doth not leave the ninety and nine in the wilderness, and go after that which is lost, until he find it?

5 And when he hath found it, he layeth it on his shoulders, rejoicing.

6 And when he cometh home, he calleth together his friends and neighbours, saying unto them, Rejoice with me; for I have found my sheep which was lost.

7 I say unto you, that likewise joy shall be in heaven over one sinner that repenteth, more than over ninety and nine just persons, which need no repentance.

Romans 5:6–10

6 For when we were yet without strength, in due time Christ died for the ungodly.

7 For scarcely for a righteous man will one die: yet peradventure for a good man some would even dare to die.

8 But God commendeth his love toward us, in that, while we were yet sinners, Christ died for us.

9 Much more then, being now justified by his blood, we shall be saved from wrath through him.

10 For if, when we were enemies, we were reconciled to God by the death of his Son, much more, being reconciled, we shall be saved by his life.

Key Text

If, when we were enemies, we were reconciled to God by the death of his Son, much more, being reconciled, we shall be saved by his life. **—Romans 5:10**

Enduring Beliefs of the Church

Unit 1: Our God and the Holy Scriptures

Lessons 1–4

Lesson Aims

After participating in this lesson, each learner will be able to:

1. Identify the paradox that Jesus is both shepherd and sacrifice.

2. Give examples of ways believers might experience Christ's rescue.

3. Make a plan to resist complacency and resolve conflict according to Christ's reconciling example.

Lesson Outline

Introduction
- A. Rescues and Rejoicing
- B. Lesson Context: Luke 15
- C. Lesson Context: Romans

I. The Seeking Shepherd (Luke 15:3–7)
- A. Lost Sheep (vv. 3–4)
  - *Missing Lamb*
- B. Found Sheep (v. 5)
- C. Communal Rejoicing (v. 6)
- D. Sinners Like Sheep (v. 7)

II. The Self-Giving Son (Romans 5:6–10)
- A. Sacrifice for Sinners (vv. 6–8)
  - *A Life for a Life*
- B. Saving Former Enemies (vv. 9–10)

Conclusion
- A. Coming Home
- B. Prayer
- C. Thought to Remember

Introduction

A. Rescues and Rejoicing

On October 13, 2010, the first of 33 men emerged from a collapsed mine in Chile. They had been trapped for nearly 10 weeks. When the rescue drill reached the underground chamber where the men had been confined, a siren announced the breakthrough. Families of the miners celebrated as the men emerged one by one. All had survived! The US president spoke of "the joy of people everywhere" as they heard the news of the successful multinational rescue effort.

Dramatic rescues capture the attention of people around the world. Such outcomes elicit great celebration. Today's lesson calls attention to the most important rescue effort of all time: Jesus' rescue mission on behalf of lost humanity.

B. Lesson Context: Luke 15

The first of our two printed texts for this lesson is drawn from a sequence of three "lost and found" parables that constitute the entirety of Luke 15. An element common to all three parables is the joy that occurs when that which was lost is found.

Jesus spoke these parables while on His final trip to Jerusalem (Luke 9:51–56). It was a lengthy journey, but the crucifixion was near. Matthew 18:12–14 is another version of today's parable.

C. Lesson Context: Romans

Paul's letter to the church in Rome was most likely written in AD 57 or 58. During Paul's third missionary journey, he spent about three months in Greece (Acts 20:1–3). This may have been the time during which he wrote this letter. He had never visited the church in Rome, but he planned to (Romans 1:8–13).

Many consider Romans to be Paul's most outstanding epistle. It is a profound doctrinal treatise, dealing with many aspects of the doctrine of salvation by grace through faith in Jesus Christ (Romans 1:5). The universal sinfulness of humanity was the issue (1:18–3:20). The remedy is "the righteousness of God" that comes to individuals through their faith in Jesus (3:21–24). The printed text leads us to explore the intersection of these facts.

I. The Seeking Shepherd

(Luke 15:3–7)

The previous chapter of Luke ends with Jesus offering a strong word of caution to count the cost before deciding to follow Him (Luke 14:25–33). His words likely shock many in the audience, especially the part about carrying a cross (14:27)!

Even so, chapter 15 begins with "Then drew near unto him all the publicans and sinners for to hear him" (Luke 15:1). Apparently, Jesus' candid language about what true discipleship means does not dissuade His audience from wanting to hear more. On the other hand, the religious leaders "murmured" against Jesus because of His willingness to welcome such "sinners" and even eat with them (15:2).

A. Lost Sheep (vv. 3–4)

3. And he spake this parable unto them, saying.

The word *them* in this phrase points us to "the Pharisees and scribes" in Luke 15:2. It is worth noting that Jesus was not the first to teach in parables (compare Judges 9:7–15; 2 Kings 14:9–10), but His authoritative use of this method characterizes much of His teaching.

4. What man of you, having an hundred sheep, if he lose one of them, doth not leave the ninety and nine in the wilderness, and go after that which is lost, until he find it?

The hypothetical setting of the parable resonates well with those of a preindustrial era, when the majority of people lived on farms. Indeed, that fact of drawing on images of common life is foundational to what makes a parable a parable. Beyond this foundation, however, there is disagreement on a precise definition.

The imagery of a shepherd leaving 99 sheep in search of 1 is startling—and that's exactly the shock effect that is intended. Much is left unsaid here. Were there other workers available to watch over the 99 during the search? How long would the shepherd be willing to search before giving up? These and other questions are neither posed nor necessary. The emphasis is God's intense concern for the lost, a concern the Pharisees lack. The expertise of these men should cause them to remember the shepherd-and-sheep imagery in their own Scriptures (compare Psalms 23; 119:176; Jeremiah 31:10; Ezekiel 34:11–16).

Missing Lamb

My daughter received a stuffed lamb as a gift at a baby shower. When she got old enough to notice the lamb, she immediately loved it. She held it every night when she was falling asleep. She chewed on its ears and nose. When she got a little older, she dressed it in doll clothes and took it to Sunday school with her. The lamb was her constant companion—until the day it disappeared.

We had gone to the park. When we came home, it was not in the car seat, the diaper bag, or the stroller. During her nap time, I left her with my husband, and then frantically drove back to the park to look for the lamb. Unfortunately, it was gone forever.

I searched for that stuffed lamb but never found it. However, the shepherd in this parable found his lost sheep. We have a "good shepherd" (John 10:14) who takes care of His flock, searching out those who are lost. In contrasting Christianity with other religions, it's been noted that while other religions feature humans' search for God, Christianity features God's search for us. Are you willing to be found, or are you hiding?

—L. M. W.

B. Found Sheep (v. 5)

5. And when he hath found it, he layeth it on his shoulders, rejoicing.

As we work our way through this parable, it is essential that we keep in mind the original audiences—plural, because there are two. The audience of Luke 15:1 is eager to hear Jesus; the audience of 15:2 is eager to criticize Him. The lamb that was *found* represents those of 15:1. Jesus came "to seek and to save" the lost (Luke 19:10), and that's exactly what He's doing here—something the audience of 15:2 disapproves.

Again, we are cautious not to fill in details that we think should be in the parable. For example, some may doubt that a sheep weighing between 100 and 200 pounds could be carried on one's *shoulders*. But that imagery is part of the shock value of the parable. The imagery is designed to get Jesus' hearers to think as they identify the characters in the story with those of real life.

C. Communal Rejoicing (v. 6)

6. And when he cometh home, he calleth together his friends and neighbours, saying unto them, Rejoice with me; for I have found my sheep which was lost.

The wording here is nearly identical to that of Luke 15:9, which describes shared joy at the recovery of a lost coin. Good news is always worth sharing. Indeed, the language of shared joy and celebration permeates the three parables of Luke 15, with nine references in total (see 15:5, 6, 7, 9, 10, 23, 24, 29, 32; see also Lesson 6). Luke 15 is one of three points in Luke's Gospel where the call to rejoice is especially stressed; the other two places are found in Luke 1–2 and Luke 6:23. The contrast in attitude with that of the dour Pharisees could hardly be more striking. To them, sinners are to be marginalized, avoided, shunned, and condemned, not sought out!

> **What Do You Think?**
> What do you find most striking about this parable?
> **Digging Deeper**
> What about God's character is revealed in what stands out to you?

D. Sinners Like Sheep (v. 7)

7. I say unto you, that likewise joy shall be in heaven over one sinner that repenteth, more than over ninety and nine just persons, which need no repentance.

Jesus now gives the application of His brief parable, which applies to the two main groups listening to Him: the "sinners" and the religious leaders. The one sheep that had strayed represents *one sinner* who has strayed from the Father in heaven. When that sinner repents (changes course to return to the Lord), there is *joy* in *heaven*.

Again, we resist the temptation to press other ideas into the lesson that Jesus is teaching. For example, we realize that everyone has sinned and is in need of repentance (Acts 2:38; Romans 3:23; etc.). Therefore, how can Jesus properly compare one sinner who *repenteth* with a fictitious group *which need no repentance?*

What Jesus is doing is reflecting the self-image of the *ninety and nine just persons*—the religious leaders who speak against Him and His actions. It is not that these leaders need no repentance; rather, they believe that they do not need to repent. This makes their spiritual condition even worse (John 9:39–41). Those who have truly repented should not feel superior to the unrepentant. If anything, their compassion should increase, for they know the freedom from sin that repentance brings. They should desire to see others experience that same freedom.

A shepherd's concern for one lost sheep, while touching, pales in comparison to God's desire to reach lost people. It is clear from Jesus' words elsewhere, especially in John 10:1–18, that He is the shepherd who has come to rescue lost sheep. Luke records the following words of Jesus, spoken while in the house of the transformed Zacchaeus: "For the Son of man is come to seek and to save that which was lost" (Luke 19:10).

> **What Do You Think?**
> Which group do you more easily see yourself in—the "sinners" or the "just persons"?
> **Digging Deeper**
> How does this parable invite you to respond?

II. The Self-Giving Son

(Romans 5:6–10)

Romans 5 begins with one of Paul's favorite methods of argumentation: the use of the word *therefore* to summarize a point in the sense of "consequently" or "accordingly." Thus, it behooves us to take a quick look at the reason for this "therefore" before we consider what flows from it.

The reasoning behind the "therefore" of Romans 5:1 is Paul's citing Abraham as an example of someone whose faith "was counted unto him for righteousness" (Romans 4:3). Paul closes the chapter by building a bridge from Abraham to the followers of Jesus. Just as righteousness was "imputed" to Abraham by faith (4:20–22), so it will be imputed to those who "believe on him that raised up Jesus our Lord from the dead" (4:24). That faith allows us to have "access . . . into this grace wherein we stand" (5:2). Our printed text expands on the wonder of God's grace by contrasting our position before God prior to Jesus' death with where we now stand because of His death.

A. Sacrifice for Sinners (vv. 6–8)

6. For when we were yet without strength, in due time Christ died for the ungodly.

The verse's opening *for when* signals additional information to the "therefore" of Romans 5:1. The additional information deals with an intersection of *time* and our lack of *strength.* Paul first pictures the desperation of our condition before Jesus' atoning death on the cross: *we were yet without strength.* This is not measuring physical strength, but spiritual. Sin renders every human incapable of saving oneself. It is another way to say what Paul states in Romans 3:23, that "all have sinned, and come short of the glory of God." By this standard, the most righteous of human beings is as much in need as the wickedest.

The adjective translated *ungodly,* used to describe humanity's condition, is fairly rare in the New Testament (other occurrences in Romans 4:5; 1 Timothy 1:9; 1 Peter 4:18; 2 Peter 2:5; 3:7; and Jude 4, 15). This refers to a life lived without regard for God-honoring beliefs and practices. No one is exempt from being so characterized.

The solution to our sad condition is this: *Christ died for the ungodly.* The timing of that event was carefully planned by God, as Galatians 4:4 establishes: "When the fulness of the time was come, God sent forth his Son" (compare Mark 1:15; Romans 4:25; Ephesians 1:10).

Christ's dying for the ungodly is His substitutionary death on the cross, an essential element of the gospel message (1 Corinthians 15:3). The prophecy of Jesus' death in Isaiah 53 is perhaps the most powerful description of that event in Scripture, even though Isaiah issued it several hundred years before Jesus came to earth. Romans 5:1 notes the peace with God that we have through Jesus. Here in verse 6, Jesus' death is connected to that peace, as expressed in Isaiah's prophecy (Isaiah 53:5).

Paul's insight is that while the enemies of Jesus had nothing but malice in their hearts, God had planned all along for His Son's death to be the means of salvation for humanity. The high priest spoke better than he knew when he declared that it was better for one man to die than to have an entire nation perish (John 11:49–53).

What Do You Think?

In what ways do you think people value individual strength or power?

Digging Deeper

What is the significance of Christ dying for us when we were "yet without strength" (Romans 5:6)?

7. For scarcely for a righteous man will one die: yet peradventure for a good man some would even dare to die.

One issue within this verse is the difference between a *righteous* person and a *good* person. Some suggest that the righteous person describes an especially pious individual who possesses a "holier-than-thou" attitude. He may be highly respected, but he is not the kind of person for whom someone would be willing *to die.* The good person would be someone whose good deeds make her a much more likable individual, and, thus, a person for whom others would be more likely to die.

Others suggest that there is basically no difference between the righteous person and the good person, and that Paul is making the same claim in two different ways. The first part of the verse states Paul's claim in a negative way; the second states it positively. Regardless of the exact distinction between the "righteous man" and the "good man," the gist of Paul's statement is that people are not likely to give their lives on behalf of even the best of human beings.

8. But God commendeth his love toward us, in that, while we were yet sinners, Christ died for us.

Reading this verse with the previous two, we can see the contrast Paul desires to make. It is not so much between the righteous person and the good person as it is between the good (and righteous) people of verse 7 and the ungodly people of verse 6. If the chances of someone dying for a good or righteous person are so slim, then the chances of someone dying for an ungodly person are laughable. Herein lies the contrast.

We see the incredible *love* God has shown to all humanity—all of whom are *sinners*—in the fact that *Christ died for us*. Self-help is out of the question; before receiving His salvation, we are all dead in our sins (Ephesians 2:1, 4–5). We need a Savior!

Paul himself never lost his sense of wonder and gratitude for Jesus' death. The grace that resulted saved him from a sinful past that included the persecution and murder of Christians (Acts 9:1–2; 22:4–5; 26:9–11; 1 Corinthians 15:9). He referred to himself as the "chief" of sinners but also the recipient of "exceeding abundant" grace (1 Timothy 1:14–15).

What Do You Think?

What is more surprising: that Christ died for us, or that this happened while we were still sinners?

Digging Deeper

What is the significance of Christ dying for sinners?

A Life for a Life

A little girl was walking with her father down a sidewalk along a busy street. They came to a crosswalk and started to cross. Halfway across the street, the girl caught sight of a balloon floating above them and stopped just as a car barreled down the street toward her. Seeing the danger, her father ran to push her out of the path of the car to safety. Tragically, the car hit her father, killing him instead.

The girl grew up with the memory of the accident and the knowledge that her father gave his own life for hers. Initially, she felt shame that he had died because of her inattention and carelessness. It was not until she had her own child that she realized the depth of her father's love. She would willingly do the same for her baby. Only when she realized that was she able to be free from shame.

Jesus willingly sacrificed His life for each of us, thereby paying the debt for our sin. How will you live in the knowledge of that love daily, free from the guilt and shame of sin? —L. M. W.

B. Saving Former Enemies (vv. 9–10)

9. Much more then, being now justified by his blood, we shall be saved from wrath through him.

Romans 5 begins with Paul's declaration that we are "justified by faith" (Romans 5:1). Here, he adds that we are *justified by* Jesus' *blood*. To be *justified* is both to be pardoned from all sin (and thus reconciled to God) and to be counted as righteous. Because Jesus died in our place, we are free from condemnation (3:25; 4:25; 8:1). In this vein, some describe "justified" as being treated "just as if I'd never sinned."

The means of our justification is Jesus' blood. The blood of Jesus given at the cross is the price paid to cleanse us from our sins (Acts 20:28; Ephesians 1:7; 2:13; 1 Peter 1:18–19; etc.). Just as God saw the blood on the houses of the Israelites in Egypt and declared, "When I see the blood, I will pass over you" (Exodus 12:13), He will "pass over" us when He sees the blood of Jesus covering us (1 Corinthians 5:7). We will not be judged according to our sins. Rather, we will *be saved from* God's *wrath* (compare Romans 1:18).

10. For if, when we were enemies, we were reconciled to God by the death of his Son, much more, being reconciled, we shall be saved by his life.

How to Say It

Colossians	Kuh-*losh*-unz.
Corinthians	Ko-*rin*-thee-unz (th as in thin).
Ezekiel	Ee-*zeek*-ee-ul or Ee-*zeek*-yul.
Jeremiah	Jair-uh-*my*-uh.
Pharisees	*Fair*-ih-seez.
Zacchaeus	Zack-*key*-us.

This verse continues a pattern from verses 6 and 8, above: *when we were* most unfit for saving, *God* in Jesus Christ took the necessary action to save us. Building on this idea, Paul introduces another term to picture the impact of Jesus' death: *reconciled*. This Greek word occurs six times in the New Testament, and the first two of those are right here. Three more occurrences are in 2 Corinthians 5:18–20, which goes into more depth about the concept of reconciliation (compare 1 Corinthians 7:11).

To be considered *enemies* of God is terrifying—or it should be. Many passages of Scripture speak of God being with us and for us (Psalm 23:4; Matthew 1:23; Romans 8:31; etc.). But there are also passages that speak of His being against sinners (Jeremiah 21:13; Ezekiel 13:8; 21:3; etc.). In the verse before us, Paul declares that it is God who has taken the initiative to remove what results in this enmity: the sin barrier. That means of reconciliation is *the death of his Son* (see also Colossians 1:19–22). This introduces the concept of Christ's "intercession," covered in more depth in Romans 8:34 and Hebrews 7:25.

What Do You Think?

What does Jesus' *death* accomplish? What does Jesus' *life* accomplish?

Digging Deeper

What does this teach us about the importance of both Jesus' death and resurrection?

Visual for Lesson 3. *Display this visual as you ask, "Explain how Jesus is both our seeking Shepherd and sacrificial lamb."*

Conclusion

A. Coming Home

A homecoming is often a time of great joy. Think of those miners in Chile whose dramatic rescue was recounted in the Introduction. But such earthly celebrations pale in comparison to celebrations in heaven over the repentance of a sinner, an enemy of God. The angels themselves join the celebration!

Strictly speaking, Paul does not use homecoming language in Romans 5. But the reconciliation made possible through Jesus' death is what allows a spiritual homecoming. Those who accept Jesus' sacrifice according to the biblical plan of salvation become reconciled to God. The sin barrier no longer stands. They are at peace with Him. They have come back to their Creator, back to where they belong. They are home spiritually and are destined for the eternal home being prepared for all faithful followers of Jesus (John 14:1–3).

For many, "coming home" is a vital part of the Christmas season. The real message of Christmas is that our heavenly Father has provided a way for every person to "come home" to Him: the gift of Emmanuel, God with us (Matthew 1:23). God wants to be for us! He proved that desire in the death of His Son. Everyone in rebellion against God is a lost sheep. But Christ specializes in finding lost sheep. What is your part in being His hands and feet in that regard?

B. Prayer

Father, in this season of gift-giving, we acknowledge that You have given the gift of all gifts in Your Son, Jesus. We look beyond the manger to the cross and empty tomb, declaring with gratitude that "Christ died for us." In Jesus' name we pray. Amen.

C. Thought to Remember

Jesus is both the seeking Shepherd
and the sacrificial Lamb.

Involvement Learning

Enhance your lesson with KJV Bible Student *(from your curriculum supplier) and the reproducible activity page (at www.standardlesson.com or in the back of the* KJV Standard Lesson Commentary Deluxe Edition*).*

Into the Lesson

Recount a time that you got lost. It could be a scary experience as a child or even as a parent losing a child. You could share a time when you got lost in a town or neighborhood. Perhaps you lost your group at an event or large gathering. Take a few minutes to share your experience. Ask others to share their own "lost" experiences.

Take a minute or two to debrief what was common about these experiences.

Lead into Bible study by saying, "We all have experienced the feeling of being lost. Today, we will study a parable from Jesus along with a teaching from Paul that shows us the extent to which God reaches out to those who are 'lost' spiritually."

Into the Word

Divide the class in half, designating one half as the *Luke Group* and the other half as the *Romans Group.* Distribute handouts of the questions below for in-group discussions.

Luke Group. Read Luke 15:3–7. 1–What are the main themes in this text? 2–How is God's redemption evident in it? 3–How does the parable demonstrate God's love and grace?

Romans Group. Read Romans 5:6–10. 1–What are the main themes in this text? 2–How is God's redemption evident in it? 3–What does this text teach us about the significance of Christ's sacrifice?

After allowing several minutes for discussion, have the groups present their findings.

Say, "In today's study, we see that Jesus is both our shepherd and our sacrifice. This is a paradox that we must explore and understand." Divide the *Luke Group* into two groups, assigning one group Romans 5:6–10 and the other Hebrews 9:26–28. Divide the *Romans Group* into two groups, assigning one group Luke 15:3–7 and the other John 10:11–18. Ask groups to read their assigned passages and discuss how they portray Jesus as either shepherd or sacrifice, noting key insights and thoughts. While the groups are working, write on the board *Shepherd* and *Sacrifice* as the headers of two columns. Then write the assigned Scripture references as rows that extend across the two columns. After calling time, ask the groups to come back together and invite them to share their findings. Write key insights in the chart on the board.

Option. Distribute copies of the "God's Love and Grace" exercise from the activity page, which you can download. Have learners complete it individually in a minute or less before checking answers with a partner.

Ask the following questions for whole-class discussion: 1–How do these passages reveal the surprising nature of Jesus' roles? 2–What does it mean for Jesus to be both shepherd and sacrifice in our lives? 3–How do we, as believers, experience Christ's rescue in daily life?

Into Life

Encourage your students to spend one minute in self-reflection to identify areas where complacency may be present in their lives. Ask them to take another minute to reflect on how that complacency can cause conflict and to consider how Christ's reconciling example can inspire change.

Discuss together, "How does knowing that Jesus is both shepherd and sacrifice motivate you to be reconciling instead of complacent?"

Have participants pair up. Ask partners to read Ephesians 4:29–32 and Matthew 5:23–24, then plan together ways to resolve conflict based on Christ's example. Their plans should also include a way to be accountable to each other.

Option. Distribute copies of the "Testimonies of Christ's Rescue" exercise from the activity page. Have learners complete it as a take-home activity. Remember to begin the next class by asking for volunteers to share insights regarding the activity.

Close in prayer, asking for guidance, wisdom, and a desire to follow Christ's example.

December 28
Lesson 4 (KJV)

The Holy Spirit

Devotional Reading: Ephesians 3:14–21
Background Scripture: John 3:5–8; 14:16–17, 26; 15:26–27; 16:7–15;
Acts 2:1–21, 32–33; 1 Corinthians 12:1–13

Romans 8:12–17, 26–27

**12 Therefore, brethren, we are debtors, not
to the flesh, to live after the flesh.
13 For if ye live after the flesh, ye shall die:
but if ye through the Spirit do mortify the
deeds of the body, ye shall live.
14 For as many as are led by the Spirit of
God, they are the sons of God.
15 For ye have not received the spirit of bond-
age again to fear; but ye have received the Spirit
of adoption, whereby we cry, Abba, Father.
16 The Spirit itself beareth witness with our
spirit, that we are the children of God:
17 And if children, then heirs; heirs of God,
and joint-heirs with Christ; if so be that we
suffer with him, that we may be also glorified
together.**

**26 Likewise the Spirit also helpeth our infir-
mities: for we know not what we should pray
for as we ought: but the Spirit itself maketh
intercession for us with groanings which can-
not be uttered.
27 And he that searcheth the hearts
knoweth what is the mind of the Spirit, because
he maketh intercession for the saints according
to the will of God.**

Key Text

The Spirit itself beareth witness with our spirit, that we are the children of God. —**Romans 8:16**

Enduring Beliefs of the Church

Unit 1: Our God and the Holy Scriptures

Lessons 1–4

Lesson Aims

After participating in this lesson, each learner will be able to:

1. Describe the Spirit's work as an "advocate" in the lives of believers.

2. Give reasons to trust the Spirit's witness about believers' standing before God.

3. Make a plan to deal with fear in favor of living confidently as God's Spirit-led children.

Lesson Outline

Introduction
- A. Real Brother
- B. Lesson Context

I. Flesh and Spirit (Romans 8:12–14)
- A. Owe the Flesh (v. 12)
- B. What Leads to Death (v. 13a)
- C. What Leads to Life (v. 13b)
- D. What Results (v. 14)

II. God's Children (Romans 8:15–17)
- A. Not Slaves (v. 15a)
- B. Adopted (v. 15b)
- C. Confirmed (v. 16)
  - *Welcome to the Family*
- D. Heirs with Jesus (v. 17)

III. Helped by the Spirit (Romans 8:26–27)
- A. To Pray (v. 26)
  - *Advocating for a Friend*
- B. Through Intercession (v. 27)

Conclusion
- A. God's Real Children
- B. Prayer
- C. Thought to Remember

Introduction

A. Real Brother

When my friend Chris was 10, his family adopted a 5-year-old boy named Mark. At first, Mark was afraid that his new parents would send him away. He tried to behave perfectly so they would keep him.

A few weeks after becoming part of Chris's family, Mark broke one of Chris's toys. Mark started to shake and cry. Chris gave him a big hug and asked why he was trembling. Mark replied, "Because Daddy will be mad that I broke your toy." Chris assured Mark that their dad wouldn't be angry. Mark replied, "But you're the real son." Chris pulled Mark closer and whispered, "You're his real son now too. You're my real brother." Chris still remembers the tension in his brother's arms melt away. The barrier was broken. Mark finally knew that he was part of the family.

B. Lesson Context

The context for last week's lesson on Romans 5 applies to this lesson as well, so that information need not be repeated here.

Romans 6–8 is Paul's rebuttal against false applications of the gospel message he has been preaching. Believers cannot continue in sin because Jesus' death released them from sin's dominion. Believers are united with Christ in His death (Romans 6:3–11), which frees them from slavery to sin, death, and the law (6:11; 7:1–6; 8:1–2; Galatians 2:19). They also receive the gift of the Holy Spirit (Romans 5:5). Since God has freed believers from sin's mastery, they are to see themselves instead as God's servants (6:12–23). This is crucial because a conflict rages in every believer (7:21–23).

The Holy Spirit lives inside of believers (Romans 8:9–11), and His will stands in opposition to the will of sin (8:5–7; Galatians 5:16–17). There is no neutral ground: one either sides with the Holy Spirit and follows His orders, or one submits again to sin's desires. Those sinful desires lead only to death (Romans 8:6a; Galatians 5:19–21). But the Spirit guides believers to "life and peace" (Romans 8:6b), and God will raise them from the dead just like Jesus (8:10–11).

The apostle Paul wrote about 25 percent of the New Testament. But nearly half of the New Testament references to the (Holy) Spirit occur in his letters. Clearly, the person and work of the Holy Spirit is a vital doctrine for him—and should be so for us.

I. Flesh and Spirit

(Romans 8:12–14)

A. Owe the Flesh (v. 12)

12. Therefore, brethren, we are debtors, not to the flesh, to live after the flesh.

The word *therefore* indicates that Paul is concluding a line of thought as he points out implications of the topic to this point. A quick look back at Romans 8:1–11 reveals that Paul has been demonstrating the absolute incompatibility between the realm of *the flesh* and the realm of the Spirit. We have to decide which we are indebted to.

The word translated "flesh" is one of Paul's favorites—he uses it over 100 times in his letters, about one-third of those in Romans alone! But Paul doesn't use this word to refer to the same thing in every context. Furthermore, the term "the body" is virtually synonymous with "the flesh" in many cases, so it's useful to consider them together. In six instances Paul uses the words translated "flesh" and "body" together in the same verse to compare or contrast one with the other in various ways (Romans 8:13 [below]; 1 Corinthians 6:16; Colossians 1:22, 24; 2:11, 23). Here's a thumbnail sketch of those two terms, plus "world," categorized in three senses each:

Sense:	Positive	Neutral	Negative
Flesh:	Galatians 2:20	1 Corinthians 15:39	Ephesians 2:3
Body:	Romans 7:4	Romans 6:12	Romans 8:13
World:	Romans 1:20	Romans 1:8	Colossians 2:20

As you can see, we have some careful reading to do to determine how Paul is using "flesh" or "body" in any given text. Considering the seven verses that immediately precede the one we are now reading, the sense is decidedly negative.

Those seven verses of Romans 8:5–11 reflect Paul's portrayal elsewhere of "flesh" and "Spirit" as opposing categories (Galatians 3:3; 4:29; 6:8; etc.). The same opposing categories present themselves in places where "body" is contrasted with "Spirit" (Romans 8:10, 13 [below]).

Visual for Lesson 4. *Display this visual as you ask the discussion question associated with Romans 8:16.*

Another way we speak of "the flesh" in a negative sense is when it is equated with "the world," when in turn the world is contrasted with the Holy Spirit (1 Corinthians 2:12). The listed passages and others reflect a complex reality: even though we have been saved from the sinful principles of this world, we still live in it. And we may encounter the world insisting that we are in debt to it in terms of meeting the various appetites of the flesh.

While the mind can recognize sin and delight in God's law (Romans 7:22–25), the flesh is unruly, tempted by the sins of the world (7:14, 23). Its desires are oriented toward the things that God disdains, and one cannot please God while submitting to the flesh (8:7–8). But believers are empowered to resist the flesh's desires. We will see how as we consider additional verses below.

B. What Leads to Death (v. 13a)

13a. For if ye live after the flesh, ye shall die.

Here we note a shift from the first-person plural "we" of the previous verse to the more pointed second-person plural "ye" as Paul states the central reason why not to *live after the flesh,* fulfilling its desires. It's because the flesh, as used in this context, stands in opposition to God's desires (Romans 8:7; Galatians 5:17). Allowing the desires of the flesh to control one's life leads to death.

But this is nothing new; Paul here is reiterating a point that he makes throughout the letter. This point is most memorably summarized in Romans 6:23 as "the wages of sin is death" (see also Romans 2:6–8; 6:16, 21; 7:5). Paul is not referring to physical death, but to the outcome of the final judgment, where one's eternal fate is sealed (Acts 17:31; Romans 2:15–16; 1 Corinthians 4:5; 2 Corinthians 5:10). The one who lives to gratify the desires of the flesh will pay the highest price.

Paul was not alone in affirming the end-time judgment. The Gospels record Jesus teaching about the judgment (Matthew 12:36; 25:31–46; John 12:48). Other New Testament authors refer to it as well (Hebrews 9:27; 2 Peter 3:7; Revelation 20:11–15).

C. What Leads to Life (v. 13b)

13b. But if ye through the Spirit do mortify the deeds of the body, ye shall live.

The alternative to living after the flesh is to *mortify the deeds of the body.* Yet Paul does not suggest that his readers can be saved by their own strength, as if salvation were by works. Rather, believers are empowered by the life-giving *Spirit* to resist their temptations and to subdue the desires of their carnal natures (Romans 8:4). Paul similarly encouraged the Galatians in this regard (Galatians 5:16–18, 24–25).

Paul draws the death/life and law/Spirit contrasts from the covenant texts of the Old Testament. In Deuteronomy 30:15–20, Moses renews the covenant that began at Sinai (Exodus 19–24) and tells the Israelites, "See, I have set before thee this day life and good, and death and evil" (Deuteronomy 30:15). Keeping the covenant would bring the people life and prosperity, while breaking it would bring them death and disaster. While the Israelites failed to keep the covenant, God promised through Jeremiah that He would make a new covenant with His people. In the new covenant, God would write His laws on their hearts and enable them to obey Him (Jeremiah 31:31–34). Paul refers to believers as ministers of this new covenant (2 Corinthians 3:6) and identifies the Holy Spirit as the one who circumcises the hearts of God's people (Romans 2:29). Under this new covenant, believers have the help they need to live in ways that please God (7:6).

How to Say It

Abba	*Ab*-buh.
Colossians	Kuh-*losh*-unz.
Corinthians	Ko-*rin*-thee-unz (*th* as in *thin*).
Deuteronomy	Due-ter-*ahn*-uh-me.
Ephesians	Ee-*fee*-zhunz.
Galatians	Guh-*lay*-shunz.

What Do You Think?

What do you think it looks like to live by the Spirit and not according to the flesh?

Digging Deeper

How does Galatians 5:16–18 contribute to your previous response?

D. What Results (v. 14)

14. For as many as are led by the Spirit of God, they are the sons of God.

The word *for* that begins this verse indicates a reason for or expansion on something stated previously. In this case, the verse now before us expands on what "ye shall live" of the previous verse means: it means to be considered as *the sons of God.* It is essential to recognize that Paul is not excluding women here. While this Greek term can be rendered either "sons" or "children," the force of the male term "sons" evokes common ideas about the rights of male children in the ancient world. In both Jewish and Greco-Roman contexts, sons would inherit their fathers' estates. Paul likely uses this term (rather than another Greek word for "children") because of its association with inheritance, a point that he will make more explicit in verse 17.

Another grammatical feature to notice is that while the verse before this one is stated in the active voice (in terms of something the readers must do), the verse now before us is stated in the passive voice (in terms of something the readers must allow to be done to them). That "something" is to be *led by the Spirit of God* (compare Galatians 4:6; 5:18). Opinions differ on exactly what form this leading takes. But most all agree that the picture is, at the least, that of a Spirit-dominated life.

II. God's Children
(Romans 8:15–17)

A. Not Slaves (v. 15a)

15a. For ye have not received the spirit of bondage again to fear.

The *for* introducing this verse again signals an expansion of the prior point. Here Paul explains his statement linking the experience of the Spirit's leading to one's status as a son of God. Paul doesn't want his readers to conclude that embracing a Spirit-dominated life is just to exchange one negative *bondage* for another negative bondage. Thus Paul emphasizes, as he has before, that believers have been freed from slavery to sin, death, the law, and judgment (Romans 6:6–22; 7:6; 8:2).

But there's more to the story! This is only a statement of what believers *do not* end up with. The next half-verse finishes the thought by stating what believers *do* receive (compare Hebrews 2:15).

> **What Do You Think?**
> What is it like to know that you are no longer bound to fear?
> **Digging Deeper**
> In what ways do you struggle to believe that you are freed from fear?

B. Adopted (v. 15b)

15b. But ye have received the Spirit of adoption, whereby we cry, Abba, Father.

The earlier description of opposites was "the flesh" versus "the Spirit"; now the description of opposites is "the spirit of bondage" versus *the Spirit of adoption.* Adoption was a common and important practice in the ancient world. Infant mortality rates were high, and many children who survived infancy died at young ages from accidents or diseases. Men would often adopt adult males as their heirs to preserve family lines and secure caretakers for their old age. An adopted son would take the father's family name and would have all the rights of a natural-born child. There is even some evidence that adopted sons had special rights against disownment, so that they were always a part of the family.

The reality of the adopted heirs' inclusion in God's family inspires them (us) to *cry, Abba, Father.* Paul here uses an Aramaic term and immediately translates it with the Greek equivalent. While some suggest that *Abba* is a child's term of endearment (like "Daddy"), the relevant literature from the time does not support this conclusion. Adults often used this term for their fathers without any childish affection implied. However, this misunderstanding does not diminish the significance of this cry. To call God one's own father was the kind of honor usually reserved for demigods. Paul proclaims that the one true God has given this honor to human beings as He adopts them into His family.

C. Confirmed (v. 16)

16. The Spirit itself beareth witness with our spirit, that we are the children of God.

Paul here emphasizes the Spirit's role in testifying to the believer's new status (compare 2 Corinthians 1:22; Ephesians 1:13). This testimony is delivered to the believer's own *spirit,* but Paul does not explain precisely what he means by this. It is likely that Paul refers back to the cry in Romans 8:15b, above. Some commentators suggest that the expression comes from a baptism ritual, but the evidence for this possibility is weak. It is more likely that Paul refers to the believer's inner sense of assurance, a gift from the Holy *Spirit* within them.

Here, instead of the Greek word for *son* (which he uses in Romans 8:14, above), Paul uses the term for *children.* This is a more comprehensive word that includes both males and females.

> **What Do You Think?**
> How should our lives look different, knowing we are children of God?
> **Digging Deeper**
> How does 1 John 3:1–2 contribute to your consideration of this?

Welcome to the Family

My brother and his wife spent years preparing to adopt children who were in the foster care system in the United States. Finally, they received a call about a sibling group of three children. The soon-to-be parents quickly made plans to visit. Before long, the kids had made the trip across several states to live with their new parents.

Almost a year went by before adoption day finally arrived. Everyone was somewhat nervous with excitement when a judge publicly declared the news: the children were officially adopted! They were no longer "in the system." They were given new last names and legally welcomed into the family that they were already emotionally part of.

Just as a judge, with authority, "bore witness" to the official adoption of my nieces and nephew, the Holy Spirit "bears witness" to our adoption as children in the family of God. We have a new title as heirs, and we can truly call Him "Father." What promises are now yours because of your adoption into His family? —B. R.

D. Heirs with Jesus (v. 17)

17. And if children, then heirs; heirs of God, and joint-heirs with Christ; if so be that we suffer with him, that we may be also glorified together.

Paul makes explicit here what he implies in Romans 8:14, above: those who are God's *children* are His *heirs*. They have become part of God's family and will receive an inheritance as *joint-heirs with Christ*, who is "appointed heir of all things" (Hebrews 1:2). But what exactly are we to inherit? It's tempting to answer that question quickly by turning to other well-known texts that speak of eternal life. But let's not be too hasty in doing that before we let the verse at hand have its say. In this regard, we focus on the phrase *heirs of God*. There is ambiguity in the original language as to what exactly this means. Several passages throughout Paul's writings and beyond speak of the promises that are ours as heirs, including God's "promise in Christ" and "hope of eternal life" (Ephesians 3:6; Titus 3:4–7; compare James 2:5). While this remains broad and rather ambiguous, the main thrust is joyful hope.

At the same time, our inheritance comes with a cost: those who desire to be *glorified together* with Christ must also *suffer with him*. The suffering that Paul has in mind here is likely the persecutions Jesus faced, which believers will also experience if they live like Jesus (Mark 13:13; 2 Corinthians 1:5; Colossians 1:24; 1 Peter 4:12–14; etc.). This suffering will result in sharing in glory with Christ. We will experience resurrection, our bodies being transformed and perfected like Jesus' body was (Romans 8:11; Philippians 3:21). God will free His creation from bondage to death and decay (Romans 8:18–22).

What Do You Think?

What does it mean to share in Christ's sufferings?

Digging Deeper

How do Philippians 3:1–7 and 1 Peter 4:12–19 inform your understanding of suffering with Christ?

III. Helped by the Spirit

(Romans 8:26–27)

A. To Pray (v. 26)

26. Likewise the Spirit also helpeth our infirmities: for we know not what we should pray for as we ought: but the Spirit itself maketh intercession for us with groanings which cannot be uttered.

In Romans 8:18–25, Paul describes how the whole cosmos looks forward to God's renewal of creation and how believers must wait with patient hope for that day.

Arriving now at Romans 8:26, Paul explains how *the Spirit* helps us as we wait. The word translated *infirmities* often refers to physical sickness or disease (Matthew 8:17; Acts 28:9; etc.). But here that word seems to speak of human limitations in a broad, general sense. This is a weakness that we cannot overcome in and of ourselves. The prayer task mentioned in Ephesians 6:18 is the challenge; the fact that we don't even know *what we should pray for as we ought* is the reality. Both texts note the involvement of the Holy Spirit. The text at hand states that the Spirit makes up for our limitations by making *intercession for us*. That concept refers to someone advocating on behalf of another.

Some interpreters have understood *groanings which cannot be uttered* as a reference to the gift of tongues (see 1 Corinthians 14:1–19). But Paul says here that it is the Holy Spirit who delivers such *groanings*, not the human believer. The Spirit communicates with God the Father on behalf of all believers with expressions that humans cannot mimic or understand.

What Do You Think?

In what ways might your prayers change, recognizing that the Spirit intercedes for you?

Digging Deeper

What weaknesses or infirmities do you desire the Spirit's help with?

Advocating for a Friend

In a volunteer role, I have the privilege of teaching English to asylum seekers. My work involves teaching them the basics of English communication so that they may seek jobs, find housing, and obtain additional assistance available to them.

One day a student stayed after class to ask me about a letter he received from the state. He didn't understand the letter's contents and needed to call the helpline mentioned in the letter. He asked if I would be willing to make the call for him.

I spent several minutes on the phone as an advocate between my student and the state representative. She explained what he needed to know and do; I then broke the information down in terms he could understand.

We might say that we can't speak the language of heaven (2 Corinthians 12:2–4), so the Holy Spirit does it for us as a go-between or intermediary. When you pray, do you acknowledge the Spirit's role in that regard? —B. R.

B. Through Intercession (v. 27)

27. And he that searcheth the hearts knoweth what is the mind of the Spirit, because he maketh intercession for the saints according to the will of God.

Paul emphasizes the unique connection between *the Spirit* and *God* the Father as well as the effectiveness of the Spirit's advocacy. Interceding *according to the will of God*, the Spirit is not trying to convince the Father of something the Father does not wish to do. On the contrary, the Spirit prays for those things that the Father desires for us. They are thus aligned in their purpose, and believers can trust that God will answer those prayers.

Conclusion

A. God's Real Children

Unfortunately, some cultures view adopted children as having a kind of second-class status. While most parents love their adopted children as full members of their families, one can find accounts on social media of parents treating adopted children as inferior to their biological children.

When we have a faulty view of adoption, we can easily miss the radical nature of Paul's claim that God has given us the Spirit of adoption. Believers are not second-class children. Rather, we are fully integrated into God's family, given both His name and His Spirit. God begrudges us nothing; instead, He makes us joint heirs with Christ, promising us a share in His inheritance. Nor does Christ begrudge our inclusion in His family. On the contrary, He joyfully calls us His brothers and sisters and willingly shares His rightful inheritance with us. Adoption into God's family is not a legal fiction but a spiritual reality.

God also shows His love for His adopted children by sending us His Spirit as our advocate. He changes us so that we look more like Jesus, and one day He will resurrect our bodies just like He resurrected Jesus. We are never alone, never inferior or illegitimate children in God's eyes. We are God's real sons and daughters.

B. Prayer

Heavenly Father, thank You for making us Your children and giving us your Spirit to intercede for us. In Jesus' name. Amen.

C. Thought to Remember

We are God's real children!

Involvement Learning

Enhance your lesson with KJV Bible Student *(from your curriculum supplier) and the reproducible activity page (at www.standardlesson.com or in the back of the* KJV Standard Lesson Commentary Deluxe Edition*).*

Into the Lesson

Have participants identify a vulnerable population or an endangered animal species. Consider researching ahead of time to find one that might be in your area. Divide participants into small groups. Distribute index cards of the following questions to find out what learners know about advocating for this population: 1–Which organizations or foundations serve this purpose? 2–What are some things people do to help, serve, or bring awareness about this group? 3–Would any of the participants say they are an advocate for this cause? If so, how? 4–Why are advocates helpful to this group?

Bring the groups back together to present their findings in a whole-class discussion.

Lead into Bible study by saying, "An advocate is someone who speaks up for someone or something that cannot speak for themselves or struggles to be heard. As we study, consider in what ways the Holy Spirit is an advocate for us."

Into the Word

Ask a volunteer to read Romans 8:12–13. Write the following headers on the board: *In the Flesh* and *In the Spirit.* Have participants name behaviors and attitudes that can be displayed by living in either of these ways. For inspiration, recommend that they refer to Galatians 5:19–23. After several items are listed in each column, ask participants to identify ways that these attitudes and behaviors lead to life or death—physically, relationally, and spiritually.

Ask a volunteer to read Romans 8:14–17. Divide the class into two groups: **Children of God Group** and **Heirs of God Group.** Distribute handouts (you create) of the questions below for in-group discussion.

Children of God Group. Read Romans 8:14–15. 1–How does this passage define what it means to be a child of God? 2–How do Matthew 7:7–11 and Hebrews 12:7–11 add to this? 3–Based on these passages, what is an implication of being called a child of God?

Heirs of God Group. Read Romans 8:16–17. 1–How does this passage explain what it means to be an heir of God? 2–How do Galatians 3:26–4:7 and Ephesians 1:3–14 add to this? 3–Based on these passages, what is an implication of being called an heir of God?

After calling time, bring the groups back together to share their findings. As a whole class, create a list of why believers can trust the Spirit's witness about their standing before God.

Ask a volunteer to read Romans 8:26–27. Refer to the definition of *advocate* used earlier in the lesson. Talk about how the Holy Spirit is an advocate for believers. Distribute an index card and envelope to each learner. Give them a minute to write down an area in their lives where they feel weak, inadequate, or helpless. Then encourage them to place the card inside the envelope, seal it, and write the words of these two verses on the envelope. Invite them to put the envelope in a place where it will be seen regularly during the coming week. Encourage them to read the above verses aloud as a reminder to live confidently as a Spirit-led child of God.

Alternative. Distribute copies of the "Intercessor Inquiry" exercise from the activity page, which you can download. Have learners work in pairs to complete as indicated.

Into Life

Lead a brief brainstorming session by challenging learners to list ways to live confidently as believers. Divide the group into pairs. Challenge pairs to make a plan to deal with their fears so they can live confidently as God's children.

Option. Distribute the "I Am a Child of God" exercise from the activity page. Have learners complete it individually in a couple of minutes before discussing conclusions with a partner.

January 4
Lesson 5 (KJV)

Sin and Forgiveness

Devotional Reading: Isaiah 59:1–8
Background Scripture: Genesis 3:1–24; 1 John 1:5–2:6

1 John 1:5–10

5 This then is the message which we have heard of him, and declare unto you, that God is light, and in him is no darkness at all.

6 If we say that we have fellowship with him, and walk in darkness, we lie, and do not the truth:

7 But if we walk in the light, as he is in the light, we have fellowship one with another, and the blood of Jesus Christ his Son cleanseth us from all sin.

8 If we say that we have no sin, we deceive ourselves, and the truth is not in us.

9 If we confess our sins, he is faithful and just to forgive us our sins, and to cleanse us from all unrighteousness.

10 If we say that we have not sinned, we make him a liar, and his word is not in us.

1 John 2:1–6

1 My little children, these things write I unto you, that ye sin not. And if any man sin, we have an advocate with the Father, Jesus Christ the righteous:

2 And he is the propitiation for our sins: and not for ours only, but also for the sins of the whole world.

3 And hereby we do know that we know him, if we keep his commandments.

4 He that saith, I know him, and keepeth not his commandments, is a liar, and the truth is not in him.

5 But whoso keepeth his word, in him verily is the love of God perfected: hereby know we that we are in him.

6 He that saith he abideth in him ought himself also so to walk, even as he walked.

Key Text

If we say that we have no sin, we deceive ourselves, and the truth is not in us. If we confess our sins, he is faithful and just to forgive us our sins, and to cleanse us from all unrighteousness. **—1 John 1:8–9**

Enduring Beliefs

of the Church

Unit 2: Grace and Reconciliation

Lessons 5–8

Lesson Aims

After participating in this lesson, each learner will be able to:

1. Summarize the gospel using the terms *light* and *darkness* as used in 1 John.

2. Explain the significance of confession.

3. Celebrate Christ's pardon from sin by walking in the light and seeking fellowship with other believers.

Lesson Outline

Introduction

A. Talk vs. Walk

When our children were younger, one of our sons, then a preteen, burst into the house to report a fire he had seen in a vacant lot nearby. We immediately contacted the fire department and managed to contain the fire with a garden hose before firefighters arrived. Upon arrival, the fire chief expressed his gratitude to our son. Later, they awarded him a certificate in recognition of his alertness and for preventing what could have been a much larger disaster.

As parents with experience raising seven children, we understood that initial reports might not always be accurate. Upon questioning him, it became clear that the details of his account were untrue. His body language contradicted his words, indicating that something was amiss. Eventually, he admitted to accidentally starting the fire while playing with a lighter he'd found. He felt relieved after confessing.

The next step was challenging for our son and us, yet it was necessary. We visited the home of the fire chief, who lived in our neighborhood, where our son "came clean" about the incident. The chief scolded him and required the return of the certificate. Following the reprimand, the chief forgave him, cautioning him about the potential severity of his actions. In today's lesson, we examine the implications of when our talk (what we say we believe) conflicts with our walk (how we conduct ourselves).

B. Lesson Context

In his Gospel, the apostle John avoided using his own name, instead identifying himself as the disciple whom Jesus loved (John 19:26; 20:2; 21:7). This profound love significantly influenced John's life and writing. The dozens of uses of the word *love* found in the Gospel that bears his name exceeds that of the other three Gospels combined!

No one knows exactly when John wrote his Gospel and his three epistles. Our best guess is the latter part of the first century. This places John's writings several decades after he experienced the love of Jesus personally—an experience he wanted others to accept as true (1 John 1:1–5).

Visual for Lesson 5. *Display this visual as you ask, "What is the connection between confessing sin and walking in the light of God?"*

There are four listings of apostles in the New Testament, and John's name occurs in the first third of the 12 names in all listings (Matthew 10:2–3; Mark 3:16–19; Luke 6:14–16; Acts 1:13). Regarding his personal experience with Jesus, John is recognized as having been one of the "inner circle" of disciples. We see this designation in his being one of only three disciples to have witnessed Jesus' transfiguration. This was a profound experience, as he saw Jesus' face and attire radiantly shining, emitting a brilliant white light similar to the sun (Matthew 17:1–8; Mark 9:2–8; Luke 9:28–35). Some commentators propose that that event profoundly influenced John's use of light and darkness metaphors in his writings, including the passage we examine today. While this may be speculation, the profound imagery is no less poignant in John's writings.

In the opening verses of the epistle we call 1 John, the writer emphasizes his tangible interactions with Jesus. This emphasis may be a response to false teachings that were beginning to take shape. One such teaching was Docetism. Docetism taught that Jesus did not possess a physical form but merely appeared to. This belief stemmed from the notion that material substance was inherently evil, making it inconceivable for the divine to be associated with it. But John will have none of this! His in-person interactions with Jesus form the basis of all he has to say in this letter.

I. True Fellowship

(1 John 1:5–7)

A. God Is Light (v. 5)

5. This then is the message which we have heard of him, and declare unto you, that God is light, and in him is no darkness at all.

The correct understanding of this verse depends on how that little preposition *of* is understood. It could be understood as referring to *the message which we have heard* **about** *him* or *the message we have heard* **from** *him.* The immediate context and other usages in this letter indicate that "of" signifies "from" in this instance, as it does also in 1 John 2:27 and 3 John 7 in the *King James Version.*

The message to which John refers was not a revelation to a singular individual. Rather, the plural pronoun *we* suggests it was confirmed by many witnesses. While the Gospels do not provide a direct quote of Jesus speaking the particular message *God is light, and in him is no darkness at all,* it is understood that not all of Jesus' words and actions were documented (John 21:25). In fact, the phrase "God is light" is found nowhere else in the Bible (compare Psalm 104:2; 1 Timothy 6:16; etc.). This statement indicates that light is not just a characteristic of God but a fundamental part of His being, similar to how "spirit" and "love" are essential attributes (John 4:24; 1 John 4:8).

Those in the original audience who were familiar with the Hebrew Bible—what we now know as the Old Testament—would have interpreted John's use of light and darkness metaphors as representing good and evil, respectively, as they saw parallels with texts such as Isaiah 5:20; 50:10; 59:9; and Micah 7:8. John uses "light versus dark" imagery also in John 1:5; 3:19; 8:12; 12:35, 46; and 1 John 2:8–9. His audience dare not miss the message: spiritual darkness and light are incompatible. If God embodies light, it logically follows that God possesses no aspect of darkness.

B. Walking in the Light (vv. 6–7)

6. If we say that we have fellowship with him, and walk in darkness, we lie, and do not the truth.

This verse introduces the first of five consecutive, and six total, *if we* clauses in today's text (1 John 1:6–10; 2:3). To *have fellowship with* God implies a profound relationship or communion with Him. However, a lifestyle that is inconsistent with God's nature and expectations results in a false representation—a *lie*. Such a lie may or may not fool other people, but it won't fool God. To *walk in darkness* is to sin habitually (Acts 26:18; 2 Peter 2:4). Sin has consistently severed the bond between God and humanity (Genesis 3:24; Isaiah 59:1–2; etc.).

The true nature of a person's beliefs, declarations, and position of the heart is revealed through behavior that aligns with Jesus' teachings (John 13:35; 14:15, 23). These actions do not result in salvation but result from it (Ephesians 2:8–10; James 2:14–19). The internal transformation becomes visible externally, guided by the work of the Spirit (2 Thessalonians 2:13; 1 Peter 1:2). An emerging heresy of the time claimed that the actions of a person's physical body could not taint a person's spirit. We're not sure if John is opposing this particular heresy as he writes. But he leaves no doubt that it's "either-or," not "both-and."

What Do You Think?

What evidence would point to someone walking "in darkness"?

Digging Deeper

How can you become aware of whether you are in danger of walking in darkness?

7. But if we walk in the light, as he is in the light, we have fellowship one with another, and the blood of Jesus Christ his Son cleanseth us from all sin.

We come to the second of the five consecutive *if we* clauses. We might assume that *walking in the light* would represent a renewal of fellowship with God. That's true, but it's not John's aim here. Rather, John challenges the reader by stating that walking in the light is not separate from having *fellowship with one another*. Fellowship with God and with other believers go (or should go) hand in hand (Psalm 55:14; Isaiah 2:5; John 13:34–35; etc.).

The light of God reveals sin (John 3:20; Ephesians 5:11–13). As such, it also reveals our need for cleansing from that sin. That's exactly what *the blood of Jesus Christ* does in paying the penalty for sin we owe. John comforts his audience in this regard (compare Hebrews 9:12–14, 22; 13:12). This serves as a reminder that salvation is not achieved by our own efforts to walk in the light; instead, it is the cross of Christ that pays sin's penalty, enabling that walk.

What Do You Think?

What does it look like to "walk in the light"?

Digging Deeper

How might you encourage fellow believers to walk in the light?

Light and Dark

My husband and I served as missionaries in Ukraine in the 1990s. During those years, Ukraine was experiencing a financial crisis after the fall of the Soviet Union. Inflation was high, and resources were low. To cope, the government restricted the amount of electricity, water, and gas people could use, which resulted in rationing utilities.

The impact of this rationing resulted in hours of darkness every night. We were never sure exactly when the power would turn off, but we knew it would happen around dinner time. We scrambled to get things done before the lights went off, but inevitably, the outages caught us off guard. I still remember the feeling of being right in the middle of writing an email or putting dinner on the table when suddenly we were plunged into absolute darkness, without even the light from street lamps or the hum of appliances to fill the pitch-black silence. What a relief when, several hours later, the electricity suddenly turned back on. What had been a darkness so deep we could not see our hands in front of our faces became a blinding light. Not a bit of darkness remained.

Light is a "something"; darkness is not. Instead, darkness is a "lack of something." Light drives out darkness. If you're experiencing a darkness of the soul right now, what is missing? —L. M. W.

II. Necessary Confession
(1 John 1:8–2:2)

A. Our Sin and Us (vv. 8–10)

8. If we say that we have no sin, we deceive ourselves, and the truth is not in us.

We now arrive at the third of the five consecutive *if we* clauses. Some commentators view this verse as addressing an error that certain false teachers have been promoting. By claiming to be in the light while behaving contrary to it, they deny their sinfulness. This amounts to self-deception; not only do false teachers fool others, but they also fool themselves.

We should not miss the fact that *truth* is extremely important to John. The word *truth* appears (in Greek) more than 100 times in the New Testament as a whole, with more than 40 percent of them occurring in John's Gospel and epistles. This is noteworthy given the relatively small percentage of the New Testament that these books comprise.

9. If we confess our sins, he is faithful and just to forgive us our sins, and to cleanse us from all unrighteousness.

In the fourth of five consecutive *if we* clauses in today's text, John highlights the stark contrast between the self-deluded people of the previous verse and those who have received forgiveness from God. Whereas sin was stated in the singular there, here it is plural: *sins*. Some commentators propose that this distinction underscores the idea that those who admit to their personal sins are fully aware of the seriousness of their condition apart from God's pardon (compare 1 Timothy 1:15).

The language used implies that sins are confessed to God, who is the one who forgives sins (see Psalm 32:5; Luke 11:4; compare James 5:16). Furthermore, the forgiveness offered by God transcends mere pardon; it involves a cleansing of the believer from all acts of unrighteousness (1 Corinthians 6:11; Titus 2:14; and 1 John 1:7, above).

10. If we say that we have not sinned, we make him a liar, and his word is not in us.

This is the fifth consecutive *if we* clause in our lesson (a sixth appears in 1 John 2:3). Again, some commentators see a corrective to claims by false teachers. Opinions along that line vary on how this "if we" clause differs from the one in 1 John 1:8, above. One proposal sees that verse opposing denials of humanity's sinful nature, whereas the verse now before us is seen to deny having engaged in sinful behaviors at the individual level. Ultimately, however, we must conclude that (1) sin is a real thing, (2 we are guilty of committing it, and (3) to disbelieve makes God *a liar* in our eyes as we sink deeper into self-deception.

> **What Do You Think?**
> In what ways do we tend to say that we have not sinned?
>
> **Digging Deeper**
> How can relationships help us recognize our need for God's forgiveness?

B. Our Sin and God (2:1–2)

1. My little children, these things write I unto you, that ye sin not. And if any man sin, we have an advocate with the Father, Jesus Christ the righteous.

The term *little children* is a favorite way for John to address his audience; he uses this designation also in 1 John 2:12, 28; 3:7, 18; 4:4; and 5:21. It occurs on the lips of Jesus as well, but only in John's Gospel (John 13:33). A slightly different Greek word, translated "children" (without "little"), is much more common, occurring about 100 times in the New Testament; John uses this word as well (1 John 5:2; 2 John 1, 4, 13; 3 John 4). John appears to view his role as that of a father figure to his readers.

John explains Jesus' ongoing role in heaven as *an advocate with the Father*. The word translated *advocate* is also a term unique to John, occurring in the New Testament only here and in John 14:26; 15:26; and 16:7. It refers to a mediator

How to Say It

Docetism	Doe-*set*-iz-um.
epistles	ee-*pis*-uls.
Gnosticism	***Nahss***-tih-*sizz*-um.
heresy	*hair*-uh-see.

or intercessor who speaks on behalf of another. After Jesus offered Himself as the sacrifice for sin and rose from the dead, He took His place at the Father's right hand. There, He continuously advocates (intercedes) for believers (Romans 8:34; Hebrews 7:25). The unique sinlessness and righteousness of Jesus enables our purification from sin (2 Corinthians 5:21).

2. And he is the propitiation for our sins: and not for ours only, but also for the sins of the whole world.

John builds on his previous statements with the rare word *propitiation,* which means "something that turns away wrath." This term appears twice in this epistle (here and 1 John 4:10). Closely related words are found in Romans 3:25 and Hebrews 9:5 (as nouns) as well as Luke 18:13 and Hebrews 2:17 (as verbs). The foundation of Jesus' serving as our mediator lies in His sinless offering of Himself on the cross, which paid the penalty for the sins of all who would believe. This doctrine is often referred to as "substitutionary atonement" (compare John 1:29; Colossians 1:20).

III. Obedient Walk

(1 John 2:3–6)

A. Proof of Knowledge (vv. 3–5)

3. And hereby we do know that we know him, if we keep his commandments.

Here, we have a sixth *if we* clause in the second half of this verse. Keeping *his commandments* is evidence *that we know him.* Perhaps John has in mind Jesus' answer to the question about the greatest commandment (Matthew 22:36–39; Mark 12:28–31; see John 13:34; 15:12). Love is the hallmark by which Jesus indicated the world would recognize His followers. Additionally, the apostle Paul regarded love as the law's fulfillment (see Romans 13:10; Galatians 5:14).

Regardless of the specific interpretation of "commandments" in this context, John implies that following the commandments is not the way to salvation; it serves as evidence of that relationship. This aligns with teachings found throughout Scripture (Galatians 2:16, 21; 3:11; Hebrews 7:19). Moreover, John's emphasis on the certainty believers in Christ possess contrasts starkly with the uncertainty propagated by false teachers (compare John 14:15; 15:10).

> **What Do You Think?**
> What role does action play in our life of faith?
>
> **Digging Deeper**
> In what ways are we dependent upon Jesus Christ, our advocate?

4. He that saith, I know him, and keepeth not his commandments, is a liar, and the truth is not in him.

John now elaborates on his earlier remark (1 John 1:6, above), drawing it to a logical conclusion. This might be summed up by the old axiom that actions speak louder than words. Anyone who professes to know God yet whose life contradicts God's commandments is making a false claim.

Some commentators suggest that John is addressing the heresy of Gnosticism here. The followers of this heresy claim exclusive enlightenment, secret knowledge. However, their conduct fails to align with the elevated knowledge they claim to possess.

5. But whoso keepeth his word, in him verily is the love of God perfected: hereby know we that we are in him.

John continues to distinguish between those who adhere to *his word* and those who do not. The central element in the statements in this verse is *the love of God.* Three main interpretations of what this love entails have been proposed: the love of God could signify (1) His love for individuals, (2) an individual's love for God, or (3) a divine type of love that individuals have for one another. Evidence exists for each of the three alternatives. But given John's portrayal of this love as a distinctive sign, it is likely that he is referring to the divine love among believers (see John 13:35). This form of love is poured into a person's heart by the Spirit when one comes to faith in Christ (see Romans 5:5).

We also acknowledge differing opinions regarding the interpretation of the word *perfected* in this verse and in 1 John 4:12, 17. This word is used in

John 4:34; 5:36; and 17:4 to refer to something that is finished (in terms of having reached a goal). Given the nature of the fallen world in which we live, our growth in love for one another will be perfected in an ultimate and final sense only after Jesus returns. Until then, we continue to grow and mature in our expressions of that love.

The Christian's Uniform

When my children were in elementary school, administrators there decided to require uniforms for all students. As a parent, I appreciated the school system's attempt to standardize the students' appearance in order to prevent comparisons and judgments regarding clothing choices. I understood that the administration hoped to eliminate the bullying that could occur between students who could afford expensive, designer clothes and those who could not.

However, parents and administrators quickly realized that students still personalized their looks by the style of shoes they chose, the hairstyles they sported, and the socks they wore. Even things such as hair ties became status symbols. Students followed the human desire to identify themselves as part of certain groups by the way they accessorized their uniforms.

Such desires can result in both positive and negative outcomes. Positively, believers validate their identity as Christians by the way they express love for one another. That expression is our "uniform," identifying us as believers. However, a problem can present itself in the way we "accessorize" that uniform, particularly if the accessories end up overshadowing the uniform itself. What dangers do you need to be aware of in that regard?

—L. M. W.

B. Proof of Abiding (v. 6)

6. He that saith he abideth in him ought himself also so to walk, even as he walked.

To *walk even as he walked* is to follow Christ's example (John 13:15; 1 Peter 2:21). The author fronts this conclusion by using a Greek word translated as "abide"; he uses this word 23 times in this letter, and this is the first. In doing so, he speaks of a close, ongoing connection. Those who abide in Jesus will live consistently in ways that reflect His love and teaching.

What Do You Think?

What outward fruit should we expect to see in Christ-followers?

Digging Deeper

How does Galatians 5:13–26 align with these passages from 1 John?

Conclusion

A. Talk = Walk

My experience as an airline supervisor required me to interact with passengers. Some attempted to board the plane with household pets by falsely claiming they were service animals. With no official registry for service animals, our team had to assess each case based on the animal's behavior. Disruptions like barking led to denied boarding.

This situation is akin to what John addresses in his letter: distinguishing the true claims from the false. John uses a firm, fatherly tone to stress that claiming to live in the light while walking in darkness is deceitful. The message is straightforward: one's walk must match one's talk. Jesus highlighted that, on Judgment Day, many will profess to know Him by citing a list of their deeds. However, their lack of a genuine relationship with Christ will result in their condemnation (Matthew 7:21–23).

This is a powerful reminder! In our spiritual walk, Jesus is our standard. When we compare our lives to Christ's example, we must ask ourselves whether we see a reflection of Him or a contradiction. This self-assessment and willingness to correct our course when necessary is crucial to authentic faith.

B. Prayer

Heavenly Father, we are grateful for Jesus' light. Thank You for the reminder that when we abide in You, we walk in the light. May the world know that we are Christians by our "walk" being aligned with our "talk." In Jesus' name we pray. Amen.

C. Thought to Remember

Praise God for the light of the gospel!

Involvement Learning

Enhance your lesson with KJV Bible Student *(from your curriculum supplier) and the reproducible activity page (at www.standardlesson.com or in the back of the* KJV Standard Lesson Commentary Deluxe Edition*).*

Into the Lesson

Ask participants to discuss the significance of light in the physical world, providing examples such as its role in plant growth, its ability to reveal hidden objects, and its part in vitamin D production and energy levels. Contrast how darkness affects the world. Next, invite the participants to consider light metaphorically and share their thoughts. Examples might include guidance, purity, revelation, hope, unity, and comfort. Conclude your discussion by contrasting the metaphorical ideas of "light" with the metaphorical ideas of "darkness."

Alternative. Distribute copies of the "Light and Darkness" exercise from the activity page, which you can download. Have learners work in pairs to complete as indicated. Discuss if time allows.

Lead into Bible study by saying, "John often employs the metaphors of light and darkness in his writings to create a clearer mental image for his readers. In today's lesson, we'll explore a passage where John uses light to represent God and the daily life of Christians while portraying sin and unrighteousness as darkness."

Into the Word

Divide the class into two groups, designating one the **Truth Trackers** and the other the **Assurance Alliance.** To each participant, distribute a copy of the lesson text you prepared, a highlighter, and a pen. Assign the following activities for group discussion.

Truth Trackers. Read 1 John 1:5–10. Highlight all the statements that about truth with one color (light). Use a different color to highlight statements about falsehood (darkness).

Assurance Alliance. Read 1 John 2:1–6. Highlight in one color everything the text instructs believers to do. Use a different color for assurances or promises mentioned in the passage.

After five minutes, ask each group to summarize their findings on a separate sheet of paper.

Reconvene for whole-class discussion. Have volunteers from each group read their Scripture passage aloud and share the group summary.

Option. Engage the two groups in a role-playing exercise to explore what it means to walk in the light in real-life scenarios. Have groups discuss how they would respond to the following situations based on the text from 1 John.

1. A family member wants to do something that contradicts your beliefs. How would you navigate this while maintaining love and respect for them?
2. A friend is seeking guidance during a crisis, feeling hopeless and guilty about a mistake. How can you use assurances from 1 John to encourage and help them find a path forward?

Present these questions for further whole-class discussion: 1–What does "walk in the light" mean, as mentioned in 1 John 1:7? 2–Based on John's text, why is confession important? 3–How does knowing that Jesus is our advocate influence how we respond to our failures and others' sins?

Into Life

Say, "One way to walk in the light is to maintain fellowship with other believers." Give participants time to brainstorm concrete ways to walk in the light and stay in fellowship. Distribute index cards to learners. After allowing time to reflect on the brainstormed ideas, ask, "What is one thing you can do this week to walk in the light and seek fellowship with another believer?" Invite learners to write their ideas on the card. Challenge them to follow through with the plan throughout the week.

Alternative. Distribute copies of the "Walking in the Light" activity from the activity page. Have learners work with a partner to complete as indicated. After calling time, invite pairs to share their poem with the whole class.

Conclude class with a prayer, thanking God for the light He provides for us to walk in and for the forgiveness of sins we have in Christ.

Repentance and Faith

Devotional Reading: Mark 1:14–20
Background Scripture: Isaiah 1:10–21; Ezekiel 18:20–23, 27–32

Luke 15:11–24

11 And he said, A certain man had two sons:

12 And the younger of them said to his father, Father, give me the portion of goods that falleth to me. And he divided unto them his living.

13 And not many days after the younger son gathered all together, and took his journey into a far country, and there wasted his substance with riotous living.

14 And when he had spent all, there arose a mighty famine in that land; and he began to be in want.

15 And he went and joined himself to a citizen of that country; and he sent him into his fields to feed swine.

16 And he would fain have filled his belly with the husks that the swine did eat: and no man gave unto him.

17 And when he came to himself, he said, How many hired servants of my father's have bread enough and to spare, and I perish with hunger!

18 I will arise and go to my father, and will say unto him, Father, I have sinned against heaven, and before thee,

19 And am no more worthy to be called thy son: make me as one of thy hired servants.

20 And he arose, and came to his father. But when he was yet a great way off, his father saw him, and had compassion, and ran, and fell on his neck, and kissed him.

21 And the son said unto him, Father, I have sinned against heaven, and in thy sight, and am no more worthy to be called thy son.

22 But the father said to his servants, Bring forth the best robe, and put it on him; and put a ring on his hand, and shoes on his feet:

23 And bring hither the fatted calf, and kill it; and let us eat, and be merry:

24 For this my son was dead, and is alive again; he was lost, and is found. And they began to be merry.

Acts 2:38–39

38 Then Peter said unto them, Repent, and be baptized every one of you in the name of Jesus Christ for the remission of sins, and ye shall receive the gift of the Holy Ghost.

39 For the promise is unto you, and to your children, and to all that are afar off, even as many as the Lord our God shall call.

Key Text

This my son was dead, and is alive again; he was lost, and is found. And they began to be merry.

—Luke 15:24

Enduring Beliefs

of the Church

Unit 2: Grace and Reconciliation

Lessons 5–8

Lesson Aims

After participating in this lesson, each learner will be able to:

1. Summarize the actions of the younger son and the father in the parable.
2. Explain why each of us must welcome others returning to God.
3. Commit to sharing God's generosity with others.

Lesson Outline

Introduction
- A. Leaving Home
- B. Lesson Context

I. Jesus' Parable (Luke 15:11–24)
- A. Son's Request (vv. 11–16)
- B. Son's Return (vv. 17–20a)
- C. Father's Response (vv. 20b–24)
  - *Wait Until Your Dad Gets Home*

II. Apostle's Teaching (Acts 2:38–39)
- A. The Gift (v. 38)
- B. The Promise (v. 39)
  - *A Long Way in the Wrong Direction*

Conclusion
- A. Homecoming
- B. Prayer
- C. Thought to Remember

Introduction

A. Leaving Home

At age 16, armed with a job, car, and license, I experienced true independence for the first time. I exercised this freedom by telling my parents I would no longer join them at their church. Instead, I intended to explore and find a religion of my own. To my surprise, my parents did not resist. But what I initially viewed as rebellion transformed into a genuine quest for truth.

Each Sunday, my girlfriend and I would explore churches of different doctrinal convictions and styles of worship. The search led us to a particular church where visitors were encouraged to complete a visitor's card. I completed a card to have something to "contribute" to the offering plate since I needed my money for gas. The card led the pastor to our home and me to a relationship with Christ. My parents proudly sat in the congregation the day I was baptized. What I had mistaken for a departure from my roots was, in truth, a journey toward Christ.

In today's lesson, we will revisit one of the most beloved but often misunderstood Bible passages: the story of the prodigal son.

B. Lesson Context

In Luke 15 (see also Lesson Context for Lesson 3), tax collectors and sinners gather to hear Jesus. Nearby, Pharisees—adherents of the Law of Moses and their traditions—murmur their disapproval (compare Mark 7:1–8). This setting underscores the meal-sharing tradition in first-century Judaism as a sign of acceptance (see Mark 2:16; 1 Corinthians 5:9–11; Galatians 2:11–14).

Jesus' use of parables was a teaching method and a profound way to convey spiritual truths. These parables, often simple earthly narratives, were vehicles for deep spiritual meanings. While the exact number of parables Jesus taught is a topic of discussion, it's widely agreed that He presented at least 30 unique ones. Figurative language, in which "this" stands for "that," predominates in parables. A failure to recognize figurative language is to repeat the errors of Jesus' disciples and the Pharisees (Matthew 16:5–12; Mark 7:18; John 10:6; etc.).

Acts 2 depicts Pentecost, when the Holy Spirit came and filled believers, causing many to speak in foreign tongues (Acts 2:1–12). In Acts 2:14–39, Peter addresses the Jews gathered to behold this miraculous sight, sharing the good news of Jesus. Peter quotes an Old Testament prophecy stating that God's Spirit would be poured out on "all flesh" (Acts 2:17; Joel 2:28), and that "whosoever shall call on the name of the Lord" will be saved (Acts 2:21; Joel 2:32). While Peter likely did not have Gentiles in mind yet, as this was prior to his vision and encounter with Cornelius (see Acts 10), he perhaps meant at least that God's Spirit would not be limited to prophets, priests, and kings. It is possible that Luke had the Gentiles in mind while writing this account, perhaps showing that just as Jesus' followers are charged to take the gospel to Jerusalem, Samaria, and the rest of the world (1:8), so would God's Spirit be given to all those He calls and who turn to Him in faith.

I. Jesus' Parable

(Luke 15:11–24)

Jesus speaks this parable against the religious leaders and their attitude, as evidenced in Luke 15:2. They undoubtedly realize Jesus' intent to challenge their position, as Luke 20:19 later indicates.

A. Son's Request (vv. 11–16)

11. And he said, A certain man had two sons.

The way Jesus starts this narrative signals its nature as a parable. Just as when a story begins with "in a land far, far away," listeners recognize that what Jesus is about to relate is not a historical account. In the Gospel of Luke, several parables begin with the introduction of *a certain man* (Luke 12:16; 14:16; etc.). A distinctive feature of these parables is their lack of named characters, setting them apart as figurative rather than historical. This storytelling technique enables listeners to place themselves within the narrative. It also makes it less obvious that Jesus is the one highlighting their sin.

The emphasis of this parable is frequently placed on the prodigal son. Nonetheless, Jesus presents three characters: a father and his *two sons.* Every character plays a role in the narrative, allowing listeners to identify with at least one.

12. And the younger of them said to his father, Father, give me the portion of goods that falleth to me. And he divided unto them his living.

Then as now, inheritance is passed along to descendants only after the death of the testator (Hebrews 9:16). However, an advisory in a Jewish non-biblical text to not do otherwise suggests that there were instances where an inheritance was indeed distributed before death (Sirach 33:19–23).

According to the Law of Moses, the eldest son was entitled to a double share of his father's estate (Deuteronomy 21:17; compare Genesis 25:31). Given the declaration that (1) this man has two sons and that (2) the one making the request is *the younger of them,* this means that (3) the son desires one-third of his father's *living.* Jesus doesn't find it necessary to specify exact ages; He merely mentions the request of the younger son.

The audience of Pharisees and scribes knows that such an outlandish request is indicative of a rebellious son who is subject to the death penalty (see Deuteronomy 21:18–21). But the father doesn't go there; instead, he grants the younger son's desire. This response from the father likely strikes Jesus' audience as unorthodox and unexpected.

What Do You Think?

What might have compelled the father to give the younger son his share of the inheritance?

Digging Deeper

How might the father have felt after this series of events?

13. And not many days after the younger son gathered all together, and took his journey into a far country, and there wasted his substance with riotous living.

The younger son, having gained possession of his inheritance (*substance*), moves a significant distance away from his father. The specifics of how the money was squandered are not detailed, though Luke 15:30 may suggest one such avenue.

Visual for Lesson 6. *Display this visual during the lesson conclusion and ask volunteers how they want to celebrate God's forgiveness.*

14. And when he had spent all, there arose a mighty famine in that land; and he began to be in want.

In great contrast to the comfort in which he was raised, the son becomes impoverished as bankruptcy coincides with *a mighty famine.* The two lacks join to deal a severe hit on the son; food shortages cause food prices to rise as the law of supply and demand asserts itself (compare 2 Kings 6:24–25; 7:1, 16).

15. And he went and joined himself to a citizen of that country; and he sent him into his fields to feed swine.

Driven by his situation, the young man seeks employment. Scripture expects those physically capable of working to earn their food (Proverbs 10:4–5; 12:11; 19:15; 2 Thessalonians 3:10; 1 Timothy 5:8). Moreover, Jesus introduces an additional cultural layer to the narrative: the man indentures himself into the service of a Gentile, *a citizen of* another *country.* The conclusion that the citizen is a Gentile is established by the fact that he has *swine,* animals considered unclean according to the Law of Moses (Leviticus 11:7; Deuteronomy 14:8).

16. And he would fain have filled his belly with the husks that the swine did eat: and no man gave unto him.

The man's dire hunger serves the purpose of bringing him to a new depth of desperation—now, even the pigs' food seems enticing to him. In Jewish tradition, Gentiles were considered unclean, leading Jews to abstain from dining with them (see Acts 10:28; 11:3; Galatians 2:12). Desiring the pigs' food was another thing entirely.

B. Son's Return (vv. 17–20a)

17. And when he came to himself, he said, How many hired servants of my father's have bread enough and to spare, and I perish with hunger!

This is a critical turning point in the story. The young man, having reached his lowest point, regained his clarity of mind. Self-examination is a recurring motif in Scripture, invariably serving as the initial step toward repentance (2 Corinthians 13:5; Galatians 6:4; Revelation 2:5; etc.).

18. I will arise and go to my father, and will say unto him, Father, I have sinned against heaven, and before thee.

Repentance requires returning to his *father* and admitting wrongdoing. However, his offense, as is the case with all transgressions, is chiefly *against* God, as implied by the term *heaven.* Undoubtedly, the listeners well acquainted with God's laws recognize the son's conduct as dishonoring his father and thereby breaking the law of God (Exodus 20:12; Matthew 15:4).

19. And am no more worthy to be called thy son: make me as one of thy hired servants.

Declaring himself unworthy of sonship, the young man's sentiments are deeply rooted in the honor and shame dynamics prevalent in that era. By squandering his inheritance, he has tarnished his father's reputation. Legally, his father is no longer obligated to provide for him. Thus, he resolves to request the bare essentials from his father through the position of a servant. Even this status will be preferable to starving as he watches pigs feed.

> **What Do You Think?**
>
> When do you think the younger son was at his lowest?
>
> **Digging Deeper**
>
> What experiences enable you to relate to the younger son?

20a. And he arose, and came to his father.

The younger son's repentance will be meaningless if he remains where he is. Hence, the penultimate act of his repentance is to get his feet moving toward home.

C. Father's Response (vv. 20b–24)

20b. But when he was yet a great way off, his father saw him, and had compassion, and ran, and fell on his neck, and kissed him.

The narrative transitions to the father's perspective. Apparently, the *father* has been eagerly awaiting his son's return. The father's joy is a motif that echoes across the parables of the lost sheep and the lost coin just before (Luke 15:1–10). To the audience, the sight of an elderly Jewish man running likely seems unusual and undignified. Yet, his act underscores the father's profound longing to be reconciled with his son.

21. And the son said unto him, Father, I have sinned against heaven, and in thy sight, and am no more worthy to be called thy son.

The son's reaction echoes that of David in Psalm 51:4 as *the son* humbles himself before his *father*. It's easy to imagine that the son has rehearsed his apology many times during the long journey back.

> **What Do You Think?**
> What circumstances of repentance and return call for public confession of sin? Why?
>
> **Digging Deeper**
> Do the circumstances depend on whether it is a sin of commission or a sin of omission?

22. But the father said to his servants, Bring forth the best robe, and put it on him; and put a ring on his hand, and shoes on his feet.

Before the son can suggest becoming a servant as he has planned, *the father* interrupts by embracing him as a son instead (compare John 15:15; Galatians 4:6–7). The finest *robe,* likely the father's own, and the *ring* both signify the father's acceptance of the young man as a son again, with the ring perhaps also symbolizing authority (compare Genesis 41:42).

23. And bring hither the fatted calf, and kill it; and let us eat, and be merry.

The father's subsequent command suggests he plans to host a celebration. Traditionally, a family reserves a fattened *calf* for significant events (example: Genesis 18:7), such as when a young man reaches adulthood. Since the son's previous actions and disrespect toward his father had undoubtedly spread through the village, it is appropriate for the father to organize a festivity to spread a counteracting message. As a bit of speculation, the pronoun *us* may indicate that the neighbors are invited to witness the son's transformation and the father's demonstration of love, acceptance, and forgiveness.

24. For this my son was dead, and is alive again; he was lost, and is found. And they began to be merry.

This celebration mirrors the rejoicing in this chapter's parables of the lost sheep (Luke 15:6) and the lost coin (15:9). From the father's point of view, his son's departure had led him to mourn as though he had lost him to death. The son's return symbolizes a reversal of that.

> **What Do You Think?**
> Can you think of an example of radical forgiveness in your life, such as is exhibited by the father?
>
> **Digging Deeper**
> What enables the father to respond with lavish grace and love?

Wait Until Your Dad Gets Home

When I was a little girl, I loved to change outfits throughout the day, discarding clothing all over my bedroom floor without a thought. When my mom would see my messy room, she would demand that I clean it up—immediately. I usually obeyed. But when I didn't, then came Mom's dreaded words: "Just wait until your dad gets home."

Knowing I was going to be in trouble with my dad was enough to leave my stomach in knots for the rest of the day. However, my fearful expectations rarely matched reality. Although my father was stern, his rebuke and discipline were not as terrifying as I had feared.

To the prodigal (which means "wastefully extravagant"), the best-case scenario upon returning to his father was to become a servant. The worst case would have been to be cut off entirely. The reality, however, was nothing less than unmerited, unexpected grace, mercy, forgiveness, a homecoming celebration, and a restored relationship.

How should this parable affect how you consider approaching the Lord with your own confessions of sin? Will you make excuses and try to justify yourself? Or will you accept responsibility and repent? Before you answer, see 1 Samuel 15:13–21; Psalm 51; and Luke 18:9–14. —B. R.

II. Apostle's Teaching

(Acts 2:38–39)

A. The Gift (v. 38)

38a. Then Peter said unto them, Repent, and be baptized every one of you in the name of Jesus Christ.

Peter's declaration is in response to a question the crowd poses following his address to them. The previous verse depicts the people's realization of guilt that prompts the question, "Men and brethren, what shall we do?" (Acts 2:37). In reviewing the two imperatives *repent, and be baptized,* we conclude that other elements are implied that only later will be stated explicitly. First, notice that faith isn't mentioned. But given the requirement for repentance, faith must be present as well. The implicit connection between repentance and faith will be made explicit later (Acts 20:21; Hebrews 6:1).

Also unexplored at this point are various elements regarding baptism. Jews are familiar with the use of water in ceremonial cleansings and would naturally make a mental connection with baptism (Ezekiel 36:25–26; Mark 7:3–4; John 2:6; 3:25). Various instances of baptism are recorded in Acts (Acts 2:41; 8:36–39; 9:17–18; 10:44–48; 16:15, 30–33; etc.), but only later will more robust explanations of baptism receive treatment (Galatians 3:27; Colossians 2:12; 1 Peter 3:21; etc.).

Likewise, the phrase *in the name of Jesus Christ* implies allegiance to God in its fullest sense. What is implied here is made explicit in Matthew 28:19, which specifies baptism "in the name of the Father, and of the Son, and of the Holy Ghost." Taken together, all these elements signify the beginning of a new relationship.

38b. for the remission of sins, and ye shall receive the gift of the Holy Ghost.

Peter highlights two blessings for those who respond as he has just directed. Forgiveness, another word for *remission of sins,* is possible because of Christ's sacrifice on the cross. There, He paid sin's price for us (Romans 3:9–26; Hebrews 1:3; 1 Peter 2:24; etc.) and cleared our debt completely (Colossians 2:14). This act initiated the new covenant, under which God has pledged to forget our sins and lawless actions (Jeremiah 31:34; Luke 22:20; Hebrews 10:17–18). The Holy Spirit, promised by Jesus (John 14:26; 15:26; 16:7), empowers believers to support the Christian community and embody virtues like love, joy, and peace (1 Corinthians 12:4–11; Galatians 5:22–23). Additionally, the Spirit assists in prayer and affirms an individual's salvation (Romans 8:16, 26; see Lesson 4).

B. The Promise (v. 39)

39. For the promise is unto you, and to your children, and to all that are afar off, even as many as the Lord our God shall call.

The promise of the previous verse is not only to those asking the question of Acts 2:37 (*you*) but also *to your children,* which reflects Isaiah 44:3. The same promise *to all that are afar off* reflects wording in Ephesians 2:13, referring to Gentiles.

Peter likely does not yet understand the full implication of his words at the time, given his surprise at the inclusion of Gentiles in Acts 10:44–46. This issue sparked significant debate in the first-century church, prompting the gathering of a council in Jerusalem to deliberate on whether Gen-

How to Say It

Colossians	Kuh-*losh*-unz.
Ephesians	Ee-*fee*-zhunz.
Galatians	Guh-*lay*-shunz.
Gentiles	*Jen*-tiles.
Pentecost	*Pent*-ih-kost.
Pharisees	*Fair*-ih-seez.
prodigal	*praw*-dih-gull.

tiles needed to embrace the practices of Judaism in becoming followers of Christ (Acts 15:1–29).

A Long Way in the Wrong Direction

Last year, some friends and I took a weekend trip to the beach. The car ride down was filled with excitement. The ride back was a different story. We were tired, sunburned, and not a little reluctant to get back to our normal routines. At some point, Jen took an exit, thinking it was a shortcut to drop off our friend Dot. After about an hour, she realized the shortcut had taken us 50 miles in the wrong direction!

As soon as we realized the mistake, we found the first safe place to turn around and head back the right way. We can laugh about it now, but at the time, it wasn't very funny. One wrong turn was all it took.

Until we recognize our need for Christ, our lives are like that car going a long way in the wrong direction. When we hear the good news of the gospel, we are awakened to our need to repent—to turn around—and begin heading in the way of Christ. As followers of Jesus, we are called to be road signs that tell those around us, "You're going the wrong way! Repent! There is hope and healing for your life!" How well is your life functioning as a "road sign" for others? —B. R.

Conclusion

A. Homecoming

I recall the most bountiful spread of food from my childhood at our annual church homecoming. This is a tradition that, as a child, I looked forward to more than any other Sunday. Everyone dressed up and brought their finest homemade dishes and pies to share. After the service, we gathered at a long table under a shady tree for a meal, followed by an afternoon of worship. Although many faces were unfamiliar to me during these homecoming celebrations, their ties to our little church granted them a place at our table.

The two segments of today's lesson share a common element of God's love for and inclusion of those once far off. Jesus' parable in Luke 15:11–32 emphasizes the joy over the repentant return of the wayward. The prodigal son represents the publicans and sinners who gathered to hear Jesus speak (Luke 15:1). The elder brother (not considered in today's texts, see Luke 15:25–30) represents the attitude of Jesus' opponents, the Pharisees and scribes (15:2). Acts 2:38–39 communicates a similar theme, calling for repentance, expressing what the repentant shall receive. Though initially addressing Jews, this passage (in light of the rest of Scripture) points toward the inclusion of the Gentiles to come. The message of Acts 2:38–39 is relevant to those who had departed and returned as well as to those who had always been far off until first being brought near.

In churches everywhere, individuals step into a congregation for the first time, while others return after a lengthy absence. God greets each one with a welcoming embrace, and there is jubilation in heaven for every soul that repents. In the parable, God is depicted as the father, and those of us who have remained in the church are invited to join our Heavenly Father in welcoming the repentant with open arms as well. When we see the prodigal return—or the unbeliever come to faith for the first time—may we be compelled by our Father's love to offer them a seat at the table and welcome them home as our brother or sister in Christ!

> **What Do You Think?**
> Do you find it more difficult to welcome new believers or those who return after a time of rebellion?
>
> **Digging Deeper**
> How do these Scripture passages encourage you to welcome both well?

B. Prayer

Heavenly Father, we are grateful for Your boundless grace and mercy. Teach us to seek Your forgiveness wholeheartedly and extend that grace to others. Grant us wisdom that we may avoid learning lessons "the hard way." We pray this in the name of Jesus. Amen.

C. Thought to Remember

The Father eagerly waits to welcome us home!

Involvement Learning

Enhance your lesson with KJV Bible Student *(from your curriculum supplier) and the reproducible activity page (at www.standardlesson.com or in the back of the* KJV Standard Lesson Commentary Deluxe Edition*).*

Into the Lesson

Write the phrase *Coming Home* on the board. Distribute index cards to each participant and ask them to recall when they or someone close moved away from their hometown. Invite them to reflect on their first return visit. What specific details stand out from that experience? Encourage each learner to write down a few memorable aspects of the homecoming on the cards provided.

Be ready to share a personal example from your own experiences. After allowing time for reflection, ask a few volunteers to share what they wrote on their cards. Invite them to explain why certain details were significant. Highlight to the class how we each assign different meanings or varying levels of importance to specific information.

Lead into Bible study by saying, "Today's lesson explores the well-known parable of the prodigal son. One intriguing element of this story is the vivid detail about the father's actions and the specific gifts he presents to his son upon their reunion. Jesus employs earthly language through this parable to convey a heavenly message about how the Father welcomes us into His home."

Into the Word

Have a volunteer read Luke 15:11–16 aloud. Write *Prodigal Son* and *The Father* as two headers on the board. Ask participants to list characteristics, actions, or phrases from the passage that describe each character. Write their responses on the board.

Have a volunteer read Luke 15:17–24 aloud. Ask participants to list characteristics, actions, or phrases from the passage that describe each character. Write responses on the board under the appropriate header.

Add two more headers to the board: *Peter* and *God*. Have a volunteer read Acts 2:38–39 aloud. Ask participants to list Peter's instruction and God's promise from these two verses.

Divide into two groups: **Returners** and **Welcomers.** Distribute the following questions and prompts to the groups for in-group discussion.

Returners Group. 1–What does the son's journey teach about repentance and reconciliation? 2–Identify other Bible verses for support.

Welcomers Group. 1–What does the father's response reveal about God's love? 2–Identify other Bible verses that support your answers.

Reunite the class and have a volunteer from each group share their findings.

Distribute copies of the lesson text (you prepare) and two different colors of highlighters or pens to each participant. Instruct them to use one color to highlight Acts 2:38 and a different color for Acts 2:39. Then, allow participants time to examine the text from Luke, using the verse 38 color to highlight verses corresponding to the command to repent. Have them use the other color for verses reflecting the promise in Acts 2:39. Discuss: 1–What parallels did you find between Acts 2:38–39 and the parable in Luke? 2–How do these verses help you understand why we should be welcoming toward those returning to God?

Alternative. Distribute copies of the "Journey Home" exercise from the activity page, which you can download. Have learners work in pairs to complete as indicated. Share as time allows.

Into Life

Point out the actions on the board the father took to show his love. Discuss how this relates to God's generosity. Distribute index cards to each participant and ask them to write one way to demonstrate God's generosity to others. Invite them to commit to act on what they wrote during the week.

Split the class into small groups to pray together, seeking God's assistance in implementing their planned actions throughout the week.

Option. Distribute the "Prayer of Celebration" exercise from the activity page. Have participants complete it individually as a take-home.

Prayer and Humility

Devotional Reading: Psalm 141
Background Scripture: Nehemiah 1:4–11; Daniel 6:10;
Matthew 6:5–15; Luke 18:1–14; John 17:1–26

Genesis 18:25–27

25 That be far from thee to do after this manner, to slay the righteous with the wicked: and that the righteous should be as the wicked, that be far from thee: Shall not the Judge of all the earth do right?

26 And the LORD said, If I find in Sodom fifty righteous within the city, then I will spare all the place for their sakes.

27 And Abraham answered and said, Behold now, I have taken upon me to speak unto the Lord, which am but dust and ashes.

Luke 18:9–14

9 And he spake this parable unto certain which trusted in themselves that they were righteous, and despised others:

10 Two men went up into the temple to pray; the one a Pharisee, and the other a publican.

11 The Pharisee stood and prayed thus with himself, God, I thank thee, that I am not as other men are, extortioners, unjust, adulterers, or even as this publican.

12 I fast twice in the week, I give tithes of all that I possess.

13 And the publican, standing afar off, would not lift up so much as his eyes unto heaven, but smote upon his breast, saying, God be merciful to me a sinner.

14 I tell you, this man went down to his house justified rather than the other: for every one that exalteth himself shall be abased; and he that humbleth himself shall be exalted.

1 John 5:14–15

14 And this is the confidence that we have in him, that, if we ask any thing according to his will, he heareth us:

15 And if we know that he hear us, whatsoever we ask, we know that we have the petitions that we desired of him.

Key Text

I tell you, this man went down to his house justified rather than the other: for every one that exalteth himself shall be abased; and he that humbleth himself shall be exalted. —**Luke 18:14**

Enduring Beliefs
of the Church

Unit 2: Grace and Reconciliation

Lessons 5–8

Lesson Aims

After participating in this lesson, each learner will be able to:

1. List the characteristics of prayer from the lesson's Scripture texts.

2. Discern which occasions call for bold prayer and which occasions call for humble prayer.

3. State a way to ask God for good things while humbly sharing the gospel with friends and neighbors.

Lesson Outline

Introduction
- A. God, I Need You!
- B. Lesson Context

I. Bold Prayer (Genesis 18:25–27)
- A. Abraham's Petition (v. 25)
- B. The Lord's Promise (vv. 26–27)

II. Humble Prayer (Luke 18:9–14)
- A. Jesus' Parable (vv. 9–10)
- B. The Pharisee (vv. 11–12)
- C. The Tax Collector (vv. 13–14)
  No Excuses

III. Confident Prayer (1 John 5:14–15)
- A. Our Request (v. 14)
- B. God's Response (v. 15)
  Praying for a Miracle

Conclusion
- A. The Foundation of Prayer
- B. Prayer
- C. Thought to Remember

Introduction

A. God, I Need You!

I knew, maybe for the first time in my life, that I really needed help. As a logistics analyst in a large textile firm, my role was to purchase all the necessary components of the clothing we produced and make sure they arrived at the production facility on time. Things were not going well. As I struggled to keep track of everything, I was terrified that I would fail. Who could help? I was not sure anyone could.

On the way to work one day, I began to pray. For the first time, these prayers came from a place of desperation. Within a couple of months, something had changed. The job was still difficult and fast-paced. But my experience of the job was different. Fear had been replaced with peace. I realized that God cares to listen to the prayers of His children.

B. Lesson Context

The word *pray* occurs in 348 verses in the Bible in 74 different forms. Today's lesson takes us into three of those instances. We take care, however, to remember that these three textual segments occur within the broader context of the Bible as a whole. While there are times when prayer is at best a waste of time (Jeremiah 7:16; 11:14; 14:11; 1 John 5:16b; etc.) and at worst an improper substitute for action that God is expecting us to take (see Exodus 14:15), in the many circumstances where prayer is an appropriate action, there are various postures we might take, which the passages below depict.

I. Bold Prayer

(Genesis 18:25–27)

In Genesis, God selects Abraham for a unique task and relationship. Those involve a promise to make him a great nation, to bless him, and to bless all the families of the earth through him (Genesis 12:1–3). Following God's call, Abraham (known as Abram at the time) journeys to a new land with his wife, Sarah (Sarai), and their nephew, Lot (12:4–9). Through many circumstances, Abraham comes to know God more and to trust Him—

Genesis 16:1–4 recording a notable failure—even when it looks impossible for the promises to be fulfilled. The three verses of our first text take us to Abraham's reaction to God's decision to destroy Sodom and Gomorrah.

A. Abraham's Petition (v. 25)

25. That be far from thee to do after this manner, to slay the righteous with the wicked: and that the righteous should be as the wicked, that be far from thee: Shall not the Judge of all the earth do right?

Abraham and the Lord are having a dialogue about the fate of the two cities just noted. This is of special concern to Abraham because his nephew, Lot, lives in Sodom (Genesis 14:12). Sodom has an evil reputation (13:13), and the Lord plans to destroy the city (18:20–21). Being startled by the Lord's plan, Abraham begins to voice his objection in the verse now before us.

Exactly what it is that should *be far from* the Lord in the current context is located between the two occurrences of that phrase. Abraham is making a bold appeal to the Lord to rethink the forthcoming destruction. Their conversation is predicated on the recognition that Sodom's fate has not yet been decided. But rather than telling the Lord what to do, Abraham asks the Lord to *do right*. The key question is, what is right? The basis of Abraham's appeal is the Lord's identity and character. Since He is the one who sets the standard for right and wrong—and indeed *is Himself* that standard—it is impossible for Him to do anything but what is right.

B. The Lord's Promise (vv. 26–27)

26. And the Lord said, If I find in Sodom fifty righteous within the city, then I will spare all the place for their sakes.

Abraham had begun his appeal by asking the Lord what He would do if 50 *righteous* people could be found living in Sodom (Genesis 18:24). The verse before us now is the Lord's answer.

27. And Abraham answered and said, Behold now, I have taken upon me to speak unto the Lord, which am but dust and ashes.

Surprisingly, even after this initial agreement, *Abraham* does not stop. He continues to intercede boldly for the inhabitants of Sodom. He goes on to inquire regarding successively lower numbers of righteous people: 45, 40, 30, 20, and then 10! At each point, the Lord agrees to spare the whole city for the sake of the righteous.

Before continuing, however, Abraham recognizes the audacity of his plea. He has *taken upon* himself *to speak unto the Lord* even though Abraham is *but dust and ashes*. To identify oneself in this way is an act of extreme humility. These terms also occur in circumstances of humiliation and contrition (Job 30:19; 42:6; Ezekiel 27:30). God is attentive to the man's concerns. Implicit in this recognition is a second one: Abraham knows that the Lord, as God, knows what is wise. He also knows that the Lord cares to listen because the Lord initiated this conversation (Genesis 18:20).

Thus, Abraham's bold intercession is dependent on three things. First, he appeals based on the Lord's character. Second, he recognizes his own inferior status. In other words, in his boldness, he is humble. Third, he feels confident to approach the Lord because of the relationship that they share (Genesis 18:17–19).

What Do You Think?

Would you have been as bold as Abraham in his situation?

Digging Deeper

What caused Abraham to have such faith to pray boldly?

II. Humble Prayer

(Luke 18:9–14)

At the point of our lesson's second passage, Jesus has been on the way to Jerusalem since Luke 9:51. He has announced His pending death twice (Luke 9:21–22, 43–45) and will do so a third time shortly after the parable of today's study (18:31–34). On this journey, Jesus teaches what His kingdom is like and who will have a place in it. The parable below helps to fill out that picture, connecting the preceding parable—also about prayer—with the story that follows, which emphasizes the need for humility.

Visual for Lesson 7. *Display this visual after the lesson conclusion during a time of personal reflection.*

A. Jesus' Parable (vv. 9–10)

9. And he spake this parable unto certain which trusted in themselves that they were righteous, and despised others.

Up until chapter 18 of his Gospel, Luke introduces most of Jesus' parables with a minimal note that He was addressing "them" (Luke 5:36; 6:39; 8:4; 12:16; 14:7; 15:3). At one point, Peter is even confused about whom the parable is for (12:41).

But chapter 18 is different. There are two parables here; the first one is addressed to the disciples (Luke 18:1, tracking the identity of "them" back to 17:22), and the second begins in the verse now at hand. The description fits the Pharisees well, although Luke does not state that explicitly. By leaving the identification a bit vague, perhaps Luke is allowing the readers to consider whether they fit this description.

10. Two men went up into the temple to pray; the one a Pharisee, and the other a publican.

The opening lines of the parable set the context for a regular activity for devout Jews in Jesus' time (Acts 3:1). *The temple* was the place where people went to be in the presence of God, to worship, and to seek forgiveness for their own sins and the sins of the nation. Pharisees of the first century are respected for their dedication to the Law of Moses. They studied Scripture and were committed to lives of holiness and worship. Their presence at the temple for prayer is exactly what Luke's audience expects.

The publican or tax collector, on the other hand, is despised. These individuals are viewed as traitors as they collude with the Roman authorities to exact tax revenue from the Jewish population. They are often dishonest (like Zacchaeus in Luke 19:1–10) and classified along with notorious sinners (Luke 5:30; 7:34; 15:1). No one would expect such a person to make an appearance at the temple.

B. The Pharisee (vv. 11–12)

11. The Pharisee stood and prayed thus with himself, God, I thank thee, that I am not as other men are, extortioners, unjust, adulterers, or even as this publican.

Jesus shares the Pharisee's prayer first. The standing position is normal (Mark 11:25). That he prays *with himself* may mean that he intentionally separates himself from the rest of the worshippers. His attitude in prayer is made clear by what he goes on to say.

Thanking *God* is appropriate content for prayer, of course (Psalms 106:47; 136:2, 26; Jeremiah 33:11; etc.). However, for the Pharisee, what is seemingly a prayer of gratitude is actually one of pride. He is thankful not for God but for himself. He makes sure that God knows he is *not as other men are.*

The Pharisee mentions particular groups that he will have nothing to do with: *extortioners, unjust,* and *adulterers.* It is unquestionably good that the Pharisee does not engage in the actions that these characterizations imply. But his foundation for avoiding these activities is his image as a "self-made man"—in other words, he has a bad case of believing that God owes him divine approval. This results from (or results in) an attitude of superiority to people he views as unrighteous. He even makes it a

How to Say It

Abraham	*Ay*-bruh-ham.
Abram	*Ay*-brum.
Gethsemane	Geth-*sem*-uh-nee (*G* as in *get*).
Gomorrah	Guh-*more*-uh.
Sodom	*Sod*-um.
Zacchaeus	Zack-*key*-us.

point of wagging a finger at a person who is particularly unrighteous: the *publican*.

12. I fast twice in the week, I give tithes of all that I possess.

The Pharisee then reminds God (and himself) of his good deeds. Both fasting and tithing are characteristics of the devout. Fasting is a good thing when it is practiced with godly motives (see Joel 2:12; contrast Zechariah 7:4–5). Tithing (giving a tenth of one's income) is also expected (see Leviticus 27:30; contrast Malachi 3:8–10). Outwardly, this Pharisee meets or exceeds the expectations. But Matthew 23:13–36 reveals the Pharisees' legalism, their works-righteousness mentality, and their hypocrisy (see also Luke 11:37–52). Although this Pharisee has worked hard both to abstain from sinful actions and to do what is required, the result is pride and self-importance. He's not praying so much as he is bragging.

What Do You Think?

How can we avoid "bragging" in our prayers like the Pharisee?

Digging Deeper

What misaligned speech habits can you identify in your own prayers?

C. The Tax Collector (vv. 13–14)

13. And the publican, standing afar off, would not lift up so much as his eyes unto heaven, but smote upon his breast, saying, God be merciful to me a sinner.

The publican also prays in a standing position, but the similarities end there. He exhibits no self-congratulatory "thanks." The fact that he is *standing afar off* indicates hesitation to approach the holy God. Like the Pharisee, he is separated from the other faithful supplicants, but with a different motive. Jesus' extended description of the publican's physical positioning helps the reader understand his distinct motivation for this separation.

The words of his prayer correspond to his physical demeanor; he prays for mercy, aware that he is *a sinner*. He has nothing to offer; he realizes that his deeds will not make him worthy. Rather, he depends on God's mercy for forgiveness.

We can pause here to remind ourselves that what Jesus is teaching is nothing new. God's approval of the publican's humility is well reflected in Isaiah 66:2b and elsewhere. To beat one's *breast* is an outward sign of this inward disposition, one of internal distress (Jeremiah 31:19; Luke 23:48; etc.).

A final interesting feature is the relative lengths of the two prayers: more than 30 words for the Pharisee but only 7 words for the publican. The latter is consistent with passages such as Ecclesiastes 5:2b and Matthew 6:7. We ought to be wary of where wordiness can lead!

What Do You Think?

What is the most important part of the publican's prayer?

Digging Deeper

How might you incorporate such aspects of humble prayer into your prayers?

No Excuses

A video on social media showed a man standing before a judge to answer for a burglary charge. The judge looked at the man closely, recognizing him as a boy she had gone to middle school with. When the recognition became mutual, he began to cry. Holding his head in his hands, he repeated, "Oh my goodness, oh my goodness!"

The judge said she remembered his kindness, intelligence, and friendship from their younger days. She expressed her sadness that he had made some poor decisions. The man was subsequently convicted and sentenced to prison. When released 10 months later, the judge was right there waiting for him. They embraced and renewed their friendship as she encouraged him to take a better path in life, and he vowed to do so.

Relationships break when offenses are committed. As true as that is for human-to-human connections, it is all the more so with God-to-human relationships. God, the ultimate judge, has provided the means for restoring our broken relationship through Jesus, but it's not automatic. Our choice is either to be a self-justifying Pharisee or to be an admitted sinner. "To this man will I look, even to him that is poor and of a contrite spirit, and trembleth at my word" (Isaiah 66:2b). Be sure to make the right choice. —L. M. W.

14. I tell you, this man went down to his house justified rather than the other: for every one that exalteth himself shall be abased; and he that humbleth himself shall be exalted.

Jesus concludes the parable by giving His evaluation of the prayers. And this isn't the only time in the Gospels where Jesus draws the sharp distinction between those who exalt themselves and those who humbly realize their situation and need (Matthew 23:12; Luke 14:11).

This outcome would have been surprising to Jesus' audience. A hated publican who is *justified* ahead of a devout Pharisee? What a reversal! This follows a pattern in Luke's Gospel, beginning with Mary's song (Luke 1:46–55), where the humble, poor, and despised are exalted by God, and the proud, rich, and strong are brought low.

III. Confident Prayer

(1 John 5:14–15)

As he did in his Gospel (John 20:31), the apostle John explicitly states his purpose in writing the letter we call 1 John: it is so that those who believe can know that they have eternal life (1 John 5:13). Throughout this letter, John encourages and challenges his audience to walk in the light, obey God's commands, and be confident in their standing before God. As the letter moves toward its conclusion, John applies this confidence to prayer.

A. Our Request (v. 14)

14. And this is the confidence that we have in him, that, if we ask any thing according to his will, he heareth us.

Confidence has been a consistent theme in John's letter. He wants Christians to reach the day of judgment with confidence in their standing before God (1 John 2:28; 3:21; 4:17). Now, at the end of the letter, John encourages his audience to have confidence when they pray.

This confidence is possible only *in him*—in God (1 John 5:6–12). It is available to Christians because they believe in the name of the Son of God (5:13). It also allows them to know that God listens. There is, however, a condition to this confidence. Previously, John had said that Christians would receive their requests if they obeyed God's commands (3:22). Here, the condition is *if we ask . . . according to his will.*

This raises (at least) two important questions. First, if prayers that are heard are prayers that are already *according to his will,* then why pray? Won't such things happen anyway? The interaction between prayer and God's will is complicated and cannot be adequately covered here. But John and Jesus clearly expected Christians to pray, and in some way, God hears and responds to believer's prayers (John 14:13–14; 15:7, 16; 16:23–24).

Second, how can Christians know God's will in order to ask accordingly? It seems that what John envisions here is the Christian's will, desires, and requests being conformed to God's through prayer. We can follow Jesus' example. At Gethsemane, he prayed, "Abba, Father, all things are possible unto thee; take away this cup from me: nevertheless not what I will, but what thou wilt" (Mark 14:36).

The opposite of confident prayer is seen in James 1:6–7: "But let him ask in faith, nothing wavering. For he that wavereth is like a wave of the sea driven with the wind and tossed. For let not that man think that he shall receive any thing of the Lord."

B. God's Response (v. 15)

15. And if we know that he hear us, whatsoever we ask, we know that we have the petitions that we desired of him.

John explains what it means that God hears the Christian's request: *we know that we have the petitions that we desired of him.* God's hearing leads to acting. This is a persistent motif in Scripture (Exodus 3:7; 1 Kings 3:12; 2 Kings 20:5; Luke 1:13; etc.). If our request aligns with God's will, a positive answer is assured. Therefore, John encourages his readers to approach God confidently in prayer knowing that He cares, hears, and acts.

What Do You Think?

What is the difference between appropriate and inappropriate confidence in prayer?

Digging Deeper

How does 1 John 5:14–15 describe appropriate confidence?

Praying for a Miracle

"Chaplain, please pray that God will save my baby! Pray for a miracle!" the dad begged me. I looked at his tiny son, attached to machines keeping him alive. My head said this baby would not live. I had a flash of shame for doubting that God would save him, but God had not spared the physical lives of many children with whom I had worked over the years. I looked into the father's eyes to see both hope and fear.

"Okay," I answered, pushing my own doubt aside. "Let's pray for a miracle for your baby." We laid our hands on the blanket covering the tiny body and prayed that God would heal the child. The father confidently approached the throne of God with his request.

You may be wondering if a miracle did indeed take place. I will not reveal the answer to that question because God's response is not the point of the story. The point, rather, is that our prayer was evidence of our confidence that God would do His will in this situation. Do you approach God in prayer with this kind of confidence? —L. M. W.

Conclusion

A. The Foundation of Prayer

These three passages of today's lesson address prayer from distinct angles. In Genesis, Abraham makes his request in terms of appealing to God's character; Abraham does so while acknowledging his own subordinate status. In the Gospel of Luke, the publican acknowledges his status as a sinner as he seeks God's mercy. In 1 John, Christians are encouraged to pray with confidence because of their relationship with God, conformity to God's will, and God's disposition to listen to His children.

God's character is the constant in these three passages. It must serve as the foundation for prayer today. Abraham's rhetorical question, "Shall not the Judge of all the earth do right?" has never lost its validity. Abraham's bold appeal is consistent both with the Lord's character and with Abraham's desire to do what was right.

Christians can pray confidently because God delights in our prayers and wants to grant our requests (but see the cautions cited in the Lesson Context at the beginning of this lesson). Christians can pray boldly by aligning their requests with what God has revealed about His desires. Christians also are to pray humbly because we know that God is God, and we are not.

As we pray today, we will do well to follow the examples in this lesson. More important than the physical posture one assumes in prayer is one's heart posture. Additionally, prayer is an important means by which the human will is conformed to the divine will. The better we know God, the more we seek God, the more our prayers will be answered because they will align with who God is and what God wants to do in the world. Certain circumstances may call for more boldness or more humility depending on the context. Yet humble, confident boldness that is grounded in God's character should undergird all our prayers.

What Do You Think?

What type of prayer do you find infrequent in your life: bold, humble, or confident?

Digging Deeper

What examples in Scripture might inspire your growth in that area?

B. Prayer

Lord, You are worthy of all praise. We come to You seeking your mercy and knowing that You care to hear and answer our petitions. Conform our wills to Yours. In Jesus' name. Amen.

C. Thought to Remember

Pray humbly and boldly with confidence.

Involvement Learning

Enhance your lesson with KJV Bible Student *(from your curriculum supplier) and the reproducible activity page (at www.standardlesson.com or in the back of the* KJV Standard Lesson Commentary Deluxe Edition*).*

Into the Lesson

Write this statement on the board:

Boldness and humility seldom exist in the same person at the same time.

Divide the class into two groups for debate. Give the groups at least five minutes to prepare. Have one group support the statement. Have the other group take the position that the statement is false.

Call the groups together, asking each group to present their best opening argument. Alternate between the groups until both have given the answers they want to share.

Discuss with the class, "Now that you've heard both sides, decide whether you agree or disagree with the statement. What makes it possible for both boldness and humility to coexist in the same person? What makes it difficult?"

Alternative. Distribute copies of the "Contrasts Defined" exercise from the activity page, which can be downloaded. Have learners work in pairs to complete as indicated. After calling time, ask the pairs to share what they've discussed.

Lead into Bible study by telling the class, "Today's lesson will concentrate on prayer and highlight ways both boldness and humility can be present as we pray. Think about your own prayers as we study."

Into the Word

Divide the class into three groups: **Bold Prayers Group, Humble Prayers Group,** and **Confident Prayers Group.** Distribute handouts of the questions below for in-group discussions.

Bold Prayers Group. Study Genesis 18:16–33. 1–What was God's intent? 2–How did Abraham respond? 3–What clues do we find for Abraham's motives? 4–How is Abraham an example here?

Humble Prayers Group. Study Luke 18:9–14. 1–Why did Jesus tell the parable? 2–List contrasts between the two characters in the story. 3–What made the prayer of one more acceptable than the prayer of the other? 4–How can Christians avoid pride in their prayers?

Confident Prayers Group. Study John 1:5–14. 1–How is the praying described here bold? 2–How is the praying described here humble? 3–How does this passage encourage us to pray? 4–How can we ensure that our prayers align with God's will?

Allow the groups several minutes to complete their study before asking them to present their findings to the whole class. You may want to put notes on the board about boldness and humility while the groups are sharing.

Summarize by asking the following questions in whole-class discussion: 1–What situations call for bold prayers? 2–What circumstances prompt humble prayers? 3–How can boldness and humility characterize all prayers?

Into Life

Send participants back to the three groups used earlier in the lesson. Ask the groups to brainstorm two lists: *Bold Prayers* and *Humble Prayers.* Invite participants to jot down phrases one might use with either prayer. After a few minutes, bring the groups back together to share their lists. Expand the discussion by asking: "What situations call for each kind of prayer?"

Draw a continuum on the board with the word *bold* on one end and *humble* on the other. Distribute note cards and pencils. Encourage learners to take notes as you discuss. Discuss: 1–Where's the best place for a Christian to land on this continuum? 2–Where do you fall? 3–What steps can you take to achieve a better blend of the two qualities? 4–How can we be both bold and humble in asking God for things in our prayers?

Option. Distribute copies of the "Prayers Examined" exercise from the activity page. Have learners complete the activity during the week and share their conclusions at the start of the next class.

January 25
Lesson 8 (KJV)

Call and Growth

Devotional Reading: Colossians 2:1–7
Background Scripture: John 1:40–42; Ephesians 4:11–16; Philippians 3:12–16; Colossians 1:9–11; Hebrews 6:1–3

Matthew 4:18–20

18 And Jesus, walking by the sea of Galilee, saw two brethren, Simon called Peter, and Andrew his brother, casting a net into the sea: for they were fishers.

19 And he saith unto them, Follow me, and I will make you fishers of men.

20 And they straightway left their nets, and followed him.

Matthew 16:16–18

16 And Simon Peter answered and said, Thou art the Christ, the Son of the living God.

17 And Jesus answered and said unto him, Blessed art thou, Simon Barjona: for flesh and blood hath not revealed it unto thee, but my Father which is in heaven.

18 And I say also unto thee, That thou art Peter, and upon this rock I will build my church; and the gates of hell shall not prevail against it.

John 21:15–18

15 So when they had dined, Jesus saith to Simon Peter, Simon, son of Jonas, lovest thou me more than these? He saith unto him, Yea, Lord; thou knowest that I love thee. He saith unto him, Feed my lambs.

16 He saith to him again the second time, Simon, son of Jonas, lovest thou me? He saith unto him, Yea, Lord; thou knowest that I love thee. He saith unto him, Feed my sheep.

17 He saith unto him the third time, Simon, son of Jonas, lovest thou me? Peter was grieved because he said unto him the third time, Lovest thou me? And he said unto him, Lord, thou knowest all things; thou knowest that I love thee. Jesus saith unto him, Feed my sheep.

18 Verily, verily, I say unto thee, When thou wast young, thou girdedst thyself, and walkedst whither thou wouldest: but when thou shalt be old, thou shalt stretch forth thy hands, and another shall gird thee, and carry thee whither thou wouldest not.

2 Peter 3:14–15, 18

14 Wherefore, beloved, seeing that ye look for such things, be diligent that ye may be found of him in peace, without spot, and blameless.

15 And account that the longsuffering of our Lord is salvation; even as our beloved brother Paul also according to the wisdom given unto him hath written unto you.

---

18 But grow in grace, and in the knowledge of our Lord and Saviour Jesus Christ. To him be glory both now and for ever. Amen.

Key Text

He saith unto him the third time, Simon, son of Jonas, lovest thou me? Peter was grieved because he said unto him the third time, Lovest thou me? And he said unto him, Lord, thou knowest all things; thou knowest that I love thee. Jesus saith unto him, Feed my sheep. **—John 21:17**

Enduring Beliefs
of the Church

Unit 2: Grace and Reconciliation
Lessons 5–8

Lesson Aims

After participating in this lesson, each learner will be able to:

1. List significant events in the life of Peter after Jesus called him.
2. State why Jesus might have continued to express confidence in Peter despite his shortcomings and weaknesses.
3. Write a note encouraging another believer who wants to grow in faith.

Lesson Outline

Introduction

A. From Fisherman to Disciple

In 1986, a severe drought lowered the water level of the Sea of Galilee, resulting in shorelines once covered in water becoming visible. On its western shores, two brothers discovered the remains of a once-buried fishing boat. Informally dubbed the "Jesus Boat," the vessel is about 27 feet long and 7 feet wide. Researchers have dated it to within approximately 100 years of the life of Jesus, causing many to hypothesize that it could be the type of boat used by first-century fishermen.

Today's lesson explores the life, call, and ministry of one such first-century fisherman, Simon Peter. He left the waters (and fishing boats) of the Sea of Galilee to become a disciple of Jesus. Peter's discipleship to Jesus was full of ups and downs, yet God used Peter to ensure the growth and spread of the first-century church.

B. Lesson Context

Simon Peter was from Bethsaida (John 1:44), a village on the northern shore of the Sea of Galilee. Here, he worked as a fisherman with his brother Andrew (Mark 1:16). Their fishing operation was a partnership with James and John, the sons of Zebedee (Luke 5:10). Peter was married (Mark 1:30; 1 Corinthians 9:5). At some point, Peter, his wife, and at least one other family member moved to Capernaum (Matthew 8:5–14), a town approximately five miles southwest of Bethsaida.

The New Testament notes three names for Peter. His Hebrew name is *Simon* or the variant *Simeon* (Mark 1:16; Acts 15:14). Later, Jesus calls him *Peter,* a designation based on an ancient Greek word meaning "rock" or "stone" (Matthew 16:18; Mark 3:16); this is his most frequently occurring name in the New Testament, found over 160 times. The third name is *Cephas,* an Aramaic word for "stone" (John 1:42; 1 Corinthians 1:12; 3:22; etc.).

I. Peter's Call

(Matthew 4:18–20)

A. Two Fishermen (v. 18)

18. And Jesus, walking by the sea of Gali-

lee, saw two brethren, Simon called Peter, and Andrew his brother, casting a net into the sea: for they were fishers.

The *sea of Galilee* is a large freshwater lake in the northern region of Palestine. The New Testament gives two other names for this body of water: "the lake of Gennesaret" (Luke 5:1) and "the sea of Tiberias" (John 6:1). It was the location of a significant fishing industry. Regarding the designation *Simon called Peter* and his involvement in that industry, see the Lesson Context, above.

Jesus is living in Capernaum at this time (Matthew 4:13). That town is located on the northwest shore of the Sea of Galilee, so His *walking by the sea* is unsurprising.

B. One Mission (vv. 19–20)

19–20. And he saith unto them, Follow me, and I will make you fishers of men. And they straightway left their nets, and followed him.

Jesus' call seems abrupt. Why would these fishermen drop *their nets* immediately for Jesus? We should note that at this time, Jesus was not unknown to the two brothers. During Andrew's time as a disciple of John the Baptist, Andrew encountered Jesus; after that, Andrew told Simon, "We have found the Messias, . . . the Christ" (John 1:41).

Jesus' command to *follow me* is not simply an invitation to join His walk along the shore. Instead, it is a summons to become His student and disciple. This relationship is not initiated by the application of the would-be disciple but by the invitation of the master, as we see here.

As disciples of Jesus, the brothers will take on a new task: they will no longer be fishermen on the lake. Instead, they will become *fishers of men*, seeking other people to become disciples of Jesus. Accepting Jesus' call, therefore, requires a significant cost. Peter later says that he had "forsaken all" to follow Jesus (Matthew 19:27). The lives of these fishermen will never be the same again.

II. Peter's Proclamation

(Matthew 16:16–18)

Jesus' early ministry focuses on the region of Galilee, where He ministers to crowds and faces testing from religious leaders (Matthew 15:29–16:4). These events form the backdrop of His teaching to the disciples (16:5–12). As this segment of our lesson opens, Jesus and the disciples have traveled to the region of Caesarea Philippi (16:13), about 25 miles north of the Sea of Galilee.

In this remote area, Jesus and the disciples experience a retreat-like atmosphere and relief from crowds. While there, Jesus asks the disciples, "Whom say ye that I am?" (Matthew 16:15). What comes next is Peter's response.

What Do You Think?

In what ways has Jesus called you to follow and trust Him in the upcoming week?

Digging Deeper

How can you follow that call at work, with your family, or in your neighborhood?

A. Recognized the Son (v. 16)

16a. And Simon Peter answered and said, Thou art the Christ.

Simon Peter answers for the whole group. The title *Christ* is the Greek equivalent of the Jewish title "Messiah." Both designations mean "the anointed one." Numerous Old Testament texts point to the Messiah's arrival and reign (Psalm 110; Isaiah 11; Micah 5:2; Zechariah 9:9; etc.). Many first-century Jews expect the Messiah to be a political figure chosen by God to save their nation, sit on the throne of David, and rule over an earthly empire. But Jesus will be a leader in God's unique terms (compare John 6:15).

What Do You Think?

How would you respond to the question, "Who is Jesus to you?"

Digging Deeper

How will your answer to that question affect your daily living?

16b. The Son of the living God.

The second part of Peter's confession reveals why

he believes that Jesus is fulfilling messianic expectations. Inherent in the two parts of Peter's confession is a recognition of both Jesus' power (the ability to do something) and authority (the right to do something) as God the Father confirms these (Matthew 3:17; 28:18; compare Luke 4:36).

B. Revealed by the Father (vv. 17–18)

17. And Jesus answered and said unto him, Blessed art thou, Simon Barjona: for flesh and blood hath not revealed it unto thee, but my Father which is in heaven.

Peter is *blessed* for having recognized and acknowledged the identity and mission of *Jesus,* although Peter still misunderstands the nature of that mission (Matthew 16:21–22). The phrase *flesh and blood* contrasts created human beings with Jesus' uncreated *Father which is in heaven* as the source of Peter's awareness (compare Galatians 1:11–12).

The designation *Simon Barjona* should not be thought of as a first name and a last name as we use personal identifiers today. Regarding the name *Simon,* see the Lesson Context. The first three letters of *Barjona* mean "son of" (compare John 1:42). Putting the two together results in a very formal address, emphasizing the importance of the situation.

18a. And I say also unto thee, That thou art Peter, and upon this rock I will build my church.

The interpretation of this verse has been the subject of much discussion throughout church history. The main issue is to determine to whom or what *this rock* refers.

Theory 1: The rock is Jesus Himself. Supporting this proposal is the fact that Jesus refers to Himself as the chief cornerstone (Matthew 21:42). Peter himself acknowledges that fact (1 Peter 2:4–8). However, the word image in the text before us would be odd since Jesus would be referring to Himself as both the church's foundation (*rock*) and its builder (*I will build*).

Theory 2: Peter himself is the rock. The word *Peter* is Greek for "rock" or "stone." Thus, the idea is that Jesus is using a play on words. The book of Acts details Peter's leadership in the first-century church (Acts 2:14–41; 4:1–31; etc.). In this regard, Peter's leadership is the "rock" on which the growth and expansion of the church was based (10:1–11:21).

Theory 3: Peter's confession is the rock. The Bible tells us that confessing Jesus as Savior and Lord is vital (Matthew 10:32; Romans 10:9; 1 John 4:15; etc.). After denying the Lord before the crucifixion, Peter "re-confessed" Christ (John 21:15–18, below).

The Greek word translated *church* occurs only here and in Matthew 18:17 in the four Gospels. Jesus Himself is the one who inaugurates this community of God's people. They are to be committed to Him. Jesus is and always will be the head of the church (Ephesians 1:22).

18b. And the gates of hell shall not prevail against it.

The meaning of the word translated as *hell* is tricky. The use of the word in Acts 2:31 seems to imply the general location of the dead, similar to the Hebrew word *Sheol* in the Old Testament, often translated "grave" (examples: Psalms 6:5; 89:48). Elsewhere in the New Testament, the word translated "hell" refers to a place of torment as we usually think of this word—the destination of the wicked after they die (Luke 16:23). The phrase *the gates of hell* refers to the domain and power of death. Even death itself cannot permanently hold back the community of God's people.

How to Say It

Aramaic	*Air*-uh-*may*-ik.
Barjona	Bar-*jo*-nuh.
Bethsaida	Beth-*say*-uh-duh.
Caesarea Philippi	Sess-uh-*ree*-uh Fih-*lip*-pie or *Fil*-ih-pie.
Capernaum	Kuh-*per*-nay-um.
Eusebius	You-*see*-be-us.
Gennesaret	Geh-*ness*-uh-ret (G as in *get*).
Messianic	Mess-ee-*an*-ick.
Messias	Mes-*sigh*-us.
Palestine	*Pah*-luh-*stein*.
Sheol	*She*-ol.
Tiberias	Tie-*beer*-ee-us.
Zebedee	*Zeb*-eh-dee.

III. Peter's Ministry

(John 21:15–18)

Our next section of Scripture takes place following Jesus' resurrection. By this time in the post-resurrection timeline, Jesus has appeared to many of His disciples and followers (John 20:11–29). He appears again to seven disciples at the Sea of Galilee (21:2), directing them to a large catch of fish before inviting them to breakfast (21:12).

A. One Question, Repeated (vv. 15–17)

15a. So when they had dined, Jesus saith to Simon Peter, Simon, son of Jonas, lovest thou me more than these?

After breakfast, *Jesus* turns the meeting into an opportunity to teach. *Simon Peter* had previously boasted of his commitment and devotion to Jesus (Matthew 26:33; Mark 14:29; Luke 22:33; John 13:37). He even resorted to violence to prove it (18:10). But his pledge of devotion proved to be bluster. Jesus' question probes Peter's heart and loyalties.

What does the word *these* refer to? Is it the boats and fishing equipment? Is it the other disciples? Or does it mean, "Do you love me more than these other disciples love me?" A definitive answer is impossible to glean from the text as written. We may conclude that Jesus means *these* as a general reference point: "Do you love me supremely, more than anything or anyone else?"

> **What Do You Think?**
>
> What are some "lesser loves" that can distract us from loving Jesus supremely?
>
> **Digging Deeper**
>
> What diagnostic questions can we ask to ensure these loves do not displace our love for Jesus?

15b. He saith unto him, Yea, Lord; thou knowest that I love thee.

Peter assures Jesus of his *love,* even reminding the *Lord* that *thou knowest* this fact. However, Jesus had correctly predicted that Peter's previous declarations of commitment would prove false (John 13:37–38).

15c. He saith unto him, Feed my lambs.

As the Good Shepherd, Jesus has laid down His life (John 10:15). If Peter loves Jesus, he will lead in the same way, protecting and providing for the *lambs* who are God's people (compare 1 Peter 5:1–4).

16. He saith to him again the second time, Simon, son of Jonas, lovest thou me? He saith unto him, Yea, Lord; thou knowest that I love thee. He saith unto him, Feed my sheep.

With only slight variation, the exchange is repeated. We imagine Peter is puzzled; he has already answered Jesus' question. But Peter does so once more.

17. He saith unto him the third time, Simon, son of Jonas, lovest thou me? Peter was grieved because he said unto him the third time, Lovest thou me? And he said unto him, Lord, thou knowest all things; thou knowest that I love thee. Jesus saith unto him, Feed my sheep.

A third time, Jesus questions Peter's love. For Peter to feel *grieved* at this repetition is understandable. Does Jesus doubt his answer? Or is Peter's distress the result of seeing a connection between these three questions and his three denials of Jesus (John 18:15–18, 25–27)?

Peter's response includes an acknowledgment that not only does Jesus know Peter's inner thoughts, but Jesus also knows *all things*—a recognition of Jesus' deity (compare John 2:25).

Demonstration of Love

My husband and I had been dating for roughly six months before he said, "I love you." I'll never forget the inflection in his voice. We had been talking and laughing when it just seemed to come out of the blue!

His proclamation of love was a turning point in our relationship. It was not the same as our expressing how much we loved reading or eating ice cream. There was a particular weight to that phrase in the context of our budding relationship. Love for each other would require mutual action in terms of selflessness, work, and even sacrifice. Our love has lasted 20 years, but the weightiness of those three words remains.

It wasn't enough that Peter spoke of his love for

Visual for Lesson 8. *Display this visual as you ask the discussion question associated with 2 Peter 3:18.*

Jesus; Peter needed to demonstrate it. He would show this through his taking care of God's people. Peter's love for Jesus would fuel his life's mission as a leader of the first-century church. How does your love for Jesus motivate your actions? What does His love compel you to do? —B. R.

B. One Future, Predicted (v. 18)

18a. Verily, verily, I say unto thee.

The phrase *verily, verily* is characteristic of John's Gospel, occurring there more than two dozen times (and never in the other three Gospels). It emphasizes the absolute certainty of what is about to be said.

18b. When thou wast young, thou girdest thyself, and walkedst whither thou wouldest: but when thou shalt be old, thou shalt stretch forth thy hands, and another shall gird thee, and carry thee whither thou wouldest not.

Jesus prophesies that the freedom of movement Peter enjoyed while *young* would someday be lost. One interpretation of the phrase *thou shalt stretch forth thy hands* is that it refers to the practice of crucifixion. The phrase thus might allude to how Peter would meet his death. Tradition is unclear regarding that method. In about AD 90, the first-century church leader Clement of Rome states that Peter was martyred (1 Clement 5:2–4). Later tradition from the church historian Eusebius holds that Peter was crucified in Rome during the reign of Nero (AD 54–68). Regardless of the method of Peter's death, Jesus promised that the apostle would glorify God because of it (John 21:19).

IV. Peter's Teaching

(2 Peter 3:14–15, 18)

Some commentators believe that the apostle Peter composed the letter we call 2 Peter in Rome shortly before his death (compare 2 Peter 1:13–15). Therefore, the epistle serves as his final word to believers. If the word *Babylon* in 1 Peter 5:13 is a code word for Rome, this lends further support to his presence in that city.

A. Living at Peace (vv. 14–15)

14. Wherefore, beloved, seeing that ye look for such things, be diligent that ye may be found of him in peace, without spot, and blameless.

We must back up a few verses to determine the antecedent of *such things*. The answer is found in 2 Peter 3:12, where the word translated *look for* here in verse 14 occurs again as "looking for," the object being "the coming of the day of God." While believers *look for such things*, we must remain *diligent* in all aspects of our faith.

What Peter is saying is nothing new. The challenge to live *in peace* is also found in 1 Corinthians 7:15 and James 3:18. *Without spot* of impurity and *blameless* from sin are echoed together in 1 Timothy 6:14. Although nothing new, these imperatives bear repeating!

15. And account that the longsuffering of our Lord is salvation; even as our beloved brother Paul also according to the wisdom given unto him hath written unto you.

The *longsuffering of our Lord* refers to the delay of the bodily return of Jesus to bring judgment. The Lord is patient, "not willing that any should perish, but that all should come to repentance" (2 Peter 3:9).

Peter calls on the authority of the *beloved brother Paul* to emphasize the harmony of their teachings. We do not know the specific teaching by Paul that Peter has in mind. But we know that Paul wrote to believers in Rome regarding God's patience for salvation (Romans 2:4; 3:25; 9:22;

etc.). He also wrote regarding the need for righteous living in light of spiritual freedom (Galatians 5:1–26; etc.). Peter directs his readers to accept Paul's teachings since the *wisdom* they contain has been *given unto him* by revelation from God (1:11–12; Ephesians 3:3).

B. Growing in Grace (v. 18)

18. But grow in grace, and in the knowledge of our Lord and Saviour Jesus Christ. To him be glory both now and for ever. Amen.

The letter ends with words of exhortation and praise. The promise of Christ's return impels us to use that certainty as a touchstone for how we are to live. We *grow in grace* as we react to God's unmerited favor given through our faith in *our Lord and Saviour Jesus Christ* (see 2 Peter 1:2).

An increase *in the knowledge* of Him implies more than knowing facts—it includes a relationship with Him as characterized by following His commands for righteous living (2 Peter 1:5–6; compare John 14:15). To be saved is a state of being justified; after that happens, what comes next is the lifelong process of sanctification.

Peter concludes with a doxology—a praise of, and attribution of *glory* to, Christ Jesus. By one count, there are more than a dozen doxologies in the New Testament (Ephesians 3:21; etc.).

> **What Do You Think?**
> In which areas of life do you need to grow most in Christ as you await His return?
>
> **Digging Deeper**
> Who is another believer you can ask to support you in this endeavor?

Free Time for French

I am trying to learn to speak French, and I decided that the best (and most fun) way to learn would be through an app on my phone. While it has helped me study parts of the French language, I still have a long way to go before I am fluent.

To give myself more learning opportunities, I've made one significant change: I have reduced my social media usage. By removing this distraction, I'm hopeful that it will help me focus on my studies. I'm using all my free time to learn French!

The letter of 2 Peter reminds us that we are responsible for our spiritual growth and maturity. Just as I face daily choices to study or not to study, we face daily choices regarding how we choose to live. Only by our personal decisions and the guidance of the Holy Spirit will we grow and mature in our Christian discipleship. What changes do you need to make to facilitate further growth? —B. R.

> **What Do You Think?**
> In what ways does Peter's story of discipleship mirror your own?
>
> **Digging Deeper**
> How will you use your own discipleship story to invite others to join you on the journey of discipleship to Jesus?

Conclusion

A. The Journey of Discipleship

Peter's life of discipleship took him from being a fisherman in Galilee to being a leader of the first-century church. He grew from being "unlearned and ignorant" (Acts 4:13) to being the author of the two letters that bear his name in the New Testament. But his growth process wasn't a straight line that always trended upward! Neither will ours be.

Even so, Jesus calls all who would claim to be His disciples to grow in His grace and knowledge—there are no exceptions. Peter's story is encouraging in that regard. And as we grow, we will find it natural to invite others to join us on this journey as well. Expect it!

B. Prayer

Heavenly Father, give us a heart for transforming growth in Your Son through Your Holy Spirit! Forgive us for times when we fail You. Empower us to recognize opportunities to invite others to become Your Son's disciples as well. In His name we pray. Amen.

C. Thought to Remember

Discipleship is a journey of growth.

Involvement Learning

Enhance your lesson with KJV Bible Student *(from your curriculum supplier) and the reproducible activity page (at www.standardlesson.com or in the back of the* KJV Standard Lesson Commentary Deluxe Edition*).*

Into the Lesson

Write the following phrases on the top of the board as headers of three columns: *Favorite Food, Favorite Hobby, Ambition*. Then, write the following words on the side of the board as labels of three rows: *Child, Teenager, Adult*. Introduce the activity by saying, "People's interests often change as they grow up. For example, their favorite food might change as they grow from a child to an adult." Invite volunteers to share their responses to the various categories to complete the chart. After completing the chart, ask, "What conclusions can you draw about how people change as they grow into adulthood?"

Option. Distribute copies of the "Transformation" exercise from the activity page, which you can download. Have learners work in pairs to complete as indicated.

Lead into the Bible study by saying, "There are many examples of how people or things change as they grow. In today's study, let the example of Peter's spiritual journey cause you to reflect on your journey of discipleship."

Into the Word

Ask a volunteer to read aloud Matthew 4:18–20. Have participants work in small groups with classmates who have similar careers. For example, all the medical workers should be placed in one group and all the technology workers in another. Instruct groups to rewrite Matthew 4:18–20 using their names, workplaces, careers, and a tool they use at their jobs. Challenge groups to consider how Jesus might refer to their career in His invitation to discipleship. Ask, "What is a phrase, like 'fishers of men' that would be specific to your jobs and reflect life as a disciple of Jesus?"

Ask a volunteer to read aloud Matthew 16:16–18. Write the following questions on the board as headers of two columns: *Who is Jesus? Who is Simon?*

Invite volunteers to list titles Simon used for Jesus and write those titles in the first column. Then, have the class identify the designations Jesus used for Simon in this passage and write those designations in the second column. Distribute a pen and sheet of paper to each participant. Ask them to work with a partner to write down five titles for Jesus that are personally significant. Encourage them to add Scripture references where appropriate.

Ask a volunteer to read aloud John 21:1–18. Divide participants into two groups: **Denial Group** (Matthew 26:69–75) and **Confession Group** (John 21:15–18). Invite each group to reenact their assigned text before the whole class. Ensure that each group chooses a narrator to read through the Scripture passages. Direct each group to alternate their reenactment between each denial and each confession. After completing the reenactments, ask the class how John 21:1–18 reveals Jesus' love for and confidence in Peter.

Ask a volunteer to read aloud 2 Peter 3:14–15, 18. Divide participants into groups of three and ask each group to answer the following questions in small-group discussion: 1–List all of the instructions Peter gives in these verses. 2–Why did Peter think it was important for believers to practice these things? 3–What would it look like to follow these instructions today? After five minutes, reconvene the class and ask a volunteer from each group to share insights with the whole class.

Into Life

Distribute a note card and pen to each participant and challenge participants to think of another believer who wants to grow in faith. Invite participants to write a short note to that person. The note should include at least one positive aspect of that believer's faith journey and one aspect of encouragement for that believer.

Option. Distribute copies of the "Journey of Discipleship" activity from the activity page. Have learners complete during the week as indicated.

February 1
Lesson 9 (KJV)

The Christian Church

Devotional Reading: Acts 2:42–47
Background Scripture: Matthew 16:13–20;
Ephesians 1:15–23; 2:13–22; 5:22–27

Mark 4:26–32

26 And he said, So is the kingdom of God, as if
a man should cast seed into the ground;
27 And should sleep, and rise night and day, and
the seed should spring and grow up, he knoweth
not how.
28 For the earth bringeth forth fruit of herself;
first the blade, then the ear, after that the full corn
in the ear.
29 But when the fruit is brought forth, imme-
diately he putteth in the sickle, because the harvest
is come.
30 And he said, Whereunto shall we liken the
kingdom of God? or with what comparison shall we
compare it?
31 It is like a grain of mustard seed, which, when
it is sown in the earth, is less than all the seeds that
be in the earth:
32 But when it is sown, it groweth up, and beco-
meth greater than all herbs, and shooteth out great
branches; so that the fowls of the air may lodge
under the shadow of it.

Ephesians 4:4–6, 11–18

4 There is one body, and one Spirit, even as ye are
called in one hope of your calling;
5 One Lord, one faith, one baptism,
6 One God and Father of all, who is above all,
and through all, and in you all.

11 And he gave some, apostles; and some, proph-
ets; and some, evangelists; and some, pastors and
teachers;
12 For the perfecting of the saints, for the work of
the ministry, for the edifying of the body of Christ:
13 Till we all come in the unity of the faith, and
of the knowledge of the Son of God, unto a perfect
man, unto the measure of the stature of the ful-
ness of Christ:
14 That we henceforth be no more children,
tossed to and fro, and carried about with every
wind of doctrine, by the sleight of men, and cun-
ning craftiness, whereby they lie in wait to deceive;
15 But speaking the truth in love, may grow
up into him in all things, which is the head, even
Christ:
16 From whom the whole body fitly joined
together and compacted by that which every joint
supplieth, according to the effectual working in the
measure of every part, maketh increase of the body
unto the edifying of itself in love.
17 This I say therefore, and testify in the Lord,
that ye henceforth walk not as other Gentiles walk,
in the vanity of their mind,
18 Having the understanding darkened, being
alienated from the life of God through the igno-
rance that is in them, because of the blindness of
their heart:

Key Text

But speaking the truth in love, may grow up into him in all things, which is the head, even Christ: From whom the whole body fitly joined together and compacted by that which every joint supplieth, according to the effectual working in the measure of every part, maketh increase of the body unto the edifying of itself in love.

—Ephesians 4:15–16

Enduring Beliefs

of the Church

Unit 3: The Church and Its Teachings

Lessons 9–13

Lesson Aims

After participating in this lesson, each learner will be able to:

1. Summarize the parables of Mark 4:26–32.
2. Explain the purpose of unity in the Spirit.
3. Make a plan for seeking reconciliation within the church and between the church and its surrounding community.

Lesson Outline

Introduction

A. Rapid Growth

B. Lesson Context

I. Parables of the Kingdom (Mark 4:26–32)

A. Scattered Seeds (vv. 26–29)

B. Smallest Seed (vv. 30–32)

II. Work of the Kingdom (Ephesians 4:4–6, 11–18)

A. Unified under Jesus (vv. 4–6)

B. Properly Led (vv. 11–13)

United We Stand

C. Secure in Truth (vv. 14–16)

Tossed Around

D. Showing Transformation (vv. 17–18)

Conclusion

A. Recognizing Two Kinds of Growth

B. Prayer

C. Thought to Remember

Introduction

A. Rapid Growth

My home state, Nebraska, enjoys a worldwide reputation for growing corn. It is estimated that cornfields in the state total nearly ten million acres. For me, moving to Nebraska from California, this was astounding. In central Nebraska, one can drive miles in the summer and see nothing but corn fields.

What was especially impressive to me was how fast this crop can grow. Farmers plant, and seedlings emerge in May. The corn stalks quickly become knee-high, then waist-high, then over-the-head-high. With plenty of moisture and fertilizer, corn stalks can grow an inch a day or more. I was told that sometimes you can hear the corn growing, which is true. If you stand in a corn field during peak growth season in the evening, you will hear popping as leaves emerge from the stalk.

Jesus and the people of His time and place did not have corn as we have it today. But they had other plants that grew rapidly in the fertile and well-watered fields of the Galilee region. Jesus told many parables involving farming and sowing seeds. This lesson reveals one reason why.

B. Lesson Context

Jesus is known for His use of parables when teaching. While Jesus' parables are unique, this teaching method was well-known in the ancient world. For Jesus, a parable is usually an illustration that compares something well-known in the experience of the hearers to less understood spiritual truths. His illustrations were drawn from the everyday lives of His audience.

Many parables teach about the "kingdom of God" (in Matthew, "kingdom of heaven"). We see their comparative nature in their introduction, "The kingdom of heaven is likened unto . . ." (example: Matthew 13:24). Some parables are narratives, telling a little story (example: Luke 15:4–7). Others are observational, giving spiritual application to an easily pictured scenario (example: 6:39).

The kingdom parables often have applications regarding Jesus' intentions for the church. This lesson looks at two such parables in Mark.

I. Parables of the Kingdom

(Mark 4:26–32)

A. Scattered Seeds (vv. 26–29)

26. And he said, So is the kingdom of God, as if a man should cast seed into the ground.

Mark 4:1–34 features four parables, and this verse begins the third. As we read about *a man* who casts *seed into the ground,* we remind ourselves that people of Jesus' day had no mechanical devices to spread seed like we have now. Rather, seed was broadcast by hand. This required skill to minimize wasted seed. After harvest, seed was saved to be ready for the spring planting. What was saved could have been eaten, but farmers knew that without that seed, there would be no future harvest.

27. And should sleep, and rise night and day, and the seed should spring and grow up, he knoweth not how.

Once *the seed* is planted, the farmer's job is done for a while. He sleeps and gets up according to his routine. The seed needs no help to spring and grow up. However, while the farmer can observe this, he doesn't know how it works. He just expects it to happen.

In a world before modern scientific advances, there was great wonder about seeds and how they were able to replicate the plants they came from (compare Genesis 1:11–12). For seeds to be sown and then produce a good crop was seen as a blessing of the Lord (26:12). So, too, for Jesus: the growth of the kingdom is accomplished by God.

28. For the earth bringeth forth fruit of herself; first the blade, then the ear, after that the full corn in the ear.

In the verse before us, Jesus describes a seed becoming a mature plant. From *the earth* (dirt), the germinated seed becomes *fruit of herself* without help from the farmer. The word *corn* is used in an older sense to indicate grain crops in general. Grain crops produce kernels that can be dried and ground into flour, providing a necessary ingredient for bread until the next harvest.

Plant growth begins with a *blade* emerging from the ground, and sprouts indicate that the planting has succeeded. This becomes a stalk that produces an *ear,* the seed head of the plant. This grain head matures and, if the conditions are right, will be *full* of grain like the seed from which it came.

29. But when the fruit is brought forth, immediately he putteth in the sickle, because the harvest is come.

The stalks of grain don't just keep growing on and on, year after year. Their seed has been planted for a purpose: *the harvest.* And so it is with the kingdom of God (compare Isaiah 17:4–6; Matthew 13:1–23; Revelation 14:14–18). And as the ancient farmer didn't understand how a seed could result in a mature stalk of wheat, so too it is with the kingdom of God.

B. Smallest Seed (vv. 30–32)

30–31. And he said, Whereunto shall we liken the kingdom of God? or with what comparison shall we compare it? It is like a grain of mustard seed, which, when it is sown in the earth, is less than all the seeds that be in the earth.

In these verses, Jesus introduces a new parable. Unlike the previous parable, the one we now consider has parallels in the other two synoptic Gospels (Matthew 13:31–32; Luke 13:18–19). Again, the parable is about *the kingdom of God.* The vital need for such illustrations is seen in the fact that "The time is fulfilled, and the kingdom of God is at hand" (Mark 1:15).

Like wheat, the mustard plant grows from seed after being planted (Matthew 13:31). Mustard seeds are tiny, as small as one millimeter in diameter. These were the smallest seeds with which Jesus' hearers would have been familiar, thus symbolic of the smallest item in their everyday world. This imagery is so powerful that Jesus will use it again later (17:20; Luke 17:6).

> **What Do You Think?**
>
> What word image would you use to tell a modern-day parable about the kingdom of God?
>
> **Digging Deeper**
>
> What truth regarding the kingdom of God would your parable convey?

32. But when it is sown, it groweth up, and

becometh greater than all herbs, and shooteth out great branches; so that the fowls of the air may lodge under the shadow of it.

Mustard plants can grow from tiny seeds to large shrubs in a single growing cycle of approximately 90 days. Some people have seen mature mustard plants around the Sea of Galilee that reached 10 feet tall. Though not technically "trees" by modern definition, they have considerable *branches*, giving a tree-like appearance. These leafy branches provide shade and can support the weight of small birds (compare Luke 13:19).

Like the previous parable, this one is about the kingdom of God. These parables refer prophetically to the church and its astounding growth. Beginning with a core of disciples, Jesus' followers became the church on Pentecost. The book of Acts describes the rapid numerical growth of the first-century church following Jesus' ascension (Acts 2:41–47; 4:4; 6:7). Today, estimates number those who identify as Christian at more than two billion.

What Do You Think?

In what ways have you seen God work through something small or humble to achieve His will?

Digging Deeper

How has the kingdom of God surprised you? How should it?

II. Work of the Kingdom

(Ephesians 4:4–6, 11–18)

In the first three chapters of this letter, Paul discusses the church's foundation in the plan of God (Ephesians 1:11–12); Paul explains Christ's role in breaking down the dividing wall between Jews and Gentiles (2:14); and he calls his readers to recognize that Christ is the head of His church, and the church is His body (1:22–23). These points are all at odds with a divided church. Therefore, chapter 4 begins Paul's expression of the vital, unitary nature of the church.

A. Unified under Jesus (vv. 4–6)

4. There is one body, and one Spirit, even as ye are called in one hope of your calling.

The church grows as more people are added to the kingdom of God. This growth creates challenges to unity as various cultures interact. Ephesians 4, however, teaches about the doctrines of the church that are to remain unchanging. Neither growth nor unity is to be emphasized at the expense of the other. The apostle Paul stresses unity by teaching on the "seven ones" in Ephesians 4:4–6. These are points of doctrine that cannot be dismissed if the growing church is to be what God intends.

One body speaks of the church (compare Romans 12:4–5; Ephesians 5:23; Colossians 1:18). Paul has much to say about diversity within the unified body of Christ in 1 Corinthians 12:12–31. That passage also tells us how the *one Spirit*—the Holy Spirit—relates to that unified body. Christians are unified in having received the Holy Spirit through faith and repentance (Acts 2:38; Galatians 3:14).

The church has *one hope* to which it is called (see Ephesians 1:18; 4:1). Believers have this hope through our belief in the bodily resurrection of Jesus Christ (see 1 Corinthians 15:19; 1 Peter 1:3) and future eternal life with the Lord in heaven (Romans 6:22). After Paul left Ephesus, he testified to his "hope and resurrection of the dead" (Acts 23:6).

5. One Lord, one faith, one baptism.

We come now to the fourth, fifth, and sixth of the "seven ones." *One Lord* refers to the Lord Jesus Christ, the head of the church (Ephesians 3:11; 5:23). *One faith* involves our common assent regarding the person and work of Jesus (John 20:30–31; Acts 16:31).

Paul emphasizes that the *one baptism* is for both Jews and Gentiles: a baptism into Christ. This emphasis aligns with Paul's corrective to the Corinthians regarding different baptisms (1 Corinthians 1:12–15; compare 12:13).

6. One God and Father of all, who is above all, and through all, and in you all.

We come to the seventh and final "one." Paul describes the *one God* by four uses of the word *all*. God is the *Father of all* in terms of creation (see Malachi 2:10; Ephesians 3:14–15). For God to be *above all* speaks to His transcendent nature. He exists outside of His creation. This means there is nothing above the Lord God in power or authority (see Psalms 97:9; 113:4–6; 1 Timothy 6:16).

As we come to the phrases *through all* and *in you all*, we may be confused about the difference between the two (compare Romans 11:36). The preposition *through* indicates "means," "agency," or "intermediacy," as in "by means of," in this context (as it does in Colossians 1:20; 1 John 4:9). The preposition *in*, for its part, indicates "location." This speaks to God's immanence, or presence everywhere (compare Jeremiah 23:23–24; Acts 17:27–28).

> **What Do You Think?**
> Which of Paul's "seven ones" do you struggle with the most? Why?
> **Digging Deeper**
> Which encourages you the most? Why?

B. Properly Led (vv. 11–13)

11. And he gave some, apostles; and some, prophets; and some, evangelists; and some, pastors and teachers.

Christ provides servant-leaders for His church. In this verse, Paul is not teaching about spiritual gifting but about Christ's gifts to the church: *apostles, prophets, evangelists, pastors,* and *teachers*. The gifts are people.

An apostle was appointed by Christ to be authoritative in the first-century church. Transforming Jesus' followers into a functioning church required strong leadership, and the apostles had that authority. Only apostles or those closely associated with an apostle were recognized as legitimate authors of the books that make up the New Testament.

Prophets speak for God to strengthen the church (Acts 11:27–28; 15:32; 21:10–11). The household of God is "built upon the foundation of the apostles and prophets, Jesus Christ himself being the chief corner stone" (Ephesians 2:20; compare 1 Corinthians 12:28).

Evangelists are mentioned in the New Testament only here and in Acts 21:8 and 2 Timothy 4:5. They proclaim the good news about Jesus, a task essential yet today (see Matthew 28:19–20; Romans 10:14).

Regarding the categories of pastors and teachers, there is some debate regarding whether these are two distinct roles or just one role (as in the hyphenated "pastor-teacher"). The Greek word translated "pastors" occurs 18 times in the New Testament (here and in Matthew 9:36; 25:32; 26:31; Mark 6:34; 14:27; Luke 2 [four times]; John 10 [six times]; Hebrews 13:20; and 1 Peter 2:25). In those other 17 instances, the translation is always "shepherd(s)." Pastors are shepherds who attend to God's people as a "flock" over which they had been made "overseers" (Acts 20:28).

Teachers instruct on how to understand God and how to live a godly life based on the Scriptures (Colossians 1:28; 2 Timothy 3:16). Noteworthy is the fact that the role of teacher is in Paul's "top three list" in 1 Corinthians 12:28. Paul explains the reason these leadership roles are necessary in the next verse.

12. For the perfecting of the saints, for the work of the ministry, for the edifying of the body of Christ.

The servant-leader roles complement one another in a common purpose: *perfecting the saints*. The leaders bring the believers in their congregations to spiritual maturity to share in *the work of the ministry* (compare Hebrews 5:11–6:3). *Edifying* means to build (construct an edifice). Church leaders should never be tearing down members, but building them up. Church leadership is about *the body of Christ*, the church.

> **What Do You Think?**
> Who has been the most influential in helping equip you to serve Christ?
> **Digging Deeper**
> How will you help equip others to serve?

13a. Till we all come in the unity of the faith.

This ministry of edification is not easy. Anyone who teaches in a church knows there will be differences of opinion that can become nasty divisions. Paul's vision is that the church will be guided by the great "seven ones" of Ephesians 4:4–6, thereby coming to *the unity of the faith* (compare Ephesians 4:3). We usually understand the word *faith* in terms of words such as *trust, assent,* or *belief that* as focused on the person and work of Christ Himself (see John 8:24; 20:31; Romans 4:5; etc.). But that is not the sense here. The inclusion of the definite article "the" in the phrase "the faith" has the sense of a body of doctrine to be believed and accepted as true (Acts 6:7; Titus 1:13; Jude 3).

13b. And of the knowledge of the Son of God, unto a perfect man, unto the measure of the stature of the fulness of Christ.

In addition to being unified in the faith, the goal is to be unified in *the knowledge of the Son of God.* This goal is repeated from Ephesians 1:17. Paul stresses such knowledge also in 2 Corinthians 2:14; 4:6.

United We Stand

"But Mom said I could!" the child yelled at her dad, who had just denied her request. Sound familiar? Children become quite skilled at playing their parents off against each other, lining up a positive response from one parent as ammunition for gaining permission from the other parent as well.

This "divide and conquer" method can turn parent against parent and weaken family relationships. It is not the child's responsibility to maintain unity, though. Parents are responsible for that. When parents are divided, the children can sense it. The result is a sense of anxious unease and lack of security.

The same thing applies to the church. The spiritually mature leaders have the responsibility to maintain unity. When that doesn't happen, those who are spiritually immature can sense it; they end up insecure and anxious. What can you do to maintain and strengthen the unity among your congregation? —L. M. W.

How to Say It

Colossians	Kuh-*losh*-unz.
Ephesians	Ee-*fee*-zhunz.
Pentecost	*Pent*-ih-kost.
Synoptic	Sih-*nawp*-tihk.

C. Secure in Truth (vv. 14–16)

14. That we henceforth be no more children, tossed to and fro, and carried about with every wind of doctrine, by the sleight of men, and cunning craftiness, whereby they lie in wait to deceive.

People seem attracted to teachers who will support preconceived ideas—what they want to hear rather than what they need to hear (see 2 Timothy 4:3). But those who move on to maturity in Christ are less susceptible to deceptive forces (compare 1 Corinthians 14:20; James 1:6). The danger here is not that of sincere but mistaken people. Instead, the threat is from professional tricksters. The descriptions here have a sense of false teachers who are peddling lies in ways that make money for themselves (compare 2 Corinthians 11:12–13).

Tossed Around

When my son was a baby, we tightly buckled him in his car seat. His neck struggled to assert control over his head movements as his head rolled side to side or tipped forward, tossed around by centrifugal and gravitational forces as we drove. We believed that he would soon gain control of his neck and head as he grew.

We were right. He grew up to be a fine young adult despite the wobbly beginning. The boy who could barely hold his head up for more than 15 seconds is now part of a world-class drum corps at college. He carries a heavy set of five drums onto the field and plays while marching. His steady development has resulted in him becoming a man who understands his role on the team and carries it out with excellence.

We were all spiritual infants at some point, subject to being tossed around by the forces of the world. Some of us have grown out of that stage and on to spiritual maturity. Others haven't. Which category are you in? To find out, read Hebrews 5:11–6:3. —L. M. W.

15. But speaking the truth in love, may grow up into him in all things, which is the head, even Christ.

Truth is what we are to speak; *in love* is how we

are to speak it. Both must characterize our speech for spiritual growth to occur. The outcome of teaching truth in love is spiritual maturity that results in unity (see 1 Corinthians 3:2; 1 Peter 2:2; etc.).

> **What Do You Think?**
> What practical ways can you keep truth and love balanced in your interactions?
>
> **Digging Deeper**
> How will you ensure that such interactions result in the maturity and unity of the body of Christ that is the church?

16. From whom the whole body fitly joined together and compacted by that which every joint supplieth, according to the effectual working in the measure of every part, maketh increase of the body unto the edifying of itself in love.

Paul returns to his metaphor of the church as *the body* of Christ (see expanded metaphor in 1 Corinthians 12:12–31; compare Colossians 2:19). Our physical bodies are made up of compatible parts. They are designed to work together as each serves its function. Just as every part is important, so it is to be in the church. This is why divisions—whether based on false doctrines, personal animosity, or whatever—cause the church to self-destruct. Instead, the goal should be edifying, building the church into a community that loves God and others. This will never happen without an overwhelming spirit of love for one another in the church. You cannot work for the destruction of others if you love them.

D. Showing Transformation (vv. 17–18)

17–18. This I say therefore, and testify in the Lord, that ye henceforth walk not as other Gentiles walk, in the vanity of their mind, Having the understanding darkened, being alienated from the life of God through the ignorance that is in them, because of the blindness of their heart.

Today's text ends with a stark warning: past practices (*walk*) and beliefs (*mind*) must remain in the past. In so doing, they will not allow paganism, the ways of the *Gentiles,* to influence the church. Paul has more to say about all this in Romans 1:18–32; 6:6; Ephesians 4:19–24; and Colossians 3.

Conclusion

A. Recognizing Two Kinds of Growth

The parables Jesus told give the impression of rapid growth of the kingdom of God. As with seeds to mature plants, this may seem mysterious to us at times. Astounding church growth may be happening in places we don't expect. May we rejoice whenever we hear stories of unbelievers coming to faith in Christ!

But the numerical growth of people brings growth in the number of opinions and interpretations. This can lead to divisions (compare 1 Corinthians 1:10–17; 3:1–9; 11:17–22). The solution is found in the "seven ones" of Ephesians 4:4–6. These still define the basis for church unity.

B. Prayer

Heavenly Father, we confess Your Son to be the head of the church. Use us to raise His name high so that everyone will be drawn to You. Help us not forget that growth of the church means the salvation of more people and their experience of new life in You. In Jesus' name we pray. Amen.

C. Thought to Remember

Christ intended and designed His church to grow in number and unity.

Visual for Lessons 9 & 13. *Display this visual as learners pair up to discuss how they can show love through action.*

Involvement Learning

Enhance your lesson with KJV Bible Student *(from your curriculum supplier) and the reproducible activity page (at www.standardlesson.com or in the back of the* KJV Standard Lesson Commentary Deluxe Edition*).*

Into the Lesson

Write the following words as headers on the board: *Season*, *Emotion*, *City*, *Machine*, and *Insect*. Lead a whole-class brainstorming session by inviting learners to list items in each category. Write responses on the board under the correct header. Then, have participants choose one of the responses listed on the board. Challenge them to describe that response by comparing it to something else. For example, say, "Autumn is like a fresh apple from a tree: colorful and crisp." After one minute, ask volunteers to share their descriptions.

Lead into the Bible study by saying, "Some things are difficult to understand if you haven't seen or experienced them before. Even for believers, the kingdom of God and the purpose of the church are complicated subjects to grasp. In today's lesson, pay attention to how Jesus and Paul explain the importance of these concepts."

Into the Word

Ask a volunteer to read aloud Mark 4:26–32. Divide the class into two groups: **Growing Grain Group** and **Mustard Seed Group.** Direct the Growing Grain Group to reread Mark 4:26–29 and the Mustard Seed Group to reread Mark 4:30–32. Distribute handouts (you create) to each group containing the following questions for in-group discussion: 1–What are the word images in your assigned verses? 2–What are possible interpretations of these images? 3–In what ways do these verses describe the kingdom of God?

Allow a few minutes for both groups to share their findings. Ask the following question for whole-class discussion: "What symbols or concepts do these parables have in common?"

Alternative. Distribute copies of the "Grow, Grow, Grow" exercise from the activity pages, which you can download. Have learners work in pairs to complete the first two sections as indicated.

Ask a volunteer to read Ephesians 4:4–6, 11–13 aloud. Write these headers on the board: *One* and *Many*. Direct participants identify all the things in Ephesians 4:4–6 described as "one" and write those things on the board under the correct header. Then, have learners review Ephesians 4:11–13 and list the roles referenced as "many."

Ask the following questions for whole-class discussion: 1–What is the significance of the responses in the first column? in the second column? 2–What would happen to the church if the items in the first column were in the second column and vice versa?

Ask a volunteer to read aloud Ephesians 4:14–18. Instruct participants to work in small groups to rewrite these verses as a modern-day parable. Direct groups to use the following questions to assist in thinking: 1–What is Paul's main point in these verses? 2–What aspect of the kingdom of God is Paul trying to convey? After calling time, have groups present their parables to the whole class.

Alternative. Have participants complete the third section of the "Grow, Grow, Grow" exercise from the activity page.

Into Life

Group participants in pairs. Have pairs brainstorm a response to this question: "How can focusing on the truths in Ephesians 4 help us resolve or remove disagreement?"

Distribute a sheet of paper and a pen to each pair. Challenge them to develop a twofold strategy for seeking reconciliation. Part one will develop a plan for seeking reconciliation within the church. Part two will develop a plan for seeking reconciliation between the church and its surrounding community. After ten minutes, ask volunteers to share their plans. Ask pairs how they might implement this plan in the upcoming weeks.

Option. Distribute the "Strategy of Unity" activity from the activity page. Have learners complete as a take-home activity.

February 8
Lesson 10 (KJV)

Baptism and the Lord's Supper

Devotional Reading: John 1:29–34
Background Scripture: Acts 2:38, 41; Romans 6:1–14;
1 Corinthians 11:23–29

Matthew 3:13–17

13 Then cometh Jesus from Galilee to Jordan unto John, to be baptized of him.

14 But John forbad him, saying, I have need to be baptized of thee, and comest thou to me?

15 And Jesus answering said unto him, Suffer it to be so now: for thus it becometh us to fulfil all righteousness. Then he suffered him.

16 And Jesus, when he was baptized, went up straightway out of the water: and, lo, the heavens were opened unto him, and he saw the Spirit of God descending like a dove, and lighting upon him:

17 And lo a voice from heaven, saying, This is my beloved Son, in whom I am well pleased.

Matthew 28:19–20

19 Go ye therefore, and teach all nations, baptizing them in the name of the Father, and of the Son, and of the Holy Ghost:

20 Teaching them to observe all things whatsoever I have commanded you: and, lo, I am with you alway, even unto the end of the world. Amen.

1 Corinthians 11:23–29

23 For I have received of the Lord that which also I delivered unto you, That the Lord Jesus the same night in which he was betrayed took bread:

24 And when he had given thanks, he brake it, and said, Take, eat: this is my body, which is broken for you: this do in remembrance of me.

25 After the same manner also he took the cup, when he had supped, saying, This cup is the new testament in my blood: this do ye, as oft as ye drink it, in remembrance of me.

26 For as often as ye eat this bread, and drink this cup, ye do shew the Lord's death till he come.

27 Wherefore whosoever shall eat this bread, and drink this cup of the Lord, unworthily, shall be guilty of the body and blood of the Lord.

28 But let a man examine himself, and so let him eat of that bread, and drink of that cup.

29 For he that eateth and drinketh unworthily, eateth and drinketh damnation to himself, not discerning the Lord's body.

Key Text

Go ye therefore, and teach all nations, baptizing them in the name of the Father, and of the Son, and of the Holy Ghost: Teaching them to observe all things whatsoever I have commanded you: and, lo, I am with you alway, even unto the end of the world. Amen. —**Matthew 28:19–20**

Enduring Beliefs
of the Church

Unit 3: The Church and Its Teachings

Lessons 9–13

Lesson Aims

After participating in this lesson, each learner will be able to:

1. List the directives found in Matthew 28:19–20.
2. Explain the vital roles of baptism and the Lord's Supper in the Christian community.
3. Make a plan to bring the good news of Jesus to those with spiritual, economic, and social needs.

Lesson Outline

Introduction
- A. The Table that Unites
- B. Lesson Context

I. Tradition of Baptism (Matthew 3:13–17)
- A. Jesus and John (vv. 13–15)
- B. Father, Son, and Spirit (vv. 16–17)

II. Making Disciples (Matthew 28:19–20)
- A. From All Nations (v. 19a)
  - *Catch the Spirit*
- B. By Baptizing and Teaching (vv. 19b–20)

III. Tradition of Communion (1 Corinthians 11:23–26)
- A. The Bread, Christ's Body (vv. 23–24)
- B. The Cup, Christ's Blood (vv. 25–26)
  - *A Taste of Home*

IV. Warning Disciples (1 Corinthians 11:27–29)
- A. Have Proper Motives (v. 27)
- B. Examine Yourselves (vv. 28–29)

Conclusion
- A. God's Gifts for God's People
- B. Prayer
- C. Thought to Remember

Introduction

A. The Table that Unites

A team of American college students and I attended a church service in a village 20 miles outside Mbale, Uganda. The worship band played hand drums and the harp-like *a'dungu*. Children's choirs sang enthusiastic songs. A preacher read from a Bible in the Luganda language.

At the climax of the service, a tray was brought out with a freshly baked loaf of bread and an assortment of glasses filled with red juice. After a time of prayer, we all ate the bread and drank from the cups. Even though we lived thousands of miles apart and spoke different languages, the experience reminded me that we are one body in Christ. It was a precious time of unity as we feasted together and celebrated the promises of our Lord and Savior.

B. Lesson Context

From its beginning, the church has observed two practices that mark its identity: baptism and the Lord's Supper. Both practices have antecedents in the first-century Jewish world.

Christian baptism has its roots in ritual cleansing practiced by Jews, a tradition that predates the first-century church. The Law of Moses prescribes cleansing with water for religious and physical purification (examples: Leviticus 14:8–9; 15:5–13; 17:15). But the Old Testament prophets promised a new baptism, a cleansing from impurity and sin (Ezekiel 36:25; Zechariah 13:1).

In the Second Temple period, washings for purification were a part of Jewish life (compare Mark 7:1–4; John 2:6; etc.). During this time, it is thought that converts to Judaism underwent a "proselyte baptism" for joining the Jewish community. Ritual washing was necessary because Gentiles were considered unclean; rules prevented them from entering the inner courts of the temple or participating with Jews in local worship.

The second practice in today's lesson is the Lord's Supper, also called Communion. The Gospels record the events of a "Last Supper"—the meal Jesus shared with His disciples the night before His crucifixion (Matthew 26:17–

30; Mark 14:12–26; Luke 22:7–23; John 13:1–30). Although the apostle Paul was not present at that dinner, he shares an account of the same meal (1 Corinthians 11:23–26).

Readers are meant to connect the Last Supper to the observance of Passover, a remembrance of God's liberation of the ancient Hebrews from their enslavement in Egypt (see Exodus 12:2–11; Deuteronomy 16:1–8). Celebrants would eat lamb, bitter herbs, and bread without yeast (Numbers 9:11). Likewise, the New Testament describes Christ as a Passover lamb (1 Corinthians 5:7; compare John 1:29; Revelation 5:6). Thus, this meal and Christ's sacrifice on the cross serve as the fulfillment of Passover: through the giving of Jesus' body and blood, freedom and forgiveness of sins are available to all.

I. Tradition of Baptism

(Matthew 3:13–17)

John the Baptist is a prophetic figure preaching in the wilderness of Judaea, where he calls people to "repent . . . for the kingdom of heaven is at hand" (Matthew 3:1–2). John preaches like the Old Testament prophets: "Prepare . . . the way of the Lord" (Isaiah 40:3, quoted in Matthew 3:3). His ministry presumes that all people need confession and forgiveness, alongside water baptism (3:6). John anticipates that another is coming, one who will "baptize . . . with the Holy Ghost, and with fire" (3:11).

A. Jesus and John (vv. 13–15)

13. Then cometh Jesus from Galilee to Jordan unto John, to be baptized of him.

Because He grew up in Nazareth of *Galilee* (Matthew 2:22–23), Jesus travels south to Judaea and the banks of the *Jordan* River. This is where *John* the Baptist is baptizing and preaching about the coming Messiah (see 3:1–12; Mark 1:1–8; John 1:19–28). Jesus' trip is not a sightseeing journey; He comes *to be baptized* by John.

14. But John forbad him, saying, I have need to be baptized of thee, and comest thou to me?

John, however, knows Jesus' identity (compare Luke 1:44). John identifies himself—a mere man—as one needing *to be baptized*, but by Jesus. John had predicted the arrival of one "whose shoe's latchet I am not worthy to unloose" (John 1:27). The words of his question are incredulous: *comest thou to me?* This is not a rebuke but a surprise. John reveals humility, for he considers himself unworthy to baptize Jesus, as God's anointed king.

15. And Jesus answering said unto him, Suffer it to be so now: for thus it becometh us to fulfil all righteousness. Then he suffered him.

Jesus replies to John's reticence by encouraging the baptism *now*. The word *suffer* reflects old English, "to allow." The immediacy of Jesus' baptism is necessary because of what it achieves and signifies.

In contrast to other baptisms performed by John, Jesus' baptism requires no repentance of sin. The perfect Son of God has no need for repentance (compare 2 Corinthians 5:21; Hebrews 4:15; 1 Peter 2:22; 1 John 3:5). But Jesus' baptism will *fulfil all righteousness* as an act of obedience to the wishes of His heavenly Father.

Jesus' baptism has three implications. First, it initiates His public ministry. Second, Jesus' ministry fulfills messianic expectations and supports John's preaching of repentance. Third, through baptism, Jesus identifies with the people He comes to save: sinful humans in need of repentance (compare Luke 19:10; Hebrews 2:17–18; 1 Peter 2:21–24).

> **What Do You Think?**
> How will you explain the necessity of Jesus' baptism?
>
> **Digging Deeper**
> When have you found it necessary to fulfill expectations and obey the righteous requirements of God?

B. Father, Son, and Spirit (vv. 16–17)

16a. And Jesus, when he was baptized, went up straightway out of the water.

The Gospels do not dwell on the method of Jesus' baptism, only that *he was baptized* by John in the Jordan River (Mark 1:9; Luke 3:21; compare John 1:32). Since the Greek word for "baptize" is the same as "wash," flowing water is a fitting image of cleansing (every other person coming to John was repenting for sins).

What Do You Think?

What makes baptism like and unlike other ways we might "wash" with water?

Digging Deeper

If you are baptized, what details of your baptism show God's favor and welcome?

16b. And, lo, the heavens were opened unto him, and he saw the Spirit of God descending like a dove, and lighting upon him.

Scripture speaks of the opening of *the heavens* as a way to indicate divine revelation (Ezekiel 1:1; Acts 10:11–13; Revelation 4:1; etc.). The opening of heaven here leads to two miraculous occurrences.

First, Jesus sees *the Spirit of God descending like a dove.* It is not necessarily the case that any actual bird is present, since the wording does not require one. The Gospel of John recounts the event from the viewpoint of John the Baptist, who also witnesses the descending Spirit (John 1:32). The Spirit is not a bird, but a dove is the most fitting comparison for what Jesus and John see.

The coming of the Spirit *upon* Jesus is a powerful representation of God's approval. It shows His status as God's servant (compare Isaiah 11:1–2; 42:1). Jesus receives the Holy Spirit so that He might fulfill the mission of His heavenly Father. Later, Jesus will empower followers to receive the same Spirit (John 20:22; Acts 1:4–5).

In the Old Testament, the Spirit of God authorizes a person for a particular task or mission (Exodus 31:1–5; 1 Samuel 16:13; etc.). Jesus is also authorized for a mission, and the arrival of the Spirit in this way is something new.

17. And lo a voice from heaven, saying, This is my beloved Son, in whom I am well pleased.

The second miraculous occurrence is *a voice from heaven*—an indication that words come from God. The verse does not say whether others hear or recognize the voice. The proclamation of Jesus as *my beloved Son* shows that the voice belongs to the Father. Therefore, this scene has all three persons of the Trinity: God the Father is *well pleased*, giving approval of His Son and His ministry; Jesus displays obedience and willingness to follow the will of His heavenly Father (compare John 4:34; 6:38); and the Spirit descends to authorize and empower Christ's work (compare Luke 4:14, 18–19).

Two texts of the Old Testament, Psalm 2:7 and Isaiah 42:1, help us to understand Jesus' identity and what He will do. Psalm 2 looks forward to when the Messiah will defeat God's enemies and bring God's rule through an appointed king. Isaiah 42 describes the servant of the Lord, who will make God known to the nations. He will not rule by raising a shout, but he will serve with gentleness (Isaiah 42:2).

The Father's words identify Jesus by these two themes. Jesus is the promised king. He will establish His rule, not by conquest but by giving of Himself. By submitting to death on the cross, Jesus will make the mercy of God available to all, and He will reign as king (see Revelation 5:12–13).

II. Making Disciples

(Matthew 28:19–20)

Following Jesus' resurrection, He brings the disciples to a mountaintop in Galilee (Matthew 28:16). Jesus proclaims His universal rule: "All power is given unto me in heaven and earth" (28:18).

A. From All Nations (v. 19a)

19a. Go ye therefore, and teach all nations.

Since Jesus possesses all authority, He commands the disciples to *go* and *teach* to continue their ministry of God's kingdom (compare Matthew 10:7). Their task is disciple-making, teaching others of the resurrected Christ. Jesus had focused His earthly ministry on the people of Israel (Matthew 10:5–6; 15:21–24). But now Jesus expands the ministry of the kingdom to include people from *all nations* (see Matthew 8:11; Luke 13:29).

Catch the Spirit

As a college student, I joined a singing team that partnered with my college's office of advancement. We traveled nationwide, singing songs, performing skits, and sharing personal testimonies. The school commissioned us to be ambassadors to encourage prospective students and their families to "catch the spirit" of our institution. As audiences "caught the spirit" from our performance, we hoped it would lead them to attend our school.

Jesus commissions His earliest disciples to serve as ambassadors for His kingdom. That same commission stands for us today: share the good news of Jesus with all people. But do your actions reflect your status as an ambassador for Christ Jesus? Consider what creative ways to reach people in conversations about Jesus. You may be surprised when they "catch" new life in Christ! —B. R.

B. By Baptizing and Teaching (vv. 19b–20)

19b. Baptizing them in the name of the Father, and of the Son, and of the Holy Ghost.

In this verse, Jesus does not explain every aspect of baptism but says it should occur *in the name* of the triune God: *Father, Son,* and *Holy Ghost.* Christians through the ages have understood the task of baptizing in various ways, but have always enacted it as a welcome of God for those who would come to Him.

Baptism signifies entry into the community of God's people and identifies a person as "in Christ" (Romans 6:3–4; Galatians 3:26–27; Colossians 2:11–12). Paul uses baptism to connect believers to the ancient Hebrews, who "passed through the sea" and were "baptized unto Moses" (1 Corinthians 10:1–2). Baptism accompanies repentance and the gift of the Holy Ghost (see Acts 2:38; 19:4–6). And through baptism, believers obey Jesus and identify with the community of God's people.

20a. Teaching them to observe all things whatsoever I have commanded you.

Teaching does not end when someone becomes a disciple. Discipleship requires a lifelong commitment to obey Christ. He alone is the foundation of faith (1 Corinthians 3:11). Through teaching one another, disciples receive Christ as Lord and learn to abide by the words, "walk ye in him" (Colossians 2:6–7).

> **What Do You Think?**
> Why do you think that Jesus mentions the "teaching" of future disciples after He mentions their baptism?
>
> **Digging Deeper**
> In what specific ways could you be more engaged in the teaching of new believers at your church?

20b. And, lo, I am with you alway, even unto the end of the world. Amen.

Matthew first presents the birth of Jesus as fulfillment of prophecy: "They shall call his name Emmanuel, . . . God with us" (Matthew 1:23; quoting Isaiah 7:14). Now Matthew concludes his Gospel with Jesus' assurance that He will always be with followers as they carry out the task of making disciples, *even unto the end of the world.*

III. Tradition of Communion

(1 Corinthians 11:23–26)

Paul plants a church in Corinth during his second missionary journey. However, the church develops problems: factionalism, immorality, rivalry, and false doctrine. At the heart of these is a sense of individual entitlement within the congregation. A lack of concern for one another causes a crisis in how they practice the Lord's Supper.

Like other early Christians, the Corinthians observe the Lord's Supper as part of a worship service and fellowship meal. But apparently, their meals begin before everyone arrives, leaving some hungry and others drunk (1 Corinthians 11:17–22). This demonstrates disrespect for the message of unity, which should be evident when celebrating the selfless sacrifice of Jesus.

A. The Bread, Christ's Body (vv. 23–24)

23a. For I have received of the Lord that which also I delivered unto you.

The apostle provides his source of tradition: *the Lord* (compare Galatians 1:12). Paul communicated with Jesus' followers in Jerusalem, where he would have learned what Jesus did during His last meal with the disciples.

23b. That the Lord Jesus the same night in which he was betrayed took bread.

Paul recounts the events of the "Last Supper" of *the Lord Jesus.* He describes it as the *night* in which Jesus *was betrayed.* The memory of Jesus' betrayal is strong (compare Mark 3:19). It set into motion the dramatic events of the Friday of Holy Week.

This *bread* is unleavened bread consumed during Passover (compare Luke 22:15). Before leaving Egypt, the Israelites ate bread without yeast—

Visual for Lesson 10. *Display this visual as you discuss the commentary associated with 1 Corinthians 11:26.*

a signal of sudden deliverance—and received instructions to observe this annual festival (Exodus 12:15, 17; see Lesson Context).

24. And when he had given thanks, he brake it, and said, Take, eat: this is my body, which is broken for you: this do in remembrance of me.

The Greek word *eucharisteo* is behind the phrase *he had given thanks*. This is why some refer to the Lord's Supper as the Eucharist (a meal of thanksgiving). It is appropriate, when we observe the Lord's Supper, to give thanks to God for the sacrifice of Christ.

Jesus links the bread of this meal with His physical *body*. Although churches may use different versions of communion bread, the symbol of breaking bread points to Jesus' sacrifice. Jesus anticipates this when He calls the bread *broken for you*.

B. The Cup, Christ's Blood (vv. 25–26)

25. After the same manner also he took the cup, when he had supped, saying, This cup is the new testament in my blood: this do ye, as oft as ye drink it, in remembrance of me.

The cup symbolizes Christ's *blood* shed on the cross. Blood is a token of life and sacrifice throughout the Old Testament (Genesis 9:4–5; Leviticus 9:18; etc.). Blood that is spilled is a sign of death and the seriousness of sin. The spilling of blood can accompany the making of a covenant—a binding agreement between two parties (see Exodus 24:8).

Jesus' words inaugurate this new agreement, the same covenant prophesied in Jeremiah 31. The new covenant restores the relationship between God and His people: instruction shall be written on their hearts and sins forgiven (Jeremiah 31:31–34). Thus, sharing the cup prompts *remembrance* of forgiveness through Christ. Like the group of Israelites who made a covenant with God (Exodus 19:3–8), the Lord's Supper is for a forgiven people, those saved by His blood. This is the essence of *the new testament*, the new covenant.

What Do You Think?

What does it look like when God writes on the hearts of those who receive Christ's sacrifice (Jeremiah 31:31–34)?

Digging Deeper

What are some other ways Jesus has provided new hope for a restored relationship between God and humans?

26. For as often as ye eat this bread, and drink this cup, ye do shew the Lord's death till he come.

When we *eat this bread* and *drink this cup*, we partake in a meal of remembrance, thanksgiving, and anticipation. We remember *the Lord's death*, give thanks for the new covenant, and anticipate that Christ will one day *come* again.

A Taste of Home

In my work with a local nonprofit, I teach English to asylum seekers. Most students come from African countries. Cultural differences make assimilation full of challenges.

During one class, we discussed favorite foods. One student mentioned that his favorite dish is fufu, a West African cuisine. Others agreed, and one announced that a local grocery store sold the vegetables for making fufu. For these students, fufu is a reminder of the beloved culture of their home countries. In short, it is a "taste of home."

The Lord's Supper invites us to *remember* Christ's sacrifice and His promise to return. The meal gives us "spiritual sustenance" as we look back at what Jesus has done and look forward to what He will do next. What do you remember when you eat this meal? How might it alter your routine to consider the Lord's Supper a "taste of home"? —B. R.

IV. Warning Disciples

(1 Corinthians 11:27–29)

A. Have Proper Motives (v. 27)

27. Wherefore whosoever shall eat this bread, and drink this cup of the Lord, unworthily, shall be guilty of the body and blood of the Lord.

The rebuke to *whosoever shall eat . . . and drink . . . unworthily* addresses the Corinthians' abuses and mishandling of the meal. Their mishandling had severe consequences (1 Corinthians 11:29–30).

To participate *unworthily* is to become guilty of disrespect for Jesus, the behavior of Jesus' enemies during His trial (Luke 23:11, 13–21; John 19:2–3). The way the Corinthians observe the Lord's Supper makes a mockery of Christ's death, disrespecting *the body and blood* of the crucified *Lord.*

B. Examine Yourselves (vv. 28–29)

28. But let a man examine himself, and so let him eat of that bread, and drink of that cup.

Paul advises self-examination to avoid unworthy participation. Elsewhere, he invites the Corinthians to examine whether "Jesus Christ is in you" (2 Corinthians 13:5–6). This occurs through reflection on actions and attitudes, prompting confession and repentance of selfishness and sin—especially wrongs against other members of the family of faith.

29. For he that eateth and drinketh unworthily, eateth and drinketh damnation to himself, not discerning the Lord's body.

Paul warns against failure to discern *the Lord's body.* This phrase can refer to the elements of the Lord's Supper and also the assembly of Christ's followers—the church (1 Corinthians 10:16; 12:27; Ephesians 4:12). The connection anticipates Paul's usage of the metaphor to represent the church (1 Corinthians 12:12).

To partake in the Lord's Supper is to participate alongside the body of the church (compare 1 Corinthians 10:17; Ephesians 4:4). The meal helps us to contemplate Christ's love, remember our identity as a forgiven people, and celebrate Christ's redemption. All are sinners in need of a Savior, and there are no privileged diners at the Lord's table.

> **What Do You Think?**
> What steps do you take to ensure that you are not guilty of treating Christ's sacrifice in an unworthy manner?
>
> **Digging Deeper**
> How is the pursuit of God's wisdom helpful in this regard (see James 3:17)?

Conclusion

A. God's Gifts for God's People

Baptism is the ritual entry to the life of faith. It includes a public testimony of God's gifts of grace and the Holy Spirit. We follow Jesus' example when we undergo baptism, and the "Great Commission" of Matthew 28 challenges us to invite all people to become His disciples.

The Lord's Supper is a meal of remembrance, thanksgiving, and anticipation. Instead of happening once for each person, it is celebrated regularly. The meal beckons us to examine our relationships with God and others. We share the meal with believers as the unified body of Christ, those who remember His sacrifice and look forward to His return.

There are differences among believers when we practice baptism and the Lord's Supper. But neither Christ nor Paul anticipates either to be cause for division. We should carefully study these practices so that, with our church, we might understand their purpose in worship and ministry. We can practice both with an attitude of humility and joy, recognizing that they are from God and for God's people.

B. Prayer

Heavenly Father, thank You for the gifts of baptism and the Lord's Supper. Through baptism, we experience unity with You and other believers. In the Lord's Supper, we remember Your sacrifice. Empower us, through Your Spirit, to participate in a worthy manner. In Your name we pray. Amen.

C. Thought to Remember

Baptism and the Lord's Supper are unifying gifts for God's people.

How to Say It

Eucharist	*You*-kuh-rist.
proselyte	*prahss*-uh-light.

Involvement Learning

Enhance your lesson with KJV Bible Student *(from your curriculum supplier) and the reproducible activity page (at www.standardlesson.com or in the back of the* KJV Standard Lesson Commentary Deluxe Edition*).*

Into the Lesson

Before class, prepare a grab bag containing small items that symbolize something else. Possible examples include a wedding ring, a red rose, a flag, a cross necklace, and an image of a dove.

Divide the class into small groups and ask a volunteer from each group to grab an item from the bag. Challenge each group to determine what the item symbolizes and whether the symbol accurately conveys the reality it represents. Continue the process until all items in the bag have been selected. Lead a whole-class discussion on the nature of symbols and their limitations.

Lead into Bible study by saying, "Today we will study two practices of the Christian church. The symbolic elements of these practices help us understand more significant spiritual realities."

Into the Word

Divide the class into three groups: **Example of Jesus Group, Directives of Jesus Group,** and **Communing with Jesus Group**. Distribute handouts (you create) of the following questions for in-group discussion.

Example of Jesus Group. Read Matthew 3:13–17 and answer these prompts: 1–Summarize John's reaction to Jesus' request for baptism. 2–Explain the reason Jesus gave for approaching John for baptism. 3–In what ways does Jesus' explanation apply to us? In what ways does it differ? 4–What happened after Jesus was baptized, and what did it signify?

Directives of Jesus Group. Read Matthew 28:19–20 and answer these questions: 1–What directive(s) did Jesus give His disciples? 2–How does each directive in these verses relate to the next one? 3–What significance is there to the order of the directives? 4–What role does baptism play in your church?

Option. Using a concordance or online Bible search tool, find New Testament references to the words *baptize* or *baptism*. What do you conclude about baptism after reading these verses?

Communing with Jesus Group. Read 1 Corinthians 11:23–29 and answer these questions: 1–What significance did Jesus give to each element in the Lord's Supper? 2–What is accomplished in us through participation in the meal? 3–What directive did Jesus give for those who wish to participate in this meal? 4–What role does the Lord's Supper play in your church?

Option. Review 1 Corinthians 11:17–34; 12:12–30; and 14:1–39. What issues had affected the Corinthians's observance of the Lord's Supper?

After calling time, have groups present their findings for whole-class discussion. Summarize findings by developing conclusions on the roles of baptism and the Lord's Supper in the church.

Into Life

Ask a volunteer to reread aloud Matthew 28:19–20. Lead a discussion on ways your congregation can "go" and "teach" others about God's kingdom. Say, "One way to introduce people to God's kingdom is to first address their spiritual, economic, or social needs." Brainstorm ways your congregation can bring the good news of Jesus to people with spiritual, economic, or social needs. Write responses on the board.

Option 1. Ask a volunteer to read aloud 1 Corinthians 10:16–17 and 12:13–15. Direct the class to brainstorm ways in which the celebration of the Lord's Supper demonstrates the unity of the church as the body of Christ. Write responses on the board.

Option 2. Distribute copies of the "Pictures of Baptism" exercise from the activity page, which you can download. Have learners work in pairs to complete as indicated.

Option 3. Distribute copies of the "A Plan for Remembering" activity from the activity page. Have learners work in groups to complete as indicated.

February 15
Lesson 11 (KJV)

The Lord's Day

Devotional Reading: Psalm 118:19–24
Background Scripture: Genesis 2:2–3; Matthew 12:1–14; 28:1–10

Exodus 20:8–11

8 Remember the sabbath day, to keep it holy.
9 Six days shalt thou labour, and do all thy work:
10 But the seventh day is the sabbath of the Lord thy God: in it thou shalt not do any work, thou, nor thy son, nor thy daughter, thy manservant, nor thy maidservant, nor thy cattle, nor thy stranger that is within thy gates:
11 For in six days the Lord made heaven and earth, the sea, and all that in them is, and rested the seventh day: wherefore the Lord blessed the sabbath day, and hallowed it.

Romans 14:4–6

4 Who art thou that judgest another man's servant? to his own master he standeth or falleth. Yea, he shall be holden up: for God is able to make him stand.
5 One man esteemeth one day above another: another esteemeth every day alike. Let every man be fully persuaded in his own mind.
6 He that regardeth the day, regardeth it unto the Lord; and he that regardeth not the day, to the Lord he doth not regard it. He that eateth, eateth to the Lord, for he giveth God thanks; and he that eateth not, to the Lord he eateth not, and giveth God thanks.

Revelation 1:10

10 I was in the Spirit on the Lord's day, and heard behind me a great voice, as of a trumpet.

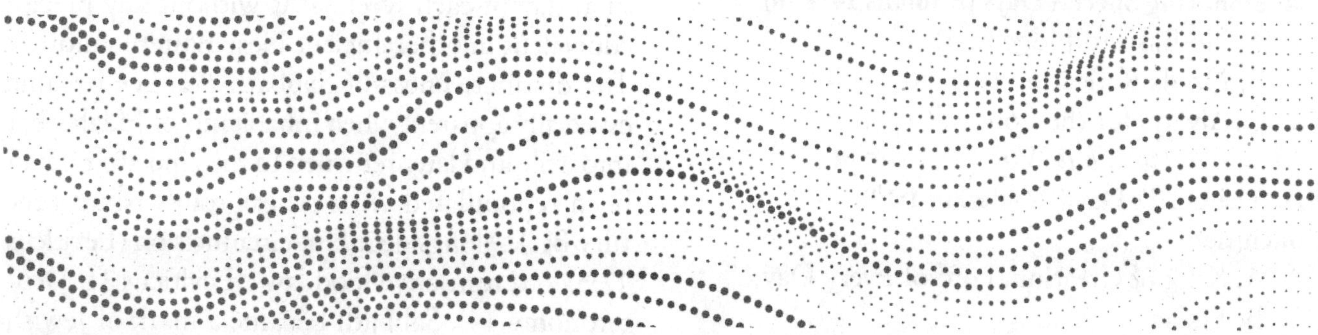

Key Text

In six days the Lord made heaven and earth, the sea, and all that in them is, and rested the seventh day: wherefore the Lord blessed the sabbath day, and hallowed it. **—Exodus 20:11**

Enduring Beliefs
of the Church

Unit 3: The Church and Its Teachings
Lessons 9–13

Lesson Aims

After participating in this lesson, each learner will be able to:

1. Summarize Exodus 20:8–11.
2. Compare and contrast the Old Testament command to honor the Sabbath with the practices of worship in the early church.
3. List ways to bring rest and worship together in the upcoming week.

Lesson Outline

Introduction
- A. The Great Birthday Debate
- B. Lesson Context

I. The Sabbath Day (Exodus 20:8–11)
- A. Keep It Holy (v. 8)
- B. Not for Labor (vv. 9–10)
- C. Created by God (v. 11)
  - *Resting Well*

II. Honoring Special Days (Romans 14:4–6)
- A. No Basis to Judge (v. 4)
- B. Needs Reflection (v. 5)
- C. Always for the Lord (v. 6)
  - *Not How, but Why*

III. The Lord's Day (Revelation 1:10)

Conclusion
- A. King of Creation, Lord of Every Day
- B. Prayer
- C. Thought to Remember

Introduction

A. The Great Birthday Debate

I have never liked birthday celebrations. I can't keep track of dates; I can't find the right words for a card; and I don't even like cake.

But when I got married, I learned that my opinion was not popular—not by a long shot. I think I knew that beforehand, but my wife would never let me impose my anti-birthday views on others. In her family, birthdays were a time when a person felt valued, when other priorities could be postponed.

You can probably guess which side my kids chose in the "great birthday debate." I have to admit, it gives me pause to see our birthday traditions evolve each year. I witness that the simple acts of *remembering* and *doing something* change my son or daughter's perspective. They wake with abundant joy to face a day of attention, and I think they've started to chip away at my indifference. I suppose we could honor one another on *any day,* but it sure helps when it's on the calendar.

B. Lesson Context

The giving of the Sinai covenant comes at a key point in the history of Israel. The Ten Commandments or *Decalogue* (which means "ten words") convey wisdom from God. By following these commands, the Israelites were invited to live at peace with one another and with the God who had just freed them from servitude in Egypt (Exodus 19:4–6).

The fourth of these commandments, Sabbath, describes a practice of refraining from work on the final day of each week. It is without any precise equivalent in other ancient Near Eastern cultures. The distinctiveness of Sabbath practice became especially apparent when inhabitants of Judah went into exile and later returned to the land after it had been repopulated with other groups (sixth century BC). Alongside infant circumcision (Leviticus 12:3) and restrictive food laws (Leviticus 11; Deuteronomy 14), Sabbath became a mark of Jewish identity in the Persian, Greek, and Roman periods and the centuries before the birth of Jesus.

But as Christianity, which began as a Jewish movement, grew to include many Gentiles, a question that the earliest of churches had to answer was, *When shall we meet?* Christian "voluntary associations," which is how churches were seen by Romans, chose to meet before dawn on the first day of the week (Sunday rather than Saturday). Outsiders noticed the habit of Christians to gather on Sunday mornings. For instance, Pliny the Younger—a second-century Roman authority trying to root out the Christians in his region—reports to the emperor Trajan that Christians gather before dawn on a particular day, when they sing hymns to Christ.

I. The Sabbath Day

(Exodus 20:8–11)

A. Keep It Holy (v. 8)

8. Remember the sabbath day, to keep it holy.

The Ten Commandments are a concise summary of Israel's covenant obligations. Israelites would speak of the Mosaic Law as a blessing and a gift, not as an onerous set of expectations. And Israel's poets, the psalmists, find "delight" in keeping God's law, for the statutes of God are a guide and a fount of understanding, not a burden (Psalms 1:2; 19:7–11; 119:70, 77; etc.). Much later, a Pharisee-turned-ambassador of Christ, the apostle Paul, will write, "I delight in the law of God after the inward man" (Romans 7:22).

"Keep the sabbath" is wording that will appear in Exodus 31:14, 16; but the main verb of the verse before us is *remember.* Since something that is *holy* is set aside for God's use, the Israelites must give attention to *the sabbath day* for the purpose of reserving it for God to use. Other things can be set aside for sacred use: a space for God's presence to manifest, parts of a sacrifice designated for God, or even the altar for sacrifices (Exodus 19:23; 29:27, 36–37).

But exactly what does it mean to remember a day and, in so doing, consecrate a day for God? We find the answer from the origin of Sabbath, which is explained by two related contexts. First, Sabbath, the last of a seven-day week, caps off and concludes the activity of God's creation of the universe (Genesis 2:1–3; compare Exodus 20:11, below). Second, Sabbath observance recalls God's rescue of the Israelites from oppression in Egypt, where rest was not allowed (see Deuteronomy 5:15). Thus, the imperative *remember the sabbath day* invites people to credit God for His supreme work of bringing order to creation and His deliverance of His people from "rest-less" oppression. Only God can give order, purpose, and freedom, both to the cosmos and to the covenant people with whom He dwells.

> **What Do You Think?**
> In what ways do you set aside a day of the week for sacred use and worship?
>
> **Digging Deeper**
> What challenges do you face when doing so? What barriers keep you from remembering and setting aside a day?

B. Not for Labor (vv. 9–10)

9. Six days shalt thou labour, and do all thy work.

The kind of remembrance that retains Sabbath for God's use is not just "remember that Sabbath exists" or "remember that Saturday comes after Friday." God provides a framework that will require active preparation during the *six days* before each Sabbath. Each of the six days that are not Sabbath are also set aside, but for *labour.* As in the collection of manna, which required extra *work* before the Sabbath, the Israelites must prepare (Exodus 16:21–30).

To the ancient audience, an incentive to work is already obvious. For tribal nomads, work is always at hand. And to anyone who does not tend livestock or work in an agrarian economy, the labor of ancient Israelites would seem endless: tarry long enough, and animals will suffer; fail to gather firewood, and your family might freeze; stop producing fabric, and you will soon have no clothes. But because the work of living is endless, the radical invitation of this verse is to restrain from work so that each day is not the same.

The invitation is a generous gift. For a group who had just emerged from slavery and unrelenting labor, God demonstrates that faithfulness to His command and His rule will not result in want.

Visual for Lesson 11. *Ask learners to consider their own habits of rest. How can this lesson inform their weekly practices?*

10. But the seventh day is the sabbath of the Lord thy God: in it thou shalt not do any work, thou, nor thy son, nor thy daughter, thy manservant, nor thy maidservant, nor thy cattle, nor thy stranger that is within thy gates.

To be deliberately unproductive for a day each week is an act of trust. It requires extra work in advance so that the Sabbath is not a day without food or water. Yet God knows that humans will look for loopholes. God prevents the redistribution of duties onto others (children, servants, even animals), a temptation to maintain the mere appearance of personal observance while making everyone else's life harder. The call is for a total cessation of labor, from the highest to the lowest, even during the busiest seasons of harvest (Exodus 34:21).

The concern for any *stranger that is within thy gates* is explained later in Exodus 22:21, which recounts the experience of God's people as foreigners in Egypt. The inclusion of the foreigner is an extension of the gift of Sabbath. Whereas Pharaoh oppressed the Hebrews (foreigners to the Egyptians), the Israelites shall invite foreigners to share in Sabbath and find respite from work.

The regular cessation of work might be healthy for people and animals, or it might even lead to greater productivity during the workweek, but the text cites none of these rationalizations for Sabbath. Neither do the instructions cite human enjoyment, for the Sabbath belongs to *the Lord thy God*. Yet by ordering working lives before God and keeping the agreement struck at Sinai, the Israelites shall be promised a series of abundant blessings (see Deuteronomy 28:1–14). The blessings that only God can bring are far more important than the lost labor of a day.

C. Created by God (v. 11)

11. For in six days the Lord made heaven and earth, the sea, and all that in them is, and rested the seventh day: wherefore the Lord blessed the sabbath day, and hallowed it.

This verse explains the basis for Sabbath: God's ordered cosmos began with an ordered creation. The very first verse of the Bible, Genesis 1:1, describes the creation of *heaven and earth* (compare Genesis 2:4). God is the creative maker who separates, orders, and gives purpose to each domain: *earth, the sea, and all that in them.*

God *rested the seventh day* from the work of creation, not because He had grown tired or needed a break from strenuous activity. That might be why humans rest, but not why God rests. God rests because creation is His kingdom, and He sits enthroned above it all. Just as God finds rest in His temple on Mount Zion (Psalm 132:13–14), God rests on the seventh day as the grand finale to creation.

Thus, Israel shall remember the Sabbath and celebrate God's role as the Creator. By placing God at the center of their lives—which is the only way to accommodate a recurring day without productive work—Israel can be shaped by the habit of observing Sabbath and setting it aside for God's purposes.

What Do You Think?

How might God's decision to rest after His act of creation affect your understanding of a weekly day of rest?

Digging Deeper

Compare Deuteronomy 5:15; how does this verse contribute to your understanding?

Resting Well

One summer, I worked in a vineyard in France. Each workday began at sunrise and continued until sunset. By the time the sunlight faded, our hands were bruised from picking, our fingers were red from grape sap, and our legs were tired from lifting heavy buckets of the season's bounty.

At dusk, we set down our tools, climbed into a three-wheeled cart, and went for a hot meal. We spent evenings enjoying one another's company, giving thanks, eating local food, and, on occasion, enjoying the fruit of our toil: freshly pressed juice!

Instructions about work and Sabbath remind me of the delicate work-rest balance of the vineyard. We worked hard; we also rested well. What do your current rhythms of work and rest look like? How are they honoring God and His creation? —N. V.

II. Honoring Special Days
(Romans 14:4–6)

A. No Basis to Judge (v. 4)

4. Who art thou that judgest another man's servant? to his own master he standeth or falleth. Yea, he shall be holden up: for God is able to make him stand.

Many centuries after the giving of the Sinai covenant, the apostle Paul writes to Christ-followers who gather within households in the city of Rome (Romans 16:5). He faces a new situation. Instead of speaking to an exclusively Jewish audience (who would be included under the Sinai covenant), Paul writes to Jews and Gentiles—those who have given their allegiance to God's Messiah, Jesus. The Gentile Christians have neither become Jews nor adopted all the same practices.

Paul cannot point to stipulations of the Sinai covenant as if these are agreed-upon foundations for universal behavior, but neither shall Paul say that any part of Scripture is irrelevant or outdated. To that he would say, "God forbid" (Romans 3:4, 6, 31). When necessary, Paul is unafraid of demanding strict adherence to a code of conduct (13:13; 1 Corinthians 5:1–5; etc.). But is that how Paul should regulate the observance of sacred days for mixed-ethnic communities of early Christians?

Paul asks a rhetorical question: *Who art thou that judgest?* We know that Paul wants his audience to avoid a particular kind of judging here since there are other times when he speaks of judging in a positive sense (1 Corinthians 5:12; 6:1–6; etc.). Paul does not say to give up discriminating right from wrong. But he wants his audience to give up acting like a final authority over matters that call for individual discernment, certain topics he calls "doubtful disputations" (Romans 14:1). If we condemn others for these—write people off as hopeless—we risk condemning ourselves when we fall short (2:1–4). Specifically, Paul describes food laws and calendar observances as requiring individual scrutiny (14:2, 5).

Only one person can be our ultimate judge: Christ Himself. Paul uses an example from his audience's everyday experience: for any *man's servant,* what the *master* deems appropriate is what really matters (*he standeth or falleth*). In other letters, Paul speaks of perseverance for the last days as standing "fast in the Lord" (Philippians 4:1; 1 Thessalonians 3:8), standing "by faith" (2 Corinthians 1:24), or standing "fast in one spirit" (Philippians 1:27). Just earlier in Romans 5:2, Paul mentions the "grace wherein we stand." Thus, the fuller meaning behind *make him stand* is "make a person fit to be judged favorably on the last day." God can do that, but not us.

B. Needs Reflection (v. 5)

5. One man esteemeth one day above another: another esteemeth every day alike. Let every man be fully persuaded in his own mind.

In his letter to the Romans, Paul first mentions diet as a matter of personal decision (Romans 14:2), and here he adds calendar observances as another way that individual habits may dif-

How to Say It

Decalogue	*Dek*-uh-log.
Deuteronomy	Due-ter-*ahn*-uh-me.
Galatians	Guh-*lay*-shunz.
Gentiles	*Jen*-tiles.
Leviticus	Leh-*vit*-ih-kus.
Patmos	*Pat*-muss.
Sinai	*Sigh*-nye or *Sigh*-nay-eye.

fer. Observance of special days would, naturally, include the Sabbath (as explicitly specified in Colossians 2:16). The word translated *esteemeth* is the same as the word translated "judgest" in the previous verse. The difference is, whereas Paul is against judging people by these matters, here he presumes that his audience will judge the days—judging days, not people.

Paul does not specify the identity of those "weak in the faith" or "strong" (Romans 14:1; 15:1). These labels do not appear to neatly divide Jewish from Gentile Christians, since only Jewish Christians would have any history of Sabbath practice and observing food laws. Instead, Paul generalizes: some have set aside Sabbath and food laws while others keep them. But the standard is the same for all, Jewish or Gentile. Each is accountable before God (compare Ephesians 4:4–6).

The phrase *let every man be fully persuaded in his own mind* speaks to individual discernment and confidence before God, no matter the choice in such cases. Paul permits differences within the churches. God will accept both the weak and the strong.

> **What Do You Think?**
> How can we determine which beliefs are essential (no room for compromise) and which are nonessential?
>
> **Digging Deeper**
> How does this quote inform your approach: "In essentials, unity; in non-essentials, liberty; in all things, charity"?

C. Always for the Lord (v. 6)

6. He that regardeth the day, regardeth it unto the Lord; and he that regardeth not the day, to the Lord he doth not regard it. He that eateth, eateth to the Lord, for he giveth God thanks; and he that eateth not, to the Lord he eateth not, and giveth God thanks.

Because all servants should be submitted before their mutual *Lord,* Paul precludes any from issuing judgments or blanket demands on other faithful servants, those who maintain a different religious calendar or diet. If a person *regardeth* one *day* as sacred to the Lord, the decision comes by heartfelt devotion. Because honoring Sabbath means respecting God's rule over space and time, Paul allows that some may deem "every day alike" (Romans 14:5, above), thereby signaling devotion to the creator of each day. The repetition of *(un)to the Lord* conveys the sole criterion for faithfulness in these matters.

Paul's allowance for individual discernment is harmonious with Christ's words: "The sabbath was made for man, and not man for the sabbath. Therefore the Son of man is Lord also of the sabbath" (Mark 2:27–28). Jesus defends a freedom for His disciples to go about their mission without hindrance, at His command. Because Jesus is Lord and ruler of creation, He is free to judge the manner in which His disciples shall honor Him.

Paul pairs together the issues of revering days and observing dietary restrictions, showing that he has a greater goal in mind. Paul's desire is for the peace and unity of Christian communities—and unity does not mean uniformity. He advises selfless consideration before others, giving no reason for any to find offense (Romans 14:13–15). In the end, what matters is life together under the rightful king's rule, for "the kingdom of God is not meat and drink; but righteousness, and peace, and joy in the Holy Ghost" (14:17).

Not How, but Why

Our Christmas Eve meal is a long-standing tradition. Several generations of my family gather around a large table to eat honey-roasted ham, farm eggs, and thick-cut fries—a feast lovingly prepared over several days. It has been this way for as long as I can remember.

However, when I was six I realized that a decadent meal is not a universal habit for Christmas Eve. Some families enjoy a full roast dinner, but others prefer something far simpler. It finally made sense when my mother explained that what matters most is not *how* something is celebrated but *why* it is celebrated—and *for whom.*

The Old Testament goes into great detail regarding the *how, when,* and *where* of celebrations and observances, yet Paul downplays those in favor of the *why.* We do not celebrate certain days because we think it's necessary for everyone else to follow our lead. We celebrate them because they are important to us, our families, and for our personal relationship with God. —N. V.

III. The Lord's Day

(Revelation 1:10)

10. I was in the Spirit on the Lord's day, and heard behind me a great voice, as of a trumpet.

Another early Christian writer—John, while on the island of Patmos (Revelation 1:9)—uses a phrase that comes to distinguish the weekly observances of Christians: *the Lord's day.* On this occasion, John describes being *in the Spirit,* meaning a trancelike state of prayerful meditation before God.

The phrase *the Lord's day* appears here alone in the entire New Testament. But elsewhere, Christians are already said to be gathering on "the first day of the week" for the sharing of a meal (Acts 20:7). The same wording is repeated in the texts of all four Gospels (Matthew 28:1; Mark 16:2; Luke 24:1; John 20:1, 19). The Evangelists all say that Jesus' resurrection occurred on "the first day of the week"—that is, Sunday.

Christians of the first and second centuries developed a reputation for meeting before dawn on Sunday, the resurrection morning that began God's new creation (see 2 Corinthians 5:17; Galatians 6:15). Because the Sabbath is a practice that honors the Creator, it is only fitting that Jesus—who was with the Father from the beginning, coequal, and responsible for all that was made (John 1:1; Colossians 1:15–17)—is honored in this observance.

What Do You Think?

In what ways do your congregation's Lord's Day services honor God as Triune: Father, Son, and Holy Spirit?

Digging Deeper

How do the service's various practices lead you into a deeper worship of God?

Conclusion

A. King of Creation, Lord of Every Day

What does the Sabbath mean for Christians today? Answers to this question have needlessly divided congregations and families who seek to devote time and space to God. A consistent thread runs from the gift of Sabbath, to the discernment of early churches, to the earliest Christians who designate Sunday for celebratory songs: God is king of creation, and Christ the Lord is worthy of praise.

For those who worship the Creator in reverent submission, the fitting response is to place God at the center of all life, to orient everything else around a mission to serve the king. Sabbath honors the rhythms of God's productive creation, even as God's people join Him in productive work on days that are not Sabbath. According to Paul, we now have the freedom to act with confidence, as Christ's own servants. Perhaps we may find that a particular day should be reserved for prayer, and we clear space for God by setting aside all distractions. Perhaps, like the earliest Christians, we find that rising early to gather on Sunday will make us peculiar.

But whatever our king expects of us, our duty is not to go about asserting ourselves as the final judge. We can anticipate that, in the splendor of God's kingdom, there are servants of Christ whose "orders from the king" differ from ours. If we seek peace together, as Paul teaches, we shall communicate best through humble actions, the kindnesses that point back to Christ as Lord of our lives.

What Do You Think?

How will you seek peace with believers who may have different interpretations of the significance of Sabbath?

Digging Deeper

In what ways has this lesson informed your interpretation of God's gifts of rest and worship?

B. Prayer

Lord, You order time and space. We worship You as Lord of our lives. Show us how to devote our time to Your kingdom's purposes in both work and rest. Amen.

C. Thought to Remember

All our time should be devoted to God.

Involvement Learning

Enhance your lesson with KJV Bible Student *(from your curriculum supplier) and the reproducible activity page (at www.standardlesson.com or in the back of the* KJV Standard Lesson Commentary Deluxe Edition*).*

Into the Lesson

Write on the board the following letters, with each letter being the header of a column:

R E S T

Ask, "What does it mean to rest?" Divide the class into four groups and assign each group one letter from the word *rest*. Distribute a sheet of paper and pen to each group and ask them to write down words or phrases beginning with their assigned letter that describe the meaning of *rest*. After calling time, ask volunteers to share their responses and write them on the board.

Lead into the Bible study by saying, "Today we're going to study what God has taught His people regarding the need for rest. We'll review how that teaching connects with our practices of worship."

Into the Word

Begin this section with a brief background on the history of Sabbath observances in the church. If possible, ask a learner to prepare this five-minute report before class.

Divide the class into three groups: **Exodus Group**, **Romans Group**, and **Revelation Group.** Distribute handouts (you create) with the following questions for in-group discussion.

Exodus Group. Read Exodus 20:8–11. 1–What did God command of His people? 2–What rationale did He give for this command?

Romans Group. Read Romans 14:4–6. 1–Does Paul forbid making one day of the week special? Why or why not? 2–What rule does Paul give for observing a particular day? 3–What hint in this text suggests Paul is speaking to a controversy between Jewish and Gentile Christians?

Revelation Group. Read Revelation 1:10. 1–Which day of the week is John referring to in this verse? 2–How, if at all, does this help us determine our day of worship?

Option. Distribute copies of the "First Day" exercise from the activity page, which you can download. Have learners work in small groups to complete as indicated.

Ask a volunteer from each group to report on their findings, augmenting their reports with information you have prepared based on the lesson commentary. Then, ask the following questions for whole-class discussion: 1–What are the significant differences between the Old Testament command to honor the Sabbath and the practice of Lord's Day worship in the New Testament church? 2–What are the significant similarities between the two? (Option: Write the following headers on the board: *Differences, Similarities.* Write responses on the board as participants respond.)

Conclude the section by asking, "What do these texts teach us about how we should approach rest and worship?" Direct the class to work together to define the words *rest* and *worship*. Write definitions on the board.

Into Life

Write the following phrases on the board:

Ways We Like to Rest
Ways We Like to Worship

Ask volunteers to respond to each phrase. Write responses on the board. Then, ask, "In what ways is our rest a form of worship, and how can we bring these two needs together?"

Place participants into pairs and distribute an index card and pen to each person. Ask participants to write down ways they can combine rest and worship. Direct them to share results with their partner. Have participants choose one item on their list that they will accomplish in the upcoming week.

Alternative. Distribute copies of the "Some Christians Say" activity from the activity page. Have learners work in pairs to complete as indicated.

February 22
Lesson 12 (KJV)

Stewardship and Mission

Devotional Reading: Zechariah 8:18–23
Background Scripture: Deuteronomy 8:17–18; Acts 26:12–20;
2 Corinthians 8:1–15; 9:1–15

Acts 1:6–8

6 When they therefore were come together, they asked of him, saying, Lord, wilt thou at this time restore again the kingdom to Israel?

7 And he said unto them, It is not for you to know the times or the seasons, which the Father hath put in his own power.

8 But ye shall receive power, after that the Holy Ghost is come upon you: and ye shall be witnesses unto me both in Jerusalem, and in all Judaea, and in Samaria, and unto the uttermost part of the earth.

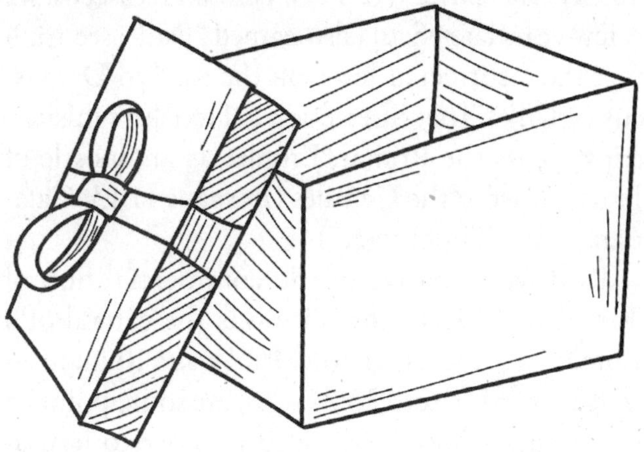

2 Corinthians 8:3–9

3 For to their power, I bear record, yea, and beyond their power they were willing of themselves;

4 Praying us with much intreaty that we would receive the gift, and take upon us the fellowship of the ministering to the saints.

5 And this they did, not as we hoped, but first gave their own selves to the Lord, and unto us by the will of God.

6 Insomuch that we desired Titus, that as he had begun, so he would also finish in you the same grace also.

7 Therefore, as ye abound in every thing, in faith, and utterance, and knowledge, and in all diligence, and in your love to us, see that ye abound in this grace also.

8 I speak not by commandment, but by occasion of the forwardness of others, and to prove the sincerity of your love.

9 For ye know the grace of our Lord Jesus Christ, that, though he was rich, yet for your sakes he became poor, that ye through his poverty might be rich.

Key Text

Ye know the grace of our Lord Jesus Christ, that, though he was rich, yet for your sakes he became poor, that ye through his poverty might be rich. **—2 Corinthians 8:9**

Enduring Beliefs

of the Church

Unit 3: The Church and Its Teachings

Lessons 9–13

Lesson Aims

After participating in this lesson, each learner will be able to:

1. Identify characteristics of the generosity highlighted in 2 Corinthians 8:3–9.
2. Explain the context of Paul's financial collection among Gentile churches of the first century.
3. State one way he or she will practice generosity in the upcoming week.

Lesson Outline

Introduction

A. Epic Generosity

B. Lesson Context

I. Jesus and the Apostles (Acts 1:6–8)

A. Disciples' Question (v. 6)

B. Jesus' Response (vv. 7–8)

II. Paul and the Church (2 Corinthians 8:3–9)

A. Facts (vv. 3–4)

Giving Gladly

B. Results (vv. 5–6)

C. Challenge (v. 7)

D. Test (vv. 8–9)

Excelling in Generosity

Conclusion

A. More than Money

B. Prayer

C. Thought to Remember

Introduction

A. Epic Generosity

One of the world's favorite stories is Victor Hugo's *Les Misérables*. First as a novel and later as a musical stage play, it has fascinated audiences for generations.

Les Misérables is the story of Jean Valjean, a poor man imprisoned for stealing a loaf of bread. Finally released from prison, he is given refuge by a bishop of the church. Valjean repays the man's generosity by stealing his silverware! But when the police capture Valjean, the bishop says that the silverware was a gift to the man. Stunned by the bishop's gracious generosity, Valjean becomes a changed man—a person of humble, heroic generosity.

Perhaps what makes *Les Misérables* so beloved is that it illustrates the grace of God. Though we have rejected God's generosity, He still offers us forgiveness by His grace. Having received that forgiveness, a person can never be the same. God's gracious generosity begets the same generosity in His people.

B. Lesson Context

The two texts for today's lesson are dated almost three decades apart. Jesus was crucified during the Passover observance of AD 30, rose from the dead, and appeared physically to His followers for some 40 days thereafter (Acts 1:3) before His ascension. A few years later, Saul (also named "Paul"; see 13:9) met the resurrected Jesus on the road to Damascus (9:1–19). That interaction led to Paul's mission trips across the Roman Empire as an apostle of Jesus Christ to the Gentiles (Romans 11:13; Galatians 2:8; 1 Timothy 2:7).

Paul was a native of the commercial hub of Tarsus of Cilicia. That city was the capital of a Roman province; therefore, Paul was a Roman citizen by birth (Acts 22:22–29). At some point in his younger days, he decided to move to Jerusalem to study under Gamaliel (22:3). After Paul's experience on the road to Damascus, he founded churches in various Roman cities. As people responded to his gospel message, Paul found himself continually needing to bridge the cultural gap between Christ-followers of Gentile background and those of Jewish descent.

We might say, then, that as the first chapter of the book of Acts features the apostles being given their mission and preparing for it, the chapters that follow reveal how that mission was carried out. There were issues regarding aspects of the Law of Moses concerning doctrine and practice as Jews and Gentiles came together. This struggle is most evident in the famous Jerusalem Council in about AD 51 (Acts 15).

The consensus reached at that council served to welcome believers of Gentile background into the church on the basis of the grace of Jesus Christ, not on adherence to the Law of Moses (Acts 15:5–11). This acknowledgment of God's plan was vitally important for establishing the inclusive nature of the church. The importance of that acknowledgment became apparent as certain events unfolded over the following years. One such event is the subject of today's lesson.

I. Jesus and the Apostles

(Acts 1:6–8)

The book of Acts begins with a dialog between Jesus and His apostles at the Mount of Olives before He ascends to heaven. Within the 40-day time period of His appearance to His disciples (see Lesson Context), Jesus directs them to remain in Jerusalem and "wait for the promise of the Father," the Holy Spirit (Acts 1:4–5). But as the conversation continues, the disciples reveal a misunderstanding they hold and a desire for something they should not have.

A. Disciples' Question (v. 6)

6. When they therefore were come together, they asked of him, saying, Lord, wilt thou at this time restore again the kingdom to Israel?

After hearing Jesus' directive to remain in Jerusalem, the disciples *come together* to ask Him the question we see here. They are convinced that He is the promised Messiah (Matthew 16:16; John 1:41). Their question reflects the expectations of many first-century Jews regarding the timing and nature of the Messiah's task.

Several Old Testament texts likely are the primary drivers of these expectations: Genesis 49:10;

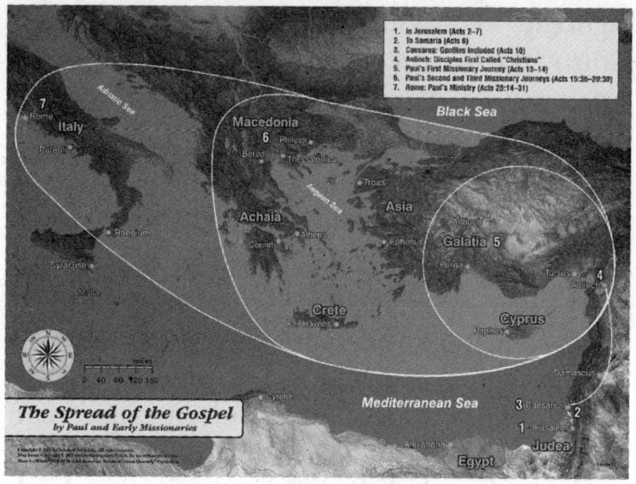

Visual for Lesson 12. *Display this visual as you discuss the events surrounding the spread of the gospel in the first century.*

Numbers 24:17–19; and Isaiah 11:1–6. These texts can be interpreted in one sense to lead the reader to conclude that the Messiah would overthrow the Roman occupiers as He ascended to the throne of David (compare Luke 24:21; John 6:14–15). Thus God is expected to *restore again the kingdom to Israel.*

The disciples, therefore, mistakenly anticipate that Jesus will lead a political and militaristic revolt. What better leader could they hope for than the one who has overcome death?

B. Jesus' Response (vv. 7–8)

7. And he said unto them, It is not for you to know the times or the seasons, which the Father hath put in his own power.

Jesus responds, but not in the way the disciples hope. He does not address their concern for Israel's restoration. Instead, Jesus tells them that they are not to be concerned with knowledge of *the times* and *the seasons* of such things. This privileged knowledge is for God *the Father* only (Mark 13:32). Earlier, Jesus exhorted the disciples to keep watch, but not to the point of becoming distracted by setting dates for His return (Matthew 24:36–44; 25:13). God is omniscient, meaning that He is all-knowing, including knowledge of things hidden from human understanding.

8a. But ye shall receive power, after that the Holy Ghost is come upon you.

Jesus redirects the disciples' focus and

highlights their unique task as they wait for His return. The Gospel of Luke ends with Jesus' command that the disciples remain in Jerusalem until they receive "power from on high" (Luke 24:49). The verse before us moves from the abstract to the specific: the source of that *power* is to be *the Holy Ghost.* One cannot help but see parallels between Jesus' prediction here and the message of John the Baptist regarding a forthcoming baptism "with the Holy Ghost and with fire" intimated by Jesus (Matthew 3:11; Luke 3:16). Both messages echo events on the Day of Pentecost (Acts 2:1–3).

8b. And ye shall be witnesses unto me both in Jerusalem, and in all Judaea, and in Samaria, and unto the uttermost part of the earth.

The Holy Spirit's empowerment becomes the starting point for the church. The noun *witness* can be interpreted in at least two ways, depending on context. In one sense, the word *witness* refers to someone who has observed something—a spectator, observer, or eyewitness. In a second sense, the noun *witness* can refer to someone who testifies to something, as in a deposition. Jesus' disciples are already witnesses in the first sense, having seen firsthand His ministry, crucifixion, and Him personally after His resurrection. But now they are to be witnesses in the second sense as they take the gospel to *Jerusalem, . . . Judaea, . . . Samaria*, and *unto the uttermost part of the earth* (compare Matthew 28:19–20; Acts 8:1–25).

Many commentators have noted that this sequence of places outlines the gospel's geographic growth as recorded in the book of Acts. Peter first preaches the gospel *in Jerusalem* on the Day of Pentecost (Acts 2). The movement then expands into *Judaea,* the region in which Jerusalem is located, and then to the region of *Samaria* to the north (8:1). Initially, only those believers who were not apostles left Jerusalem. But those believers took the gospel message with them (8:4–8; 11:19–21).

The phrase *uttermost part of the earth* emphasizes that Jesus wants His disciples to take His message of salvation to all people and all the world. To do so would be a significant undertaking. Further, Jesus gave them no specifics regarding how they would work to complete this task. The instructions would come on an "as needed" basis (examples: Acts 8:26; 10:9–20; 16:6–10; 18:9). For the disciples and witnesses to follow through on this task, they must show each other care, hospitality, and financial generosity.

What Do You Think?

What practical steps will you take in the week ahead to become a more effective witness for the Lord?

Digging Deeper

What training and resources will you need to assist you in this endeavor?

How to Say It

Achaia	Uh-*kay*-uh.
Berea	Buh-*ree*-uh.
Corinth	*Kor*-inth.
Corinthians	Ko-*rin*-thee-unz (*th* as in *thin*).
Gamaliel	Guh-*may*-lih-ul or Guh-*may*-lee-al.
Macedonia	Mass-eh-*doe*-nee-uh.
Macedonians	Mass-eh-*doe*-nee-uns.
omniscient	ahm-*nish*-unt.
Philippi	Fih-*lip*-pie or *Fil*-ih-pie.
Tarsus	*Tar*-sus.

II. Paul and the Church

(2 Corinthians 8:3–9)

The next segment of Scripture to study takes us into the middle of a relief project being managed by the apostle Paul. This fundraising initiative is mentioned several times in the New Testament. In Paul's first letter to the Corinthian church (written about AD 56), he instructed his readers to make weekly contributions to the fund so that it would be ready when he visited (1 Corinthians 16:1–4). Paul wrote 2 Corinthians about a year later. The collection of this gift provides the backdrop for Paul's teachings on stewardship found in 2 Corinthians 8. The timeline indicates that the relief project was a plan spread over several years, given that Paul did not arrive back in Jerusalem until AD 58 (Acts 21:17; 24:17).

A. Facts (vv. 3–4)

3. For to their power, I bear record, yea, and beyond their power they were willing of themselves.

To make his case to the church at Corinth that they should complete the gift, Paul presents the example of the churches of Macedonia in 2 Corinthians 8:1, which is the antecedent of the words *their* and *they* in the verse before us. Macedonia is the region located directly north of Corinth, and it includes the cities of Philippi, Thessalonica, and Berea (Acts 16:12; 17:1, 13; etc.). When Paul writes to the church in Rome a short time later, he mentions Achaia as well on this same subject (Romans 15:26); this is the province where Corinth is located.

The Macedonian churches had been experiencing "a great trial of affliction" and "deep poverty" (2 Corinthians 8:2; see 1:8), which might have included persecution (see 7:5). But amazingly, the relief collection is not *for* them, but *from* them! Despite their suffering, those congregations have demonstrated joy that has yielded a gift of rich generosity (8:2). In effect, Paul uses the example of the Macedonian Christians to set a standard.

Paul does not give the specific financial amount offered by the Macedonian churches. Instead, he classifies their giving into two categories. First, their giving was *to their power,* an amount to be expected (compare 1 Corinthians 16:2). The second category, however, goes above and beyond the first: their giving was *beyond their power.* This giving level reveals that God was at work in and through their sacrificial generosity.

Further, the fact that they *were willing of themselves* indicates that they gave without coercion from Paul. Their generosity was a free response to having received God's gift of grace (see 2 Corinthians 8:1).

> **What Do You Think?**
> Who has been, for you, an example of sacrificial generosity?
> **Digging Deeper**
> Which of that person's habits of generosity would you like to implement?

Giving Gladly

When I think of my parents, I think of their radical generosity. From my perspective, it feels like their financial giving outweighs their income! They give gladly, and the Lord multiplies their gifts for a powerful effect on the church. I frequently ask the Lord to develop in me a generous heart, a heart like my parents'.

The power of financial generosity is not the amount given but the status of the giver's heart—one that offers willingly and joyfully in service to the Lord. How will you cultivate such a heart? As you ponder that question, think of your generosity as a direct response to the gift of grace that you have received! —N. V.

4. Praying us with much intreaty that we would receive the gift, and take upon us the fellowship of the ministering to the saints.

Not only do the Macedonian churches give freely, but they also plead with Paul and his companions to *receive* the churches' generous financial *gift.* As used here, the word *praying* refers to requests not to God but to other people—in this case, to Paul and his traveling companions (*us*). For believers in one area to provide aid to believers in other provinces is not without precedent (Acts 11:29–30).

The key theme in this verse and this chapter is the *fellowship* of God's people. This refers to a complete sharing of life with another and the unity God's people experience as they abide in Christ, receive God's gift of grace, and freely respond to that gift for the mission of the church (examples: Philippians 1:3–6; 4:14–18). Similar terminology is used to describe the earliest life of the church in Acts 2:42–47. There, we see the believers worshiping, sharing meals, and providing for one another's needs.

One way to demonstrate unity and fellowship among God's people is through *ministering* through financial giving. As believers experience unity, they are willing to meet the financial needs of others. In doing so, God's people embody Jesus' commands to follow Him and care for other believers in Christ (Matthew 25:34–40).

Both the recipients and the givers of the gift are

the saints—the people of God set apart by His grace (compare 2 Corinthians 9:1). Although Paul does not here identify the recipient(s) of this gift, they are poverty-stricken believers in Jerusalem (Acts 24:17; Romans 15:25–28; 1 Corinthians 16:3).

> **What Do You Think?**
> In what ways can you practice fellowship with other believers?
> **Digging Deeper**
> Does unity result in fellowship, or is it the other way around? Why?

B. Results (vv. 5–6)

5. And this they did, not as we hoped, but first gave their own selves to the Lord, and unto us by the will of God.

The phrase *not as we hoped* should be understood to signify a mismatch between what Paul and his traveling companions (*us*) expected and what happened. Knowing of the precarious situation of the Macedonians, Paul's expectations of their ability to give had been in line with that reality. Therefore, he is truly surprised by their overwhelming generosity —one that happened because they *first gave their own selves to the Lord.* That initial commitment was not to the offering but to Christ. The Macedonians had experienced Christ's love and grace, which, in turn, led them to give their whole lives in service to Him and to His people. Their commitment was both the prerequisite and motivating factor for their sacrificial giving to support the mission of the first-century churches. This level of commitment comes only *by the will of God,* as modeled by Jesus, who gave Himself on the cross.

6. Insomuch that we desired Titus, that as he had begun, so he would also finish in you the same grace also.

Having summarized the generosity of the Macedonian church, Paul now challenges his Corinthian readers. The challenge is based on the fact that the Macedonian churches have already finished their giving project, but the Corinthians have not.

A key player in helping the Corinthians do so is *Titus,* a "partner and fellowhelper" of the apostle Paul (2 Corinthians 8:23). He is mentioned by name nine times in this book—more than in all the other New Testament books combined. Collecting funds for the poverty-stricken Jerusalem church seems to be a primary task for Titus (8:16–9:5).

Paul refers to the anticipated financial gift from the Corinthians as *the same grace.* Their gift is not being coerced (more on this below). Instead, it will be their response of grace for having received the grace of God themselves.

C. Challenge (v. 7)

7a. Therefore, as ye abound in every thing, in faith, and utterance, and knowledge, and in all diligence, and in your love to us.

Paul has much to say elsewhere about *faith, utterance, knowledge, diligence,* and *love.* Regarding just the Corinthians, we can list 1 Corinthians 1:5; 12:8; 13:1–2, 13; 14:6; and 16:1–2 on those topics.

7b. See that ye abound in this grace also.

Even though the Corinthians excelled in several qualities, completing the offering was an opportunity for them to still *abound* in one more quality —*grace.* Growing in this regard involves the tangible *grace* of financial giving.

> **What Do You Think?**
> How is the term *grace* a suitable descriptor of the gift of giving?
> **Digging Deeper**
> In what ways can believers grow in the grace of giving?

D. Test (vv. 8–9)

8. I speak not by commandment, but by occasion of the forwardness of others, and to prove the sincerity of your love.

Regarding certain situations, the apostle Paul gives commands to the Christians in Corinth (examples: 1 Corinthians 5:7, 13), and sometimes he merely advises (example: 7:6). The imperative "See that ye abound in this grace also," just studied in 2 Corinthians 8:7b (above), seems like a command at first. But Paul hastens to ensure his exhortation is not misconstrued: *I speak not by command.* Perhaps the clarification is because previously, he had been much more direct to them regarding their giving (1 Corinthians 16:1–2). Paul desires that the Corinthian believers be generous to other believers in need, but he wants the Corinthians to give out of cheerful love, not compulsion.

Paul notes the reason for his bringing up the example of the Macedonian churches. The word translated *forwardness* is also translated as "diligence" in 2 Corinthians 8:7, above, and that is the sense here. The Macedonians' *diligence* in showing financial generosity was the *occasion* for him to use as an example to the Corinthians. If the Corinthians are similarly diligent, they will *prove the sincerity of* their *love* (compare 2 Corinthians 8:24).

Excelling in Generosity

My congregation regularly contributes to a fund to meet the needs of families in the community. Hundreds of thousands of dollars have been donated to this fund to address housing, food, and education needs.

However, not all acts of generosity are related to money. On the first Sunday of each month, a "repairs café" appears in our neighborhood where people can bring broken household items to be repaired. Those having fix-it skills generously share their time and talents to help others. Generous communities are powerful witnesses, and I'm encouraged to see my neighbors excel in the art of showing generosity through their time, skills, and labor.

Financial giving is one way we can respond to the gift of God's grace. But in addition, how can you excel in other forms of generosity? If you need a biblical example, see Acts 9:36, 39. —N. V.

9. For ye know the grace of our Lord Jesus Christ, that, though he was rich, yet for your sakes he became poor, that ye through his poverty might be rich.

Paul appeals to the example of the *Lord Jesus Christ.* Before the incarnation, Jesus *was rich* in ways we cannot grasp. As the divine Son, He is equal with God from eternity (John 1:1–2). These eternal riches did not stop the divine Son from becoming a servant, humbling Himself and becoming *poor* for the sake of humanity (Philippians 2:5–8). Through His self-sacrifice, Jesus inaugurated the riches of the Father's salvation by making atonement for sin (Ephesians 1:7; Hebrews 2:17).

Conclusion

A. More than Money

The Bible reveals God's expectations regarding how people are to treat each other. One such expectation concerns meeting the needs of the poverty-stricken. The Law of Moses had clear rules in this regard (examples: Leviticus 19:10; Deuteronomy 15:11). And the issue is no less present under the new covenant (examples: Matthew 25:34–46; Galatians 2:10).

Even so, money and its giving are touchy subjects at church, causing many to avoid discussing the topic. The oft-heard complaint, "They're always asking for money!" has soured many people away from church. Perhaps we should take a different approach to giving, one that acknowledges financial generosity as, first and foremost, a privileged response to God's grace.

Our generosity results from first acknowledging the generosity of God. Our God is a giving God, demonstrated through His gift of salvation. When we show generosity to others, we are following God's lead. Our acts of generosity are acts of worship, bearing witness to our testimony of Christ and His great love for us.

What Do You Think?

How will you be generous with your time and resources in the upcoming week?

Digging Deeper

How does the example in Acts 2:42–47 inspire you in this regard?

B. Prayer

Heavenly Father, You showed us generosity when You gave us Your gift of grace through Your Son, Jesus. May our thankfulness for this gift be revealed in our heartfelt gifts in return. In Jesus' name we pray. Amen.

C. Thought to Remember

Generosity is our response to God's grace.

Involvement Learning

Enhance your lesson with KJV Bible Student *(from your curriculum supplier) and the reproducible activity page (at www.standardlesson.com or in the back of the* KJV Standard Lesson Commentary Deluxe Edition*).*

Into the Lesson

Distribute five small items to each participant. Possible items include pennies, clothespins, or individually wrapped candies. Lead into the activity by explaining that the whole class will play a game with these items. Participants should try to give away all five items in their possession to other participants by the end of three minutes. However, each participant can only give one item at a time to another person. When everyone is ready, say, "Go!" Call time at the end of three minutes. Reconvene the class and ask participants to assess the number of items they still possess. Ask, "Why was it difficult or nearly impossible to win this game?"

Lead into the Bible study by saying, "Generosity is much easier when we realize how much we have been given! In today's lesson, we will study the chain of generosity—one that begins with God in Christ Jesus and extends to all His followers."

Into the Word

Divide participants into groups of three and distribute a pen and sheet of paper to each group. Direct groups to read Acts 1:6–8 and imagine themselves as Jesus' first-century disciples and write down a five-to-six-sentence testimony that recounts their time and experience as "witnesses" to Jesus. (Option: Challenge groups to read 1 John 1:1–4, then consider what the disciples had seen, heard, and touched as they followed Jesus.) After five minutes, ask groups to share with the class what they have written. Conduct a whole-class discussion regarding how this passage can help Jesus' disciples define *mission.*

Alternative. Distribute copies of the "Gospel Effect" exercise from the activity pages, which you can download. Have participants work in small groups to complete as indicated.

Ask a volunteer to prepare and present a three-minute presentation on the historical context of the church in Corinth and the financial offerings of the Macedonian congregations. The presentation should address the following questions: 1–What part of "Jerusalem, . . . Judaea, . . . Samaria, and . . . the uttermost part of the earth" (Acts 1:8) does Macedonia belong to? 2–How is the example of the Macedonians a testimony to the faithfulness and generosity of the disciples? Encourage the presenter to use the material from the Lesson Context.

Ask a volunteer to read aloud 2 Corinthians 8:1–5. Invite participants to identify words in these verses that reflect the abundant and exceptional giving from the Macedonians. Write these words and phrases on the board.

Ask a volunteer to read aloud 2 Corinthians 8:6–9. Divide participants into three groups: **Self Group, Others Group,** and **Jesus Group.** Direct the **Self Group** to study verse 7 and discuss the strengths that Paul recognized in the Corinthian church and why these are good qualities. Have the **Others Group** read verse 8 and discuss why it is sometimes appropriate to compare ourselves to others. Assign verse 9 to the **Jesus Group** and ask them to discuss Jesus' example of a generous life.

After calling time, let each group summarize their conclusions to the class. Then, as a whole class, discuss how these verses help to define Christian stewardship and mission.

Into Life

Write the word *Generosity* as a header on the board. Lead a brainstorming session to determine ways to practice generosity every day. Distribute an index card and pen to each learner. Direct them to write down how they will practice generosity throughout the upcoming week. Allow time at the beginning of the next class for volunteers to share their experiences.

Option. Distribute copies of the "Pass It On" activity from the activity page. Challenge participants to complete as indicated throughout the coming week.

Loving God, Loving Others

Devotional Reading: Proverbs 28:18–22
Background Scripture: Romans 15:1–7; Philippians 2:1–8; Colossians 3:12; 4:1

Mark 12:28–34

28 And one of the scribes came, and having heard them reasoning together, and perceiving that he had answered them well, asked him, Which is the first commandment of all?
29 And Jesus answered him, The first of all the commandments is, Hear, O Israel; The Lord our God is one Lord:
30 And thou shalt love the Lord thy God with all thy heart, and with all thy soul, and with all thy mind, and with all thy strength: this is the first commandment.
31 And the second is like, namely this, Thou shalt love thy neighbour as thyself. There is none other commandment greater than these.
32 And the scribe said unto him, Well, Master, thou hast said the truth: for there is one God; and there is none other but he:
33 And to love him with all the heart, and with all the understanding, and with all the soul, and with all the strength, and to love his neighbour as himself, is more than all whole burnt offerings and sacrifices.
34 And when Jesus saw that he answered discreetly, he said unto him, Thou art not far from the kingdom of God. And no man after that durst ask him any question.

James 2:14–17

14 What doth it profit, my brethren, though a man say he hath faith, and have not works? can faith save him?
15 If a brother or sister be naked, and destitute of daily food,
16 And one of you say unto them, Depart in peace, be ye warmed and filled; notwithstanding ye give them not those things which are needful to the body; what doth it profit?
17 Even so faith, if it hath not works, is dead, being alone.

Key Text

To love him with all the heart, and with all the understanding, and with all the soul, and with all the strength, and to love his neighbour as himself, is more than all whole burnt offerings and sacrifices. **—Mark 12:33**

Enduring Beliefs
of the Church

Unit 3: The Church and Its Teachings
Lessons 9–13

Lesson Aims

After participating in this lesson, each learner will be able to:

1. Identify the two greatest commandments according to Mark 12:28–34.

2. Give examples of practices inspired by James 2:14–17 that embody these commandments.

3. Make a plan to see and address the immediate needs of your surrounding community.

Lesson Outline

Introduction
- A. Keep the "Main Thing" the Main Thing
- B. Lesson Context

I. Right Belief (Mark 12:28–34)
- A. Inquiry for Jesus (v. 28)
- B. Explanation of the Law (vv. 29–31)
  - *All In*
- C. Expansion of the Reply (vv. 32–33)
- D. Evidence of Wisdom (v. 34)

II. Right Action (James 2:14–17)
- A. Rhetorical Question (v. 14)
- B. Obvious Example (vv. 15–16)
- C. Confident Assertion (v. 17)
  - *More Than Just Bumper Stickers*

Conclusion
- A. The Most Important Thing
- B. Prayer
- C. Thought to Remember

Introduction

A. Keep the "Main Thing" the Main Thing

When I was in college studying theology and biblical studies, it was common for me and my peers to get into discussions about matters of biblical interpretation. Occasionally these got rather heated, with advocates on either side of an issue growing vehement as they tried to convince the others of their position. While we continued to see one another as brothers and sisters in Christ, I would be lying if I said it wasn't a struggle to remember to "keep the main thing the main thing." Learning lots of exciting things about our faith each week through various readings and lectures, it was all too easy to fall into "majoring on the minors" when we got into discussions. Often we were tempted to see each other as opponents to shoot down with arguments and ideas, rather than as fellow believers worthy of love and kindness. But love should always take first place in our thoughts, words, and actions.

Today's lesson texts remind us how to live out our faith from a center of love for God and others.

B. Lesson Context

The setting of Mark 12:28–34 is the temple in Jerusalem during Jesus' final week. He spends much of that week teaching in the temple environs (Mark 11:15–17, 27; 12:35; etc.). Earlier, Jesus expressed His opposition to the economics of temple practices when He drove out the moneychangers who had turned the temple into a commercial center rather than a place of prayer (11:15–17). This, along with His teaching, enraged the temple authorities (11:18).

Consequently, those authorities sought to undermine Jesus' credibility with the people by questioning His allegiances and debating Him publicly. Should His popularity wane by being discredited, the authorities could act against Jesus without incurring the people's anger. If His answers questioned the authority of Rome, He could be handed over to the Romans for execution. Either way, the authorities wanted to undermine Jesus' credibility because they perceived Him as a threat to their own powerful positions (compare John 11:48).

Concerning the book of James, there are four or five men named James in the New Testament. The author of the book that bears his name is the James of Matthew 13:55. Thus, he is the half-brother of Jesus. We see the influence of this James in Acts 15:13–21.

James writes his letter to the "diaspora": religiously and ethnically Jewish people who are dispersed and scattered, many of whom have come to see Jesus as the fulfillment of the hope of Israel (James 1:1). He is evidently concerned with his readers' actions. In providing a solution to the areas of concern, he exhorts his readers to live in light of the gospel they profess (James 1:21–22, 27; 2:8, 24). James's identification of the "royal law" is the same that Jesus quoted in Mark 12:31: love your neighbor as yourself (James 2:8).

I. Right Belief

(Mark 12:28–34)

Just prior to our lesson passage, a succession of inquisitors had peppered Jesus with questions in order to cast doubt on His authority and discredit His ministry (Mark 11:27–33; 12:13–27). These opponents represented all elements and levels of Jewish religious authority in Jerusalem—chief priests, scribes, elders, Pharisees, Herodians, and Sadducees.

A. Inquiry for Jesus (v. 28)

28. And one of the scribes came, and having heard them reasoning together, and perceiving that he had answered them well, asked him, Which is the first commandment of all?

One of the scribes seems impressed with how Jesus has been answering His interrogators. The man approaches Jesus with respect; the parallel account in Matthew 22:36 includes the use of the title "master" (compare Mark 12:32, below). He wonders how Jesus might answer a question often debated among the rabbis: Of all the commandments, which is the *first* one *of all?*

Traditionally, rabbis counted over 600 commands in the Law of Moses. It is not surprising, then, that a debate might arise concerning which ones were the most important. If one were to create a "top ten" list, the task might seem easy: the most important ones are the Ten Commandments, of course! Some Jewish scholars, like the first-century Philo of Alexandria, thought those 10 summarized all the commands in the law. He believed they articulated two primary responsibilities: one pertaining to God (piety) and the other pertaining to people (justice).

Categorizing those commandments in this twofold way is not uncommon at the time. But does the Law of Moses suggest a hierarchy of importance whereby one commandment can be singled out as being *the first commandment of all?*

B. Explanation of the Law (vv. 29–31)

29. And Jesus answered him, The first of all the commandments is, Hear, O Israel; The Lord our God is one Lord.

Given His straightforward reply, Jesus recognizes that this is not a trick question designed to trap Him (compare Mark 12:15). There is no hesitation in identifying the *first of all the commandments* as Jesus quotes the opening words of Deuteronomy 6:4. This is often called "the Shema" (the Hebrew word for "hear"). This is ancient Israel's foundational confession. As evidence of its centrality, some devout Jews in Jesus' time recited the Shema twice a day.

Just before voicing the Shema to the Israelites, Moses charged them to follow God as they entered the promised land. This included fearing God and keeping His commands, so that things might go well with them (Deuteronomy 6:1–3). The Shema proclaims God's singularity.

How to Say It

Adonai (Hebrew)	Ad-owe-*nye*.
Deuteronomy	Due-ter-*ahn*-uh-me.
Diaspora	Dee-*as*-puh-ruh.
Elohim (Hebrew)	El-o-*heem*.
Herodians	Heh-*roe*-dee-unz.
pantheon	*pan*-thee-on.
Pharisees	*Fair*-ih-seez.
Sadducees	*Sad*-you-seez.
Shema (Hebrew)	Shih-*mah*.
Yahweh (Hebrew)	*Yah*-weh.

Following the Shema, Moses reminded the people of how God had delivered them from Egyptian bondage. This deliverance emphasized the importance of remembering the Lord their God and keeping His commands (Deuteronomy 6:12–25).

The Shema is the foundation of obedience to God's commands. There is not a multiplicity of gods (a pantheon; compare Deuteronomy 6:14). The one, true God has more than one designation in the Hebrew language (*Elohim, Yahweh,* and *Adonai*), but He alone is God.

30. And thou shalt love the Lord thy God with all thy heart, and with all thy soul, and with all thy mind, and with all thy strength: this is the first commandment.

Jesus continues the quotation as He moves to Deuteronomy 6:5. We note that this is not a second commandment since the phrase *this is the first commandment* serves as the second bookend to the one that began Mark 12:29. The word *mind* is not in the original "with all" list, and so it has been added by Jesus (compare Matthew 22:37; Luke 10:27). While each of these aspects of the human person is distinct and unique, they also overlap in various ways. These terms collectively emphasize the whole person. This realization is more important than carefully defining each one to distinguish it from the others. The primary theme of Deuteronomy 6:5; Matthew 22:37; Mark 12:30; and Luke 10:27 is just this: we are to devote our whole selves, everything we are and have, toward loving God.

> **What Do You Think?**
> What examples in your life point toward a life wholly devoted to loving God?
>
> **Digging Deeper**
> Name characters from Scripture whom you admire for their devotion.

All In

Before I met my husband, I went on a few dates with a guy in college. I worked at the college bookstore at the time, and he would often come in to talk to me while I worked. Sometimes, he'd purchase a piece of chocolate and slip it to me before he left. I thought he was wonderful.

Before long, I realized it had been quite a few days since he'd called me or stopped by my work. Just as I began to think the relationship was over, he came into the bookstore to chat and slip me another piece of chocolate. I was enthralled once again. Soon, however, the pattern of silence continued. The roller-coaster ride of emotions involved was difficult to navigate, and I finally told him it was over. It became evident that he was not "all in."

Jesus said that the greatest commandment was to be all in regarding our love for God. In the past, I have been like that college guy, stopping in to talk to God and slip Him a little praise once in a while. But He is worthy of all the love of our hearts, minds, souls, and strength! Are you "all in" in your love for the Lord? How will you show Him today that you are? —B. R.

31. And the second is like, namely this, Thou shalt love thy neighbour as thyself. There is none other commandment greater than these.

The scribe asks which commandment is first. But Jesus provides two answers. While distinct, the second commandment is intrinsically connected to the first. One cannot truly *love thy neighbour as thyself* without first loving God. In practice, they form one commandment. The intrinsic connection is seen in the fact that our fellow human beings have been created in the image of God, just as we have been (see 1 John 4:7–12, 20).

Jesus' statement here matches Leviticus 19:18. Within the book of Leviticus, this commandment appears as part of the Holiness Code, which is found in Leviticus 17–26. Some commentators suggest that Leviticus 19:18 serves as a kind of summary statement for the Holiness Code. To love one's neighbor is to treat them with the respect and holiness demanded in the legislation recorded in Leviticus 17–26.

Together, these two commandments provide the foundation for the rest of God's commands. Those who fail at keeping these two have no hope of fulfilling the rest of the law. An anecdote notes an occasion when a Jew known as Hillel the Elder (lived about 40 BC–AD 10) was challenged by a Gentile to summarize the entirety of the Law of Moses in a single sentence. His reported response was, "What you yourself hate, do not do to your neighbor; this is the whole Law, the rest is commentary. Go and learn it."

Inherent in the command of love toward our neighbors is to love them as we love ourselves. Rather than grounds for selfishness, love of self here carries the sense of seeking our own good (compare Ephesians 5:28–29). We don't harm ourselves; we take care of ourselves. Just so, we ought to treat others as we would want to be treated (Matthew 7:12; Luke 6:31). When Jesus gives this charge in His Sermon on the Mount, He adds that this is a summary of the law and prophets (Matthew 7:12).

What Do You Think?

Which part of Jesus' twofold answer do you find most difficult to obey?

Digging Deeper

In what ways are the two parts of the greatest commandment interconnected?

C. Expansion of the Reply (vv. 32–33)

32–33. And the scribe said unto him, Well, Master, thou hast said the truth: for there is one God; and there is none other but he: And to love him with all the heart, and with all the understanding, and with all the soul, and with all the strength, and to love his neighbour as himself, is more than all whole burnt offerings and sacrifices.

While agreeing with and restating the answer Jesus gives, the scribe adds something to what Jesus said: the man claims that loving God and neighbor is more important than *all whole burnt offerings and sacrifices* of the Levitical system. Jesus' declaration, "I will have mercy, and not sacrifice" (Matthew 9:13; 12:7, quoting Hosea 6:6), wasn't intended to suggest doing away with the Levitical system but to ensure that people understood which command was relatively more important.

A relativizing of the sacrificial system makes sure that it doesn't take precedence over loving God and loving neighbor. There was always a danger of inappropriately prioritizing the temple and its sacrifices (Isaiah 1:11–17; Jeremiah 7:4–11; etc.). During Jesus' final week, He condemns the Pharisees and scribes for missing "the weightier matters of the law" (Matthew 23:23).

What Do You Think?

How does one's motive affect the meaning of one's actions?

Digging Deeper

Whose actions in Scripture came from poor motives? Whose came from good motives?

D. Evidence of Wisdom (v. 34)

34. And when Jesus saw that he answered discreetly, he said unto him, Thou art not far from the kingdom of God. And no man after that durst ask him any question.

Jesus is apparently impressed with the scribe's answer and affirms what the man perceives. As Jesus informs him that he is *not far from the kingdom of God,* Jesus is not saying that the man is *in* the kingdom of God. He is near to it but not yet there. This implies that he still lacks something. He has grasped something essential, and he very well may be closer to the kingdom than others within earshot.

The series of questions the religious leaders asked Jesus comes to an end with this dialogue. Jesus' response is profound and unassailable. Those looking to undermine Him are silenced.

II. Right Action

(James 2:14–17)

Verses prior to our printed passage tie this section of the lesson to the passage above from Mark 12. James 2 begins with a discussion of favoritism. James indicts his readers for showing preference for the rich over the poor, even citing the "royal law" as Jesus did in Mark 12:31 (Leviticus 19:18). James claims his readers will do well to "love thy neighbour as thyself" (James 2:8). On the contrary, if they show favoritism, they are lawbreakers, failing to love their neighbors as themselves (2:9). This discussion continues as the writer digs deeper to drive home the points just made in 2:1–13.

A. Rhetorical Question (v. 14)

14. What doth it profit, my brethren, though a man say he hath faith, and have not works? can faith save him?

James raises two rhetorical questions that introduce the larger question of when faith becomes ineffective. When is faith unable to save? James says there is no profit in *faith* when it does not have works—when it lies inactive. As Paul says in Galatians 5:6, the highest priority is faith working through love. A faith without works is a faith that is failing to love God and our neighbors. Examples of such works follow.

> **What Do You Think?**
> In what ways does this passage from James challenge your understanding of faith?
> **Digging Deeper**
> How does Hebrews 11 inform your understanding of James 2:14?

B. Obvious Example (vv. 15–16)

15. If a brother or sister be naked, and destitute of daily food.

This verse begins a second hypothetical example in this chapter. In the first one, in James 2:2–4, the writer condemned favoritism based on economic status. His second example focuses on someone in abject poverty. More specifically, this is someone in the congregation—*a brother or sister*—who is without adequate clothing or food. What does saving faith do in such a situation?

16. And one of you say unto them, Depart in peace, be ye warmed and filled; notwithstanding ye give them not those things which are needful to the body; what doth it profit?

James highlights the sort of callousness of heart that neglecting the poor entails. The example is so embarrassing; it's difficult to imagine such a reality being an issue among believers. Yet this seems to be the situation among those to whom James writes his letter. The rich are honored, but the poor are despised. The rich are loved, but the poor are neglected. Instead of showing love as they ought, certain people have become lawbreakers while ingratiating themselves to the rich (James 2:6–9).

The apostle John writes similarly (1 John 3:17–18). James calls the second commandment as noted in Mark 12:31, above, the "royal law" (James 2:8). Honoring the royal law means loving others enough to include feeding and clothing brothers and sisters in need. When we fail to do so, we fail to love our neighbors. Faith that does not result in such works does not *profit*. Another way to say that comes next.

> **What Do You Think?**
> Where is your faith, or your community's life of faith, characterized by a lack of action?
> **Digging Deeper**
> What specific opportunities exist to shift in the direction of a more active faith?

C. Confident Assertion (v. 17)

17. Even so faith, if it hath not works, is dead, being alone.

Here, James offers an initial concluding statement in response to his rhetorical question in James 2:14, above. Faith that is void of good *works* is not authentic faith. Such a faith, *being alone*, is *dead*.

It is important not to misread James here. He is not contradicting what is affirmed elsewhere in the New Testament, namely, that we are saved by grace through faith—not by works, as the apostle Paul establishes in Ephesians 2:8–9. Christianity is not based on salvation by faith plus works, but is instead a system that requires a faith that produces (or results in) works. In other words, salvation is not "F + W," but is "F → W."

We were created to do good works, "which God hath before ordained that we should walk in them" (Ephesians 2:10). What Paul stresses in this passage to the Ephesians is that our salvation is not of our own doing, but a gift of God. Rather than contradicting this, James adds clarity to what that faith entails. It is a faith that is alive (rather than *dead*) and united to good works (not *alone*). James 2:26 restates these ideas, driving home this point as crucial: "For as the body without the spirit is dead, so faith without works is dead also."

Having an active faith is a theme throughout the book of James. He charges his readers to be not just hearers but doers (James 1:22–25). He expresses that wisdom and understanding are evident in deeds done in humility and characterized by mercy and good fruit (3:13, 17). Failing to do the good we know we ought to do is sin (4:17). He highlights prayer as an example of faith working itself out in action (5:13–16).

More Than Just Bumper Stickers

Our church in Mississippi gives out bumper stickers to all of its members. The bumper stickers include the church's name and this declaration: "We love people." I have one on the back of my car. It's easy to spot other members of our church out on the roads when we all proudly display the same sticker on our vehicles.

That phrase "We love people" is a mission statement for our church. But the statement alone does not mean anything unless it is followed by action. The way our church loves people is by serving them. For example, we feed hundreds of food-insecure children every summer through our lunch initiative. We find ways to love the service members of our community by showing up with meals and gifts of appreciation. We clean the bathrooms in our local schools and offer snacks and treats to the teachers several times a month. Our hope is that our neighbors will know we love them as we seek to love them well.

Just displaying the bumper stickers on our cars is not enough; a hollow, inactive faith is a contradiction in terms. We have to prove the validity of our faith with meaningful, loving action. —B. R.

Conclusion

A. The Most Important Thing

The Law of Moses established many specific things that God desired of His people living under that covenant. But the people were pleasing to God only when those required actions were motivated and accompanied by love for God and love for those created in His image. Having these priorities rightly aligned enables us yet today to live rightly in other, subsidiary matters. Jesus made this abundantly clear in Mark 12.

Visual for Lessons 9 & 13. *Point to this visual as you conclude, tying together both Scripture passages in this lesson.*

Similarly, James 2 reveals that as critical as faith is, it means nothing if it is void of proper action. Bringing these passages together, true faith and right response to God comes down to love lived out daily.

When Jesus was asked what the greatest commandment was, He gave a twofold reply. That's because one cannot be the case without the other. The two replies are interlinked in an inseparable way. We cannot love God without loving our neighbor, and we cannot love our neighbor properly without loving God first (1 John 3:16–17). True faith is expressed in such good works.

To love God and neighbor is the best sacrifice we offer to God; it is the gift of our whole selves to God and to others. We offer ourselves as living sacrifices worked out in love for God and others—even our enemies (Romans 12:1, 9–11, 20–21).

B. Prayer

Blessed are You, Father, for pouring Your love upon us through Jesus' payment of sin's price on the cross. Fill us with Your love that our whole selves might love You and love our neighbors. We pray in the name of Jesus. Amen.

C. Thought to Remember

Love God and love others.

Involvement Learning

Enhance your lesson with KJV Bible Student *(from your curriculum supplier) and the reproducible activity page (at www.standardlesson.com or in the back of the* KJV Standard Lesson Commentary Deluxe Edition*).*

Into the Lesson

Write the words *Love* and *Faith* as headers on the board. Ask participants what comes to mind for each word and write their responses on the board. Lead a whole-class discussion on love and faith and the relationship between the two for a believer. To encourage discussion, ask, "How has your faith been strengthened by loving others?"

Alternative. Distribute copies of the "Faith and Love" exercise from the activity page, which you can download. Have learners work in pairs to complete as indicated. After calling time, discuss answers as a whole class.

After either activity, lead into Bible study by saying, "Today, we will study Jesus' teaching regarding the most important commandments: the directives to love God and love others. Then we will turn to the book of James to see how our actions demonstrate our faith in and love for God."

Into the Word

Distribute a handout (you create) with the following questions for a true/false pre-test. Allow one minute to complete with closed Bibles:

1–One of the scribes approached Jesus with a question.
2–The "first" commandment is "Love thy neighbour as thyself."
3–Jesus said that loving God and one's neighbor as oneself is not more important than burnt offerings and sacrifices.
4–James says that if faith lacks works, it is "dead."

[Answers: 1–true; 2–false; 3–false; 4–true]

After the minute is up, ask a volunteer to read Mark 12:28–34 and James 2:14–17 aloud so that participants can check their responses.

Divide the class into two groups: **God and Neighbor Group** and **Faith and Works Group.** Distribute handouts (you create) of the following prompts and questions to each group for discussion.

God and Neighbor Group. Read Mark 12:28–34. 1–What is the significance of God's people being commanded to love the Lord God with their heart, soul, mind, and strength? 2–Summarize the relationship between loving God and loving others.

Faith and Works Group. Read James 2:14–17. 1–What is the significance of James's description of faith without works as "dead"? 2–Summarize the relationship between faith and works.

After calling time, reconvene the class and ask a volunteer from each group to summarize their group's response. Conclude by asking volunteers to summarize the connections between faith, love, and good works.

Into Life

Write on the board the following questions:

1. *What are the immediate needs of our surrounding community?*
2. *What groups or organizations in our community are already addressing these needs?*
3. *How can our congregation join with those groups or organizations?*

Place learners in small groups and distribute a sheet of paper and pen to each group. Ask them to discuss each question and write their answers on the paper. Then direct each group to write a proposal for how the class can see and address the immediate needs of the surrounding community.

After 15 minutes of group work, ask a representative from each group to present their proposal to the class. After each group has presented, have the entire class vote on which proposal the class should pursue in the upcoming weeks. Nominate a representative to bring the proposal before the congregation's leadership for support and guidance.

Alternative. Distribute the "Plan of Action" exercise from the activity page. Have class members work on it in pairs. If time is short, use the exercise as a take-home activity.

Social Teachings of the Church

Special Features

Lessons

Unit 1: Fulfilling Our Obligations to Neighbors

Unit 2: Fulfilling Our Obligations to Family and Community

Unit 3: Fulfilling Our Obligations to God and Society

Quarterly Quiz

Use these questions as a pretest or as a review. The answers are on page iv of This Quarter in the Word.

Lesson 1

1. Daniel defiled himself with the king's food. T/F. *Daniel 1:8*

2. Godliness is profitable for _______ things. *1 Timothy 4:8*

Lesson 2

1. God directs the Israelites to be openhanded with the poor. T/F. *Deuteronomy 15:8*

2. Jesus says, "I was an hungred, and ye gave me no _____." *Matthew 25:42*

Lesson 3

1. Simon Peter was in which city when Cornelius sent for him? (Caesarea, Joppa, Jericho) *Acts 10:32*

2. Those who belong to Christ are both Abraham's seed and _____. *Galatians 3:29*

Lesson 4

1. Isaiah prophecies that in the last days, people will beat their "swords into ______." *Isaiah 2:4*

2. In God, we "live, and move, and have our ______." *Acts 17:28*

Lesson 5

1. Paul teaches that if Christ has not been raised, then our faith is _________. *1 Corinthians 15:17*

2. What instrument will sound when the dead are raised? (flute, lyre, trumpet) *1 Corinthians 15:52*

Lesson 6

1. Paul teaches that "higher powers" have been ________ by God. *Romans 13:1*

2. How are believers to respond to "every ordinance of man"? (resist, punish, submit) *1 Peter 2:13*

Lesson 7

1. Jesus placed what or whom "in the midst of them"? (seed, chair, child) *Mark 9:36*

2. One must receive the kingdom of God "as a little child." T/F. *Mark 10:15*

Lesson 8

1. Israel was commanded to "love the Lord thy God" with the totality of which parts? (choose three: heart, soul, energy, might) *Deuteronomy 6:5*

2. In marriage, a man and a woman become "______ flesh." *Matthew 19:5*

Lesson 9

1. The Lord commanded Jonah to go to which "great city"? (Jericho, Joppa, Nineveh) *Jonah 3:2*

2. Which creature caused the shade plant to wither? (whale, bird, worm) *Jonah 4:7*

Lesson 10

1. God commands, "Seven days shalt thou labor, and do all thy work." T/F. *Exodus 20:9*

2. Which designation does Paul give to Thessalonians who were "disorderly, working not at all"? (lazy, helpless, busybodies) *2 Thessalonians 3:11*

Lesson 11

1. God told the Israelites to leave portions of the harvest in the field. T/F. *Deuteronomy 24:19*

2. The apostle Paul teaches believers to be "rich in good ______." *1 Timothy 6:18*

Lesson 12

1. David and his companions ate the shewbread in the days of which priest? (Abiathar, Zechariah, Nathan) *Mark 2:26*

2. According to Jesus, the Sabbath was made for man. T/F. *Mark 2:27*

Lesson 13

1. Jesus promises, "I am with you _____, even unto the end of the world." *Matthew 28:20*

2. Believers are to provoke one another toward love and good ______. *Hebrews 10:24*

Quarter at a Glance

by Brenner S. Carlson

God instructs His people to relate in particular ways to their friends, neighbors, family, governmental structures, and even the structured rhythm of our days. He cares about how we treat our bodies, what we consume, and how we use our time. This quarter contemplates a kingdom perspective regarding our responsibilities, relationships, and commitments.

Obligations to Neighbors

The first unit of lessons explores the relationship between God's people and their neighbors inside and outside the church. This unit begins by studying the Israelites' exile in Babylon and looking at Daniel's exercise of faith in a hostile environment (Daniel 1:8–17; see lesson 1). The lesson also considers mental and spiritual health alongside care for our physical bodies (1 Timothy 4:7–8).

Other lessons in this unit teach that Christian love is not simply an intellectual exercise but an intentional action. For example, God's people love others when they care for the poor, welcome others in Christ, and look forward to days of peace (Deuteronomy 15:4–11; Acts 10:9–15, 30–35; Isaiah 2:2–4; see lessons 2–4). Jesus' teaching breaks social expectations as He invites His followers to extend their hands to all people, not flinching at anyone who might grasp them in return (Matthew 25:42–45, lesson 2).

Obligations to Family and Community

The second unit examines the scope of the Christian life from its foundations in Jesus' resurrection to its application in the household. We belong to God through faith in Jesus' life, death, and resurrection. Therefore, God's way of doing things shapes our households, allegiances, and submission to authority (Mark 12:17; Romans 13:6–8; 1 Peter 2:13–17; see lesson 6).

God values children. They model Christian values and perspective (Mark 9:36–37, 42; 10:13–16; see lesson 7). Jesus asks us to learn from them and diligently instruct them in God's ways (Deuteronomy 6:3–9; see lesson 8). Our households are strong when we love God with the whole of our lives and honor the marriage covenant (Matthew 19:3–9). God calls his people to implement His commandments and values, which alter our attitudes toward children, our spouses, and governmental structures' power, authority, and prestige.

Obligations to God and Society

The final unit studies the mission of God's people in life and society. The unit launches with the story of the prophet Jonah, whose reluctant evangelism to the people of Nineveh prompts a conversation with God about who is worthy of receiving the good news (Jonah 3:1–5, 4:6–11; see lesson 9). Learners are encouraged to consider how to reach out to neighbors from various cultural backgrounds.

> *We belong to God through faith in Jesus' life, death, and resurrection.*

God created humans as social beings who carry out His work (Genesis 2:15). Work is good and necessary for a fulfilled life in God. The unit discusses work-rest balance through the topic of Sabbath-keeping. This study also weighs our call to work for and support our communities rather than parasitizing them for individual gain (Exodus 20:9; Mark 2:18–28; 2 Thessalonians 3:6–12; see lesson 10).

God calls His followers to provide for the needy, assist the widow and orphan, and encourage one another as we gather for worship and fellowship (Deuteronomy 24:14-21; Hebrews 10:22–25; see lessons 11 and 13). The Christian life is neither boundlessly relaxed ease nor endless labor (Mark 2:27; see lesson 12). God urges us toward mission, labor, justice, service, rest, worship, and community as healthy rhythms of life.

Get the Setting

by Joshua Seth Houston

Alexander the Great's conquest in the third century BC spread Greek culture throughout the world. After his death, the Roman Empire became the dominant world power, controlling much of region around the Mediterranean Sea. Culturally, however, Greek philosophy and religion remained prominent. This period, therefore, is called the Greco-Roman period.

The Greco-Roman world was, by God's standards, immoral. It celebrated sexual immorality, encouraged power attainment by any means necessary, and perpetuated social injustice.

Sexual Immorality

The Greco-Roman world was notorious for sexual immorality. Same-sex relationships were common. Relationships were often abusive. Powerful men frequently had multiple partners, and sexual relationships with enslaved people were normative.

However, God introduces a sexual ethic for His church—an ethic different from the world's. The sexual ethic presented in the New Testament honored sexuality as a gift to be enjoyed within the confines of heterosexual marriage. The apostle Paul encourages believers to "flee from sexual immorality" and warns that those who dishonor this ethic will face consequences (1 Corinthians 6:9–10, 18). Jesus calls His followers to a high standard of purity and regard for human dignity.

Several centuries later, the sexual ethic of the New Testament influenced cultural norms and became law under the emperor Justinian I (reigned AD 527–565). He declared male homosexuality and pederasty illegal. During the same era, prostitution diminished.

Power

The relationship between religion and government is complex. Ancient rulers often paraded themselves as oppressors and power-hungry tyrants. The Roman emperor, Nero (reigned AD 54–68), allegedly killed his mother, first wife, and second wife, all to gain or maintain power. Jesus acknowledged the tendency of Gentile rulers to "exercise dominion over" their subjects (Matthew 20:25). The Jews were not immune to this either. In 172 BC, Menelaus—a man outside Aaron's lineage—bribed his way into the high priesthood to gain political authority (2 Maccabees 4:23–29).

In His teachings, Jesus emphasized a different approach to power. He taught that the first shall be last and the last shall be first (Matthew 20:16). Instead of striving for control, Jesus' followers acknowledge Him as Lord and submit to His leadership and command (Revelation 17:14).

Social Injustice

Greco-Roman class structures ranged from senatorial to enslaved people. Slavery occurred for a variety of reasons. Some people became enslaved through war, while others sold themselves into slavery to pay off debts. Scholars estimate up to 40 percent of the Roman population in the first century were enslaved.

Slavery was normative in the first century, but that does not mean God condoned it. God created all humans in His image and calls us to treat one another fairly. Jesus taught that the second greatest commandment is to love others as ourselves (Matthew 22:39). The apostle Paul taught the Galatian church that "there is neither bond nor free . . . for ye are all one in Christ Jesus" (Galatians 3:28).

God calls His people to behave differently than the secular culture, whether Greco-Roman or modern-day (Ephesians 4:17). First-century Christians understood they belonged to a kingdom not of this world (John 18:36). To maintain citizenship in this kingdom, God asked them to reject the unholiness of their society. To do this, they dedicated themselves to Scripture and lived according to its standards (Acts 2:42). We too are called to keep ourselves "unspotted from the world" (James 1:27).

Mon, May 18	**A Feast of Finest Wine**	John 2:1–11
Tue, May 19	**Celebrate God's Blessings**	Genesis 21:1–8
Wed, May 20	**Playing Children Signal God's Grace**	Zechariah 8:1–5
Thu, May 21	**Release from Human Rules**	Colossians 2:16–23
Fri, May 22	**A Time for Feasting and Joy**	Matthew 11:7–11, 16–19
Sat, May 23	**Rejoice and Be Glad**	Jeremiah 31:10–14
Sun, May 24	**The Lord of the Sabbath**	Mark 2:18–28
Mon, May 25	**Let Us Sing to the Lord**	Psalm 95
Tue, May 26	**Gladness in the House of the Lord**	Psalm 122
Wed, May 27	**Members of the Body of Christ**	Romans 12:1–8
Thu, May 28	**A Holy Day of Rejoicing**	Nehemiah 8:9–12
Fri, May 29	**Restoring Healthy Relationships**	Matthew 18:15–20
Sat, May 30	**Fellowship Through Common Property**	Acts 4:32–37
Sun, May 31	**Inspiring Love and Good Deeds**	Hebrews 10:19–25

Answers to the Quarterly Quiz on page 226

Lesson 1—1. False. 2. all. **Lesson 2**—1. True. 2. meat. **Lesson 3**—1. Joppa. 2. heirs. **Lesson 4**—1. plowshares. 2. being. **Lesson 5**—1. vain. 2. trumpet. **Lesson 6**—1. ordained. 2. submit. **Lesson 7**—1. child. 2. True. **Lesson 8**—1. heart, soul, might. 2. one. **Lesson 9**—1. Nineveh. 2. worm. **Lesson 10**—1. False. 2. busybodies. **Lesson 11**—1. True. 2. works. **Lesson 12**—1. Abiathar. 2. True. **Lesson 13**—1. always. 2. works.

This Quarter in the Word

Mon, Mar. 2	**Work and Discipline**	Proverbs 12:1–2, 10–14
Tue, Mar. 3	**The Temple of the Body**	1 Corinthians 6:12–20
Wed, Mar. 4	**The Discipline of Right Choices**	1 Corinthians 9:19–27
Thu, Mar. 5	**God Is Always with Me**	Psalm 139:1–12
Fri, Mar. 6	**Fearfully and Wonderfully Made**	Psalm 139:13–24
Sat, Mar. 7	**The Superior Training in Godliness**	1 Timothy 4:7–12
Sun, Mar. 8	**Pure in Mind and Spirit**	Daniel 1:8–17
Mon, Mar. 9	**God Will Defend the Needy**	Psalm 12
Tue, Mar. 10	**Do Not Be Afraid to Give**	Luke 12:13–21, 33–34
Wed, Mar. 11	**Treat the Neighbor with Justice**	Leviticus 19:11–18
Thu, Mar. 12	**The Royal Law of Love**	James 2:8–13
Fri, Mar. 13	**Everyone Is Our Neighbor**	Luke 10:25–37
Sat, Mar. 14	**Compassion for Those in Need**	Deuteronomy 15:4–11
Sun, Mar. 15	**Seeing Christ in Those Around Us**	Matthew 25:41–45
Mon, Mar. 16	**Souls Bound Together**	1 Samuel 18:1–5
Tue, Mar. 17	**Abide in God's Love**	1 John 4:7–16
Wed, Mar. 18	**Loving God and Each Other**	1 John 4:17–21
Thu, Mar. 19	**All Peoples Will Worship God**	Isaiah 56:3–8
Fri, Mar. 20	**Living Together in Unity**	Psalms 133–134
Sat, Mar. 21	**Children of God Through Faith**	Galatians 3:25–29
Sun, Mar. 22	**God Accepts Us All**	Acts 10:9–15, 30–35

Mon, Mar. 23	**A Kingdom Not of This World**	John 18:28–38
Tue, Mar. 24	**The Lord's Peace**	Numbers 6:22–26
Wed, Mar. 25	**God Is Exalted Among the Nations**	Psalm 46
Thu, Mar. 26	**God Guides the Destiny of Nations**	Amos 9:7–12
Fri, Mar. 27	**Glory and Honor of the Nations**	Revelation 21:21–27
Sat, Mar. 28	**The Nations Shall Gather to God**	Isaiah 2:1–5
Sun, Mar. 29	**All Peoples Are Kin**	Acts 17:22–28
Mon, Mar. 30	**Many Dwellings in the Father's House**	John 14:1–4
Tue, Mar. 31	**Encouraging Words of Hope**	1 Thessalonians 4:13–18
Wed, Apr. 1	**I Know That My Redeemer Lives**	Job 19:23–27
Thu, Apr. 2	**Awake and Sing for Joy**	Isaiah 26:12–19
Fri, Apr. 3	**Give Thanks to the Lord**	Psalm 118:15–24
Sat, Apr. 4	**Christ Is Risen from the Dead**	1 Corinthians 15:13–20
Sun, Apr. 5	**Death Is Swallowed Up**	1 Corinthians 15:50–58
Mon, Apr. 6	**Wise and Righteous Counsel**	Proverbs 11:3–6, 8–11, 14
Tue, Apr. 7	**Our Ultimate Allegiance Is to God**	Acts 5:26–32
Wed, Apr. 8	**Godly Leaders Will Give an Account**	Hebrews 13:16–21
Thu, Apr. 9	**Just Rulers Fear God**	2 Samuel 23:1–7
Fri, Apr. 10	**The Ways of a Godly King**	Deuteronomy 17:14–20
Sat, Apr. 11	**The Things That Belong to God**	Mark 12:13–17
Sun, Apr. 12	**Show Honor, Love, and Righteousness**	1 Peter 2:13–17
Mon, Apr. 13	**A Heritage from the Lord**	Psalm 127
Tue, Apr. 14	**My Child, Be Eager to Learn**	Proverbs 2:1–6
Wed, Apr. 15	**Do Not Despise the Little Ones**	Matthew 18:7–14
Thu, Apr. 16	**Obedience That Is Acceptable Before God**	Colossians 3:20–25
Fri, Apr. 17	**Praise from Infants**	Matthew 21:8–9, 15–17
Sat, Apr. 18	**Good Deeds of Children**	Proverbs 20:7–12
Sun, Apr. 19	**Let the Little Children Come**	Mark 9:33–37; 10:13–16

Mon, Apr. 20	**By Wisdom a House Is Built**	Proverbs 24:1–6
Tue, Apr. 21	**Growing in Divine and Human Favor**	Luke 2:40–52
Wed, Apr. 22	**Submit to One Another**	Ephesians 5:21–33
Thu, Apr. 23	**Choose Whom You Will Serve**	Joshua 24:15–21
Fri, Apr. 24	**We Will Serve the Lord**	Joshua 24:22–28
Sat, Apr. 25	**An Inseparable Union**	Matthew 19:3–9
Sun, Apr. 26	**Teach Your Children God's Ways**	Deuteronomy 6:3–9
Mon, Apr. 27	**Seek the Welfare of the City**	Jeremiah 29:3–7
Tue, Apr. 28	**God's Own People**	1 Peter 2:4–12
Wed, Apr. 29	**Pray for Those in Authority**	1 Timothy 2:1–8
Thu, Apr. 30	**God Is Sovereign over the Nations**	Psalm 33:10–22
Fri, May 1	**Our Citizenship Is in Heaven**	Philippians 3:17–21
Sat, May 2	**A Season of National Repentance**	Jonah 3:1–5
Sun, May 3	**God's Compassion for All**	Jonah 4:6–11
Mon, May 4	**God Ordains Productive Work**	Genesis 2:4–10, 15
Tue, May 5	**Commit Your Work to the Lord**	Proverbs 16:1–3, 8–9
Wed, May 6	**Caring for the Work of God's Hands**	Psalm 8
Thu, May 7	**The Sabbath Is a Perpetual Covenant**	Exodus 31:12–17
Fri, May 8	**Working on the Sabbath**	John 5:8–11, 16–17
Sat, May 9	**Supporting Oneself and Others**	Acts 20:31–35
Sun, May 10	**Work Quietly and Diligently**	2 Thessalonians 3:6–12
Mon, May 11	**Work Diligently Before God**	Proverbs 10:1–5, 15–16
Tue, May 12	**The Workers and Their Wages**	Matthew 20:1–16
Wed, May 13	**God Demands Justice for All**	Amos 5:6–15
Thu, May 14	**Wait Patiently for God's Justice**	James 5:1–11
Fri, May 15	**Serving with Enthusiasm**	Colossians 3:12–17
Sat, May 16	**Justice for the Worker**	Deuteronomy 24:14–21
Sun, May 17	**Contentment, Humility, and Generosity**	1 Timothy 6:6–8, 17–19

Chart Feature

New Testament Epistles: *Highlights from This Quarter*

Epistle	Writer	Occasion	Date
Romans	Paul	Written in anticipation of a visit to Rome; Paul requests the house churches of Rome to collectively support his planned journey to Spain	AD 57–58
1 Corinthians	Paul	Written from Ephesus in anticipation of Paul's return to Corinth, after he receives word of divisions and selfishness among the believers living there; addresses questions received in a letter from the Corinthian church	AD 55–57
Galatians	Paul	Written to address false teachers who claim that circumcision is required for Gentile converts joining the family of faith	AD 48–49 (some arguing mid-50s)
Ephesians	Paul	Written while Paul is imprisoned in Rome; shares many themes with Colossians	AD 60–63
1 Thessalonians	Paul	Written to commend the young Thessalonian church for enduring persecution; addresses questions about ethics and eschatology	AD 50–51
2 Thessalonians	Paul	Written to address confusion about the day of the Lord and the need to hold to the teachings of God	AD 50–51
1 Timothy	Paul	Written to encourage Paul's protégé, Timothy, to stand firm in his leadership against false teaching	AD 63–65
Hebrews	Unknown	A sermon calling followers of Christ to understand Jesus' sacrifice as the fulfillment of promises to God's people	AD 67–70 (perhaps even later)
James	James, the half-brother of Jesus	Written from Jerusalem to encourage Jewish Christians scattered throughout the world to put faith into action	AD 45–62
1 Peter	Peter	Written to believers who endure persecution as strangers and aliens in a world that does not recognize Jesus as Lord	AD 60–69

*Dating the occasional letters of the New Testament is often difficult and subject to revision as new information emerges. The dates on this chart represent the best approximation from scriptural and other historical evidence.

Sheet 5—Spring 2026, *Adult Resources*, Standard Lesson Quarterly® Curriculum

Lesson 5

The Best Lesson I Ever Taught

Teacher Tips by Ronald L. Nickelson

It turned out to be the best Bible lesson I ever taught. How do I know it was the best? Because as class ended, one of the participants rushed up to me and exclaimed, "That was the best class ever!" What follows is a description of the teaching methods I utilized during that hour of study.

The What and the Why

The lesson was on Matthew 7, and I customized it to address a specific need. Church members were frequently misusing Matthew 7:1, which says, "Judge not, that ye be not judged." Our assumptions made addressing sinful behaviors difficult. I focused the lesson on both biblical interpretation and application.

The Preparation

First, I created the handout below from relevant New Testament passages found within the lesson. The wavy lines down the middle were to help participants avoid the impression that every passage on the left had a counterpart directly across from it on the right. Second, I printed the same passages on index cards and gave one card to each person in the class. Tip: Always feel free to customize Standard Lesson content to your specialized needs.

DON'T JUDGE	DO JUDGE
Matthew 7:1–3 (Luke 6:37)	Matthew 7:15–20
Romans 2:1–4	Matthew 12:33
Romans 14:1–4, 10, 13	John 7:24
1 Corinthians 4:5	1 Corinthians 5:12b, 13b
1 Corinthians 5:12a, 13a	1 Corinthians 6:1–6
2 Corinthians 10:7	1 Corinthians 10:14–15
Colossians 2:16	1 Corinthians 11:13
James 4:11–12	2 Timothy 3:1–6

Two Methods, One Mistake

My initial teaching method was reading aloud. I had participants take turns looking up the passages on the index cards and then reading them to the class. I naïvely believed we would all instantly adopt the nuanced biblical viewpoint(s) on "judging" present in the texts and abandon our prior assumptions and understanding. My mistake!

The difficulty in this lesson arose specifically around the verb *judge*. I quickly realized my simplistic "read and believe" strategy wasn't working. I needed to start asking questions. An example interchange went like this:

Me: When you punish your child for misbehaving or violating rules, aren't you judging that child?

Participant: No. What the child did is a statement of fact, not a judgment.

Me: But doesn't that fail to distinguish what the child did (a statement of fact) from your judgment that the behavior was wrong?

The Outcome

When objections and disagreement arose throughout the discussion, I met students with further questions. These questions were designed to make participants think, causing them to wrestle with the content in new ways. And wrestling is the ultimate value of every lesson.

To customize lessons yourself, first identify the needs of your class. Then, brainstorm fun ways to interact with the material or visuals you might create. (You can purchase beautifully designed lesson visuals from www.standardlesson.com.) Additionally, ask yourself questions about the material as you prepare: what attracts, confuses, or challenges you?

March 8
Lesson 1 (KJV)

Watching Our Consumption

Devotional Reading: Titus 1:5–9
Background Scripture: Daniel 1:8–20; 1 Corinthians 9:19–27; 1 Timothy 4:7–12

Daniel 1:8–17

8 But Daniel purposed in his heart that he would not defile himself with the portion of the king's meat, nor with the wine which he drank: therefore he requested of the prince of the eunuchs that he might not defile himself.

9 Now God had brought Daniel into favour and tender love with the prince of the eunuchs.

10 And the prince of the eunuchs said unto Daniel, I fear my lord the king, who hath appointed your meat and your drink: for why should he see your faces worse liking than the children which are of your sort? then shall ye make me endanger my head to the king.

11 Then said Daniel to Melzar, whom the prince of the eunuchs had set over Daniel, Hananiah, Mishael, and Azariah,

12 Prove thy servants, I beseech thee, ten days; and let them give us pulse to eat, and water to drink.

13 Then let our countenances be looked upon before thee, and the countenance of the children that eat of the portion of the king's meat: and as thou seest, deal with thy servants.

14 So he consented to them in this matter, and proved them ten days.

15 And at the end of ten days their countenances appeared fairer and fatter in flesh than all the children which did eat the portion of the king's meat.

16 Thus Melzar took away the portion of their meat, and the wine that they should drink; and gave them pulse.

17 As for these four children, God gave them knowledge and skill in all learning and wisdom: and Daniel had understanding in all visions and dreams.

1 Timothy 4:7–8

7 But refuse profane and old wives' fables, and exercise thyself rather unto godliness.

8 For bodily exercise profiteth little: but godliness is profitable unto all things, having promise of the life that now is, and of that which is to come.

Key Text

Exercise thyself rather unto godliness. For bodily exercise profiteth little: but godliness is profitable unto all things, having promise of the life that now is, and of that which is to come. —**1 Timothy 4:7b–8**

Social Teachings

of the Church

Unit 1: Fulfilling Our Obligations to Neighbors

Lessons 1–4

Lesson Aims

After participating in this lesson, each learner will be able to:

1. List the components of Daniel's proposal and its results.

2. Outline ways to cultivate mental, physical, and spiritual health by seeking true and wholesome things.

3. Make an inventory of daily habits and plan adjustments to honor God with time, diet, and attention.

Lesson Outline

Introduction

A. Consequences of Neglect

B. Lesson Context

I. Firm Resolve (Daniel 1:8–10)

A. Daniel's Favor (vv. 8–9)

Wearing White

B. Official's Concern (v. 10)

II. Agreeable Arrangement (Daniel 1:11–14)

A. Trial Proposed (vv. 11–12)

B. Comparison Accepted (vv. 13–14)

III. Clear Results (Daniel 1:15–17)

A. Contrast in Appearance (v. 15)

B. Change in Provisions (v. 16)

C. Blessings from God (v. 17)

IV. Preferred Path (1 Timothy 4:7–8)

A. Avoid Foolishness (v. 7a)

B. Pursue Godliness (v. 7b)

C. Reap Benefits (v. 8)

Physical and Spiritual Nourishment

Conclusion

A. The Ultimate Goal

B. Prayer

C. Thought to Remember

Introduction

A. Consequences of Neglect

When I was a teenager, taking care of my body seemed effortless. As an athlete on the cross-country team, exercise was built into my routine. I could eat whatever I wanted without feeling any adverse effects, so I didn't pay attention to what I ate.

Several decades, two children, and a stint in graduate school later, I wish I could still say the same. While it brings me joy, most of my work is done at a desk, in front of a screen. The demands of family and church take up whatever time I have left, and I find myself neglecting the care my body needs. On a trip with our church's youth group last summer, I struggled physically. At that point, it occurred to me that while I spend a lot of energy studying, writing, and teaching about God, I hardly put any effort into caring for the body God gave me. That neglect was getting in the way of serving God. It is impossible to separate my physical body and my service to God. As both texts for this lesson show, neither should be ignored.

B. Lesson Context

The book of Daniel is divided into two parts: chapters 1–6 consist of narratives about Daniel and his companions in service to various kings, while chapters 7–12 consist of Daniel's visions. Because of these visions, the book is found in the "prophecy" section of the Bible. Today's lesson comes from the first half of the book.

The epistle of 1 Timothy was written more than 500 years after Daniel's time. Timothy was a traveling companion and coworker of Paul's. In this letter, Paul gives Timothy instructions regarding the situation in the church at Ephesus, particularly in countering false teachings that threaten to muddy the good news of the gospel and cause distress within the church.

I. Firm Resolve

(Daniel 1:8–10)

A. Daniel's Favor (vv. 8–9)

8. But Daniel purposed in his heart that he

would not defile himself with the portion of the king's meat, nor with the wine which he drank: therefore he requested of the prince of the eunuchs that he might not defile himself.

In ancient Near Eastern understanding of the human body, the *heart* was thought to be the seat of thought and intellect, while the gut was the seat of the emotions. Daniel's choice should not be understood as an emotional reaction but rather as a thoughtful decision.

Daniel and his companions are forcibly removed from their families and brought to the court of King Nebuchadnezzar (Daniel 1:1–3). The intention behind bringing them to the palace was to "reprogram" them, so to speak. At the palace of King Nebuchadnezzar, they are trained to serve in the royal court, a process meant to thoroughly assimilate them into the culture of their conquerors (1:3–5). To begin this process, *the prince of the eunuchs* gives Daniel and his friends new names (1:6–7). Daniel's refusal of the food prescribed to him is an attempt to hold on to his identity as a servant of God instead of as a servant of his conqueror.

It is not clear, however, what it is about the king's royal food that may *defile* Daniel. The Law of Moses forbids eating certain kinds of *meat,* but other kinds are perfectly acceptable (Leviticus 11:1–46; Deuteronomy 14:1–21). *Wine* is not forbidden (Numbers 6:20; 18:12; 1 Samuel 1:24; Psalm 104:14–15; etc.), though it is spoken of in negative terms when excess is involved (Isaiah 28:7; 5:11, 22; Proverbs 20:1). Daniel may be avoiding food and drink associated with pagan temple offerings and thus idolatry (compare 1 Corinthians 8). But under this theory, the vegetarian alternative he proposes in verse 12 would be equally suspect since flour is also offered to pagan idols.

Part of Babylon's success was its practice of assimilating bright, educated young men from among the peoples the empire conquered. If the best and brightest from these conquered people groups ate Babylonian foods, practiced Babylonian customs, worshiped Babylonian gods, and loyally served the Babylonian king, they would have no reason to cause costly uprisings. They would be thoroughly invested in Babylon's well-being. This is the reality that Daniel is trying to resist.

The Hebrew word translated here as *defile* is used elsewhere in the context of ritual purity in connection to blood (Isaiah 59:3) or impure offerings (Malachi 1:7, 12). Some commentators interpret the use of the word to indicate that Daniel is concerned with the ritual purity of the *king's meat* and requests a vegetarian diet as a way of ensuring that he will not accidentally consume impure meat.

Daniel's decision is less about maintaining ritual purity through diet and more about maintaining a sense of identity by refusing to be completely assimilated into the empire that conquered his people. Daniel chooses to use his body and the food he eats as a way of honoring God.

What Do You Think?

How do we decide which issues and situations call for setting a boundary in service to God and which do not?

Digging Deeper

Describe a time that you honored a boundary to stay faithful to God's will. What did you learn from the experience that could help others?

Wearing White

It was the first week of a new job. I was nervous, excited, and keen to make a good first impression. One morning, I chose to wear my favorite white trousers. On the way to work I picked up a breakfast bowl with egg and tomato. As I sat down at my desk, I managed to spill all the contents onto my white trousers. The accident happened just minutes before a business meeting with senior leaders.

Panic set in as I rushed to the restroom to assess the damage. I learned a valuable lesson: when you wear white, you are more conscious of where you sit and what you eat (or at least you should be) to avoid staining or spoiling your trousers. Daniel knew he belonged to the Lord and was clothed in the fear and favor of the Lord. He knew that being God's servant required one to be set apart. Consider what you regularly consume with your body, mind, and spirit. Where might you make adjustments to serve the Lord more faithfully, just as Daniel did? —N. V.

Visual for Lesson 1. *Have this visual displayed prominently as a backdrop as you allow one minute for silent reflection on the question.*

9. Now God had brought Daniel into favour and tender love with the prince of the eunuchs.

For the first time in the book of Daniel, *God* is credited as the active force. Daniel's situation echoes the relationship between Joseph and the prison warden (Genesis 39:20–23). In both cases, the person who obeys and follows God finds favor and approval from others.

The sentiment expressed by the *prince of the eunuchs* is more than a feeling of sympathy toward Daniel. The Hebrew word translated *tender love* is also translated as "mercies" in Daniel 9:9, 18, and that is the sense here. The phrase evokes ideas of faithfulness and loyalty. Moreover, the two Hebrew words translated as *favour* and *tender love* appear together throughout Scripture to describe God's commitment to His people (Psalms 25:6; 40:11; 51:1; 69:16; 103:4; Isaiah 63:7; Jeremiah 16:5; Lamentations 3:22; Hosea 2:19; Zechariah 7:9).

B. Official's Concern (v. 10)

10. And the prince of the eunuchs said unto Daniel, I fear my lord the king, who hath appointed your meat and your drink: for why should he see your faces worse liking than the children which are of your sort? then shall ye make me endanger my head to the king.

The *prince of the eunuchs* does not give Daniel an immediately desirable answer. It's not a flat refusal, but it points out that if things go wrong, more people than Daniel will suffer the consequences. What Daniel is requesting—to reject a visible and substantial sign of allegiance and assimilation—could be dangerous. The desires of kings are not to be taken lightly. The death penalty is a very real possibility (example: Daniel 6). What we might think to be hyperbole on the part of the official seems to be a genuine fear to him.

The main concern seems to be that by refusing the food and *drink* appointed by the king, Daniel and his companions will be eating inferior food. The prince of the eunuchs anticipates this will render them visibly less healthy than *the children which are of your sort.*

The word *sort* is difficult to translate since this is the only place in the Old Testament where the underlying Hebrew word occurs. The old Greek version, the Septuagint, translates this with a word that means "to bring up together." This most likely refers to fellow Judeans who are being trained up at court.

In the end, by not giving a flat refusal, the prince of the eunuchs gives Daniel tacit permission to continue pursuing his request. As a loyal servant, he cannot promote Daniel's request. Nevertheless, the favor and tender love that God kindled in him causes the prince of the eunuchs to allow Daniel to continue pursuing his request without interference.

II. Agreeable Arrangement

(Daniel 1:11–14)

A. Trial Proposed (vv. 11–12)

11–12. Then said Daniel to Melzar, whom the prince of the eunuchs had set over Daniel, Hananiah, Mishael, and Azariah, Prove thy servants, I beseech thee, ten days; and let them give us pulse to eat, and water to drink.

The translators of the *King James Version* determined that the word *Melzar* is a proper name; later studies propose that the meaning of the word *Melzar* is "overseer," "steward," or "guard." So it is possible that the word is used as a common noun to refer to a guard in service to *the prince of the eunuchs*. In the Old Testament, the underlying word is used only here and in Daniel 1:16.

Although Daniel is now speaking with a different person, he is continuing the same request. The addition of *Hananiah, Mishael, and Azariah* underscores the fact that Daniel is making this dietary request for his community. Unless individuals only eat what they grow, kill, or forage entirely, food is always sourced in the context of connections between people or groups. Our modern, detached system of purchasing food can cause us to forget those connections. Daniel chooses to use diet as a means of maintaining his identity, including his connection to his people and God. It is fitting that he does this in the company of his fellows.

By asking for *ten days* to test his dietary request, Daniel acknowledges the warning the prince of the eunuchs has given (Daniel 1:10, above). Daniel also offers an alternative to the king's food: *pulse*. The Hebrew word used here is rare, occurring only here and in Daniel 1:16 (below), where it appears with a slightly different spelling. It is related to the Hebrew word for *seed*. It could refer to a diet of seeds, meaning legumes and grains. It could also indicate things that grow from seeds, including fruits and vegetables. This diet resembles what God gave humans to eat in the Garden of Eden (Genesis 1:29).

We do not assume that Daniel requests an entirely vegetarian diet. In Daniel 10:3, he temporarily stops eating meat, so it must be concluded that he consumes meat more or less regularly.

No matter what we assume the "king's meat" and "pulse" to be, there remains a strong contrast between what Daniel is ordered to eat and what he is requesting to eat. The portion of the royal food and wine are symbols of power and privilege. Even if it is just a fancy loaf of bread, it is something that can presumably be obtained only by the king's permission. It is, therefore, a tangible way in which the king demonstrates his power. By contrast, requesting the humble "pulse" and water could be seen as an act of solidarity with those conquered of Judah. Perhaps this food is more in keeping with what inhabitants of Judah who had not been whisked away to court have available to eat. Again, the key point is that Daniel uses the food he eats, and thus his body, as a way to honor God.

How to Say It

Azariah	Az-uh-*rye*-uh.
Babylon	*Bab*-uh-lun.
Babylonian	Bab-ih-*low*-nee-un.
Ephesus	*Ef*-uh-sus.
eunuchs	*you*-nicks.
Hananiah	Han-uh-*nye*-uh.
Melzar	*Mel*-zar.
Mishael	*Mish*-a-el.
Nebuchadnezzar	*Neb*-yuh-kud-*nez*-er.

What Do You Think?

How should Christians respond to a policy that goes against their convictions?

Digging Deeper

How do you square the example of Daniel with Acts 5:27–29; Romans 13:1–7; Titus 3:1–2; and 1 Peter 2:13–17?

B. Comparison Accepted (vv. 13–14)

13. Then let our countenances be looked upon before thee, and the countenance of the children that eat of the portion of the king's meat: and as thou seest, deal with thy servants.

Daniel essentially places the outcome of his request in Melzar's hands. This keeps the experiment behind the scenes while also ensuring that Melzar will feel confident in the outcome.

14. So he consented to them in this matter, and proved them ten days.

Melzar gives his permission. *Ten days* is a very short amount of time for such an experiment. It is unlikely that Melzar expects a significant change in their appearances—especially a negative one.

III. Clear Results
(Daniel 1:15–17)

A. Contrast in Appearance (v. 15)

15. And at the end of ten days their countenances appeared fairer and fatter in flesh than all the children which did eat the portion of the king's meat.

Despite expectations, Daniel and his companions all appear much healthier than those who *did eat the portion of the king's meat.* The *ten days* should not have made that big of a difference. Although God is not explicitly stated to be active in the situation, this is clearly divine intervention.

B. Change in Provisions (v. 16)

16. Thus Melzar took away the portion of their meat, and the wine that they should drink; and gave them pulse.

Having passed the test, Daniel and his companions are granted a dietary exemption on an ongoing basis.

C. Blessings from God (v. 17)

17. As for these four children, God gave them knowledge and skill in all learning and wisdom: and Daniel had understanding in all visions and dreams.

This verse sets the stage for the narratives to follow. *God* is once again explicitly active, granting Daniel and his fellows *knowledge and skill* beyond what they were brought to court to learn. This is particularly true regarding Daniel's *understanding in all visions and dreams.* The text makes it clear that Daniel will succeed in the Babylonian court, not because he earned it, but because God wills it.

What Do You Think?

In what ways has God blessed you beyond what you have asked or imagined? (Ephesians 3:20–21)

Digging Deeper

How do you use these blessings to serve God and others?

IV. Preferred Path
(1 Timothy 4:7–8)

A. Avoid Foolishness (v. 7a)

7a. But refuse profane and old wives' fables.

This verse begins an expansion of the discussion in 1 Timothy 1:3–7, where Paul warns Timothy about false teachings and teachers that have their origin in legends and myths (compare Titus 1:14). Paul's caution against *profane and old wives' fables* here employs an imperative verb, which means it is an order, not a suggestion. This is the first imperative in a paired exhortation; the other appears in the second half of the verse.

B. Pursue Godliness (v. 7b)

7b. And exercise thyself rather unto godliness.

The second half of the paired imperative instructs Timothy to *exercise* himself. Paul uses athletic imagery, but the training he has in mind is not that of the athlete in pursuit of peak physical performance. Instead, Paul instructs Timothy to take the same drive and passion that an athlete devotes to his body and apply it to pursuing *godliness* (compare 1 Corinthians 9:24). It's not enough to merely avoid evil; one must pursue holiness.

What Do You Think?

What are some ways a Christian can train for godliness?

Digging Deeper

How do these ways compare with the training we do for our physical bodies?

C. Reap Benefits (v. 8)

8. For bodily exercise profiteth little: but godliness is profitable unto all things, having promise of the life that now is, and of that which is to come.

The phrase *profiteth little* is sometimes wrongly interpreted to mean that there is nothing to be gained from taking care of the body. The Greek word used here indicates that something is small in comparison to something else (compare 1 Timothy 5:23). In other words, it is "not nothing." There is something to be gained from *bodily exercise.* The physical body is a gift from God. Jesus cared for His physical body (Mark 6:31; 11:12–13), and so should we.

On the other hand, genuine *godliness* is beneficial both in the present and in eternity. The godly life yields peace, harmony, and contentment that cannot be found by any other means. And unlike physical health, spiritual health lasts forever. Death cannot conquer it.

Physical and Spiritual Nourishment

Years ago, a friend and I decided to complete a metabolic program together. The 28-day plan promised to revive our metabolisms if we abstained from processed food and regularly ate nutrient-dense foods instead. The idea was to make a strategic lifestyle change.

The concept was based on the analogy of burning logs. Just as proper fuel enables the fire to continue burning, human metabolism thrives on the right kinds of food. Though initially skeptical, after 28 days, I achieved a level of physical fitness of which I had previously only dreamed. I was energized, experienced mental clarity, and slept better.

More significant than the physical discipline I gained, however, was the spiritual fitness that also resulted. I was able to spend more time in prayer, worship, and reading the Bible. The result was growth in my closeness to God. As I attended more carefully to the food I consumed, I ended up doing the same regarding spiritual food. What habits will you adopt to help build your spiritual fitness as well as your physical health? —N. V.

Conclusion

A. The Ultimate Goal

Both texts for this lesson deal with the connection between bodies and honoring God. In Daniel 1:8–17, Daniel and his companions resisted total assimilation into Babylonian culture and religion. This resistance took the form of tactfully refusing to eat the food and drink the wine given to them. Instead, Daniel requested water and food that was more in line with God's desires. Through God's intervention, his request was granted, and the resulting trial period was successful. Daniel and his companions resisted being fully assimilated, maintaining their connection to their people and God.

Strong connections can be formed through food and other kinds of consumption. These connections may be relational. They may be philosophical or societal. Being mindful of what you consume and its effects on both your body and soul will be noticed by others. Daniel and his friends used their bodies to honor God. For us, this can take the physical forms of eating healthy foods, exercising, getting enough rest, and being proactive about preventative care.

The text of 1 Timothy 4:7–8 puts this into a spiritual perspective. While celebrating the goodness of God's creation, Paul instructed Timothy to make the pursuit of godliness his highest priority. The language he used alluded to athletes' training (compare 1 Corinthians 9:24–27). This reminded Timothy that pursuing God gains a believer far more than focusing primarily on the body ever could. Living within misaligned cultures, it can be easy to allow the pursuit of bodily health to rise above its proper place in our priorities. Paul's words remind believers that faithfulness to God matters more. Read together, Daniel 1 and 1 Timothy 4 encourage us to honor our bodies so that we might honor God.

What Do You Think?

What questions will you ask to evaluate whether your consumption honors God?

Digging Deeper

How do these questions differ regarding dietary consumption? media consumption? material consumption?

B. Prayer

Heavenly Father, You created all things and pronounced them good. Thank You for making us in Your image. Help us honor that image so that we may bring glory to You in all that we are and in all that we do. In Jesus' name we pray. Amen.

C. Thought to Remember

Honor God by honoring your body.

Visuals FOR THESE LESSONS

The visual pictured in each lesson (example: page 236) is a small reproduction of a large, full-color poster included in the *Adult Resources* packet for the Spring Quarter. Order No. 9780784740132 from your supplier.

Involvement Learning

Enhance your lesson with KJV Bible Student *(from your curriculum supplier) and the reproducible activity page (at www.standardlesson.com or in the back of the* KJV Standard Lesson Commentary Deluxe Edition*).*

Into the Lesson

Write *Healthy* and *Unhealthy* as headers on the board. As students enter class, ask them to write down foods that fall into either category. After class begins, review the list and ask volunteers to explain the ramifications of a diet consisting of only foods from one category. Include the benefits and consequences of such choices.

Option. Invite participants to list foods they like and foods they dislike. Ask them to give reasons for their liking or disliking these foods. (Be sure to include your own examples.)

Say, "We often think of 'consumption' as referring to dietary consumption. However, there are other ways that humans consume." Ask volunteers to list other forms of consumption. Responses might include media consumption, financial consumption, service consumption, or product consumption.

Lead into Bible study by saying, "Today's lesson deals with an issue of consumption as it relates to physical and spiritual health. We will see how the example of Daniel and the teachings of the apostle Paul inform the relationship between consumption and spiritual health."

Into the Word

Ask a volunteer to read aloud Daniel 1:8–17. Use the following prompts for whole-class discussion: 1–Describe the cultural and social pressures that Daniel and his friends faced. 2–What do you think it would have been like to be in Daniel's shoes? 3–How would you have responded to the pressures they faced? 4–What would help you act as boldly as Daniel acted? 5–Why do you think Daniel and his friends wanted to avoid the king's food and drink? 6–Do you think Daniel and his friends knew God would reward their decision? Why or why not? 7–What would be a modern-day parallel to Daniel's story?

Option. Distribute copies of the "The Holy Life" exercise from the activity page, which you can download. Have learners work on it individually before sharing conclusions with a partner.

Ask another volunteer to read aloud 1 Timothy 4:7–8. Use the following prompts for whole-class discussion: 1–In what ways are physical fitness and spiritual fitness similar and dissimilar? 2–Why are both physical health and spiritual health important? 3–What do we need to live spiritually healthy and godly lives?

Assign participants to pairs or small groups. Distribute a pen and index card to each participant. Ask groups to brainstorm and write down a list of "spiritual exercises" based on 1 Timothy 4:7–8. Some examples might include prayer, Bible study, serving others, worship, etc. After five minutes, reconvene the class and have volunteers share their responses. Write responses on the board under the heading *Spiritual Exercises.*

Into Life

Distribute an index card and pen to each learner and ask them to write an hour-by-hour inventory of an average day. Then direct them to circle habits or activities on the inventory that improve physical or spiritual health. Ask learners to work with a partner to answer the following questions: 1–How does this inventory reveal your priorities? 2–What habits or activities serve to improve your physical health, spiritual health, or both? 3–What changes would you like to make in the upcoming week so that you will honor God with your time, diet, and attention? Encourage learners to write those changes into their itinerary agenda.

Alternative. Distribute copies of the "My Spiritual Fitness Plan" exercise from the activity page. Direct learners to complete the activity as a take-home. To encourage completion, promise to discuss their reactions next week.

Close with prayer, asking God to strengthen your desires to improve spiritual fitness.

March 15
Lesson 2 (KJV)

Giving to the Community

Devotional Reading: Exodus 20:12–17
Background Scripture: Deuteronomy 15:1–11; Matthew 25:31–46; Luke 10:25–37; James 1:27; 2:14–17

Deuteronomy 15:4–11

4 Save when there shall be no poor among you; for the LORD shall greatly bless thee in the land which the LORD thy God giveth thee for an inheritance to possess it:

5 Only if thou carefully hearken unto the voice of the LORD thy God, to observe to do all these commandments which I command thee this day.

6 For the LORD thy God blesseth thee, as he promised thee: and thou shalt lend unto many nations, but thou shalt not borrow; and thou shalt reign over many nations, but they shall not reign over thee.

7 If there be among you a poor man of one of thy brethren within any of thy gates in thy land which the LORD thy God giveth thee, thou shalt not harden thine heart, nor shut thine hand from thy poor brother:

8 But thou shalt open thine hand wide unto him, and shalt surely lend him sufficient for his need, in that which he wanteth.

9 Beware that there be not a thought in thy wicked heart, saying, The seventh year, the year of release, is at hand; and thine eye be evil against thy poor brother, and thou givest him nought; and he cry unto the LORD against thee, and it be sin unto thee.

10 Thou shalt surely give him, and thine heart shall not be grieved when thou givest unto him: because that for this thing the LORD thy God shall bless thee in all thy works, and in all that thou puttest thine hand unto.

11 For the poor shall never cease out of the land: therefore I command thee, saying, Thou shalt open thine hand wide unto thy brother, to thy poor, and to thy needy, in thy land.

Matthew 25:42–45

42 For I was an hungred, and ye gave me no meat: I was thirsty, and ye gave me no drink:

43 I was a stranger, and ye took me not in: naked, and ye clothed me not: sick, and in prison, and ye visited me not.

44 Then shall they also answer him, saying, Lord, when saw we thee an hungred, or athirst, or a stranger, or naked, or sick, or in prison, and did not minister unto thee?

45 Then shall he answer them, saying, Verily I say unto you, Inasmuch as ye did it not to one of the least of these, ye did it not to me.

Key Text

The poor shall never cease out of the land: therefore I command thee, saying, Thou shalt open thine hand wide unto thy brother, to thy poor, and to thy needy, in thy land. —**Deuteronomy 15:11**

Social Teachings

of the Church

Unit 1: Fulfilling Our Obligations to Neighbors

Lessons 1–4

Lesson Aims

After participating in this lesson, each learner will be able to:

1. List categories of generosity from Deuteronomy 15:4–11 and Matthew 25:42–45.
2. Explain why believers should demonstrate generosity without expectation.
3. Implement a plan to grow in a personal capacity to express generosity.

Lesson Outline

Introduction
- A. Endless Blessings
- B. Lesson Context: Deuteronomy
- C. Lesson Context: Matthew

I. Giving to Neighbors (Deuteronomy 15:4–11)
- A. Promise of Blessing (vv. 4–6)
- B. Reminder of Generosity (vv. 7–10)
- C. Command of Benevolence (v. 11)
  English Lessons

II. Giving to the Lord (Matthew 25:42–45)
- A. Showing Compassion (vv. 42–43)
- B. Questioning Timing (v. 44)
- C. Revealing Meaning (v. 45)
  Jesus at the Grocery Store

Conclusion
- A. Open Hands, Hearts, and Eyes
- B. Prayer
- C. Thought to Remember

Introduction

A. Endless Blessings

I live on a farm. My family primarily raises cattle and sheep, though we also raise chickens. In the past, we enjoyed raising hogs, goats, and horses. To make money with cattle and sheep, one must sell them appropriately. You must consider timing, weight, breeding quality, and other marketing factors. When we sell an animal, that animal is gone for good. We will never have it back. The finality of it makes selling livestock difficult.

Chickens, on the other hand, differ because they produce eggs. We can take the eggs, knowing more will appear tomorrow. No matter how often we collect the eggs, the chickens will lay more if they are healthy.

Sometimes, we reject generosity because we fear we will face a lack. However, generosity is like chickens and eggs. Our giving does not equate to permanent depletion. As you think about today's lesson, consider the blessings of God. God supplies the needs of His people; therefore, what we are gifted is to be used generously.

B. Lesson Context: Deuteronomy

The title *Deuteronomy* is a combination of two Greek words meaning "second law." Moses spoke and wrote the words in this book after the Israelites served their 40-year sentence in the wilderness (Numbers 32:13; Deuteronomy 2:7; 8:2). A new generation replaced the previous one, and that new generation needed to hear the Law of Moses for themselves. Thus *Deuteronomy* refers to the second giving of the law (compare the Ten Commandments in both Exodus 20 and Deuteronomy 5).

Law codes directly shape (and are shaped by) culture. They articulate societal norms and expectations. Throughout the ancient Near East, law codes included common themes such as repayment of debts, release of enslaved people, and establishing land rights. The Law of Moses speaks to similar themes. It also calls for the release of debts, people, and land, although on a different timeline (Leviticus 25:10; Deuteronomy 15:1–2).

The Law of Moses bears striking similarities to other codes of the ancient world, including the

Code of Hammurabi. But the combination of political, governmental, and spiritual leadership within the Law of Moses is ultimately unique. The one true God is the spiritual leader and king. He calls His people to reflect His holiness and generosity.

C. Lesson Context: Matthew

Roughly fourteen centuries pass before the nation that received the Law of Moses receives the Gospel of Matthew. In that long interval, the Law of Moses received various "creative" reinterpretations (compare Matthew 23:13–26; Mark 7:8–13). Matthew and other New Testament writers document the birth, life, death, resurrection, and ascension of Jesus. These events transitioned God's people from the rules of the old covenant to the expectations of the new. Does this transition mean that the Law of Moses is without value today? Do practitioners of the new covenant need to uphold the expectations of the old? Today's lesson explores one aspect of these questions.

I. Giving to Neighbors

(Deuteronomy 15:4–11)

A. Promise of Blessing (vv. 4–6)

4. Save when there shall be no poor among you; for the Lord shall greatly bless thee in the land which the Lord thy God giveth thee for an inheritance to possess it.

The term *save* is a difficult translation. In certain contexts it means "no," "nothing," "only," or "yet." The solution here is to see its connection with the preceding verses, which discuss the cancelation of debts for the Israelites every seventh year. God's intention is to *bless* His people. So the first part of this verse reminds the Israelites of God's ultimate goal: *there shall be no poor among you*. The possibility of extinguishing poverty exists because God is poised to bless the people *greatly* in their obedience.

The Israelites dwell *in the land* only because God *giveth* it. Their *inheritance* was set in motion when God made His covenant with Abraham (Genesis 17:7–8; Deuteronomy 7:7–8). They now have all they *possess* because of their relationship with God and His great blessings.

> **What Do You Think?**
> What does *inheritance* mean to you? What kind of things do you hope you will inherit?
>
> **Digging Deeper**
> How does the hope of an inheritance change your perspective, goals, or direction? How does the idea of leaving an inheritance affect those things?

5. Only if thou carefully hearken unto the voice of the Lord thy God, to observe to do all these commandments which I command thee this day.

God's promise of blessing is conditional. The Israelites must obey His commands. The blessings promised for their careful obedience are protection, procreation, and prosperity (Deuteronomy 28:1–14). However, if the people of Israel disobey God's commands, He will bring curses upon them (28:15–68). Those curses include disease, famine, and domination by foreign nations (28:21–22, 25).

Unfortunately, this warning is not one the Israelites ultimately heed. Future generations struggle to *carefully hearken unto* God's words and *observe* all His commands. Evidence of God's adherence to the conditions of His promise (and its consequences) appears frequently throughout the book of Judges. Judges 2:11–19 establishes a cycle in which the Israelites do evil in the sight of the Lord; the Lord allows other nations to oppress them, they call out to God for deliverance, God

How to Say It

Corinthians	Ko-rin-thee-unz (th as in thin).
Colossians	Kuh-losh-unz.
Deuteronomy	Due-ter-*ahn*-uh-me.
Ephesians	Ee-fee-zhunz.
Hammurabi	*Ham*-muh-*rah*-bee.
Isaiah	Eye-*zay*-uh.
Israelites	*Iz*-ray-el-ites.
Leviticus	Leh-*vit*-ih-kus.
Synoptic	Sih-*nawp*-tihk.

Visual for Lesson 2. *Point to the visual and say, "Jesus teaches that we serve Him when we meet the needs of other people."*

raises a judge to lead His people, the judge is successful, and then the judge dies and the people rebel again. The cycle repeats over and over again (compare Judges 3:7–11; 4:1–6:1; 6:1–8:35).

6. For the LORD thy God blesseth thee, as he promised thee: and thou shalt lend unto many nations, but thou shalt not borrow; and thou shalt reign over many nations, but they shall not reign over thee.

God promises to bless, and lying is outside of His holy nature (Numbers 23:19; Titus 1:2; Hebrews 6:18). If God promises something, He will do it. The promises stated here are of abundance and preeminence. Up to this point in history, the descendants of Abraham have lived as either nomads or slaves; however, God promised he would make Abraham into a "great nation" (Genesis 12:2). The Israelites stand on the cusp of having enough prosperity to lend to other nations, never having to borrow, and having the power to rule. With God's blessing, Israel could become the ancient Near East's most prosperous nation.

B. Reminder of Generosity (vv. 7–10)

7. If there be among you a poor man of one of thy brethren within any of thy gates in thy land which the LORD thy God giveth thee, thou shalt not harden thine heart, nor shut thine hand from thy poor brother.

If indicates a prescription for times when the Israelites encounter poverty. As such, the instructions now move the narrative from the envisioned ideal to a future reality. That reality will include the continuous presence of *poor* people (compare Matthew 26:11). In this case, God points to someone who is *thy brethren*, meaning a fellow Israelite, one's neighbor, a brother, or a friend. This person lacks the financial means to survive, and God calls His people to notice and offer aid (compare 1 John 3:17). God reminds His hearers that the land they dwell in was gifted to them. He then appeals to their hearts. Instead of callousness and selfishness, God calls for compassion and generosity.

Provision for "strangers" dwelling among the Israelites is addressed later in this book (examples: Deuteronomy 10:18–19; 14:28).

What Do You Think?

Have you ever experienced a "hardening" of your heart toward a poor or needy person? Did it cause you to "shut your hand"? Explain.

Digging Deeper

What helps you "thaw" your heart and keep it soft toward others?

8. But thou shalt open thine hand wide unto him, and shalt surely lend him sufficient for his need, in that which he wanteth.

God's expectation that His people hold material things loosely does not change in the transition from the old covenant to the new (Matthew 5:42; 2 Corinthians 9:9; etc.). God is the provider, and His children should consider all they have as gifts (Psalm 145:16; James 1:17; compare Psalm 37:21–22; Proverbs 28:20, 22; 1 Timothy 6:9). When holding this perspective, benevolence flows naturally.

The verb *lend* here includes the idea "to give a pledge," implying a security deposit of some kind to ensure that the money will be repaid (compare Deuteronomy 24:10). It is tempting to avoid lending to the poor because they do not possess the means to repay. Thus the need for a security deposit. Unfortunately, history shows this practice is subject to abuse (Exodus 22:25–27; Amos 2:8). But God says His people have the responsibility to lend if it is within their power to do so.

The caveat *sufficient for his need* directs lenders concerning how much they should give. The term *wanteth* means "to lack" or "to be without." It is not a comment on what a person might desire beyond basic needs but rather a fundamental deficiency. God's people are to take care of each other.

9. Beware that there be not a thought in thy wicked heart, saying, The seventh year, the year of release, is at hand; and thine eye be evil against thy poor brother, and thou givest him nought; and he cry unto the LORD against thee, and it be sin unto thee.

The seventh year is the Sabbath year (Leviticus 25:1–7). God declares that every seven years, all debt is forgiven—this is *the year of release*. Suppose an individual asks for a loan of $10,000 with a repayment plan of $100 per month. If the plan is followed as outlined, the debtor will repay the loan in approximately 8 years. According to the Sabbath-year system, however, the loan must be forgiven at the end of the seventh year (Deuteronomy 15:1). The discrepancy might well discourage lenders. God realizes the possibility of such an attitude and speaks to it. He warns that withholding aid from someone who needs it may be considered *evil* and sinful because it shows something *wicked* in their hearts. When a needy person goes to God with a complaint against the generosity of God's people, God takes it seriously.

10. Thou shalt surely give him, and thine heart shall not be grieved when thou givest unto him: because that for this thing the LORD thy God shall bless thee in all thy works, and in all that thou puttest thine hand unto.

It is one thing to lend money out of obligation. It is another thing to lend money with a happy heart, knowing the funds may not be repaid. God's commands extend beyond the letter of the law to the action of the heart. The phrase *shall not be grieved* refers to the internal attitude of the giver. God's people are not to be saddened by sharing their means with others. They are not to feel like they are losing or must give unwillingly. When God's people follow His ways, He provides for their needs and blesses *all* they do—abundance in work, skill, and finance flows from generosity.

What Do You Think?

Have you ever gone against "business sense" and given generously to someone even though it was a "bad deal"?

Digging Deeper

Compare 2 Thessalonians 3:10 with Deuteronomy 15:9–10. How do you reconcile the New Testament teaching with the Law of Moses?

C. Command of Benevolence (v. 11)

11. For the poor shall never cease out of the land: therefore I command thee, saying, Thou shalt open thine hand wide unto thy brother, to thy poor, and to thy needy, in thy land.

On the surface, this statement looks like a blatant contradiction of God's words just a few verses earlier (see Deuteronomy 15:4). Some commentators believe *the poor shall never cease out of the land* is a foreshadowing of Israel's refusal toward complete obedience. Others say it is a reminder that sin breeds poverty. No one can deny that hard times exist in this world. Therefore, 15:4 refers to the ideal, and this verse faces a harsh reality.

Open and *wide* are purposefully repetitive. God essentially says, "Throw open your lives" in compassionate generosity. The image of an open hand contrasts starkly with the idea of a clenched fist. God calls His people to a broad, unobstructed benevolence. This is the opposite of the closed hand of Deuteronomy 15:7, above.

The repetitive use of the term *thy* emphasizes ownership, which indicates responsibility. There is a relationship to consider: the underprivileged live alongside the wealthy and successful. They are part of the same *land*. The issue is personal. Caring for the destitute is not a social issue left to governmental leaders to solve. It is a personal issue in which God's chosen people are called to act.

English Lessons

English was my favorite subject in school. I loved everything about words—spelling bees, vocabulary, diagramming sentences, and writing research papers. On warm, sunny days, I didn't want to play outside; I wanted to read books. It was natural for me to become an English teacher. I delighted in sharing the English language with high schoolers.

These days, I share my love for English with students from all around the world. They move to my city with minimal English language experience, and it is my joy to teach them.

God gives more than enough of everything to go around. Even if your wealth isn't material in nature, you have treasure. Like me, it might be language. Or you may have a special skill, like sewing. Maybe you are a builder or an athlete. What has God given you to share? How can you use your "wealth" to bless others? —B. R.

II. Giving to the Lord

(Matthew 25:42–45)

The literary context for this passage begins in Matthew 25:31, where Jesus identifies Himself as the "Son of man" who comes in glory. He then describes an elaborate sorting (25:32–45). In judgment, Jesus separates the "sheep" from the "goats" (25:32–33). The goats face an eternal punishment and must depart from His presence (25:41). Today's passage focuses on the reason for their separation.

A. Showing Compassion (vv. 42–43)

42. For I was an hungred, and ye gave me no meat: I was thirsty, and ye gave me no drink.

Jesus is outside Jerusalem, on the Mount of Olives, when He makes this statement to His disciples (Matthew 24:3). He speaks in first-person and boldly declares that when *I was* hungry and thirsty, no one assisted. Like an undercover boss, the King comes incognito, and people fail to respond. The passage unfolds in an "I was" and "you did not" formula that pairs a needful condition with a subsequent reaction.

43. I was a stranger, and ye took me not in: naked, and ye clothed me not: sick, and in prison, and ye visited me not.

Under both the old and new covenants, God requires His people to care for others, with equal treatment (Leviticus 19:34). He calls His people to act with commonsense humanity. Through the prophet Isaiah, God urges true religion and fasting to be practiced by freeing captives, feeding the hungry, housing the exposed, and covering the naked (Isaiah 58:6–8). When Jesus sent His disciples out to preach God's kingdom and heal the sick, He declared, "Freely ye have received, freely give" (Matthew 10:8). Hospitality results from a generous spirit. The author of Hebrews writes, "Be not forgetful to entertain strangers: for thereby some have entertained angels unawares" (Hebrews 13:2).

What Do You Think?

Have you ever encountered Jesus through an interaction with someone?

Digging Deeper

Share an example of a time when you extended kindness to someone as though serving the Lord.

B. Questioning Timing (v. 44)

44. Then shall they also answer him, saying, Lord, when saw we thee an hungred, or athirst, or a stranger, or naked, or sick, or in prison, and did not minister unto thee?

Those condemned rebut, "But when did we ever see You like this?!" How could they be held responsible for something they did not know? Surely if they had seen Jesus in such a terrible condition, they would have come to His aid. If they had seen the *Lord* naked, *in prison*, or *sick*, they would have done something.

C. Revealing Meaning (v. 45)

45. Then shall he answer them, saying, Verily I say unto you, Inasmuch as ye did it not to one of the least of these, ye did it not to me.

The faithfulness of God's people hinges on their treatment of *the least of these.* Judgment does not consider our knowledge, fame, or fortune. It is based on the help we give to others as an indicator of the grace we ourselves receive. To neglect those who are suffering is to neglect the Lord.

Considering our treatment of God's people as though we serve God Himself is the closest the Synoptic Gospels come to identifying the church as the body of Christ (compare Ephesians 5:23, 29; Colossians 1:18, 24). The ways we're called to help are not extravagant. They are based upon responding to obvious needs. We are held responsible for how we react to what we know and see. James writes, "Therefore to him that knoweth to do good, and doeth it not, to him it is sin" (James 4:17).

> **What Do You Think?**
> How is it possible that the hungry, thirsty, naked, sick, and imprisoned represent Jesus?
>
> **Digging Deeper**
> To whom is Jesus referring when He mentions "the least of these"?

Jesus at the Grocery Store

As I walked into the grocery store one day, I noticed a young girl sitting on the ground in the parking lot. I thought it was odd, but I quickly moved on. She was still there when I left.

I looked at her intently. She wasn't begging for anything, and she wasn't talking to anyone. She was just sitting on the pavement with her shoulders slumped. She seemed sad. For a split second, I wished I had some cash or a gift card to give her. But I kept walking and loaded my groceries into the car.

Before I arrived home, Jesus' words in Matthew 25 were racing through my mind. Was it *Him* sitting there on the ground? How could it be? In my mind, Jesus doesn't have piercings or colorful hair. He doesn't look like a teenage girl.

How often do we miss Jesus because He looks like people we quickly dismiss? If we genuinely recognized Jesus in the eyes of the people we see on the street, how would our response toward them change? —B. R.

Conclusion

A. Open Hands, Hearts, and Eyes

God calls His people to pay particular attention to orphans, widows, the poor, the needy, and foreigners. He gives similar-sounding laws as those prescribed in the nations around Israel (consider the Code of Hammurabi; see Lesson Context) but adds a significant layer of generosity to His commands. God wants His people to see and comprehend needs and then be moved by compassion into action. He wants us to serve one another as though we are serving Him. Jesus radically teaches that compassion for the poor and needy is one way to recognize true disciples.

Our God is full of incredible generosity. We reflect His glory and charitable nature when we give. Benevolence helps us remember that our abundance and blessing come from the Lord. As God's children, we need not worry about lack or loss. Our heavenly Father provides for our needs. Therefore, if it is within our means to help another person, we are to do so. The help Jesus calls us toward is not difficult or complicated. It is simple and reflects His heart, compassion, grace, and love. We are to be openhanded.

God loves a cheerful giver (2 Corinthians 9:7). He does not consider the gifts and blessings He bestows as something that harms or bankrupts Him. Instead, God blesses His children because He loves them. He desires His people to reflect His nature. God calls us to live with open hearts.

Jesus asks us to see and serve others as if we are seeing and serving Him. This requires new eyes of compassion. There is no room for prejudice, racism, judgment, or favoritism among the people of God. Jesus does not want His people to have an "everyone for themselves" mentality. He calls His people to vibrantly compassionate community life. The poor, needy, hungry, thirsty, migrant, homeless, shirtless, sick, and imprisoned all deserve our loving kindness, care, and attention. Although society might reject these people, God sees them as children created in His image. The care we extend impacts the inheritance we receive. God calls us to live with open eyes.

B. Prayer

Father God, give us loving hearts open wide to all people. Protect us from the sin of selfishness. Open our hands in generosity. Help us remember that everything we have comes as a gift from You. In Jesus' name we pray. Amen.

C. Thought to Remember

Give out of your rich inheritance!

Involvement Learning

Enhance your lesson with KJV Bible Student *(from your curriculum supplier) and the reproducible activity page (at www.standardlesson.com or in the back of the* KJV Standard Lesson Commentary Deluxe Edition*).*

Into the Lesson

Invite learners to share a time when they experienced generosity. Expect many monetary examples. Prepare personal examples in advance and share them as needed to keep the conversation moving.

Option. Create a list of generous acts and write them on small slips of paper. Consider including biblical characters known for their generosity. Place the slips in a hat. Divide your class into two teams. Have one person from each team draw a slip of paper and act out the generous act or character without speaking. Set a one-minute timer for each actor. Award points for correct guesses. The team with the most points wins.

Lead a discussion about generosity as an attitude of gracious giving. Ask learners to share times when they have received or participated in generosity outside the financial realm. Be prepared with personal illustrations as well. You may want to write a class definition of *generosity* on the board.

As you transition into the Bible study, say: "In today's lesson, God commands His followers to be generous. Let's discover why generosity is an important characteristic of a Christ-follower."

Into the Word

Read Deuteronomy 15:4–11 out loud. Divide learners into small groups. Ask groups to discuss the following questions: 1–What is the central message of Deuteronomy 15:4–11? 2–How does the promise of blessing in verse 10 motivate generous giving? 3–How can the principle of canceling debts be applied in modernity? 4–How do you "open your hand" to those in need in the modern world? List practical examples. 5–How does this passage challenge our understanding of wealth and possessions? 6–What does it mean to be a good steward? Ask groups to reconvene and allow a representative from each group to share highlights with the class.

Invite a volunteer to read Matthew 25:42–45 out loud. Using the same small groups, ask participants to discuss the following: 1–Define *neighbor* in your own words. 2–How does the biblical concept of neighbor differ from your common understanding? 3–How do consumerism and materialism impact our ability to practice generosity? 4–What are the potential consequences of neglecting the poor and needy in our society? Bring the groups back together to share their conclusions.

Option. Distribute copies of the "Neighborly Case Study" exercise from the activity page, which you can download. Have learners work in pairs to complete before discussing their findings with the whole group.

Into Life

Write the following as the headers of two columns on the board:

Traditional Neighbors / Biblical Neighbors

Invite participants to list definitions or examples of neighbors for each column. Ask: "How can we cultivate a heart of generosity toward others?"

Lead a brainstorming session of ways learners can expand who they serve as a neighbor in their daily lives. Write their ideas on the board beneath the column headings already listed.

Distribute an index card and a pen to each participant. Ask them to write down a "neighbor" to whom they can show generosity this week. Under the name, encourage them to write down one specific way they plan to express generosity to that person and when.

Alternative. Distribute copies of the "Won't You Be My Neighbor?" activity from the activity page. Have learners work in pairs to complete as indicated.

Close your class time with a prayer. Say, "Lord, You are gracious, kind, and full of generosity. Teach us how to be openhanded with others as You are openhanded with us. Give us opportunities to grow in generosity this week. Amen."

Welcoming Others in Christ

Devotional Reading: Colossians 3:1–11
Background Scripture: Ruth 1:1–18; John 4:5–10;
Acts 10:1–11:18

Acts 10:9–15, 30–35

**9 On the morrow, as they went on their jour-
ney, and drew nigh unto the city, Peter went up
upon the housetop to pray about the sixth hour:
10 And he became very hungry, and would
have eaten: but while they made ready, he fell
into a trance,
11 And saw heaven opened, and a certain
vessel descending unto him, as it had been a
great sheet knit at the four corners, and let
down to the earth:
12 Wherein were all manner of fourfooted
beasts of the earth, and wild beasts, and creep-
ing things, and fowls of the air.
13 And there came a voice to him, Rise,
Peter; kill, and eat.
14 But Peter said, Not so, Lord; for I have
never eaten any thing that is common or
unclean.
15 And the voice spake unto him again the
second time, What God hath cleansed, that call
not thou common.**

**30 And Cornelius said, Four days ago I was
fasting until this hour; and at the ninth hour I
prayed in my house, and, behold, a man stood
before me in bright clothing,
31 And said, Cornelius, thy prayer is heard,
and thine alms are had in remembrance in the
sight of God.
32 Send therefore to Joppa, and call hither
Simon, whose surname is Peter; he is lodged in
the house of one Simon a tanner by the sea side:
who, when he cometh, shall speak unto thee.
33 Immediately therefore I sent to thee;
and thou hast well done that thou art come.
Now therefore are we all here present before
God, to hear all things that are commanded
thee of God.
34 Then Peter opened his mouth, and said,
Of a truth I perceive that God is no respecter
of persons:
35 But in every nation he that feareth him,
and worketh righteousness, is accepted with
him.**

Galatians 3:28–29

**28 There is neither Jew nor Greek, there is
neither bond nor free, there is neither male nor
female: for ye are all one in Christ Jesus.
29 And if ye be Christ's, then are ye Abra-
ham's seed, and heirs according to the promise.**

Key Text

There is neither Jew nor Greek, there is neither bond nor free, there is neither male nor female: for ye are all one in Christ Jesus. **—Galatians 3:28**

Social Teachings
of the Church

Unit 1: Fulfilling Our Obligations to Neighbors

Lessons 1–4

Lesson Aims

After participating in this lesson, each learner will be able to:

1. Recount the events of Peter's interaction with Cornelius.
2. Explain Galatians 3:28–29 in light of Acts 10.
3. Make a plan to initiate conversations across the wider family of God to dismantle walls of division.

Lesson Outline

Introduction
- A. Equal Worth, Equal Access
- B. Lesson Context: Acts
- C. Lesson Context: Galatians

I. Extraordinary Vision (Acts 10:9–15)
- A. Descending Sheet (vv. 9–12)
- B. Declaring Clean (vv. 13–15)
  Fiddleheads

II. Eminent Visitors (Acts 10:30–35)
- A. The Angelic Messenger (vv. 30–33)
- B. The Preaching Apostle (vv. 34–35)

III. Equal Value (Galatians 3:28–29)
- A. All Are One (v. 28)
  Nursing Qualifications
- B. All Are Heirs (v. 29)

Conclusion
- A. Breaking Down Walls
- B. Prayer
- C. Thought to Remember

Introduction

A. Equal Worth, Equal Access

In 1863, President Abraham Lincoln delivered a two-minute speech at the dedication of the National Cemetery in Gettysburg, Pennsylvania. The speech, now known as the "Gettysburg Address," contains several phrases that have become iconic in American culture. Boldly, Lincoln declares that "all men are created equal." His words echo the Declaration of Independence, where the phrase appears as one of Thomas Jefferson's "self-evident truths." Jefferson himself probably borrowed the statement from earlier philosophers. In fact, historians found examples of the phrase as early as 1381!

However, neither Jefferson nor Lincoln nor any other philosophers originated the concept of equality. Human equality was established by our Creator God, who formed everyone in His image (Genesis 1:26–27). We all possess equivalent worth in God's sight. The concept of *equal worth* is bound up in the notion of *equal access* to God's grace. Today's lesson explores that connection.

B. Lesson Context: Acts

The church birthed on the day of Pentecost stemmed from a core of believers with Jewish backgrounds (Acts 2:5). The twelve apostles, seven deacons in Jerusalem (6:5–6), Paul and Barnabas (14:1), and Jesus Himself were all ethnically Jewish or converts to Judaism. Most Jews in the Roman Empire kept themselves apart from Gentiles, forming distinct communities in their cities. Observant Jews saw Gentiles as unclean pagans who endangered Jewish religious and moral purity. They would not eat with Gentiles nor visit their homes (10:28).

Jewish faith drew a significant number of non-Jewish people. Some of these Gentiles became "proselytes," complete converts to Judaism who were circumcised and followed the Law of Moses (Acts 2:10; 6:5; 13:43). Other Gentiles worshiped God but did not become total converts. These people were called "devout," or those who "feareth God" (13:16, 26; 17:4, 17).

C. Lesson Context: Galatians

The book of Galatians is a fiery letter from the

apostle Paul to the church at Galatia. Paul wrote it to clarify the relationship between Jewish and Gentile Christians. Arguments arose debating whether Gentiles must follow the Law of Moses and be circumcised into the Jewish faith to be faithful Christians. Paul posits that Jesus fulfilled the law and Gentiles were not bound to follow it. Paul's knowledge of Hebrew law and tradition, paired with his sincere love for Gentile believers, created the necessary opening for God to bring unity to a diverse community.

I. Extraordinary Vision

(Acts 10:9–15)

A. Descending Sheet (vv. 9–12)

9. On the morrow, as they went on their journey, and drew nigh unto the city, Peter went up upon the housetop to pray about the sixth hour.

The word *they* refers to a group of three men sent from Cornelius to find Peter and bring him back to Caesarea (Acts 10:7–8). The journey took the men a little less than a day. They came near *the city* of Joppa around *the sixth hour*. Our time keeping equivalent is "around noon."

The author notes that simultaneous to the group approaching their destination, Peter *went up* to the roof of Simon's house *to pray*. The roofs of this period were typically flat and functioned almost like an extra room. Tenants commonly used them for storage, worship, and socializing, especially during hot summer days.

> **What Do You Think?**
>
> Is it a good idea to set specific times each day for prayer? Why, or why not?
>
> **Digging Deeper**
>
> How do Daniel 6:10 and Acts 3:1 help frame your response?

10. And he became very hungry, and would have eaten: but while they made ready, he fell into a trance.

Peter, ready for his midday meal, becomes *very hungry*. His hosts begin to prepare food. Before refrigeration, most dishes had to be freshly made, so Peter's appetite had time to grow during the preparations. While he waits, Peter falls into a *trance*. This state is separate from his hunger.

11. And saw heaven opened, and a certain vessel descending unto him, as it had been a great sheet knit at the four corners, and let down to the earth.

In the trance, Peter experiences a vision. He sees *heaven opened*. In the first century, people associated the sky with the dwelling place of God. Seeing it "opened" suggests God's presence and power (compare Jesus' baptism in Matthew 3:13 and Stephen's vision in Acts 7:56).

The text lets us "see" the vision from Peter's perspective. At first, he watches a mysterious *vessel* that descends from the sky. The vessel turns out to be a large *sheet* lowered by its *four corners*. This sheet, made of linen, was a standard tool in the ancient world. It served several purposes, from providing shade to covering one's body while sleeping.

12. Wherein were all manner of fourfooted beasts of the earth, and wild beasts, and creeping things, and fowls of the air.

The sheet's contents, a collection of live animals, surely surprise Peter. Our text's mention of *all manner* of creatures may reflect the wording of the creation account (Genesis 1:20, 24). The

How to Say It

Abraham	*Ay*-bruh-ham.
Barnabas	*Bar*-nuh-bus.
Caesarea	Sess-uh-*ree*-uh.
centurion	sen-*ture*-ee-un.
Cornelius	Cor-*neel*-yus.
Deuteronomy	Due-ter-*ahn*-uh-me.
Ephesians	Ee-*fee*-zhunz.
Galatia	Guh-*lay*-shuh.
Galatians	Guh-*lay*-shunz.
Gentiles	*Jen*-tiles.
Joppa	*Jop*-uh.
Judaism	*Joo*-duh-izz-um or *Joo*-day-izz-um.
Pentecost	*Pent*-ih-kost.
patriarch	*pay*-tree-ark.
proselytes	*prahss*-uh-lights.
Simon	*Sy*-mun.

Visual for Lesson 3. *Point to the visual and ask, "How can we show God's impartial love to someone different from us this week?"*

animals on the sheet include all kinds of *beasts*, *creeping things* (probably rats, insects, or reptiles), and birds. While the text does not name any specific species, the collection includes animals that were "unclean" according to the Law of Moses (see commentary below).

B. Declaring Clean (vv. 13–15)

13. And there came a voice to him, Rise, Peter; kill, and eat.

Peter's vision continues as a *voice* commands him to slaughter the animals for a meal. This command comes as a shock to the apostle. While the Law of Moses acknowledges that God created all creatures as "good" (Genesis 1:25), it also lays out clear instructions regarding which animals are appropriate for food (Leviticus 11; Deuteronomy 14:3–12). Animals like cows and sheep are considered "clean" (Leviticus 11:3). Other animals, such as lizards and rats, are deemed "unclean" (11:29–30). Certain types of birds are also unclean (Deuteronomy 14:12-18). Eating, and in some cases even touching, an unclean animal is forbidden for observant Jews (Leviticus 5:2; 7:21).

If an animal species was named "unclean," it did not necessarily mean it was physically dirty or that it was somehow more "sinful" than other animals. It can be helpful to think of "cleanness" as a visible representation of God's unique holiness. A person had to be clean (pure) to approach God's holy spaces or participate in corporate worship (Exodus 19:10; Leviticus 7:21; 15:31; Numbers 19:13, 20). One of the ways the Jewish people showed their commitment to God and displayed their status as His special people was by committing to "clean" practices and foods (Leviticus 20:26). This applied not only to the food they ate but also to the clothes they wore (19:19). In Peter's day, most Jews avoided any risk of uncleanness by refusing association with Gentiles, who regularly ate and touched unclean things (John 18:28; Acts 10:28).

14. But Peter said, Not so, Lord; for I have never eaten any thing that is common or unclean.

Peter understands that *the voice* in verse 13 is God's voice, so he addresses Him as *Lord*. Peter's response confirms that at least some of the animals on the sheet are *unclean*.

The apostle strongly protests that he has never *eaten any thing* that would violate the Law of Moses. The Old Testament depicts Jews' refusal to eat unclean food as an act of faithfulness (compare Ezekiel 4:12–15; Daniel 1:1–17).

The word translated *common* here is translated "defiled" in Mark 7:2 and "unholy" in Hebrews 10:29. In this case, it reflects the sense of something outside of God's boundaries for His people.

15. And the voice spake unto him again the second time, What God hath cleansed, that call not thou common.

The voice of the Lord responds to Peter with a final word. Despite Peter's reservations, *God* is the one who decides what or who is unclean. If God chooses, He can designate something as *cleansed* that was previously declared *unclean*. This statement is consistent with Jesus' assertion that all foods are clean since the accurate measure of cleanness is based on a person's heart (Mark 7:19).

Further, God's words remind us of His promise to create a new, "cleansed" people for Himself, who are willing and able to live out His commands (Ezekiel 36:25–28). Under this new covenant, God's holy people are not distinguished by a diet or a set of practices. Instead, they are marked by a complete inward transformation (Jeremiah 31:33; compare Hebrews 8:10).

The vision repeats twice more, highlighting its importance (Acts 10:16).

Fiddleheads

In Maine, we have a springtime delicacy called "fiddleheads." They are edible ferns. When I was a little girl, my mom would cook them for me. They were a delicious treat.

I recently showed my children some fiddleheads growing in the woods. "You *eat* those?" they exclaimed. My kids struggle to eat green vegetables on a good day, so their palates are suspicious. I considered their question. After all, fiddleheads do look funny.

Peter and other Jews of his time were conditioned to sort food, actions, and even people into categories. But God called Peter to change his thinking. Today, we still tend to see some people the way my children look at fiddleheads. But God calls us to remove our biases (Acts 10:34). What biases do you hold that need to change?

—B. R.

> **What Do You Think?**
> What makes you pure, clean, or holy? What evidence do you have of your cleansing?
> **Digging Deeper**
> What transformation have you experienced since becoming a Christian?

II. Eminent Visitors

(Acts 10:30–35)

A. The Angelic Messenger (vv. 30–33)

30. And Cornelius said, Four days ago I was fasting until this hour; and at the ninth hour I prayed in my house, and, behold, a man stood before me in bright clothing.

The men from Caesarea bring Peter to *Cornelius*. He receives the apostle enthusiastically (Acts 10:17–29) and recounts his experience from Acts 10:3–6. *Fasting* was a common practice for both Jews and God-fearing Gentiles, often used to express devotion or underline a specific request to God (Psalm 35:13; Daniel 6:18; Acts 14:23). At *the ninth hour*, or about three o'clock, a man dressed *in bright clothing* appears, whom Cornelius recognizes as an angel (Acts 10:22; compare John 20:12).

> **What Do You Think?**
> How should we react to claims of angelic visitations today?
> **Digging Deeper**
> How do Galatians 1:8; Colossians 2:18; and Hebrews 1:1–2 inform your response?

31. And said, Cornelius, thy prayer is heard, and thine alms are had in remembrance in the sight of God.

Cornelius doesn't share his prayer request. Whatever his *prayer*, the angel tells him it was *heard*. That is, the Lord acknowledged Cornelius' words and was ready to give him an answer (compare Luke 1:13).

Alms refers to money given for the relief of those experiencing poverty. The angel tells Cornelius that God sees and remembers the care he's given the needy. God calls His people to hold concern for the poor and to give generously (Deuteronomy 15:11; see lesson 2).

32. Send therefore to Joppa, and call hither Simon, whose surname is Peter; he is lodged in the house of one Simon a tanner by the sea side: who, when he cometh, shall speak unto thee.

The angel gives instructions: Cornelius is to send for *Peter*. Then he provides the ancient equivalent of an address. Simon is a *tanner*. Tanners made their living by curing animal skins in stinky liquid to turn them into leather. We can, therefore, deduce that Simon's family lived on the outskirts of town, where sea breezes might carry the smells away. Presumably, Peter would be easy to find. The angel implies that Peter has an essential message for Cornelius.

33. Immediately therefore I sent to thee; and thou hast well done that thou art come. Now therefore are we all here present before God, to hear all things that are commanded thee of God.

Cornelius, a centurion, was a man of action and authority (compare Luke 7:8). He wasted no time in sending for Peter. In the meantime, he gathered the members of his household, who were also "devout" Gentiles (Acts 10:2), to hear what the man of God had to say (10:24).

What Do You Think?

Have you ever purposefully gathered a group in your home to hear a traveling teacher or missionary?

Digging Deeper

How might you increase your enthusiasm toward sharing the good news with your community?

B. The Preaching Apostle (vv. 34–35)

34. Then Peter opened his mouth, and said, Of a truth I perceive that God is no respecter of persons.

Although Peter initially struggles to understand the vision he saw (Acts 10:11–15, 17), Cornelius's story helps him grasp its significance. God's command to not call anything "common" is not about unclean food (10:15), but about people—specifically the Gentiles. Peter's resulting conclusion, which he shares with Cornelius, changes the course of the church forever.

Firstly, Peter declares that *God is no respecter of persons.* This saying means that God does not hold preference toward or partiality for any one people group over any others. While such words surprised a first-century Jewish audience, this theme runs throughout the Old Testament (Exodus 12:49; Numbers 15:15–16). It continues into the New Testament (Romans 2:11; Ephesians 6:9).

35. But in every nation he that feareth him, and worketh righteousness, is accepted with him.

Secondly, Peter concludes that membership in the people of God is not limited to any one *nation* or ethnicity. Instead, every person who reveres the Lord and lives by faith in *righteousness* finds acceptance as one of His people. Acceptance was joyous news for Cornelius and his family. Peter boldly declared God's inclusion of them in God's plan for repentance and salvation (compare Acts 11:18)!

III. Equal Value

(Galatians 3:28–29)

A. All Are One (v. 28)

28. There is neither Jew nor Greek, there is neither bond nor free, there is neither male nor female: for ye are all one in Christ Jesus.

Roughly 20 years after Peter met Cornelius, the apostle Paul revisits the theme of Gentile inclusion in his letter to the Galatians. Some members of the Galatian church taught that Gentiles had to be circumcised to receive salvation (Galatians 5:2–4; 6:12; compare Acts 15:1–11). Paul, however, argues that faith in Jesus grants full status as a member of God's family (Galatians 3:26–4:7). In the above verse, he teaches that all distinctions between people groups disappear when viewed through the lens of salvation *in Christ Jesus.*

The verse considers three specific contrasts: ethnicity, social status, and gender. These categories broadly sum up the way first-century Roman society classified people. They may also reflect the structure of a typical daily prayer that an observant Jewish man might recite. During the prayer, the man would thank God that he was not a Gentile, slave, or woman since tradition limited each of those groups from full participation in temple worship.

In contrast, Paul reminds the Galatians that faith in Christ does not hinge on a person's heritage. Although they may begin as a *Jew* or a *Greek*, their ultimate, unified identity ends as *one.* The Jew/Greek comparison may be first in Paul's list because it was the most controversial at the time (compare Acts 11:1–3; 15:11–12).

The following comparison is one of social status: *there is neither bond nor free.* Slavery was widespread in the Roman Empire, and if someone was not *free*, it affected nearly every aspect of their life. Even so, Paul teaches that this earthly standing does not affect a person's status in Christ.

The third comparison is that of gender. Even though gender was instituted at creation and called "good" (Genesis 1:27; 5:2), the distinctions of *male* and *female* are also irrelevant when it comes to being children of God (Galatians 3:26).

Though Paul does not address every possible category of difference, his point is clear: salvation through faith in Jesus is equally accessible to all people groups. Every believer is as "Christian" as any other: we *are all one* when we clothe ourselves with Christ (Galatians 3:27). There is one Lord for all humankind (Romans 10:12).

> **What Do You Think?**
> List modern-day classifications in the categories of ethnicity, social status, and gender.
>
> **Digging Deeper**
> Who do you struggle to welcome into God's family by faith? How might you overcome your prejudice?

Nursing Qualifications

My grandmother was a nurse in the 1940s. In those days, nursing was a woman's job. The pressed and starched uniform, replete with a cap and apron, was made exclusively for women. There may be many reasons why this was the mindset of the day. Still, time and experience have taught modern society that men are just as capable of being compassionate nurses as their female counterparts. One of the kindest nursing aids my grandmother ever had was a young man in his early twenties who gently carried her fragile body to bed after a bad fall.

Just as nursing no longer sees a gendered distinction in professional capabilities, Paul reminds his readers that God makes no distinction between people who may join His family. All sizes, shapes, socioeconomic classes, genders, and ethnicities become one in Jesus. God breaks down the barriers we often put up to separate and segregate. Are there assumptions you make about who belongs in the family of God? How might you erase lines God never intended for you to draw? —B. R.

B. All Are Heirs (v. 29)

29. And if ye be Christ's, then are ye Abraham's seed, and heirs according to the promise.

Being a descendant of Abraham, or of *Abraham's seed*, was a vital self-identifier for Jews in the first century (Luke 1:55, 73; 3:8; John 8:37, 39). Paul accepts this identification and then includes Gentiles in it. They too are *heirs* of the promise given to the patriarch (Ephesians 3:6). This status comes through Christ as the "seed" (Galatians 3:16) and our adoption as God's "sons" (4:5; Romans 8:15–17). As children of God, we inherit all of God's promises. While Paul's opponents thought of Abrahamic heritage in a biological sense, Paul speaks of it spiritually. Through faith in Jesus, Abraham's blessing includes people of all backgrounds (Galatians 3:9).

Conclusion

A. Breaking Down Walls

The account of Peter and Cornelius is the longest single narrative in the book of Acts. The length of the account highlights the importance of what their experiences represent: the acceptance of Gentiles into the new covenant.

While the Bible teaches that Jesus meant for the gospel to be shared with all people (Mark 16:15; Luke 24:47; Acts 1:8), the first-century church struggled to overcome divisions. They needed a reminder that anyone, through faith in Christ, could become a full member of God's people. Today, new sources of division rear their ugly heads in the church. Christians argue and divide over politics, worship styles, and preaching preferences.

The events of Acts 10 show how Peter and Cornelius shifted their understanding and widened their acceptance of each other to achieve unity in Christ. God did not impose their cooperation but led them to conclusions that broke the cultural walls between them. Paul's words in Galatians 3 emphasize the stripping away of divisive categories and focusing on the commonality that comes from faith in Christ Jesus. If we focus on Jesus and recognize that He alone is the Lord of the church, our divisions may melt away.

B. Prayer

Lord God, forgive us for the times we've failed to consider every believer in Christ as an equal member of Your family. Unite us to see no distinctions in Your salvation. In Jesus' name we pray. Amen.

C. Thought to Remember

Christ's salvation is available to all people without distinction.

Involvement Learning

Enhance your lesson with KJV Bible Student *(from your curriculum supplier) and the reproducible activity page (at www.standardlesson.com or in the back of the* KJV Standard Lesson Commentary Deluxe Edition*).*

Into the Lesson

Begin the session by discussing a time you held a preconceived notion about someone or something that turned out to be completely wrong. Explain your idea, how you realized it was incorrect, and what its impact was on you.

Invite participants in your class to share their own experiences. Ask them to include a preconceived notion they held, how they realized it was wrong, and how it impacted their lives. Encourage a supportive and nonjudgmental sharing environment. Consider having several personal examples to share, if needed. After the discussion, ask your class: "How do we challenge our preconceived notions to embrace diversity"?

To lead into Bible study, say: "Today we are exploring the story of Peter and Cornelius. In it, God challenges their preconceived notions and reveals a new understanding of His plan for salvation."

Into the Word

Read Acts 10:9–15, 30–35 out loud with your class. Then divide the class in half, designating one half as *Jews* and the other half as *Gentiles.* Create a physical barrier between the two groups. Then have each group discuss the following question from the perspective of their group names: What historical and cultural barriers existed between the Jews and Gentiles during the first century? Refer to Leviticus 11 and Deuteronomy 15:4–11.

Remove the barrier and bring the groups back together to share their findings. Have them discuss the challenges and opportunities involved in overcoming divisions. Then return to the story of Peter's vision in Acts 10:9–15. Talk about how Peter and Cornelius overcame their division. Ask: 1–How does the Holy Spirit play a role in breaking down barriers between people? 2–What are some modern barriers that divide people? 3–How can Christians be agents of reconciliation and unity?

Read Galatians 3:28–29 out loud. As a group, identify common barriers to unity with the church and society today (examples: race, gender, social status, political views). Write ideas on the board. Then ask: 1–How do you see these barriers in light of Acts 10? 2–How does Galatians 3:28–29 address these challenges? 3–How might we live out the principles of Galatians 3:28–29 in our daily lives?

Alternative. Distribute copies of "Word Study" from the activity page, which you can download. Have participants work in pairs to complete as indicated. Then ask students to discuss the concluding questions with a small group.

Option. Distribute copies of "Identity and Belonging" from the activity page. Give learners one minute to complete it individually. Then ask them to share their thoughts with a partner.

Into Life

Summarize the lesson with a comment like: "All believers, regardless of their background, are equal before God and united as one body." Remind learners that dismantling walls of division in a community and the broader family of God comes with time and practice. Brainstorm as a class some ways you can promote unity. Consider the following ideas:

- Organize a meal where people may share stories and experiences.
- Start a book club to discuss books that address diversity.
- Arrange a community-wide Bible study.
- Collaborate on community service initiatives to foster a sense of shared purpose.
- Invite experts or community leaders to share their experiences of unity and division.
- Participate in a church or community collaborative event to foster relationships.

As a class, make a plan to implement one idea, including a set timeline. Close in prayer, praising Christ for uniting believers in Him.

March 29
Lesson 4 (KJV)

Waiting for God's Peace

Devotional Reading: Revelation 5:8–14
Background Scripture: Isaiah 11:6–10; John 18:28–38;
Ephesians 4:4–6, 13–19

Isaiah 2:2–4

**2 And it shall come to pass in the last days,
that the mountain of the LORD's house shall be
established in the top of the mountains, and
shall be exalted above the hills; and all nations
shall flow unto it.**
**3 And many people shall go and say, Come
ye, and let us go up to the mountain of the
LORD, to the house of the God of Jacob; and
he will teach us of his ways, and we will walk
in his paths: for out of Zion shall go forth the
law, and the word of the LORD from Jerusalem.**
**4 And he shall judge among the nations,
and shall rebuke many people: and they shall
beat their swords into plowshares, and their
spears into pruninghooks: nation shall not
lift up sword against nation, neither shall they
learn war any more.**

Acts 17:26–28

**26 And hath made of one blood all nations
of men for to dwell on all the face of the
earth, and hath determined the times before
appointed, and the bounds of their habitation;**
**27 That they should seek the Lord, if haply
they might feel after him, and find him, though
he be not far from every one of us:**
**28 For in him we live, and move, and have
our being; as certain also of your own poets
have said, For we are also his offspring.**

Key Text

Many people shall go and say, Come ye, and let us go up to the mountain of the LORD, to the house of the God of Jacob; and he will teach us of his ways, and we will walk in his paths: for out of Zion shall go forth the law, and the word of the LORD from Jerusalem. —**Isaiah 2:3**

Social Teachings of the Church

Unit 1: Fulfilling Our Obligations to Neighbors

Lessons 1–4

Lesson Aims

After participating in this lesson, each learner will be able to:

1. Summarize the main points of Isaiah's prophecy.

2. Explain how God's peace is already present in the world but not fully manifest until Jesus returns.

3. Create a plan for fostering peace in a specific context where unresolved conflict exists.

Lesson Outline

Introduction
- A. Yearning for Peace
- B. Lesson Context: Isaiah in Judah
- C. Lesson Context: Paul in Athens

I. Final Peace Among Nations (Isaiah 2:2–4)
- A. Mountain for All (v. 2)
- B. Identification of Authority (v. 3)
- C. Freedom from War (v. 4)
  - *There Is a Place*

II. Divine Origin of Nations (Acts 17:26–28)
- A. Creator's Actions (v. 26)
  - *Honoring God*
- B. Humanity's Response (v. 27)
- C. Humanity's Awareness (v. 28)

Conclusion
- A. Promised Peace
- B. Prayer
- C. Thought to Remember

Introduction

A. Yearning for Peace

Throughout history, war is a constant reality. Examples of conflict are not hard to find; you can pick any century. In modern times, many of us grow weary of seeing headlines about wars and threats of war on a regular basis. We live in a world that is often gripped by terrorism and violence. Nevertheless, most people desire peace. We yearn for it. But how can such peace arrive? Where will it come from?

The Bible tells us that true, lasting peace will only come from God. The total peace He promises has two aspects. The first is peace between us and God. The second is peace between humans, nations, and people groups. The first aspect has already been achieved through Jesus (Romans 5:1). This week, our Scripture texts reveal the path toward the second aspect.

B. Lesson Context: Isaiah in Judah

Isaiah began prophesying at the end of the reign of Uzziah, king of Judah, in about 740 BC (Isaiah 1:1; 6:1). During Isaiah's lifetime, the kingdom of Judah faced threats from within and without. Whether the danger came from war with the massive Assyrian Empire (7:17) or injustice and violence within Judah itself (1:21–23), the future of its capital, Jerusalem, was uncertain.

The beginning of the book of Isaiah warns Judah against an even deeper conflict: a war of rebellion that the people were waging against God. The people of Jerusalem led lives filled with unrighteousness, idolatry, and oppression; the once "faithful city" had become a "harlot" (Isaiah 1:21). Isaiah explains that the Judeans will have no peace with other nations or among their own people until they first accept God's terms of peace. Thus, Isaiah calls Judah to repent (1:16–17). Amid promises of fearsome judgment, however, Isaiah also announces a message of hope: Jerusalem would once again become a "city of righteousness" through God's redeeming work (1:26–27). The first of today's texts (which has a parallel in Micah 4:1–3) picks up on this theme.

C. Lesson Context: Paul in Athens

On his second missionary journey (AD 52–54), Paul traveled through the region of Macedonia (modern-day northern Greece). During this journey, he planted churches in the cities of Philippi and Thessalonica (Acts 16:6–15; 17:1–9). Due to persecution in Thessalonica, Paul fled to Athens, some 300 miles to the south (17:14–15).

As Paul walked around Athens, he became distressed by all the city's idolatry (Acts 17:16). He responded by engaging fellow Jews, God-fearing Gentiles, and others in conversation about Jesus. Paul's teaching drew the attention of local philosophers, who invited him to speak at the Areopagus, the space in which the city's political council met (17:19). The Areopagus council likely had authority over which religious teachings were allowed into the city. These men had a rich knowledge of Greek philosophy but almost no familiarity with Hebrew Scripture. Today's passage comes as Paul addresses this new, highly educated audience with the gospel.

I. Final Peace Among Nations

(Isaiah 2:2–4)

A. Mountain for All (v. 2)

2. And it shall come to pass in the last days, that the mountain of the LORD's house shall be established in the top of the mountains, and shall be exalted above the hills; and all nations shall flow unto it.

After a first chapter filled with dire warnings for Judah to repent (see Lesson Context), the Lord promises that something incredible will happen during *the last days*. The breadth of this oracle is astounding: *all nations* will come to *the Lord's house*, that is, the temple in Jerusalem. They will come not as enemies, ready to mount an attack, but as disciples, ready to learn and have a relationship with God.

It is not immediately clear what Isaiah means by "the last days." The original audience likely understood such days to be a part of the future history of the nation. Several Old Testament prophets refer to this as a time when God's glory and authority will be revealed to Israel and the world more universally (Jeremiah 49:39; Hosea 3:5; Micah 4:1; etc.).

The imagery of *the Lord's house* located high on the top of *the mountain* indicates the temple's relative importance. At the time of Isaiah's prophecy, other fictitious gods were commonly worshiped and offered sacrifices on mountains and hills as well (Isaiah 65:7; compare 2 Kings 15:4). The elevated location of the Lord's house on *the top of the mountains* indicates the Lord's holiness above all other gods and authorities (compare Psalm 3:4; Isaiah 27:13; 56:7; 66:20; Micah 4:7). God had commanded the people of Israel to destroy such sites upon entrance into the promised land of Canaan (Deuteronomy 12:2), but the vision in the verse before us is that of a singular, holy mountain naturally elevated above all others. The last days will make clear that the Lord alone is God and that the God of Israel is the only true God.

The New Testament references the language of "last days" to describe the messianic era, as God speaks to us through Jesus the Son (Hebrews 1:2). Both Jesus' own physical body and the church as the body of Christ are described as the new temple (John 2:21; 1 Corinthians 3:16–17; 2 Corinthians 6:16). Understood in this light, we can read Isaiah's prophecy as a promise that the nations will come to learn from Jesus through the church. Through its obedience to God and its proclamation of the truth, the church will make known the mystery of God to the nations (Ephesians 3:9–11).

B. Identification of Authority (v. 3)

3a. And many people shall go and say, Come ye, and let us go up to the mountain of the LORD, to the house of the God of Jacob.

When *many people* realize the nature of *the mountain of the Lord* as defined above, they will be drawn toward it and to the God who dwells there (compare Micah 4:2). Further, they will also draw each other to the mountain, encouraging each other to *go up* and approach God together. The image is one of people who no longer oppress each other or encourage each other to pursue idolatry but help each other serve the one true God. The image of *many people* from various nations worshipping *the God of Jacob* may have shocked its original audience. Still, Isaiah underscores the promise by later prophesying that even Israel's historical enemies of Egypt and Assyria would experience blessing and become the people of God (Isaiah 19:25).

Jesus echoes this verse's imagery when He tells His disciples that "repentance and remission of sins should be preached in his name among all the nations, beginning at Jerusalem" (Luke 24:47; compare Matthew 28:19–20; Acts 1:8).

3b. And he will teach us of his ways, and we will walk in his paths: for out of Zion shall go forth the law, and the word of the LORD from Jerusalem.

A logical prerequisite for being able to *walk in* God's *paths* is learning *his ways* (compare Psalm 86:11). *The law* was given to Israel to guide them as they lived before God in the land He gave to them. Initially, God designed His law to identify people who were distinct in bearing witness to Him as the one true God. Israel was to be a "kingdom of priests" with the unique honor of displaying God's character to a watching world (Exodus 19:6). When the nations saw Israel flourish because of its people's obedience, they would inquire and want to share in that life with them (Deuteronomy 4:5–8). Sadly, prophets like Isaiah and Jeremiah indicate that this beautiful display was not what happened in history. Instead, Israel and Judah often subverted their priestly role through idolatry and oppressive behavior toward others.

In the verse before us, God promises that, once again, people would follow *the word of the Lord*. Israel would truly become a light to the nations by broadcasting that word to all (compare Isaiah 42:6). The Gospel of Luke returns to this image, with the prophet Simeon announcing that Jesus Himself would be that "light" to heal the relationship between God and the nations (Luke 2:32).

What Do You Think?

What steps do you need to take to learn God's ways better?

Digging Deeper

How do Proverbs 6:23; John 14:15; Colossians 1:10; and 1 John 2:5; 5:3 inform your response?

C. Freedom from War (v. 4)

4a. And he shall judge among the nations, and shall rebuke many people.

The word translated *rebuke* can take the sense of "arbitrate," though other shades of meaning are possible (compare Isaiah 11:3–4; 37:4; Jeremiah 2:19; Micah 4:3; 6:2). God Himself will be the one to decide what is true, good, and righteous as He executes justice between people groups in the world (compare Isaiah 32:1). Yet while *many people* from *among the nations* will seek God and learn from His word, many others will not. God will deal with such people according to their folly, violence, and injustice.

4b. And they shall beat their swords into plowshares, and their spears into pruninghooks.

In each of our three verses from Isaiah, we can see a pattern of *parallelism*. Parallelism, which appears frequently in Hebrew poetry, happens when words in one line of a verse reflect the words in another line to communicate a larger point. In this partial verse, we see parallelism communicating God's promise to establish a permanent peace between Himself and humanity.

swords . . . . plowshares
↓ ↓
spears . . . . .pruninghooks

At this point, a further promise emerges: when the nations are in fellowship with God, they will have peace with one another. At the proper time, they will take their weapons, both *swords* and *spears*, and turn them into farming instruments. The destructive tools of warfare will become tools of peaceful creation (contrast Joel 3:10). Nations will be free to seek ways to flourish together.

4c. Nation shall not lift up sword against nation, neither shall they learn war any more.

When every *nation* becomes devoted to God's reign, there will no longer be a need for conflict between them. They will be transformed from self-interested, violent people groups into participants in the kingdom of God. Each nation will be filled with peace, justice, and righteousness. Such nations no longer need to pursue conquest and domination over each other. There will no longer be a need to learn the ways of *war*. There will no longer be any cause for fear from other people (Micah 4:4). When God reigns, peace will reign too.

While we can be sure that the Lord is at work within the church and the wider world, we recognize that the world will not fully know this peace until Jesus returns and all people worship Him.

What Do You Think?

In what ways is the message of the gospel one of peace (see Romans 5:1; 2 Peter 3:14)?

Digging Deeper

How can we direct our gospel witness to move people from all nations toward peace with God?

There Is a Place

Stellenbosch, South Africa, is home to some of the most beautiful landscapes in the world. Towering mountains surround acres of luscious green vineyards, plentiful orchards of citrus produce, and vast expanses of farmland that extend for miles. Places such as these remind me that there will be a future kingdom with lasting peace. It will be far better and more beautiful than anything on earth. God's people will flourish and prosper there, surrounded by all that is good, true, and beautiful. Thankfully, we'll never have to leave.

This is not just wishful thinking—quite the opposite! Many prophetic visions in Scripture speak of a place where war and suffering cease and where people will live in a perfect relationship with each other and the Creator. This calls the people of God to live not with dread or fear toward the future but in hopeful expectation of what is to come. In what ways are you advancing the kingdom of God toward that ultimate reality to come? —N. V.

II. Divine Origin of Nations

(Acts 17:26–28)

A. Creator's Actions (v. 26)

26. And hath made of one blood all nations of men for to dwell on all the face of the earth, and hath determined the times before appointed, and the bounds of their habitation.

Many of Paul's listeners in Athens would have been trained in philosophy (Acts 17:18; see Lesson Context). With this in mind, Paul adapts his usual mode of sharing the gospel. Rather than beginning with obvious references to Hebrew Scripture, as he might with a Jewish audience (example: 17:1–4), some commentators propose that Paul adopts a common three-part form of classical debate:

I. Points of Reference
(common ground; Acts 17:22–23)
II. Points of Relevance
(importance of the topic; Acts 17:24–28)
III. Points of Disturbance
(how Christianity differs; Acts 17:29–31)

Well into his second point by verse 26, Paul draws on his knowledge of Hebrew Scripture to strengthen his argument while also referencing concepts found in Greek philosophy. He affirms the creation of humanity from *one blood*, affirming all peoples' descent from Adam and Eve (Genesis 3:20). Much of Paul's Greek audience, influenced by a philosophy called Stoicism, would have already agreed that all humanity came from divine origin (though they may not have been completely sure which god was the creator!). Paul's statement regarding *times* and *bounds* may reflect texts such as

How to Say It

Aratus	*Air*-uh-tus.
Areopagus	Air-ee-*op*-uh-gus.
Epimenides	Ep-ih-*men*-ih-deez.
Macedonia	Mass-eh-*doe*-nee-uh.
Philippi	Fih-*lip*-pie or *Fil*-ih-pie.
Stoicism	*Stoe*-uh-siz-um.
Thessalonica	*Thess*-uh-lo-***nye***-kuh (*th* as in *thin*).
Uzziah	Uh-*zye*-uh.

Visual for Lesson 4. *Display this visual as you discuss the lesson conclusion and associated questions.*

Deuteronomy 32:8 and Isaiah 10:13. This language would have resonated with adherents of Stoicism, who held that all of history was guided by one powerful, driving force.

Honoring God

I live in one of the oldest and busiest cities in the world. Walking down the street is like a history lesson as I pass majestic Victorian-era architecture and buildings that once housed kings. The architecture that remains from past centuries is a powerful, visible reminder that we are all part of something bigger than ourselves. I often find myself wondering what my own life would have been like had I lived in this city a century ago. Would the pace of life be any slower? Would things be simpler, or would they be equally complex?

When I consider the journey that my city has been on in the last millennium, I am reminded of Acts 17:26. God has "marked out" a special time and space for the people of our city to glorify Him. It's like a parent saying to a child, "Here's a canvas I made for you, and here are the paintbrushes. Go and create something that honors me!" Is that the way you approach your tasks? —N. V.

B. Humanity's Response (v. 27)

27. That they should seek the Lord, if haply they might feel after him, and find him, though he be not far from every one of us.

God created the earth to be inhabited (Genesis 1:28). He allowed all kinds of nations to flourish in different times and places (see Acts 17:26, above). But *why* did God create nations in this way? Paul explains that God did this in order for the nations to *feel after him, and find him.*

It is important to recognize that God is not playing a game of hide-and-seek in this regard. Although God transcends both time and space, He is concurrently *not far from every one of us*—this speaks to what is called His "immanence." This word describes His close presence and activity within the created world. God has always worked among nations to heal the broken relationship between humanity and Himself. His works are designed to create opportunities for people from every nation to seek Him.

Can people from every nation find God? Paul thinks they can. God has not left Himself without a witness through nature and history (see Acts 14:17; Romans 1:19–20). At the same time, people from all nations can be ignorant, blinded, and self-deceived by their own sin (1:18). Idolatry has darkened their sensibility to the true God. Paul even notes that the Athenians ignorantly worshiped what they called "the unknown god" (Acts 17:23).

Nevertheless, the true God never left them. God is present among the nations. Indeed, God is present to every person. The transcendent God is also the "right here, right now" God.

What Do You Think?

In what ways have you experienced the immanence and transcendence of God?

Digging Deeper

How would you explain the significance of these attributes of God to an unbeliever?

C. Humanity's Awareness (v. 28)

28. For in him we live, and move, and have our being; as certain also of your own poets have said, For we are also his offspring.

As Paul addresses the council, he confirms his statements about God by quoting their *own poets.* We might imagine that Paul's audience was surprised to hear an expert in Jewish law quoting

Greek poets. It should be amazing to *us* how widely read Paul is! It was compelling enough for at least part of the council to want to hear more of what Paul had to say in the future (see Acts 17:32–33).

Paul's first quote may come from Epimenides, a sixth-century BC philosopher-poet who writes that in Zeus, "We live and move and have our being." He then follows immediately by quoting the third-century BC poet Aratus, who describes Zeus with the words: "We are truly his offspring." Paul adapts these quotes to align with the Scriptural truth that God created and sustains all of humanity (see Genesis 2:7; Job 12:10; Psalm 104:29; etc.).

It is important to note that Paul is not arguing that Zeus and the God of Scripture are equal or even similar. Rather, he finds common ideological ground with the philosophers before claiming that the Lord is unique (Acts 17:29–31). This common ground indicates that some people and nations can understand truths about God, even if their ideas about Him are misguided in many ways. In effect, Paul says, "Hey, even some of your own people have figured out this part." Paul uses the council's own way of thinking as a springboard for the gospel. In this way, Paul's line of argument in verse 28 proves his words in verses 26 and 27!

What Do You Think?

What common starting points from contemporary secular culture can you draw on to introduce people to the gospel?

Digging Deeper

How can you be a better "student" of contemporary secular culture in this regard?

Conclusion

A. Promised Peace

When we suffer, or see others suffering, from the devastating effects of conflicts between nations, any hope for lasting peace may seem unrealistic. Christians might be tempted to imagine that God has left the nations to fend for themselves. But today's texts tell a different story.

The Lord promises in Isaiah 2:2–4 that, eventually, people will end their conflicts with each other when they embrace His ways. Peace between humanity and God will ultimately result in peace between nations. Christians can rest assured that peace has been established between God and people through Jesus Christ (Romans 5:1; 2 Peter 3:14). Yet while God's reign of peace has begun, it is not yet fully complete. Until Jesus returns, there will always be wrongs to make right in the world. As His disciples, we are called to be peacemakers (Matthew 5:9; James 3:18). Through Christ's power, the church can be a shining example of peace in the world, starting within our own relationships. We must seek to live peaceably with everyone as far as it depends on us to do so (Romans 12:18). By leading the way in peacemaking, the church can truly be a light to the nations.

Although conflicts sometimes appear too deep to heal, Acts 17:24–26 reminds us that God has made each of these different groups for the purpose of seeking Him. Like Paul before the Areopagus council, we can use these differences as a launchpad to share the hope of the gospel.

One day, people from every nation and region, from every ethnic group and language, will stand before the throne of God and enjoy God's peace (Revelation 7:9–12). This will happen when God renews all things, and the new heaven and new earth appear (21:1–4). Finally, all the kingdoms of this world will become one kingdom in our Lord.

What Do You Think?

How will you practice peacemaking, thereby being a light to others of the gospel?

Digging Deeper

How can your class or congregation be agents of God's peace in your neighborhood? town or city? country?

B. Prayer

Lord God, we pray for peace among the nations. Work among the nations through us, God, to move them toward peace and toward You. May they seek Your face. In Jesus' name we pray. Amen.

C. Thought to Remember

Nations will find peace only when they find God.

Involvement Learning

Enhance your lesson with KJV Bible Student *(from your curriculum supplier) and the reproducible activity page (at www.standardlesson.com or in the back of the* KJV Standard Lesson Commentary Deluxe Edition*).*

Into the Lesson

Write on the board the following letters, with each letter being the header of a column:

P E A C E

Introduce the activity by asking, "What does it mean to find and experience peace?" Divide the class into five groups and assign each group one letter from the word *peace*. Distribute a sheet of paper and pen to each group and ask them to write down words or phrases beginning with their assigned letter that describe the experience of *peace*. After calling time, ask volunteers to share their responses and write them on the board. (Do not erase the header because it will be used during the Into Life section.)

Ask the following questions in whole-class discussion: 1–How have you experienced peace? 2–Why does peace seem elusive?

Lead into Bible study by saying, "Today's study will teach us that God is the author of peace. Through Christ, we can have peace with God, and, as a result, we can have peace with each other. Let's see what we can learn about the path of that peace."

Into the Word

Divide the class into two groups: **Isaiah Group** and **Paul Group**. Distribute handouts (you create) with the following questions for in-group discussion. Encourage groups to use study Bibles, lesson commentary, or online resources to complete the handout.

Isaiah Group. Read Isaiah 2:2–4. 1–What is the historical context of Isaiah's prophecy? 2–What does he prophesy will happen "in the last days"? 3–In what ways will the nations respond to other nations? to the Lord? 4–How would this prophecy have encouraged Isaiah's original audience? 5–How does Isaiah's prophecy encourage us?

Paul Group. Read Acts 17:26–28. 1–What is the historical context of Paul's speech? 2–What does Paul say is the reason that God made the nations? 3–How does Paul cite ancient poets and philosophers to reinforce his teaching points? 4–How would Paul's speech persuade the citizens of Athens? 5–How does Paul's speech encourage us?

After the activities, ask a volunteer from each group to report on their findings, augmenting their reports with information you have prepared based on the lesson commentary. Then ask the following questions for whole-class discussion: 1–What is the connection between these two passages? 2–What do these passages teach us about peace? 3–What do these passages teach us about God's priorities for the world? 4–What do these passages teach us about the ultimate end of the earth's nations?

Conclude the section by asking, "How do you see God's peace present in the world, knowing that it won't be fully manifest until Jesus' return?" After volunteers share their responses, ask volunteers to share how believers might live faithfully until that day comes.

Into Life

Return to the header from Into the Lesson. Lead a whole-class brainstorming session to list situations where people have unresolved conflict and need to experience God's peace. Each situation must begin with one of the letters of the header. Write responses under the appropriate letter.

Challenge learners to choose one of the responses where they could make a difference. Ask learners to create a plan for fostering peace in their chosen situation. Place learners into pairs to pray for each situation and ask for God's wisdom regarding the next steps.

Option. Distribute copies of the "Let There Be Peace on Earth" exercise from the activity page. Have learners complete it as a take-home activity.

Option. Distribute copies of the "And Let It Begin with Me" activity from the activity page. Have learners work in pairs or small groups to complete as indicated.

April 5
Lesson 5 (KJV)

Resurrection: The Future Hope

Devotional Reading: Luke 24:1–12
Background Scripture: Luke 24:1–12; 1 Corinthians 15:3–20, 50–58;
Revelation 22:1–5

1 Corinthians 15:13–20, 51–58

**13 But if there be no resurrection of the
dead, then is Christ not risen:
14 And if Christ be not risen, then is our
preaching vain, and your faith is also vain.
15 Yea, and we are found false witnesses of
God; because we have testified of God that he
raised up Christ: whom he raised not up, if so
be that the dead rise not.
16 For if the dead rise not, then is not Christ
raised:
17 And if Christ be not raised, your faith is
vain; ye are yet in your sins.
18 Then they also which are fallen asleep in
Christ are perished.
19 If in this life only we have hope in Christ,
we are of all men most miserable.
20 But now is Christ risen from the dead,
and become the firstfruits of them that slept.**

**51 Behold, I shew you a mystery; We shall
not all sleep, but we shall all be changed,
52 In a moment, in the twinkling of an eye,
at the last trump: for the trumpet shall sound,
and the dead shall be raised incorruptible, and
we shall be changed.
53 For this corruptible must put on
incorruption, and this mortal must put on
immortality.
54 So when this corruptible shall have put
on incorruption, and this mortal shall have put
on immortality, then shall be brought to pass
the saying that is written, Death is swallowed
up in victory.
55 O death, where is thy sting? O grave,
where is thy victory?
56 The sting of death is sin; and the
strength of sin is the law.
57 But thanks be to God, which giveth us
the victory through our Lord Jesus Christ.
58 Therefore, my beloved brethren, be ye
stedfast, unmoveable, always abounding in the
work of the Lord, forasmuch as ye know that
your labour is not in vain in the Lord.**

Key Text

Now is Christ risen from the dead, and become the firstfruits of them that slept. **—1 Corinthians 15:20**

Social Teachings

of the Church

Unit 2: Fulfilling Our Obligations to Family and Community

Lessons 5–8

Lesson Aims

After participating in this lesson, each learner will be able to:

1. Identify the "mystery" of 1 Corinthians 15:51.
2. Explain how Christ's resurrection brings believers comfort.
3. Compose a letter encouraging other believers that trials of this life are not God's final word.

Lesson Outline

Introduction

A. Groundbreaking News

B. Lesson Context

I. The Resurrection (1 Corinthians 15:13–20)

A. False Witness (vv. 13–15)

B. Futile Hope (vv. 16–19)

Hopeful or Hopeless?

C. Faithful Firstfruits (v. 20)

II. The Mystery (1 Corinthians 15:51–57)

A. Changed People (vv. 51–53)

B. Victorious Promise (vv. 54–57)

Unforeseen Losses

III. The Work (1 Corinthians 15:58)

Conclusion

A. Comma, Not Period

B. Prayer

C. Thought to Remember

Introduction

A. Groundbreaking News

The 1969 book *On Death and Dying*, by Elisabeth Kübler-Ross (1926–2004), proved revolutionary in identifying grief stages. The author named five parts of the grief cycle: *denial, anger, bargaining, depression,* and *acceptance.* These are typical stages experienced by a person diagnosed with a terminal illness. As a result of her research, Kübler-Ross pioneered hospice care for the terminally ill and served as an advocate for grieving families. Kübler-Ross received numerous honorary degrees for her insights. By July 1982, she had taught her grief model to approximately 125,000 students in various learning institutions.

Today we will consider the subject of death and dying too. As we do, we remember that the ultimate expert is Jesus. His experience of death and resurrection changed things forever.

B. Lesson Context

Corinth was a great commercial center in the first-century Roman Empire. It was situated between two seas on a very narrow strip of land in southern Greece: the Aegean to the east and the Adriatic to the west. A popular trade route grew between the two harbors because it was cheaper and less dangerous for merchants to freight their cargo overland than to sail around the Peloponnesian Peninsula.

Paul traveled to Corinth from Athens during his second missionary journey between AD 51–54. His initial visit lasted around 18 months (Acts 18:11). Then Paul traveled to Ephesus, where he made a brief stop before proceeding to Jerusalem. He returned to Ephesus on his third missionary journey and, while there, wrote a letter to the church in Corinth. We now refer to that letter as 1 Corinthians. (Paul mentions being in Ephesus in 1 Corinthians 16:8.)

Among an array of issues causing tension and debate within the Corinthian church was the resurrection of the dead. Some believers were still impacted by their pagan background and philosophical ways of thinking. The Greeks considered the body and soul as entirely separate entities. Plato and Socrates viewed the body as a "prison" for the soul. They even had a saying to express their philosophical disdain for physical mortality: *Soma Sema,* which means "the body [is] a tomb." Greek philosophers believed in the immortality of the soul but not a resurrection of the body (Acts 17:32).

Paul begins 1 Corinthians 15 by reminding the Corinthian church of the gospel he preached to them and that they received. The foundation of the gospel is Jesus' death, burial, and resurrection (1 Corinthians 15:1–4). Paul then lists some of the appearances Jesus made after His resurrection, including His appearance to Paul, "as of one born out of due time" (15:5–8). In the first portion of our printed text, Paul describes the devastating consequences that result if Jesus' resurrection did not occur.

I. The Resurrection

(1 Corinthians 15:13–20)

A. False Witness (vv. 13–15)

13. But if there be no resurrection of the dead, then is Christ not risen.

Some members of the church of Corinth disputed the reality of future *resurrection* (1 Corinthians 15:12). Paul reasons that, if their belief is true, then either Jesus' crucified body is still in Joseph's tomb, or there's credibility to the rumor that Jesus' disciples stole it (Matthew 28:12–15). Thus, Paul begins to examine their faulty logic.

14a. And if Christ be not risen, then is our preaching vain.

Paul sets forth what we might call a "chain reaction of consequences." These if-then statements emphasize the importance of Christ's resurrection on the Christian faith. In this verse, Paul says if Jesus didn't rise, then Paul's preaching and that of others like him amounts to nothing at best. It is downright deceptive at worst.

The heart of the gospel is that Jesus "died for our sins" and "rose again the third day according to the scriptures" (1 Corinthians 15:3–4). Paul likely had in mind passages such as Psalm 16:8–11 that claim God's "Holy One" will not "see corruption" (compare Acts 2:25–28, 31; 13:33–37). Paul is saying that if there is no resurrection and Jesus is not alive, then the Old Testament Scriptures presenting the Messiah in these terms are also worthless.

14b. And your faith is also vain.

A hypothetical deception such as this says something negative against both the preachers and those who accept their message. They (and we) put faith in a lie if Jesus is not raised.

15. Yea, and we are found false witnesses of God; because we have testified of God that he raised up Christ: whom he raised not up, if so be that the dead rise not.

The chain-reaction argument continues. If Jesus is not risen, then those who boldly proclaim Jesus' resurrection are *false witnesses of God.* They violate the ninth commandment (Exodus 20:16; compare Proverbs 19:5, 9).

The collection of people who become false witnesses if Christ is not raised includes Cephas, the rest of the twelve disciples, a group of 500 believers, James, all of the apostles, and Paul himself (1 Corinthians 15:5–8). Two of those witnesses, Cephas and John, did not hesitate to voice their unshakable convictions before the Sanhedrin: "We cannot but speak the things which we have seen and heard" (Acts 4:20).

What Do You Think?

If Christ did not rise, what else is in vain or false? Who does a false resurrection affect, and in what ways?

Digging Deeper

How does considering the resurrection false deepen your understanding of its significance?

B. Futile Hope (vv. 16–19)

16–17. For if the dead rise not, then is not Christ raised. And if Christ be not raised, your faith is vain; ye are yet in your sins.

As if to underscore the seriousness of his argument, Paul repeats words from verses 13–14 above. Then he adds an independent clause: *ye are yet in your sins.* Paul's argument personally affects his listeners. Presuming Christ did not rise, then they are holding to useless faith, and the hope of forgiveness and new life is gone.

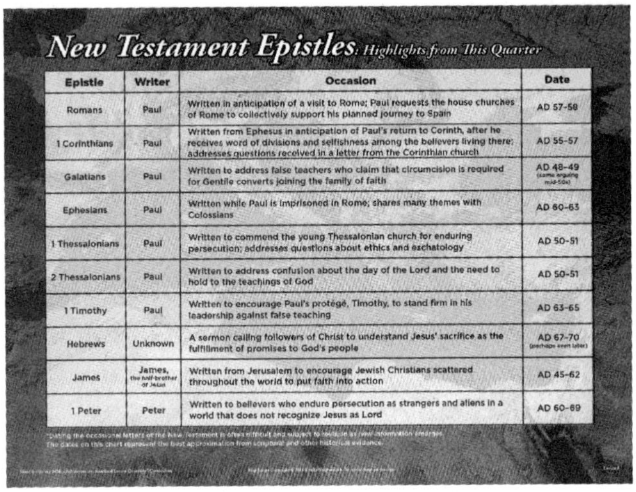

New Testament Epistles: Highlights from This Quarter

Epistle	Writer	Occasion	Date
Romans	Paul	Written in anticipation of a visit to Rome; Paul requests the house churches of Rome to collectively support his planned journey to Spain	AD 57–58
1 Corinthians	Paul	Written from Ephesus in anticipation of Paul's return to Corinth, after he receives word of divisions and selfishness among the believers living there; addresses questions received in a letter from the Corinthian church	AD 55–57
Galatians	Paul	Written to address false teachers who claim that circumcision is required for Gentile converts joining the family of faith	AD 48–49 (some arguing mid-50s)
Ephesians	Paul	Written while Paul is imprisoned in Rome; shares many themes with Colossians	AD 60–63
1 Thessalonians	Paul	Written to commend the young Thessalonian church for enduring persecution; addresses questions about ethics and eschatology	AD 50–51
2 Thessalonians	Paul	Written to address confusion about the day of the Lord and the need to hold to the teachings of God	AD 50–51
1 Timothy	Paul	Written to encourage Paul's protégé, Timothy, to stand firm in his leadership against false teaching	AD 63–65
Hebrews	Unknown	A sermon calling followers of Christ to understand Jesus' sacrifice as the fulfillment of promises to God's people	AD 67–70 (perhaps even later)
James	James, the half-brother of Jesus	Written from Jerusalem to encourage Jewish Christians scattered throughout the world to put faith into action	AD 45–62
1 Peter	Peter	Written to believers who endure persecution as strangers and aliens in a world that does not recognize Jesus as Lord	AD 60–69

*Dating the occasional letters of the New Testament is often difficult and subject to revision as new information emerges. The dates on this chart represent the best approximation from scriptural and other historical evidence.

Visual for Lesson 5. *Utilize this chart throughout the quarter to enhance lesson contexts and historical timelines.*

Jesus' death and resurrection are inseparable. Jesus "was delivered for our offences, and was raised again for our justification" (Romans 4:25). Without the resurrection, Jesus' crucifixion is nothing more than the death of a self-deceived, self-named Messiah. In this scenario, He, too, is a false witness of God. The ultimate tragedy of such an alternative is that humans are, therefore, still dead in *sins*.

18. Then they also which are fallen asleep in Christ are perished.

Paul moves from the tragic results of "no resurrection" for living Christians to addressing the dire consequences for Christians who have already died. The Greek word translated *asleep* is used in both biblical and non-biblical literature. It can mean literal, ordinary sleep or figuratively represent the idea of passing away. In the New Testament, the former usage appears four times (example: Luke 22:45) and the latter thirteen times (example: Acts 13:36). We see one sense confused with the other in the case of Lazarus (John 11:11–15).

19. If in this life only we have hope in Christ, we are of all men most miserable.

Earlier in the letter, Paul lists *hope* among the three qualities that "abideth" (1 Corinthians 13:13). He writes, "We are saved by hope" in Romans 8:24. Hope for the future sets Christians apart from "others which have no hope" (1 Thessalonians 4:13).

In this context, Paul refers to hope as a "confident expectation." It is not the same as today's concept of "wishful thinking." Paul's point is that because Jesus conquered death, we have a "blessed hope" that eagerly awaits His return in glory (Titus 2:13).

Everything the Scriptures say about true Christian hope is null and void if Jesus is not risen from the dead. Christian hope is based upon the reality of Jesus' resurrection. If that foundation crumbles, our hope crumbles with it. That Jesus has risen, never to die again, instills in His followers a "lively hope" (1 Peter 1:3). Jesus' resurrection gives the Christian faith a power and distinctive that no other religion provides. If Jesus' resurrection is untrue, that distinctive is destroyed.

What Do You Think?

What is the greatest gift resulting from Jesus' resurrection?

Digging Deeper

How does a false claim of resurrection affect the Christian concept of hope?

Hopeful or Hopeless?

I walked with my son every afternoon during the spring of 2020. As you probably remember, it was a challenging year. Many things felt dead and broken. Suffering, frustration, disappointment, and discouragement filled the atmosphere. Loneliness prevailed.

As a purposeful break from online school and the confines of our home, we trekked outside. My son picked the route, and it became "our walk." Our habit led to noticing the slow and steady process of winter turning into spring. Dead branches set buds. Buds opened to leaves and flowers. Bulbs bloomed with vibrancy and life. We challenged each other to behold new things and new colors every day. It became an encouraging and fruitful game. As spring proclaimed resurrection and renewal, we felt hope blossom in our souls. When was the last time you chose to be hopeful instead of hopeless? How can you purposefully share the hope of new life with those around you?—B. R. T.

C. Faithful Firstfruits (v. 20)

20. But now is Christ risen from the dead, and become the firstfruits of them that slept.

The gloom of the previous verses is replaced with Paul's declaration that *Christ is risen.* Paul supplements his declaration with a noteworthy affirmation: Christ is *the firstfruits of them that slept.* The term *firstfruits* is derived from the Law of Moses. After the harvest, the people of Israel were to bring the first portion of their crops to the priest as an offering to the Lord (Leviticus 23:9–11). There was even a specific "day of firstfruits" (Exodus 23:16; Numbers 28:26–31).

This practice emphasized two realities. The first: harvests come from the Lord. The Israelites are just tenants or stewards of the land God gave them, and He blesses them with harvests. The second reality is that more harvests will follow; the *first* fruits are just that—the rest is yet to come.

Paul links the implications of God's provision and bountiful harvest to Jesus' resurrection. As the first soul God raised, Jesus paved the way for other souls to follow. The harvest of souls is by the power of the Lord of the harvest (Luke 10:2). That power brought Jesus back from the dead (Romans 8:11; Hebrews 13:20), so a bountiful future harvest could become a reality.

Additionally, Jesus' resurrection guarantees more to come. People were raised from the dead before Jesus (examples: 1 Kings 17:17–24; Luke 7:14–15). God's sovereign power also performed these miracles, but those individuals eventually died again. Jesus' resurrection is permanent. It is the prototype of what is to come, the hope of eternal life.

II. The Mystery

(1 Corinthians 15:51–57)

In 1 Corinthians 15:21–50, Paul teaches about sin, death, and the possibility of being made alive in Christ. He proclaims Jesus' triumph over death, His ultimate rule with authority and power, and the heavenly inheritance available to those who align with Him. Paul challenges the Corinthians to consider their behavior (to "awake to righteousness, and sin not" in 15:34). Then Paul anticipates questions about the characteristics of a resurrected body. He explains that humans begin in "a natural body" but gain eternity in a "spiritual" one (15:44) and then points out that people must "bear the image of the heavenly" to "inherit the kingdom of God" (15:49–50). Paul's teaching points to Jesus' ultimate and complete victory over death.

A. Changed People (vv. 51–53)

51. Behold, I shew you a mystery; We shall not all sleep, but we shall all be changed.

The Greek word that is translated as *mystery* in this verse occurs 27 times in the New Testament, most often by Paul (20 times). When Paul uses the term "mystery," he is not speaking of an unsolvable problem with no resolution. His definition indicates a vital spiritual truth that was hidden for a time but is now revealed (Romans 11:25). In the text before us, the mystery he's talking about concerns what the future holds for Christians. *Sleep* is a euphemism for death (see commentary on 1 Corinthians 15:18, above). Paul says the collective experience will not be death but rather *change.* His teaching here is consistent with what he writes elsewhere on the subject, especially in 1 Thessalonians 4:13–18 regarding the connection between our resurrection and the return of Jesus.

52. In a moment, in the twinkling of an eye, at the last trump: for the trumpet shall sound, and the dead shall be raised incorruptible, and we shall be changed.

The phrase *in the twinkling of an eye* indicates an event that will happen suddenly. Scripture highlights the suddenness of God's judgment (examples: Psalm 73:19; Isaiah 29:5–6; 30:13; 47:11; Jeremiah 6:26; 18:22; Mark 13:35–36). The idea that the change will be instantaneous, not gradual, also predominates. Although God is "longsuffering . . . not willing that any should perish" (2 Peter 3:9), when the time comes for His judgment

How to Say It

Adriatic	Ay-dree-*at*-ic.
Aegean	A-*jee*-un.
Corinth	Kor-inth.
Corinthians	Ko-*rin*-thee-unz (*th* as in *thin*).
Peloponnesian	*Pell*-uh-puh-*ne*-shen.
Sanhedrin	*San*-huh-drun or San-*heed*-run.

to be carried out at the return of Jesus, it will happen quickly.

A feature of the Lord's return will be the sounding of a *trump[et]*. A trumpet blast is associated with the coming of God's judgment throughout Scripture (Isaiah 27:13; Joel 2:1; Matthew 24:31; 1 Thessalonians 4:16; compare Revelation 8:2–9:14).

In 1 Thessalonians 4:16, Paul states that the trumpet's sound will be accompanied by a shout from Jesus and the voice of the archangel. At that time, *the dead shall be raised incorruptible*, no longer subject to the problems and limitations of a broken, sin-cursed world. When Jesus returns, the remainder of the "crop" following the "firstfruits" of His resurrection will be "harvested." *And we shall be changed!*

The alteration of our beings applies to both believers and unbelievers. Jesus speaks of a resurrection of the good and the evil, the former being a "resurrection of life" and the latter being a "resurrection of damnation" (John 5:28–29; compare Daniel 12:2–3). In this sense, resurrection will apply to both the "just and unjust" (Acts 24:15).

What Do You Think?

What types of change can believers expect when the time comes to inherit the kingdom of God?

Digging Deeper

Compare the use of a trumpet blast in Isaiah 27:13; Joel 2:1; Matthew 24:31; 1 Thessalonians 4:16; and Revelation 8:2–9:14.

53a. For this corruptible must put on incorruption.

Our physical bodies are perishable; they are *corruptible*. Since "flesh and blood cannot inherit the kingdom of God" (1 Corinthians 15:50), a radical transformation is required. That transformation will happen at the resurrection. The corruptible will give way to *incorruption*.

53b. And this mortal must put on immortality.

We must take care to understand this phrase correctly. When we *put on immortality* we will not become gods ourselves. To believe otherwise is to confuse the word *immortality* with the word *eternality*. The former means "without end"; the latter means "without beginning or end"—an incommunicable attribute belonging only to God.

B. Victorious Promise (vv. 54–57)

54. So when this corruptible shall have put on incorruption, and this mortal shall have put on immortality, then shall be brought to pass the saying that is written, Death is swallowed up in victory.

The word *mortal* reminds us of words like *mortuary* and *mortician*, which have close associations with death. But such vocabulary has no place in our promised transformation.

The saying *Death is swallowed up in victory* is likely drawn from Isaiah 25:8. The second half of that verse features God's promise to wipe away all tears. We see the promise's ultimate fulfillment in the glimpses of heaven given in Revelation 7:17 and 21:4. The absence of tears in heaven is a byproduct of Jesus' *victory* over death.

55. O death, where is thy sting? O grave, where is thy victory?

Paul personifies *death* and the *grave* and addresses them to highlight Jesus' triumph. He adapts the words from Hosea 13:14. Death and the grave cannot respond to Paul's challenge, for death is a defeated enemy.

56. The sting of death is sin; and the strength of sin is the law.

God warned Adam that *death* was the consequence of disobedience (Genesis 2:17). "The wages of sin is death," writes Paul in Romans 6:23. Additionally, God's *law*, as seen most clearly in the Ten Commandments, gives *strength* to *sin* by making sins undeniable (Romans 7:7–11). Sin ensures we can never measure up to the standards set by God's law.

57. But thanks be to God, which giveth us the victory through our Lord Jesus Christ.

The death and resurrection of *our Lord Jesus Christ* gives us *victory*. The threats mentioned in the previous verse are all dismantled. The cross and empty tomb of Jesus are victorious (Romans 8:1–4, 11, 34). Gratitude rises for all God has accomplished. We say with Paul, *thanks be to God*.

Unforeseen Losses

One year, I taught a group of high school students who experienced loss on a scale I have never witnessed before or since. This tight-knit group of friends spent weekends at each other's houses, attended church together, and sat in the same classes daily. The losses came in waves and changed them forever.

There were about 15 students in the class. Three lost a parent suddenly. When the first student's parent died, the class mourned for weeks. They felt like family, having personally spent time in that home. The second loss happened months later, but just as unexpectedly. Devastated, they asked, "How could this happen *again*?" Then fear surfaced, "What if my parent is next?" Unbelievably, the same devastating loss struck the class a third time.

Nothing shakes the foundations of our faith like an unforeseen loss. Bereavement blindsides its victims, laying a minefield of grief. Because of Christ's resurrection, however, death does not have the final word. How does the hope of resurrection change your perspective on death? How do you keep an eternal mindset? —B. R.

What Do You Think?

What does it mean for death to lose its sting and the grave to lose its victory?

Digging Deeper

How does death's defeat shift your outlook on sickness, dying, hospice care, grief, and bereavement?

III. The Work

(1 Corinthians 15:58)

58. Therefore, my beloved brethren, be ye stedfast, unmoveable, always abounding in the work of the Lord, forasmuch as ye know that your labour is not in vain in the Lord.

The word *therefore* links the crucial truths of Jesus' resurrection to the mechanics of how the Corinthians (and all Christians) are to live. Stated differently, it links doctrine with practical counsel. The doctrine of our future resurrection is the foundation for present-moment kingdom service. Thus, Christians are called to remain *stedfast* and *unmoveable* in commitment to *the work of the Lord.*

What Do You Think?

How does Jesus' resurrection help you to be steadfast, unmovable, and work with faithfulness for the Lord?

Digging Deeper

How does the mystery attached to Jesus' resurrection increase your sense of joy, wonder, and celebration this Resurrection Day?

Conclusion

A. Comma, Not Period

The Lesson Introduction noted the work of Elisabeth Kübler-Ross and her contributions to the psychological study of death and dying. Despite her extensive research and writing on the topic, she named death the "greatest mystery in science." Paul also used the word *mystery* in conjunction with death (1 Corinthians 15:51). There is much we cannot fully comprehend as humans in a fallen world.

Death is indeed a mystery. It is not a friend; it is an enemy. The good news is that Christ's cross and empty tomb defeat death for all time (1 Corinthians 15:26; 2 Timothy 1:10; Revelation 20:14). Death's defeat is what Easter Sunday celebrates! Loss still hurts; of that, there is no question. But the power of death is vanquished by the resurrection. Because Jesus is risen, death is not the period at the end of life's "sentence"; it is only a comma. As Christians, we believe the "comma" of death is just a pause leading to something far greater than anything this world can ever provide.

B. Prayer

Father, thank You for the hope of Jesus' resurrection. Thank You for the comfort it brings us to know that death is not the end. We praise You for the promise of eternal life in Jesus. May we live differently, knowing the trials of this life are not the final word. In Jesus' name we pray. Amen.

C. Thought to Remember

Christ is risen!

Involvement Learning

Enhance your lesson with KJV Bible Student *(from your curriculum supplier) and the reproducible activity page (at www.standardlesson.com or in the back of the* KJV Standard Lesson Commentary Deluxe Edition*).*

Into the Lesson

Divide your class into groups of three. Ask each group to do an internet search to find an example of a great victory. Examples may come from history, current news, a sports or personal achievement story, an industry advancement, etc. Encourage groups to find a picture that represents their victory. After a few minutes, facilitate group sharing. Ask volunteers to present their examples and pictures to the whole class.

Alternative. Before class, select several examples of victories. Create a slideshow of pictures representing these victories. Use your slideshow as an introduction to the class. Ask students to identify the victory each picture portrays. Then discuss for each example: "Who, or what, was the enemy in this scenario? How was that enemy overcome?"

Lead into Bible study by saying, "Today we will examine the greatest victory of all time. We will consider the wonderful comfort this victory provides to all who believe in Jesus."

Into the Word

Prepare a handout in advance. Cite today's Scripture at the top: 1 Corinthians 15:13–20, 51–58. Then create a section labeled "Discover the Victory." Include the following prompts:

1–List all the promises in this text.
2–What is the "mystery"?
3–What is the victory?
4–What does the resurrection provide believers? (Use specific phrases from the text in your answer.)
5–How does Paul ask believers to respond to the truths in this passage, and why?

Create a second section labeled "Tell Me More." List the following terms:

1–"fallen asleep" (v. 18)
2–"firstfruits" (v. 20)
3–"mystery" (v. 51)
4–"law" (v. 56)

Read 1 Corinthians 15:13–20, 51–58 out loud as a class. Then distribute the prepared handout and pens. Ask students to work together in groups of two or three. Instruct them to use Bible-study references or online tools to complete the handout. Assign specific sections to groups if needed for time.

Option. Distribute copies of the "What Happens When" exercise from the activity page, which you can download. Have learners work in groups to complete it as indicated.

After about 10 minutes, call all groups together. Encourage groups to share their answers by leading discussion with the whole class.

Then purposefully shift the discussion and state that Jesus' resurrection is the foundation of the Christian faith. Ask members to share answers to the following questions with a partner: 1–What word or phrase from today's text stands out in a new way? 2–How does Christ's resurrection bring you comfort?

Into Life

Write *Trials / Encouragement* as the headers of two columns on the board. Conduct a brainstorming session by having learners name trials, such as loss, death, health diagnoses, or financial stress. Write their responses on the board. Continue brainstorming by inviting members to create a second list of encouraging words, phrases, and verses from today's text.

Distribute cards and pens. Instruct learners to write a letter to another believer whom they know is enduring a trial. Ask them to include the message that the trials of this life are not God's final word. Invite them to include encouraging words, phrases, or verses from today's lesson.

Option. Distribute copies of the "Send Words of Hope" activity from the activity page. Have learners complete the activity in small groups.

End the session by singing a favorite praise song or hymn about Jesus' resurrection.

Authority: Belonging to God

Devotional Reading: Proverbs 31:4–9
Background Scripture: Mark 12:17; Romans 13:1, 6–8; 1 Peter 2:13–17

Mark 12:17

17 And Jesus answering said unto them, Render to Caesar the things that are Caesar's, and to God the things that are God's. And they marvelled at him.

Romans 13:1, 6–8

1 Let every soul be subject unto the higher powers. For there is no power but of God: the powers that be are ordained of God.

6 For for this cause pay ye tribute also: for they are God's ministers, attending continually upon this very thing.
7 Render therefore to all their dues: tribute to whom tribute is due; custom to whom custom; fear to whom fear; honour to whom honour.
8 Owe no man any thing, but to love one another: for he that loveth another hath fulfilled the law.

1 Peter 2:13–17

13 Submit yourselves to every ordinance of man for the Lord's sake: whether it be to the king, as supreme;
14 Or unto governors, as unto them that are sent by him for the punishment of evildoers, and for the praise of them that do well.
15 For so is the will of God, that with well doing ye may put to silence the ignorance of foolish men:
16 As free, and not using your liberty for a cloke of maliciousness, but as the servants of God.
17 Honour all men. Love the brotherhood. Fear God. Honour the king.

Key Text

Jesus answering said unto them, Render to Caesar the things that are Caesar's, and to God the things that are God's. And they marvelled at him. **—Mark 12:17**

Social Teachings of the Church

Unit 2: Fulfilling Our Obligations to Family and Community

Lessons 5–8

Lesson Aims

After participating in this lesson, each learner will be able to:

1. Identify the major themes that unite Mark 12:17; Romans 13:1, 6–8; and 1 Peter 2:13–17.
2. Analyze God's directive for relating to civil authorities who rule justly.
3. Commit to honoring God by praying for elected leaders.

Lesson Outline

Introduction

A. Higher Authority
B. Lesson Context: General
C. Lesson Context: Mark
D. Lesson Context: Romans
E. Lesson Context: 1 Peter

I. Teaching on Authority (Mark 12:17)

II. Tribute to Authority (Romans 13:1, 6–8)

A. Source of Authority (v. 1)
Who's Really in Charge?
B. Payment of Debt (vv. 6–7)
C. Fulfillment of Law (v. 8)

III. Submission to Authority (1 Peter 2:13–17)

A. Doing Good (vv. 13–15)
B. Behaving Properly (vv. 16–17)
The Highest Respect

Conclusion

A. The Highest Authority
B. Prayer
C. Thought to Remember

Introduction

A. Higher Authority

When I was in kindergarten, my dad had a rule against taking our toys out of the house. He feared we would lose them. One day I took a toy to school. When I got home, I began to tell my father what I had done. Before I could explain, he yelled at me and sent me to my room.

A few minutes later, he opened the door with tears in his eyes, knelt beside me, and asked for my forgiveness. My mother told him that I had taken the toy as a present for another kid. This child had little money, and he brought nothing to show and tell. I told my dad I thought Jesus wanted me to share with the boy. My father looked at me and said, "Yes, He did, pal. I was unfair to you. I'm so sorry." My dad was always quick to admit his mistakes.

Every earthly father derives his title and role from our heavenly Father (Ephesians 3:14–15). God charges every father with the duty and authority to train, guide, and protect his children. Scripture commands children to obey their parents (6:1), but the authority of earthly parents is not absolute. Similarly, Scripture asks believers to respect governmental authority while offering ultimate submission to the Lord.

B. Lesson Context: General

The Gospel of Mark and the epistles of Romans and 1 Peter contain some of the sharpest statements in the New Testament about how Christ-followers should relate to their governments. These passages guide us as we walk out our duties to God and nation. Two aspects of first-century context are helpful for modern readers in this regard.

First, the intended audiences of these texts lived under the dominion of a foreign empire. The Roman emperor held total authority. He ruled locally through a structure of governors and other officials. Roman citizens possessed a few rights, but most of the emperor's subjects had minimal legal protections and no say in the political processes that affected them. Public objection toward ruling powers was considered seditious, and officials responded swiftly with overwhelming force.

Consequently, the populace possessed few avenues for political or cultural change.

Second, the earliest Christians viewed spreading the gospel as their primary responsibility. Therefore, they avoided actions that might hinder their message. They discouraged behaviors that would dishonor the faith community in the eyes of unbelievers—the apostles aimed at discipleship, not political revolution.

C. Lesson Context: Mark

The Gospel of Mark contains a series of stories with a consistent structure: (1) Jesus' opponents pose a tricky or controversial question, hoping He will stumble in His response, but (2) Jesus gives a response that challenges, frustrates, or silences them (Mark 2:18–22; 2:23–28; 3:1–6; 7:1–13; 11:27–33; 12:13–17; 12:18–27; 12:28–34). The opponents aimed to trick Jesus, harm His reputation, and subvert His authority (12:13). These opponents came from religious sects like the Pharisees and Sadducees, as well as political groups like the Herodians. Conflicts between members of religious sects or philosophical schools were common in the ancient world—as the old saying goes, "Nothing makes better friends than a common enemy."

D. Lesson Context: Romans

Paul wrote this letter to introduce himself to the followers of Christ in Rome. He explained the gospel message, corrected rumors, and addressed misconceptions regarding his character and message. One distortion of his teaching was that Paul encouraged his converts to "do evil" so that "good may come" (Romans 3:8). Paul provided examples of upright behavior in response (Romans 12–15).

E. Lesson Context: 1 Peter

The epistle of 1 Peter was most likely written from Rome in the early AD 60s. During this time, the evil Emperor Nero reigned (AD 53–68). Therefore, we detect a coded reference to the city of Rome as Peter greets his readers from "the church that is at Babylon" (1 Peter 5:13; compare Revelation 14:8; 16:19; 17:5; 18:2). The Babylonian empire brought about the exile of the southern kingdom of Judah (586 BC). In Jewish literature contemporary to 1 Peter, Babylon represented decadence, immorality, and opposition to God. Some Jews, like the authors of 4 Ezra and 2 Baruch (non-biblical books from the collection known as the Apocrypha), also used "Babylon" as a code name for Rome. The author of Revelation calls Rome "Babylon" too.

Peter addresses his letter to "the strangers scattered throughout Pontus, Galatia, Cappadocia, Asia, and Bithynia" (1 Peter 1:1). By using the term "strangers," Peter encourages Christ's followers to perceive themselves primarily as citizens of God's kingdom, even as he addresses the responsibility owed to their earthly government.

How to Say It

Bithynia	Bih-*thin*-ee-uh.
Cappadocia	Kap-uh-*doe*-shuh.
Felix	*Fee*-licks.
Festus	*Fes*-tus.
Herodians	Heh-*roe*-dee-unz.
Judean	Joo-*dee*-un.
Pharisees	*Fair*-ih-seez.
Pilate	*Pie*-lut.
Pontus	*Pon*-tuss.
Sadducees	*Sad*-you-seez.
Septuagint	Sep-*too*-ih-jent.

I. Teaching on Authority

(Mark 12:17)

17. And Jesus answering said unto them, Render to Caesar the things that are Caesar's, and to God the things that are God's. And they marvelled at him.

The conflict here is prompted by the question of whether or not it is "lawful to give tribute to Caesar" (Mark 12:14). Jesus' questioners are the Pharisees and Herodians (12:13). Although these groups do not typically work together, in this case, they both desire to discredit Jesus no matter how He responds. If Jesus answers *yes,* the Pharisees can say Jesus violates the Law of Moses. If He answers *no,* the Herodians—whose power comes from Rome—can charge Him with treason.

Jesus answers by requesting a coin (Mark 12:15–16). After His opponents verify Caesar's image on it, Jesus directs them to *render to Caesar* what is due him. Using the coin recognizes Caesar's earthly authority and the benefits they receive from Caesar's civil government. One may consider here the advantages that empires provide like military order, safe roads, and superior buildings. With the enjoyment of these assets comes a certain obligation. Then Jesus continues, the people are also to give *to God* the things owed Him. Believers owe God honor, respect, obedience, and worship. Caesar is not the ultimate authority nor a deity.

Despite His opponents' attempt to trick Him, Jesus answers with all wisdom and grace. His answer gives Roman listeners no room to claim that Christ-followers are disloyal to the state. God's people are responsible for their earthly citizenship as well as their heavenly citizenship.

What Do You Think?

Do you consider paying taxes a part of your spiritual integrity? Why, or why not?

Digging Deeper

How do you faithfully approach your earthly citizenship? In what ways does earthly citizenship reflect on your heavenly citizenship?

II. Tribute to Authority

(Romans 13:1, 6–8)

A. Source of Authority (v. 1)

1. Let every soul be subject unto the higher powers. For there is no power but of God: the powers that be are ordained of God.

Paul addresses how believers should relate to earthly authorities (compare Titus 3:1). To be *subject unto* means to be ranked under another. We are to submit because *God* ordains all earthly *powers*. Just prior to this directive, Paul stresses the importance of believers living peaceably among themselves and under government (Romans 12:9–21). The thoughts in this verse are a logical extension of those requirements.

Yet Paul is not demanding total obedience to the whims of every evil or tyrannical ruler. The primary decision is whether the directives of an earthly ruler conflict with the directives of God. Paul was beaten and imprisoned multiple times for allegedly unlawful conduct (Acts 16:22–24; 22:22–29; 2 Corinthians 11:23–25). When the commands of human authorities conflicted with his duties as God's servant, Paul obeyed God. An even clearer example of this concept is the response of Peter and the other apostles to the Sanhedrin in Acts 5:29: "We ought to obey God rather than men" (compare Acts 4:19).

What Do You Think?

Do you struggle with power and with those who exercise power over you? In what ways is submission difficult?

Digging Deeper

In what circumstances is it appropriate to go against earthly authority? Give specific examples.

Who's Really in Charge?

One day I conducted an experiment in my English class. I sat in the back, quietly watched, and took notes in a notebook. With no one obviously leading from the front, student leaders emerged. Hesitantly, one student walked to the board and outlined a lesson. Then another student challenged his leadership and tried to take over. Students quickly chose their favorite "teacher" and loudly protested the opposing leader.

I stayed out of the negotiations but made sure violence did not erupt. The experiment was an illustration related to a novel we were reading. I remained the authority in the class, but I relinquished some of it for the sake of the lesson. I did not agree with everything the would-be leaders said or did, but I let them have authority for the sake of their learning.

We sometimes forget that God is still the authority "in the room." When governmental leadership makes decisions we don't understand, it is easy to feel like God has lost control. He hasn't; He just gives authority to others in some measure, like I did for my class. As believers, we must honor others, submit to authority, and let God worry about the details. How can we better exemplify Christlike behavior in our attitude

Visual for Lesson 6. *Point to the visual and say, "Christians submit to earthly authority for the Lord's sake. All authority belongs to God."*

toward authority? How can we serve others well regardless of who is in power? —B. R.

B. Payment of Debt (vv. 6–7)

6. For for this cause pay ye tribute also: for they are God's ministers, attending continually upon this very thing.

The double *for* may be considered "this is also" or "for because." It sets up Paul's reasoning. To find the antecedent of *this cause,* we look to the verses just before the one at hand. Paul states that governing powers serve the populace by upholding "good" behavior and punishing "evil" (Romans 13:3–4). Then he appeals to the reader's conscience (13:5). Since the governing authorities *are God's ministers,* then shouldn't one's conscience require that they be supported? The fact that they do their jobs on a full-time basis (the sense of *attending continually upon this very thing*) further buttresses Paul's line of thought.

Tribute refers to taxes. In any era, taxes feel like (and are) a burden. The extortion committed by corrupt tax collectors in the first century did not help. Despite the injustice of imperial taxation, Paul invites his audience to view paying their taxes not just as a legal obligation but as a moral one as well. A primary element of God's bestowal of authority on local and national leaders is to maintain peace, safety, and order.

The Greek word translated *ministers* is different from the word translated "minister" twice in Romans 13:4. In the earlier two instances, the word is the source of our word *deacon.* But the word here rendered as "ministers" only sometimes refers to those devoted to religious service (Romans 15:16; Hebrews 1:7; 8:2). The old Greek version of the Old Testament, known as the Septuagint, uses it this way often (consider Numbers 4:37, 41; Isaiah 61:6), but the term applies to service in broad senses as well (2 Kings 4:43; 6:15). In the New Testament, the term also describes someone who performs duties toward others for the sake of the Lord (Philippians 2:25; Hebrews 1:7, 14; 8:2; 10:11; etc.). It leans toward those committed to civic good, as in "public servants."

7. Render therefore to all their dues: tribute to whom tribute is due; custom to whom custom; fear to whom fear; honour to whom honour.

The big picture here concerns how to act on one's debts (which is the sense of the word *dues*). Paul approaches this topic in terms of four categories. The first is *tribute,* which refers to direct taxes (compare Luke 20:22; 23:2). The second category is *custom,* which relates to custom duties and fees, or what may be called indirect taxes. Secular authorities require taxes to function.

Leadership positions deserve the deference inherent in the words *fear* and *honour,* the last two categories. In the Old Testament, *fear* is sometimes used for reverence toward human beings (Deuteronomy 2:25; 1 Chronicles 14:17). But throughout the Bible, the word also describes the holy awe one experiences in the presence of God or His miraculous work (2 Samuel 23:3; 2 Chronicles 19:7; Acts 9:31; Romans 3:18). *Honour* refers more generally to the respect given to others, whether political leaders (1 Peter 2:17), parents (Mark 7:10), spouses (1 Peter 3:7), widows (1 Timothy 5:3), or God (Revelation 4:11).

What Do You Think?

How do you discern whether someone deserves your "fear" and "honour"?

Digging Deeper

In what practical ways do you show reverence and respect toward government and community?

C. Fulfillment of Law (v. 8)

8. Owe no man any thing, but to love one another: for he that loveth another hath fulfilled the law.

This verse is connected to the previous seven by the concept of obligation. Paul expands believers' responsibility beyond the political and secular realms. The only debt not to be paid off that aligns with God's kingdom is the commitment *to love one another*. The requirement to love one another renews continually, with every encounter.

Paul uses both *one another* and *another*. Some commentators argue that the debt of *love* is owed only to fellow believers, as consistent with Paul's use of the phrase "one another" in other writings (example: Galatians 5:13). But the second half of this verse indicates we are to love people in general. This matches Jesus' parable of the good Samaritan (Luke 10:25–37). Believers are called to a wide target of love.

Paul continues by offering a reason for exhibiting love: it meets the law's requirement (Leviticus 19:18; compare Mark 12:31). Paul sets the groundwork for the "acceptance" he will specify in Romans 14.

III. Submission to Authority

(1 Peter 2:13–17)

A. Doing Good (vv. 13–15)

13a. Submit yourselves to every ordinance of man for the Lord's sake.

Writing from Rome, Peter calls believers to respectful citizenship. His directive is truly remarkable, given the persecution by Nero at the time (see Lesson Context). Even so, Peter emphasizes the authority of governmental directives by stating that the people should obey *every ordinance* (compare Romans 13:1; Titus 3:1). But such submission is not absolute. Peter makes this clear when he explains his act of civil disobedience in Acts 5:29.

As believers follow the laws of the earthly kingdoms in which they reside, their submission will be *for the Lord's sake*. How this happens is explained as Peter continues.

13b–14. Whether it be to the king, as supreme; Or unto governors, as unto them that are sent by him for the punishment of evildoers, and for the praise of them that do well.

Following the general instruction of the previous half-verse, Peter names two offices of earthly authority. First, the *king, as supreme* refers to whoever rules as the overarching authority. As Peter writes, that person is Nero in Rome. Second, *governors* are regional managers. During Peter's time, governors oversaw all the minor Roman provinces. Judean governors mentioned in the New Testament are Pilate (Matthew 27:2, 11; Luke 3:1), Felix (Acts 23:24–26), and Festus (Acts 24:27; 26:32).

A primary task of government is protecting the innocent from *evildoers* (compare Romans 13:3–5). A congenial by-product of living a law-abiding life is the resulting *praise of them that do well*. Such praise is not a primary goal to be sought, however (compare John 12:43; 2 Corinthians 10:12); rather, it is a desirable by-product that reflects well on God. Peter thus calls believers to consider how their behavior serves as a witness of God to an unbelieving world. God's reputation is at stake! This matches what Jesus says in Matthew 10:18.

15. For so is the will of God, that with well doing ye may put to silence the ignorance of foolish men.

Peter appeals to God's *will* to stress that believers are to be models of proper living. Naysayers of the Christian faith accused Jesus and His followers of sedition and hostility (Luke 23:2; Acts 24:5). By living in ways that benefit their fellow citizens, Christ-followers *silence* false accusations. Their careful submission to civil authority aids the church's mission and protects the faithful. Peter assumes an overlap between the moral framework of believers and their presence within society.

What Do You Think?

If you and your church were suddenly removed from your community, would you be missed?

Digging Deeper

In what specific ways do you model right living and "well doing"? Share examples of upright behavior that "silence[s]" the "foolish."

B. Behaving Properly (vv. 16–17)

16. As free, and not using your liberty for a cloke of maliciousness, but as the servants of God.

This verse calls to mind what might be called a "spectrum of behavior." At one extreme end of the spectrum stands "Legalism," which stresses rule-keeping as the model behavior that best reflects on God. This position is refuted by Acts 15:1; Galatians 5:3; Colossians 2:20–23; etc. At the other extreme end of the spectrum stands "License." This position as the model of behavior is refuted by Galatians 5:13; 2 Peter 2:19; etc. The proper view stands midway between the two extremes. It is called "Liberty." *Liberty* is affirmed by John 8:34; Romans 6:14; 14:1–6; 2 Corinthians 3:17; Galatians 2:4; 5:1–13; etc.

What Do You Think?

Where do you land on the spectrum of Legalism, License, and Liberty?

Digging Deeper

How should Christians exercise their liberty (consider Romans 14:1-6 and Galatians 5:1-13)?

17. Honour all men. Love the brotherhood. Fear God. Honour the king.

Peter concludes with a series of short exhortations. The four statements summarize the previous verses. Give honor to everyone, extend extravagant love to fellow believers, direct awe and reverence to God, and esteem governmental leaders.

The Highest Respect

African students highly respect the title and position of *teacher*. They treat teachers the way North Americans treat doctors. This took some adjustment when I began instructing asylum seekers from Africa. I was used to the (very low) level of respect I received as a high school teacher.

One way my international students show respect is in the title they give me. They call me *Teacher*. This is not because they do not know my name; they call me Teacher because they respect my position. To their way of thinking, my authority is worthy of the utmost honor. If the class gets loud, some students demand respect on my behalf; this never happened in my high school classes!

When we conceptualize all authority as originating from God's design, we may honor and respect the positions held even if we do not agree with all of the decisions made. What are some ways you can be better at giving honor and respect to those in authority? How might this give glory to God? —B. R.

Conclusion

A. The Highest Authority

As citizens of God's kingdom, we owe allegiance to God above all. Where a government's laws conflict with God's law, believers must follow God. Yet the God who created the world oversees and sanctions the nations. They exist at His discretion and derive their authority from Him. Therefore, believers are also to submit to earthly governments. By obeying human leaders, Christ's followers honor God, submit to His cosmic order, and strengthen their witness to those outside the church.

Citizens in Western democracies are blessed with "due process," among other things. Such citizens have opportunities that ancient Christians could only imagine. But no matter the kind of government under which we live, Scripture's commands remain the same: love and care for neighbors, resist evil, and model upright citizenship. Honor others, especially those in high positions, while loving all people well. In other words, reflect the character of God.

B. Prayer

Father God, teach us to balance life in this world with our citizenship in Your kingdom. Guide us in Your will as we fulfill our responsibilities to earthly authorities and fellow humans. In so doing, may we be the fragrance of Jesus Christ on earth. In Jesus' name we pray. Amen.

C. Thought to Remember

Respect the government, honor God.

Involvement Learning

Enhance your lesson with KJV Bible Student *(from your curriculum supplier) and the reproducible activity page (at www.standardlesson.com or in the back of the* KJV Standard Lesson Commentary Deluxe Edition*).*

Into the Lesson

Write the title *Government* on the board and then add two columns labeled *Times I'm Grateful* and *Times I'm Frustrated.* Divide class members into groups of four to six members and say, "Brainstorm a list of specific times you are grateful for the government and times you are frustrated by the government." After calling time, ask volunteers to share their group's ideas with the whole class.

Alternative. Draw a continuum on the board with the word *Adversary* at one end and *Friend* at the other. Add the number zero under "Adversary," one through three between the terms, and four under "Friend." Ask class members to think about their feelings regarding the government. Then ask, "Where would you place yourself on this continuum?" Record participants' answers by placing their names along the continuum and then ask, "Why do you place yourself there?"

Alternative. Distribute copies of the "Obey the Government?" exercise from the activity page, which you can download. Have learners work in small groups to complete as indicated.

Lead into the Bible study by saying, "Today let's consider how Mark 12:17; Romans 13:1, 6–8; and 1 Peter 2:13–17 ask us to respond to government."

Into the Word

Ask learners to divide into groups of three or four—hand out notebook paper and pens. Ask volunteers to take turns reading Mark 12:17; Romans 13:1, 6–8; and 1 Peter 2:13–17 out loud. Then instruct groups to write two "Standards of Conduct" documents—one for governing officials and another for citizens under jurisdiction. Ask learners to include verse references and specific phrases from today's texts as part of their standards.

Option. Extend the conversation in the same groups. Distribute a handout (you create) with the following prompts and questions for small-group discussion: Consider Mark 12:17. 1–What did Jesus mean when He differentiated between "things that are Caesar's" and "things that are God's"? 2–Do you think Jesus means that Christians should pay taxes even when those taxes support activities or initiatives contrary to Christian belief? Why or why not? Consider Romans 1:8 and 1 Peter 2:16–17. 3–Why did Paul and Peter add these instructions? 4–How might obeying these directives make it easier to obey specific governmental instructions? More challenging? 5–Can the government do anything to make obeying the apostles' instructions impossible? 6–Consider your actions and attitudes toward elected officials. How are Christians to conduct themselves?

When time is up, invite a representative from each group to share their "Standards of Conduct" documents. Record common ideas among the groups. Discuss unique responses.

Alternative. Distribute copies of the "What Is a Believer to Do?" exercise from the activity page. Have learners work in small groups to complete as indicated.

Into Life

Invite the class to brainstorm a list of government officials by name. Include local, regional, and national leaders. Write the list on the board.

Divide learners into pairs and distribute index cards and pens. Ask pairs to choose three or four names from the board and write specific petitions for them. Ask pairs to pray together quietly for their list.

Conclude the session by praying out loud as a class for the governmental positions and leaders you identified. Begin by asking a volunteer to open your prayer time. Then instruct learners to pray aloud as they feel led and comfortable. Let them know you will close. Challenge learners to continue their prayers for these leaders throughout the week.

April 19
Lesson 7 (KJV)

Children: Gift and Model

Devotional Reading: Psalm 8
Background Scripture: Matthew 18:1–6; Mark 9:36–37, 42; 10:13–16; Luke 2:1–20

Mark 9:36–37, 42

36 And he took a child, and set him in the midst of them: and when he had taken him in his arms, he said unto them,

37 Whosoever shall receive one of such children in my name, receiveth me: and whosoever shall receive me, receiveth not me, but him that sent me.

---

42 And whosoever shall offend one of these little ones that believe in me, it is better for him that a millstone were hanged about his neck, and he were cast into the sea.

Mark 10:13–16

13 And they brought young children to him, that he should touch them: and his disciples rebuked those that brought them.

14 But when Jesus saw it, he was much displeased, and said unto them, Suffer the little children to come unto me, and forbid them not: for of such is the kingdom of God.

15 Verily I say unto you, Whosoever shall not receive the kingdom of God as a little child, he shall not enter therein.

16 And he took them up in his arms, put his hands upon them, and blessed them.

Key Text

Verily I say unto you, Whosoever shall not receive the kingdom of God as a little child, he shall not enter therein. **—Matthew 10:15**

Social Teachings
of the Church

Unit 2: Fulfilling Our Obligations to Family and Community

Lessons 5–8

Lesson Aims

After participating in this lesson, each learner will be able to:

1. Summarize Jesus' interactions with children in Mark 9 and 10.

2. Assess daily habits against the backdrop of Jesus' invitation to become "like children."

3. Repent of ways he or she has been like the disciples, rebuking (even internally) the "least of these."

Lesson Outline

Introduction

A. Role Models

B. Lesson Context: Historical

C. Lesson Context: Children

I. Jesus and a Child (Mark 9:36–37, 42)

A. Welcoming, Part 1 (vv. 36–37)

Childlike Trust

B. Warning, Part 1 (v. 42)

II. Disciples and Children (Mark 10:13–16)

A. Welcoming, Part 2 (vv. 13–14)

B. Warning, Part 2 (vv. 15–16)

Messy Kingdom

Conclusion

A. Greatness Is Childlikeness

B. Prayer

C. Thought to Remember

Introduction

A. Role Models

"Being a role model is the most powerful form of educating," said John Wooden, a well-known and successful NCAA basketball coach. "Modeling" is the process of teaching skills and behaviors through observable actions and imitation. It is more than being told how to do something; consider that "actions speak louder than words." Therefore, role models positively influence our lives by sharing their wisdom, knowledge, and experience through observational learning. They live alongside us and teach by demonstrating exemplary attitudes, behaviors, skills, and habits. A role model can make a big difference in a young, impressionable life.

In today's text, Jesus speaks and models His lesson to the disciples. As the most significant role model in history, we seek to learn and imitate His values and ways.

B. Lesson Context: Historical

Our text lands between Peter's confession of Jesus, "Thou art the Christ" (Mark 8:29), and the triumphal entry (11:1–10). Sandwiched between these events are clarifying motifs defining God's kingdom as upside down and backward to natural human instinct. Examples of these motifs are the high cost of discipleship (10:21–22), the difficulties of wealth (10:24–31), and a redefinition of greatness (10:36–45). Throughout this section, Jesus exalts the weak and lowly while humbling the powerful and proud.

Just prior to today's text, Jesus and His disciples traveled the 25 miles between Caesarea Philippi and Capernaum (Mark 8:27; 9:33). Caesarea Philippi was a town in the hill country at the base of Mount Hermon. Capernaum was a small fishing village that Jesus used as the home base of His ministry on the northern shore of the Sea of Galilee (Matthew 4:13). Capernaum is mentioned in all four Gospels and named more than any other town in the New Testament except Jerusalem. It is where the centurion asks for Jesus' help and where He heals the paralytic who was dropped through the roof (Matthew 8:5; Mark 2:1–12). In contrast,

Scripture mentions Caesarea Philippi only twice: in Matthew 16:13 and its parallel in Mark 8:27.

C. Lesson Context: Children

In the Greco-Roman world of the first century AD, children held little significance. Adults viewed them as lacking reason and requiring training. The aim of their training was to learn their parents' business and duties. Their value was in their contribution to the family. In the extreme, children were considered property—to be nurtured or disposed of as the head of household determined. The same was true in Jewish households, but God also taught His people to consider children as a blessing (Psalm 127:3–5). God instructed parents to teach Israel's faith to their children and train them properly in behavior and wisdom (Deuteronomy 11:19; 31:12–13; Proverbs 22:6). Still, they had little power or status.

I. Jesus and a Child

(Mark 9:36–37, 42)

Today's passage begins with the disciples settling into their lodging for the night. As they do so, Jesus confronts them, asking about a dispute. The disciples are ashamed and do not answer. But of course, Jesus knows their argument was about status (Mark 9:33–34). Jesus replies to their concealed debate by teaching that those who want to be first must be last and servants of all (9:35). Then Jesus proceeds to teach through a practical demonstration. (Matthew 18:2–6 and Luke 9:47–48 are parallel passages to the first segment of our lesson.)

A. Welcoming, Part 1 (vv. 36–37)

36. And he took a child, and set him in the midst of them: and when he had taken him in his arms, he said unto them.

Jesus begins His illustration by bringing *a child* into the room and situating him where all 12 disciples can see. Jesus' unusual actions do not stop there. He proceeds to embrace the child as a father would, a detail not mentioned in the parallel texts of Matthew 18:2 and Luke 9:47. Jesus physically models the verbal point He is about to make, teaching through "an enacted parable."

> **What Do You Think?**
> Do you learn best by reading/hearing verbal instructions, watching someone demonstrate, or trying things yourself?
>
> **Digging Deeper**
> Why do you think modeling is more effective than telling someone what to do? Share examples of modeling.

37a. Whosoever shall receive one of such children in my name, receiveth me.

This verse is essential for understanding true discipleship. There is a relationship between how believers see people, accept and serve them, and the welcoming of Jesus Himself.

The 12 disciples and Jesus are most likely conversing in Aramaic, the everyday conversational language of first-century Jews and a later version of Hebrew (Mark 5:41; 15:34; John 1:42; Acts 21:40; 22:2; etc.). In Aramaic, the word for "child" is the same as the word for "servant." Therefore, Jesus' illustration points toward acceptance of the young, childlike, and lowly in social status.

Jesus begins two sequences with this verse. One has a positive outcome, and the other has a negative result. The positive sequence begins with those willing to receive both Jesus and children. As Jesus adds words to His provocative gesture, He calls on His *name*, expressing His authority as king. What Jesus offers here is not a general maxim of life apart from any other belief or truth. Instead, He specifically connects a particular outlook on life to following Him. When one submits to Jesus as Lord, there is an expectation of inclusion, unity, and a warm welcome for all. Jesus is doing something beyond merely affirming the humane impulse to honor children. He is redefining fundamental values essential to life in God's kingdom. Because Jesus is King, His followers must pursue a new way of thinking and acting that points away from status-seeking and toward radical inclusion of all people regardless of rank.

37b. And whosoever shall receive me, receiveth not me, but him that sent me.

The positive sequence continues. To *receive* Jesus is to receive the one who *sent* Him—the heavenly

Father. Jesus' words expand the disciples' view in a sort of chain reaction. When believers welcome the poor and humble, they act in warm hospitality toward the Lord Himself. When they embrace Jesus, they mysteriously also receive the Father. Equating the receipt of Jesus with receiving the one who sent Him reflects a shared purpose of the Father and Son. The three distinct persons of the Trinity—Father, Son, and Holy Spirit—are one in divine nature and exist together in constant relationship with mutual submission. Truly, there is no greater glory than theirs!

Yet, throughout Mark's Gospel, Jesus personally models lowliness. The 12 disciples' argument about their relative positions of greatness indicates that they don't yet understand—they don't get it. Our God possesses unequaled authority but reaches down in love for the lowly and unworthy. To undeniably know God and belong to God, we must follow Jesus' modeling and humbly extend the gospel message to everyone, just as He does (Matthew 25:34–40; 28:19–20). When we do, we reflect the values of His kingdom.

The parallel texts of Matthew 10:40–42 and Luke 9:48 expand on the cause and effect of believers' welcoming actions. Matthew teaches that heavenly reward comes for those who serve the poor and needy. Luke emphasizes Jesus' perspective that to be great, one must be willing to serve.

What Do You Think?

What does Jesus mean when He talks about receiving people in His name?

Digging Deeper

How do we actively receive children, immigrants, the poor, and the needy in our communities?

Childlike Trust

Our daughter loves swings. We cherish a framed picture of her swinging on a playground as a preschooler. The sun is shining on her face, and there is wonder in her eyes. Her expression holds no worry, stress, or fear of the future. She is smiling as though everything is right with the world. The picture conveys trust. As only a child can, she holds full confidence that all is well.

Playfulness comes with childlike trust. When there is nothing to fear, joy has room to grow uninhibited. Unfortunately, for many adults, the worries and cares of life choke out the space for delight, trust, and joy to flourish. Jesus said His kingdom belongs to those who approach it like children.

When was the last time you surrendered your worries to the Lord? When was the last time you let childlike, playful joy overtake you? Does wonder characterize your spiritual life? How can you become more childlike in your approach to the things of God? —B. R.

B. Warning, Part 1 (v. 42)

42. And whosoever shall offend one of these little ones that believe in me, it is better for him that a millstone were hanged about his neck, and he were cast into the sea.

This section moves into the negative sequence. As Jesus holds the child in His arms, He pronounces a dire warning. Those who cause the small, weak, or vulnerable to stumble spiritually face severe judgment. The Greek word translated *offend* in this verse holds connotations of entrapment or tripping someone up. In other contexts, it refers to interfering with faith in Jesus, prompting someone to give up on faith or causing a person to sin (Romans 14:13–21; 1 Corinthians 8:13). The word is repeated several times in the verses following this one to emphasize how important it is to remove roadblocks from the path of faith (Mark 9:43, 45, 47). It likely has the same force here, warning the disciples to keep the path to Jesus clear.

A more significant issue to which this verse is attached is Jesus' aim at peaceful camaraderie in shared ministry (Mark 9:50). We recall that the specific concern running through the conversation is an incorrect focus upon power and status that leads to argument and posturing (9:33–34). All those turning to Jesus, speaking out in His name, and serving for His sake are not to be hindered or rejected (9:38–41). He calls for a straight and open path to Him for all who desire to come.

Jesus compares blocking someone's approach to Him with having a *millstone* hung around one's *neck*. This shocking illustration depicts weighty judgment. By its very nature, the image causes us to stop and consider the consequences of our actions. A *millstone* is a large, round stone disk on which grain is ground into flour. It has a hole carved in the center so that it may be rotated upon a stationary stone underneath. This allows the grain between the stones to be crushed and ground.

A millstone represents a weight far more than any human can hope to carry. To be *cast into the sea* with a millstone around one's neck means certain death by drowning. By most estimations, not many things are worse than this consequence, yet Jesus states this idea is *better* than being a stumbling block!

Jesus continues, suggesting that anything that prohibits the disciples from following Him must be radically removed from their lives (Mark 9:43–50). He uses hyperbolic examples like cutting off their hands or feet if they cause them to stumble, or even gouging out their eyes (9:43, 45, 47). Jesus' reasoning is that of free entrance into God's kingdom, a clear path toward eternal life, rather than the unpalatable alternative of finding oneself in hell (9:47–48).

What Do You Think?

How does hyperbole (overstatement or exaggeration) assist in teaching a difficult concept?

Digging Deeper

Where else does Jesus use hyperbole? Make a list of examples.

II. Disciples and Children

(Mark 10:13–16)

As Mark 10 opens, Jesus and His disciples leave Capernaum and enter the region of Judea to the south. They cross the Jordan River, and Jesus ministers to those in Perea. Crowds begin to gather, and Jesus teaches them (Mark 10:1). Mark 10:10 mentions Jesus returning to "the house" with His disciples and continuing to teach them. Matthew 19:13–15 and Luke 18:15–17 are parallel passages to this segment of our lesson text.

A. Welcoming, Part 2 (vv. 13–14)

13. And they brought young children to

Visual for Lesson 7. *Display this visual as you ask volunteers to share what they can learn from the faith of a child.*

him, that he should touch them: and his disciples rebuked those that brought them.

When we read that Jesus' *disciples rebuked those that brought* Him *children* for blessing, we may wonder whether the word *disciples* refers only to the original Twelve or if it includes others who also travel with Jesus (Mark 3:13–19). The New Testament uses the word *disciples* both ways (compare Matthew 27:57; Mark 8:34; Acts 6:2). The distinction is evident in places where the Twelve are designated as "apostles" (examples: Mark 6:30; Luke 6:13). Mark 10:32 uses the term "they" for 3 different groups: the disciples, others who followed Jesus, and the twelve.

The Greek term utilized here for the word *children* often refers to preteens, anyone who has not yet entered puberty. The age range is rather broad since Matthew 2 uses it for the infant Jesus, and Mark 5:39–42 uses the same word for a 12-year-old girl. No matter the age of their children, parents naturally want God's best for them. So, parents approach Jesus and the Twelve, asking that Jesus *touch* their children. The action reminds us of kingly and rabbinical blessings where the leader places his hands on the child's head and speaks a benediction (see Genesis 48:12–20). Perhaps, too, they heard the news of Jairus' daughter and the power transferred to the hemorrhaging woman by touching Jesus' garment (Mark 5:22–42).

The disciples presume to decide who gets access to Jesus and who doesn't. The Greek word translated *rebuked* here occurs nine times in Mark's Gospel. It shows up in this passage, used by the disciples, but Jesus also reproves evil spirits with it (Mark 1:25; 9:25). He uses it to strictly order people to keep to themselves the knowledge of who He is or what He has done (3:12; 8:30). Jesus reprimands the very wind and waves with it, and they cease (4:39). Back and forth, Peter and Jesus each use the word after Jesus teaches that He must suffer, be killed, and rise again after three days (8:31–33). Finally, when a blind beggar tries to get Jesus' attention, a crowd uses the term to silence him (10:48). In all cases, the use of the word is intended to change and/or prevent something. Perhaps the disciples saw themselves as protecting Jesus' time and efforts. Even though they've learned from Him for three years, they still don't "get it"!

> **What Do You Think?**
> Why did the disciples criticize those who brought children to Jesus?
> **Digging Deeper**
> What do you think parents hoped Jesus' touch would do for their children?

14. But when Jesus saw it, he was much displeased, and said unto them, Suffer the little children to come unto me, and forbid them not: for of such is the kingdom of God.

Jesus was likely just a short distance away and saw everything. The text describes Jesus' reaction as indignant or angry. The word translated *much displeased* is used only three times in the Gospel of Mark. Here is the first instance, and the second involves the disciples' extreme displeasure at the request of James and John for the most powerful places in Jesus' kingdom (Mark 10:41). The third instance is Mark 14:4, which describes a reaction to the woman who breaks the alabaster jar of ointment on Jesus' head. Putting all three together, we get a picture of what upsets or angers people. Jesus is irritated at an attitude that seems to value one person over another. The other two instances focus on earthly values: status and money. Jesus wants His disciples to see that the wrong priorities work against the values of *the kingdom of God.*

The disciples find themselves countermanded. Jesus' chastisement is sharp. He expresses the correction both positively and negatively for emphasis. Positively, He instructs the disciples to let the children *come* to Him. The term *suffer* here means "let" or "allow." Then He says, *forbid them not.* This saying is framed negatively: do not keep these children away—because *the kingdom* belongs to them.

Why does God's kingdom belong to people who are like children? Because those who bring no status or standing as they come to God are ready to receive His kingdom as a gift. In vulnerability, they come to their provider with open hands and hearts.

B. Warning, Part 2 (vv. 15–16)

15. Verily I say unto you, Whosoever shall not receive the kingdom of God as a little child, he shall not enter therein.

Jesus asks His disciples to pay close attention: Entrance into *the kingdom of God* is not granted through power and prestige but rather by becoming like a *child* in some sense. Worldly perspectives place a premium on earning things. Children are unable to do much of that, but they are good at receiving gifts! Childlike delight, gratitude, and open arms are some attitudes to have when receiving the kingdom of God.

Thus, Jesus continues to shift the disciples' conceptualization of status, procurement, and belonging. Jesus speaks the phrase *the kingdom of God* 15 times in the Gospel of Mark. The repetition indicates its importance. In this instance, Jesus teaches that no one can do God favors in exchange for entry into His place of dominion. Instead, we all must come like vulnerable, humble children who need provision (Matthew 7:9–11). Those clinging to the illusion of their own status will not enter God's kingdom (Mark 10:23–26). But those who receive the kingdom as a gift will enter it by Jesus' compassionate grace.

> **What Do You Think?**
> What does it mean to receive the kingdom of God like a little child?
> **Digging Deeper**
> How can we be childlike in faith without being childish?

16. And he took them up in his arms, put his hands upon them, and blessed them.

The discourse ends with Jesus repeating His point yet again through action. As He did in Mark 9:36, Jesus takes the children into His *arms*. His embrace both blesses them and powerfully communicates complete inclusion and love. The act of blessing by the laying on of hands began way back in Genesis with Israel's ancestors (example: Genesis 48:9, 13–16). Consider the words of Numbers 6:24–26, "The Lord bless thee, and keep thee: The Lord make his face shine upon thee, and be gracious unto thee: The Lord lift up his countenance upon thee, and give thee peace." The Lord shone upon these children with presence, touch, and speech. His words and actions together expressed an emphatic promise that those who have the outlook of children belong in the kingdom of God.

Messy Kingdom

When I was a child, my parents ran a bus route that picked up inner-city children for church on Sunday mornings. Dozens of kids piled onto the bus, and we whisked them away to Sunday school and children's church. We took them home too. The aftermath on the bus always shocked me. Kids left clothing, Sunday school papers, gum, candy wrappers, and blankets behind when they got off the bus. And church classrooms held much of the same. The fact is that kids are messy.

We all come to Jesus with our messes too. Regardless, He welcomes us with open arms. It is easy to act like the disciples, attempting to "shield" Jesus from the messiest among us. But Jesus doesn't need protection; He welcomes all who come to Him. Our messes don't scare Him. Have you held back, afraid to approach Jesus with your mess? Have you blocked others from approaching Him with their messes? In what ways might we demonstrate Jesus' love and welcome to all? —B. R.

Conclusion

A. Greatness Is Childlikeness

Culture teaches us that the "good life" is for the smart, powerful, and accomplished. This concept is a constant refrain heralded by academia, work environments, media, and social circles. Even our children express this outlook—bragging about how good they are at something, how well they do in school, or how much bigger they are than younger siblings. This behavior points to social and cultural values that promote competition and comparison to determine who's in and who's not. Jesus' point is quite the opposite.

Jesus teaches a nonhierarchical mindset among His followers. He challenges His disciples to recalibrate their values and embrace a new kingdom mindset. Jesus encourages unity, service, and childlike faith. He calls His people to accept entry into His kingdom with the delight of a child receiving a gift. To be sure, there are childish attitudes and actions we must avoid, correct, or otherwise put behind us (1 Corinthians 13:11; 14:20; Ephesians 4:14; Hebrews 5:13–14; 1 Peter 2:2). Knowing what those are and how to grow beyond them while honoring and embracing Jesus' viewpoint is our continuing challenge.

How might you adjust your goals, vantage points, and perceptions to better align with Jesus' directives? In what ways might you embrace childlikeness, vulnerability, innocence, and trust on a day-to-day basis?

B. Prayer

Heavenly Father, we thank You for welcoming us into Your kingdom as You welcomed the little children. Teach us to depend on You as a child depends on an adult. In Jesus' name we pray. Amen.

C. Thought to Remember

The kingdom of God belongs to the childlike.

How to Say It

Aramaic	*Air*-uh-*may*-ik.
Caesarea Philippi	Sess-uh-*ree*-uh Fih-*lip*-pie or *Fil*-ih-pie.
Capernaum	Kuh-*per*-nay-um.
centurion	sen-*ture*-ee-un.
Deuteronomy	Due-ter-*ahn*-uh-me.
Perea	Peh-*ree*-uh.

Involvement Learning

Enhance your lesson with KJV Bible Student *(from your curriculum supplier) and the reproducible activity page (at www.standardlesson.com or in the back of the* KJV Standard Lesson Commentary Deluxe Edition*).*

Into the Lesson

Read each of the following statements out loud. Invite class members to share whether they agree or disagree with each statement. Welcome all opinions and remind members to listen to each other's thoughts.

1–Children should be seen and not heard.
2–Children are a blessing.
3–Children are a burden.
4–Children bring a delightful perspective.
5–Children are worth my time and effort.

Alternative. Display the following open-ended sentence: "Kids are great at . . .". Have learners discuss in pairs before sharing with the whole class.

Lead into Bible study by saying, "Children hold a special perspective on life. Jesus loved and included them in His teaching. Today we will see how He used them as models for our faith."

Into the Word

Ask volunteers to read Mark 9:36–37, 42, and 10:13–16 aloud. Then divide members into small groups to discuss the following questions: 1–What did Jesus want the disciples to understand from His actions and His words? 2–Would you describe Jesus' actions and teachings as "child-centric" or "adult-centric"? Why?

Option. Distribute copies of the "Jesus and the Children" exercise from the activity page, which you can download. Instruct learners to work in pairs and complete the page as indicated. To conclude the activity, have pairs present their findings while you write their answers on the board.

In the same groups as before, ask learners to respond to the following questions: 1–How does Mark 9:30–35 add to our understanding of what Jesus is teaching in 9:36–37, 42? 2–How does the phrase "in my name" limit and/or deepen the meaning of what Jesus is teaching here? 3–In 10:14–15, could Jesus be talking about more than children? Why or why not?

Invite learners to use commentary from the lesson, internet resources, or study Bibles to help them find their answers. After several minutes, discuss their conclusions as a whole class.

Option. Assign each group one or two of the following categories:

Parents / School teachers / Church leaders / Grandparents / Singles / Children's ministers / Adult believers

Distribute a pen and index card to each group. Ask them to write a sentence describing what people in their assigned category might learn from Mark 9:36–37, 42 and 10:13–16. Allow ample time for small group work. Then ask a volunteer from each group to share their sentence while you write them on the board.

Into Life

Ask participants to brainstorm ways believers can exhibit childlike faith. After one minute, ask volunteers to share their ideas. Write their responses on the board. Then ask, "How can we develop a childlike attitude?" Write these answers next to the previous list.

Distribute a pen and index card to each learner, and ask them to identify people, besides children, whom they consider to be "the least of these." Encourage learners to repent of ways they have rebuked, even internally, the "least of these."

Alternative. Distribute copies of the "Jesus and Me" activity from the activity page. Have learners complete it in pairs as indicated.

Conclude class by asking participants to pray with a partner, using the following prompts. Invite them to pray silently or quietly out loud.

1–Thank You, God, for the children in our lives.
2–Forgive us, God, for putting up barriers that keep people from You, especially those we consider "less than" or "the least of these."
3–Help us, God, to approach You the way children do—with childlike faith.

April 26
Lesson 8 (KJV)

Family: Distinct and Obedient

Devotional Reading: 2 Samuel 7:25–29
Background Scripture: Matthew 19:3–9; Ephesians 6:1–4;
2 Timothy 1:3–5

Deuteronomy 6:3–9

3 Hear therefore, O Israel, and observe to do it; that it may be well with thee, and that ye may increase mightily, as the LORD God of thy fathers hath promised thee, in the land that floweth with milk and honey.

4 Hear, O Israel: The LORD our God is one LORD:

5 And thou shalt love the LORD thy God with all thine heart, and with all thy soul, and with all thy might.

6 And these words, which I command thee this day, shall be in thine heart:

7 And thou shalt teach them diligently unto thy children, and shalt talk of them when thou sittest in thine house, and when thou walkest by the way, and when thou liest down, and when thou risest up.

8 And thou shalt bind them for a sign upon thine hand, and they shall be as frontlets between thine eyes.

9 And thou shalt write them upon the posts of thy house, and on thy gates.

Matthew 19:3–9

3 The Pharisees also came unto him, tempting him, and saying unto him, Is it lawful for a man to put away his wife for every cause?

4 And he answered and said unto them, Have ye not read, that he which made them at the beginning made them male and female,

5 And said, For this cause shall a man leave father and mother, and shall cleave to his wife: and they twain shall be one flesh?

6 Wherefore they are no more twain, but one flesh. What therefore God hath joined together, let not man put asunder.

7 They say unto him, Why did Moses then command to give a writing of divorcement, and to put her away?

8 He saith unto them, Moses because of the hardness of your hearts suffered you to put away your wives: but from the beginning it was not so.

9 And I say unto you, Whosoever shall put away his wife, except it be for fornication, and shall marry another, committeth adultery: and whoso marrieth her which is put away doth commit adultery.

Key Text

These words, which I command thee this day, shall be in thine heart: and thou shalt teach them diligently unto thy children, and shalt talk of them when thou sittest in thine house, and when thou walkest by the way, and when thou liest down, and when thou risest up. —**Deuteronomy 6:6–7**

Social Teachings
of the Church

Unit 2: Fulfilling Our Obligations to Family and Community

Lessons 5–8

Lesson Aims

After participating in this lesson, each learner will be able to:

1. List the main points of Deuteronomy 6:3–9.
2. Explain the context of Jesus' teaching in Matthew 19:3–9.
3. Write a letter to encourage the faith of a younger believer.

Lesson Outline

Introduction
- A. The Crossroads of Life
- B. Lesson Context

I. Receiving the Law (Deuteronomy 6:3–9)
- A. Blessing for Obedience (v. 3)
  - *Repeat, Repeat, Repeat*
- B. Right Response to the Lord (vv. 4–5)
- C. Internal Inscription (v. 6)
- D. External Repetition (vv. 7–9)
  - *The Treasure of Traditions*

II. Applying the Law (Matthew 19:3–9)
- A. The Question (v. 3)
- B. The Response (vv. 4–6)
- C. The Rebuttal (v. 7)
- D. The Clarification (vv. 8–9)

Conclusion
- A. Walking the Walk
- B. Prayer
- C. Thought to Remember

Introduction

A. The Crossroads of Life

Born and raised in the middle of scenic nowhere, North Dakota, the greatest degree of religious and philosophical variety I encountered growing up was the difference between Protestants and Roman Catholics. When I lived in Chicago for three years, I encountered a great diversity of ideas. I interacted with Muslims, Mormons, Christians of various denominations, and countless secular philosophies. This experience forced me to ask one fundamental question: "How should a person live?"

Across history, this question has been answered in as many ways as there are people. Myriad philosophies, religions, and walks of life from thousands of years past are on offer, and the internet allows anyone access. But in the cacophony of all these ideas, the question stands: How should the follower of God live? This is just the question that the book of Deuteronomy answered for the Israelites when God renewed His covenant with them, and they prepared to enter the promised land.

B. Lesson Context

Deuteronomy has been described as a "farewell speech." The people of Israel were about to enter the promised land. Although Moses had led them since their freedom from Egypt, they were to enter a land forbidden to Moses (Deuteronomy 3:25–27). Even on the eve of his death, Moses prepared the people to move on without him.

Deuteronomy begins with a summary of the people's journey to that point in the text (1:1–4:43) before shifting into a list of laws and commandments (4:44–28:68), the renewal of the covenant (29:1–30:20), and then the final deeds and death of Moses (31:1–34:12). Many of the laws and commandments found in this middle section of Deuteronomy, where our passage occurs, are similar to the earlier books in the Pentateuch (first five books of the Bible). But specific commandments are worth repeating on the eve of Israel's transition.

The second passage in today's lesson, Matthew 19:3–9, describes proper application of the Law of Moses. By the time of Jesus, some 15 centuries had passed since the Law of Moses was given. But people still had questions regarding its application.

Various branches of first-century Judaism—particularly the Pharisees and the Sadducees—regularly debated the interpretation of the Law of Moses. This situation is no different: Jesus is challenged to provide His interpretation of a particular subject in the Law of Moses. The sparring partners here are Pharisees, but the Pharisees were not a united front.

I. Receiving the Law

(Deuteronomy 6:3–9)

A. Blessing for Obedience (v. 3)

3. Hear therefore, O Israel, and observe to do it; that it may be well with thee, and that ye may increase mightily, as the Lord God of thy fathers hath promised thee, in the land that floweth with milk and honey.

Our text from Deuteronomy begins the third part of a three-part exhortation. The first of those three parts affirms God as the source of the commandments (Deuteronomy 5:32–33). The second affirms Moses as God's spokesman of the commandments (6:1–2). The third, now before us, focuses on the people as doers in obedience to the commandments (*observe to do it*). The reason for doing so follows. For the Israelites, the reward they seek is the fulfillment of the promise to the patriarchs (*thy fathers*). This verse reinforces the importance of the ensuing blessing; acquiring that which had been promised to their forefathers depends on obedience.

How to Say It

Baal	*Bay*-ul.
Deuteronomy	Due-ter-*ahn*-uh-me.
Hillel	*Hill*-el.
Marduk	*Mar*-duke.
patriarchs	*pay*-tree-arks.
Pentateuch	*Pen*-ta-teuk.
Pharisees	*Fair*-ih-seez.
phylacteries	fih-*lak*-ter-eez.
Sadducees	*Sad*-you-seez.
Shammai	*Sham*-eye.

Note that it is not enough simply to *hear* the word. One must *do* what is heard (compare James 1:22–23). Those who built the golden calf were the same people who had just received the commandments from Sinai (Exodus 24:3; 32:1–6). The Israelites were expected to keep these words close and to live them out. Simply being a part of the chosen people was not enough; they had to keep God's commandments.

What Do You Think?

What steps can we take to help us remember and obey the Lord's commands?

Digging Deeper

What Scripture texts have you found most helpful in this regard? Why?

Repeat, Repeat, Repeat

Repetition is a crucial part of education. As a mathematics teacher, my husband believes that the number one way to ensure children not only retain but understand the material is through repetition. It secures new learning into long-term memory. It disciplines the mind and cements concepts so that students are more likely to master a subject.

For many of us, repetition sounds incredibly boring. Regardless, it has shown time and again to be an effective strategy for both learning and habit formation. The Israelites were to talk about God's law throughout each day to remind them of God's love—and how they were to respond to such love. God calls His people to live in constant awareness of His commandments, which are to be treasured, and with good reason: "That it may be well with thee, and that ye may increase mightily."

How might you go beyond simply reading Scripture to internalizing it so that it shapes your daily life?

—N. V.

B. Right Response to the Lord (vv. 4–5)

4. Hear, O Israel: The Lord our God is one Lord.

Because the Hebrew verse does not contain any verbs for "is," the exact rendering of the verse has been subject to much discussion. (The need to supply the word *is* for smooth English is indicated by that word's appearing in italics in most editions of the *King James Version*.) As it appears in Hebrew, the verse literally reads, "Hear, Israel, the Lord, our God, the Lord, one." Some students suggest that the word for *one* may also be rendered *alone*; however, "one" is the most accepted translation. Certainly, the oneness of God that this verse declares implies that He alone is God, and there is no other.

This doctrine is affirmed elsewhere in Scripture (Psalm 18:31; Isaiah 44:8; 45:22; 1 Corinthians 8:4–6; Ephesians 4:6). Such a belief stands in stark contrast to the pagan religions of the Old Testament world, which are characterized by belief in many gods. The fact that the singular God has clearly revealed His will eliminates the guesswork and uncertainty accompanying belief in many gods.

The church father Augustine (AD 354–430) cites this same verse in asserting that the Trinity is one God while affirming that the Father, Son, and Spirit are personally distinct. If Israel would obtain the promises to the patriarchs, they must have the same faith as Abraham, Isaac, and Jacob: faith that the one God who covenanted with them would see His plans to fruition—and that one God alone! It was not Baal who brought Abraham to Canaan. It was not Marduk who split the Red Sea. The God of Israel alone—the only God there is—did so.

Visual for Lesson 8. *Display this visual as you lead a whole-class brainstorming session regarding how families can walk in God's ways.*

5. And thou shalt love the LORD thy God with all thine heart, and with all thy soul, and with all thy might.

This allegiance is established abstractly in this verse: to love the Lord with one's whole *heart, soul,* and *might.* Notice that in this most fundamental of beliefs, the Bible does not prescribe particular rituals or deeds that fulfill what God desires. Instead, it provides the foundational principles that can be applied anywhere in life. This, the appropriate human response to God, is what Jesus declared "the first and great commandment" (Matthew 22:38): to love Him without any reservation, to love Him with the totality of one's being. Indeed, on this and the command to love one's neighbor "hang all the law and the prophets" (22:40).

C. Internal Inscription (v. 6)

6. And these words, which I command thee this day, shall be in thine heart.

This verse reinforces the universal scope of the blessing by commanding it to be *in thine heart* at all times. This is not a command to fixate on or compulsively repeat the prayer as a reflex, but rather that it should be so familiar as to inform everything one thinks and does. To love God with the devotion described in the previous verse implies keeping His *words* treasured within one's *heart.* The psalmist recognized the importance of this when he wrote, "Thy word have I hid in mine heart, that I might not sin against thee" (Psalm 119:11). The commandments of God are to be internalized, not superficially listened to and then ignored.

D. External Repetition (vv. 7–9)

7. And thou shalt teach them diligently unto thy children, and shalt talk of them when thou sittest in thine house, and when thou walkest by the way, and when thou liest down, and when thou risest up.

It is not enough, however, for the people of God to discipline themselves. If the Israelites did not educate their *children* on how to think about God, then their pagan neighbors would happily do so. Later rabbis interpreted the "children" referenced here as students, suggesting that, at least in later Judaism, one's responsibility for instructing the next generation did not apply exclusively to one's progeny. Similarly, while the book of Proverbs refers to the recipient of its wisdom as "my son," we understand it as applicable to all (Proverbs 1:8; 2:1; 3:1; etc.).

The verse now before us is not an exhaustive list of the times the Israelites should educate their children about this blessing. Instead, the examples show its extensiveness: this imperative ought to permeate one's entire life.

What Do You Think?

How will you help encourage and strengthen a younger believer in their faith journey?

Digging Deeper

Which is better: to shelter younger believers from exposure to the world or to allow the exposure to test and strengthen their faith? Explain.

The Treasure of Traditions

My mother is an excellent cook. Growing up, my parents encouraged my brother and me to order meals from the adult menu and not the children's menu in an effort to teach us to enjoy various foods and develop a mature palate.

It sure worked! As part of our wedding presents, my mother gave us each a recipe book full of her treasured culinary secrets and foundational elements of hospitality. To this day, it is one of the best presents I have ever received. Her years of cooking experience are distilled onto pages and passed down to the next generation.

God gives His people His own recipe to fullness in Deuteronomy 6:3–9. He teaches His people to treasure His commandments, pass them on to future generations, and even "write them" on their hearts. What is something passed down through generations that is still important in your journey of faith today? —N. V.

8–9. And thou shalt bind them for a sign upon thine hand, and they shall be as frontlets between thine eyes. And thou shalt write them upon the posts of thy house, and on thy gates.

Notably, the text does not command to *bind* these things on the hands and between the eyes of one's children, but on one's own *hand* and *between* one's own *eyes*. Leading by example is the ultimate form of education.

The list in these two verses is also not exhaustive. These are examples of how one might establish visual reminders of this prescribed attitude. The failure to erect such reminders is not a sin, but to heed it is wisdom. The purpose of this verse is to encourage endurance in the attitude outlined in the previous verses. When times get difficult, it is easy to forget this way of looking at the world. One way to mitigate human forgetfulness is with external reminders.

The command to bind these commandments to one's hand and head may be metaphorical (compare Proverbs 6:20–21). Still, many ancient people would wear clothing and accessories inscribed with invocations of deities as protectors. Hebrew examples invoking the Lord have also been found in the archeological record, suggesting that they may have worn clothing or jewelry with writing on them. This definitely seems to be the case in Matthew 23:5, where Jesus criticized the Pharisees for wrong motives in their use of phylacteries—small boxes containing Scripture verses worn on arms and foreheads (compare Exodus 13:9).

What Do You Think?

What steps can you take today to implement the principle of verses 8–9?

Digging Deeper

How will you ensure that your witness does not become holier-than-thou showmanship?

II. Applying the Law

(Matthew 19:3–9)

The New Testament passage for today's lesson takes us into the third year of Jesus' earthly ministry. Matthew structures his Gospel account in terms of five discourses, and the fourth of those has just ended as Jesus shifts His ministry efforts from Galilee to Judea on the eastern side of the Jordan River (Matthew 19:1).

A. The Question (v. 3)

3. The Pharisees also came unto him, tempting him, and saying unto him, Is it lawful for a man to put away his wife for every cause?

Opposition has been growing, and these *Pharisees,* like those of Matthew 16:1, do not have Jesus' best interests at heart. So they test His interpretation of the Law of Moses. We should note that Jesus has already addressed this issue in Matthew 5:31–32.

Their issue specifically seems to concern Deuteronomy 24:1 and its divorce clause regarding "uncleanness in her." The Pharisees were themselves divided over the interpretation here between the conservative school of Shammai and the more liberal school of Hillel, two famous rabbis from the late first century BC. Those of Shammai were narrowly focused regarding their interpretation of the law: it must be followed to the very letter. To them, "uncleanness" meant "unchastity"—period. Those of Hillel were looser in their interpretation; in a rather uncontrolled way, they pretty much allowed the husband in a marriage to determine what "uncleanness" meant in his situation. Unlike the squabbling factions of His contemporaries, however, Jesus is no simple rabbi or interpreter.

B. The Response (vv. 4–6)

4. And he answered and said unto them, Have ye not read, that he which made them at the beginning made them male and female.

Jesus' strategy is to go back to Genesis, where God's original intent for marriage is recorded. It starts with acknowledging the *male and female* distinctive of Genesis 1:27; 5:2.

5. And said, For this cause shall a man leave father and mother, and shall cleave to his wife: and they twain shall be one flesh?

Jesus quotes Genesis 2:24, marking the establishing of a new family unit by means of marriage. A *man* living in his parents' household leaves his original situation to make a new household with *his wife.* The relationship between man and wife overrides what was previously the most important relationship, that of parents to their son or daughter. Jesus' invocation of this verse in this context reinforces the sacredness of the marriage relationship: with marriage, a new family unit is born. This is not a relationship to be established or treated lightly (Malachi 2:16).

6. Wherefore they are no more twain, but one flesh. What therefore God hath joined together, let not man put asunder.

This verse contains the thrust of Jesus' response: God has made *one flesh* by joining together a man and a woman. To rend them apart amounts to the destruction of God's established order. Thus Jesus' declaration aligns more with that of the school of Shammai rather than Hillel (see above). But this does not make Jesus a follower of Shammai. Rather, as the Son of God—and very God Himself—Jesus possesses special authority to interpret the Law of Moses as only God can.

C. The Rebuttal (v. 7)

7. They say unto him, Why did Moses then command to give a writing of divorcement, and to put her away?

The Pharisees' rejoinder is valid enough: the fact of the matter is that ordinances for divorce *do* exist in the Law of *Moses* (Deuteronomy 24:1–4; compare 22:13–30; Jeremiah 3:1). If these ordinances are not applicable in the universal scope of space or time, then how did they find their way into Scripture? Perhaps the Pharisees think they have caught Jesus in a trap: Jesus has been stating the ideal situation; but the Pharisees counter by noting the reality of divorce and its justification.

D. The Clarification (vv. 8–9)

8. He saith unto them, Moses because of the hardness of your hearts suffered you to put away your wives: but from the beginning it was not so.

Jesus does not deny what *Moses* allowed. Instead, Jesus contrasts the doctrine of marriage with God's permission of divorce as a concession. In the beginning, God joined man and woman together in marriage, a union never intended to be broken (except by death; see 1 Corinthians 7:39). Divorce is not the result that God intends for marriage relationships. However, because of the fall and resulting human sin, it is a "permission" that God gives.

Jesus reorients the conversation toward the

original aim of God's plan: although an exception exists, it should not be normalized (compare 1 Corinthians 7:10–11). This is not to say that situations involving adultery (see next verse) or abusive relationships should be preserved in every circumstance. Rather, Christians ought to strive first and foremost toward the ideal that God has established while acknowledging the contingency if this aim should fail.

9. And I say unto you, Whosoever shall put away his wife, except it be for fornication, and shall marry another, committeth adultery: And whoso marrieth her which is put away doth commit adultery.

In the Gospels, Jesus frequently says, "Ye have heard it said . . . but I say unto you . . ." (Matthew 5:21–22, 27–28, etc.). These pairs are often called "antitheses." But notice here that instead of overturning a former saying, Jesus strengthens the grounds of what was said. Here, Jesus affirms what God had ordained through Moses: divorce is permissible in very particular conditions. However, He prioritizes God's plan over the contingent allowances that God granted to hardhearted humanity.

The final clause speaks of the spiritual reality of marriage: a man who marries a woman who is, in the eyes of God, still married to her first husband commits *adultery* since she is still married in God's sight. A marriage relationship is brought into being with God, and He will not easily admit its dissolution.

> **What Do You Think?**
> What are some unhelpful or possibly dangerous interpretations of Matthew 19:3–9 concerning considerations of divorce?
>
> **Digging Deeper**
> What questions should a believer ask when considering divorce?

Conclusion

A. Walking the Walk

Christians are called to receive and apply God's will. If we are to be distinct in the world—as families and as individuals—we must be marked by faithful obedience. Central to this is acknowledging that a whole-person love of God is the most fundamental part of the Christian life, even as it was to believers under the old covenant. It should undergird all thoughts and animate every action that a believer takes. One example of exhibiting such love for God is to submit to His desires as they relate to marriage.

It is not just in matters of marriage that one's love for God can be displayed, however. The commandment "thou shalt love the Lord thy God" can and should manifest in every decision and action in the life of a Christian. Love for God can look like obeying God's wishes for human life as expressed in the Bible and especially in the person of Jesus Christ, the incarnation of God Himself.

As we faithfully receive and live out God's law, we must remember that it is not for us alone. We are to spur one another on and instruct younger believers growing up in the faith (Hebrews 10:24). Human nature inclines away from God and toward its own desires. We must receive God's law—and establish external reminders of this commitment so as to combat human forgetfulness—so that it dwells in our hearts and forms our actions to live in alignment with it.

> **What Do You Think?**
> How can believers live as a people who are distinct from the world?
>
> **Digging Deeper**
> In what ways can this be true regarding our family relationships? our habits? our finances? our treatment of neighbors?

B. Prayer

Heavenly Father, God of Moses and Jesus, help us to love You with all our hearts, all our souls, and all our might. Help us to love You in our homes and outside of our homes. Help us to love You with all our words and in all our deeds. In Jesus' name we pray. Amen.

C. Thought to Remember

Love God in and through everything you do.

Involvement Learning

Enhance your lesson with KJV Bible Student *(from your curriculum supplier) and the reproducible activity page (at www.standardlesson.com or in the back of the* KJV Standard Lesson Commentary Deluxe Edition*).*

Into the Lesson

Write the commands *Hear!* and *Obey!* on the board. Begin the class by saying, "Few words are more necessary than these two. These two words can be tangible reminders that we must hear the Word of God and not forget it. These are key ideas that God wanted Moses to emphasize to His people. God still wants these ideas emphasized today." Lead a whole-class discussion regarding ways we can hear and obey God's Word.

Alternative. Ask learners to raise their hands if they wish they knew more Scriptures by heart. Then say, "Let's take the opportunity to do that right now as we work on 'the first commandment' as Jesus stated in the Gospels." Ask learners to repeat the following after you: "Thou shalt love the Lord thy God with all thy heart, and with all thy soul, and with all thy mind, and with all thy strength." Pause after each comma to signal learners to repeat the phrase you just vocalized.

After either activity, transition to Bible study by saying, "Now let's find out why Deuteronomy 6:3–9 is so important to memorize and what it means for God's people of all eras."

Into the Word

Read Deuteronomy 6:3–9 aloud, then divide the class into two groups: **Parent/Grandparent Group** and **Children Group**. Read Deuteronomy 6:7 aloud again and say: "We are going to act out conversations we might have about God with our children and grandchildren. "

Invite someone from the **Parents/Grandparents Group** to pose a question or make a statement about obeying God; then let a volunteer from the **Children Group** respond. Alternate back and forth, allowing all learners to voice a question or answer. If they have trouble knowing what to say, give each group the appropriate handout (you prepare).

Parents/Grandparents Group: 1–What are some of the commandments God wants us to obey? 2–What do you know about God's promises? 3–Why does God want us to love Him with the totality of our being?

Children Group: 1–Why does God say we're supposed to love Him with the totality of our being? 2–What is the reason for God's commandments? 3–Why should we go to great lengths to remember these commandments?

Option. Distribute copies of the "Reminders!" exercise from the activity page, which you can download. Have learners complete it individually in a minute or less before discussing responses in small groups.

Wrap up by saying: "Our love of God and our obedience to Him should undergird every action we take, including how we approach our relationships with others."

Divide learners into pairs or triads. Ask a volunteer to read aloud Matthew 19:3–9. Distribute handouts (you create) with the following questions for small-group discussion: 1–Why did the Pharisees use marriage and divorce as topics to test Jesus? 2–What is the reason for Jesus' strategy of going back to the Genesis account? 3–How does Jesus' answer in verses 8–9 challenge the beliefs of the Pharisees? 4–What is the connection between Matthew 19:3–9 and Deuteronomy 6:3–9?

Into Life

Distribute a sheet of paper and a pen to each learner. Direct them to write a letter to a young believer growing in faith. Suggest that the letter encourage the young believer in their faith and celebrate the work of the Holy Spirit.

Alternative. Distribute copies of the "Letters of Encouragement" exercise from the activity page. Invite learners to complete the page throughout the upcoming week. To encourage completion, say that you will ask for volunteers next week to share how this exercise challenged or inspired them.

May 3
Lesson 9 (KJV)

Christian Expectation of Grace

Devotional Reading: Revelation 5:1–5
Background Scripture: Jonah 1–4; Galatians 3:1–13

Jonah 3:1–5

1 And the word of the LORD came unto Jonah the second time, saying,

2 Arise, go unto Nineveh, that great city, and preach unto it the preaching that I bid thee.

3 So Jonah arose, and went unto Nineveh, according to the word of the LORD. Now Nineveh was an exceeding great city of three days' journey.

4 And Jonah began to enter into the city a day's journey, and he cried, and said, Yet forty days, and Nineveh shall be overthrown.

5 So the people of Nineveh believed God, and proclaimed a fast, and put on sackcloth, from the greatest of them even to the least of them.

Jonah 4:6–11

6 And the LORD God prepared a gourd, and made it to come up over Jonah, that it might be a shadow over his head, to deliver him from his grief. So Jonah was exceeding glad of the gourd.

7 But God prepared a worm when the morning rose the next day, and it smote the gourd that it withered.

8 And it came to pass, when the sun did arise, that God prepared a vehement east wind; and the sun beat upon the head of Jonah, that he fainted, and wished in himself to die, and said, It is better for me to die than to live.

9 And God said to Jonah, Doest thou well to be angry for the gourd? And he said, I do well to be angry, even unto death.

10 Then said the LORD, Thou hast had pity on the gourd, for the which thou hast not laboured, neither madest it grow; which came up in a night, and perished in a night:

11 And should not I spare Nineveh, that great city, wherein are more than sixscore thousand persons that cannot discern between their right hand and their left hand; and also much cattle?

Key Text

Then said the LORD, Thou hast had pity on the gourd, for the which thou hast not laboured, neither madest it grow; which came up in a night, and perished in a night: and should not I spare Nineveh, that great city.

—Jonah 4:10–11a

Social Teachings
of the Church

Unit 3: Fulfilling Our Obligations to God and Society

Lessons 9–13

Lesson Aims

After participating in this lesson, each learner will be able to:

1. Identify the reason for Jonah's anger.
2. Describe how God's desire to extend grace to Nineveh expresses impartiality.
3. List ideas for extending God's grace to neighbors from various cultural and ethnic backgrounds.

Lesson Outline

Introduction

A. I'm the Judge!
B. Lesson Context: Historical
C. Lesson Context: Literary

I. The Prophet's Message (Jonah 3:1–5)

A. Directive from the Lord (vv. 1–2)
B. Proclamation of Jonah (vv. 3–4)
C. Response of the Ninevites (v. 5)
Powerful Motivator

II. The Prophet's Anger (Jonah 4:6–11)

A. Divine Provision (vv. 6–7)
B. Divine Questioning (vv. 8–9)
Flying Off the Handle
C. Divine Corrective (vv. 10–11)

Conclusion

A. Our Graciously Patient God
B. Prayer
C. Thought to Remember

Introduction

A. I'm the Judge!

His drug of choice was adrenaline. He recklessly and repeatedly drove his motorcycle at high speeds—a decision that resulted in numerous wrecks and serious bodily harm. He squandered his money on expensive vehicles, alcohol, and drugs. He jeopardized his family's financial stability and threatened to leave them without a father and husband. Although I considered him a friend, I grew angry at his irresponsible decision-making and selfish desires.

One day, my anger bubbled to the surface. He had lost weight and felt good about it. He approached me, saying, "I'm looking good, don't you think?"

"Well, it's generally good to put on some muscle, too, don't you think?" I retorted.

In that moment, I felt justified. *This man is a jerk*, I thought. *He doesn't care about anyone else, so why should I be kind to him?* Now, I realize I angrily judged him and concluded he did not deserve kindness and respect.

The question, "Who's the just judge?" is central in today's study of the prophet Jonah. The prophet angrily judges God and the people of Nineveh. But are his conclusions accurate?

B. Lesson Context: Historical

Jonah's ministry is difficult to date. The closest approximation we may make is that he prophesied about events that occurred during the reign of Jeroboam II, the king of Israel from 793 to 753 BC (2 Kings 14:23–29). The designation "Israel" in this context refers to the northern kingdom that formed following the division of the original nation of Israel. This division occurred after King Solomon's death, around 930 BC (1 Kings 12:20).

In the eighth century BC, before the reign of Jeroboam, military conflicts existed between Israel and Assyria. The Assyrians were known for their brutal violence. Assyrian kings boasted about their power and commissioned visual displays of their cruelty as propaganda, reminding enemies of the futility of resistance.

Nineveh was a major city in the Assyrian

Empire. It became the empire's capital in about 700 BC during the reign of Sennacherib. Jonah prophesied more than 50 years before Nineveh became the seat of government. The city is first mentioned in the Bible when a descendant of Noah's son Ham built it (Genesis 10:11).

During Jeroboam's reign, Israel experienced prosperity, though it was short-lived. Their fortune was due in part to internal turmoil in Assyria. However, people remembered past conflicts, and soldiers involved in those wars may have been alive during Jonah's lifetime. Jonah's hometown of Gathhepher was in northern Israel (2 Kings 14:25), and this region likely experienced direct conflict with the Assyrians. Eventually, the Assyrian Empire regained strength and, in 722 BC, attacked the northern kingdom of Israel.

C. Lesson Context: Literary

The book of Jonah opens with the Lord commanding Jonah to go to Nineveh and preach against it (Jonah 1:1–2). The Lord observed the city's wickedness. Jonah, however, disobeyed the Lord's command. He traveled to Joppa and boarded a west-bound ship to Tarshish (1:3).

The Lord sent a storm to intercept Jonah and the ship. To save the vessel, the sailors lightened its load (Jonah 1:5; compare Acts 27:18). Their efforts failed, leading the crew to cast lots to determine the responsible party for the sudden storm (Jonah 1:6–7). Their process pointed to Jonah (1:7). Jonah revealed that he fled the presence of "the Lord, the God of heaven" (1:9–10). He directed the ship's crew to throw him overboard as a last-ditch effort to calm the storm. They agreed to do so only after requesting that Jonah's God not hold them guilty of murder (1:14).

Rather than let Jonah drown in the sea, the Lord prepared "a great fish" to swallow him (Jonah 1:17). For three days and three nights, Jonah remained in the fish. He acknowledged his situation and prayed to the Lord (2:1). Jonah promised to make good on his vow to preach the Lord's salvation to Nineveh (2:2–9). After three days, God directed the fish to vomit Jonah onto dry land (2:10). The prophet followed the Lord's command to go to Nineveh.

I. The Prophet's Message

(Jonah 3:1–5)

A. Directive from the Lord (vv. 1–2)

1–2. And the word of the Lord came unto Jonah the second time, saying, Arise, go unto Nineveh, that great city, and preach unto it the preaching that I bid thee.

The expression *the word of the Lord came* appears throughout the Old Testament to introduce a message from God (Genesis 15:4; 2 Samuel 7:4; Ezekiel 7:1; etc.). This verse is *the second time* in this book that Jonah receives a word from the Lord. Jonah 1:1–2 contains the first (see Lesson Context).

While the verse before us does not specify the exact message that Jonah is to *preach,* its content is likely still related to the "wickedness" of *Nineveh* (Jonah 1:2). The point is clear: Jonah does not control the message of his *preaching;* it comes directly from the Lord.

B. Proclamation of Jonah (vv. 3–4)

3. So Jonah arose, and went unto Nineveh, according to the word of the Lord. Now Nineveh was an exceeding great city of three days' journey.

The book of Jonah identifies *Nineveh* as a "great city" (Jonah 1:2; 3:2). The verse before us elaborates on the description. The Hebrew phrase translated as *exceeding great* may be understood literally as "great to God." Most commentators interpret this to mean Nineveh was so large and influential that it held significant importance, even to God.

The claim that Nineveh's size requires a *three days' journey* faces criticism. The supposition is that no ancient city could be so vast. This skepticism draws various responses. One response is that the three days include the time needed for Jonah to stop and preach. The book of Jonah describes the city's population as more than 120,000 people (Jonah 4:11, below). For Jonah to preach in every neighborhood, it could easily require three days.

Additionally, the reference to *three days* invites comparisons to Jonah's painful three-day ordeal in the "great fish" (Jonah 1:17). Sadly, his prophetic mission to Nineveh will feel even more painful (see 4:1–4, below).

4. And Jonah began to enter into the city a day's journey, and he cried, and said, Yet forty days, and Nineveh shall be overthrown.

Though *Nineveh* is a "city of three days' journey" (Jonah 3:3, above), Jonah only travels *a day's journey* before delivering his message. The proclamation is very brief—just five words in Hebrew. Notably, there is no mention of Nineveh's sins or any reference to the true God behind the message.

In ancient Near Eastern cultures, many nations and cities worshipped patron deities believed to oversee the territories. In this instance, Jonah does not reference the Lord's authority. He proclaims the message of judgment and offers no hope, only a declaration of doom.

The Hebrew word translated *overthrown* suggests a change in direction or status (examples: Joshua 7:8; 8:20; Job 19:19; Hosea 11:8; Joel 2:31). This can include the significant alteration a city might experience through destruction (examples: Genesis 19:29; Jeremiah 20:16; Amos 4:11). Jonah's message indicates imminent judgment without providing any explanation. The city will undoubtedly change, but not in the way Jonah expects.

What Do You Think?

How do we respond to the charge of "being judgmental" when we communicate the message of God's judgment?

Digging Deeper

How should we balance communicating God's love and mercy with His justice and holiness?

C. Response of the Ninevites (v. 5)

5. So the people of Nineveh believed God, and proclaimed a fast, and put on sackcloth, from the greatest of them even to the least of them.

A proclamation from *the people of Nineveh* follows Jonah's message. A *fast* can signify deep sorrow and lament (examples: Judges 20:26; Esther 4:3; Joel 1:14). Wearing *sackcloth,* a coarse and rough fabric, is an expression of grief (examples: Genesis 37:34; 2 Kings 19:1; Job 16:15). Together, fasting and sackcloth represent turning toward God (example: Daniel 9:3; compare Psalm 35:13).

Ninevites of every social class, *from the greatest of them even to the least,* express their grief and repentance. There is no guarantee that their actions will prevent the predicted disaster. However, they willingly do what is required to save themselves. They believe Jonah's message and hope for a different outcome because of their penitent response. This is not the first time in the book of Jonah that non-Israelites (Gentiles) respond faithfully to the *God* of Israel (compare Jonah 1:16).

Jesus highlights the skepticism of the religious leaders of His time by referring to the Ninevites' belief and repentance (Matthew 12:41). While Jesus' ministry primarily focused on Israel, their response led to His condemnation (11:20–24). In contrast, Gentiles positively received Jonah's preaching despite no record of him performing any miracles.

What Do You Think?

Why are sorrow and lament appropriate responses when we are confronted with our sin (see Psalms 51:17; 119:136; 2 Corinthians 7:10; James 4:7–9)?

Digging Deeper

How do Psalm 30:11–12; Romans 8:1, 34; Hebrews 7:25; and 1 John 3:20 offer encouragement in this state?

Powerful Motivator

As a high school English teacher, I observed particular habits in my students. One notable pattern emerged around the six-week mark of a nine-week quarter. When faced with the possibility of failing, students would ask about their grades. Their question was always the same: "What can I do to avoid failing?" Students who were once indifferent to their grades suddenly became very concerned. The threat of a failing grade was a powerful motivator.

Similarly, the warning of judgment prompted Nineveh to heed Jonah's prophetic message. When imminent destruction was on the table, they repented for their sins and believed in God.

God gave us the Holy Spirit and Scripture to motivate and empower us to live as His children.

Are you attentive to God's guidance in convicting your heart of sin and leading you toward greater holiness? —B. R.

II. The Prophet's Anger

(Jonah 4:6–11)

When Jonah's message reaches the king of Nineveh, he responds by clothing himself in sackcloth and sitting in ashes (Jonah 3:6). He issues a decree that all Ninevites should abandon their wicked ways and turn to God (3:7–9). The people obey his directives, and God promises not to destroy the city (3:10). God's decision infuriates Jonah, and he asks the Lord to take his life (4:1–3). The Lord responds, "Doest thou well to be angry?" (4:4). Angry and sulking, Jonah goes outside the city, builds a small booth (4:5), and waits to see whether the Lord will change His mind.

A. Divine Provision (vv. 6–7)

6. And the LORD God prepared a gourd, and made it to come up over Jonah, that it might be a shadow over his head, to deliver him from his grief. So Jonah was exceeding glad of the gourd.

This verse contains the first and only appearance of the title *LORD God* in the book of Jonah. *LORD* (with small caps) translates God's proper name, often transliterated "Yahweh." This name is first recorded in Exodus 3:13–14 when Moses asks how to refer to the deity he encounters. The name means "I am who I am" or "I will be what I will be." It conveys God's reliability to be Himself, not fickle or changing like people or pagan gods. The Hebrew word translated *God* is "Elohim." While Elohim is one of the primary names for the true God of the Old Testament, the same word refers to "gods" in a general sense (examples: Exodus 12:12; 20:3). Thus, the composite name *LORD God* unites a generic word meaning "god" with the unique personal name of Israel's one true God.

According to the book of Jonah, God *prepared* four objects to interact with Jonah: a "great fish" (1:17), a "gourd" (4:6), a "worm" (4:7), and a "vehement east wind" (4:8). This verse introduces the second of these four items. The Lord God temporarily supplements the booth Jonah built for protection from the sun with a rapidly growing *gourd*. The exact type of plant this Hebrew word represents is unknown. One possibility is that it refers to a castor oil plant, which can grow to about eight feet and features large leaves.

Jonah feels *exceeding glad* for the shade. The Hebrew word translated *grief* refers elsewhere to Nineveh's "wickedness" and "evil" (Jonah 1:2; 3:8, 10), the troublesome storm at sea (1:7), and Jonah's own negative feelings (4:1). God's love for Jonah's perceived enemies continues to displease Jonah. While Jonah enjoys the shade, he mourns the Lord's merciful response to Nineveh.

7. But God prepared a worm when the morning rose the next day, and it smote the gourd that it withered.

This verse identifies the third of four objects *prepared* by *God* to teach Jonah (see commentary on Jonah 3:6, above). God directs *a worm* to consume the same plant He established to shade Jonah. This action illustrates God's sovereign control over the world; He possesses the power to give life and bring about destruction. Ironically, it is not the destruction of Nineveh that Jonah witnesses; instead, the natural protection from the sun God provided is destroyed.

B. Divine Questioning (vv. 8–9)

8. And it came to pass, when the sun did arise, that God prepared a vehement east wind; and the sun beat upon the head of Jonah, that he fainted, and wished in himself to die, and said, It is better for me to die than to live.

By the time the sun *did arise*, the plant no longer

How to Say It

Assyria	Uh-*sear*-ee-uh.
Assyrians	Uh-*sear*-e-unz.
Gathhepher	Gath-*he*-fer.
Jeroboam	Jair-uh-*boe*-um.
Jonah	*Jo*-nuh.
Joppa	*Jop*-uh.
Nineveh	*Nin*-uh-vuh.
Ninevites	*Nin*-uh-vites.
Sennacherib	Sen-*nack*-er-ib.
Tarshish	*Tar*-shish.

Visual for Lessons 9 & 11. *Point to this visual and discuss the connection between God's generosity and the ways we deal generously with others.*

provides shade. God further increases Jonah's discomfort by sending *a vehement east wind* (compare Jeremiah 18:17). Such winds are life-threatening, as they blow in sand and intensify the sun's heat. The combination of the sun and wind causes Jonah to become light-headed and dizzy, to the point that he faints. Jonah's reaction is not merely dramatic; he is physically and spiritually miserable, far from home. The exhaustion from a preaching tour he didn't ask for is worsened by the threat of heatstroke. Jonah experiences a small taste of God's judgment.

9a. And God said to Jonah, Doest thou well to be angry for the gourd?

The first six words of God's question are the same as His initial question to Jonah in verse 4. The question demonstrates God as a gracious and kind teacher who pursues Jonah, even when Jonah's values are misaligned.

9b. And he said, I do well to be angry, even unto death.

Jonah's answer is petty, defensive, and defiant. He attempts to bolster his position by asserting once again his preference for *death*. From Jonah's perspective, God is inconsistent: why would God spare the evil city of Nineveh while allowing the destruction of a harmless shade plant?

Readers quickly notice the irony. On the one hand, Jonah, a prophet of Yahweh, reacts angrily to God's mercy toward Nineveh. On the other hand, the pagan king of Nineveh, who likely does not even know the name of Israel's God, acts piously by repenting of sin (Jonah 3:6–9). Jonah's anger reveals his lack of compassion for the Ninevites.

> **What Do You Think?**
> Is it appropriate for us to be angry at God? Why, or why not?
>
> **Digging Deeper**
> How can we prevent anger from becoming hatred, bitterness, or unbelief?

Flying Off the Handle

In the early days of the United States, ax heads were made in the industrialized East and then shipped to the frontier West. When the ax heads arrived at their destination, they were fit to wooden handles. The handles were often hastily fashioned, yielding the deadly possibility that an ax head could fly off an ill-fitting handle when in use.

The suddenness of such an event became a metaphor for an outburst of anger: *flying off the handle*. Possibly, the first use of this figure of speech in print was in a satirical story titled *The Attaché*. It was published in 1844 by the Canadian humorist Thomas C. Haliburton. However, the idea goes back much further than that! God's directive for Jonah to preach in Nineveh struck deep resentment in that prophet; thus, we see him "flying off the handle" at God. Do you deal with your anger better than Jonah? See James 1:19–20. —C. R. B.

C. Divine Corrective (vv. 10–11)

10. Then said the Lord, Thou hast had pity on the gourd, for the which thou hast not laboured, neither madest it grow; which came up in a night, and perished in a night.

The Lord forcefully points out Jonah's misdirected sense of *pity*. Jonah had no ownership of the *gourd*; he neither planted nor tended to it. It was a gracious gift from the Lord. Nevertheless, Jonah was angry when it *perished*. One would hope these facts led the prophet to realize the absurdity of his misplaced pity. However, God has more to say.

11. And should not I spare Nineveh, that great city, wherein are more than sixscore thousand persons that cannot discern between their right hand and their left hand; and also much cattle?

The text indicates the population of Nineveh as *sixscore thousand*, which translates to 120,000 people. Some commentators propose that it reflects the total population of the city. A city of this size could easily accommodate twice that number. Under this view, the declaration that they *cannot discern between their right hand and their left hand* has a spiritual dimension. Spiritually, the Ninevites are deficient in distinguishing good from evil.

An alternate interpretation holds that 120,000 refers specifically to children who are not yet old enough to know right from wrong. If this interpretation is accurate, then the total population is significantly greater. However, the Hebrew word translated *persons* does not explicitly indicate children. Therefore, the number likely refers to the total population of Nineveh—a people who, until Jonah's visit, were spiritually ignorant. They were, in essence, spiritual infants.

The word translated *cattle* refers to general livestock, given its frequent translation as "beast" (Exodus 13:15; 22:19; etc.). The mention of *much cattle* serves as a reminder that God also cares for animal life (see Psalm 36:6).

The Lord's question abruptly concludes the book. The Lord presses Jonah to consider the *persons* of Nineveh and whether they should have the chance to repent. The Lord's words indicate mercy toward the undiscerning and a desire to *spare* the ignorant. The book of Jonah wraps up with a timely question: Is God not free to show mercy and compassion to whomever He desires (Psalm 145:8–9)?

What Do You Think?

What ministries can your church offer to those of the nearest "great city"?

Digging Deeper

How does ministry in a "great city" differ from ministry in a rural context? In what ways are they similar?

Conclusion

A. Our Graciously Patient God

The story of Jonah reveals God's expansive grace and mercy without partiality. God does not ignore Nineveh's wickedness; He is, of course, the just judge. However, when the people of Nineveh received the warning of destruction, they responded appropriately. In an act of compassion, God extended mercy and grace, relenting from the promised punishment.

Such manifestations of grace and mercy can surprise us. Like Jonah, we may quickly question God's willingness to extend forgiveness to our enemies—people we feel do not deserve salvation. However, God is the ultimate judge. His treatment of Nineveh exemplifies that His grace and forgiveness are available to all who will accept them. God's grace is massive, and His patience endures.

Jonah's example reveals how God pursues His people and wants to conform our desires to His. God did not immediately punish Jonah for his disobedience and rebellion. Instead, God remained in conversation with Jonah and taught him the comprehensive nature of divine grace. The Lord God is "slow to anger, and of great kindness" (Jonah 4:2) to all people who respond to His grace and mercy. How do you remain in conversation with God? Are you leaning into the divine questions Scripture and the Holy Spirit continually ask? Are you willing to let your perception and understanding shift, change, and grow as you mature in faith?

What Do You Think?

What new insights have you discovered from this study of Jonah?

Digging Deeper

How will this insight strengthen your faith in God or reveal opportunities for spiritual growth?

B. Prayer

Lord God, You are gracious and compassionate, slow to anger, and abounding in steadfast love. We repent of the times we have not reflected Your grace and mercy. Shape our hearts and desires to faithfully imitate Your compassion and kindness toward the world. In Jesus' name we pray. Amen.

C. Thought to Remember

God's grace is expansive,
and His patience is persistent.

Involvement Learning

Enhance your lesson with KJV Bible Student *(from your curriculum supplier) and the reproducible activity page (at www.standardlesson.com or in the back of the* KJV Standard Lesson Commentary Deluxe Edition*).*

Into the Lesson

Begin by asking, "When have you wanted someone else to experience the consequences of their actions?" Distribute a sheet of paper and a pen to each learner. Instruct them to create two columns by drawing a line down the middle of the paper. In the first column, ask them to list real or imaginary examples of someone who did wrong and faced consequences. In the second column, ask them to list real or imaginary examples of someone who received mercy and grace despite doing wrong.

After they have completed their lists, encourage them to compare the examples in the two columns and describe how it might feel to see someone else receive mercy and grace despite their wrongdoing.

Transition into the Bible study by saying, "It's a human tendency to desire justice for those who have wronged us. Today's study of the prophet Jonah will reveal how this tendency often overlooks the surprising and gracious ways that God works."

Into the Word

Ask one volunteer to read aloud Jonah 3:1–5 and another to read aloud Jonah 4:6–11. Divide the class into three groups. Provide each group with highlighters and handouts (you create) containing the lesson's Scripture text and the prompts and questions below.

Begin the activity by instructing each group to highlight words or phrases that describe their assigned namesake in one color. Then have them highlight in a different color any words or phrases related to the key actions taken by their namesake.

Ninevites Group. 1–Who were the Ninevites, and why might they have been considered enemies of Israel? 2–What details about the city can we discern from these Scriptures? 3–What is the significance of the Ninevites undertaking a fast and wearing sackcloth? 4–What does it mean that the Ninevites "cannot discern between their right hand and their left" (Jonah 4:11)?

Jonah Group. 1–Who was Jonah, and why might he have avoided traveling to Nineveh? 2–What was the content of Jonah's message to the Ninevites? 3–Why did Jonah think it would be better to die? 4–Was Jonah's anger justified? Why or why not?

Lord God Group. 1–What is the meaning of the title "Lord God" (Jonah 4:6), and why is the title significant in this narrative? 2–How does God show mercy to Jonah? 3–How does God show mercy to the Ninevites? 4–How do these Scripture texts depict the mercy and justice of God?

After calling time, ask a volunteer from each group to share their responses with the entire class. Conclude this section with a whole-class discussion on the following question: "Do we sometimes identify with Jonah, becoming upset with God's impartial displays of mercy? Why or why not?"

As a group, write a statement on the board summarizing how God showed grace and mercy.

Option. Distribute copies of the "Surprised or Expected" activity from the activity page, which you can download. Have learners complete it in groups of three.

Into Life

Say, "Today's study reminds us that God is impartial regarding His grace, mercy, and forgiveness. God desires for all people, regardless of their cultural or ethnic backgrounds, to come to know Him as the Lord God."

Conduct a whole-class brainstorming session on ways to extend God's grace to our neighbors. Write the responses on the board. After five minutes of brainstorming, distribute an index card and pen to each participant. Invite them to write down a plan to use the ideas on the board to extend God's grace to others in the community.

Option. Distribute copies of the "Verses of Grace" exercise from the activity page. Have learners work in pairs to complete as indicated.

May 10
Lesson 10 (KJV)

Work as Christian Duty

Devotional Reading: Ecclesiastes 9:4–10
Background Scripture: Genesis 2:15–25; 2 Thessalonians 3:6–12

Genesis 2:15

15 And the LORD God took the man, and put him into the garden of Eden to dress it and to keep it.

Exodus 20:9

9 Six days shalt thou labour, and do all thy work.

John 5:17

17 But Jesus answered them, My Father worketh hitherto, and I work.

John 9:4

4 I must work the works of him that sent me, while it is day: the night cometh, when no man can work.

Acts 20:33–35

33 I have coveted no man's silver, or gold, or apparel.

34 Yea, ye yourselves know, that these hands have ministered unto my necessities, and to them that were with me.

35 I have shewed you all things, how that so labouring ye ought to support the weak, and to remember the words of the Lord Jesus, how he said, It is more blessed to give than to receive.

2 Thessalonians 3:6–12

6 Now we command you, brethren, in the name of our Lord Jesus Christ, that ye withdraw yourselves from every brother that walketh disorderly, and not after the tradition which he received of us.

7 For yourselves know how ye ought to follow us: for we behaved not ourselves disorderly among you;

8 Neither did we eat any man's bread for nought; but wrought with labour and travail night and day, that we might not be chargeable to any of you:

9 Not because we have not power, but to make ourselves an ensample unto you to follow us.

10 For even when we were with you, this we commanded you, that if any would not work, neither should he eat.

11 For we hear that there are some which walk among you disorderly, working not at all, but are busybodies.

12 Now them that are such we command and exhort by our Lord Jesus Christ, that with quietness they work, and eat their own bread.

Key Text

I have shewed you all things, how that so labouring ye ought to support the weak, and to remember the words of the Lord Jesus, how he said, It is more blessed to give than to receive. **—Acts 20:35**

Social Teachings
of the Church

Unit 3: Fulfilling Our Obligations to God and Society

Lessons 9–13

Lesson Aims

After participating in this lesson, each learner will be able to:

1. Summarize the main points of each text.
2. Explain the purpose of work from these texts.
3. Write a personal resolution regarding work in service to God.

Lesson Outline

Introduction
- A. Valuing Work
- B. Lesson Context: Acts
- C. Lesson Context: 2 Thessalonians

I. Work Given by God (Genesis 2:15; Exodus 20:9)
- A. Commanded (Genesis 2:15)
- B. Limited (Exodus 20:9)

II. Work of God (John 5:17; 9:4)
- A. The Father (John 5:17)
- B. The Son (John 9:4)

III. Work to Meet Needs (Acts 20:33–35)
- A. Helping Oneself (vv. 33–34)
- B. Helping Others (v. 35)
  - *A Box of Diapers*

IV. Work and the People of God (2 Thessalonians 3:6–12)
- A. Be Not Idle (v. 6)
- B. An Imitable Example (vv. 7–9)
- C. Earning One's Food (vv. 10–12)
  - *Growing a Garden*

Conclusion
- A. Embracing Work
- B. Prayer
- C. Thought to Remember

Introduction

A. Valuing Work

My grandfather taught me the value of hard work. After retiring from the military, he started his own construction business, enlisting the help of his teenage grandsons. We spent our summers pouring concrete and building homes from the ground up, laboring tirelessly from sunrise to sunset. After a long day of construction work, we would return to his 80-acre farm to tend to the cattle and handle various farm duties. We repeated this routine every weekday.

My grandfather grew up during the Great Depression (1929–1939), a fact I never fully appreciated as a teenager. His father and grandfather desperately wanted to work but struggled to find employment, making my grandfather's formative years challenging. Witnessing their struggle, he developed a strong work ethic, which he passed to his grandsons by example.

In today's lesson, we will explore God's design for work, starting from creation and continuing through the life of the first-century church with application for today. While this lesson reviews a variety of Scripture texts, those of primary interest will be Acts 20:33–35 and 2 Thessalonians 3:6–12, both focusing on words from the apostle Paul.

B. Lesson Context: Acts

The book of Acts covers events from about AD 30 to 63. Our lesson segment from that book takes us almost to the end of that period.

In about AD 58, Paul traveled to Jerusalem after concluding his third missionary journey. Some members of the church in Jerusalem had fallen into poverty. Therefore, Paul's trip included collecting offerings from the churches in Macedonia and Achaia (Romans 15:25–26; 1 Corinthians 16:1–4; 2 Corinthians 8:1–4). This offering allowed Christians who were predominately of Gentile background to support the Christians in Jerusalem who were predominately of Jewish background.

Paul initially planned to sail to Syria from Greece to deliver the offering. But discovering a plot against him, he traveled by land through Macedonia (Acts 20:3). Paul aimed to arrive in

Jerusalem by Pentecost (20:16), which would mark the anniversary of the church's beginning (2:1). This would be a significant occasion for one group of Christians to receive a life-sustaining gift from fellow believers of different backgrounds.

C. Lesson Context: 2 Thessalonians

Paul took the message of the gospel to the city of Thessalonica during his second missionary journey (AD 52–54). What we know about his effort to plant a church there and the immediate aftershock of doing so are recorded in Acts 17:1–9, 13. The apostle did not start a church in every town or city he visited. But the demographics of Thessalonica made that city a good candidate for a church plant. First, the city had one or more synagogues, where Paul liked to begin voicing his message (Acts 17:2, 10, 16). Second, the city was large—by some estimates, nearly 200,000 people lived there in the Roman era. Third, Thessalonica sat astride major trade routes of land and sea.

Some commentators think that the letters we call 1 and 2 Thessalonians were the very first of the New Testament documents written. Since our study concerns 2 Thessalonians, the most immediate literary context for it is 1 Thessalonians. That letter features a mixture of expressions of Paul's gratitude, a summary of his ministry in the city, doctrinal clarifications, and instructions for daily life. The tone of 2 Thessalonians is direct, as Paul finds it necessary to review some of the same topics again.

I. Work Given by God

(Genesis 2:15; Exodus 20:9)

A. Commanded (Genesis 2:15)

15. And the LORD God took the man, and put him into the garden of Eden to dress it and to keep it.

This verse is crucial to understanding work in God's world. Occurring prior to the fall (Genesis 3), this is evidence that work is good. While the curse following humanity's disobedience renders work toilsome—marked by thorns, thistles, and sweat to bring forth food (3:17–19)—it did not start out that way. The toilsome nature of work is still with us today, but it ought not to distort our view of work itself. God Himself is a worker, demonstrated by the creation narratives in Genesis 1–2, and He calls humanity to work alongside Him (examples: Ezekiel 22:30; Matthew 28:19–20). For an interesting back and forth on the nature of work, see Ecclesiastes 2:10, 17–26; 3:9–13, 22; 4:8; 5:18–19; 8:15.

B. Limited (Exodus 20:9)

9. Six days shalt thou labour, and do all thy work.

This verse is part of the fourth of the Ten Commandments, that of remembering the Sabbath day to keep it holy (Exodus 20:8–11; see also Deuteronomy 5:12–15). Work is necessary, and so is rest (Exodus 34:21). God modeled rest from His work of creation in Genesis 2:1–3. The version of the Ten Commandments in Exodus 20 established God's rest on the seventh day after six days of work as the model for those under the old covenant.

What Do You Think?

How would you respond to someone who says that the need for work itself results from the fall?

Digging Deeper

In what ways is the need for work and rest modeled in the Old Testament?

II. Work of God

(John 5:17; 9:4)

A. The Father (John 5:17)

17. But Jesus answered them, My Father worketh hitherto, and I work.

This verse is Jesus' response to Jewish leaders who persecute Him for healing on the Sabbath (John 5:1–16). Although God rested after His work of creation (Genesis 2:1–3), His providential care continues without interruption (Psalm 121; etc.), and Jesus shows the alignment of His own priorities with those of His heavenly Father. Consistent throughout the Gospels, to heal on the Sabbath is to do the good work that His Father has been doing up to this point (Matthew 12:10–11; Mark 3:1–5; Luke 13:10–17; etc.).

B. The Son (John 9:4)

4. I must work the works of him that sent me, while it is day: the night cometh, when no man can work.

Here, Jesus uses the terms *day* and *night* to represent His own limited time on earth to do *the works of him that sent* Him, the Father. Contextually, Jesus is speaking with His disciples about a man born blind (John 9:1–2). The reason Jesus gives for why this man was born blind has nothing to do with the man's or his parents' sin; rather, it happened so that "the works of God should be made manifest in him" (9:3).

> **What Do You Think?**
> How would you summarize the main points of Christ Jesus' work?
> **Digging Deeper**
> In what ways can we join with Christ Jesus in this work? (See John 14:12.)

III. Work to Meet Needs

(Acts 20:33–35)

In our next section, Paul addresses the elders of the church in Ephesus. Speaking to them before heading to Jerusalem for the final time, he summarizes his ministry to them.

A. Helping Oneself (vv. 33–34)

33. I have coveted no man's silver, or gold, or apparel.

Much of the economy of the city of Ephesus is rooted in the renowned temple of the goddess Diana (Artemis). This temple attracted many visitors to the city and brought significant wealth to the artisans who made shrines (Acts 19:24–27). However, Paul's preaching and the resulting conversions to Christ disrupted the local economy. Those who profited greatly from the temple incited a riot in response (19:28–40).

In contrast to the motives of the silversmiths in Ephesus, Paul does not preach the gospel for material gain. Paul willingly gives up worldly possessions in order to "win Christ" (Philippians 3:8).

To a modern reader, it may seem unusual that Paul mentions clothing alongside *silver* and *gold.* However, dye and fabric were costly in antiquity, and *apparel* was often valued similarly to gold and silver (examples: Genesis 24:53; Exodus 3:22; 2 Kings 5:5). The main point is not the specific items mentioned, but rather that faith in Christ does not nullify the law of God that prohibits coveting (Exodus 20:17; Romans 7:7).

34. Yea, ye yourselves know, that these hands have ministered unto my necessities, and to them that were with me.

The phrase *ye yourselves know* mirrors how Paul started his speech to the elders (Acts 20:18). He spent at least three years in Ephesus, giving the elders ample time to know him and his character (20:31). He had the right to receive support from the churches and sometimes did (2 Corinthians 11:7–8; Philippians 4:15; contrast 1 Corinthians 9:12–14). But he needs to distinguish himself from false teachers who sought to profit from their teachings.

It is worth reiterating the reach of Paul's work and its benefits: his *hands ministered* not only to his own *necessities* (Acts 18:1–3) but also to those of his traveling companions.

B. Helping Others (v. 35)

35. I have shewed you all things, how that so labouring ye ought to support the weak, and to remember the words of the Lord Jesus, how he said, It is more blessed to give than to receive.

Physical labor is not to be for selfish gain, but to assist those in need. Paul worked with his hands to be self-supporting, thereby setting an example for others (compare John 13:15; 1 Corinthians 11:1; Philippians 3:17). His actions confirmed his words, or to put it a bit differently, his walk matched his talk. The word translated *weak* can mean someone physically ill or spiritually vulnerable (examples: Matthew 10:8; Romans 14:1).

Although *the words of the Lord Jesus* that Paul cites are not explicitly recorded in the Gospels, we must remember that the Gospels do not capture every word spoken by Jesus (see John 20:30–31). Thus, this particular quote may have been commonly known within the early church through oral tradition. Additionally, its message aligns with Jesus' teachings (Matthew 10:8; 25:34–36; Mark 10:21–22; Luke 14:12–14; etc.).

What Do You Think?

How can you use the fruit of your labor to give generously to others in the upcoming week?

Digging Deeper

How do our expressions of generosity help further God's mission in the world?

A Box of Diapers

Recently, I was made aware that someone I knew needed diapers for her baby. As soon as my husband arrived home from work, I told him about the need. His answer was immediate: "Let's go buy some."

Our children were long out of diapers, and it had been a while since we'd shopped in the baby aisle. We found the diapers and asked ourselves what size box to buy. Remembering how quickly diapers get used up, we promptly bought the largest box we could find. It was expensive, but we agreed that God had given us the resources and awareness to meet this need.

When we delivered the diapers, the mother came outside and gave me a huge hug. Her smile lit up her entire face. She struggled to speak English, but in broken speech, she conveyed her deepest thanks.

My husband and I smiled all the way home. It truly is "more blessed to give than to receive!" How can you use your work and the resources God has given you to meet the needs of those around you? —B. R.

IV. Work and the People of God

(2 Thessalonians 3:6–12)

A. Be Not Idle (v. 6)

6. Now we command you, brethren, in the name of our Lord Jesus Christ, that ye withdraw yourselves from every brother that walketh disorderly, and not after the tradition which he received of us.

The *brethren* Paul now addresses are those in the church at Thessalonica (see Lesson Context). His appeal *in the name of our Lord Jesus Christ* strikes a note of formality and utmost seriousness (compare Acts 16:18). This sense is further heightened by Paul's language of *command.* He is not offering mere suggestions or guidelines! In fact, he uses the word translated "command" a total of five times in his two short letters to the Thessalonians (here and 1 Thessalonians 4:11; 2 Thessalonians 3:4, 10, 12).

The command deals with behavior toward *every brother that walketh disorderly.* The idea is someone who lives in a haphazard way. This undoubtedly includes having a poor work ethic—laziness, if you will. Those not in this category are not to hang around with those who are. We may wonder if this consequence rises to the level of needing to "disfellowship" the errant individual for the health of the church. The New Testament establishes three categories for doing so. These are

- Doctrinal defection: 1 Timothy 1:3–11; 6:3–5
- Moral defection: 1 Corinthians 5
- Divisiveness: Romans 16:17–18; Titus 3:10–11

It seems unlikely that this situation has reached the point of needing to disfellowship under any of these patterns. A chance for repentance and forgiveness comes first (2 Corinthians 2:5–11).

B. An Imitable Example (vv. 7–9)

7. For yourselves know how ye ought to follow us: for we behaved not ourselves disorderly among you.

In contrasting himself with the disorderly person of the previous verse, Paul offers himself as an example *to follow.* His request is not unreasonable. As seen above in the commentary on Genesis 2:15, work is good. God Himself works and invites humanity to join Him.

Paul emphasizes that he is not asking his readers to do anything he will not do (and has not already done!) himself. One key distinction between the

How to Say It

Achaia	Uh-*kay*-uh.
Ephesus	*Ef*-uh-sus.
Macedonia	Mass-eh-*doe*-nee-uh.
Thessalonians	*Thess*-uh-**lo**-nee-unz (*th* as in *thin*).
Thessalonica	Thess-uh-lo-nye-kuh (*th* as in *thin*).

Visual for Lesson 10. *Display this visual as you ask the discussion questions associated with 2 Thessalonians 3:9.*

apostles and false teachers is that the former practiced what they preached and expected others to do the same (1 Timothy 6:3–10; etc.). Because Paul's actions were consistent, he could confidently ask people to follow his example, knowing it was the will of God (1 Corinthians 4:16; 11:1).

8. Neither did we eat any man's bread for nought; but wrought with labour and travail night and day, that we might not be chargeable to any of you.

The first part of this verse is an extension of the previous verse. In avoiding laziness in their manner of living, Paul and his companions had made sure to provide compensation for the food they ate.

The middle part of this verse reflects Paul's previous letter to the church (see 1 Thessalonians 2:9). Paul likely refers to his manual work as a tentmaker, through which he supports himself in Corinth (Acts 18:3). Likely for the sake of emphasis, Paul uses two nouns, *labor* and *travail,* to emphasize the extent of his efforts to avoid being a financial burden. He also uses the words *night* and *day* as another point of emphasis. This perhaps alludes to a noteworthy sacrifice of his time, working to meet his needs while preaching and teaching the gospel.

9. Not because we have not power, but to make ourselves an ensample unto you to follow us.

The word translated as *power* in English can also mean "authority" or "right," depending on the context. The two terms are related, although there is this difference: *authority* is the right to do something, while *power* is the ability to do something.

As an apostle of Christ, Paul had both power and authority. And any decision of his not to use either is not evidence of their absence. He simply chose not to exercise either. He consistently evaluated his actions and refrained if they would cause other believers to stumble (1 Corinthians 8:13; 9:1–19). In the case of the Thessalonians, it would have been of more significant benefit for them to see his *ensample* (another spelling of the word *example,* as in 1 Corinthians 10:6) of working for his bread rather than receiving it without payment.

What Do You Think?

How will your perspective and attitude toward your work serve as an example to others regarding your life in Christ?

Digging Deeper

What behaviors and tendencies do you need to change so that you might be an example in this regard?

C. Earning One's Food (vv. 10–12)

10. For even when we were with you, this we commanded you, that if any would not work, neither should he eat.

Paul places great importance on *work* and personal responsibility. A person unwilling to work is not fit to receive food to *eat.* We may safely assume that the word *any* in this command refers to those physically able to work. Historically, the church cared for those unable to work for various reasons (Acts 4:34–35; 6:1–6; etc.). Paul's instruction aims to ensure that those capable of working do their part, thereby preventing a burden from falling unfairly on others.

Growing a Garden

My sister-in-law is an avid gardener. Even in the winter, she grows seedlings under the warmth of heat lamps. When planting them in the spring, she places them strategically, where each will benefit most.

The first year she planted her garden, she offered

us a portion of her tomato harvest. I gladly took some, thinking I could cook them into salsa or tomato sauce since our family doesn't like to eat fresh tomatoes. Those tomatoes sat on our counter for days. I never got around to making salsa or sauce, and before long, they began to rot. I had to throw them out.

Because I didn't work hard for those tomatoes, it wasn't a priority for me to use them up. Now that we've started our own garden, I rarely let a single vegetable go to waste; I now know the effort that goes into growing each one. We value what we work hard to produce or achieve.

Work is part of our God-given purpose. How can you reframe your work as a gift from God? Do you need to shift your perspective toward work?

—B. R.

11. For we hear that there are some which walk among you disorderly, working not at all, but are busybodies.

Here, Paul focuses on a point initially raised in 2 Thessalonians 3:6, above. He had received reports that some individuals are not only refusing to work but are also actively interfering with the lives and work of others. Paul will have to deal with this problem more than once before the end of his ministry (1 Timothy 5:13). When some members choose to be idle and meddlesome, it burdens others and creates friction and discord. This internal strife weakens the church's witness to the outside world, undermining its mission and message (1 Thessalonians 4:11–12).

Unity among Christians is a primary goal of the New Testament church (Romans 16:17; 1 Corinthians 1:10; Ephesians 4:13; etc.). Church leaders are responsible for fostering and maintaining this unity, sometimes requiring them to address disruptive behavior directly (2 Timothy 4:2; Titus 2:15).

12. Now them that are such we command and exhort by our Lord Jesus Christ, that with quietness they work, and eat their own bread.

This verse has the cure for those who are "busybodies": stable, meaningful work. Work is a connection between God and humanity, and it should be conducted in a holy manner (Colossians 3:23–24). The ultimate goal is for everyone who is physically able to work to provide for themselves, summarized as *eat their own bread.*

Conclusion

A. Embracing Work

As fraught with difficulty as work may be in the fallen world we currently inhabit, work remains good. Given as a gift to humanity prior to the fall—and part of our purpose—we are invited to work alongside our heavenly Father and His Son, Jesus Christ. The Holy Spirit enables us to walk obediently, joining our worker God in His good work. The old axiom "We don't work to live; we live to work" helps engage our thinking on this.

Paul reminds us that work serves both to meet our own material needs and the needs of those around us. Beyond earning a living, we can leverage our work and the resources it provides to serve others.

Through our work, we follow the example of our Creator and set a positive example for others to follow. Ignoring this example can lead to disunity and a weakening of the church, diminishing its testimony to the world. However, when the church works together and supports those who are weak and unable to work, unity is strengthened, God is glorified, and the church presents a powerful testimony to the world.

What Do You Think?

Do you agree with the axiom, "We don't work to live; we live to work"? Why, or why not?

Digging Deeper

How has this lesson reframed your perspective and attitude toward work?

B. Prayer

Heavenly Father, thank You for reminding us why we are called to work. Help us embrace this message and maintain a positive attitude toward the work You have given us. We pray this in Jesus' name. Amen.

C. Thought to Remember

Those who are able should engage in good work.

Involvement Learning

Enhance your lesson with KJV Bible Student *(from your curriculum supplier) and the reproducible activity page (at www.standardlesson.com or in the back of the* KJV Standard Lesson Commentary Deluxe Edition*).*

Into the Lesson

Ask volunteers to share about their jobs. State that you're interested in *all* lines of work and clarify that being retired, a student, a homemaker, a parent, a caretaker, or another field is considered a line of work. Write responses on the board. By way of raising hands, ask the class to vote on which job they think is the busiest, most challenging, or most demanding. Ask volunteers to explain the reasons for their vote.

Alternative. Distribute copies of the "What Are You?" exercise from the activity page, which you can download. Have learners complete it individually in a minute or less before submitting responses to you. Shuffle and redistribute papers back to each participant. Ask them to take turns guessing the job their sheet describes. Finish the activity by asking, "What conclusions can we draw about the workers in our class?"

Lead into Bible study by saying, "Our work is an important part of our identity. In today's lesson, consider why God values work and how we can complete our work—in whatever context—as an act of worship and obedience to Him."

Into the Word

Ask volunteers to read Genesis 2:15 and Exodus 20:9 aloud. Divide participants into groups of three and provide each group with an index card and pen. Instruct groups to write a "job description" for human beings in service to God. The description should be based on these two Scripture texts but may include others. After calling time, ask a volunteer from each group to share the descriptions with the whole class. Ask, "How are the job descriptions described in these verses relevant to us?"

Invite volunteers to read aloud John 5:17; John 9:4; and Acts 20:33–35. Write the following headers on the board: *The Father*, *Jesus*, and *Humans*. Lead a whole-class discussion by asking the following questions for each header. Write responses under the appropriate header: 1–What is each person's work? 2–How does each person complete that work? 3–What is the purpose of that work? Conclude the activity by asking what conclusions can be drawn from these responses.

Alternative. Distribute the "All Kinds of Work" exercise from the activity page. Have small groups complete it as indicated before reviewing responses in a whole-class discussion.

Ask a volunteer to read aloud 2 Thessalonians 3:6–12. Use the Lesson Context section to give a short presentation on the context of 2 Thessalonians. (*Option.* Prior to class time, ask a participant to prepare this presentation.)

Then distribute to study pairs or triads the following questions on handouts (you create): 1–What are the main points of Paul's teaching? 2–Why does Paul identify himself as an example for the Thessalonian believers? 3–What does Paul say is the correct response to "busybodies"? 4–How does Paul's teaching inform our approach to our work?

Allow several minutes for pairs or triads to work, after which they will share conclusions in whole-class discussion.

Into Life

Begin by asking, "Based on today's study, what is the meaning and purpose of work?" Write responses on the board. Invite participants to reflect on these responses and consider how their work serves God and other people. After a minute of personal reflection, allow volunteers to share their reflections.

Distribute an index card and pen to each participant. Invite them to write down a personal resolution regarding work in service to God. Encourage them to place the index card in an easy-to-see location so that they can be reminded of the resolution throughout the upcoming work week.

Conclude class by placing learners into pairs. Direct partners to pray that God would empower them to view their work as a service to Him.

May 17
Lesson 11 (KJV)

Christian Manner of Justice

Devotional Reading: Luke 3:7–14
Background Scripture: Exodus 1:8–14; Amos 5:6–15;
Zechariah 8:16–17; 1 Timothy 6:17–19

Deuteronomy 24:14–21

14 Thou shalt not oppress an hired servant that is poor and needy, whether he be of thy brethren, or of thy strangers that are in thy land within thy gates:

15 At his day thou shalt give him his hire, neither shall the sun go down upon it; for he is poor, and setteth his heart upon it: lest he cry against thee unto the LORD, and it be sin unto thee.

16 The fathers shall not be put to death for the children, neither shall the children be put to death for the fathers: every man shall be put to death for his own sin.

17 Thou shalt not pervert the judgment of the stranger, nor of the fatherless; nor take a widow's raiment to pledge:

18 But thou shalt remember that thou wast a bondman in Egypt, and the LORD thy God redeemed thee thence: therefore I command thee to do this thing.

19 When thou cuttest down thine harvest in thy field, and hast forgot a sheaf in the field, thou shalt not go again to fetch it: it shall be for the stranger, for the fatherless, and for the widow: that the LORD thy God may bless thee in all the work of thine hands.

20 When thou beatest thine olive tree, thou shalt not go over the boughs again: it shall be for the stranger, for the fatherless, and for the widow.

21 When thou gatherest the grapes of thy vineyard, thou shalt not glean it afterward: it shall be for the stranger, for the fatherless, and for the widow.

Ephesians 6:5–9

5 Servants, be obedient to them that are your masters according to the flesh, with fear and trembling, in singleness of your heart, as unto Christ;

6 Not with eyeservice, as menpleasers; but as the servants of Christ, doing the will of God from the heart;

7 With good will doing service, as to the Lord, and not to men:

8 Knowing that whatsoever good thing any man doeth, the same shall he receive of the Lord, whether he be bond or free.

9 And, ye masters, do the same things unto them, forbearing threatening: knowing that your Master also is in heaven; neither is there respect of persons with him.

1 Timothy 6:17–19

17 Charge them that are rich in this world, that they be not highminded, nor trust in uncertain riches, but in the living God, who giveth us richly all things to enjoy;

18 That they do good, that they be rich in good works, ready to distribute, willing to communicate;

19 Laying up in store for themselves a good foundation against the time to come, that they may lay hold on eternal life.

Key Text

When thou cuttest down thine harvest in thy field, and hast forgot a sheaf in the field, thou shalt not go again to fetch it: it shall be for the stranger, for the fatherless, and for the widow: that the LORD thy God may bless thee in all the work of thine hands. —**Deuteronomy 24:19**

Social Teachings
of the Church

Unit 3: Fulfilling Our Obligations to God and Society
Lessons 9–13

Lesson Aims

After participating in this lesson, each learner will be able to:

1. Identify themes of justice in each text.
2. Contrast God's justice and impartiality with societal tendencies toward "*-isms*"(e.g., classism, racism, ableism, etc.).
3. List ways to care for others in and through our work.

Lesson Outline

Introduction
- A. Actions Speak Louder than Words
- B. Lesson Context

I. Generosity in Work (Deuteronomy 24:14–21)
- A. Fair Payment (vv. 14–15)
- B. Individual Responsibility (v. 16)
- C. Remember Past Justice (vv. 17–18)
- D. Leave Some for the Poor (vv. 19–21)
  - *Licking the Bowl*

II. Mutual Respect in Work (Ephesians 6:5–9)
- A. Obey as unto the Lord (vv. 5–7)
  - *Busy Work*
- B. Reward for Obedience (v. 8)
- C. Reciprocal Treatment (v. 9)

III. Future Rewards of Work (1 Timothy 6:17–19)
- A. Rightly Placed Hope (v. 17)
- B. Richness in Deeds (v. 18)
- C. Treasure to Come (v. 19)

Conclusion
- A. The Work of Faith
- B. Prayer
- C. Thought to Remember

Introduction

A. Actions Speak Louder than Words

At age 15, I started working at a fast-food restaurant. The job came with an unexpected perk: Bible discussions with my Christian manager. Nearly four decades later, I have forgotten most of our conversations, but an act of kindness he displayed has stayed with me. One morning, I found a man rummaging through the dumpster, looking for food and told my manager. I expected my manager to chase the man away. Instead, I was surprised. He brought the man inside, gave him a meal, and packed fresh food for him to take. That day, I saw an aspect of God's character uniquely displayed through my manager. His single act of generosity, hospitality, and respect had a more significant impact on me than any of our discussions.

B. Lesson Context

The first Scripture text from today's lesson comes from Moses' second speech in Deuteronomy to the people of Israel. The speech begins by setting forth a general set of rules for God's covenant people (Deuteronomy 4:44–11:32). The second part of the speech focuses on specific rules within God's order for a new society (12:1–26:19).

Israel's identity as God's covenant people was supposed to shape their treatment of poor and marginalized people. Moses had already reminded the Israelites that poor people would always be part of the population (Deuteronomy 15:11). As a result, he commanded an openhanded policy toward these people, requiring generous giving without resentment (15:10; see lesson 2).

The second Scripture text comes from the apostle Paul's letter to the church in Ephesus. In Ephesians 5:21–6:9, Paul includes a "household code," a common form of social teaching in that day. These codes consisted of a list of obligations and duties in household relationships (compare Colossians 3:8–14; 1 Peter 2:18–3:7). He discusses each of the common roles in a household of his time, including family members and servants. Far from simply affirming the culturally accepted social order, Paul infuses every household role with the revolutionary story of Jesus.

The final Scripture text comes from the first letter that Paul wrote to Timothy. Timothy was likely dealing with false teachers who arose in the church in Ephesus (1 Timothy 1:3–4). These false teachers glorified wealth (6:5–10). Paul outlines steps the community members can take to ensure they are not overcome by "love of money" (6:10).

I. Generosity in Work

(Deuteronomy 24:14–21)

A. Fair Payment (vv. 14–15)

14. Thou shalt not oppress an hired servant that is poor and needy, whether he be of thy brethren, or of thy strangers that are in thy land within thy gates.

The meaning of the Hebrew word translated *servant* is similar to *hireling*: a free person who works in exchange for wages (see Job 7:2). An Israelite who experienced economic difficulty might serve other Israelites as a *hired servant* (Leviticus 25:39–40). These workers committed to a set time of service. They would eventually receive their freedom (25:41; see Exodus 21:2; Deuteronomy 15:12).

God's command to treat laborers fairly does not depend on a laborer's place of origin. God expects His people not to *oppress* the *poor and needy*, whether those people are *brethren* Israelites or *strangers* (non-Israelites living within the *gates* of Israelite towns).

15. At his day thou shalt give him his hire, neither shall the sun go down upon it; for he is poor, and setteth his heart upon it: lest he cry against thee unto the LORD, and it be sin unto thee.

One obvious way to practice justice toward workers is through the timely payment of wages. The hired workers described in this verse are equivalent to day laborers. They were usually paid for their work at the end of an agreed time (compare Matthew 20:8). Their situation was the ancient equivalent of living paycheck to paycheck. It was cruel and unlawful for a landowner to withhold a day's wages from the worker (Leviticus 19:13). The text notes that causing these workers reason to cry out *to the Lord* is *sin* (compare Malachi 3:5; James 5:4).

B. Individual Responsibility (v. 16)

16. The fathers shall not be put to death for the children, neither shall the children be put to death for the fathers: every man shall be put to death for his own sin.

The principle in this verse differs from other law codes of the ancient world. The Babylonian Code of Hammurabi, for example, stated that if a builder built a house that collapsed, causing the death of the homeowner's son, the builder's son was to be killed. In contrast, the Law of Moses protects innocent family members who might otherwise be punished for a relative's actions. The given stipulation in God's law prevents a potentially endless chain of revenge.

This principle does not contradict the Scripture that speaks of God's "visiting the iniquity of the *fathers* upon the *children* unto the third and fourth generation of them that hate me" (Deuteronomy 5:9). Each person surely experiences the consequences of their sin, as do others close to them. Sin has a far-reaching effect but needs not include retribution or revenge.

C. Remember Past Justice (vv. 17–18)

17. Thou shalt not pervert the judgment of the stranger, nor of the fatherless; nor take a widow's raiment to pledge.

The three groups of people most at risk of unfair *judgment* are *the stranger* (non-Israelites living in the land), the *fatherless,* and widows (compare

Visual for Lessons 9 & 11. *Display this visual as you review the verse-by-verse commentary associated with Deuteronomy 24:14–21.*

Exodus 22:21–22; Psalms 94:6; 146:9; Jeremiah 7:6; 22:3; Ezekiel 22:7; Zechariah 7:10).

This text contains a specific statute to protect widows. Lenders could not take a widow's *raiment* as a *pledge* when lending. While the law includes rules for lenders to take clothing as collateral (Exodus 22:26–27), they are strictly forbidden to take it from the vulnerable (Deuteronomy 24:12–13).

What Do You Think?

What steps can your class take to help address the needs of immigrants, orphans, and widows in your community?

Digging Deeper

What specialized training will your class need to be effective in this ministry?

18. But thou shalt remember that thou wast a bondman in Egypt, and the LORD thy God redeemed thee thence: therefore I command thee to do this thing.

The Israelites recall their history of enslavement in the land of *Egypt*. That history, along with God's redemptive act, serves as the foundation of Israel's identity (see Deuteronomy 5:15; 7:8; 15:15; etc.). The national memory of that enslavement and redemption was supposed to motivate the Israelites to compassionate treatment of the marginalized. Israel was to *remember* that *God redeemed* them and respond by caring for the most vulnerable around them.

What Do You Think?

How has your recollection of God's redemptive acts encouraged you to keep His commands?

Digging Deeper

In what ways do you strengthen your memory of God's redemptive acts?

D. Leave Some for the Poor (vv. 19–21)

19. When thou cuttest down thine harvest in thy field, and hast forgot a sheaf in the field, thou shalt not go again to fetch it: it shall be for the stranger, for the fatherless, and for the widow: that the LORD thy God may bless thee in all the work of thine hands.

One practical way the Israelites could show justice to the most vulnerable was through practices at *harvest* time. Harvesters in a field would cut bundles of grain and bind each bundle into *a sheaf*. The poor and vulnerable could collect the leftover grain in a process called "gleaning" (compare Ruth 1:22–2:3; see also Leviticus 19:9–10; 23:22). If the harvesters *forgot a sheaf*, the text directs them to leave it for the gleaners.

This practice reminds landowners that their land and the resulting harvest belong to the Lord (Leviticus 25:23; Deuteronomy 10:14; etc.). The phrase *that the Lord thy God may bless thee* occurs three times in the book of Deuteronomy: here, in 14:29, and 23:20. In all three cases, God's blessing depends on meeting the needs of others. The Lord promises to bless those who honor His laws and treat the marginalized with respect (15:10; 28:1–12).

20–21. When thou beatest thine olive tree, thou shalt not go over the boughs again: it shall be for the stranger, for the fatherless, and for the widow. When thou gatherest the grapes of thy vineyard, thou shalt not glean it afterward: it shall be for the stranger, for the fatherless, and for the widow.

The ancient world prized olive trees for their fruit and the oil they produced. Olives also represented God's blessing (Jeremiah 31:12; Joel 2:19, etc.). Vineyards, too, were a sign of wealth and stability for their owners (Isaiah 65:21–22; Amos 9:14; etc.).

Cultivation and harvest of the *olive tree* and *vineyard* requires considerable time and energy. Landowners worked hard to prevent any wasted crops. In this verse, however, the law extends rules for gleaning to even the most valuable of harvests (compare Leviticus 19:9–10).

Licking the Bowl

When I was little, I loved to help my mom bake cakes. I would assemble all the ingredients while she prepared the bowl and mixer. After adding the ingredients to the bowl, she'd turn on the beaters, and I'd watch her whip everything together. Then came my favorite part.

After she poured the batter into a pan, she'd

offer me one of the mixing beaters to lick (though I now know you aren't supposed to eat raw cake batter!). Before she could soak the almost-empty bowl in soapy water, I'd quickly grab a spoon so I could scoop out any last remaining batter.

We often live in a way that leaves little room for any leftovers. In Deuteronomy 24, God reminds His people to "leave some batter in the bowl." We are called to live with margin and to share it with others. What would it look like for you to make room in your life to meet the needs of those around you? How could you leave space for spontaneous or intentional generosity? —B. R.

II. Mutual Respect in Work

(Ephesians 6:5–9)

A. Obey as unto the Lord (vv. 5–7)

5a. Servants, be obedient to them that are your masters according to the flesh.

The Greek word translated *servants* can refer to enslaved people, and that is the sense in this verse. In many ways, slavery in the first-century world was unlike slavery in the pre-Civil War United States. For example, enslavement in the first century was not tied to a person's race. A person could become enslaved for many reasons. Some were taken captive in war, while others sold themselves into slavery to pay off debts. Further, during the time of the apostle Paul, it was possible for enslaved people, mainly males who worked in households, to gain a level of freedom.

Paul begins this text by addressing the less powerful party in the household relationship. He directs *servants* to submit to earthly authority by being *obedient* (Colossians 3:22). Although an enslaved person is under an authority *according to the flesh*, both the master and enslaved person have one Lord: Christ Jesus (Galatians 3:28–29; Ephesians 4:4–6).

5b. With fear and trembling, in singleness of your heart, as unto Christ.

Fear of violence and cruelty was common in the lives of many enslaved people. This verse, however, does not indicate approval of such things. Intimidation and brutality have no place in a household that follows Christ (see Ephesians 6:9, below). Instead, the phrase *fear and trembling* communicates a sense of reverent respect that household members must show one another (5:21; compare 1 Corinthians 2:3; 2 Corinthians 7:15).

A servant's obedience should occur with complete sincerity of *heart* as if *unto Christ* Himself (see Colossians 3:22–24). Paul is not saying that earthly masters are a "stand-in" for God. In fact, the servants themselves model Christ through their obedience to the authorities (see Philippians 2:7). Rather, Paul teaches that the authority of the Lord Jesus should govern all relationships within the household and in society (1 Peter 2:13; compare 1 Timothy 6:1–2). In Paul's context, this teaching is revolutionary.

6–7. Not with eyeservice, as menpleasers; but as the servants of Christ, doing the will of God from the heart; with good will doing service, as to the Lord, and not to men.

The opposite of working as if *unto Christ* is working only to please people. If someone works only to win favor in the public eye, then the attitude of their heart is wrong. Labor in any context should be completed as if in service to *Christ*, who knows the thoughts and intentions of *the heart* (see Colossians 3:23). Workers are free to serve others for the sake of the Lord with an attitude of *good will*.

What Do You Think?

In what ways do you consider your work to be a service to Christ?

Digging Deeper

How will you adjust your approach to work so that others see Christ through your attitudes and actions?

Busy Work

When I was in college, I worked at my school's bookstore. My boss would often assign the task of dusting the bookshelves, something I saw as "busy work." My boss rarely assigned the task to more than one person at a time, because when we were allowed to work together, we'd inevitably begin talking instead of working. Admittedly, we were diligent in cleaning only when our boss was watching!

These days, I complete most of my work without anyone's direct oversight. I had to learn to be diligent without a supervisor present. Paul reminds us that all our labor should be done as if in service to the Lord, no matter who else is there to see it. Regardless of whether a supervisor is watching, God is watching. I want to be diligent and hardworking to please Him, no matter the task. Further, I now know that by being a faithful worker, I can display His goodness to my managers and clients. How does your view of your work change when you realize you are working for the Lord? —B. R.

B. Reward for Obedience (v. 8)

8. Knowing that whatsoever good thing any man doeth, the same shall he receive of the Lord, whether he be bond or free.

When it comes to obedience to the Lord Jesus Christ, all people, *bond or free*, are under the same authority (1 Corinthians 12:13; Colossians 3:11). All people will stand before Christ to have their works tested, and all will have an opportunity to receive a reward (Matthew 16:27; 2 Corinthians 5:10; Revelation 22:12; etc.). Therefore, all people should aim to do *good* works in response to receiving the gift of grace (see Ephesians 2:10).

C. Reciprocal Treatment (v. 9)

9. And, ye masters, do the same things unto them, forbearing threatening: knowing that your Master also is in heaven; neither is there respect of persons with him.

Paul now directs his teachings toward *masters.* In Paul's day, this turn would have surprised readers. Household codes rarely mentioned the obligations of masters to enslaved people. The apostle directs masters *to do the same things*: treat others, including those enslaved under their authority, with respect out of reverence for Christ. This was to result in fair and just treatment of enslaved people (see Colossians 4:1). One way masters could practice justice was by no longer *threatening* those under their authority.

Through these two directives, along with the commands to enslaved people in the previous verses, Paul overturns the slave-master dynamics of his day. The text promises enslaved people a reward for their work. Further, it directs enslavers to think of themselves as servants of the Lord, their *master in heaven*, and to treat others justly. Paul does not openly condemn slavery in this passage. He understood, however, that adding Christ to such an unequal relationship would bring a God-honoring shift to the culture.

III. Future Rewards of Work
(1 Timothy 6:17–19)

A. Rightly Placed Hope (v. 17)

17. Charge them that are rich in this world, that they be not highminded, nor trust in uncertain riches, but in the living God, who giveth us richly all things to enjoy.

Paul gives specific advice to Timothy for teaching those in his faith community who are *rich in this world.* These people seem to have many reasons to *trust* their own judgment, abilities, and *riches*, but these things are not guaranteed to last (Proverbs 23:5; 27:24; Luke 12:20–21; James 4:13–14). All people need to trust in the Lord.

The wealthy must also remember that God is the source of their wealth (Deuteronomy 8:18; Ecclesiastes 5:19). He is the creator and sustainer of the world, and all wealth comes from His provision and generosity (see Deuteronomy 8:17–18; 1 Samuel 2:7; etc.). This is true of both material and spiritual wealth. The church in first-century Laodicea is an example of a community that did not recognize its poor spiritual state despite having material wealth (Revelation 3:14–18).

What Do You Think?

What preventative measures can Christians employ to avoid placing trust wholly in material wealth?

Digging Deeper

How can Christians oppose cultural narratives that encourage the accumulation of material wealth?

B. Richness in Deeds (v. 18)

18. That they do good, that they be rich in good works, ready to distribute, willing to communicate.

After Paul warns the wealthy members of the community, he provides them with a positive directive. Wealthy people have an opportunity to use their resources to *do good* for the body of Christ (Galatians 6:10; Hebrews 13:16). Paul engages in wordplay by using the word *rich*, a word often associated with earthly possessions, to describe the practice of doing *good works* for others.

The phrase *ready to distribute* suggests generosity, while *willing to communicate* likely means a willingness to share. These phrases probably refer to the attitude behind a person's good works. Paul emphasizes that the wealthy should be eager to serve others, not to hold on to their material wealth. These commands align closely with his commands for giving among specific New Testament churches (Romans 15:25–27; 2 Corinthians 8:1–7).

What Do You Think?

What barriers prevent believers from showing generosity with their material wealth?

Digging Deeper

In what ways will you be "rich" in good deeds in the upcoming week?

C. Treasure to Come (v. 19)

19. Laying up in store for themselves a good foundation against the time to come, that they may lay hold on eternal life.

Some commentators believe that Paul's exhortation about *laying up* wealth *in store* reflects Jesus' teaching on storing treasures in heaven (Matthew 6:19–21; 19:21). The image of *laying up* treasure implies that when believers give to others, they are not losing their wealth but transferring it from earth to heaven. *The time to come* that Paul has in mind might be a time of economic distress in the near future, or it might be the time of Christ's return. At any rate, people who have shared their wealth with the faith community are promised a secure future, if not in this life, then through receiving *eternal life*.

Paul does not suggest that a person can earn eternal life through good works. His words are consistent, however, with James's teaching that true faith is evidenced by works (James 2:14–26). When people show generosity, they build a strong *foundation* of faith in their lives (contrast 5:1–5).

Conclusion

A. The Work of Faith

These three texts teach that God's people must display generosity, mutual respect, and rightly ordered hope. Deuteronomy 24 identifies the generosity and justice God commanded of the ancient Israelites. We ought to show generosity and act justly in our homes, neighborhoods, and workplaces. When we do so, we reflect God's character to everyone around us, including the most vulnerable.

Paul's letter to the Ephesians reminds us of the "level playing field" on which we stand before Christ. His authority governs all earthly relationships. Our faith demands that we treat others with respect, recognizing that we are all equal in Christ.

Finally, Paul's letter to Timothy encourages us to order our hopes rightly. The truth that our security comes from God, not our material possessions, remains especially relevant in the twenty-first century. As we place our hope in God, we should be openhanded and generous with our resources.

Lives that do not prioritize the world's measures of money, status, and power are living testimonies to God's life-transforming grace. Because our lives have been transformed by God, we seek to practice justice, respect all people, and share generously.

B. Prayer

Heavenly Father, help us never to neglect the most vulnerable members of our communities. Give us eyes to see how we can act justly and generously meet needs. May we do this to reflect Your love to the world. In Jesus' name we pray. Amen.

C. Thought to Remember

Serve God by serving others with justice, respect, and generosity.

How to Say It

Ephesus	*Ef*-uh-sus.
Hammurabi	*Ham*-muh-***rah***-bee.
Laodicea	Lay-*odd*-uh-***see***-uh.

Involvement Learning

Enhance your lesson with KJV Bible Student *(from your curriculum supplier) and the reproducible activity page (at www.standardlesson.com or in the back of the* KJV Standard Lesson Commentary Deluxe Edition*).*

Into the Lesson

Begin class by asking participants to brainstorm jobs. List their responses on the board. Then ask, "How can workers complete these jobs with the intention of caring for or blessing other people?" Add their answers to the board under your list.

After the activity, lead into Bible study by saying, "One central theme of Scripture is justice. God calls His people to act justly through their work and with their material resources. Today's lesson will study three texts inviting us to consider how we can use our work and resources to serve God, act justly, and bless others. Look for key truths that can help us be compassionate, just, honorable, and generous as followers of God."

Into the Word

Divide the class into four groups: **Poor and Needy Group, Fatherless Group, Foreigner Group,** and **Widow Group.** Direct each group to read Deuteronomy 24:14–21 and summarize the teaching regarding fair and just treatment of their group's namesake. After studying the text, challenge groups to write down ways that modern-day believers can demonstrate fair and just treatment to these groups. After calling time, ask for a volunteer from each group to share their findings.

Option. Distribute copies of the "Remember, Remember, Remember" exercise from the activity page, which you can download. Have learners complete it individually in a minute or less before sharing responses with a partner. After calling time, reconvene the class and ask volunteers to present their conclusions.

Ask a volunteer to read aloud Ephesians 6:5–9. Lead a five-minute presentation on the context of Ephesians 6:5–9. Ensure that participants know that slavery in the first century was unlike race-based slavery in the antebellum United States. Additionally, explain how Paul's teachings overturn the slave-master dynamics of his day.

After the presentation, ask one volunteer to summarize Paul's teachings to enslaved people and another to summarize Paul's teachings to their masters. Then, ask the following questions for whole-class discussion: 1–What truths does Paul hope each group will "know"? (*Expected answers*: Enslaved people know the Lord will reward each person according to their good works, whether enslaved or free; Masters know that God shows no favoritism and is the master of all people.) 2–How are these truths similar? 3–How can these truths encourage us to act justly and treat others fairly in our labor?

Ask a volunteer to read 1 Timothy 6:17–19 aloud. Write the phrases *Rich in This World* and *Rich in Good Works* on the board as headers. Lead a whole-class brainstorming session to identify people who fit the descriptions of each header. Write their names under the appropriate header. Ask the following questions for whole-class discussion: 1–How do the actions and attitudes of people in each category compare? 2–What actions or attitudes indicate that a person is rich in good works? 3–How will you emulate these actions or attitudes? 4–How will you use your material blessings to be rich in good works in the upcoming week?

Alternative. Distribute copies of the "Tale of Two Rulers" activity from the activity page. Have learners work in pairs to complete as indicated.

Into Life

Ask volunteers to list people they interact with in and through their work. Encourage learners to keep the names anonymous by asking them to identify the people by their roles (examples: coworkers, clients, supervisors, customers, etc.). Write responses on the board.

For each response, work as a class to brainstorm ways to care for that person in and through work. End class by praying that God will give occasions to help others in and through work.

May 24
Lesson 12 (KJV)

Christian Rhythms of Life

Devotional Reading: Ecclesiastes 2:20–25
Background Scripture: Jeremiah 31:12–13; Mark 2:18–28; 6:30–32; John 2:1–11

Mark 2:18–28

18 And the disciples of John and of the Pharisees used to fast: and they come and say unto him, Why do the disciples of John and of the Pharisees fast, but thy disciples fast not?

19 And Jesus said unto them, Can the children of the bridechamber fast, while the bridegroom is with them? as long as they have the bridegroom with them, they cannot fast.

20 But the days will come, when the bridegroom shall be taken away from them, and then shall they fast in those days.

21 No man also seweth a piece of new cloth on an old garment: else the new piece that filled it up taketh away from the old, and the rent is made worse.

22 And no man putteth new wine into old bottles: else the new wine doth burst the bottles, and the wine is spilled, and the bottles will be marred: but new wine must be put into new bottles.

23 And it came to pass, that he went through the corn fields on the sabbath day; and his disciples began, as they went, to pluck the ears of corn.

24 And the Pharisees said unto him, Behold, why do they on the sabbath day that which is not lawful?

25 And he said unto them, Have ye never read what David did, when he had need, and was an hungred, he, and they that were with him?

26 How he went into the house of God in the days of Abiathar the high priest, and did eat the shewbread, which is not lawful to eat but for the priests, and gave also to them which were with him?

27 And he said unto them, The sabbath was made for man, and not man for the sabbath:

28 Therefore the Son of man is Lord also of the sabbath.

Key Text

He said unto them, The sabbath was made for man, and not man for the sabbath: therefore the Son of man is Lord also of the sabbath. **—Mark 2:27–28**

Social Teachings
of the Church

Unit 3: Fulfilling Our Obligations to God and Society

Lessons 9–13

Lesson Aims

After participating in this lesson, each learner will be able to:

1. Summarize the significance of the Sabbath for a first-century audience.

2. Explain the diversity of Christian practices for fasting and Sabbath-keeping in light of the ministry of Jesus.

3. Make a plan to balance fasting and feasting, working and resting.

Lesson Outline

Introduction

A. Challenging Cherished Customs
B. Lesson Context: Fasting
C. Lesson Context: Sabbath

I. Question of Fasting (Mark 2:18–22)

A. Differing Practices (v. 18)
B. Fasting and Presence (vv. 19–20)
C. New and Old (vv. 21–22)
New Pot Needed?

II. Question of Sabbath (Mark 2:23–28)

A. Accusation (vv. 23–24)
B. Accommodation (vv. 25–26)
C. Account (vv. 27–28)
Tunnel Vision?

Conclusion

A. Centering Customs on Christ
B. Prayer
C. Thought to Remember

Introduction

A. Challenging Cherished Customs

Every culture has customs that are widely practiced and deeply respected. In the United States, for instance, many people enjoy flying the flag and watching fireworks displays on the Fourth of July. At Thanksgiving dinner, people anticipate eating dishes like turkey and mashed potatoes. A sudden shift in traditional expectations comes as a shock. For example, suggesting a quiet evening indoors for Independence Day feels strange. Likewise, anyone invited to a Thanksgiving meal might feel confused if they receive only rice and beans. As with all traditions, the details matter.

Jesus challenged people to rethink old customs in light of the new things God was doing. Some people interpreted His teachings as contentious or controversial. Our text today highlights two specific traditions: fasting and the Sabbath.

B. Lesson Context: Fasting

In the Old Testament, God required only one formalized day of fasting (abstaining from food) for all of Israel. He called it the Day of Atonement (Leviticus 16:29–31; 23:26–32). Yearly, everyone in Israel was to observe the Day of Atonement on the tenth day of the seventh month (in late September or early October). On this day, the high priest sacrificed collectively for all the nation's sins. His priestly act cleansed the people from impurity. The community participated through confession, prayer, and fasting.

Fasting was also associated with situations of grief, anxiety, or remorse. It was used in worship and preparation to draw near to God and to seek revelation, discernment, or help in overcoming temptation. Moses fasted for 40 days when he met God on Mount Sinai and received the Ten Commandments (Exodus 34:28). Soldiers fasted before entering battle (Judges 20:26; 1 Samuel 7:6), the nation fasted at Saul's death (31:12–13), and parents fasted in distress over the illness of a child (2 Samuel 12:16). All Israel fasted in repentance when they recommitted to God's covenant ways and heard the Mosaic law read aloud in Jerusalem after exile (Nehemiah 9:1).

We see continued evidence of fasting as a spiritual discipline in the New Testament. The prophetess Anna used fasting as a part of her perpetual worship in the temple (Luke 2:36–37). Jesus fasted for 40 days and 40 nights when the Spirit drove Him into the wilderness after His baptism (Matthew 4:2). The Pharisees were known for fasting twice weekly (Luke 18:12). Looking ahead to the practices of the early church, we see the apostles utilizing fasting in worship, for discernment, and when appointing elders (Acts 13:2; 14:23).

The passages of Matthew 9:14–17 and Luke 5:33–39 are parallels to today's text on fasting.

C. Lesson Context: Sabbath

Sabbath observance began after Israel escaped from slavery under Pharaoh in Egypt. The Law of Moses formalized the Sabbath as a commemoration of God's rest after creation (Exodus 20:8–11; see lesson 10). As a liberated community, Israel learned a new pattern of healthy living, rewriting their mindset after being enslaved (Deuteronomy 5:15). Unlike other cultures of their time, God required His people to balance labor and toil with rest to reflect on His sovereignty. Their weekly rhythm required abstaining from work on the seventh day of every week. Obedience indicated reliance on God's provision rather than human effort and achievement. Adherence to the imperative of Sabbath rest was a regular reminder of their dependence upon God.

As with fasting, observance of the Sabbath was formalized in various ways over time by different Jewish religious sects. A Jewish document called the Mishnah reflects the Pharisees' views and traditions over centuries. It was compiled in the AD 200s and lists 39 prohibited categories of labor. As with fasting, the long-term result was a religious practice that was divorced from the attitude of one's heart. What began as a careful attempt to define "work" became a weapon used against anyone who stepped over strictly marked boundaries. Well-intentioned efforts to prevent anyone from accidentally breaking the Sabbath commandment became an exercise in legalism.

Matthew 12:1–8 and Luke 6:1–5 are parallel passages to today's lesson text on the Sabbath.

I. Question of Fasting

(Mark 2:18–22)

A. Differing Practices (v. 18)

18. And the disciples of John and of the Pharisees used to fast: and they come and say unto him, Why do the disciples of John and of the Pharisees fast, but thy disciples fast not?

Our passage lands within a series of accounts depicting conflicts between Jesus' actions and Jewish religious tradition (Mark 1:21–3:6). These narratives point to a shift in faith and practice with the arrival of God's kingdom (1:15).

People inevitably compared Jesus and *John* the Baptist. They were contemporaries, and each established himself as a prominent Jewish rabbi with devoted *disciples*. Their ministries, which shared a common goal of calling Israel back to faithfulness, overlapped in time and message (Matthew 3:1–2; Mark 1:9–11, 15). Therefore, it is unsurprising that questions over observable differences between their habits arose. The Pharisees' religious practices were well-known, and apparent differences from those of Jesus prompted the question we see here.

The Pharisees consistently meet Jesus' messages with pushback and interrogation. First, they take issue with Jesus declaring forgiveness of sins, then His choice to dine with publicans and sinners (Mark 2:1–17). Now, the tension builds further as the controversy moves to fasting practices.

> **What Do You Think?**
> Do you look to the leadership, insight, and modeling of various religious teachers?
>
> **Digging Deeper**
> How might noting variations in faith and practice between Christian leaders enhance our depth of insight and understanding?

B. Fasting and Presence (vv. 19–20)

19. And Jesus said unto them, Can the children of the bridechamber fast, while the bridegroom is with them? as long as they have the bridegroom with them, they cannot fast.

Visual for Lesson 12. *At the conclusion of the lesson, point to the visual and ask, "How will you discern between fasting, feasting, working, and rest?"*

Jesus responds with a parable framed as a question. First-century Jews observed the wedding as an extended feast that could last for days. The groom's family hosted the wedding at their home. Guests gathered ahead of the bride. They waited at the groom's house while the bridegroom went to receive the bride. The groom then escorted the bride from her home to his home, where the assembled guests shared in a communal celebration. Thus, the groom's arrival signaled the start of the wedding feast, a time of unity and joy. Jesus' narrative implies that there is a time and place for fasting, but this is neither!

Jesus' use of the bridal metaphor elicits recollection of prophetic Scriptures. Jeremiah spoke of Judah's exile as an end to the joyous sound of a bride and groom's voices (Jeremiah 7:34; 16:9; 25:10). He then promised restoration of the nation and joy in glorious praise (33:11). Isaiah compared God to a groom who rejoices over His bride, Israel (Isaiah 62:5). Considering these familiar images, Jesus continues preaching that the kingdom of God is at hand (Mark 1:15).

20. But the days will come, when the bridegroom shall be taken away from them, and then shall they fast in those days.

Jesus takes the imagery into unexpected territory. No one anticipates a groom to be taken away from the wedding party. Although no custom corresponds to this description, 1 Maccabees 9:37–41 (a non-biblical text) records a violent episode of it happening. Naturally, feasting ceases if the groom is taken from the celebration. Joy turns to mourning, which appropriately expresses itself in fasting.

Jesus' veiled warning probably baffles hearers. But it also prepares them for future events. His cryptic speech foreshadows His crucifixion (Mark 8:31; 9:31; 10:33–34).

C. New and Old (vv. 21–22)

21. No man also seweth a piece of new cloth on an old garment: else the new piece that filled it up taketh away from the old, and the rent is made worse.

The conversation continues without a break, but Jesus moves to a second parable, utilizing new imagery. His example expands the subject from fasting to everything related to the kingdom of God. God's kingdom requires and implements a new paradigm.

If someone patched a torn *old* cloak with new, unshrunk *cloth*, it would tear when drying out after getting wet. In the same way, old religious practices will not hold up to new ways of doing things. Jesus' teaching indicates a necessary separation between the old and new.

22. And no man putteth new wine into old bottles: else the new wine doth burst the bottles, and the wine is spilled, and the bottles will be marred: but new wine must be put into new bottles.

To drive the point home, Jesus launches directly into a third parable. The term translated *bottles* refers to bags made from leather that store wine while it ferments. When new, such bags are flexible and stretchy. Off-gassing occurs during the fermentation process. As gas builds up, it puts pressure on the bags. New bags expand with the process. Old bags, however, are stiff and brittle. If new wine ferments in them, both wine and bag are ruined.

Jesus is warning all who will listen that the new is incompatible with the old. His ministry inaugurates the new. God's promises are being fulfilled, and new ways of doing things are in play. Jesus clarifies the establishment of a new way, a new covenant, and the arrival of God's kingdom.

What Do You Think?

What is your first reaction to new concepts, traditions, and ideas?

Digging Deeper

What is it about newness that makes you excited or causes you to push back?

New Pot Needed?

We have two citrus trees in our backyard. They occupy stately pots, and their leaves give off a most glorious fragrance. The growth of these trees is a great mystery to us. Some years, they yield bountiful lemons and limes. Others, none.

A few winters ago, we thought both trees died from frostbite. We considered adding them to the compost heap but noticed a small green shoot emerging from one stem. Instead of scrapping them, we fed and watered them. Fast-forward to the following summer, and both trees were tall, voluminous, and required replanting. Their old pots were no longer sufficient; they'd outgrown them.

Following Jesus requires new ways of thinking, seeing, and approaching daily life for spiritual growth. "The old" still has value if properly used (Romans 15:4; 1 Corinthians 10:1–11), but ultimately, the old has fulfilled its purpose and gives way to "the new" (Hebrews 7:18). Are there things you've outgrown or need to discard to move into fruitful maturity? —N. V.

II. Question of Sabbath

(Mark 2:23–28)

A. Accusation (vv. 23–24)

23. And it came to pass, that he went through the corn fields on the sabbath day; and his disciples began, as they went, to pluck the ears of corn.

This verse signals a scene and subject change. Jesus and His followers are traveling through farmland. *Corn* refers to cereal crops like wheat and barley, not the maize that North Americans associate with the word. This day, the grain is ripe and ready for consumption.

According to the Law of Moses, the poor are allowed to help themselves to unharvested grain in a neighbor's fields (Deuteronomy 23:25). This law is part of the broader way in which God requires the Israelites to act with hospitality and generosity toward one another (Leviticus 23:22). Therefore, the distinctive feature of this passage is that the action is happening on *the sabbath day.*

24. And the Pharisees said unto him, Behold, why do they on the sabbath day that which is not lawful?

Jesus' critics among *the Pharisees* jump on what they see, quickly concluding that the Law of Moses forbids the disciples' actions (Exodus 20:8–11). In their minds, the disciples were working in three ways: harvesting, threshing, and winnowing. Harvesting refers to the act of picking the grain. Threshing involves separating the grain from the hull. Winnowing is where the hulls blow away, leaving only the grain. Preparation for eating requires all three.

The Pharisees' objection is grounded in their approach to the law. In effect, they want to "build a fence" around the law by adding interpretations that, if followed, protect the faithful from ever coming near a violation (see Lesson Context: Sabbath regarding the Mishnah). We might think the disciples' efforts could hardly be called "work." For the Pharisees, however, the nature of the action matters more than the amount of effort it requires. To the Pharisees, God commanded work to cease on the Sabbath, and Jesus' disciples were working.

What Do You Think?

Do you think the Pharisees were "out to get" Jesus and His disciples? Explain.

Digging Deeper

Compare the Pharisees' question in Mark 2:24 with other passages reacting to Jesus' teaching and actions (examples: Mark 2:6–12; 3:1–6; 3:22; 6:2–3).

B. Accommodation (vv. 25–26)

25. And he said unto them, Have ye never read what David did, when he had need, and was an hungred, he, and they that were with him?

Jesus answers His opponents with an analogy from Israel's history (1 Samuel 21:1–6). As religious leaders, the Pharisees are familiar with this story. Before ruling, young David served in King Saul's court. But Saul, jealous of David's success and popularity, wanted to kill his young rival. So David fled with several of his supporters. After a tiring journey of several miles, David and his fellow fugitives were famished and exhausted.

26. How he went into the house of God in the days of Abiathar the high priest, and did eat the shewbread, which is not lawful to eat but for the priests, and gave also to them which were with him?

David went into the tabernacle, Israel's portable tent of meeting, looking for food. The purpose of the tabernacle (*the house of God*) was worship and sacrifice. Typically, food was present at these sacrifices, and a portion of it was set aside for the priesthood to eat (examples: Leviticus 7:1–21). The priest at Nob informed David there was no "common bread" there (1 Samuel 21:4). The only available food was "hallowed bread," also known as *shewbread.* Only priests were allowed to eat this bread (Leviticus 24:5–9). On this occasion, however, *the high priest* violated the rule and gave David the bread. The priest did this to meet a genuine need as it was explained to him by David (although David was not being truthful; 1 Samuel 21:2).

A small problem arises in this text with the name *Abiathar.* According to 1 Samuel 21:1, the name of the man who helped David was Ahimelech. Abiathar was his son, the only priest to escape the violent consequences of helping David (22:20). Abiathar joined David's entourage and eventually served in the tabernacle as high priest with Zadok (2 Samuel 8:17; 15:24–29). So when Jesus refers to *the days of Abiathar,* He is pointing to a general time frame. Referring to Abiathar as *the high priest* recognizes the office he eventually took and for which he was best known.

At this point we may ask ourselves, "What is the relationship between the alleged violation of the Sabbath and David's violation?" Each incident involves godly men doing something presumably forbidden to meet a valid need. The Pharisees' reliance upon tradition has blinded them to the true character of Scripture (Matthew 23:13–36).

C. Account (vv. 27–28)

27. And he said unto them, The sabbath was made for man, and not man for the sabbath.

Jesus responds again with a whole new paradigm. He says the purpose of the law is to bless humankind. God gave His law to enhance people's lives. Where its usage is misinterpreted and misapplied, the result is undue burden (Matthew 23:4; Luke 11:46). God desires good for His people, but Jesus' opponents have lost sight of the introduction to the law: "I am the Lord thy God, which have brought thee out of the land of Egypt, out of the house of bondage" (Exodus 20:2). God, who gives Israel freedom, does not intend His law to enslave and burden. The Pharisees have a decision to make: which will be their priority—human need or ritual formality?

What Do You Think?

What is more important, upholding the letter of a law or the spirit of a law?

Digging Deeper

In what circumstance would you disregard or disobey a rule for something you deem more important than that rule?

28. Therefore the Son of man is Lord also of the sabbath.

Jesus' declaration is the climax of the exchange. He refers to Himself as *the Son of man,* a self-designation that occurs more than 80 times across all four Gospels (examples: Matthew 8:20; Mark 10:45; Luke 11:30; John 1:51). This designation generally means "one who belongs to the category 'man,'" as in a human. The book of Ezekiel uses it dozens of times to delineate between a man used as the mouthpiece of God and God Himself (examples: Ezekiel 2:1; 3:17; 33:2). However, Jesus uses it differently. His use connects Him with power and authority, assuming He is the king of God's kingdom. He is the one who rules and reigns. The term resembles the figure in Daniel 7:13–14, called "one like the Son of man." This one receives authority from God to rule the world forever, served by all people, nations, and languages (7:14).

With this title, Jesus claims the authority to apply God's law. Jesus is saying, in effect, that He is the one who defines Sabbath adherence, not the Pharisees. In so doing, He strips away the trappings of religiosity and tradition and replaces them with sovereignty. Ultimately, God decides how His law applies, and Jesus says that role belongs to Him. The Sabbath and its practice are subject to Jesus' supreme authority.

Tunnel Vision?

I recently encountered a problem with my bicycle: when it was in third gear, the chain would periodically slip as if it were about to come off. The second and fourth gears were fine, but not the third. So I went online to diagnose the problem and decide what to do. Unfortunately, I misinterpreted something, and then ordered the wrong part and tool with which to fix it.

After several failed attempts at repair, I decided to consult the experts at the bicycle company. I found their contact information printed on a sticker on the bike itself. They told me what I needed; I ordered it, it came, and I installed it quickly.

I was guilty of tunnel vision. Tunnel vision is a metaphor for focusing on one thing to the exclusion of all other things. I was so focused on adhering to specific details that I knew were "right" that it took total failure to get me to go to the experts. The information I needed was right under my nose, printed on a silver sticker on the seat tube. We're all guilty of tunnel vision at one time or another. We think we know best. Do your prayers presume you already know the right answer and want God to agree with your conclusions? —R. L. N.

Conclusion

A. Centering Customs on Christ

Christians around the globe hold differing viewpoints on the practices of fasting and Sabbath-keeping. Their practices reflect tradition, doctrinal convictions, and/or personal choice.

Today's lesson gives a reason for this variety: Jesus, unlike the Pharisees, did not present set rules about fasting or the Sabbath. Instead, He pointed to their intent and His authority and presence. He taught new ways of living in God's kingdom, focusing on freedom and well-being rather than strict adherence to rules and regulations (compare Colossians 2:16). Jesus calls us to center our spiritual practices on Him as the source of life. God designed humans to follow cycles of work, rest, feasting, and fasting. Jesus, as our Lord, invites us to trust Him on this. His way offers rest from burdens, not additional weight (Matthew 11:28–30; 1 John 5:3). Life with Jesus presents opportunities for both celebration and mourning, with Scripture guiding us in what is appropriate at any given time (Romans 12:15; 1 Corinthians 5:2; 2 Corinthians 7:11). If our spiritual disciplines strengthen our dependence on Jesus, then they are beneficial, regardless of the specifics (Romans 14:22; 1 Corinthians 8:8).

Ultimately, the goal is not to find the perfect formula for any rhythm of life but to thrive in our relationship with Jesus. May He be the heartbeat, center, origin, and director of all we do.

B. Prayer

Heavenly Father, may we depend on You in every act of devotion and every rhythm of life. Whether we are feasting in joy or fasting in sadness, working or resting, may we keep our eyes fixed on You, our Lord and king. In Jesus' name we pray. Amen.

C. Thought to Remember

Christ is Lord over the rhythms of our lives.

How to Say It

Abiathar	Ah-*bye*-uh-thar.
Ahimelech	A-*him*-uh-leck.
Isaiah	Eye-*zay*-uh.
Jeremiah	Jair-uh-*my*-uh.
Maccabees	*Mack*-uh-bees.
Pharisees	*Fair*-ih-seez.
Sinai	*Sigh*-nye or *Sigh*-nay-eye.
tabernacle	*tah*-burr-*nah*-kul.
Zadok	*Zay*-dok.

Involvement Learning

Enhance your lesson with KJV Bible Student *(from your curriculum supplier) and the reproducible activity page (at www.standardlesson.com or in the back of the* KJV Standard Lesson Commentary Deluxe Edition*).*

Into the Lesson

Distribute index cards and pens to all students. Instruct learners to take one minute to write down a general schedule of what they do each day. Let them know that specific times are unnecessary; the goal is to list at least five typical daily activities between waking up and going to sleep. Then invite learners to call out items from their list while you compile their ideas on the board. Lead a conversation that identifies universal activities. Circle those items. Lead discussion on why participants believe these activities are important, and possibly even essential, to daily life.

Say, "We prioritize certain activities or habits by repeating them often and consistently. These rhythms keep us balanced and healthy. In today's lesson, look for the rhythms and habits Jesus promotes and consider their relevance to our lives."

Into the Word

Break your class into small groups. Ask a volunteer to read Mark 2:18–20 out loud. Instruct learners to compare Jesus' teaching in Mark 2:18–20 with God's message to Israel in Isaiah 58:1–12. Instruct groups to write down one way Israel misused fasting over time, and one way God redirected their practice to align with His heart.

Alternative. Distribute copies of the "A Time for Everything" exercise from the activity page, which you can download. Instruct students to complete the activity in small groups. Give several minutes for groups to complete the worksheet as indicated, or divide groups in half and ask some to focus on questions A–D and others on E–H. Then lead the whole class in a discussion about their responses.

Ask a volunteer to read Mark 2:21–22 out loud. In the same small groups, invite students to discuss the meaning of Jesus' analogy. Challenge groups to brainstorm a new analogy that expresses the same truth. Invite each group to share their idea with the whole class.

Optional. Distribute a square of "new" cloth fabric and a permanent marker to each participant. Give them a minute to silently meditate on Mark 2:21–22. As they do, write these references on the board: Isaiah 43:19; Ezekiel 36:26; 2 Corinthians 5:17; and Revelation 21:5. Ask volunteers to read these verses aloud. Then instruct individuals to select one verse to write on their fabric. (Encourage learners to protect whatever is beneath their cloth as they write.)

Ask a volunteer to read Mark 2:23–28 out loud. Have small groups look up Exodus 31:12–17. Ask participants to record the reasons God established Sabbath-keeping laws. Then read Isaiah 58:13–14. Lead a discussion pointing to the benefits of keeping the Sabbath. Direct participants to return to Mark 2:28 and say, "In light of these Old Testament passages, how would you explain this last statement by Jesus?" Give small groups a minute to discuss and then invite one representative from each group to share their conclusions publicly.

Into Life

Have small groups make a plan to balance fasting, feasting, working, and resting. Invite students to choose one meal or regular habit to fast (skip) and one meal to use as a celebratory feast this week; then choose one hour to intentionally work on a particular task and one hour to purposefully rest. Ask the class to think about how to use these special times in ways that honor the Lord and help them draw closer to Him. Ask participants to write down their plans. Inform the class that you will provide a few minutes at the beginning of the next class for them to share their experiences.

Alternative. Distribute copies of the "To Fast or Feast?" exercise on the activity page to small groups to complete as indicated. Allow a few minutes at the beginning of the next class for volunteers to share how they practiced fasting, feasting, working, and resting throughout the previous week.

May 31
Lesson 13 (KJV)

Living in Christian Community

Devotional Reading: Hebrews 1:1–6
Background Scripture: Nehemiah 8:1–12; Psalm 122:1–9; Hebrews 10:19–25

Matthew 28:18–20

18 And Jesus came and spake unto them, saying, All power is given unto me in heaven and in earth.

19 Go ye therefore, and teach all nations, baptizing them in the name of the Father, and of the Son, and of the Holy Ghost:

20 Teaching them to observe all things whatsoever I have commanded you: and, lo, I am with you alway, even unto the end of the world. Amen.

Hebrews 10:22–25

22 Let us draw near with a true heart in full assurance of faith, having our hearts sprinkled from an evil conscience, and our bodies washed with pure water.

23 Let us hold fast the profession of our faith without wavering; (for he is faithful that promised;)

24 And let us consider one another to provoke unto love and to good works:

25 Not forsaking the assembling of ourselves together, as the manner of some is; but exhorting one another: and so much the more, as ye see the day approaching.

Key Text

Let us hold fast the profession of our faith without wavering; (for he is faithful that promised).

—Hebrews 10:23

Social Teachings
of the Church

Unit 3: Fulfilling Our Obligations to God and Society

Lessons 9–13

Lesson Aims

After participating in this lesson, each learner will be able to:

1. Identify the facets of worship in these Scripture passages.
2. Evaluate whether these facets are present in the learner's life.
3. Make a plan to encourage fellow believers to live out their faith.

Lesson Outline

Introduction

A. Privileges and Responsibilities
B. Lesson Context

I. Building the Church (Matthew 28:18–20)

A. Jesus' Authority (v. 18)
B. Jesus' Command (vv. 19–20a)
Go and Teach . . . All Neighbors?
C. Jesus' Presence (v. 20b)

II. Living as the Church (Hebrews 10:22–25)

A. Approaching Rightly (v. 22)
B. Holding to Faith (v. 23)
C. Encouraging One Another (v. 24)
D. Gathering Together (v. 25)
The Monastic Life

Conclusion

A. Life in the Kingdom
B. Prayer
C. Thought to Remember

Introduction

A. Privileges and Responsibilities

My teenage children have household chores assigned to them. It is a way they contribute to our family responsibilities. Some days, my kids exceed all expectations for their tasks. On other days, however, I must remind them to complete their chores. Often, they ask, "Do we have to?"

My children's response creates the opportunity to talk about reliability, trustworthiness, and the importance of family. These chores are not just busywork. Each task, when completed, supports and strengthens the entire family. Each person's contribution is vital to the health of the whole.

Belonging to God's family also includes specific responsibilities to God and other believers. Today's lesson illustrates examples of these obligations. As we fulfill our commitments in obedience to God and our Christian brothers and sisters, we discover that life in God's family is full of challenge, meaningful work, and relationship-building. Life in community offers fulfillment and eternal hope.

B. Lesson Context

Today's lesson comes from two New Testament texts. The first is Matthew 28, which describes events following Jesus' resurrection. Mary discovers the empty tomb, brings the news to the disciples, and Jesus appears to them (Matthew 28:1–10). Religious officials pay off Roman soldiers to tell a different story (28:11–15). These events take place in and around Jerusalem. When we pick up with our text, however, the disciples are on a mountaintop in Galilee (28:16). Jesus gives them instructions for continuing ministry (28:18–20).

The second text comes from the book of Hebrews. Its unnamed author draws significantly from the Old Testament, quoting or referencing it nearly 30 times. The book's use of Old Testament passages strengthens its claims regarding Jesus and the new covenant. In particular, the author emphasizes Jesus' superiority (Hebrews 1:5–2:18), priestly status (4:14–5:10), and eternal sacrifice (9:1–10:18).

The verses just prior to today's lesson establish that believers have access to the presence of God because of the work of Jesus Christ (Hebrews 10:19–20). Jesus serves as the "high priest over the house of God" (10:21). Through Jesus, believers may approach the very throne of God (see 4:16). Hebrews describes God's house in new, spiritual terms (3:6). Jesus is not the priest of a physical building, such as the temple in Jerusalem. Instead, He is the priest over the very people of God (Ephesians 2:21–22). As members of God's family, "lively stones" that make up His house (1 Peter 2:5), we host the Spirit of God (1 Corinthians 3:16). God calls believers to live faithfully in community, to respond to Him, and to serve each other.

I. Building the Church

(Matthew 28:18–20)

A. Jesus' Authority (v. 18)

18. And Jesus came and spake unto them, saying, All power is given unto me in heaven and in earth.

The ancient Greek word *power* in this passage is translated as "authority" in other contexts (examples: Matthew 7:29; 8:9). We often think of "power" as the *ability* to do something, while "authority" refers to the *right* to do something. The two concepts are closely related, with slightly different connotations. Jesus has both power and authority in an absolute sense. He asserts His power and proclaims the dominion given Him as a precursor to His right to pass influence and authority on to His disciples. The word *all* appears throughout this section of Matthew 28, indicating that nothing is partial or half-hearted here!

The heavenly Father, who sent the Son (Galatians 4:4), grants the Son all power and authority (John 3:35; 13:3; 17:2). No place *in heaven* or on *earth* falls beyond the reach of Jesus' divine sovereignty. During His earthly ministry, Jesus exercised power over disease, natural elements like the wind and waves, and ultimately, death (Matthew 4:23–25; 8:23–27; John 11:43–44; etc.). His resurrection is definitive proof of His claim (Matthew 28:6). Jesus has possessed all power and authority from the very beginning (John 1:1–3). His resurrection confirms it (Philippians 2:8–11), and His authority will remain true forever (Revelation 1:18).

What Do You Think?

In what ways can your choices in the coming week demonstrate that Christ is the ultimate authority and power?

Digging Deeper

How can those choices also challenge popular alternative "authorities"?

B. Jesus' Command (vv. 19–20a)

19a. Go ye therefore, and teach all nations.

Having established His authority and power, Jesus commands His disciples to *go* and *teach*. They are empowered through their relationship with Him (compare Matthew 10:1, 7). The disciples' task is to teach others about the resurrected Christ. Jesus' commission in this half-verse presents non-Israelites (Gentiles) as a new mission field for the disciples. Gentiles are included by His use of the phrase *all nations*. We now refer to the directives in this verse as "disciple-making."

During His three-year earthly ministry, Jesus focused primarily on Israel (see Matthew 10:5–6; 15:21–24). He also indicated, however, that His kingdom will be inclusive, welcoming people from all backgrounds (8:11; Luke 13:29; see lesson 3). This expansion fulfills the promises of Old Testament prophets (Isaiah 42:6; 49:6; Jeremiah 3:17; Daniel 4:17; Micah 4:2; etc.). The inclusive nature of Jesus' kingdom fulfills God's promise to Abraham that "in thee shall all families of the earth be blessed" (Genesis 12:3; compare Galatians 3:8).

What Do You Think?

What is one step you can take in the coming week to help share the gospel with a nation other than your own?

Digging Deeper

What distractions might divert your attention from this goal, and how will you address these distractions?

Go and Teach . . . All Neighbors?

When I was ten years old, I was determined to follow Jesus' Great Commission. I wasn't old enough to become a missionary to all nations, but I wanted to do something concrete. With my brother's help, I started a Bible club for the kids in our neighborhood. I worked hard to prepare the "lessons" for each meeting. The "nations" might have to wait, but the kids in my neighborhood couldn't!

The club lasted only a few weeks, but I fondly remember the experience. It was a ten-year-old's imperfect way of obeying Jesus' command to teach the gospel.

Even as an adult, I find sharing the gospel with "the nations" intimidating. My neighbors feel more accessible. How can you love your neighbors and "make disciples" of them? It may not look like a weekly Bible club, but you could host events with your neighbors to share the gospel. Is there a first step God has placed on your heart for the upcoming week? —B. R.

19b. Baptizing them in the name of the Father, and of the Son, and of the Holy Ghost.

Making disciples includes *baptizing.* Baptism signifies entry into the community of God and identifies a person as being "in Christ" (Romans 6:3–4; Galatians 3:26–27; Colossians 2:11–12). Baptism is accompanied by repentance and the gift of the Holy Ghost (see Acts 2:38; 19:4–6). Through baptism, believers stand in solidarity with Jesus and publicly identify themselves as a part of God's people.

In this verse, Jesus does not explain every aspect of baptism but says it should occur *in the name* of the triune God: *Father, Son,* and *Holy Ghost.* This threefold guidance became the standard formula for the baptismal practices of the early church (compare the noncanonical Didache 7:1–3). Jesus' guidance also recalls His baptism, during which the presence of God the Father and God the Spirit was evident (Matthew 3:16–17). Becoming a disciple means identifying with Christ and learning to walk in His ways.

20a. Teaching them to observe all things whatsoever I have commanded you.

Jesus' disciples are to teach what they know—*whatsoever* they learned from Him. Jesus' words shift the disciples' role from that of students to mentors and guides. They move from *disciples* to *disciple-makers.* This change does not mean that their learning, growth, transformation, or development are over—these things continue forever in the life of a disciple—but it does shift their responsibility. They've had Jesus as their teacher, and now He gives them His authority to do the *teaching.*

It is not enough to know Jesus' teachings; He also calls believers to *observe all things* He has taught. Observing Jesus' commands means putting them into practice. Discipleship requires a lifelong commitment to both learning and obedience. Christ is the foundation of our faith (1 Corinthians 3:11). As disciples receive teaching, we come to accept Christ as Lord and learn to "walk" in Him (Colossians 2:6–7). His "yoke is easy," and His "burden is light" (Matthew 11:30). Jesus invites His followers to "learn of" Him, for He is meek and humble, a safe and restful place for our souls (11:29).

Believers do not graduate from discipleship. We must learn to follow Jesus through every stage of life. Following Him will look different depending on the season—teenager, adult, spouse, parent, grandparent, widow(er), etc. However, being a disciple of Jesus informs each transition and provides us opportunities to present the good news to others. Disciples become disciple-makers in an everlasting cycle of learning, growth, and outreach.

C. Jesus' Presence (v. 20b)

20b. And, lo, I am with you alway, even unto the end of the world. Amen.

Matthew begins his Gospel with the birth of Jesus as the fulfillment of prophecy: "They shall call his name Emmanuel, . . . God with us" (Matthew 1:23; quoting Isaiah 7:14). In this half-verse, Matthew concludes his Gospel with the promise that Jesus will always be *with* His followers. There is no place we can go from His presence (Psalm 139:7–10).

How to Say It

Amos	*Ay*-mus.
Galatians	Guh-*lay*-shunz.
Gentiles	*Jen*-tiles.
Hebrews	*Hee*-brews.
Jeremiah	Jair-uh-*my*-uh.
Zechariah	*Zek*-uh-**rye**-uh.
Zephaniah	Zef-uh-*nye*-uh.

The phrase *end of the world* refers to Christ's physical return to earth and the subsequent judgment of both the righteous and the wicked (see commentary on Hebrews 10:25, below; compare Matthew 13:39–49; 24:3).

II. Living as the Church

(Hebrews 10:22–25)

A. Approaching Rightly (v. 22)

22. Let us draw near with a true heart in full assurance of faith, having our hearts sprinkled from an evil conscience, and our bodies washed with pure water.

The following verses from the book of Hebrews feature three exhortations that guide the actions of believers. Each starts with the words *let us*. The first is in this verse: Christ-followers are encouraged to *draw near* to God (compare Hebrews 4:16). Direct access to God is available to every believer since the inner curtain of the temple was torn at Jesus' death (Matthew 27:51; Mark 15:38; Luke 23:45). We now have "boldness" to freely approach God by the blood of Jesus (Hebrews 10:19; compare 1 John 5:14–15). The book of James promises that God "draws nigh" to those who "draw nigh" to Him (4:8).

The author connects having *a true heart* with the *full assurance of faith*, meaning that we are to approach God filled with complete confidence in His fidelity. The genuine center of our person must trust in God's promises. Believers can have this kind of faith because He has proved His faithfulness to those who have walked in faith before us (Hebrews 11:1–12:3).

This verse includes imagery of a worshipper entering the temple. The phrase *hearts sprinkled* recalls the practice of sprinkling sacrificial blood upon the altar to cleanse both the people and the implements of the temple from impurity (Exodus 24:6–8; 29:16–21; see Hebrews 9:13, 18–22). God promises to "sprinkle clean water" and to give "a new heart" and "a new spirit" as part of His new covenant (Ezekiel 36:25–27; compare Hebrews 8:7–13; 10:15–18). The cleansing in question is *from an evil conscience*, which is characterized by unbelief (see Hebrews 3:12).

In contrast to the sacrifices outlined in the Law

Visual for Lesson 13. *Display this visual as you ask the Discussion Questions associated with Hebrews 10:24.*

of Moses, Jesus "offered one sacrifice for sins for ever" (Hebrews 10:12). As a result, we no longer need a ceremony involving physical blood, as we benefit from the purifying effects of Jesus' atoning blood. This is the perfect and eternal "blood of the testament" (Hebrews 9:20; compare Luke 22:20).

We also must approach God's throne with *washed bodies*. The author may be referencing the ritual cleansing that occurred before entering the tabernacle (see Leviticus 16:4). Another possibility is that the author alludes to water baptism (compare 1 Peter 3:21; see commentary on Matthew 18:19b, above). Scripture describes baptism as a washing of the person who has come to faith (Acts 22:16). It is more likely, however, that this text reveals a more significant picture, one in which baptism is only a part. Believers experience spiritual cleansing through the blood of Christ (Hebrews 9:14) and sanctification through the gift of the Holy Spirit (1 Corinthians 6:11).

B. Holding to Faith (v. 23)

23. Let us hold fast the profession of our faith without wavering; (for he is faithful that promised).

This verse includes the second *let us*. The work of Jesus, which grants us access to God the Father, is trustworthy and may be boldly declared. The author encourages us to do so *without wavering*. This message undoubtedly speaks to those considering abandoning the Christian faith to return to the Law of Moses. But these words also encourage those who are enduring periods of discouragement.

Our circumstances do not determine our faithfulness. Believers are called to remain faithful because God is *faithful* (1 Corinthians 1:9; 1 Thessalonians 5:24; 2 Timothy 2:11–13). He has been faithful to His promises in the past (see Hebrews 6:13–18; 11:11), and He continues to be faithful to us through His Son, Christ Jesus, "the author and finisher of our faith" (12:2).

> **What Do You Think?**
> How does trusting in God's faithfulness help you remain steadfast in your faith?
> **Digging Deeper**
> Can you share a time when you experienced God's faithfulness?

C. Encouraging One Another (v. 24)

24. And let us consider one another to provoke unto love and to good works.

The third *let us* encourages believers in relationships. The word *consider* means to think about something attentively. The idea pushes us outside of our personal faith lives and into a place where others gain our attention and understanding. The author exhorts believers to influence *one another* in attitude and action. Our lives should stimulate *love* among our Christian brothers and sisters (see Galatians 6:10). This is more than a gentle nudge; our lives are to motivate and incite each other toward something *good*. Christian love is not just a theoretical idea but a demonstrated act. Loving *works* should flow from our salvation.

In other words, our faith needs to make an observable difference in the lives of others. James reminds us that faith without works is dead (James 2:17, 26). The author of Hebrews provides specific examples of behaviors that show Christian love. These behaviors include practicing hospitality, caring for those who are suffering, maintaining purity in relationships, and contentment with material possessions (Hebrews 13:1–5). Loving actions should naturally emerge from trust in our loving God (compare 1 John 3:18).

> **What Do You Think?**
> In what practical ways can you encourage others in your community to live out love and good works?
> **Digging Deeper**
> What challenges might you face in this process, and how can you overcome them?

D. Gathering Together (v. 25)

25. Not forsaking the assembling of ourselves together, as the manner of some is; but exhorting one another: and so much the more, as ye see the day approaching.

The author calls God's people toward regular *assembling*. The intensity of this message is revealed by the author's using the negative. Instead of saying, "Meet together," the author urges believers to *not* forsake gathering *together*. He further reinforces the directive by admitting *some* have stopped attending gatherings.

It is unclear whether the author of Hebrews refers specifically to weekly worship services or more informal gatherings. The text does not specify the reasons for these absences, but the lack of regular commitment from some puts the entire community of believers at risk. First-century culture was hostile to Christianity, and our current culture is not much different. Regular gathering in the name of Jesus to worship, fellowship, and learn helps us function healthfully as the body of Christ (see Acts 2:42).

The *day* mentioned likely refers to the future day of judgment when Christ will return (see 1 Corinthians 1:8; 1 Thessalonians 5:1–3; 2 Thessalonians 2:1–4; 2 Peter 3:10). Expectations of judgment and redemption are rooted in Old Testament prophetic texts (Isaiah 2:12–21; 24:21–23; Joel 1:15; Amos 5:18–20; 8:9–14; Zephaniah 1:14–18; Zechariah 14:1; etc.). Anticipation of this day adds a sense of urgency to the need for believers' obedience and their commitment to the community (compare 1 Thessalonians 5:1–8). The author again emphasizes the importance of assembling by urging them to gather *so much the more* as time passes.

> **What Do You Think?**
> Why do you think gathering as a community of faith is vital for spiritual growth?
> **Digging Deeper**
> How has your experience of Christian fellowship strengthened your faith?

The Monastic Life

A group of monastics from the third century AD lived in the deserts of Egypt and Palestine. Church history calls them the Desert Fathers and Mothers. They embraced lives of poverty, self-denial, and prayer. Their commitment led them to isolation from the broader world to focus on obedience to Christ. Their example made me wonder whether a life of solitude and silence would result in an easier spiritual life.

God does not call all of us to monastic orders. Most of us are called to lives filled with noise, distraction, and multi-layered relationships. We have dependents—jobs, friends, and families. Devout followers serve and obey God wherever He guides us, whether in a quiet, monastic community or a bustling environment among crowds.

The writer of Hebrews urges us to encourage one another in faith. Do you strengthen others? Or have you isolated yourself? How can you serve as a vital and vibrant part of a faith community? How can you uplift those within your sphere of influence?

—B. R.

Conclusion

A. Life in the Kingdom

Life in God's kingdom is not a solo journey but a family endeavor. We fill various roles throughout our lives, as learners, proclaimers, mentors, guides, encouragers, worshipers, and those who serve. We participate in various activities to enhance and develop our faith. Matthew's Gospel urges disciples to participate in kingdom building by proclaiming the gospel, baptizing new disciples, and teaching the way of King Jesus. It is a call for ongoing obedience to Him, commitment to one another, and care for humanity. The facets of worship presented in Jesus' Great Commission point believers toward preaching and teaching, sacraments, public declarations of faith, and personal relationships with other believers through apprenticeship or mentoring.

The book of Hebrews provides clear instructions on how believers are to behave within a Christian community. Unity in this community is anchored in the hope we have through faith in Christ (Hebrews 6:19). Worship elements highlighted throughout today's passage include drawing near to God in confident faith, remembering our cleansing through Jesus' blood, holding onto hope with steadfastness, encouraging one another in good works of service, and regularly meeting for worship and fellowship.

Although today's texts don't use the word *worship*, a holistic life of worship is outlined within them. They pave the way for a comprehensive life as a disciple of Christ. Worship naturally occurs when God's people gather and faithfully uphold His commands. Together, we remember Jesus' sacrifice and person, celebrate His resurrection, and band together to make new disciples. We faithfully teach what Jesus taught, support one another, and urge each other toward actionable love. The people of God need one another as we follow King Jesus—the one who will one day return to judge the living and the dead (2 Timothy 4:1). Is there a facet of worship outlined in these texts that is missing from your personal practice? Have you taken an active role in both faithful discipleship and disciple-making?

B. Prayer

All-powerful God, through Your Son, you invite us to participate in building Your kingdom. Empower us through Your Spirit to make disciples. Strengthen us to live faithfully in light of Your promises. Show us how to love and serve one another as we wait for Christ's return. In Jesus' name we pray. Amen.

C. Thought to Remember

Christian community obeys God, loves others, and gathers faithfully.

Involvement Learning

Enhance your lesson with KJV Bible Student *(from your curriculum supplier) and the reproducible activity page (at www.standardlesson.com or in the back of the* KJV Standard Lesson Commentary Deluxe Edition*).*

Into the Lesson

Ask participants to share their current or past occupations or job titles. As they respond, list the jobs on the board. Ask the following questions for whole-class discussion: 1–How can people recognize what this person does? 2–What evidence or indicators support that role?

Alternative. Print copies of the "Act Like It" facilitator's page from the activity page, which you can download. Distribute one word to each participant and direct each participant to complete the activity as indicated. Conclude the activity by discussing how each person's role was revealed.

After either activity, transition into Bible study by saying, "Often, our behavior and appearance signal key aspects of our identity to others. This is also true for our Christian faith. How can people recognize that we are followers of Jesus? In today's lesson, let's explore the attributes that reveal the comprehensive life of a disciple of Christ."

Into the Word

Divide the class into three groups: **Past Group, Present Group,** and **Future Group**. Ask each group to read Matthew 28:18–20. Distribute handouts (you create) of the questions below for small-group discussion.

Past Group. 1–How have believers obeyed the commands that Jesus gave in these verses throughout church history? 2–How did Jesus' promises encourage the apostles to remain faithful to their obedience to Him?

Present Group. 1–In what ways does the modern church obey Jesus' commands? 2–How do Jesus' promises encourage us to remain faithful to our obedience to Him?

Future Group. 1–How can the church continue to obey Jesus' commands amid an ever-changing world? 2–What roadblocks must be overcome so the church can remain faithful in obedience to Christ?

After calling time, ask volunteers to share their group's responses for the whole class.

Ask a volunteer to read aloud Hebrews 10:22–25. Next, invite another volunteer to read verses 19–21 aloud for context. After that, direct participants to return to the same groups they were in during the previous activity. Assign each group one of the following Old Testament passages: Exodus 26:31–34; Leviticus 16:2–5; and Leviticus 16:32–34. Have groups discuss their assigned passage and how it relates to the text from Hebrews 10:22–25.

Continue the discussion by asking the following questions for whole-class discussion: 1–How did Jesus fulfill His purpose more effectively than a priest from the Old Testament? 2–How does understanding what our High Priest has accomplished (Hebrews 10:19–22) assist believers in living out the imperatives found in Hebrews 10:23–25?

Option. Distribute copies of the "Keep Moving" exercise from the activity page. Have participants work in small groups to complete as indicated before sharing their responses with the whole class.

Into Life

Have participants share the commands in the two Scripture passages from today's lesson. Write these commands on the board. Then distribute an index card and pen to each participant and ask them to choose one command from the board to write on their card.

State, "One way to encourage other believers to live out their faith is by practicing and demonstrating how to do so." Challenge participants to obey the command they wrote on their index cards throughout the upcoming week.

Divide participants into pairs to brainstorm ways to practice their chosen commands. Invite them to write their ideas on the back of the card.

Conclude by having partners pray for one another, asking for strength and commitment to live as followers of Jesus.

The Testimony of Faithful Witnesses

Special Features

Lessons

Unit 1: Faithful Witnesses Model God's Fidelity

Unit 2: Faithful Witnesses Say "Yes" to Jesus

Unit 3: Faithful Witnesses Spread the Good News

Quarterly Quiz

Use these questions as a pretest or as a review. The answers are on page iv of This Quarter in the Word.

Lesson 1

1. Deborah foretold that the Lord would deliver Sisera into the hand of a woman. T/F. *Judges 4:9*

2. Who killed Sisera? (Deborah, Jael, Heber) *Judges 4:21*

Lesson 2

1. Eli mistakenly thought Hannah was drunk. T/F. *1 Samuel 1:14*

2. Hannah named her son ________. *1 Samuel 1:20*

Lesson 3

1. Because of his love for David, Jonathan made a __________ with David. *1 Samuel 18:3*

2. What is the name of Jonathan's son who was spared by the king? (Melech, Michal, Mephibosheth) *2 Samuel 21:7*

Lesson 4

1. Amos worked as one of the "________ of Tekoa." *Amos 1:1*

2. Who was the king of Israel during Amos's ministry? (Uzziah, Jeroboam, Amaziah) *Amos 7:10*

Lesson 5

1. The centurion invited Jesus into his house to heal his servant. T/F. *Matthew 8:8*

2. Jesus commended the centurion for having "great ______." *Matthew 8:10*

Lesson 6

1. Who does Jesus say desires to "sift" Simon like wheat? (Sadducees, Pharisees, Satan) *Luke 22:31*

2. One of the people who questioned Peter was a relative of the man whose ear Peter had cut off. T/F. *John 18:26*

Lesson 7

1. Jesus encountered Zacchaeus in which city? (Jericho, Jerusalem, Joppa) *Luke 19:1–2*

2. Jesus declared Zacchaeus to be a son of whom? (Abraham, the devil, a Samaritan) *Luke 19:9*

Lesson 8

1. Mary pondered the events surrounding Jesus' birth "in her ________." *Luke 2:19*

2. The wedding in Cana had problems when it ran out of what? (cake, roast lamb, wine) *John 2:3*

Lesson 9

1. Thomas was also known by which name? (Didymus, Dionysius, Diotrephes) *John 11:16*

2. Thomas believed in Jesus' resurrection without seeing Jesus' resurrected body. T/F. *John 20:25*

Lesson 10

1. Stephen not only served food but also did miracles. T/F. *Acts 6:8*

2. Just before dying, Stephen had a vision of whom? (David, Moses, Jesus) *Acts 7:55*

Lesson 11

1. Saul was trained in the law of his ancestors under the teachings of ________. *Acts 22:3*

2. Saul's encounter with the Lord occurred near the city of __________. *Acts 22:6*

Lesson 12

1. Paul's grandmother was named Lois, and his mother was named Eunice. T/F. *2 Timothy 1:5*

2. Paul stated that all Scripture is useful to help believers be ________ unto all good works. *2 Timothy 3:16–17*

Lesson 13

1. Paul and Silas met Lydia in the city square. T/F. *Acts 16:13–14*

2. Which color cloth did Lydia sell? (red, blue, purple) *Acts 16:14*

Quarter at a Glance

by Brenner S. Carlson

This quarter will look at the examples of faithful witnesses from Scripture. These were people who heard the call of God, responded in faith, and testified to God's mercy and fidelity to His promises through their words and deeds.

Faithful Witnesses in Ancient Israel

Faithful witnesses in ancient Israel model God's faithfulness to His word. Deborah, a courageous judge of Israel, demonstrates her trust in God's promise to save His people by risking her life in battle (Judges 4:4–10, 14; see lesson 1). In the period following the judges, a devoted supplicant named Hannah tearfully prays to God for a child (1 Samuel 1:9–20; see lesson 2). Because of her persistence, Hannah plays a vital role in God's plan for Israel, dedicating her son to serve God. This son would become a significant figure in the monarchy of Israel.

During that time, the friendship between David and Jonathan shows the love and loyalty humans can share (1 Samuel 18:1–4; 20:16–17; etc.; see lesson 3). David maintains this commitment even after Jonathan dies (2 Samuel 21:7), modeling the faithfulness that God shows to His people. Finally, in the era of the divided kingdom, the prophet Amos confronts his own people for their refusal to heed God's warnings about impending judgment (Amos 2:11–12; 3:7–8; see lesson 4).

Faithful Witnesses Say "Yes" to Jesus

In the New Testament, we see many examples of faithful witnesses who encounter Christ and respond with a resounding "Yes!" An unnamed centurion, a servant of the hated Roman Empire, demonstrates "great faith" by trusting that Jesus will heal his servant (Matthew 8:5–13; see lesson 5). A despised tax collector named Zacchaeus subverts expectations by following Jesus and repenting of his wrongdoing (Luke 19:1–10; see lesson 7).

Even those closest to Jesus had to make their own commitments of faith. Simon Peter recognizes Jesus more clearly than any other, but that disciple still falters and needs restoration (Mark 8:27–29; Luke 22:31–34; John 18:25–27; 21:15–17; see lesson 6). Another disciple, Thomas, although known for his doubts, nevertheless expresses a faith that empowers him to share the gospel (20:24–29; 21:1–2; see lesson 9). Even Jesus' mother says "Yes" to Him; she is chosen to bear the Son of God and demonstrates persistent faithfulness to her son throughout His life (Luke 2:15–19; John 2:1–5; 19:25–27; see lesson 8).

Faithful Witnesses Share the Gospel

The gospel spreads through the work of faithful witnesses. Stephen, the first martyr, serves God even in death (Acts 6:7–10, 7:54–60; see lesson 10). His boldness in proclaiming the message leads to the scattering of faithful witnesses throughout the region, enabling the gospel to disperse further.

After approving Stephen's execution, Saul encounters the resurrected Christ (Acts 22:3–15; see lesson 11). This experience transforms him into the faithful apostle we now call "Paul." He becomes a witness, sharing his firsthand experience with Christ Jesus. One of the recipients of Paul's message is Lydia, a seller of purple cloth and a worshiper of God. After responding to Paul's message, she is baptized and demonstrates hospitality as her own faithful witness (Acts 16:11–15, 40; see lesson 13).

Paul's ministry also involves training and equipping others to proclaim the gospel. He encourages Timothy to remember the "gift of God" and the promises of Scripture that Timothy received from his mother and grandmother—promises that make one "wise" for salvation (2 Timothy 1:1–6; 3:14–16; see lesson 12).

Though the circumstances surrounding the commitments of these witnesses vary, their stories inspire us to trust and follow the way of Christ.

Get the Setting

by K. R. Harriman

Community life among first-century Jews varied significantly based on location. Where a person lived influenced their experience. Jews in Palestine dwelt differently than those in the Diaspora (those dispersed throughout the Roman Empire). Population density also influenced differences in community life with variations between rural settings, small towns, and urban communities. In some contexts, Jews freely observed their traditions; in others, they felt pressure to conform to secular Greco-Roman culture and its prevailing lifestyle.

Family: The Foundation of Community

The household was the cornerstone of the community for most first-century Jews. Immediate and extended family members often lived close to one another, sometimes even in the same living quarters. Marriages were typically arranged by family leaders, usually between families of similar socioeconomic standing. Suitable matches enhanced family stability and community status. Marital life revolved around bearing children, especially for women. Unfortunately, infant mortality rates were high, and families remained relatively small (father, mother, and one to three children). Families valued children and relied on younger generations to care for older family members.

Families in the Greco-Roman world valued the community over the individual. The culture hinged on the values of honor and shame. Men largely gained honor through their occupation, economic status, family size, and ability to show their courage and generosity. Women gained honor in modesty, subservience, and child-rearing. Contrary to the common belief, Greco-Roman women often worked outside the home in various positions. They sold goods in markets, created textiles, worked as nurses or nannies, and participated in trade guilds. Wealthy women owned workshops and businesses, assisted in manufacturing, worked as calligraphers or scribes, and, in rare cases, acted as managers of workshops.

Economic Livelihood

A father often passed down an occupation to his sons. For example, fishermen owned boats and nets and passed their tools on to the next generation—along with knowledge and expertise. There were exceptions, particularly among wealthier community members who could afford formal education, which opened up other opportunities for their children.

Certain occupations generated hostility among the Jews. Tax collectors garnered taxes on behalf of the Roman Empire. They often increased the collection amount and kept the excess for themselves. Due to unjust practices, dishonest principles, and their association with the oppressive empire, Jewish tax collectors were often despised and rejected by other Jews. Most first-century Jews in Palestine lived in poverty, so the unjust actions of tax collectors added further burdens to their already challenging lives.

Limited resources drove many economically disadvantaged individuals to seek support from benefactors or patrons among wealthier portions of the community. For example, affluent landowners provided land, money, tools, and other resources to help the poor achieve financial stability. In return, these workers became clients of their benefactors. Benefactors expected loyalty, service, and portions of their harvest from their clients. While these benefactor-client relationships could be advantageous, they often exploited the less fortunate party.

The Power of Memory

For first-century Jews, another essential aspect of community life was the power of remembrance and tradition. Retelling the stories of ancient Israel shaped every generation according to the experiences and beliefs of those who came before. Jewish parents taught God's commands, communicating them through worship traditions and household customs (see Deuteronomy 6:6–12). Ancient proverbs conveyed traditional wisdom in a way that was easy to memorize and pass on (example: Proverbs 9:10).

Mon, Aug. 17	**A Protégé with Promise**	Acts 16:1–5
Tue, Aug. 18	**Receive Instruction**	Proverbs 1:1–9
Wed, Aug. 19	**Learn from Your Parents**	Proverbs 23:22–25
Thu, Aug. 20	**A Worthy and Trusted Minister**	Philippians 2:19–24
Fri, Aug. 21	**Teach Your Children God's Ways**	Deuteronomy 4:9–13
Sat, Aug. 22	**A Father's Message**	2 Timothy 1:1–16
Sun, Aug. 23	**Continue What You Have Learned**	2 Timothy 3:10–11, 14–17
Mon, Aug. 24	**Use Your Gifts to Serve**	1 Peter 4:7–11
Tue, Aug. 25	**God Rewards Hospitality**	2 Kings 4:8–17
Wed, Aug. 26	**A Capable, Entrepreneurial Woman**	Proverbs 31:10–22
Thu, Aug. 27	**Good and Faithful Servants**	Matthew 25:14–23
Fri, Aug. 28	**The Wicked Servant**	Matthew 25:24–30
Sat, Aug. 29	**The Righteous Provide for Others**	Job 31:16–28
Sun, Aug. 30	**Lydia Welcomes Guests**	Acts 16:11–15, 40

Answers to the Quarterly Quiz on page 338

Lesson 1—1. True. 2. Jael. **Lesson 2**—1. True. 2. Samuel. **Lesson 3**—1. covenant. 2. Mephibosheth. **Lesson 4**—1. herdmen. 2. Jeroboam. **Lesson 5**—1. False. 2. faith. **Lesson 6**—1. Satan. 2. True. **Lesson 7**—1. Jericho. 2. Abraham. **Lesson 8**—1. heart. 2. wine. **Lesson 9**—1. Didymus. 2. False. **Lesson 10**—1. True. 2. Jesus. **Lesson 11**—1. Gamaliel. 2. Damascus. **Lesson 12**—1. True. 2. furnished. **Lesson 13**—1. False. 2. purple.

This Quarter in the Word

Mon, June 1	**A Leadership Example**	1 Timothy 3:1–7
Tue, June 2	**A Leader Who Cares**	Acts 9:36–42
Wed, June 3	**A Leader Who Teaches**	Acts 18:24–28
Thu, June 4	**A Leader Who Listens**	Nehemiah 2:1–8
Fri, June 5	**A Leader Who Intercedes**	Nehemiah 4:1–6
Sat, June 6	**A Leader Who Serves**	John 13:3–17
Sun, June 7	**A Leader Who Inspires**	Judges 4:4–10, 14, 21–22
Mon, June 8	**Living a Righteous Life**	Ezekiel 18:5–9
Tue, June 9	**Trusting a God Who Sees**	Genesis 16:1, 4–16
Wed, June 10	**Keeping Wise Counsel**	Proverbs 6:20–22
Thu, June 11	**Praising the LORD**	Psalm 113
Fri, June 12	**Comforting like a Mother**	Isaiah 66:9–13
Sat, June 13	**Rejoicing in God's Deliverance**	Luke 1:46–55
Sun, June 14	**Praying for Provision**	1 Samuel 1:9–20, 25
Mon, June 15	**A Praying Friend**	Romans 1:8–12
Tue, June 16	**Choose Your Friends Wisely**	1 Corinthians 15:30–34
Wed, June 17	**A Friend Closer than a Brother**	Proverbs 18:19–24
Thu, June 18	**Friends Stick Together**	Ruth 1:11–18
Fri, June 19	**Friends Love Radically**	John 15:9–17
Sat, June 20	**Sworn Friendship**	1 Samuel 20:16–17, 32–34, 42
Sun, June 21	**Grief for a Friend**	2 Samuel 1:17, 19–27

Mon, June 22	**Prophecy: Toward Restoration**	Isaiah 61:4–9
Tue, June 23	**A Shepherd Rejoices**	Luke 15:1–7
Wed, June 24	**Prophecy: The Day of the Lord**	Amos 5:16–20
Thu, June 25	**Prophecy: Let Justice Roll**	Amos 5:21–27
Fri, June 26	**Know the Shepherd's Voice**	John 10:1–9
Sat, June 27	**The Good Shepherd**	John 10:10–18
Sun, June 28	**A Prophet: Chosen**	Amos 7:10–15
Mon, June 29	**A Light to the Nations**	Isaiah 49:1–6
Tue, June 30	**A Deliverer Will Come**	Psalm 72:1–13
Wed, July 1	**Saved By Grace**	Ephesians 2:1–10
Thu, July 2	**No Longer Strangers**	Ephesians 2:11–22
Fri, July 3	**Nations Come to God's Light**	Isaiah 60:1–7
Sat, July 4	**Nations Bow to Zion**	Isaiah 60:8–14
Sun, July 5	**A Banquet Spread for All**	Matthew 8:5–13
Mon, July 6	**Peter: Bold Gospel Preacher**	Acts 2:14–21
Tue, July 7	**I Sought the Lord**	Psalm 34:1–9
Wed, July 8	**The Lord Delivers**	Psalm 34:10–22
Thu, July 9	**Peter Misunderstands**	Mark 8:27–33
Fri, July 10	**God Will Strengthen and Help**	Isaiah 41:8–13
Sat, July 11	**Peter Denies Jesus**	Mark 14:55–72
Sun, July 12	**Jesus Restores Peter**	John 21:15–19
Mon, July 13	**God Calls for Restitution**	Exodus 22:1–6
Tue, July 14	**Let the Oppressed Go Free**	Isaiah 58:3–7
Wed, July 15	**Blessings and Woes**	Luke 6:20–26
Thu, July 16	**Love, Hospitality, and Contentment**	Hebrews 13:1–6
Fri, July 17	**Put Love Into Action**	1 John 3:14–18
Sat, July 18	**Commit Your Way to God**	Psalm 37:1–5, 18–22
Sun, July 19	**Salvation for Zacchaeus**	Luke 19:1–10

Mon, July 20	**Consequences for Sin**	Genesis 3:14–20
Tue, July 21	**Spiritual Family**	Mark 3:31–35; Luke 11:27–28
Wed, July 22	**Meditating on God's Law**	Psalm 119:97–104
Thu, July 23	**Mary: the Lord's Servant**	Luke 1:26–38
Fri, July 24	**Keepsakes and Treasures**	Luke 2:15–19
Sat, July 25	**To Us a Child is Born**	Isaiah 9:3–7
Sun, July 26	**Mary Points Others to Jesus**	John 2:1–5
Mon, July 27	**Seek the Lord**	Isaiah 55:6–11
Tue, July 28	**Wait for Christ's Mercy**	Jude 20–25
Wed, July 29	**Jesus Is the Way**	John 14:1–7
Thu, July 30	**Call on the Lord**	Psalm 50:7–15
Fri, July 31	**God Is Merciful**	Deuteronomy 4:27–31
Sat, Aug. 1	**Jesus Appears to the Disciples**	John 20:19–23
Sun, Aug. 2	**Jesus Appears to Thomas**	John 20:24–29
Mon, Aug. 3	**A Great Multitude**	Revelation 7:9–10, 13–17
Tue, Aug. 4	**The Word of Their Testimony**	Revelation 12:7–11
Wed, Aug. 5	**Stephen's Arrest**	Acts 6:7–14
Thu, Aug. 6	**Delivered from Death**	Psalm 116:1–9
Fri, Aug. 7	**Precious Deaths**	Psalm 116:10–19
Sat, Aug. 8	**Stephen's Bold Message**	Acts 7:1, 44–53
Sun, Aug. 9	**Stephen's Martyrdom**	Acts 7:54–60
Mon, Aug. 10	**No Fear of God**	Psalm 36:1–9
Tue, Aug. 11	**Called By God's Grace**	Galatians 1:13–24
Wed, Aug. 12	**No Confidence in Flesh**	Philippians 3:3–9
Thu, Aug. 13	**A Stiff-Necked People**	Exodus 34:5–9
Fri, Aug. 14	**A New Creation in Christ**	2 Corinthians 5:17–21
Sat, Aug. 15	**Rejoice in God's Forgiveness**	Psalm 32
Sun, Aug. 16	**God's Chosen Witness**	Acts 22:3–15

Chart Feature

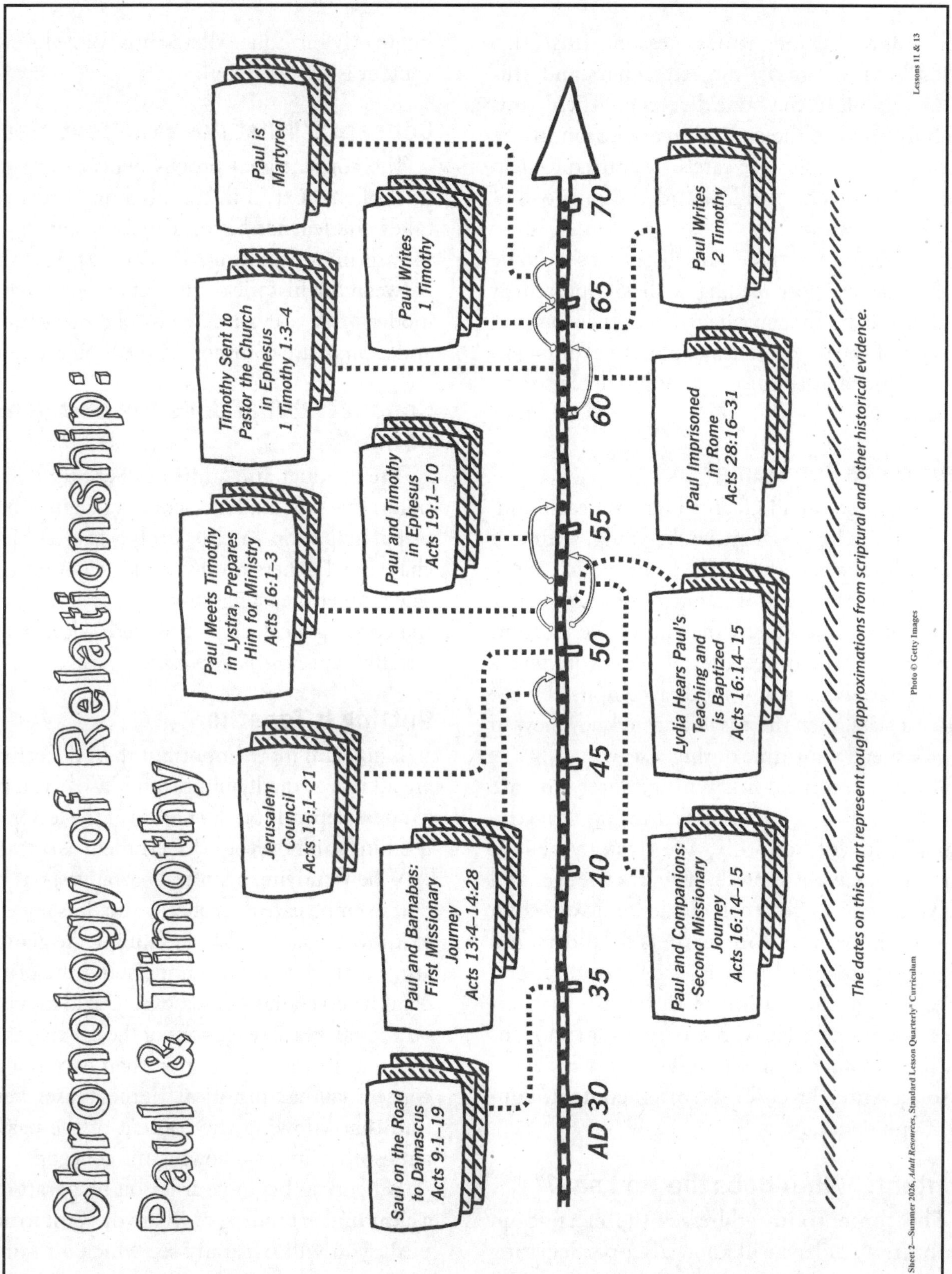

Ready, Aim, Teach

Teacher Tips by Jonathan Underwood

Standard Lesson utilizes lesson aims (also called learning goals) to get teachers and students pointed in the same direction. These aims are published at the start of every lesson in the teacher books. They are carefully crafted to help you as the teacher understand the purpose of each week's study.

Every lesson has three aims. The first should be easily met by a close reading of the Scripture text for that lesson. The second targets deeper comprehension of the lesson's theme, objective, or meaning. The third asks learners to apply the lesson in some way.

Where Are You Going?

Lewis Carroll and George Harrison each said, "If you don't know where you're going, then any road will take you there." To know which is the right road, or the right way, one must know where he or she wants to be by the end of the journey. The same is true in teaching. Unless you have a clear idea of what you want to accomplish by the end of a class, then there is no way to know how to rightly spend your time during a session.

What is your goal in teaching? Surely you are not just filling up time or skimming a particular portion of Scripture. We strongly believe our teachers want growth, new knowledge, and active discovery for their students. More than that, we know you want learners to understand the deep truths and principles of Scripture. You want active application of Scripture in their lives—whether that be hours, days, or months ahead. *Standard Lesson Commentary* aims every lesson at three levels of learning: content, concept, and conduct.

Content: "What does the text say?"

The content aim addresses the facts about Scripture a student will know after participating in your class. Verbs like *recount*, *tell*, and *identify* frequently introduce these aims. Bible knowledge content is foundational.

Concept: "What does the text mean?"

The content goal probes beneath the surface level of the text to find underlying principles. It takes the learner beyond mere knowledge and toward understanding. This aim bridges the gap between the historical truth of biblical events and modern-day relevance. Verbs like *relate*, *compare*, and *explain* are common in these objectives.

Conduct: "What does the text demand of me?"

The conduct aim addresses Scriptural application: How will students' conduct change because of participation in this study? These objectives challenge learners toward making commitments. They sometimes suggest specific actions to take in the coming week(s). Action verbs dominate this aim like *write*, *help*, and *do*.

Putting It Together

Is any aim more important than the others? Or are all three equally important? What you choose to stress depends on the nature of the lesson you're teaching, and on your discernment as a teacher.

When studying historical narratives, it is important to emphasize the concept aim. It is not enough to know the facts of David's killing the giant Goliath. Learners must also understand the principles of faith and courage that moved David to action. In other passages, like sections of the epistles, the content may be more exposition than narration, more conceptual than historical. In these cases, you may find that knowing the content of the passage is almost the same as knowing the concept.

When you begin your lesson preparation with a clear understanding of what you want to accomplish, you will naturally see which aim or set of aims you want to stress.

June 7
Lesson 1 (KJV)

Deborah, the Dutiful Judge

Devotional Reading: Matthew 20:20–28
Background Scripture: Judges 4–5

Judges 4:4–10, 14, 21–22

4 And Deborah, a prophetess, the wife of Lapidoth, she judged Israel at that time.

5 And she dwelt under the palm tree of Deborah between Ramah and Bethel in mount Ephraim: and the children of Israel came up to her for judgment.

6 And she sent and called Barak the son of Abinoam out of Kedeshnaphtali, and said unto him, Hath not the LORD God of Israel commanded, saying, Go and draw toward mount Tabor, and take with thee ten thousand men of the children of Naphtali and of the children of Zebulun?

7 And I will draw unto thee to the river Kishon Sisera, the captain of Jabin's army, with his chariots and his multitude; and I will deliver him into thine hand.

8 And Barak said unto her, If thou wilt go with me, then I will go: but if thou wilt not go with me, then I will not go.

9 And she said, I will surely go with thee: notwithstanding the journey that thou takest shall not be for thine honour; for the LORD shall sell Sisera into the hand of a woman. And Deborah arose, and went with Barak to Kedesh.

10 And Barak called Zebulun and Naphtali to Kedesh; and he went up with ten thousand men at his feet: and Deborah went up with him.

---

14 And Deborah said unto Barak, Up; for this is the day in which the LORD hath delivered Sisera into thine hand: is not the LORD gone out before thee? So Barak went down from mount Tabor, and ten thousand men after him.

---

21 Then Jael Heber's wife took a nail of the tent, and took an hammer in her hand, and went softly unto him, and smote the nail into his temples, and fastened it into the ground: for he was fast asleep and weary. So he died.

22 And, behold, as Barak pursued Sisera, Jael came out to meet him, and said unto him, Come, and I will shew thee the man whom thou seekest. And when he came into her tent, behold, Sisera lay dead, and the nail was in his temples.

Key Text

Deborah, a prophetess, the wife of Lapidoth, she judged Israel at that time. And she dwelt under the palm tree of Deborah between Ramah and Bethel in mount Ephraim: and the children of Israel came up to her for judgment. **—Judges 4:4–5**

The Testimony of

Faithful Witnesses

Unit 1: Faithful Witnesses Model God's Fidelity

Lessons 1–4

Lesson Aims

After participating in this lesson, each learner will be able to:

1. Summarize Deborah's role in the defeat of Sisera.

2. Explain how Deborah demonstrated faithfulness in difficult circumstances.

3. State one way to follow Deborah's example of heeding God's call to serve others.

Lesson Outline

Introduction

A. Supportive Greatness

B. Lesson Context

I. Deborah's Plan (Judges 4:4–10, 14)

A. The Setting (vv. 4–5)

B. The Task (vv. 6–7)

God Still Speaks

C. The Prophecy (vv. 8–10)

You'll Bring Honor

D. The Action (v. 14)

II. Jael's Action (Judges 4:21–22)

A. Violent Response (v. 21)

B. Prophetic Fulfillment (v. 22)

Conclusion

A. Emboldened Leader

B. Prayer

C. Thought to Remember

Introduction

A. Supportive Greatness

Numerous world records were broken during the 2024 Olympic Games. One was for sport climbing, set by Sam Watson (USA). Sam claimed the climbing record by completing the course in just 4.74 seconds! Amazingly, Sam also held the previous record of 4.75 seconds. He beat his own record by .01 second! Sometimes, the smallest victories require the most extraordinary dedication.

Sam is a fantastic athlete, but like anyone attempting an audacious goal, he needed help and support. Enter the role of a coach! Sam's coach enabled his growth capacity through knowledge, confidence, and courage. He emboldened Sam toward consistent training and offered encouragement when doubts crept in. Coaches are rarely seen or noticed, but their impact is esteemed when their students succeed. As you ponder today's lesson, consider the out-in-front and behind-the-scenes roles of Deborah and Jael in Israel's victory. Leadership comes in many forms.

B. Lesson Context

The book of Judges opens with the news that Joshua, Moses' successor, has died. His death signals a transition to what we now call "the period of the judges" (about 1373–1043 BC). The firm, centralized leadership that nomadic Israel knew under Moses and Joshua is gone. A theocracy remains in its place—a rule by God.

Before the tribes of Israel went to their respective portions of land, they agreed to serve God (Joshua 24:14–28). But that didn't happen; the Israelites' commitment to God faded as the generation of the conquest died. The new generation worshiped fictitious Canaanite gods such as Baal and Ashtoreth (Judges 2:10–13) as "every man did that which was right in his own eyes" (17:6; 21:25). Because of their idolatry, God handed His people over to their enemies. Oppression and hardship resulted (2:14–15).

A cyclical pattern characterizes the book of Judges: (1) obedience to God brings peace and stability to Israel; (2) the people's resolve weakens, and faithfulness to God's covenant falters; (3) a disintegration of spiritual well-being breaks down the community, leaving God's people vulnerable to repression and attacks from external enemies; (4) oppression and suffering trigger repentance; and (5) God mercifully raises a leader to deliver them from their enemies.

Typically, when we hear the noun *judge,* we think of a magistrate who renders legal decisions in a court of law. The Old Testament use of the term is much broader, however. The book of Judges uses the word *judge* to describe a leader who renders decisions for the nation. As such, the word is used to describe officials who make legal decisions in civil and criminal cases (example: Deuteronomy 25:1–2), prophets (Judges 4:4), military commanders (2:18), and even the Lord Himself (11:27). In all instances, the "judge" was to lead in accordance with the will of God.

Today's text takes us to approximately 1225 BC, where we consider the fourth of Israel's judges.

I. Deborah's Plan

(Judges 4:4–10, 14)

When Deborah succeeded Ehud as judge, she found herself in the same situation as her predecessor: "The children of Israel again did evil in the sight of the Lord" (Judges 4:1). Because of their desire to do evil, God allowed Jabin, the king of Canaan, to oppress Israel for 20 years (4:2–3).

A. The Setting (vv. 4–5)

4. And Deborah, a prophetess, the wife of Lapidoth, she judged Israel at that time.

In the most basic sense, a prophet hears from God and relays His message to the people. Men commonly held the role of prophet in ancient Israel, but several female prophets are also noted (Exodus 15:20; 2 Kings 22:14; Nehemiah 6:14; Isaiah 8:3; and Luke 2:36). *Deborah* is one such female prophet, and she is married. Here, we see the only mention in Scripture of her husband, *Lapidoth.* Nothing more is known about him.

This verse formally identifies Deborah as Israel's civil leader (*judge*).

5. And she dwelt under the palm tree of Deborah between Ramah and Bethel in mount Ephraim: and the children of Israel came up to her for judgment.

The designation *mount Ephraim* appears about 30 times in the Old Testament. It probably refers to the hilly area where the tribe of Ephraim dwelt. The distance between *Ramah* and *Bethel* is about five miles. The towns are situated approximately five and ten miles north of Jerusalem, respectively.

Trees often mark places of idol worship in the Old Testament (example: Deuteronomy 12:2). But there is no hint of that here. Instead, the mention of Deborah's *palm tree* offers a convenient landmark. The association with *Deborah* implies that she and her tree were well known.

Deborah's role as civil magistrate is revealed by the fact that the Israelites come *up to her for judgment* (compare Exodus 18:13).

B. The Task (vv. 6–7)

6. And she sent and called Barak the son of Abinoam out of Kedeshnaphtali, and said unto him, Hath not the LORD God of Israel commanded, saying, Go and draw toward mount Tabor, and take with thee ten thousand men of the children of Naphtali and of the children of Zebulun?

This verse introduces the reader to *Barak,* a military commander in Israel. His importance is seen in (1) his mention by name a dozen times in Judges, (2) the specification of the names of his father and hometown, and (3) his inclusion in "faith's hall of fame" (Hebrews 11:32).

The four points of geography mentioned here help us set the scene. There is more than one city named Kedesh in the Old Testament, but *Kedeshnaphtali* is the one located in the tribal territory of *Naphtali;* it is a city of refuge for those accused of unintentionally taking the life of another (Joshua

How to Say It

Harosheth	Huh-*roe*-sheth.
Kedesh	*Kee*-desh.
Kishon	*Kye*-shon.
Lapidoth	*Lap*-ih-doth.
Naphtali	*Naf*-tuh-lye.
Zebulun	*Zeb*-you-lun.

20:7; 21:32). *Mount Tabor* is roughly 50 miles to the north of where Deborah and Barak confer and about 11 miles southwest of the Sea of Galilee. Located just within the northern border of the tribe of Issachar, the mount's elevation (1,886 feet) does not qualify it as a "mountain" in the modern sense of the term. Therefore, picture a hill set very close to the tribal borders of *Naphtali* and *Zebulun*. A helpful New Testament title for the tribal lands at hand is "Galilee of the Gentiles" (Matthew 4:15, quoting Isaiah 9:1–2).

Deborah begins to speak the word of God to Barak. At this point, we may wonder whether the *command* to take *ten thousand* men from those two tribes means 10,000 total or 10,000 from each. The answer to that question is in Judges 4:14, below.

> **What Do You Think?**
> Consider Judges 4, 7, and 13–16. Why does God sometimes use "a cast of thousands" to accomplish His will but at other times He uses many fewer?
>
> **Digging Deeper**
> When have you participated in serving others with a large group? Small group? Independently?

God Still Speaks

Deborah wasn't just a judge; she was also a prophet. She had a unique advantage when defending against Israel's enemies: she heard God's voice. Therefore, she knew what to do and how to do it. If only all leaders had such an advantage!

While God may not call me to battle, I often find myself in tense circumstances with high stakes. Sometimes a particular decision feels like life or death. I often find myself desperate for God to speak clearly about what I should do and how to do it, especially if I am to lead others and care for their well-being.

It is easy to forget that while God may not speak in a loud, booming voice to give me obvious and specific directions about each step, I can access His will through the Holy Spirit and the study of Scripture. The more I walk with the Spirit through prayer, the more I discern His will—and perhaps most importantly, my heart desires to follow Him. Have you invited the wisdom and guidance of God into the significant decisions of your life? How are you allowing God to work through you as a leader for the sake of serving others well? —N. M. H.

7. And I will draw unto thee to the river Kishon Sisera, the captain of Jabin's army, with his chariots and his multitude; and I will deliver him into thine hand.

Deborah continues God's message to Barak: God is the *I* in this passage.

The Canaanite army is formidable. Of particular interest are its *chariots*. *Sisera* leads the force and has an advantage over Israel in terms of both quantity and quality of fighting forces. The chariots' construction includes iron (Judges 4:3). Barak and Deborah's conflict with Sisera falls between "the bronze age" (3300–1200 BC) and "the iron age" (1200–550 BC). To have chariots outfitted with iron at the time of our text (about 1225 BC; see Lesson Context) is a huge technological advantage.

Bronze chariots have defeated the Israelites in other, previous contexts (Joshua 17:16–18; Judges 1:19; 4:3). The Israelites (and Barak) have a choice: on what will they focus? Will they fixate on the strength of iron chariots or remember the strength of God (Deuteronomy 20:1)?

The Kishon River, the site of the mentioned ambush, is southwest of Mount Tabor and flows along the Jezreel Valley. Sisera's military base is Harosheth of the Gentiles (Judges 4:13), a town that hugs the river downstream. It is about 16 miles west of Mount Tabor. The villages of the Jezreel Valley are largely Canaanite, so Sisera has a "home field advantage" (consider Judges 1:27).

> **What Do You Think?**
> What is the role of fear in our lives? How does it protect, guide, or assist us? Is fear ever a good thing?
>
> **Digging Deeper**
> What role does God play in overcoming our fears? How might the Christian community assist?

C. The Prophecy (vv. 8–10)

8. And Barak said unto her, If thou wilt go with me, then I will go: but if thou wilt not go with me, then I will not go.

Barak shows his doubt. One might compare his misgivings with those of Gideon, who wanted proof that the Lord was speaking (Judges 6:36–40). Essentially, Barak asks himself, "Is Deborah really speaking the commandment of the Lord, or is she making it up?" His proof of truth will be her willingness to risk her life by accompanying the army on the expedition.

9. And she said, I will surely go with thee: notwithstanding the journey that thou takest shall not be for thine honour; for the Lord shall sell Sisera into the hand of a woman. And Deborah arose, and went with Barak to Kedesh.

Deborah agrees to go with Barak, though she warns that there is a consequence for his doubt: the *journey* will not result in Barak's *honour*; Sisera will be sold *into the hand of a woman.* The deliverance and consequence come from *the Lord.* Deborah emphasizes that it is God who is in control.

Variations of the Hebrew word underneath the translation *shall sell* appear five times in Judges (2:9, 14; 3:8; 4:2, 9). The phrase's use in these passages is illustrated by poetic parallelism in Deuteronomy 32:30: "Except their Rock had sold them, and the Lord had shut them up?" The parallel with "sold them" (the same Hebrew word as this verse's "shall sell") is the phrase "shut them up." It means God will "confine them." In other words, Sisera's destiny is not in his hands!

You'll Bring Honor

The children's film, *Mulan*, tells the story of a young woman named Fa Mulan who wants more than anything to bring honor to her family. The Chinese Imperial Army calls Mulan's father to serve in the war against invaders from the north. Mulan's father is a war veteran with old injuries that make the rigors of combat inadvisable. But he believes upholding the family's reputation and honor is more important than his health. To avoid shame, Fa Zhou answers the call to war.

In response, Mulan feels compelled to protect him. She disguises herself as a man and joins the Imperial Army. Mulan defies traditional gender roles and societal expectations. She faces adversity with creativity, courage, and strength. Mulan sets aside the customary ways a young woman might merit her family. A song in the film explains the traditional expectations: "We all must serve our Emperor/Who guards us from the Huns/A man by bearing arms/A girl by bearing sons." She rejects demureness and embraces physical strength, surprising everyone. Ultimately, the emperor voices gratitude for Mulan's service and bows to her in honor.

Today's texts also showcase honor given and received in unexpected places. By using unanticipated characters, God keeps the honor for Himself. In what ways does honor drive you? What is your reaction to honor deflected from yourself and conveyed to others? —B. R. T.

What Do You Think?

How does the concept of honor motivate you?

Digging Deeper

How does your life honor God?

10. And Barak called Zebulun and Naphtali to Kedesh; and he went up with ten thousand men at his feet: and Deborah went up with him.

Barak obeys the Lord's command to assemble an army from the tribes of *Zebulun and Naphtali*, the tribes closest to the forthcoming action. King Jabin's headquarters is in Hazor (Judges 4:2), which lies within the tribal boundaries of Naphtali, north of the Sea of Galilee.

The town name *Kedesh* occurs frequently in the Old Testament. It refers to several different towns and sometimes to a general region. It is uncertain whether this Kedesh refers to Kedeshnaphtali from which Barak was summoned in Judges 4:6 or another town in Issachar (see 1 Chronicles 6:72). It may also be synonymous with the city of Kishion mentioned in Joshua 19:20. Kedesh of Issachar would be in the right vicinity, however, near the southwestern shore of the Sea of Galilee and approximately 10 miles from Mount Tabor.

Deborah accompanies Barak just as she said she would.

D. The Action (v. 14)

14. And Deborah said unto Barak, Up; for this is the day in which the LORD hath delivered Sisera into thine hand: is not the LORD gone out before thee? So Barak went down from mount Tabor, and ten thousand men after him.

The time comes for battle. Barak advances the army when Deborah gives the command. The term *Up* is a call to action (also Judges 5:12). The Lord uses the same Hebrew word later to prod Gideon to take initiative (7:9). Again, Deborah reminds Barak of the promise God made in 4:6–7: Sisera is delivered into Israel's *hand.*

As brief as it is, the text reveals an unusual military maneuver. Barak and Israel's 10,000 soldiers are in a strong defensive position when stationed on *mount Tabor.* There, they possess the higher ground. When expecting an attack from a skilled foe, one does not usually abandon such a position! But Deborah and Barak aren't waiting for the attack. God directs the army through Deborah, and they take the initiative to strike a blow. Knowing that *the Lord [goes] out before* them is the key to the ensuing victory (compare Deuteronomy 9:3; Psalm 68:7–8).

At first glance, the flat plains beside the Kishon River favor chariots. However, the song of Deborah states that the Kishon River "swept them away" (Judges 5:21). Whether this mishap caused the defeat of Sisera's army or whether the bodies of the defeated were thrown into the river after the battle is difficult to say (compare Exodus 14:23–25).

> **What Do You Think?**
>
> How did Deborah utilize discernment?
>
> **Digging Deeper**
>
> What does discernment look like in your spiritual walk? Your day-to-day life?

II. Jael's Action

(Judges 4:21–22)

In the verses between today's lesson texts, Sisera's army is destroyed by God at the hand of Barak and the Israelite army (Judges 4:15). Sisera manages to escape, but his fortune doesn't last long. He maneuvers to the tent of an ally named Heber the Kenite (4:17). Heber's wife, Jael, invites Sisera in and offers him respite (4:18–19). Exhausted by the battle and 17-mile retreat to Harosheth, Sisera is grateful for the chance to rest safely (4:20).

Jael makes bold decisions and takes the role of leading actor in this segment. She deals with Sisera swiftly and shrewdly.

A. Violent Response (v. 21)

21. Then Jael Heber's wife took a nail of the tent, and took an hammer in her hand, and went softly unto him, and smote the nail into his temples, and fastened it into the ground: for he was fast asleep and weary. So he died.

Sisera assumes safety in Jael's tent and falls asleep. While he rests his battle-weary body, Jael takes advantage of his vulnerable position. She uses a hammer to drive a large spike into Sisera's temple. Jael does not stop with one blow. She continues until the peg is *fastened . . . into the ground.* Sisera's fall happens as Deborah prophesied: at the "hand of a woman" (Judges 4:9; see above).

Modern ethics and law make it difficult to discern the motivation for Jael's actions. She commits treason by assisting Israelite forces (compare Rahab's story in Joshua 2). Jael is sharp-witted, clever, and cunning. By offering Sisera hospitality, gaining his trust, and then turning on him, Jael ensures her safety (see next verse).

B. Prophetic Fulfillment (v. 22)

22a. And, behold, as Barak pursued Sisera, Jael came out to meet him, and said unto him, Come, and I will shew thee the man whom thou seekest.

Jael is undoubtedly aware that *Barak* is not far behind Sisera. Her people, the Kenites, actively worked against Israel at the beginning of the conflict by telling Jabin's army commander, Sisera, the location of the Israelite army (Judges 4:11–12). Therefore, it is easy to imagine that Jael fears the shift in power dynamics following Israel's conquest (4:15–16). Jael is proactive—just like she was with Sisera (4:18)—and preemptively goes out to *meet* Barak. She confidently informs him that she knows where to find Sisera, which is the aim of his current pursuit. In doing so, Jael aligns herself with the winning party. Presumably, Jael believes Barak will turn against her people when he finishes with the Canaanites. We may reasonably infer that Jael's motives align with the hope of protecting her clan.

> **What Do You Think?**
> How do you react to the violence in this story? The whole of Scripture?
> **Digging Deeper**
> Consider Matthew 5:7 and James 2:13. How do you reconcile this story with the New Testament call to mercy?

22b. And when he came into her tent, behold, Sisera lay dead, and the nail was in his temples.

The dramatic event concludes with proof of triumph: Barak enters Jael's *tent* and sees *Sisera* lying there, *dead*. Deborah's words as prophetess are verified. Barak experiences victory through indirect means. He will not return home with honor and praise pointed toward his skill and prowess. He must share the commendation of victory with a Kenite woman (see Judges 5:24–27).

Conclusion

A. Emboldened Leader

When a prophet's words demonstrate truth and accuracy, they confirm the prophet's calling and legitimacy. God proves Deborah's predictions and faithfulness throughout the narrative. Judge Deborah is an emboldened witness of God's fidelity and integrity.

As prophetess, Deborah called Barak to her palm tree to relay God's commands. She boldly informed him he was to go into battle and that God would bring about victory. Her initiative set Barak into action. Deborah remained steadfast despite Barak's doubts and courageously followed him into the war, taking her place in military leadership for the sake of her people. She reminded Barak along the way that God planned their success, serving him through exhortation. She also

Visual for Lesson 1. *Display the visual in a prominent place. Invite students to spend one minute silently reflecting on their answer to the question.*

assisted in discerning the correct timing and movement of the army (the role of both prophet and strategist). After their victory, Deborah led God's people in praise: "Praise ye the Lord for the avenging of Israel, when the people willingly offered themselves" (Judges 5:2). She proved herself a loyal and dutiful deliverer for Israel, continually giving all glory and honor to the Lord.

When the word of the Lord prompted Deborah, she responded with obedience. May her example inspire us all toward deferential submission to God's instructions. Like Deborah, may we encourage others to take God at His word.

B. Prayer

Almighty God, help us remember that the victory is Yours. Thank You for using people of all shapes, sizes, backgrounds, and skills to implement Your will. May You embolden us to answer Your call whenever and however it comes. In Jesus' name we pray. Amen.

C. Thought to Remember

God spoke a faithful word through Deborah.

Visuals FOR THESE LESSONS

The visual pictured in each lesson (example: page 351) is a small reproduction of a large, full-color poster included in the *Adult Resources* packet for the Summer Quarter. Order No. 9780784740637 from your supplier.

Involvement Learning

Enhance your lesson with KJV Bible Student *(from your curriculum supplier) and the reproducible activity page (at www.standardlesson.com or in the back of the* KJV Standard Lesson Commentary Deluxe Edition*).*

Into the Lesson

Form your class into small groups of about six members each. Ask the groups to brainstorm examples of leaders whose egos got in the way of their mission. These may come from politics or government, sports, religion, education, or business and may be current or historical. Ask groups to name specific examples rather than give summaries of the lives or careers of those they choose. After six to eight minutes, call time and ask the groups to share their examples.

Lead into Bible study saying, "Today we will look at a leader who humbly and assertively led her people to accomplish God's mission. We'll consider how to serve Him in obedience like she did."

Into the Word

Prepare a handout containing each of the following statements. (Each sentence is false; the verses noted are for your reference; therefore, do not include them on the handout.)

1. Deborah said, "God has called me to defeat our enemies." [vv. 6–7]
2. Deborah said, "Our enemies are too powerful. God doesn't want us to risk bloodshed by going into battle with them." [v. 7]
3. God hid the enemy of the Israelites from them because He knew the search would make them stronger. [v. 7]
4. Barak had little respect for Deborah, but his only choice was to obey her. [v. 8]
5. Deborah prophesied that her actions would win the battle. [vv. 6–7, 9]
6. Deborah told Barak he'd win because of his great military prowess and strong army. [v. 14]
7. The death of Sisera came about because of Barak's military prowess. [vv. 21–22]

Distribute a pen and handout to every student. Ask students to work within the same groups as above to decide whether each statement is true or false. Ask them to include a verse reference from today's text to support their answers.

Call time after eight to ten minutes, and then lead a discussion comparing each group's answers.

Alternative. Distribute copies of the "Look at the Whole Chapter" exercise from the activity page, which you can download. Have learners work in pairs to complete as indicated.

Ask your class to return to whole-group discussion and answer these questions: 1–What was God's role in the military victory? 2–What was Deborah's role in the victory? 3–What was Barak's role? Then challenge learners to complete the following sentences with a partner: 1–"Deborah showed her submission to God by . . ." 2–"God showed His power through Deborah by . . ." 3–"Deborah served her people by . . ."

After a few minutes, lead into the next section of the lesson by saying, "Let's also consider how Deborah can be an example for each one of us."

Into Life

Write these sentences on the board. Ask volunteers to read each one aloud.

1. God is honored through humble leadership.
2. God's discernment helps us fight our battles best.
3. Leadership comes in all shapes and sizes.

Send your students back to their original small groups to decide how today's Bible story illustrates these truths. Then ask class members, "What's one way that you can follow Deborah's example of heeding God's call to serve others?"

If there's time, let learners share their thoughts in small groups before calling on volunteers to share with the whole class.

Alternative. Distribute copies of the "God Is Calling" exercise from the activity page. Have learners complete it individually in a minute or less before discussing their conclusions in a small group.

Close your classroom time with prayer: "God, help us lead and serve with confidence and grace."

June 14
Lesson 2 (KJV)

Hannah, the Faithful Supplicant

Devotional Reading: Isaiah 49:13–17
Background Scripture: 1 Samuel 1:1–28; 2:1–11, 18–21; 3:1–18

1 Samuel 1:9–20, 25b

9 So Hannah rose up after they had eaten in Shiloh, and after they had drunk. Now Eli the priest sat upon a seat by a post of the temple of the Lord.

10 And she was in bitterness of soul, and prayed unto the Lord, and wept sore.

11 And she vowed a vow, and said, O Lord of hosts, if thou wilt indeed look on the affliction of thine handmaid, and remember me, and not forget thine handmaid, but wilt give unto thine handmaid a man child, then I will give him unto the Lord all the days of his life, and there shall no razor come upon his head.

12 And it came to pass, as she continued praying before the Lord, that Eli marked her mouth.

13 Now Hannah, she spake in her heart; only her lips moved, but her voice was not heard: therefore Eli thought she had been drunken.

14 And Eli said unto her, How long wilt thou be drunken? put away thy wine from thee.

15 And Hannah answered and said, No, my lord, I am a woman of a sorrowful spirit: I have drunk neither wine nor strong drink, but have poured out my soul before the Lord.

16 Count not thine handmaid for a daughter of Belial: for out of the abundance of my complaint and grief have I spoken hitherto.

17 Then Eli answered and said, Go in peace: and the God of Israel grant thee thy petition that thou hast asked of him.

18 And she said, Let thine handmaid find grace in thy sight. So the woman went her way, and did eat, and her countenance was no more sad.

19 And they rose up in the morning early, and worshipped before the Lord, and returned, and came to their house to Ramah: and Elkanah knew Hannah his wife; and the Lord remembered her.

20 Wherefore it came to pass, when the time was come about after Hannah had conceived, that she bare a son, and called his name Samuel, saying, Because I have asked him of the Lord.

25b And [they] brought the child to Eli.

Key Text

Wherefore it came to pass, when the time was come about after Hannah had conceived, that she bare a son, and called his name Samuel, saying, Because I have asked him of the Lord. **—1 Samuel 1:20**

The Testimony of

Faithful Witnesses

Unit 1: Faithful Witnesses Model God's Fidelity

Lessons 1–4

Lesson Aims

After participating in this lesson, each learner will be able to:

1. Describe Hannah's faithfulness in keeping her promise.

2. Explain how vows show the speaker's sincerity and witness to God's generosity.

3. Compose a specific expression of thanksgiving for God's gifts.

Lesson Outline

Introduction

A. Experiencing God's Mercy

We enjoy telling and retelling stories of dogged persistence. Consider Thomas Edison's countless attempts at creating a functioning light bulb, or Walt Disney's commercial failures that gave rise to an entertainment empire. Such stories inspire us to keep trying, even in the face of adversity.

But not all stories of persistence are so grandiose; many are personal. A husband and wife were desperate to have a child, but like many couples, struggled to make that hope a reality. Despite every medical intervention, it appeared their chances were slim. Fears and uncertainty clouded their prayers, and they even felt ashamed for wanting *so badly* what God had not made possible.

My friends' story has a happy ending. After nearly giving up, God granted them a healthy baby girl! Her infant cries were music to their ears. Afterward, one said, "We didn't know if we were praying for the right thing. But we knew that God would show us mercy in one way or another."

B. Lesson Context

The events of today's text occurred late in the period of the Judges, perhaps around 1100 BC. In 1 Samuel 1:1–8, Elkanah is introduced with two wives: Peninnah and Hannah. Elkanah may have been an important individual of the priestly Levitical tribe (1 Chronicles 6:23). Although Elkanah loved Hannah very much, she was unable to bear children (1 Samuel 1:8). Peninnah mocked Hannah, perhaps jealous that Elkanah gave her a greater share of their family's annual sacrifice (1:5–6). Even though Hannah was childless, Elkanah gave her a "worthy portion," the amount typically given to a firstborn son and heir (1:5; see Deuteronomy 21:15–17).

Scripture often frames the ability to conceive children as a capacity under the sole discretion of God (Genesis 29:31; 30:22; 1 Samuel 1:6). This is a perfectly reasonable perspective in an age before medical interventions. Just like the fertility of crops and the success of a harvest, the blessing of bearing children was attributed to God (Psalm 127:3–5). But this left many ancient women in a difficult social position. The anxiety and sorrow of infertility became a special place of God's intervention, often signaling the coming of a remarkable child: Isaac (Genesis 21:1–2); Jacob and Esau (25:21); Joseph (30:23–24); Samson (Judges 13:2–3); and, even later, John the Baptist (Luke 1:13, 24–25). As we examine Hannah's story, we see God's attention turned toward her. The child of her penitent prayers will be a leader for a leaderless generation.

I. Anguished Prayer

(1 Samuel 1:9–16)

A. Eli's Presence (v. 9)

9. So Hannah rose up after they had eaten in Shiloh, and after they had drunk. Now Eli the priest sat upon a seat by a post of the temple of the LORD.

Hannah and her family have traveled to *Shiloh* for an annual sacrifice. They are in the habit of traveling to this sanctuary because of a local festival (Judges 21:19) or a personal desire to make sacrificial offerings to God. The *temple* mentioned here is not Solomon's temple, which won't be built for several years, but rather the tabernacle (Joshua 18:1; Psalm 78:60; compare 2 Samuel 7:6). *Eli the priest* presides over the temporary home for the ark of the covenant (1 Samuel 3:3).

The Bible does not say how Shiloh became the first central location for the Israelites to gather for worship and sacrifice (Joshua 18:1). But the city is mentioned more than 30 times in the Old Testament (Joshua 18:8–10; 22:12; Judges 18:31; etc.) Its eventual destruction is a consequence of disobedience (Jeremiah 7:12, 14; 26:6, 9). God's later abandonment of Shiloh is a prelude to a more permanent sanctuary, a temple in Jerusalem (Psalm 132:13–16).

The eating and drinking described in this verse refer to the sacrifice Hannah's family has traveled to make. Unlike burnt offerings, which are entirely consumed and for God alone (Leviticus 1:9), other kinds of sacrifices are shared and eaten. Therefore, the family eats a portion of the sacrifice together in the presence of God. Thanksgiving and peace offerings must be eaten quickly (7:15–16).

B. Hannah's Plea (vv. 10–11)

10. And she was in bitterness of soul, and prayed unto the LORD, and wept sore.

Hannah's *bitterness of soul* is her distress at being childless (see Lesson Context). Therefore, she seeks a remedy from God, the source of life and breath (Acts 17:25). The underlying Hebrew for *wept sore* is literally, "weeping, she was weeping." This repetition of the verb emphasizes the seriousness of her grief. Hannah's husband has children with his other wife (1 Samuel 1:2). So, God's intervention is a personal request for Hannah. The family line continues without her bearing a child, but she desires fruitfulness for herself.

What Do You Think?

What does it mean to be "in bitterness of soul"? Have you ever felt like this?

Digging Deeper

Why might God allow us to experience grief, bitterness, and anguish? Consider Psalm 34:18; Matthew 5:4; and 2 Corinthians 1:3–4.

11a. And she vowed a vow, and said, O LORD of hosts, if thou wilt indeed look on the affliction of thine handmaid, and remember me, and not forget thine handmaid, but wilt give unto thine handmaid a man child.

The designation *Lord of hosts* recognizes God's absolute power: He stands above countless angels equipped to do His bidding. By contrast, the threefold use of *handmaid* admits powerlessness and subservience before the Almighty. Before God, Hannah offers her faithfulness by making a *vow*. The literal rendering of the underlying Hebrew *vowed a vow* appears elsewhere in the Bible for expressions of deep commitment (see Genesis 28:20; Numbers 21:2; 30:3–4; Deuteronomy 23:21; Judges 11:30; Ecclesiastes 5:4–5). Vow formulas are standard in ancient Near Eastern prayers, not just in Israel. Vows consist of promises to a deity in return for a benefit. A vow becomes a way to seek favor or negotiate with forces beyond human control. The Bible records mixed results in attempts like this to bargain with God (Genesis 28:20–22; compare Judges 11:30–40).

Visual for Lesson 2. *Display this visual as a focal point for prayer. Ask students to take one minute to quietly contemplate the question.*

In this case, readers may sympathize with Hannah, whose motivation is straightforward and personal. Hannah's vow is not made in haste or without a plan to fulfill what is spoken. It is a last-ditch attempt to see her problem solved. Hannah requests that God *not forget* her. She desires the token of God's attention to be the gift of a male child.

11b. Then I will give him unto the Lord all the days of his life, and there shall no razor come upon his head.

Hannah pledges her future son to God's holy service, which may be why she specifically requests a male. Her words resemble the ordinances in Exodus 13:2, 12–15, and 34:19–20, acknowledging that a firstborn belongs to God. Hannah promises a lifelong commitment to God's purposes for her child.

The additional promise never to shave his hair is an indication of a special priestly office connected with the more temporary Nazarite vow (Numbers 6:5; Judges 13:5). Hannah volunteers her hypothetical child, setting him apart as one consecrated from birth. God nowhere says that Hannah's son shall become a Nazarite as He does with Samson's mother (13:2–5). Instead, Hannah seems to draw from the sacred traditions of the Nazarite vow to reinforce her dedication to God and define the purpose of this child's life. Now, if God allows Hannah to give birth, her son will be destined to be an agent of God's righteous purposes. The logic is that by granting a child, God would receive this person back into His service. The gift that God gives is one He also directs.

Desperate Prayers

I remember times when I was so desperate for divine intervention that I wept bitterly through my prayers. One time, many years ago, we were hoping to buy a home. We rented for a while but then desired to have a place to put down solid roots. Before long, our agent found us the perfect house! It had a fenced-in backyard and plenty of space for our family. There was even a doggy door for our family pet.

After we viewed the home, I remember returning to our rental and weeping as I prayed that God would help us purchase that home. I just *knew* it would be a place where our family could thrive. God heard our prayers and worked out every detail! We spent many happy years in that home.

Have you ever cried out to God, asking Him with tears to move on your behalf? Whether we get the answer we desire or not, we may rest assured that God hears our desperation and extends compassion! —B. R.

C. Eli's Assumption (vv. 12–14)

12–13. And it came to pass, as she continued praying before the Lord, that Eli marked her mouth. Now Hannah, she spake in her heart; only her lips moved, but her voice was not heard: therefore Eli thought she had been drunken.

Hannah continues *praying . . . in her heart,* or, in other words, in silence. When Eli notices *her mouth,* he observes the movement of her lips, but he hears no sounds. It is important to note that ancient people usually prayed aloud. In fact, this is the only time that silent prayer is explicitly mentioned in Scripture (contrast with the Spirit's "groanings which cannot be uttered" in Romans 8:26).

The text does not say why Hannah makes a silent prayer and vow, except perhaps because the contents of her prayer are so personal. To fulfill the vow, she would later have to report it to her family and confirm it with Elkanah (see Numbers 30:10–13). But the wordless moving of lips prompts a predictable misunderstanding from the priest. He recently observed her family celebrating a sacrificial dinner, and therefore, he assumes Hannah consumed too much wine and is now acting inappropriately in God's sanctuary. Instead of asking questions or looking for more details, Eli jumps to a hasty conclusion.

14. And Eli said unto her, How long wilt thou be drunken? put away thy wine from thee.

Eli bases his accusation on limited information (for a similar mistaken confusion in the New Testament, see Acts 2:13–15). Therefore, he comes across as insensitive to the prayers of God's people. 1 Samuel 3 further proves Eli's lack of spiritual discernment when he cannot hear God—unlike Hannah's future son.

Eli's insensitivity is also the result of deliberate blindness. His two sons, Hophni and Phinehas, are widely known for scandalously stealing from the Lord's sacrifices (1 Samuel 2:12–17). Eli rebukes his sons privately but does not remove them (2:22–25). Ironically, Eli himself will receive the Lord's rebuke and judgment from the mouth of Hannah's son-to-be (3:11–18; compare 2:27–36; 4:11–18).

> **What Do You Think?**
> Has anyone ever misinterpreted your method of worship before the Lord?
>
> **Digging Deeper**
> How might Hannah's example help you navigate such a situation in the future?

D. Hannah's Grief (vv. 15–16)

15. And Hannah answered and said, No, my lord, I am a woman of a sorrowful spirit: I have drunk neither wine nor strong drink, but have poured out my soul before the Lord.

Hannah firmly denies the accusation, explaining that she has had *neither wine nor strong drink*. Her lack of appetite is previously noted in 1 Samuel 1:7, for she was taunted into sorrow by her rival, Peninnah. Her lack of participation in the sacrificial meal shows she was not drowning her sorrows in food and drink. Fellowship with God might feel hollow compared to her offering of tears. Her response indicates that she knows "pouring" various liquids—like water or wine—is a sacrificial act (see 1 Samuel 7:6; Isaiah 57:6). Hannah has poured out her *soul*, meaning every part of her. She may consider her spilled tears a part of her offering.

16. Count not thine handmaid for a daughter of Belial: for out of the abundance of my complaint and grief have I spoken hitherto.

Belial is a transliteration of a word that occurs 27 times in the Old Testament. "Beliar" (Greek spelling) or "Belial" also appears in the New Testament (2 Corinthians 6:15). In some contexts, this word is treated as the name of a demonic figure—akin to Satan—but the word also reflects a personification of wickedness. It can be translated as "wicked" (example: Deuteronomy 15:9), "evil" (Psalm 41:8), etc. Again, an ironic twist comes in 1 Samuel 2:12, where nearly the same description—"sons of Belial"—describes Eli's two sons. The evil that Hannah denies already resides in Eli's household.

Hannah is no such wicked person. Her prayers are earnest, and her vow pours from an abundance of sadness and emptiness. Her genuine supplication to God and persistence attest to a pure, guileless soul who submits to God's most excellent plan.

II. Kindled Hope

(1 Samuel 1:17–20)

A. Eli Blesses (v. 17)

17. Then Eli answered and said, Go in peace: and the God of Israel grant thee thy petition that thou hast asked of him.

Whether out of sincerity or embarrassment at being so wrong, Eli's response is a straightforward blessing. He is instrumental in the birth of his replacement. Numbers 6:23–27 sets a precedent for priestly blessings. So, like the Aaronic priesthood, Eli blesses Hannah in the name of the Lord. Specifically, he asks that she receive an answer to her *petition*. Either Eli guesses her request, or his ignorance does not matter. Eli has no power to grant the request, but he adds himself to the petition on Hannah's behalf, asking God to pay close attention to her prayers.

What Do You Think?

Eli blesses Hannah from his position as a priest. Who has the authority to bless in modern Christianity? Explain your answer.

Digging Deeper

Why might we need the blessing of someone else in the process of our petitions?

B. Hannah Revives (v. 18)

18. And she said, Let thine handmaid find grace in thy sight. So the woman went her way, and did eat, and her countenance was no more sad.

Variations of the phrase *find grace in thy sight* occur two dozen times in the Old Testament. The phrase appears in contexts where humans seek right standing with God or with one another (examples: Numbers 11:15; 1 Samuel 20:29). Hannah is pleased to have Eli's favor, but she is even more concerned that Eli's blessing will come to pass—that God will respond. Although Eli possesses no power to bring about the blessing he voiced, he is a priest of God, and Hannah treats him with great respect.

Hannah's decision to *eat* at this point indicates that her outlook has shifted. She is no longer focused on the jealous antagonism of her counterpart, Peninnah. Since Hannah has hope that God has heard her petitions, she can eat and return to the regular rhythms of her life.

Answer on the Way

Recently, my husband and I were waiting for a check to arrive. We didn't know exactly when it would be sent, so we checked the mailbox daily—to no avail. We felt frustrated and defeated. Finally, we contacted the sender to ask about the check, and they informed us that it was going out in the mail the following day. It hadn't left their office yet! Once we knew the check was in the mail, we no longer worried about it. We trusted that it would arrive soon.

Sometimes, we look for answers to prayer like checking the mailbox. With frustration and angst, we seek immediate answers. But having faith in God requires that we trust Him and His timing. We may rest assured that the answer—"yes" or "no"—is coming. If we trust Him, we may release worry; He's got the outcome handled. Are you trusting that the answers you seek are on the way? Are you living in the reality of provision or "staring at the mailbox" in frustration? —B. R.

C. The Lord Remembers (vv. 19–20)

19. And they rose up in the morning early, and worshipped before the LORD, and returned, and came to their house to Ramah: and Elkanah knew Hannah his wife; and the LORD remembered her.

The family's home is in Ramah, which is the shortened title of "Ramathaimzophim, of mount Ephraim" (1 Samuel 1:1). The straight-line distance between there and Shiloh is about 18 miles. To make this difficult trek, one must get underway *early* in the *morning.* Before the family departs, they offer worship to God, which is another confirmation of their devotion.

After they return home, Elkanah *knew Hannah his wife*, which is a polite way to say that the couple had intimate relations. The phrase *the LORD remembered her* does not mean that God had forgotten something, as humans might. It means that God attended to the words of her request and brought about the long-awaited result (compare Genesis 8:1; 9:15; Exodus 2:24; etc.). In this case,

How to Say It

Belial	*Bee*-li-ul.
Beliar	Beh-lee-*ar*.
Eli	*Ee*-lye.
Elkanah	*El*-kuh-nuh or El-*kay*-nuh.
Ephraim	*Ee*-fray-im.
Hophni	*Hoff*-nye.
Nazarite	*Naz*-uh-rite.
Peninnah	Peh-*nin*-uh.
Phinehas	*Fin*-ee-us.
Ramah	*Ray*-muh.
Ramathaimzophim	*Ray*-muh-***thay***-im–***zo***-fim.

it means that the couple's intimacy results in the conception of a child.

20. Wherefore it came to pass, when the time was come about after Hannah had conceived, that she bare a son, and called his name Samuel, saying, Because I have asked him of the Lord.

Like many important births in the Bible, Samuel's miraculous birth demonstrates that God's hand is on the boy's life. Although previously barren like Sarah and Rachel (see Lesson Context), Hannah receives a son despite her previous hopelessness.

Many names in Scripture signal something important about the person. The name of Hannah's son is no different. She has a particular meaning in mind. *Samuel* is a combination of two words: the two final letters *el* are a Hebrew word for "God" (*the Lord* in Hannah's explanation), and the first part of the name sounds like the Hebrew word for "ask." Hannah intended Samuel's name to remind everyone that he exists *because* . . . Hannah *asked him of the Lord.*

III. Fulfilled Vow

(1 Samuel 1:25b)

25b. And [they] brought the child to Eli.

Bringing Samuel to live in the sanctuary at Shiloh seems peculiar since Elkanah—and, by extension, his son Samuel—dwell in Ephraim (1 Samuel 1:1). But Hannah and Elkanah dedicate Samuel to the Lord in a particular way, one that requires his service in apprenticeship to the priest who blessed his birth.

Hannah upholds her end of the promise and fulfills her vow. Her faithfulness results in further blessings. 1 Samuel 2 tells us that she visits Samuel yearly (1 Samuel 2:19), Eli continues to bless her and Elkanah (2:20), and she bears five additional children (2:21). She disappears from the narrative after 1 Samuel 2:10, but her extraordinary child does not! He becomes the embodiment of his mother's faith. Samuel becomes a transitional figure in the history of ancient Israel, the end of the line of judges and the first of the prophets (Acts 3:24; 13:20; Hebrews 11:32).

What Do You Think?

Compare (1) the dedication of Samuel to holy service by Hannah and Elkanah with (2) Abraham's willingness to sacrifice Isaac (Genesis 22:1–12).

Digging Deeper

What does it take for someone to follow through with such loyalty and commitment?

Conclusion

A. Playing Our Parts

Hannah faithfully approached God with her grief, desire, and need. Because she did, God allowed her to play a role in the grand narrative of God's design. Hannah's fidelity to her vow put her son in the right place at the right time to lead Israel as a priest, judge, and prophet.

Hannah models faithfulness in prayer, bravery in the face of false accusations, and dedication to her word. She asks God for her heart's desire and then willingly returns that gift to God. Every mother knows the strength required to follow through with such a vow! May we all learn to have such faithfulness, submission, trust, and generosity in our relationships with God.

What Do You Think?

How does Hannah's faithfulness inspire you toward greater faith?

Digging Deeper

What steps do you sense God asking you to take toward deeper prayer, faith, loyalty, or courage?

B. Prayer

Heavenly Father, God of impossible things, thank You for Your miraculous provisions. May we relish them with delight while they are ours and release them back to You when required. In Jesus' name we pray. Amen.

C. Thought to Remember

God listens and gives good gifts.

Involvement Learning

Enhance your lesson with KJV Bible Student *(from your curriculum supplier) and the reproducible activity page (at www.standardlesson.com or in the back of the* KJV Standard Lesson Commentary Deluxe Edition*).*

Into the Lesson

Display the following sentence for students to notice as they arrive: "Vows don't mean much anymore." Divide the class into groups of four to six. Ask one half of the groups to come up with reasons in support of this statement. Ask the other half to list reasons against it. After a few minutes, ask a volunteer from each group to state their best reason. Alternate between the two sides until everyone agrees that their lists are exhausted. Then ask the class to decide together whether they agree or disagree with the statement.

Alternative. Play a short clip of General Douglas MacArthur's "I Shall Return Speech" during World War II. Then discuss: What happened because MacArthur kept his vow? What might have happened if he hadn't?

Lead into Bible study by saying, "Our text today narrates one of the best-known vows in all of Scripture. Let's discover what it meant for one young woman to make a vow."

Into the Word

Distribute a handout (you create) that contains the following questions based on today's text. Ask a volunteer to read 1 Samuel 1:9–20, 25b out loud. Then direct class members to work in the same groups as before. They may find answers to these questions from lesson resources or outside sources like study Bibles, the internet, etc. Give students ten minutes to jot down their answers before discussing the list of questions with the whole class.

Questions: 1–Where did Eli sit, and why? 2–Why was Hannah's anguish so severe? 3–Why would Hannah not let a razor touch her son's head? 4–What do Eli's responses to Hannah say about him? 5–Why did Eli's words comfort her? 6–What part did Eli play in allowing Hannah to fulfill her vow? 7–What do we conclude about Hannah because of her petition and vow?

Summarize, or ask a volunteer to summarize, the events described in 1 Samuel 1:21–24 and explain their significance. (Example: Samuel lived with Hannah for quite a while. He was no longer an infant, but a little boy, when she took him to Eli. Hannah and Samuel had surely developed a strong bond in that time.) Ask the class to brainstorm a list of emotions or feelings Hannah must have had as she prepared to keep her vow. Discuss, "Do you think Hannah would have taken Samuel to Eli if she hadn't made the vow?"

Option. Read Hannah's prayer of praise that is recorded in 1 Samuel 2:1–10, or play a recording of the prayer set to music. Discuss, "How is this prayer a fitting climax to the sacrifice Hannah willingly made?"

Option. Distribute copies of the "Two Prayers" exercise from the activity page, which you can download. Ask students to work in groups for eight or ten minutes to complete as indicated. Then ask volunteers to share their responses.

Into Life

Mount butcher paper on the walls of your classroom and provide felt markers or crayons for class members to use. Encourage students to use the butcher paper to write down (or draw a picture depicting) one or two specific gifts God has given them. Ask students to draw circles around each item they received as an answer to a specific prayer.

After several minutes, ask volunteers to discuss what they wrote or drew. Start with gifts that they received as a direct answer to prayer.

Option 1. Ask students to return to their groups. Instruct groups to write a song of thanksgiving to God using the tune of a familiar chorus. Ask them to include some of the specific gifts mentioned in your class discussion.

Option 2. Distribute copies of the "My Prayer" exercise from the activity page. Ask students to complete it as indicated.

Ask for a volunteer to close class with prayer.

Jonathan and David, Resolute Friends

Devotional Reading: Proverbs 27:6, 10–11, 17, 19
Background Scripture: 1 Samuel 19:1–7; 20:1–42; 2 Samuel 1:17–27

1 Samuel 18:1–4

1 And it came to pass, when he had made an end of speaking unto Saul, that the soul of Jonathan was knit with the soul of David, and Jonathan loved him as his own soul.

2 And Saul took him that day, and would let him go no more home to his father's house.

3 Then Jonathan and David made a covenant, because he loved him as his own soul.

4 And Jonathan stripped himself of the robe that was upon him, and gave it to David, and his garments, even to his sword, and to his bow, and to his girdle.

1 Samuel 20:16–17, 32–34, 42

16 So Jonathan made a covenant with the house of David, saying, Let the LORD even require it at the hand of David's enemies.

17 And Jonathan caused David to swear again, because he loved him: for he loved him as he loved his own soul.

---

32 And Jonathan answered Saul his father, and said unto him, Wherefore shall he be slain? what hath he done?

33 And Saul cast a javelin at him to smite him: whereby Jonathan knew that it was determined of his father to slay David.

34 So Jonathan arose from the table in fierce anger, and did eat no meat the second day of the month: for he was grieved for David, because his father had done him shame.

---

42 And Jonathan said to David, Go in peace, forasmuch as we have sworn both of us in the name of the LORD, saying, The LORD be between me and thee, and between my seed and thy seed for ever. And he arose and departed: and Jonathan went into the city.

2 Samuel 1:26–27

26 I am distressed for thee, my brother Jonathan: very pleasant hast thou been unto me: thy love to me was wonderful, passing the love of women.

27 How are the mighty fallen, and the weapons of war perished!

2 Samuel 21:7

7 But the king spared Mephibosheth, the son of Jonathan the son of Saul, because of the LORD's oath that was between them, between David and Jonathan the son of Saul.

Key Text

Jonathan said to David, Go in peace, forasmuch as we have sworn both of us in the name of the LORD, saying, The LORD be between me and thee, and between my seed and thy seed for ever. And he arose and departed: and Jonathan went into the city. **—1 Samuel 20:42**

The Testimony of Faithful Witnesses

Unit 1: Faithful Witnesses Model God's Fidelity

Lessons 1–4

Lesson Aims

After participating in this lesson, each learner will be able to:

1. Identify the ways David and Jonathan show loyalty to one another.
2. Explain the significance of the covenant between David and Jonathan.
3. Plan a way to show love and loyalty to a friend or community member in the week ahead.

Lesson Outline

Introduction

A. Rivals Turned Friends

B. Lesson Context

I. Unexpected Friend (1 Samuel 18:1–4)

A. In Saul's Household (vv. 1–2)

B. Saul's Heir (vv. 3–4)

Productive Friendships

II. Unwavering Alliance (1 Samuel 20:16–17, 32–34, 42)

A. Expanded Covenant (vv. 16–17)

B. Honorable Defense (vv. 32–34)

Your Cultivation Record

C. Permanent Peace (v. 42)

III. Unbroken Promise (2 Samuel 1:26–27; 21:7)

A. Lament for the Dead (1:26–27)

B. Compassion for the Living (21:7)

Conclusion

A. New Covenant Loyalty

B. Prayer

C. Thought to Remember

Introduction

A. Rivals Turned Friends

C. S. Lewis and J. R. R. Tolkien's friendship is no secret to their readers. Each was an English professor at Merton College in Oxford during the 1920s, 30s, and 40s. They met during a faculty meeting in 1926 and went on to enjoy forty years of mutual encouragement and support. Tolkien played a vital role in Lewis's Christian conversion, and Lewis pressed Tolkien to finish several important writing projects.

Although they each held literary aspirations, their initial impression of one another was sour. Their different interests and personalities—combined with initially contradictory religious beliefs—made conflict and rivalry seem inevitable. But over time, the two set aside their differences and recognized their shared passions for curriculum, language, and creative writing. The pair developed such a strong bond that Tolkien would later refer to Lewis's death as leaving a permanent wound in his heart.

Today's lesson considers another famous friendship. Their relationship shows loyalty to one another and God.

B. Lesson Context

The books of 1 & 2 Samuel introduce three key figures: Samuel, Saul, and David. The boy Samuel grew up to be an important transitional figure, taking Israel from the era of judges to the time of Israel's united monarchy (see lesson 2). He first anointed Saul, then David as king (1 Samuel 10:1; 16:13). Kings at this time (eleventh century BC) were seen especially as military protectors, able to lead their subjects in battle (example: 8:11–12).

Before Saul's disastrous rule ended, God prepared David to take over as leader in Saul's place. The secret anointing of David and plan to make him king created a potential conflict with Saul and his household, especially with Saul's firstborn son and heir, Jonathan. Jonathan had the most to lose and could have easily rejected God's choice of king.

Jonathan is first mentioned in 1 Samuel 13–14, where he proves to be an impressive captain of fighting men himself. In one exploit, Jonathan and his armor-bearer manage to single-handedly defeat about twenty Philistines, turning the tide in favor of the Israelites (1 Samuel 14:1–14). Jonathan speaks like a virtuous leader, one who knows "there is no restraint to the Lord to save by many or by few" (14:6; compare 17:45).

But God's choice of David, "a man after [God's] own heart" (1 Samuel 13:14), interrupts the dynastic rule and demonstrates that God is in charge. Both then and in the future, the rise and fall of rulers and empires is subject to God's control (see Daniel 7:27).

I. Unexpected Friend

(1 Samuel 18:1–4)

This chapter begins right after David has defeated Goliath and proved himself a heroic fighter willing to defend the reputation of God. King Saul responds by inviting the young shepherd boy to meet with him while David still holds the head of Goliath (1 Samuel 17:57)!

A. In Saul's Household (vv. 1–2)

1. And it came to pass, when he had made an end of speaking unto Saul, that the soul of Jonathan was knit with the soul of David, and Jonathan loved him as his own soul.

After David introduces himself (1 Samuel 17:58), this verse leaves the impression that more is said—perhaps an account of the duel with Goliath and David's victory. These words are enough to win over the heart of Jonathan, who is with Saul and listening. The verb *knit* means to join things together, in this case, joining *the soul of Jonathan* to *the soul of David*. This refers to Jonathan's love for the man, who has just taken it upon himself to fight a Philistine champion. Whereas Saul was willing to arm David and to give him the traditional means to fight, this proved useless (1 Samuel 17:38–39). Saul showed no willingness to lead or to fight for God's people, which confirms David's superiority as the future king.

In Hebrew, the term for *love* is broad and flexible enough to apply to numerous human relationships: father and son (Genesis 22:2), mother and son (25:28), mother and daughter-in-law (Ruth 4:15), husband and wife (Hosea 3:1), and people for their leader (1 Samuel 18:16). The last example is particularly relevant in this context, as it describes the general sentiment already growing in Israel and Judah, as the people acclaim the leadership potential of David.

What makes this expression of devotion for David unique is its source: Saul's own son from the royal household! If David proves able to win over the support of Jonathan, he must be a charismatic and compelling figure, capable of winning people over with the wisdom of his words.

2. And Saul took him that day, and would let him go no more home to his father's house.

Saul knows his kingship is ending, as God has chosen a different person to lead Israel (1 Samuel 13:14; 15:26–28). That realization colors how we read this text and provides at least two reasons for Saul's keeping David from returning *home to his father's house* in Bethlehem, only a few miles away (15:34).

On the one hand, Saul's hospitality gives the impression of graciousness; he treats David as if he is becoming one of the king's advisors by rewarding and consulting him. On the other hand, this hospitality gives Saul time to assess David's growing popularity (see 1 Samuel 18:7). Keeping David close enables Saul to control him and prevent his reputation from growing. Ultimately, Saul will try to entrap and eliminate David by sending him into battle (18:17).

B. Saul's Heir (vv. 3–4)

3. Then Jonathan and David made a covenant, because he loved him as his own soul.

The word *covenant* appears hundreds of times in the Old Testament. It refers to a formalized agreement between two parties, usually with obligations for each to fulfill. The most famous covenants of the Bible are between God and His people (examples: Genesis 9:9–11; 15:17–19; Exodus 19:5–6; 24:7–8). Covenants can also occur between two groups of people and serve as treaties of mutual benefit (example: Genesis 21:22–24, 32). In some cases, a weaker side may be forced to promise obedience and military support in exchange for safety (example: Ezekiel 17:13–14).

What stands out from the exchange between *Jonathan* and *David* is that Jonathan appears to be the stronger party, given that he is the heir to the throne. Typically, one would expect a king's son to demand support from others, perhaps pressuring a national hero to back his future kingship. Instead, the words of this verse repeat the same wording of 1 Samuel 18:1 (above): Jonathan *loved* David *as his own soul*. Jonathan is the subject, and it leaves the impression that he is the one to initiate an alliance, seemingly with little concern for his own future.

The same impression—that Jonathan was the one to initiate a covenant against self-interests—emerges from later retellings of this event (1 Samuel 20:8, 16–17). Saul will eventually hear of this and grow incensed, describing it as a conspiracy against him (22:8). In fact, Jonathan's choice to support David places him in agreement with God's call (see 16:12). The biblical text does not tell us how God worked on the heart of Jonathan, whether he learned of David's secret anointing or whether God simply gave David favor in his eyes (compare Exodus 12:36). Perhaps Jonathan perceived that the Spirit of God was upon David, empowering him for his future role as king (1 Samuel 16:13).

4. And Jonathan stripped himself of the robe that was upon him, and gave it to David, and his garments, even to his sword, and to his bow, and to his girdle.

Visual for Lesson 3. *Display this visual as you ask participants to spend one minute in silent prayer of thanksgiving for a loyal friend.*

Jonathan's gifts hold significant meaning. In ancient times, royals were identified by their fine robes, a stark contrast to David's shepherd garments. By wearing royal robes, *David* would be associated with the royal entourage, foreshadowing his later ascension. If Jonathan's *garments* identified him as the prince of Israel and successor to the throne, then giving them away is like giving up his ambition to rule.

What Do You Think?

What could be some modern equivalents of the way Jonathan expressed friendship with David? Why?

Digging Deeper

Consider both non-material things and tangible objects. Be prepared to explain the nature of the equivalence.

Productive Friendships

Years ago, we lived next door to a professional tennis doubles player. We saw her returning from practice each day, and she would frequently share insights about the rigor of training. She emphasized that finding the right partner was crucial, as well as recognizing the potential for a powerful partnership after more practice. Speed, technique, and strategy all had to align—or at least be complementary—for the pair to be effective.

Players spend hours training together to perfect their game and to learn how to anticipate a partner's moves. They learn to communicate effectively and to cover each other's weaknesses. Furthermore, partners need to be compatible off the court, willing to have one another's backs.

This prompts me to think about friendships in general and what it means to be committed to another person's success as if it were your own. What criteria are important to you in a productive friendship? —N. V.

II. Unwavering Alliance

(1 Samuel 20:16–17, 32–34, 42)

Saul tries to manipulate David by inviting him to marry into the family. David is nonetheless able to escape, and he proves fearsome to Israel's enemies (1 Samuel 18:22–30). Meanwhile, Jonathan stands up for David until Saul swears an oath that he shall not harm the man (19:1–7). However, Saul breaks his oath and again tries to kill David, sending him on the run (19:9–12). David is now at the mercy of Jonathan, who could easily reveal his location and help Saul's men find him.

A. Expanded Covenant (vv. 16–17)

16. So Jonathan made a covenant with the house of David, saying, Let the LORD even require it at the hand of David's enemies.

The word that begins this verse, *so*, refers to Jonathan's request in 1 Samuel 20:14–15, where he looks forward to a time when David will be without enemies. In exchange for helping David, Jonathan requests future kindness for his own family (1 Samuel 20:15). To solidify the commitment between the two men, Jonathan expands the scope of their initial bond.

This time, the *covenant* is between Jonathan and *the house of David*. The Hebrew word translated as "house" can mean more than just the physical structure; it also refers to the people who inhabit a home—residents of the entire household, including immediate and extended family (example: Joshua 24:15). Additionally, in the context of royal dynasties, a "house" includes future descendants and those who will rule as king (examples: 1 Kings 12:26; Isaiah 7:2). Jonathan's request acknowledges the significance of David's lineage, as it was common practice to eliminate the family of rivals after defeating or removing them (example: 2 Kings 10:11; compare Matthew 2:16–18).

To signify the seriousness of his commitment, Jonathan invokes the Lord's authority and oversight: *Let the Lord even require it*. Jonathan expects *David's enemies* to be the instruments of holding each man to this bond. For other oaths that anticipate God's intervention, see Genesis 24:3; 50:25; 1 Samuel 14:28; and Nehemiah 5:12.

17. And Jonathan caused David to swear again, because he loved him: for he loved him as he loved his own soul.

This verse concludes the narrative that began in 1 Samuel 18:1. *Jonathan* receives a commitment from *David*, and each man promises to protect the other's family. Jonathan loves David as he loves *his own soul*, demonstrating Jonathan's commitment to protecting this person who is favored by God, even at personal risk.

> **What Do You Think?**
> When have you experienced a friendship like that of David and Jonathan?
>
> **Digging Deeper**
> In what ways did your friendship demonstrate unity and love?

B. Honorable Defense (vv. 32–34)

32. And Jonathan answered Saul his father, and said unto him, Wherefore shall he be slain? what hath he done?

Saul is concerned that David is a threat to the king's throne and dynastic lineage. Jonathan's words here are a response to Saul's desperate threat: as long as David lives, *Jonathan* will not inherit the throne (1 Samuel 20:31).

33. And Saul cast a javelin at him to smite him: whereby Jonathan knew that it was determined of his father to slay David.

This attempt on Jonathan's life mirrors Saul's earlier attempt to kill David (1 Samuel 19:10). To this point, *Jonathan* was still holding out hope that *Saul* would not try to kill *David*. He did not think his father had wicked intentions (20:2). However, this attempted murder exposes Saul's anger and paranoia after Samuel had proclaimed that Saul's kingdom would be torn away (13:14; 15:26).

34. So Jonathan arose from the table in fierce anger, and did eat no meat the second day of the month: for he was grieved for David, because his father had done him shame.

How to Say It

Bethlehem	*Beth*-lih-hem.
Goliath	Go-*lye*-uth.
Mephibosheth	Meh-*fib*-o-sheth.
Philistines	Fuh-*liss*-teenz or *Fill*-us-teenz.

Now aware that his father is capable of murder, *Jonathan* grieves instead of eating and celebrating at the New Moon festival (1 Samuel 20:5, 18, 24; compare Numbers 28:11–15). Saul has crossed a line of no return, bringing *shame* upon the family.

What Do You Think?

Have you ever had to choose between loyalty to a friend and loyalty to someone else? How did you handle it?

Digging Deeper

When have you been on the receiving end of a friend's loyalty and love? How did you respond?

Your Cultivation Record

I'll never forget that scorching summer day in northern California. Our group of four friends was relaxing on the bank of the Sacramento River. Seeking relief from the heat, we decided it would be fun to use our small inflatables to float the river. The first part was slow and peaceful, but the current picked up speed as water from the mountain joined the flow. The river tossed us around, hurled us over rocks, and made us fear for our lives. Before we knew it, we were thrown upon the bank with our inflatables nowhere in sight.

To our collective horror, we had lost sight of one person: my (now) husband, Ryan. Before I could call out his name, his best friend Mark spotted him and was already swimming upstream to rescue him. I remember the look on Mark's face. He battled the current and ducked under branches to reach his friend, who was clinging to a tree near the riverbank. Mark didn't think twice about the danger to himself.

Without a doubt, Mark saved Ryan's life that day. But sacrifices in friendship don't just happen when someone is in deadly peril. Even when we aren't risking life and limb, we often have to set our personal needs aside. Are you willing to sacrifice for others, or do you think first of your own comfort and safety? —N. V.

C. Permanent Peace (v. 42)

42. And Jonathan said to David, Go in peace, forasmuch as we have sworn both of us in the name of the Lord, saying, The Lord be between me and thee, and between my seed and thy seed for ever. And he arose and departed: and Jonathan went into the city.

Jonathan carries out a plan to communicate secretly with *David* (1 Samuel 20:5–8, 18–23). Now that he has become aware of Saul's murderous rage, Jonathan takes steps to ensure David's escape. He leaves his friend with a greeting of *peace*—the Hebrew word *shalom*—and recalls their commitments. The phrase *between my seed and thy seed* repeats the terms of their promise to seek the safety of each respective family (compare Genesis 9:12; 17:7–10). After this meeting, David would remain separated from Jonathan until Jonathan's death.

III. Unbroken Promise

(2 Samuel 1:26–27, 21:7)

The remaining chapters of 1 Samuel record Saul's pursuit of David, David's sparing of Saul's life (twice), the death of Samuel, David's hiding among the Philistines, and the eventual death of Saul and his sons in battle—including Jonathan (1 Samuel 31:1–2). The book of 2 Samuel covers David's forty-year reign, but it begins with a time of mourning.

A. Lament for the Dead (1:26–27)

26. I am distressed for thee, my brother Jonathan: very pleasant hast thou been unto me: thy love to me was wonderful, passing the love of women.

After Jonathan's death, David composes a lament for both the fallen prince and his father, Saul (2 Samuel 1:19–27). A lament is a song that expresses pain, loss, and uncertainty (compare Psalm 6). This response is consistent with David's honorable treatment of God's anointed—even when the king tried to kill David (1 Samuel 24:6; 26:11).

The poetic expression of *love* in this verse can easily be misconstrued. As noted in the comments on 1 Samuel 18:1, loving relationships are often nonsexual. Although this verse compares David's love for Jonathan to *the love of women*—meaning romantic love—the point is that David and Jonathan's bond is either unlike or even stronger than the bonds of a romantic relationship. The English idiom describing close friends as "thick as thieves" expresses a similar idea. It does not mean that two friends have literally become partners in thievery, but rather that their friendship is very close.

David calls Jonathan *my brother*, which is more than just artistic expression. Their families were united when David married Saul's daughter Michal (1 Samuel 18:20–27).

27. How are the mighty fallen, and the weapons of war perished!

This concludes the lament. The phrase *weapons of war* is a reference to Saul and Jonathan, who have fallen in battle. This is an especially poignant metaphor after Saul was killed by falling upon his own sword (1 Samuel 31:4–6).

David's second anointing follows (2 Samuel 2:1–7; compare 1 Samuel 16:13; 1 Chronicles 11:1–3), but there is little room for triumph.

What Do You Think?

What line from David's song of lament in 2 Samuel 1:19–27 stands out to you? Why?

Digging Deeper

What steps can a believer take to process the grief that comes from losing a close friend?

B. Compassion for the Living (21:7)

7. But the king spared Mephibosheth, the son of Jonathan the son of Saul, because of the Lord's oath that was between them, between David and Jonathan the son of Saul.

After ascending to the throne, David, *the king*, honors his covenant with his now-deceased friend. Details of David's kindness to *Mephibosheth, the son of Jonathan* are recounted in 2 Samuel 9. This graciousness toward Jonathan's disabled son is even more remarkable given that the rest of Saul's house has been at war with David (2 Samuel 3:1). Even after Jonathan's death, David remembers and honors his commitments.

Conclusion

A. New Covenant Loyalty

Friendship, like that between David and Jonathan, doesn't just happen—it must be cultivated. The world has a way of predisposing people toward self-gain and narcissism, leaving us disinclined to connect with one another, much less show the kind of loyalty that Jonathan shows at his own expense.

But the church can become a place where people are willing to serve one another sacrificially. It begins with individuals who look beyond their own needs. Simple acts of friendship and loyalty can make a difference: inviting someone to coffee, checking in with a friend, sharing a meal, and keeping confidences are just a few examples. These simple actions can open the door to a deeper relationship wherein both people recognize the dignity of the other and serve one another under Christ.

This is not a foolproof strategy; some will not reciprocate. But Christians are called to hospitality (Romans 12:13; 1 Timothy 5:10; Hebrews 13:2; 3 John 8; see lesson 13), even generosity and love for enemies (Proverbs 25:21; Matthew 5:43–44). If kindness goes unreciprocated, it remains kindness well-spent.

What Do You Think?

In what ways has this study of David and Jonathan inspired you to develop friendships that are like family (compare Proverbs 18:24)?

Digging Deeper

What actions will you take to develop such friendships?

B. Prayer

Heavenly Father, lead us to create unshakable bonds of friendship like we see between David and Jonathan. Help us to be faithful and loyal to one another, even when it is difficult. Build us into healthy communities through which You carry out Your work. In Jesus' name we pray. Amen.

C. Thought to Remember

Honor God in your friendships.

Involvement Learning

Enhance your lesson with KJV Bible Student *(from your curriculum supplier) and the reproducible activity page (at www.standardlesson.com or in the back of the* KJV Standard Lesson Commentary Deluxe Edition*).*

Into the Lesson

Write the following open-ended sentences on the board for participants to see as they enter class:

Friendship is wonderful because . . .
Friendship is difficult because . . .
Friendship is necessary because . . .
Friendships may not last because . . .
Friendships for a lifetime are special because . . .

Divide your class into pairs or triads and ask each to choose one of the sentences to complete. After calling time, ask volunteers to share how they completed each sentence.

Lead into Bible study by saying, "Today we'll study one of the most significant examples of deep friendship we see in Scripture. We'll find ideas for nurturing our friendships."

Into the Word

Recruit three volunteers to explain the context for this week's lesson by preparing a 90-second story beginning with one of these phrases:

Let me tell you about Saul
Let me tell you about David
Let me tell you about Jonathan
Let me tell you about Mephibosheth

After their presentations, have the lesson's Scripture texts read aloud. Then ask the following question for discussion: "Why was David and Jonathan's covenant with each other significant?" Then present a brief lecture that explains David and Jonathan's whole story and provides details not included in today's printed text. Be sure to answer the question you've displayed.

Write the following phrases as headers on the board:

How David showed loyalty to Jonathan
How Jonathan showed loyalty to David

Divide the class into two groups and assign one phrase to each group. Ask them to reread the Scripture text and come up with responses to the written prompt. After several minutes, allow volunteers to share responses. Continue discussing until all the possible answers are mentioned.

Alternative. Distribute copies of the "A Friend Is . . ." exercise from the activity page, which you can download. Have participants work in pairs to complete as indicated before discussing conclusions with the whole class.

Option. Refer back to the open-ended sentences used during Into the Lesson activity. Ask class members to identify how the sentences could be completed with David and Jonathan's friendship in mind. (example: "David and Jonathan's friendship was wonderful because . . ."). Allow participants to discuss among themselves before calling time and reviewing responses with the whole class. Write summary statements for each of these new sentences on the board.

Into Life

Divide the class into small groups of three or four participants. Ask them to share with each other about a close friend, how they met, and how that relationship has grown and matured over time. Distribute an index card and pen to each participant. Ask them to write down one way to show love and loyalty to this friend in the upcoming week. After one minute, ask participants to share with their small group.

Alternative. Distribute copies of the "Showing Loyalty" exercise from the activity page. Have participants work with a partner to complete the activity as indicated.

After calling time for either activity, have groups or pairs present their responses to the whole class. Conclude class time by asking class members to remain in their small groups or pairs and pray for opportunities to serve and love their friends in the upcoming weeks.

Amos, the Courageous Prophet

Devotional Reading: Psalm 23
Background Scripture: Amos 1:1; 2:6–16; 3:1–15; 7:10–17

Amos 1:1

1 The words of Amos, who was among the herdmen of Tekoa, which he saw concerning Israel in the days of Uzziah king of Judah, and in the days of Jeroboam the son of Joash king of Israel, two years before the earthquake.

Amos 2:11–12

11 And I raised up of your sons for prophets, and of your young men for Nazarites. Is it not even thus, O ye children of Israel? saith the LORD.

12 But ye gave the Nazarites wine to drink; and commanded the prophets, saying, Prophesy not.

Amos 3:7–8

7 Surely the Lord GOD will do nothing, but he revealeth his secret unto his servants the prophets.

8 The lion hath roared, who will not fear? the Lord GOD hath spoken, who can but prophesy?

Amos 7:10–15

10 Then Amaziah the priest of Bethel sent to Jeroboam king of Israel, saying, Amos hath conspired against thee in the midst of the house of Israel: the land is not able to bear all his words.

11 For thus Amos saith, Jeroboam shall die by the sword, and Israel shall surely be led away captive out of their own land.

12 Also Amaziah said unto Amos, O thou seer, go, flee thee away into the land of Judah, and there eat bread, and prophesy there:

13 But prophesy not again any more at Bethel: for it is the king's chapel, and it is the king's court.

14 Then answered Amos, and said to Amaziah, I was no prophet, neither was I a prophet's son; but I was an herdman, and a gatherer of sycomore fruit:

15 And the LORD took me as I followed the flock, and the LORD said unto me, Go, prophesy unto my people Israel.

Key Text

The LORD took me as I followed the flock, and the LORD said unto me, Go, prophesy unto my people Israel.

—Amos 7:15

The Testimony of

Faithful Witnesses

Unit 1: Faithful Witnesses Model God's Fidelity

Lessons 1–4

Lesson Aims

After participating in this lesson, each learner will be able to:

1. Summarize the message Amos brought to Israel.

2. Compare the call and ministry of Amos to other prophets of Israel and Judah.

3. Propose a way to strengthen courage for giving witness to God's justice.

Lesson Outline

Introduction

A. Whose Words Will We Heed?

B. Lesson Context

I. Setting (Amos 1:1)

A. Who (v. 1a)

B. When (v. 1b)

II. Sin (Amos 2:11–12)

A. Raising Prophets (v. 11)

B. Rejecting Leadership (v. 12)

III. Servants (Amos 3:7–8)

A. Divine Plan (v. 7)

B. Dutiful Proclamation (v. 8)

IV. Struggle (Amos 7:10–15)

A. The Conspiracy (vv. 10–11)

B. The Challenge (vv. 12–13)

Itching, Covering, or . . . What?

C. The Charge (vv. 14–15)

When Plans Must Change

Conclusion

A. Will We Listen?

B. Prayer

C. Thought to Remember

Introduction

A. Whose Words Will We Heed?

When I served in the church nursery, I both loved and hated building block towers with the kids. It was fun to see how tall we could build the towers, but it could be frustrating when my advice went ignored. I would often suggest, "Let's make sure we build a big base." However, my building buddies were more interested in reaching the sky as quickly as possible. I would be thinking about stability; my co-architects were more interested in originality. The result was always the same: the tower would come crashing down to shouts of glee. Maybe the point for the kids was to see it fall more than to build it tall, after all?

It fascinates me that while kids love imitating adults, they also love doing things their own way. The kids in the nursery did not want building advice; they wanted to take their own approach. Adults can easily adopt a similar mindset regarding various matters. We often assume that we are in the right and feel we don't need anyone else's input, so we ignore the voices and words of those who can offer guidance. The stakes are low when building block towers for children, but the stakes are much higher in real life. Whose words will we heed?

B. Lesson Context

The book of Amos is one of 12 entries in the section of the Bible known as the Minor Prophets. These books are not "minor" in message; they are "minor" only in length when compared with the "major" prophets of Isaiah, Jeremiah, Ezekiel, and Daniel.

Amos preached in the northern kingdom of Israel in about 755 BC (see more on Amos 1:1, below). He ministered during a period of economic prosperity (3:15; 6:4–6). The national borders had been extended significantly through military campaigns (2 Kings 14:23–28). All this resulted in excessive pride and injustice among the people (Amos 6:8, 12–13).

Despite material wealth, the kingdom was in spiritual decline. The people practiced idolatrous worship at national shrines in the cities of Dan, Bethel, and Gilgal (Amos 4:4; 5:5, 26; 8:14;

compare 1 Kings 12:28–30). The people silenced voices that challenged their practices (Amos 2:11). Again, the question is: *Whose words will be heeded?*

I. Setting
(Amos 1:1)

A. Who (v. 1a)

1a. The words of Amos, who was among the herdmen of Tekoa.

This half-verse introduces the man *Amos.* Notice that he does not refer to himself as a prophet. Instead, he identifies as being *among the herdmen of Tekoa.* This statement raises two interesting points. Tekoa is a small town in the southern kingdom of Judah, about 10 miles south of Jerusalem. However, Amos primarily preaches in the northern kingdom of Israel (Amos 3:9–15; 4:1–5; 5:1; 7:10–17) and only occasionally addresses the southern kingdom of Judah (2:4–5; 6:1).

Because of the rarity of the underlying Hebrew word translated *herdmen,* his occupation is difficult to interpret. This word appears only one other time in the Bible, describing Mesha, king of Moab (2 Kings 3:4). The translation there is "sheepmaster," indicating a man of considerable means. The Hebrew term, therefore, seems to indicate not a poor shepherd but possibly a sheep breeder, likely with significant resources (see also Amos 7:14, below).

B. When (v. 1b)

1b. Which he saw concerning Israel in the days of Uzziah king of Judah, and in the days of Jeroboam the son of Joash king of Israel, two years before the earthquake.

This half-verse locates Amos's ministry during the reign of *Uzziah king of Judah* in the eighth century BC. Amos adds a second historical marker: *two years before the earthquake,* also mentioned by the prophet Zechariah, who lived several decades later (Zechariah 14:5). Some have dated the earthquake to 760 BC. However, more important than the exact date is the image of an earthquake coming just two years after Amos's preaching. At several points, Amos uses the imagery of an earthquake to describe God's coming judgment (Amos 3:14–15; 6:11; 8:8; 9:1, 5, 9).

II. Sin
(Amos 2:11–12)

A. Raising Prophets (v. 11)

11a. And I raised up of your sons for prophets, and of your young men for Nazarites.

God now speaks in the first person, highlighting two ways He has blessed and cared for Israel. In the two verses before this one, God references other blessings He has shown Israel (Amos 2:9–10).

The mention of *Nazarites* is somewhat surprising here, as they are not commonly cited as examples of God's care. Instructions are given in Numbers 6:1–21 for those who wish to "separate themselves unto the Lord" as Nazarites. They are not to drink fermented beverages, cut their hair, consume anything that comes from a vine, or be in the presence of a dead body. Samson is known as a Nazarite (Judges 13:5, 7; 16:17), and another possible example of someone who may have taken the Nazarite vow is Samuel (1 Samuel 1:11).

There are likely two reasons why God identifies Nazarites in this context. First, their austere lifestyle stands in stark contrast to the luxurious yet sinful practices of oppression and injustice (see Amos 2:8; 4:1; 6:4–6). Second, the Nazarites had consecrated themselves to the Lord. Therefore, they contrast the people of Israel, who live in a manner that contradicts their confession of the Lord as their God.

11b. Is it not even thus, O ye children of Israel? saith the LORD.

This rhetorical question proves that the Lord has guided the people with a succession of prophets and has provided Nazarites as examples of

How to Say It

Amaziah	Am-uh-*zye*-uh.
Bethel	*Beth*-ul.
Gilgal	*Gil*-gal (*G* as in *get*).
Jeroboam	Jair-uh-*boe*-um.
Joash	*Jo*-ash.
Mesha	*Me*-shuh.
Moab	*Mo*-ab.
Nazarites	*Naz*-uh-rites.
Uzziah	Uh-*zye*-uh.
Zechariah	*Zek*-uh-***rye***-uh.

consecration. The *children of Israel*, however, have abused or ignored them.

B. Rejecting Leadership (v. 12)

12. But ye gave the Nazarites wine to drink; and commanded the prophets, saying, Prophesy not.

In the previous verse, the Lord mentions the prophets before mentioning the Nazarites; in the verse before us, however, the order is reversed. This kind of structure is characteristic of Hebrew literature and serves as an aid to memorization.

Offering *the Nazarites wine to drink* was to tempt them to violate their vow of consecration (Numbers 6:2–4). To incite such a violation is no small thing! Likewise, silencing the prophets is also a serious matter. Throughout Israel's history leading up to Amos's time, many prophets had been silenced or ignored (1 Kings 18:4; 22:8–28; etc.). More will follow, and Amos himself will face similar experiences (Amos 7:10–16, below).

> **What Do You Think?**
> What might cause a community to reject or resist God's messengers?
> **Digging Deeper**
> How can we remain open to hearing God's voice and following His will?

III. Servants
(Amos 3:7–8)

A. Divine Plan (v. 7)

7. Surely the Lord God will do nothing, but he revealeth his secret unto his servants the prophets.

God's track record shows that He gives people many chances to repent before His holy nature requires retributive and corrective action (2 Peter 3:9). In Old Testament times, He voices those opportunities either personally, through an angel, or through *his servants the prophets* (2 Kings 17:13; Jeremiah 7:25; 25;4; etc.). In New Testament times, He conveys those opportunities through His Son (Hebrews 1:1–2). Offenders in either era try to stop that message by silencing the messengers (examples: Jeremiah 38:6; Acts 4:18).

> **What Do You Think?**
> Why does God choose to work through human messengers?
> **Digging Deeper**
> What does this reveal about His character and His relationship with humanity?

B. Dutiful Proclamation (v. 8)

8. The lion hath roared, who will not fear? the Lord God hath spoken, who can but prophesy?

The emphasis of this verse is on the inevitability of the Lord's word of judgment. Lions typically roar after they have captured prey, not before (Amos 3:4). Thus, the image of a roaring *lion* associated with the Lord's speech is a terrifying prediction of impending judgment. *Who will not fear,* indeed!

This word imagery reflects the Lord's roar described in Amos 1:2, which occurs right before a series of accusations directed at the surrounding nations, as well as Judah and Israel.

IV. Struggle
(Amos 7:10–15)

In Amos 7:1–9 (not in our printed text), the Lord shows Amos three visions of judgment on the northern kingdom of Israel. After each of the first two, Amos intercedes, and the Lord relents. After the third vision, however, the Lord leaves no room for intercession; He will indeed destroy the religious sites where Israel worshiped pagan deities (compare Amos 3:14; 4:4–5; 5:4–6). The Lord promises also to "rise against the house of Jeroboam with the sword" (7:9). Judgment is coming.

A. The Conspiracy (vv. 10–11)

10. Then Amaziah the priest of Bethel sent to Jeroboam king of Israel, saying, Amos hath conspired against thee in the midst of the house of Israel: the land is not able to bear all his words.

It's dangerous to challenge vested interests! Yet that is exactly what Amos has been doing. As a result, one member of the vested interests—*Amaziah the priest of Bethel*—now feels threatened enough to report his concerns to the *king of Israel.*

Throughout the book of Amos, tension has been building between God's sending of prophets and Israel's response (or lack of response) to them (Amos 1:1–2; 2:11; 3:1–8). This tension comes to a head here in 7:10–17 in a battle of credentials. The verse now before us documents the first part of the war of words between Amaziah and *Amos.*

After the nation of Israel split in 930 BC, Bethel emerged as a key sanctuary. The first king of the northern kingdom—whose name was also Jeroboam (1 Kings 12:1–24)—chose Bethel as an alternative to Jerusalem as a place of worship (12:26–33). Bethel is strategically located about 10 miles north of Jerusalem. The numerous times that Amos mentions Bethel by name speaks to its level of idolatry (Amos 3:14; 4:4–5; 5:5–6; 7:13).

11. For thus Amos saith, Jeroboam shall die by the sword, and Israel shall surely be led away captive out of their own land.

Prophets often introduced divine speech with the phrase, "Thus saith the Lord." Amos himself uses the phrase more than a dozen times (Amos 1:3, 6, 9, 11, 13; 2:1, 4, 6; 3:11, 12; 5:3, 4, 16; 7:17). In this context, Amaziah mocks Amos by reporting *For thus Amos saith,* insinuating that Amos is just making things up.

What Do You Think?

How can we ensure that our commitment to God takes precedence over cultural or societal loyalties?

Digging Deeper

How can we cultivate a posture of openness to God's Word, even when it challenges our comfort or assumptions?

B. The Challenge (vv. 12–13)

12. Also Amaziah said unto Amos, O thou seer, go, flee thee away into the land of Judah, and there eat bread, and prophesy there.

Some commentators suggest that *Amaziah* slights *Amos* by calling him a *seer* and not a prophet. However, this interpretation is unlikely since the terms often appear together in descriptions (example: 2 Samuel 24:11). The word *seer* is the older of the two words (1 Samuel 9:9). Since Amaziah doesn't

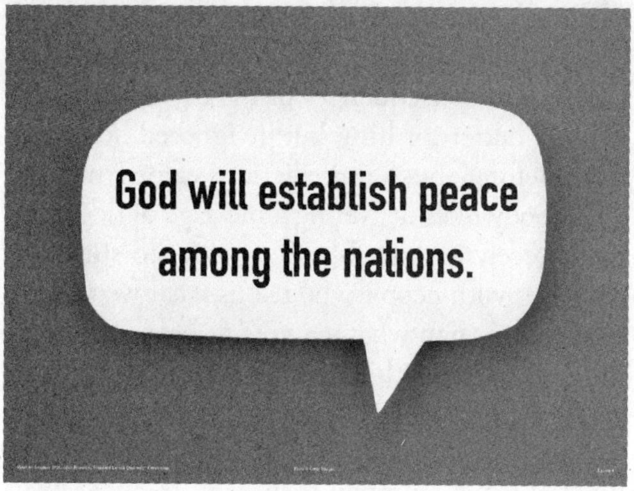

Visual for Lesson 4. *Display this visual as you ask, "Where do you notice God's work of peace among the nations?"*

acknowledge God to be the source of Amos's teaching, the use of the word *seer* here is likely sarcastic.

By referring to eating *bread,* Amaziah may imply that Amos prophesies simply for financial gain (compare Micah 3:11; Acts 16:16–20; 2 Corinthians 2:17; 1 Timothy 6:5).

13. But prophesy not again any more at Bethel: for it is the king's chapel, and it is the king's court.

Bethel is Amaziah's domain, and he does not want further interference from Amos. He invokes the authority of the king twice. The word translated *chapel* is usually translated as "sanctuary" (example: Amos 7:9). The word translated *court* refers to a dwelling place; it is translated as "house" in Amos 1:4; 2:8; 3:13, 15; 5:19 and elsewhere.

The most important aspect of both Amaziah's report to Jeroboam and his challenge to Amos is the absence of any mention of God. Amaziah does not challenge Amos's interpretation of God's message or his role as a divine spokesperson. He does not contradict Amos's accusations of sin. Instead, Amaziah is interested only in countering threats to the vested interests.

Itching, Covering, or . . . What?

Brian grew up in a dysfunctional family, which led to a rebellious phase during his teenage years. Drugs and alcohol became frequent vices for him and his friends. His grandmother noticed the troubling changes in his life and tried to take the boy under her wing. She warned him that if he continued making poor decisions, he would face severe consequences of his own doing. She wanted better for him, but he ignored her warnings. Before long, her predictions came true.

Nobody likes delivering a message of doom, let alone receiving one. It's often easier to surround ourselves with people who tell us what we *want* to hear rather than what we *need* to hear. The apostle Paul refers to this practice as having "itching ears" (2 Timothy 4:3). To refuse to listen and heed can also be likened to the stoning of Stephen when his detractors "stopped their ears" to avoid hearing the truth (Acts 7:57; compare Zechariah 7:11). Amaziah did not want to hear the "minority opinion" of Amos's prophecy of coming destruction. What he failed to understand was that Amos spoke God's words, and God's words always come true.

—L. M. W.

C. The Charge (vv. 14–15)

14. Then answered Amos, and said to Amaziah, I was no prophet, neither was I a prophet's son; but I was an herdman, and a gatherer of sycomore fruit.

We now come to the second part of the war of words between *Amos* and *Amaziah*. Amos begins his response by clarifying his occupation. By denying that he is *a prophet's son*, Amos denies that he comes from a prophetic school, such as we see in 1 Samuel 19:18–21 and 2 Kings 2:3; 4:38; 6:1–2; 9:1. This could imply that he speaks freely and is not beholden to any particular group or person in the giving of his message.

Amos has the background of a farmer. The word translated *herdman* here differs from the term translated that way in Amos 1:1, and it is quite rare; this verse is the only instance in the Old Testament where the underlying Hebrew word appears. The underlying word used in the Septuagint, the ancient Greek version, is also quite rare. Our best interpretation suggests that it refers to someone who cares for livestock. Therefore, the combination of these two rare terms may indicate that Amos was a businessman.

His additional work as a *gatherer of sycamore fruit* adds to his résumé. Trees bearing figs were common in the region during antiquity (1 Kings 10:27; 1 Chronicles 27:28; Luke 19:4). Amos does not need to prophesy for financial gain; he already has his own vocation.

What Do You Think?

How does Amos's claim in verse 14 illustrate God's ability to call and use anyone, regardless of their background or profession?

Digging Deeper

In what ways does this idea challenge conventional ideas about leadership or ministry?

When Plans Must Change

The year 2020 brought significant and unexpected changes to my family. Our oldest daughter was planning to attend Bible college on a scholarship, and we were preparing to launch her, our first child, into adulthood. In the midst of those preparations, the Christian college where my husband and I worked closed its doors forever. As a result, both of us found ourselves out of jobs, and our daughter's scholarship vanished. We had to switch gears quickly; we were both looking for work at a time when all organizations had stopped hiring due to the onset of the COVID-19 pandemic.

I took a chance and applied to a competitive residency program for hospital chaplaincy. I did not have all the right qualifications. After submitting my application, I learned that the deadline had already passed. However, God worked behind the scenes, and I was accepted into the program.

This opportunity shifted my life onto a new path that focused on ministry. Despite the challenges of navigating such an abrupt change, I quickly realized that I would love my new career and sensed that God was using me in this role. He transformed a difficult situation and changed my life.

Amos also seemed to have his life well planned. He owned sheep, goats, and orchards. He knew what he would be doing for the rest of his life. Then, God stepped in and changed his plans. When God changes your plans—and He surely will, in some way—how will you respond? Will you resist, or will you embrace the change as an opportunity for greater service to the kingdom of God? —L. M. W.

15. And the LORD took me as I followed the flock, and the LORD said unto me, Go, prophesy unto my people Israel.

Amos does not seem eager to become a prophet. He is not looking for an opportunity to speak out against Amaziah, Jeroboam, or the *people* of northern *Israel*. God took the initiative and asked Amos to *Go* and speak. This idea is supported by Amos 7:14, where Amos clearly states that his motivation for prophesying was not for financial gain.

Additionally, it is important to note that Amos is not a political operative or rabble-rouser. Rather, he is a divine spokesperson. This heightens the seriousness of Amaziah's resistance to Amos. Amaziah opposes not merely an individual prophet or even a school of prophets; he opposes the Lord, Israel's God. As Amaziah functions as a representative of his king and the nation of northern Israel, their rejection of Amos's messages is essentially a rejection of God's message.

What Do You Think?

How should we respond when we sense a call from God, even if it feels beyond our abilities?

Digging Deeper

What questions can you ask to help you discern God's call?

Conclusion

A. Will We Listen?

The message of Amos went unheeded. Soon after his ministry ended, Assyria began to make incursions into the territory of Israel and its neighboring regions. Less than 40 years later, in 722 BC, northern Israel would fall and be exiled (2 Kings 17). As with the message of other prophets, the choice was between only two courses: either repent or die. Nearly all the prophets had their message rejected, the prominent exception being Jonah (see Jonah 3).

Because of their nation's relative prosperity and religious fervor, Jeroboam and Amaziah assumed that God was on their side. Amos challenged this assumption, warned of judgment, encouraged repentance, and offered hope for the future.

To say that we read the words of God in the book of Amos seems obvious. After all, we read the prophecies with the advantage of hindsight; we see the prophecies fulfilled. But at the time the prophecies were given, it was a challenge to determine who was speaking the truth. That challenge still exists today, which is why Jesus warns His followers against false teachers (Matthew 7:15; 24:24). We do well to examine the teaching we hear in light of what Scripture says (compare Revelation 22:18–19).

The book of Amos offers another method for distinguishing a teacher of truth from a teacher of fiction. That method is to examine motivation—what's in it for the teacher? When we compare Amos's motivations with those of Amaziah, we see polar opposites. When Amos spoke against the religious, economic, and political status quo, he was risking his life by questioning Israel's assumption that God was happy with their behaviors and beliefs. To speak against a holy place in antiquity was to invite the death penalty (example: Jeremiah 26:1–15). On the other hand, Amaziah's perceived risk was an upset of the status quo, in which he had a vested interest. The New Testament witnesses to the same concern (2 Corinthians 2:17; 4:1–2).

For modern readers, the account of Amos also encourages us to reflect on how we hear the word of God today. Are we willing to listen? Will we accept God's challenge? Are we so committed to our religious, economic, and political status quo that we become unwilling to give an ear to anything that questions it? The fact that God speaks is a sign of God's grace. He wants to communicate with us. Will we have ears to hear?

B. Prayer

Heavenly Father, help us be open to Your challenge and quick to repent of sin. Give us ears to hear Your words and hearts committed to obeying. In Jesus' name we pray. Amen.

C. Thought to Remember

Listen to the Lord's words of challenge,
"Repent and obey."

Involvement Learning

Enhance your lesson with KJV Bible Student *(from your curriculum supplier) and the reproducible activity page (at www.standardlesson.com or in the back of the* KJV Standard Lesson Commentary Deluxe Edition*).*

Into the Lesson

Write the following scrambled word on the board:

UISJTEC

Ask participants to raise their hands when they have unscrambled the word. (The correct answer is "justice.")

After revealing the correct answer, ask participants to share with a partner what comes to mind when they hear the word *justice*. Invite volunteers to share their thoughts with the class. Next, pose the question, "When have you seen an injustice in the news or experienced an injustice in your life?" Allow time for whole-class discussion.

Lead into Bible study by saying, "The news reveals examples of injustice. Today we'll examine the life and message of a prophet who spoke out against violations of God's justice."

Into the Word

Begin this section with a brief background on the historical context of the prophet Amos and the northern kingdom of Israel. If possible, ask a participant to prepare a five-minute report before class. Encourage the presenter to use the material from the Lesson Context.

Divide the class into two groups: **People and Places Group** and **Mission and Vision Group**. Distribute handouts (you create) with the following prompts or questions for in-group discussion based on the lesson's Scripture text. Encourage the group to use lesson resources, study Bibles, or internet sources to write the explanations.

People and Places Group. Identify and explain the significance of the following people and places: Tekoa, Israel, Judah, Uzziah, Jeroboam, Nazarites, Amaziah, and Amos.

Mission and Vision Group. 1–What was Amos's occupation before receiving God's call? 2–Why did God send Amos to prophesy? 3–What was Amos's message to Israel? 4–How was that message received? 5–How did the response to Amos's message compare to the responses to other prophets of God?

Ask volunteers from each group to report on their findings, augmenting their reports with information you have prepared based on the lesson commentary. Then ask the following questions for whole-class discussion: 1–Why was Amos's message met with resistance? 2–Why didn't Israel's leaders recognize the message as coming from God? 3–In what ways might Israel's leaders have felt threatened by Amos's message? 4–Why might a call for justice be perceived as a threat by those in power?

Option. Distribute copies of the "Song for Justice" activity from the activity page, which you can download. Have participants work in small groups to complete as indicated. After calling time, ask a volunteer from each group to share their group's song ideas with the whole class.

Into Life

Ask participants to work in small groups to brainstorm a list of perceived injustices that require God's justice to be corrected. Distribute a pen and a sheet of paper to each group to jot down ideas. After creating their list, instruct each group to choose one item and make a second list of ways that God's people can promote God's justice and righteousness in response to that injustice.

Ask the class, "Which of these injustices can our class address in a meaningful way?" Challenge the class to develop a plan to give witness to God's justice in the context of the listed injustice. Next, ask, "How can we strengthen our courage for giving witness to God's justice?" Write responses on the board.

Option. Distribute copies of the "Justice Acrostic" exercise from the activity page. Have participants work in small groups to complete as indicated. After calling time, ask volunteers to share their group's summary with the whole class.

July 5
Lesson 5 (KJV)

The Believing Centurion

Devotional Reading: Acts 10:19–22, 30–35
Background Scripture: Matthew 8:5–13; Luke 7:1–10

Matthew 8:5–13

5 And when Jesus was entered into Capernaum, there came unto him a centurion, beseeching him,

6 And saying, Lord, my servant lieth at home sick of the palsy, grievously tormented.

7 And Jesus saith unto him, I will come and heal him.

8 The centurion answered and said, Lord, I am not worthy that thou shouldest come under my roof: but speak the word only, and my servant shall be healed.

9 For I am a man under authority, having soldiers under me: and I say to this man, Go, and he goeth; and to another, Come, and he cometh; and to my servant, Do this, and he doeth it.

10 When Jesus heard it, he marvelled, and said to them that followed, Verily I say unto you, I have not found so great faith, no, not in Israel.

11 And I say unto you, That many shall come from the east and west, and shall sit down with Abraham, and Isaac, and Jacob, in the kingdom of heaven.

12 But the children of the kingdom shall be cast out into outer darkness: there shall be weeping and gnashing of teeth.

13 And Jesus said unto the centurion, Go thy way; and as thou hast believed, so be it done unto thee. And his servant was healed in the selfsame hour.

Key Text

When Jesus heard it, he marvelled, and said to them that followed, Verily I say unto you, I have not found so great faith, no, not in Israel. **—Matthew 5:10**

The Testimony of

Faithful Witnesses

Unit 2: Faithful Witnesses Say "Yes" to Jesus

Lessons 5–8

Lesson Aims

After participating in this lesson, each learner will be able to:

1. Identify the centurion's appeal to Jesus.
2. Explain why the centurion's "great faith" is astonishing.
3. List ways to practice intercessory prayer and appeals to Jesus as an act of faith in God's power.

Lesson Outline

Introduction

A. Please Fix It, Daddy!

B. Lesson Context

I. Expressing Need and Faith (Matthew 8:5–9)

A. Centurion's Request (vv. 5–6)

B. Jesus' Offer (v. 7)

C. Centurion's Response (v. 8)

D. Centurion's Position (v. 9)

Officer's Orders

II. Instructing Others (Matthew 8:10–12)

A. Jesus' Surprise (v. 10)

B. Inclusion of Outsiders (v. 11)

Banquet Table

C. Exclusion of Insiders (v. 12)

III. Healing from a Distance (Matthew 8:13)

Conclusion

A. According to Your Faith

B. Prayer

C. Thought to Remember

Introduction

A. Please Fix It, Daddy!

My young children run to me when something is amiss. They fully expect that I can fix whatever has gone wrong: a broken toy, a skinned knee, or a swing that won't push itself. In their eyes, I am the big, experienced adult who has been there for them since they were born. In their eyes, I seem completely trustworthy and capable of doing whatever they need. (They're still young enough to be enchanted by my capacity!) This trust is constant—whether they are behaving well or poorly, whether they are healthy or sick, whether I am full of energy or exhausted.

If children can place this radical trust in an earthly father, how much more might the children of God run to a faithful and capable heavenly Father! Yet, we often hesitate to bring specific requests or intercessions. We waver when we feel unworthy of attention, or that our situation is too much. But like the centurion in Matthew 8:5–13, we can trust God's capability and willingness to act. God will respond when we come to Him, full of faith. He does not tire.

B. Lesson Context

Today's lesson comes shortly after the Sermon on the Mount. In Matthew 5–7, Jesus gives an authoritative interpretation of the Torah (or Jewish Law), explaining the ethics of God's kingdom. The sermon includes Jesus' self-identification as "Lord," to whom everyone owes obedience and allegiance (Matthew 7:21–23). Jesus compares His teachings to a foundation stone (7:24). His words are like the ground on which one might stand; they ensure the stability of whoever lives by them (7:24–27).

As Jesus descends from the mount, a "leper" approaches Him (Matthew 8:2). The Torah—which Jesus just showed authority to interpret—contains purity laws that regulate contact with those who are sick. Anyone with visible disease struggled day-to-day, facing the prospect of making others ritually impure. The man's request for cleansing reveals faith in Jesus' authority over sickness and death. Thus, when Jesus responds by cleansing the man with a touch, Jesus accepts ritual impurity (8:3). Simultaneously, He displays the capacity to heal the diseases that the Law of Moses carefully regulated. Jesus demonstrates healing with a touch, setting the stage for a second healing without physical contact.

I. Expressing Need and Faith

(Matthew 8:5–9)

A. Centurion's Request (vv. 5–6)

5. And when Jesus was entered into Capernaum, there came unto him a centurion, beseeching him.

Capernaum was the town that Jesus chose as the base of His Galilean ministry (Matthew 4:13). It was the home of Simon Peter and probably more of the disciples (17:25). The name "village of Nahum" is fitting for Jesus' ministry. *Nahum* means "comfort" in Hebrew, and comfort is the very thing Jesus came to bring Israel (see Isaiah 40:1: "Comfort ye, comfort ye my people"). The village's name is also a reminder of the biblical prophet who prophesied judgment against Nineveh and Assyria (Nahum 1–3).

A *centurion* was an officer in the Roman army. He led between sixty and one hundred troops. Since Rome had no legion in Galilee or Judaea at the time, this centurion was probably part of the auxiliary force under Herod Antipas. Auxiliaries were non-citizen troops, mainly recruited from the free population of the empire. This man might have been from Galilee, Phoenicia, or Syria—thus, neither a Roman citizen nor Jewish.

The centurion approaches Jesus as a supplicant and subordinate, *beseeching* Jesus for a favor. In a parallel account in Luke (7:1–10), the centurion does not approach Jesus directly but sends Jewish elders on his behalf. An indirect approach is another way to emphasize his perceived position as inferior to Jesus.

6. And saying, Lord, my servant lieth at home sick of the palsy, grievously tormented.

The centurion calls Jesus *Lord.* The title carries some ambiguity in meaning, as it can refer to a human ruler, serve as an honorific title like "mister," or even represent the name of God. Using the term "lord" or "master" allowed God-fearers (non-Jewish followers of God) to avoid pronouncing the revered name—Yahweh. Throughout Matthew's Gospel, *Lord* frequently refers to God (Matthew 1:20; 2:13; 4:7; etc.). Only one chapter prior to today's text, Jesus uses *Lord* as a title for Himself (7:21–22). Therefore, it is significant that the centurion—an outsider and representative of imperial power—approaches Jesus as a supplicant and repeats this title. At a minimum, the term bestows honor and indicates authority.

The centurion does not bring his *servant* to be healed. Leaving the servant at home indicates the extent of the centurion's faith. His approach presumes that Jesus is capable of healing without even seeing the man.

The word rendered *servant* is ambiguous and could refer to a child or enslaved person. One viable possibility, in this case, is that the "servant" is the centurion's son from a woman to whom he is not legally married—perhaps the child of an enslaved or lower-status woman. Roman soldiers in this era were officially forbidden to marry during their term of service. Yet, in practice, the authorities often looked the other way. Therefore, soldiers in long-term localized service sometimes had unlicensed or unofficial families. In such cases, the soldier could formally adopt the legally unrecognized children after completing his term of service. With the centurion's higher rank and long-term assignment, this interpretation fits the parallel in Luke's Gospel, which adds that the sick person is "dear unto him" (7:2–10).

What Do You Think?

To whom do you go when someone you care for is suffering? What kind of help do you seek?

Digging Deeper

Is it easy for you to ask for help? What character traits must be developed in us before we can easily ask for assistance?

B. Jesus' Offer (v. 7)

7. And Jesus saith unto him, I will come and heal him.

Jesus practices what He preaches. During the

Visual for Lesson 5. *Point to the visual and say, "How might you practice confident faith in Jesus' authority and abilities?"*

Sermon on the Mount, He teaches love—even for enemies (Matthew 5:43–44). Since God gives good gifts to the righteous and the wicked (5:45), Jesus encourages His followers that the one who seeks and asks will also find and receive (7:8).

Christ's kingdom differs from the patterns of earthly conquest. Rather than resisting someone who could easily be seen as an enemy or an oppressor, Jesus serves him and offers blessing. In Luke's retelling of the story, Jewish elders testify on the centurion's behalf, showing that he is no enemy or oppressor. They vouch for him, saying he is "worthy . . . for he loveth our nation, and he hath built us a synagogue" (Luke 7:4–5).

The Greek grammar underlying this verse could be rendered as a question, "Shall I come and heal him?" The basic meaning is the same; Jesus is willing to go and to heal at the centurion's request. The wording includes the personal pronoun *I*, which is grammatically unnecessary except to serve an emphatic purpose. Jesus clarifies what the centurion is implying: "You want *me* to come to heal him?" In this respect, Jesus' answer is like the leading question He will pose to the young man in Matthew 19:17 ("Why callest . . . *me* good? there is none good but one, that is, God"). Every word Jesus speaks reflects His identity, status, and authority.

C. Centurion's Response (v. 8)

8. The centurion answered and said, Lord, I am not worthy that thou shouldest come under my roof: but speak the word only, and my servant shall be healed.

The centurion repeats the title *Lord*, which picks up on the emphasis in Jesus' initial reply. The centurion accentuates faith in Jesus' authority, declaring that Jesus *only* needs to *speak the word*. From the beginning of Scripture (Genesis 1), God creates through word alone. God only needs to say, "Let there be light," and it appears (1:3). Thus, intentionally or not, the centurion's faith links Jesus to the Creator, whose voice of authority brings life.

It is often argued that the centurion's unworthiness *that [Jesus] shouldest come under [his] roof* anticipates the unwillingness of a Jew to enter the home of an unclean Gentile. However, this idea exaggerates Jewish purity regulations in the first century. Contracting ritual impurity is not sinful; in some cases, it is mandated by the expectations of the Law. For instance, the death of a close relative requires a burial—which, according to the traditional interpretation of Deuteronomy 21:23, must be completed within twenty-four hours. Nearly all first-century Jews spent the majority of their lives in a state of ritual impurity. Only those entering holy spaces, like the temple courts, needed to purify themselves. Merely entering a Gentile house, therefore, would be a nonissue. Jewish texts and rabbinic materials presume that Jews enter Gentile households without concern, even to eat with non-Jews (provided the menu does not include forbidden foods).

Therefore, when the centurion claims unworthiness, it is on grounds other than his Gentile status. It again suggests great humility and recognition of Jesus' high standing relative to his own.

D. Centurion's Position (v. 9)

9. For I am a man under authority, having soldiers under me: and I say to this man, Go, and he goeth; and to another, Come, and he cometh; and to my servant, Do this, and he doeth it.

The centurion describes his knowledge of *authority* and experience as a military leader. He knows that soldiers obey his orders, which creates an analogy that explains Jesus' position in the cosmic hierarchy. Jesus has the authority to command the powerful, unseen forces of heaven in the same way that the centurion directs the troops under his jurisdiction.

The centurion uses the phrase *under authority* to describe himself. His commands carry weight because he speaks with the authority of the emperor. Likewise, Jesus' authority over cosmic forces is entirely sanctioned and supported by the Father in heaven. As Jesus says in Matthew 28:18, "All power is given unto me in heaven and in earth" (compare John 5:36).

What Do You Think?

Is there a unique part of your job, worldview, or skillset that sheds light on how faith works?

Digging Deeper

How might you share the analogies and examples of faith from your life and experience with others?

Officer's Orders

An army runs on authority. Soldiers must obey orders from superiors. Massive consequences occur when commands are ignored or disobeyed. General orders include the following: leaving a post *only* when relieved by another, sounding an alarm in the case of an emergency, and remaining alert while on duty. Soldiers are expected to carry out the directives of a commander—not second-guess or question the strategy.

This pattern was evident in the Roman army, which remains one of history's most successful fighting and ruling forces. A centurion served within a hierarchy. Above him were the legate, tribune, and prefect ranks; and under his authority were hundreds of common soldiers. Although everyone served the emperor, soldiers and their commanding officers were loyal to one another. Good officers care for their men.

The centurion in Matthew 8:5–13 obviously cares for his servant. His concern drives him to the source of ultimate authority: Jesus. The centurion's understanding of command bolsters his faith and his decisive action. Are you a leader with influence? Are you using your influence for the benefit of those under your care? Where is the line that indicates it is time to turn and seek God's superior capabilities and limitless authority? —B. R. T.

II. Instructing Others
(Matthew 8:10–12)

A. Jesus' Surprise (v. 10)

10. When Jesus heard it, he marvelled, and said to them that followed, Verily I say unto you, I have not found so great faith, no, not in Israel.

Jesus expresses amazement at the centurion's *faith*. *Faith* here is more than mere belief; it includes concepts like "trust" or "fidelity." The centurion identifies Jesus' authority and submits himself entirely. He trusts that Jesus can and will respond with favor. And Jesus finds this conviction astonishing—it displays a level of trust and submission that Jesus has not seen, even *in Israel*.

Despite having the witness of the law—an advantage that the apostle Paul calls "the oracles of God" (Romans 3:2)—the residents of *Israel* do not exhibit this measure of trust and submission. The centurion's active faith surprises Jesus; as a Gentile, the centurion enjoys none of those advantages. The centurion's faith recognizes the presence and authority of God in the person of Jesus.

What Do You Think?

What is it about the centurion's faith that amazes Jesus?

Digging Deeper

Have you ever marveled at someone else's faith? What was so astonishing to you?

B. Inclusion of Outsiders (v. 11)

11. And I say unto you, That many shall come from the east and west, and shall sit down with Abraham, and Isaac, and Jacob, in the kingdom of heaven.

Jesus uses the centurion's faith as an object lesson. He explains that outsiders who submit to Jesus in this manner will be welcomed into *the kingdom of heaven* with the covenantal patriarchs.

The kingdom of heaven refers to the rule of God that is active on earth. It includes the resurrection of the dead and the promised restoration of the people of Israel. Remarkably, Jesus teaches that God includes outsiders, like this centurion, among the faithful. In the new era of justice and life, *many* will be rewarded and treated as heirs to the covenant, even alongside *Abraham*, *Isaac*, and *Jacob*.

The outsiders *come from* places far from Israel: *the east and west*. These directional terms depict widespread inclusion. People from nations at the ends of the earth will find a place in God's kingdom. This is like the psalmist who uses the phrase "as far as the east is from the west" to poetically describe infinite space (Psalm 103:12). Jesus' words do something similar. They expand His listener's expectations of kingdom access.

To *sit down with* the patriarchs hints at a forthcoming great feast. Jesus pushes His disciples to increase their holy imagination of who will be present at the wedding banquet of the Lamb (Revelation 19:6–9).

What Do You Think?

Consider the parable of the great banquet (Luke 14:16–24). Who comes to the feast?

Digging Deeper

How does imagining these banquet guests shift your understanding of the "many" who will come from the "east and west" to sit with the patriarchs?

Banquet Table

I sat at the end of a long rectangular table. It butted up against several others, creating a long line. Tables filled the lawn beside ours, and chattering picnic-goers happily sat alongside them all. Food covered another set of tables: barbecued pork, rolls, vegetables, salads, casserole dishes, fruit platters, and every kind of dessert you might imagine. It was an epic potluck to close out the summer and kick off the school year for our church.

Suddenly, the words of Psalm 23 floated through my mind, "Thou preparest a table before me . . ." (23:5). But instead of being surrounded by my enemies, I was surrounded by my family and closest of friends. I felt gratitude rush through my heart for this provision, invitation, and abundance.

At the same time, movement caught my eye, and I turned my head to see a family hesitating at the edge of our gathering. They looked unsure. Quickly, I alerted my family to clean up their plates. I went to the other family and assured them we'd made space. I invited them to take our place at the table. Later, the family admitted they were considering whether to leave, but the invitation encouraged them to remain. When did you last invite a stranger to sit at God's banqueting table? How might you increase your imagination of who belongs and how to make room for them?

—B. R. T.

C. Exclusion of Insiders (v. 12)

12. But the children of the kingdom shall be cast out into outer darkness: there shall be weeping and gnashing of teeth.

On the other hand, the unfaithful *children* will be expelled. Their consequence for disobedience, lack of faith, and apathy is exclusion from the benefits of *the kingdom*: they will be *cast out*. Just imagine the shock of Jesus' comment. Those who expect inclusion as a matter of privilege must beware. Jesus says that insiders who anticipate their family history or religious affiliation as granting automatic entry into the kingdom must watch out—they could find themselves outside the fold, in *darkness*. There are serious consequences for unfaithfulness and infidelity. Jesus' teaching follows the prediction of Amos 5:18–20, which warns that the day of the Lord's judgment will be "darkness, and not light" for the house of Israel.

Weeping and gnashing of teeth recalls figurative imagery used frequently in Psalms. David describes mockers who conspire against him and gnash their teeth (Psalm 35:15–16). In the same context, these teeth-gnashers are at a feast, which connects to Jesus' words about sitting with the patriarchs (see earlier comments on Matthew 8:11). In another psalm, the wicked scheme against the righteous (Psalm 37:12). Although they gnash their teeth, God will bring them and their plans to nothing (37:20). And in Psalm 112, the righteous look forward to an enduring future, with exaltation and honor (112:9). In contrast, those misaligned with God will see honor given to others, be "grieved" by it, "gnash with [their] teeth," and then "melt away" (112:10). Thus, Jesus' phrase reflects the bitterness and anger of the wicked who look upon the salvation of the righteous. It warns God's people against having an inhospitable and faithless mindset, which can only lead to ruin.

What Do You Think?

What is the fundamental difference between "children of the kingdom" and "children of God"?

Digging Deeper

Have you ever expected to receive something because you felt it was your right or privilege and ended up disappointed? Explain.

III. Healing from a Distance

(Matthew 8:13)

13. And Jesus said unto the centurion, Go thy way; and as thou hast believed, so be it done unto thee. And his servant was healed in the selfsame hour.

Jesus acts with the divine authority that the centurion expected of Him. He proclaims healing to the servant from a distance, which occurs in an instant—the *selfsame hour*. He immediately dismisses the centurion, telling him to *go thy way*.

Jesus' declaration *as thou hast believed, so it be done unto thee* is especially important. Jesus does not act unilaterally. In Matthew 13:58, Jesus will refuse to perform miraculous healings when His audience is lacking faith. But for the centurion, abundant faith determines what he receives from Jesus. God responds in direct reaction to the centurion's petition.

Jesus does not respond to the centurion's outward appearance, social status, ethnic identity, or even membership in the covenant community. Instead, He looks at his faith. Jesus' interaction with the centurion is an example of God's ability to grant the "desires of thine heart" to those who pray in accordance with His will (Psalm 37:4). It puts flesh and bone to John's words: "If we ask any thing according to his will, he heareth us" (1 John 5:14). Those who trust God can seek, ask (with confidence), and receive a righteous reward.

Conclusion

A. According to Your Faith

The centurion in today's lesson gives us a refreshing example of approaching God properly. Our methodology is critical as we intercede for those who are suffering. The centurion showcases essential aspects of a faithful petition: acknowledge Jesus as Lord, submit to God's authority, and do so with great humility. The centurion also appeals to the Lord's mercy. He holds complete confidence in Jesus' ability to alleviate suffering, even from a distance. This story demonstrates that we can be confident like the centurion—in Christ's authority over sickness, death, and every power.

This story shows that faith sees beyond the physical to perceive spiritual realities that are deep and salient. Faith perceives Jesus' divine jurisdiction; faith gives us boldness to act with adept confidence; faith makes us children of God.

B. Prayer

Heavenly Father, teach us to approach You like the centurion. May we boldly intercede on behalf of those who suffer. Grant us complete faith in Your authority. In Jesus' name we pray. Amen.

C. Thought to Remember

Jesus holds complete authority.

How to Say It

Assyria	Uh-*sear*-ee-uh.
Capernaum	Kuh-*per*-nay-um.
centurion	sen-*ture*-ee-un.
Gentile	*Jen*-tile.
Herod Antipas	*Hair*-ud An-tih-pus.
rabbinic	ruh-*bin*-ihk.
Syria	*Sear*-ee-uh.

Involvement Learning

Enhance your lesson with KJV Bible Student *(from your curriculum supplier) and the reproducible activity page (at www.standardlesson.com or in the back of the* KJV Standard Lesson Commentary Deluxe Edition*).*

Into the Lesson

Open the class time by saying, "Every day we encounter appeals. We request things from others, and they request things from us. Every appeal is made, granted, or denied on specific grounds."

Write a list of common appeals on the board. Examples might include a bank loan application, job application, marriage proposal, request for financial assistance, or prayer for healing. Ask the class to come up with examples of appropriate and inappropriate grounds on which to make each appeal.

Alternative. Distribute copies of the "Anatomy of an Appeal" exercise from the activity page, which you can download. Have learners work in groups of three as indicated.

Transition into the Bible study by saying, "Today's passage helps us see how God is pleased with appeals made on faithful grounds."

Into the Word

In preparation for class, compile a list of general grounds for appeal. Examples might include *influence, justice, love, money, power, popularity*, or *punishment*. Write them on small slips of paper and place them in a hat. Also prepare the following script:

Centurion: "Lord, my servant lieth at home sick of the palsy, grievously tormented."

Jesus: "I will come and heal him."

Centurion: "Lord, I am [appeal]. Speak the word only, and my servant shall be healed."

Jesus: "Verily I say unto you, I have not found so great faith, no, not in Israel."

Ask for two volunteers willing to play the roles of Jesus and the centurion. Ask them to perform the script 4–6 times, drawing a slip from the hat each time. Ask the centurion to creatively plug in the grounds for appeal from the drawn slip. (Example: "Lord I am greatly *influential*—I can put in a good word for you with the emperor!")

Lead a discussion considering which appeals make sense with Jesus' final reply. Ask why most of the reasons the centurion might have appealed to Jesus seem to fall short.

Ask learners to take a minute to read Matthew 8:5–13 silently to themselves. When the minute is up, say to the class, "Jesus not only granted the centurion's appeal, He 'marvelled' at it. Jesus perceived a uniquely 'great faith' behind this request." Then ask, "What was so remarkable about the centurion's appeal to Jesus?"

Option. Distribute copies of the "Tale of Two Appeals" exercise from the activity page along with pens of different colors. Have learners complete the activity individually as indicated and then discuss it in small groups.

Into Life

Explain that even though the centurion's appeal is not a template for all intercessory prayer, it is instructive as an example of "great faith" that pleases Jesus. Pass out index cards and pens to each learner and then ask them to pair up. As they do, write this on the board:

Lord, my [relation] [statement of problem]. Lord, I [statement of humility]. But say the word, and my [relation] will [statement of request].

Ask learners to take a minute to write a short intercessory prayer using this fill-in-the-blank script that is modeled after the centurion's appeal (Matthew 8:6, 8). (Example: "Lord, my friend is struggling with his mental health. Lord, I cannot alleviate his suffering as much as I wish I could. But say the word, and my friend will experience some relief today.")

Ask learners to share their prayers with their partner if they are comfortable. Then encourage them to pray quietly together.

Option. Ask the class to share how the "statement of humility" affected their thinking process and what or how they prayed.

Simon Peter, the Restored Disciple

Devotional Reading: Isaiah 40:26–31
Background Scripture: Mark 8:27–29; Luke 22:7–38;
John 18:15–18, 25–27; 21:15–17

Mark 8:27–29

27 And Jesus went out, and his disciples, into the towns of Caesarea Philippi: and by the way he asked his disciples, saying unto them, Whom do men say that I am?

28 And they answered, John the Baptist: but some say, Elias; and others, One of the prophets.

29 And he saith unto them, But whom say ye that I am? And Peter answereth and saith unto him, Thou art the Christ.

Luke 22:31–34

31 And the Lord said, Simon, Simon, behold, Satan hath desired to have you, that he may sift you as wheat:

32 But I have prayed for thee, that thy faith fail not: and when thou art converted, strengthen thy brethren.

33 And he said unto him, Lord, I am ready to go with thee, both into prison, and to death.

34 And he said, I tell thee, Peter, the cock shall not crow this day, before that thou shalt thrice deny that thou knowest me.

John 18:25–27

25 And Simon Peter stood and warmed himself. They said therefore unto him, Art not thou also one of his disciples? He denied it, and said, I am not.

26 One of the servants of the high priest, being his kinsman whose ear Peter cut off, saith, Did not I see thee in the garden with him?

27 Peter then denied again: and immediately the cock crew.

John 21:15–17

15 So when they had dined, Jesus saith to Simon Peter, Simon, son of Jonas, lovest thou me more than these? He saith unto him, Yea, Lord; thou knowest that I love thee. He saith unto him, Feed my lambs.

16 He saith to him again the second time, Simon, son of Jonas, lovest thou me? He saith unto him, Yea, Lord; thou knowest that I love thee. He saith unto him, Feed my sheep.

17 He saith unto him the third time, Simon, son of Jonas, lovest thou me? Peter was grieved because he said unto him the third time, Lovest thou me? And he said unto him, Lord, thou knowest all things; thou knowest that I love thee. Jesus saith unto him, Feed my sheep.

Key Text

[Jesus] saith unto him the third time, Simon, son of Jonas, lovest thou me? Peter was grieved because he said unto him the third time, Lovest thou me? And he said unto him, Lord, thou knowest all things; thou knowest that I love thee. Jesus saith unto him, Feed my sheep. —**John 21:17**

The Testimony of

Faithful Witnesses

Unit 2: Faithful Witnesses Say "Yes" to Jesus

Lessons 5–8

Lesson Aims

After participating in this lesson, each learner will be able to:

1. Recount the major events of Peter's life.
2. Explain how Peter's life demonstrates God's ability to use people in spite of their failings.
3. List ways that personal shortcomings can become opportunities to depend on Christ.

Lesson Outline

Introduction
- A. Broken Made Beautiful
- B. Lesson Context

I. Identity of the Messiah (Mark 8:27–29)
- A. What People Say (vv. 27–28)
- B. What the Disciples Say (v. 29)
  - *Who Is Jesus?*

II. Failing of a Follower (Luke 22:31–34)
- A. Jesus' Encouragement (vv. 31–32)
- B. Assertion of Devotion (v. 33)
  - *Are Ye Able?*
- C. Prediction of Denial (v. 34)

III. Prediction Realized (John 18:25–27)
- A. Second Denial (v. 25)
- B. Third Denial (vv. 26–27)

IV. Reinstating a Leader (John 21:15–17)
- A. First Exchange (v. 15)
- B. Second Exchange (v. 16)
- C. Third Exchange (v. 17)

Conclusion
- A. Time to Change the Story
- B. Prayer
- C. Thought to Remember

Introduction

A. Broken Made Beautiful

Kintsugi is a centuries-old Japanese technique of pottery repair. The process involves using a special lacquer mixed with gold, silver, or platinum to repair damages to broken or cracked pieces. Other methods of ceramic restoration aim to hide the damage or make it less noticeable as if the object were "like new." Kintsugi, however, highlights the imperfections and brokenness of the pottery, transforming them into a new artifact. The restoration process transforms the damaged pottery into something whole, with the lacquered repairs serving as a visual reminder of the item's history and use. Rather than obscuring the damage, this technique celebrates it, making the once-broken pieces beautiful and usable for many more years.

Similarly, God's work of salvation brings healing and reconciliation to sinful humanity. Today's account demonstrates how God restored one of the first apostles, Peter. Through Christ's forgiveness and restoration, Peter's story becomes more beautiful than he could have imagined.

B. Lesson Context

Peter was a fisherman from Bethsaida, a village on the northern shore of the Sea of Galilee (John 1:44). Here, Peter worked with his brother Andrew (Mark 1:16). While fishing on the Sea of Galilee, Peter and his brother are called by Jesus to follow Him and become "fishers of men" (Matthew 4:18–22; Mark 1:16–20; Luke 5:1–11; John 1:35–42).

We also know that Peter was married (Mark 1:30; 1 Corinthians 9:5). At some point, Peter, his wife, and at least one other family member moved to Capernaum (Matthew 8:5–14), a town approximately five miles southwest of Bethsaida.

The New Testament notes three names for Peter. His Hebrew name is *Simon* or the variant *Simeon* (Mark 1:16; Acts 15:14). Later, Jesus calls him *Peter*, a designation based on an ancient Greek word meaning "rock" or "stone" (Matthew 16:18; Mark 3:16); this is his most frequently occurring name in the New Testament, found over 160 times. The third name is *Cephas*, an Aramaic word for "stone" (John 1:42; 1 Corinthians 1:12; 3:22; etc.).

I. Identity of the Messiah

(Mark 8:27–29)

This first passage of Scripture comes from the third and final year of Jesus' ministry. He has just fed the five thousand (Mark 6:30–44). As a result, the people try to "take him by force, to make him a king" (John 6:15). When He refuses to accept such an earthly crown, many stop following Him (6:66).

Over the next several months, Jesus is on the move. He goes westward to Phoenicia (Mark 7:24–30) and then to the southeast to the eastern side of the Sea of Galilee and into the Decapolis (Matthew 15:29; Mark 7:31–37).

Then Jesus and the disciples cross the lake to Dalmanutha, where they face the Pharisees (Mark 8:10–12). Following this encounter, Jesus returns to Bethsaida on the other side of the lake (8:22). From there, Jesus and His disciples travel north.

A. What People Say (vv. 27–28)

27a. And Jesus went out, and his disciples, into the towns of Caesarea Philippi.

Without the constant distraction of crowds or opposition, Jesus prepares His *disciples* for the next phase of His ministry. They visit the *towns* in Caesarea Philippi, an area nearly 30 miles northeast of the Sea of Galilee, overlooking the northern end of the Jordan River valley.

During this period, several towns are named "Caesarea" in honor of the Roman emperor. A more prominent Caesarea, for example, is Caesarea Maritima on the Mediterranean coastline. However, the town where Jesus and His disciples gather is called *Caesarea Philippi,* named in honor of Philip II (also known as Philip the Tetrarch), the son of Herod the Great and brother of Herod Antipas.

27b. And by the way he asked his disciples, saying unto them, Whom do men say that I am?

Answering the question "Who is Jesus?" is a fundamental issue that everyone, especially the *disciples,* must face. Where does Jesus come from? What is His purpose? The answer to these questions shapes how we respond to Him.

28. And they answered, John the Baptist: but some say, Elias; and others, One of the prophets.

The disciples report the various opinions and rumors circulating about Jesus. Some believe that He is *John the Baptist,* who had already been killed by Herod (Mark 6:14–29; compare Matthew 14:1–12; Luke 9:7–9). Others think that Jesus might be *Elias* (Elijah), the Old Testament prophet known for speaking out against a king (see 1 Kings 21). The Old Testament prophesied that a person like Elijah would someday return (Malachi 4:5–6), a prophecy that was fulfilled through the ministry of John the Baptist (see Matthew 17:10–13).

The disciples do not mention the possibility that Jesus could be the promised Messiah. Even so, there seems to be some inclination in that direction (see Matthew 9:27; 15:22; John 4:29).

B. What the Disciples Say (v. 29)

29a. And he saith unto them, But whom say ye that I am?

Now the question becomes pointed and personal: *But whom say ye that I am?* Have the disciples come to a conclusion about Jesus' identity?

Who Is Jesus?

One of my earliest memories involves my dad reading bedtime stories from a children's Bible. The intricate illustrations in that Bible are still vividly etched in my mind. The stories he read and the spiritual instruction he provided became the foundation of my faith.

As I grew older, I realized that simply knowing Bible stories and memorizing verses was not enough. It was insufficient to rely solely on my parents' beliefs about Jesus. I needed to form my own conclusions and be able to answer the question, "Who is Jesus?" for myself.

While knowing how others answer that question is valuable, what matters most is how you respond. How do you answer the question, "Who is Jesus?" —B. R.

29b. And Peter answereth and saith unto him, Thou art the Christ.

The title *Christ* is the Greek equivalent of the Jewish title "Messiah" (John 1:41; 4:25). Both designations mean "the anointed one." Numerous Old Testament texts point to the Messiah's arrival and reign (Psalm 110; Micah 5:2; Zechariah 9:9; etc.).

First-century Jewish expectations regarding this figure were diverse. Some believed the Messiah would be a prophet like Moses or Elijah, performing miraculous deeds to lead Israel to righteousness. Others hypothesized that this figure would be a high priest like Aaron, coming to purify the temple and sanctify the people. The prevailing belief among most first-century Jews was that this person would be a political figure, a nationalistic king, who would sit on the earthly throne of David and rule over an earthly empire.

What Do You Think?

Why is confessing Jesus as Christ important for an individual believer and the church?

Digging Deeper

How can we help others move from having a general idea of who Jesus is to truly knowing Him as Christ?

II. Failing of a Follower

(Luke 22:31–34)

It is Thursday night of Jesus' final week, "the day of unleavened bread, when the passover [lamb] must be killed" (Luke 22:7). Jesus' arrest, trial, and crucifixion looms. He shares one final meal with His disciples, using the opportunity to teach them about their role in service to Him (22:8–30).

A. Jesus' Encouragement (vv. 31–32)

31. And the Lord said, Simon, Simon, behold, Satan hath desired to have you, that he may sift you as wheat.

Jesus singles out *Simon* Peter and makes him a representative of the trials the other disciples will encounter. His representative role is communicated by the fact that the word translated *you* is plural in Greek.

The role of *Satan* is similar to that in the opening chapters of the book of Job: a heavenly official who accuses and tests God's people (Job 1:6–12; 2:1–6; compare Zechariah 3:1; Luke 4:1–13; Revelation 12:10). The warning that Satan *may sift you as wheat* evokes the image of separating valuable wheat kernels from the useless chaff (compare Matthew 3:12; Luke 3:17; Amos 9:9). The text does not specify what the "wheat" represents. Instead, Jesus' point is that Peter will undergo a season of trial as Satan tempts him away from faithfulness to Christ.

32. But I have prayed for thee, that thy faith fail not: and when thou art converted, strengthen thy brethren.

Jesus has *prayed* to strengthen Peter's faith and devotion. This is not the only time Jesus prays for His followers (John 17:6–26; 10:27–29; etc.). Even today, the risen Christ is our "advocate" with the Father (1 John 2:1).

The Greek term translated *faith* encompasses more than simply "doctrinal belief." The term can also convey meanings such as "loyalty," "fidelity," and "faithfulness" (compare usage in Luke 18:8; Acts 14:22; etc.). Although Jesus knows that Peter will soon deny Him (Luke 22:34, below; see 22:54–62), He prays for Peter to experience only a temporary failure of faith rather than a complete disavowal.

The Greek term translated *converted* often has the sense of turning away from a wrong course, which aligns with the concept of repentance (examples: Luke 1:16–17; 17:4; Acts 3:19; 26:18). Jesus assures Peter that he will be restored. Peter's experience will ultimately *strengthen* the *faith* of others (compare 1:15–26; 2:14–40; 8:14–25; 15:7–11).

What Do You Think?

Have you ever experienced a time when your faith was tested? How did it affect your relationship with God?

Digging Deeper

How does knowing that Jesus intercedes for us (like He did for Peter) encourage you in your struggles?

B. Assertion of Devotion (v. 33)

33. And he said unto him, Lord, I am ready to go with thee, both into prison, and to death.

Peter has been with Jesus since the beginning of His public ministry (see Lesson Context). He is the most outspoken of the disciples, and he tends to speak with the most conviction (examples: Matthew 14:22–33; Mark 10:23–31; Luke 8:43–48; John 6:67–70). Peter's association with Jesus leads him to boldly assert his devotion to the *Lord*, even unto *death* (compare John 13:37).

Peter now understands the possibility that Jesus might experience imprisonment and death. This marks a shift in perspective from his previous confessions (see Matthew 16:21–22; Mark 8:31–32).

Are Ye Able?

The church I grew up attending sang hymns as part of its worship services. I came to recognize at least two categories of hymns: the bright, uplifting kind and the dark, melancholy kind. The melancholy hymns included titles like "Almost Persuaded" and "'Are Ye Able,' said the Master."

Without a doubt, I can say that the dark, melancholy hymns had far more influence on my journey to becoming a Christian than did the bright, uplifting ones. The words of the dark ones were eerily convicting. Consider these lyrics:

"Are ye able," said the Master
  "To be crucified with me?"
"Yea," the sturdy dreamers answered,
  "To the death we follow Thee."

Over the years, I often wondered what made such hymns so convicting. Then one day I found the answer in an article about learning styles. The article said that there were, broadly speaking, two ways to learn: from our own mistakes ("learning by experience") or from others' mistakes ("learning by wisdom"). I'm more attracted to the latter style by nature, and the melancholy hymns served me admirably in that regard. Consider Peter's mistaken bravado in Luke 22:33 as echoed in the words of "Are Ye Able."

But that's just me. What about you? How can you set yourself on a path of learning via wisdom rather than experience? —R. L. N.

C. Prediction of Denial (v. 34)

34. And he said, I tell thee, Peter, the cock shall not crow this day, before that thou shalt thrice deny that thou knowest me.

The word *cock* refers to a male rooster, a bird known for its tendency to *crow* during the early

Visual for Lesson 6. *Display this visual during the lesson conclusion and ask, "How is God's mercy on display in the example of Peter?"*

hours of the morning. This reference to a rooster's crowing also highlights the illegality of Jesus' trial. According to Jewish legal tradition, a trial for a capital offense cannot be conducted at night. Such clandestine judicial meetings are often seen as corrupt and unjust.

Although the rooster's crowing is typically associated with the break of a day, in this context, it does not signal a new day. Jewish custom marks the beginning of a day at sunset, not sunrise. Thus Jesus predicts that Peter's denial will happen on the same *day* as the nighttime meal, during the overnight hours leading up to dawn.

The verb *deny*, having the sense of "renounce," also appears in Luke 9:23, where Jesus says, "If any man will come after me, let him deny himself, and take up his cross daily, and follow me." When we consider this verse alongside the current passage, two choices become clear: either (1) deny oneself and affirm Christ, or (2) affirm oneself and deny Christ. It is impossible to affirm both oneself and Christ simultaneously.

III. Prediction Realized

(John 18:25–27)

After Jesus is arrested and taken by the soldiers and Jewish officials, Peter and another disciple, likely John, follow the crowd into the high priest's courtyard (John 18:15–16). As Peter enters, a servant girl accuses, "Art not thou also one of this man's disciples?" (18:17a). Peter denies this and joins the others who are warming themselves by the fire (18:17b–18).

A. Second Denial (v. 25)

25. And Simon Peter stood and warmed himself. They said therefore unto him, Art not thou also one of his disciples? He denied it, and said, I am not.

A second accusation against *Simon Peter* arises, essentially the same as the first. John's account of this event is more concise than the other Gospels (compare Matthew 26:69–75; Mark 14:66–72; Luke 22:54–62).

B. Third Denial (vv. 26–27)

26. One of the servants of the high priest, being his kinsman whose ear Peter cut off, saith, Did not I see thee in the garden with him?

The third accusation comes from *one of the servants* who was *in the garden* named Gethsemane earlier that night during Jesus' arrest (see Mark 14:32, 43–46). This servant is related to Malchus, a servant of the high priest, whose right ear Peter cut off (Matthew 26:51; Mark 14:47; Luke 22:50; John 18:10). Fortunately, due to Jesus' mercy, the injury was not fatal (Luke 22:51). Thus, this servant has good reason to believe that Peter was *with* Jesus!

27. Peter then denied again: and immediately the cock crew.

The Gospels of Matthew, Mark, and Luke all note that *Peter* wept after his third denial and the rooster crow (Matthew 26:75; Mark 14:72; Luke 22:62). Jesus' prediction has come true, and Peter responds to this realization with shame, anguish, and remorse. At this point, there is nothing he can do to change what has happened.

How to Say It

Aramaic	*Air*-uh-*may*-ik.
Bethsaida	Beth-*say*-uh-duh.
Dalmanutha	Dal-muh-*new*-thuh.
Decapolis	Dee-*cap*-uh-lis.
Gethsemane	Geth-*sem*-uh-nee (*G* as in *get*).
Malchus	*Mal*-kus.
Phoenicia	Fuh-*nish*-uh.
Tetrarch	*Teh*-trark or *Tee*-trark.

What Do You Think?

How can we strengthen our faith to stand firm in difficult situations?

Digging Deeper

How can we help strengthen the faith of other believers in a similar situation?

IV. Reinstating a Leader

(John 21:15–17)

The next section of Scripture takes place following Jesus' resurrection. By this time, the risen Jesus has appeared to many disciples and followers (John 20:11–29). He appears again to seven disciples at the Sea of Galilee (21:2), directing them to a large catch of fish before inviting them to breakfast (21:12).

A. First Exchange (v. 15)

15a. So when they had dined, Jesus saith to Simon Peter, Simon, son of Jonas, lovest thou me more than these?

After breakfast, *Jesus* turns the meeting into a teaching moment. *Simon Peter* had previously boasted of his commitment and devotion to Jesus (Luke 22:33, above). But his pledge of devotion proved to be bluster. Jesus' question probes Peter's heart and loyalties.

What does the word *these* refer to? Is it the boats and fishing equipment? Is it the other disciples? Or does it mean, "Do you love me more than these other disciples love me?" We may conclude that Jesus means *these* as a general reference point: "Do you love me supremely, more than anything or anyone else?"

15b. He saith unto him, Yea, Lord; thou knowest that I love thee.

Peter assures Jesus of his *love*, even reminding the *Lord* that *thou knowest* this fact. Jesus had correctly predicted that Peter's previous declarations of commitment would prove false (John 13:37–38; compare 18:25–27, above).

15c. He saith unto him, Feed my lambs.

As the Good Shepherd, Jesus laid down His life (John 10:15). If Peter loves Jesus, he will lead in the same way, protecting and providing for the *lambs* who are God's people (see Luke 22:32; 1 Peter 5:1–4; compare Luke 15:3–7).

What Do You Think?

How can you actively show your love for Jesus in your relationships, work, and service to others?

Digging Deeper

What challenges might arise when trying to do so?

B. Second Exchange (v. 16)

16. He saith to him again the second time, Simon, son of Jonas, lovest thou me? He saith unto him, Yea, Lord; thou knowest that I love thee. He saith unto him, Feed my sheep.

With only slight variation, the exchange is repeated.

C. Third Exchange (v. 17)

17. He saith unto him the third time, Simon, son of Jonas, lovest thou me? Peter was grieved because he said unto him the third time, Lovest thou me? And he said unto him, Lord, thou knowest all things; thou knowest that I love thee. Jesus saith unto him, Feed my sheep.

Jesus questions Peter's love a third time. For Peter to feel *grieved* at this repetition is understandable. Does Jesus doubt his answer? Or is Peter's distress the result of seeing a connection between these three questions and his three denials (John 18:15–18, 25–27)? Just as Peter denied Jesus three times, Jesus allows Peter to affirm his love three times. Peter responds by being as absolute in his affirmation of love as he was in his denial.

Peter's response acknowledges that not only does Jesus know Peter's thoughts, but He also knows *all things*—a recognition of His deity (John 2:25).

Conclusion

A. Time to Change the Story

Following Jesus' ascension, Peter demonstrated his love for Christ and commitment to God's people. He played a key role in the first-century church (Acts 1:21–22; 2:14; 3:12; 4:8–20; 10:47–48). His declaration of commitment to Christ, even while imprisoned, came to fruition (5:17–42; 12:1–11). He grew from being "unlearned and ignorant" (4:13) to being the author of the two letters in the New Testament that bear his name. Although we don't know the circumstances of Peter's death, tradition suggests that he was crucified in Rome.

Peter's story following Jesus' ascension is an important milestone marking his spiritual maturity. But we must not miss the formative issues of today's lesson. The most significant aspect of Peter's story may not be its beginning or ending but rather the remarkable turning point in the middle.

Peter faced a painful low point in his life when he denied his Savior. We too will experience painful lows on our road to spiritual maturity—every Christian does. When such a low happens, the primary issue is how we respond. Peter heard Jesus speak of four possible outcomes in hearing the Word (see Matthew 13:1–9). Three of those are quite negative, but they need not be considered irreversible. God redeemed Peter's failure and used his weakness to strengthen his faith. The same can happen with us.

What Do You Think?

What areas in your life do you need to surrender to God so that He can use your weaknesses for His glory?

Digging Deeper

What steps can you take this week to surrender those areas to God?

B. Prayer

Heavenly Father, You are our Healer. You restore brokenness. Thank You for the testimony of Peter. We need Your healing power, and we pray that You will restore, renew, and strengthen us so that we may help others and direct them to You. In Jesus' name we pray. Amen.

C. Thought to Remember

Never underestimate what God can do with our weaknesses.

Involvement Learning

Enhance your lesson with KJV Bible Student *(from your curriculum supplier) and the reproducible activity page (at www.standardlesson.com or in the back of the* KJV Standard Lesson Commentary Deluxe Edition*).*

Into the Lesson

Before class begins, write the following open-ended sentences on the board for class members to see as they arrive:

1. *Bad times are good when . . .*
2. *Good times are bad when . . .*
3. *Defeat leads to success when . . .*
4. *Success leads to defeat when . . .*

Divide the class into four small groups and assign each group one of the sentences to complete. After five minutes of group work, reconvene the class and invite volunteers to share how their group completed the assigned sentence. Then facilitate a whole-class discussion by asking the following questions: 1–What defines "good times" and "bad times"? 2–Which has taught you more: defeat or success? 3–Why does failure sometimes lead to greater success? Lead to Bible study by saying, "Today's study will investigate one of the most successful Christ-followers in history. As we will see, his successes came after experiencing deep failure."

Into the Word

Announce a Bible-marking activity. Provide copies of today's Scripture texts for those who prefer not to write in their Bibles. Distribute handouts (you create) with these instructions:

- Write a plus sign (+) next to verses depicting a "high" moment in Peter's life.
- Write a minus sign (–) next to verses depicting a "low" moment in Peter's life.
- In the margins, jot down possible thoughts Peter might have had during each interaction with Jesus.
- Write an "A" next to words or phrases that indicate Peter's affirmation of Christ's deity.
- Write a "C" next to words or phrases that illustrate how Peter committed himself to Christ.
- Write a "D" next to words or phrases that show how Peter denied having a relationship with Christ.
- Write an "M" next to words or phrases that describe how Peter accepted the mission he received from Christ.

Slowly read the Scripture aloud (or ask volunteers to do so) at least twice and as many as four times. As the Scripture is read, class members should mark their copies in the ways noted.

After calling time, summarize findings by asking the following questions for whole-class discussion: 1–In what ways was Peter's life a success? In what ways was it a failure? 2–How would you predict Peter's story would end if the biblical account concluded with his denial of Christ? 3–In what ways does Peter's life surprise you? 4–Can you think of other individuals from the Bible who turned their lives around after a dramatic encounter with God? 5–What does this tell you about how God has worked in the past and continues to work today?

Option. Distribute copies of the "The Life of Peter" exercise from the activity page, which you can download. Have learners work in pairs to complete as indicated.

Into Life

Distribute an index card and pen to each participant. Ask them to write down potential shortcomings a believer might experience. After one minute, collect the cards, shuffle them, and redistribute them, giving one card to each class member. Direct participants to write down ways the shortcomings listed on their cards can become opportunities for believers to depend on Christ. After calling time, invite volunteers to share the shortcomings on their cards and discuss how they believe those shortcomings can create opportunities to practice dependence on Christ.

Option. Distribute copies of the "Feed the Sheep" exercise from the activity page. Have learners complete it individually in a minute or less before discussing conclusions with a partner.

Zacchaeus, the Repentant Tax Collector

Devotional Reading: Luke 6:31–38
Background Scripture: Luke 19:1–10

Luke 19:1–10

1 And Jesus entered and passed through Jericho.

2 And, behold, there was a man named Zacchaeus, which was the chief among the publicans, and he was rich.

3 And he sought to see Jesus who he was; and could not for the press, because he was little of stature.

4 And he ran before, and climbed up into a sycomore tree to see him: for he was to pass that way.

5 And when Jesus came to the place, he looked up, and saw him, and said unto him, Zacchaeus, make haste, and come down; for to day I must abide at thy house.

6 And he made haste, and came down, and received him joyfully.

7 And when they saw it, they all murmured, saying, That he was gone to be guest with a man that is a sinner.

8 And Zacchaeus stood, and said unto the Lord; Behold, Lord, the half of my goods I give to the poor; and if I have taken any thing from any man by false accusation, I restore him fourfold.

9 And Jesus said unto him, This day is salvation come to this house, forsomuch as he also is a son of Abraham.

10 For the Son of man is come to seek and to save that which was lost.

Key Text

When Jesus came to the place, he looked up, and saw him, and said unto him, Zacchaeus, make haste, and come down; for to day I must abide at thy house. **—Luke 19:5**

The Testimony of
Faithful Witnesses

Unit 2: Faithful Witnesses Say "Yes" to Jesus

Lessons 5–8

Lesson Aims

After participating in this lesson, each learner will be able to:

1. Summarize Zacchaeus's character development.

2. Explain the significance of Jesus' willingness to stay at Zacchaeus's house.

3. Make a list of personal attitudes and behaviors that Jesus' love compels them to change.

Lesson Outline

Introduction
- A. Favorite Story
- B. Lesson Context

I. Viewing from a Distance (Luke 19:1–4)
- A. Entering and Passing (v. 1)
- B. Status and Wealth (v. 2)
- C. Stature and Curiosity (vv. 3–4)
  - *Pining for a Clear View*

II. Interacting Up Close (Luke 19:5–10)
- A. Unmerited Attention (vv. 5–7)
- B. Change of Heart (v. 8)
- C. Seeking of the Lost (vv. 9–10)
  - *Met by Mercy*

Conclusion
- A. "Yes" That Brings Change
- B. Prayer
- C. Thought to Remember

Introduction

A. Favorite Story

"Zacchaeus was a wee little man . . .". So begins a popular children's Sunday school song about this Bible story. As a child, I loved the story of Zacchaeus. I remember the first time I heard it—I leaned in to catch every word. The anticipation! The drama! The tree climbing! When I was little, I loved to climb trees and was delighted that one of my favorite activities showed up in the Bible. Even better—Zacchaeus did it to see Jesus! I sympathized with Zacchaeus's inability to see over the crowd. Most of all, I loved this story because Jesus knew Zacchaeus's name.

As an adult, I climb fewer trees but still sit up straighter whenever I hear or read Zacchaeus's story. I still marvel that Jesus knew Zacchaeus's name—and also knows mine. However, these days, it is Zacchaeus's response to Jesus that catches my attention. The story challenges me now: What kind of fruit is my faith bearing? To what lengths will I go to see and follow Jesus?

B. Lesson Context

Jesus and His disciples journeyed to Jerusalem for the final Passover that they would observe together (Luke 9:51; 18:31–33). Along the way, Jesus taught (17:22–37; 18:31–34), told parables (18:1–8; 18:9–14), handled questioning people (17:20–21; 18:18–30), and healed (17:11–19; 18:35–43). Jericho was their last stop before reaching the capital city. It was only about 15 miles northeast of Jerusalem and situated in the Jordan River valley. It had a warm climate and freshwater springs; Jericho was an oasis for weary travelers.

Luke groups together three special encounters with Jesus—a "certain ruler" (Luke 18:18–30), a blind beggar (18:35–43), and Zacchaeus (19:1–10). Each of them sought out Jesus as He traveled. In the first scenario, the man was wealthy and privileged but went away unfulfilled. The crowd who witnessed the exchange questioned, "Who then can be saved?" (18:26). In the second, the man had nothing but audacity and perseverance. Jesus was moved on his behalf, and his faith healed him—he received his sight and followed Jesus (18:43)! Zacchaeus's story is the third encounter in this sequence.

Zacchaeus was "chief among the publicans" in Jericho (Luke 19:2). As such, he led those who implemented taxes, collected tolls, and performed customs duties. Lead publicans were tax collectors who hired other collectors and set collection policies. Tax collectors held a position of prominence or authority, but with this came hard feelings from the general populace. Tax collectors frequently overcharged to make a profit. They were despised and mistrusted, seen as collaborators with oppressive Rome, and considered dishonest (Mark 2:15–16). Roman authorities auctioned contracts to the highest bidders—groups or individuals—to collect local tolls and tariffs. Whoever won the contract was on the hook for the contracted amount. Therefore, collections officers often took bribes and passed overages onto ordinary citizens, protecting themselves while ensuring contracts were paid.

I. Viewing from a Distance

(Luke 19:1–4)

A. Entering and Passing (v. 1)

1. And Jesus entered and passed through Jericho.

This verse indicates a scene change. Jesus and His disciples are traveling from Galilee to Jerusalem for the Passover (see Lesson Context). While outside *Jericho*, Jesus heals a blind beggar (Luke 18:35–43). Then they move into the city, presumably walking along the main thoroughfare.

B. Status and Wealth (v. 2)

2. And, behold, there was a man named Zacchaeus, which was the chief among the publicans, and he was rich.

Luke uses the word *behold* to capture his audience's attention and introduce a new character. Unlike the encounter with the rich young ruler (Luke 18:18–25), Luke introduces *Zacchaeus* by name. His name is the Greek form of a Hebrew word that means "innocent," "pure," or "clean." Luke also names Zacchaeus's occupation. He is *the chief* tax collector in Jericho (see Lesson Context).

Additionally, Luke highlights Zacchaeus's wealth. In doing so, Luke connects Zacchaeus's story with the rich ruler Jesus and His disciples met before arriving in Jericho.

> **What Do You Think?**
> Why does Luke include the details of Zacchaeus's profession and socioeconomic status? What effect do these details have on the story?
>
> **Digging Deeper**
> In what ways might such information about someone bear on your work as a disciple-maker (Matthew 28:19–20)?

C. Stature and Curiosity (vv. 3–4)

3. And he sought to see Jesus who he was; and could not for the press, because he was little of stature.

The Greek word translated here as *he sought* is essential to Luke's Gospel, appearing more than two dozen times in various forms (examples: Luke 5:18; 12:31; 15:8; 17:33). Perhaps the most memorable of these instances is, "Ask, and it shall be given you; seek, and ye shall find; knock, and it shall be opened unto you" (11:9).

Zacchaeus wants *to see* Jesus. He has no problem with his eyes but is struggling in another way—he is short in *stature,* and the crowd (*the press*) is dense (Luke 12:1; 14:25). A growing multitude now fills the narrow streets of Jericho and prevents Zacchaeus from catching a glimpse of Jesus.

Luke implies that Zacchaeus wants to learn about this well-known prophet so that he can evaluate Him, but Zacchaeus's height is a barrier to reaching his goal. He can't see over the crowd. Therefore, he is forced to use other means to achieve his objective.

4. And he ran before, and climbed up into a sycomore tree to see him: for he was to pass that way.

Zacchaeus sets aside his dignity with two actions: running and climbing. He is eager to beat the crowd to the next likely spot that Jesus will be. Powerful men do not run; they have other people do it for them—running errands, sending messages, and securing invitations. It is significant that Zacchaeus wants to see Jesus for himself and is willing to risk looking undignified in the process. His actions indicate that his interest is more than idle curiosity. He positions himself ahead of Jesus and prepares for the approach.

The *sycomore* tree is a species of fig native to the Middle East and Africa. It has a wide, short trunk and low branches. We may imagine Zacchaeus climbing it quickly. Grown men typically do not climb trees, and Zacchaeus's action may have been humbling. His posture in this moment is neither haughty nor concerned with outward appearance (compare Luke 18:14).

> **What Do You Think?**
> Have you ever done anything undignified to "catch a glimpse" of Jesus? Why, or why not?
>
> **Digging Deeper**
> How do humility, enthusiasm, and childlikeness deepen the significance of Zacchaeus's actions?

Pining for a Clear View

Growing up, my friends and I were obsessed with a famous boy band. We followed them on every tour, watched all their online videos, knew all their song lyrics, and even researched their personal lives. Yes, it was a little strange and over-the-top, and I look back as a nearly 30-year-old with great relief that I eventually outgrew the fascination.

One afternoon we discovered that the band was recording at a studio only 10 miles from my parent's house. To say we were excited would be an understatement. So we traveled to the recording studio, and to our delight, only a small crowd was gathered outside. We didn't have a clear view, however, so a friend and I walked around the side of the property, climbed over a few walls, pushed through the bushes, and eventually found ourselves at a fence beside the garden. From there, our view was unhindered—one of the band members was only ten meters away! Mission complete!

I look back and admire the determination of my 15-year-old self. Like Zacchaeus, I went to great lengths to get a glimpse of a person I was curious about. Have you ever gone to great lengths to see someone famous? —N. V.

II. Interacting Up Close

(Luke 19:5–10)

A. Unmerited Attention (vv. 5–7)

5. And when Jesus came to the place, he looked up, and saw him, and said unto him, Zacchaeus, make haste, and come down; for to day I must abide at thy house.

This is one of many examples in Luke's Gospel where Jesus exhibits supernatural knowledge, which can be rightly expected of God alone (compare Luke 5:22; 6:8; 7:36–50; 8:46; 19:29–34; 22:7–13). Astonishingly, Jesus stops and calls *Zacchaeus* by name.

Jesus does not compare schedules or ask if today is convenient for guests—He tells Zacchaeus to hurry *down* and invites Himself over. In fact, Jesus presents His stay with Zacchaeus as something that *must* happen. The Greek expression translated "must" regularly signifies something that has to take place to fulfill God's purpose (examples: Luke 2:49; 9:22; 17:25; 24:44). Jesus' visit to the man's *house* is a divine necessity.

Jesus initiates the invitation as if He is the host. He is authoritative in the exchange and dignifies Zacchaeus by designating the man's home as the place where He and His disciples will receive refreshment. Jesus is not afraid to associate with this unpopular man. His words are urgent—it will happen *to day*.

6. And he made haste, and came down, and received him joyfully.

Zacchaeus obeys Jesus immediately. He doesn't

How to Say It

Galatians	Guh-*lay*-shunz.
Jericho	*Jair*-ih-co.
Les Misérables	Lay Mee-zher-*abh*.
sycomore	*si*-kuh-mor.
Valjean	Vahl-*szohn*.
Zacchaeus	Zack-*key*-us.

act flustered or annoyed at having an unexpected houseguest (or 13!). Instead, he responds to Jesus' message with joy.

Zacchaeus's eagerness to catch a glimpse of Jesus from up in the tree has paid off, so he climbs back *down* to ground level and meets Jesus, face to face. This is no longer a momentary encounter; Jesus likely will remain in his company for the length of a meal and travel respite.

> **What Do You Think?**
>
> Being "hospitable" is one mark of a mature believer (Titus 1:8). What is your response to spur-of-the-moment invitations?
>
> **Digging Deeper**
>
> How might Romans 12:13 and 1 Peter 4:9 shift your response or encourage you toward change?

7. And when they saw it, they all murmured, saying, That he was gone to be guest with a man that is a sinner.

The crowd continues to be an obstacle. *They* are not happy with Jesus' choice to stay with Zacchaeus. Therefore, they grumble. The onlookers' condemnation is clear; they consider Zacchaeus a *sinner*. Zacchaeus holds no respect within his community. As a notorious tax collector, the crowd regards Zacchaeus as disloyal to God and His people (see Lesson Context). They are shocked to think Jesus would associate with him.

Throughout Luke's Gospel Jesus receives criticism for His affiliation with "publicans and sinners" (Luke 5:30; 7:34; 15:1–2). In going home with Zacchaeus, Jesus is doing the right thing, not the popular thing.

> **What Do You Think?**
>
> Why does Jesus' choice to be Zacchaeus's guest bother the crowd? What judgment do they make? Why?
>
> **Digging Deeper**
>
> How are you like the grumbling crowd? What judgments do you make against "sinners"?

B. Change of Heart (v. 8)

8. And Zacchaeus stood, and said unto the Lord; Behold, Lord, the half of my goods I give to the poor; and if I have taken any thing from any man by false accusation, I restore him fourfold.

By standing to speak, *Zacchaeus* emphasizes the importance of his pronouncement. He begins by calling Jesus to attention and then attributes to Him the respectful title of *Lord*. Zacchaeus affirms an attitude of humility and reverence toward Jesus. Then he declares an intention toward restitution.

Zacchaeus announces to Jesus (and the city of Jericho) the actions he will take to fix the damage he has caused. He begins by halving his wealth and pledging it to *the poor*. In doing so, he aligns with the wisdom and goodness taught through Jewish Scripture: "He that hath a bountiful eye shall be blessed; for he giveth of his bread to the poor" (Proverbs 22:9).

He promises to restore monies *taken* by false accusation. Since the tax collection system was not standardized, extortion ran rampant, and bribery was common. Zacchaeus says he will pay four times the amount (*fourfold*) of anything he took unfairly. This amount echoes the restitution required by the Law of Moses for stealing livestock (Exodus 22:1). By stating his intentions in this way, Zacchaeus acknowledges that he gained his wealth unethically. He openly confesses that he has done wrong and is ready to make reparations.

Perhaps Zacchaeus's desire to see Jesus with his own eyes has opened and healed his sight in ways beyond the physical (compare Mark 4:12). Zacchaeus acknowledges his wrongs and declares a shift in priorities. He will turn to generosity, offering alms instead of being greedy, as is typical of his profession. Zacchaeus chooses righteousness over wealth, one of the significant obstacles to inheriting God's kingdom (compare Luke 18:18–30).

C. Seeking of the Lost (vv. 9–10)

9a. And Jesus said unto him, This day is salvation come to this house.

Jesus responds to Zacchaeus's speech with profound blessing. A physical miracle is not needed, but a spiritual one has occurred as *this day* Zacchaeus receives *salvation*. Zacchaeus does not need to wait for some far-off time to experience the justice and mercy of God's kingdom. He participates in it immediately.

Jesus includes *this house*, the entirety of Zacchaeus's household, in the receipt of saving grace. In the first century, a household's faith hinged on the beliefs and lifestyle of its leader. In the same way that everyone in Zacchaeus's household would have been affected by his reputation and dishonest behavior, tainted in the eyes of the community, they are also restored through his repentance.

9b. Forsomuch as he also is a son of Abraham.

Jesus' words continue, reinstating Zacchaeus's place within the family of faith. The Jews in Jericho see Zacchaeus as someone cut off from God's people, a traitor because he collaborated with the Romans. Jesus' words offer Zacchaeus restoration, belonging, and forgiveness. As a *son of Abraham*, the inheritance of God's kingdom is his. God's promise is to bless all nations through Abraham's seed (Genesis 22:18; compare Galatians 3:29). Zacchaeus is now reclaimed as a part of God's people according to God's promise. With Jesus' pronouncement, the meaning of Zacchaeus's name, "clean," regains its accuracy. Jesus makes a way for Zacchaeus to return to his true self: a son of God, pure and forgiven.

10. For the Son of man is come to seek and to save that which was lost.

The phrase *Son of man* appears more than 80 times across all four Gospels (see Matthew 8:20; Mark 10:45; Luke 11:30; John 1:51). It also shows up frequently in the Old Testament. In Hebrew, "Son of man" literally reads "son of Adam," meaning "human being." In the Old Testament, the phrase often highlights the difference between humans and God (consider Numbers 23:19; Psalm 8:4; Isaiah 51:12). God addresses the prophet Ezekiel as "Son of man" 93 times (examples: Ezekiel 2:1; 3:17; 33:2)! In Daniel, there is a heavenly figure seen and described "like the Son of man" (Daniel 7:13). This figure receives authority from God to rule the world forever, served by all people, nations, and languages (7:14).

By Jesus' time, "Son of man" carried connotations of judgment and deliverance. The Son of man was considered a servant of God and sometimes the Messiah. Jesus uses the title for Himself and, in so doing, pairs His humanity and divinity. In this passage, Jesus uses the title to claim the authority to *seek* and *save*.

Seeking and saving are strong themes throughout Luke. The parables of the lost coin, the lost sheep, and the prodigal son illustrate these themes exceptionally (Luke 15:1–7; 8–10; 11–32). Jesus welcomes Zacchaeus back into the fold, for He came "not to call the righteous, but sinners to repentance" (5:32). Jesus' choice to become Zacchaeus's guest reveals the nature of His ministry.

What Do You Think?

How does Zacchaeus's story enhance your concept of seeking and saving the lost?

Digging Deeper

How do Luke 15:3–7, 8–10, and 11–32 influence your answer? What is the church's role? Yours? God's? The lost's?

Met by Mercy

In my opinion, the best musical of all time is *Les Misérables*. It is roughly based on Victor Hugo's famous novel of the same name. The novel and musical masterfully tell the story of Jean Valjean, a troubled former prisoner in search of a better life during the struggle of the French Revolution.

An unforgettable scene early in the musical paints a profound picture of mercy and grace. Valjean, newly released from prison, meets a bishop who gives him a place to sleep. However, Valjean steals silverware from the bishop during the night and escapes. When the police discover him on the road laden with silverware that is evidently not his, they return him to the bishop. Expecting to be rearrested and condemned, Valjean instead meets mercy as the bishop insists that he gave the silverware as a gift. To add emphasis, the bishop also offers two silver candlesticks, saying, "Would you leave the best behind?" As Valjean leaves, the bishop sings, "You must use this precious silver to become an honest man."

Jean Valjean is so staggered by this display of mercy and grace that he turns to a life of radical service and generosity toward others. The candlesticks become a precious and solemn reminder of lavish mercy.

Similarly, Zacchaeus is transformed by a merciful encounter with the Lord. Jesus' love touches his life and transforms him from lostness to one found in perfect, eternal love. How have you experienced mercy? How might you extend radical mercy to others? —N. V.

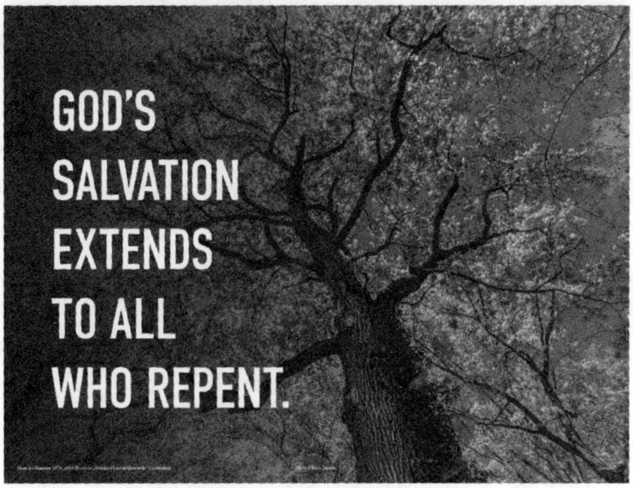

Visual for Lesson 7. *Display the visual in a prominent place. Ask students to spend one minute offering God gratitude for His great mercy.*

Conclusion

A. "Yes" That Brings Change

Saying "Yes!" to Jesus is not the same as liking a post or retweeting a comment on social media. It is not as simple as catching a glimpse of a passing hero. The "yes" we give to Jesus changes our lives. It requires obedience within a new way of life. Kingdom perspective shifts how we think and act, changes priorities, and helps us relate generously with our neighbors, communities, and the world. A "yes" to Jesus halts old habits that actively harm others.

As many new things are, Jesus' way may be initially uncomfortable. His way often requires significant lifestyle shifts and sacrifices. Like Jesus' response to the rich ruler in Luke 18, we must admit that following God is hard (Luke 18:24), especially for the wealthy. Jesus says it is "easier for a camel to go through a needle's eye, than for a rich man to enter into the kingdom of God," but Zacchaeus models hope and possibility for all of us (18:25). Although the rich ruler presumably struggles to gain salvation or misses it altogether, Zacchaeus's story powerfully models Jesus' words, "The things which are impossible with men are possible with God" (18:27).

Jesus offers Zacchaeus and his household saving grace—but how difficult it must have been for Zacchaeus to face each person he had harmed! How difficult it must have been to return the money he previously considered his rightful possession! After all, Zacchaeus hadn't broken societal rules; he had worked within the cultural system surrounding him. And yet, after welcoming Jesus into his life, Zacchaeus is called to something better and higher than the culture in which he lives. He is called to a new generosity and righteousness—as are we.

As followers of Jesus, we are called to repair, as best we can, the harm we have done to others. This restitution includes reversing course regarding the evil in which we passively participate. Is there someone in your circle whom you have not treated with generosity? Have you neglected to pay someone back or taken credit for another's effort, creativity, or work? What is necessary to repair that damage? And on a larger scale—is there a system in which you have participated that causes harm to others? What is Jesus calling you to do to restore righteousness within your community? Whom might you invite into the generous, hospitable, gospel welcome of Jesus?

B. Prayer

Lord, we come before You with contrite hearts. We have not loved our neighbors as ourselves. We have failed to act with generosity in the work of reconciliation and restoration. Help us, like Zacchaeus, to live out our faith in You with immediate boldness and resolve. When it is uncomfortable, empower us by Your love. In Jesus' name we pray. Amen.

C. Thought to Remember

Jesus still seeks and saves the lost.

Involvement Learning

Enhance your lesson with KJV Bible Student *(from your curriculum supplier) and the reproducible activity page (at www.standardlesson.com or in the back of the* KJV Standard Lesson Commentary Deluxe Edition*).*

Into the Lesson

Open class by inviting participants to recall a time they were close to a celebrity. Ask learners to describe their proximity. (Examples: from a stadium seat at a concert, spotting them in a public place, seeing them across a restaurant, or getting their autograph.) Then ask students to share what they imagine might happen if that person showed up at their house at dinnertime.

Alternative. Distribute copies of the "Seen and Known" exercise from the activity page, which you can download. Allow one minute for students to complete the written section individually and then ask students to share their responses with a partner.

Say, "It means so much when we are acknowledged by someone important to us. In today's lesson, we will consider the intentional ways Jesus interacted with Zacchaeus."

Into the Word

Ask a volunteer to read Luke 19:1–3 out loud. Ask learners to quickly identify five things they know about Zacchaeus from these verses. Write their responses on the board. (*Expected answers*: lives in Jericho, male, chief publican, wealthy, and short.) Divide students into five small groups, one for each trait. Instruct groups to discuss ways their trait might hinder or help Zacchaeus follow Jesus.

Ask a volunteer to read Luke 19:4–6 out loud. Ask for another volunteer and position them on an elevated surface in one corner of the room (consider using a sturdy chair, table, stepstool, or step ladder). Ask learners, "What is the advantage of [volunteer]'s position?" (*Expected answer*: they can see everything.) Then ask, "What is the disadvantage?" (*Expected answer*: they're alone/disconnected.) Instruct the volunteer to come back and sit in the common area with the class. Ask the group, "How does [volunteer]'s position in the group change their perspective?" (*Possible answer*: they become a passive participant.) Finally, ask another class member to lead the volunteer to a private corner to talk. Ask the group, "How is this interaction different from being a part of the group?" (*Possible answer*: it is personal and active.)

Alternative. Distribute copies of the "Proximity" exercise from the activity page. Ask learners to complete the exercise as instructed in small groups.

Divide the class into the same small groups as before. Ask a volunteer to read Luke 19:7–10 out loud. Assign one of the following Scripture passages to each small group: Luke 5:17–25; 5:27–32; 6:6–11; 7:36–39; and 15:1–7. Ask groups to read their passage and answer these questions: 1–Who or what are the Pharisees criticizing? 2–What is scandalous about Jesus' behavior? After a minute or two, ask a volunteer from each group to summarize their answers. Then ask the class, "What do these passages have in common with Luke 19:7–10?"

Into Life

Say, "Romans 2:4 indicates that God's goodness is intended to lead us to repentance, just as we see Zacchaeus repent in response to Jesus' goodness." Ask participants to take a minute to quietly reflect on the people and circumstances Jesus has used to "seek and save" them.

Option. Distribute index cards and pens. Ask participants to draw a simple timeline of their life and then mark critical moments on it where they notably experienced God's goodness.

Ask learners to make a mental list of personal attitudes and behaviors that Jesus' love has compelled them to change. Return students to small groups and ask them to share at least one transformed attitude or behavior as a personal testimony of God's faithfulness.

Alternative. Distribute copies of the "Then and Now" exercise from the activity page. Encourage students to complete the exercise individually during the week. Let students know you will make time during the next class to share their responses.

Mary, the Loyal Mother

Devotional Reading: Revelation 12:1–6
Background Scripture: Luke 1:26–56; 2:15–19; John 2:1–5; 19:25–27

Luke 2:15–19

15 And it came to pass, as the angels were gone away from them into heaven, the shepherds said one to another, Let us now go even unto Bethlehem, and see this thing which is come to pass, which the Lord hath made known unto us.

16 And they came with haste, and found Mary, and Joseph, and the babe lying in a manger.

17 And when they had seen it, they made known abroad the saying which was told them concerning this child.

18 And all they that heard it wondered at those things which were told them by the shepherds.

19 But Mary kept all these things, and pondered them in her heart.

John 2:1–5

1 And the third day there was a marriage in Cana of Galilee; and the mother of Jesus was there:

2 And both Jesus was called, and his disciples, to the marriage.

3 And when they wanted wine, the mother of Jesus saith unto him, They have no wine.

4 Jesus saith unto her, Woman, what have I to do with thee? mine hour is not yet come.

5 His mother saith unto the servants, Whatsoever he saith unto you, do it.

John 19:25–27

25 Now there stood by the cross of Jesus his mother, and his mother's sister, Mary the wife of Cleophas, and Mary Magdalene.

26 When Jesus therefore saw his mother, and the disciple standing by, whom he loved, he saith unto his mother, Woman, behold thy son!

27 Then saith he to the disciple, Behold thy mother! And from that hour that disciple took her unto his own home.

Key Text

Mary kept all these things, and pondered them in her heart. **—Luke 2:19**

Image © Getty Images

The Testimony of

Faithful Witnesses

Unit 2: Faithful Witnesses Say "Yes" to Jesus

Lessons 5–8

Lesson Aims

After participating in this lesson, each learner will be able to:

1. Recount how Mary expressed her trust in Jesus.

2. Explain Mary and Jesus' loyalty to one another.

3. Write a prayer of trust to Jesus, expressing faith amidst uncertainty in present life circumstances.

Lesson Outline

Introduction

A. Hidden Treasure
B. Lesson Context: Luke
C. Lesson Context: John

I. Mother's Amazement (Luke 2:15–19)

A. Visited at the Manger (vv. 15–18)
B. Pondered in Her Heart (v. 19)
Keepsakes and Memories

II. Mother's Request (John 2:1–5)

A. The Setting (vv. 1–2)
B. The Need (vv. 3–5)
Known Well

III. Mother's Future (John 19:25–27)

A. New Son (vv. 25–26)
B. Responsible Caretaker (v. 27)

Conclusion

A. Steadfast "Yes"
B. Prayer
C. Thought to Remember

Introduction

A. Hidden Treasure

My children love a good mystery, and we often listen to podcasts as a family when we travel. It is common for us to choose enigmatic tales. One such recent story involved the so-called eighth wonder of the world—Prussia's Amber Room. The Amber Room was built between 1701 and 1714 for King Frederick I of Prussia. It was given to Peter the Great, the Tzar of Russia, and moved to the Catherine Palace near St. Petersburg in 1716.

The Amber Room was considered one of Russia's most beloved artifacts for 200 years, a cultural treasure. But the Nazis stole the room in 1941. It was reconstructed in Germany and then disassembled and packed up for protection from the war in 1944. No one has seen it since. Historians believe it was stored in crates in the basement of a castle museum that collapsed from wartime bombing.

In pictures of the replica, the Amber Room glows with golden light. It is a wonder to behold. Unfortunately, its beauty was stolen and hidden, resulting in great loss.

Today's lesson tells of a different kind of hidden treasure—the identity, capabilities, and calling of the Lord, Jesus Christ. It focuses on Jesus' mother, Mary, and how she trusted the slow unfolding of Jesus' person and work.

B. Lesson Context: Luke

Luke 2:1 sets Jesus' birth narrative during the reign of Caesar Augustus (27 BC–AD 14). Augustus was a powerful ruler, and his supporters heralded him as the "savior of the world" because he brought peace to the Roman Empire. Luke tells us that Caesar Augustus decreed a census. The purpose of such a decree was to determine who was subject to taxation and military service. The census required that people return to their familial hometowns. It also served as a reminder that Rome ruled the world, especially for those who lived in small, far-off provinces like Palestine. Thus, Mary and Joseph journeyed the 90 miles from Nazareth in north Galilee southward to Bethlehem. There, they had a baby!

Luke's Gospel provides many details about

Visual for Lesson 8. *Point to the visual and say, "Mary's loyalty teaches us to trust God amidst life's amazements and disappointments."*

Mary and her experience—more than any other Gospel. Luke records the angel Gabriel's visit and Mary's miraculous conception (Luke 1:26–38). He also describes Mary's visit to her cousin Elisabeth's home and the special reception she received (1:39–45). Luke records Mary's worshipful song of praise to God (known as the Magnificat) and her example of faithful trust in God's plan (1:46–55).

C. Lesson Context: John

Today's texts from the Gospel of John act as bookends to Jesus' life and ministry. They focus on two times that Jesus' mother is mentioned. The first is at a wedding in Cana, and the second is at Jesus' crucifixion. The first passage has no parallel texts in the synoptic Gospels. Parallel texts for the second are found in Matthew 27:55–56; Mark 15:40–41; and Luke 23:49.

I. Mother's Amazement

(Luke 2:15–19)

A. Visited at the Manger (vv. 15–18)

15. And it came to pass, as the angels were gone away from them into heaven, the shepherds said one to another, Let us now go even unto Bethlehem, and see this thing which is come to pass, which the Lord hath made known unto us.

A group of *shepherds* receive a heavenly visitation. It is the third time an angelic messenger appears in Luke's narrative (Luke 1:11–20; 1:26–38; 2:9–13). These declare a Savior newly born.

As the *angels* return to *heaven*, the shepherds deduce that the city mentioned (Luke 2:11) is *Bethlehem* (1 Samuel 16:1, 13). They decide to seek out the sign and *go* and *see* the Christ child. They recognize that the message they've received came from the *Lord*.

What Do You Think?

Have you ever heard about something you just couldn't wait to go and see for yourself? What made it necessary to not just take someone else's word for it?

Digging Deeper

What investigation methods do you use to safeguard against "false news"?

16. And they came with haste, and found Mary, and Joseph, and the babe lying in a manger.

A *manger* is a feeding trough for cattle. Mary and Joseph used it as a crib out of necessity (Luke 2:7). What a strange sign for the shepherds to receive (2:12)! Yet it proves to them the identity of Jesus, the infant Lord (2:11).

17. And when they had seen it, they made known abroad the saying which was told them concerning this child.

The shepherds' sight of the baby in the manger is enough to confirm what they heard from the angels. Immediately, they become evangelists, spreading the good news to the surrounding towns and villages (compare Luke 2:10).

18. And all they that heard it wondered at those things which were told them by the shepherds.

The shepherds' witness is effective. People hear and respond. The story the shepherds tell includes heavenly messengers, unlikely recipients, incredible directions, and a humble infant Savior lying in a feeding trough. The story sounds far-fetched, but it is accurate and makes the hearers marvel.

B. Pondered in Her Heart (v. 19)

19. But Mary kept all these things, and pondered them in her heart.

In contrast, *Mary* stays quiet. Like creating an interior scrapbook, she takes mental notes of each moment, memory, and visitor as she experiences God's plan unfolding. Mary considers the miracle of it *all* and then tucks the memories away in her *heart*.

Imagine the things Mary *pondered*: angels, visions, dreams, her husband's obedience, a miraculous pregnancy and subsequent birth, tales of more angels, and shepherds who know what she knows—this is no ordinary baby!

> **What Do You Think?**
> How do you purposefully mark special milestones or experiences in your spiritual walk?
>
> **Digging Deeper**
> What are you more likely to do with spiritual news or experience: "make [it] known abroad" like the shepherds or quietly contemplate it like Mary? Why?

Keepsakes and Memories

My daughter recently got married. Before the wedding, her sister and I opened our old cedar chest to look for memorabilia from my marriage 25 years ago. As I pulled out layer after layer of various keepsakes, we marveled at the tiny dresses she and her sister wore when they were babies. We smiled at the little blue sweater my son wore for his two-year-old pictures.

At the bottom of the chest lay our guest book, white candles, and dried flowers. We thumbed through wedding photos and then dug around some more to find the specific thing I was looking for: the cake cutter my husband and I used at our wedding. My daughter wanted to use it for hers.

Seeing all these special things took me back to when I was young. I saved only the most critical things but kept more than that in my heart. Looking at the keepsakes I realized that, like Mary, I have a lifetime of memories to ponder.

Consider Isaiah 43:18; Philippians 3:13–14; and 2 Peter 1:9; what biblical criteria do you use to decide which memories are worth storing in your heart and which are not? —L. M. W.

II. Mother's Request

(John 2:1–5)

John 1 expresses the beginning of Jesus' ministry from an external perspective, focusing on Him as an adult coming into the fullness of His ministry. John 2 turns to the vantage point of Jesus' mother, who has intimately known Him all His life.

A. The Setting (vv. 1–2)

1. And the third day there was a marriage in Cana of Galilee; and the mother of Jesus was there.

The *mother of Jesus* (who is never specifically named in John's Gospel) attends a wedding in Cana, a small town less than 10 miles from Nazareth. Her attendance at the event makes it probable that she has a family connection with someone in the wedding party. It is possible she came early to help. At the least, the marriage involves close family friends.

Jesus' mother's presence serves as essential background information for the episode that follows.

2. And both Jesus was called, and his disciples, to the marriage.

If Mary is related to the bride or groom, Jesus is too. Therefore, Jesus' presence may be a family expectation at the event. Jesus' *disciples* are present with Him. Thus far in John's Gospel, we know that the band of disciples includes Andrew (John 1:40), Peter (1:42), Philip (1:43), Nathanael (1:49), and the unnamed disciple of John the Baptist (1:35–40). The unnamed disciple might be John the Evangelist, the author of this Gospel. If John is present, then it is likely that his brother, James, is in attendance too (compare Matthew 4:21–22).

Weddings in first-century Judea lasted for seven days after the bride and groom finalized their vows. The invitation to this *marriage* was not to an after-

How to Say It

Bethlehem	*Beth*-lih-hem.
Caesar Augustus	*See*-zer Aw-*gus*-tus.
Magnificat	Mag-*nif*-ih-cot.
Magdalene	*Mag*-duh-leen or Mag-duh-*lee*-nee.

noon ceremony but rather an extensive feast. Those *called* to the celebration could expect an abundant time of joy, food, wine, desserts, music, and dancing at the groom's family home. Jesus and His disciples accept the invitation to participate. Nathanael is from Cana (John 21:2), so he is likely acquainted with the family hosting the wedding.

The scene is set for the first of seven miraculous signs that point to Jesus' identity as the Messiah (John 2:1–11; 2:13–22; 4:46–54; 5:1–15; 6:1–14; 9:1–38; 11:1–45).

B. The Need (vv. 3–5)

3. And when they wanted wine, the mother of Jesus saith unto him, They have no wine.

A near catastrophe occurs: the *wine* runs out. Since the customs of honor and status naturally led to comparisons with other families and local wedding celebrations, no bridegroom wanted to be considered miserly for scrimping on the event. Tradition and public image pushed wedding feasts toward extravagance. The tendency would be to provide a lavish experience that made others in the village consider the bridegroom a generous provider. As in any era, communities have long corporate memories! The host (the groom's family) was responsible for providing all food and drink for the duration of the celebration. To fail to do so was shameful. Therefore, a shortage of wine was an embarrassing problem!

Jesus' *mother* informs Him of the situation, and her message conveys more than simple information—it bears weight, urgency, and concern with the reputation of her family and friends. Some commentators think Mary wants *Jesus* and His company to leave to minimize the family's embarrassment. However, given what follows, this explanation is unlikely. Mary thoroughly knows who Jesus is and that He has the power and authority to fix the situation.

Bearing in mind the potential that this wedding is for a portion of Jesus' relatives, the pressure behind Jesus' mother's words could have been intense. A sharp edge of obligation to her tone could explain Jesus' response (see below).

4. Jesus saith unto her, Woman, what have I to do with thee? mine hour is not yet come.

Jesus responds in three parts. First, He acknowledges His mother as *Woman*. This designation sounds disrespectful to modern ears, but it was not inappropriate to refer to a lady in this manner in the first century. Jesus also uses this same term in addressing His mother in John 19:26 (see below). Although not disrespectful, the moniker does create a separation between Jesus and His mother.

Second, He asks a question. The Greek phrase underlying the translation *what have I to do with thee?* is an idiomatic expression used in both the Old and New Testaments. It can function as a stern rebuke (Judges 11:12). It can also be a neutral equivalent to, "What does this have to do with me?" (2 Samuel 16:10; 2 Kings 3:13). The question can be either direct or rhetorical. It appears that Jesus is reconfiguring His familial relations with the query. The question builds on His reference to His mother as "Woman." As Jesus begins a new season of life and ministry, every relationship is transformed. With His mission before Him, His blood relations become secondary.

Third, Jesus refers to His *hour*. The Gospel of John frequently mentions Jesus' "hour" (John 7:30; 8:20; 12:23, 27; 13:1; 16:32; 17:1). The term refers to the moment when Jesus' complete identity will be revealed, His passion undergone, and His glory exposed. Jesus mentions this "hour" at critical moments in His personal life. Here, He states that ultimate revelation and fulfillment remain in the future. Jesus' comment may be a reminder to His mother that God the Father chooses when and what is revealed about Him in any situation.

> **What Do You Think?**
> As a parent or grandparent, do you know things about your children or grandchildren that others don't know?
> **Digging Deeper**
> Do you ever ask them to get involved in things because you know they could help—and you know they wouldn't naturally step in themselves?

5. His mother saith unto the servants, Whatsoever he saith unto you, do it.

Despite Jesus' brusque response, Mary is not

dissuaded. She trusts that Jesus will do something helpful. Mary instructs the household *servants* to follow Jesus' lead. During large celebrations such as these, the bridegroom might hire a coordinator or steward to manage the event. Mary speaks to those serving the household and guests, behind the scenes. Although her words are specific to the situation, they hold the key to Christian discipleship; it is wisdom to *do* the things Jesus says to do! You never know when a miracle may be right around the corner.

Mary shows great faith in Jesus and plays a significant role in the first miracle of His public ministry. Jesus goes on to turn six pots of water into wine—"good wine" (John 2:10). Imagine Mary's delight as she witnesses yet another marvel! The "ruler of the feast" is impressed with the bridegroom's provision (2:9–10). Presumably, the wedding feast runs its course, and the celebrants finish their week with joy. Jesus' glory—His divinity—manifests in this miracle. Those who follow Him grow in belief (2:11).

Known Well

When my children were in school, we attended many band concerts. While sitting through one, my son and I started playing a game together. We each tried to be the last audience member clapping after a song. We enjoyed the game thoroughly, and eventually he said, "It's not brave to be the *last one*. What's brave is being the *first one* to clap." After that, our game changed, and we carefully gauged when it was appropriate to begin the clapping.

Eventually, my son also started playing in band. He often sat across the theater from my husband and me, waiting with his friends for their turn to play. Sometimes, I heard one lone clap start or end the applause, and I laughed as I searched the crowd for my son. When I found him, we shared a conspiratorial smile. We knew each other, and we knew our game.

Similarly, Mary knew her son. She knew how He would react when He discovered the wine ran out, and she knew He could do something about it. Because of this, she witnessed a miracle. How well do you know Jesus? What might you learn from Mary's confidence in Him? —L. M. W.

III. Mother's Future

(John 19:25–27)

A. New Son (vv. 25–26)

25. Now there stood by the cross of Jesus his mother, and his mother's sister, Mary the wife of Cleophas, and Mary Magdalene.

Near to Jesus' *cross*, several women gather. Interestingly, three of the four are named Mary. The group is comprised of female followers of Jesus who remain present with Him despite the brutality, pain, and suffering they witness.

Matthew's Gospel states that the women were there to minister to Jesus, poised to care for His needs (Matthew 27:55–56). In contrast to John's perspective, Matthew and Mark state that the women stand at a distance to watch (27:55; Mark 15:40). Mark's Gospel adds that "many other women" were also there (15:41), so perhaps we may imagine quite a crowd. The women had followed Jesus from Galilee (Luke 23:49). Luke's Gospel adds the detail that the women "bewailed and lamented" Jesus (Luke 23:27).

What a difficult scene for Jesus' *mother*! Yet she stands in solidarity with Him, enduring.

> **What Do You Think?**
> Have you witnessed someone passing? What was it like?
>
> **Digging Deeper**
> Are you willing to remain present with someone who is suffering? To witness injustice?

26. When Jesus therefore saw his mother, and the disciple standing by, whom he loved, he saith unto his mother, Woman, behold thy son!

Here, John mentions another disciple: the one *whom [Jesus] loved*. It is very common to identify this disciple as John himself. The "beloved disciple," as many endearingly refer to him, is mentioned at a few key points throughout John's Gospel. Most famously, the one "whom Jesus loved" leaned against Jesus at the Passover table (John 13:23) and had a conversation with Him about Jesus' betrayer (13:25–26).

Seeing the two figures together, Jesus addresses

his *mother*. On the formal, attention-getting salutation *Woman*, see John 2:4, above (compare 4:21 and 8:10). Then He asks Mary to see (*behold*) or consider this *disciple* a *son*.

B. Responsible Caretaker (v. 27)

27. Then saith he to the disciple, Behold thy mother! And from that hour that disciple took her unto his own home.

Jesus turns His attention to the *disciple*. This man is to *see* (behold) or consider Mary his *mother*.

More important than identifying the disciple's name who is "standing by" (John 19:26) is to reflect on Jesus' words to him. This man takes Jesus' saying as a direct order and obediently accommodates Jesus' mother's care. From this moment, the two are asked to think about each other as family; Mary gains a *home*.

Jesus' request is at least partially a practical measure. Jesus' (legal, but not biological) father, Joseph, is likely no longer living. Therefore, as the eldest son, Jesus is responsible for His mother's care. We do not know why Jesus asks someone outside His immediate family to look out for Mary because we do know Jesus has other brothers (Matthew 12:46; 13:55; Mark 3:31; 6:3; Luke 8:19; John 7:3–5). What is clear, however, is Jesus' love for both the disciple and His mother. He desires to see them in a supportive relationship. As Mary loses one son, she gains another.

Jesus is in the business of reconfiguring familial relations (Luke 14:26; John 2:4; see commentary above). John 1:11 says that Jesus "came unto his own, and his own received him not." Here, John says that the disciple *took her unto his own home*. The verbal parallel is likely intentional. Jesus' work is nearly finished (John 19:30). Ultimately, He creates a new family built around response to His ministry rather than bloodlines. In doing so, Jesus fulfills the mission of John 1:12—He gives power to those who receive Him to become children of God, vital parts of God's family. This disciple and Jesus' mother demonstrate a new kingdom reality and familial relationship on two levels. The first is practical—the disciple cares for Mary in his home (compare 1 Timothy 5:4). The second is spiritual—they are indeed related as a part of God's family.

Conclusion

A. Steadfast "Yes"

Mary's "yes" to God included cherishing her son's identity through tender, exciting, and excruciating circumstances. She trusted God to sustain her journey and Jesus as her son and divine Lord. Mary held Jesus as He took His first breaths, and she was there with Him as He took His last. She was with Him as much as possible in between, even witnessing His first miracle. Mary observed Jesus' earthly life in all its humble humanity and divine activity. She kept watch and cherished the glorious (albeit painful) unfolding of God's perfect plan: the salvation of the world through Jesus Christ, our Lord.

Mary's consistent "yes" models a beautiful pathway through uncertainty for us. She believed so fiercely in God's provision that she submitted her whole life to obedience and wonder. From the beginning, Mary collected and purposefully remembered the signs God sent that proved His prophetic word was true. She didn't waiver in her belief. Mary's love and loyalty were rewarded by continued care and belonging in God's family.

Mary was a model disciple. She knew the significance of Jesus' life and trusted that He could make a difference in times of need. Jesus was a model son. He did all He could to provide care and support for His mother.

What Do You Think?

In what ways does Mary's witness or specific "yes" to God inspire you toward greater loyalty to Jesus?

Digging Deeper

What promises from God are you incubating? What keeps you steadfast in your belief?

B. Prayer

Father God, may we remain committed to You in the highs and lows of life. In Jesus' name we pray. Amen.

C. Thought to Remember

Loyalty to Jesus means a life of sacrificial love.

Involvement Learning

Enhance your lesson with KJV Bible Student *(from your curriculum supplier) and the reproducible activity page (at www.standardlesson.com or in the back of the* KJV Standard Lesson Commentary Deluxe Edition*).*

Into the Lesson

Invite each student to find three photographs on their cell phone that represent significant moments with a loved one. (Alternatively, ask in advance for students to bring three printed photographs to class.) Divide students into small groups of three or four. Have them take turns sharing their photos with their small group, talking about the significant memories associated with each picture. Encourage them to tell why the person is important to them and why the memories are special.

Lead into Bible study by saying, "Photographs don't tell the whole story of our lives, but they can hold memories of people and events that impacted, changed, and defined us. In today's lesson, we're going to consider glimpses—metaphorical photographs or snapshots—of a very special relationship. As we look at these 'pictures,' pay attention to the impact of this relationship on both Jesus and His mother."

Into the Word

Ask a volunteer to read Luke 2:15–19. Ask the small groups to consider and discuss how they would explain the phrase: "kept all these things." Ask, "How and why do we keep precious moments in our lives?" Challenge students to imagine how Mary might have done this in her time and culture. (*Possible answers*: saving Jesus' baby blanket, keeping a little straw from the manger, retelling the story every year on Jesus' birthday, etc.)

Option. Provide a scrapbook page, scissors, glue, magazines with Christmas images, stickers, extra paper, and pens to each small group. Ask students to design a page for Jesus' baby book.

Alternative. Distribute copies of the "Same News, Different Experiences" exercise from the activity page, which you can download. Give groups a few minutes to work on it and share their responses.

Ask a volunteer to read John 2:1–5. Have groups imagine the scene as if Jesus was an ordinary man and not the Son of God. Ask groups to write a short script of the dialogue between Mary and Jesus. Challenge groups to consider how ordinary people might try to resolve, complain, or worry about the lack of wine at the wedding feast. After five minutes, ask two volunteers from each group to act out their dialogue. Then say, "But Mary and Jesus both knew that He was the Son of God, and that made all the difference." Ask the whole class: What truths and implications were Mary and Jesus aware of that aren't explicitly stated in the passage? (*Possible responses*: Mary could not fix the problem herself, but Jesus could; Mary could trust Jesus to somehow restore the bridegroom's honor, etc.)

Ask a volunteer to read John 19:25–27. Ask small groups to discuss the following question and create a group "Top Ten" list: If you knew you would die tomorrow, what are the ten most important things you would want to say or do? Then ask, "What does John 19:25–27 reveal about what was important to Jesus?" (*Expected responses*: Taking care of others, honoring His mother, entrusting His mother to His friend, etc.)

Alternative. Distribute copies of the "Perspectives" exercise from the activity page. Give groups time to combine their responses.

Into Life

Say, "Life can be full of unexpected twists and turns. Mary's steadfast dedication to trusting God through all things models strong faith."

Distribute index cards and pens. Instruct students to write to Jesus a prayer of trust, expressing faith amidst uncertainty in their present life circumstances. Allow a minute for participants to silently reflect and begin writing their prayers, then encourage them to elaborate throughout the week ahead.

August 2
Lesson 9 (KJV)

Thomas, the Hesitant Believer

Devotional Reading: Psalm 91:1–6
Background Scripture: John 11:14–16; 14:5–8; 20:24–29; 21:1–2

John 11:14–16

14 Then said Jesus unto them plainly, Lazarus is dead.

15 And I am glad for your sakes that I was not there, to the intent ye may believe; nevertheless let us go unto him.

16 Then said Thomas, which is called Didymus, unto his fellowdisciples, Let us also go, that we may die with him.

John 14:5–8

5 Thomas saith unto him, Lord, we know not whither thou goest; and how can we know the way?

6 Jesus saith unto him, I am the way, the truth, and the life: no man cometh unto the Father, but by me.

7 If ye had known me, ye should have known my Father also: and from henceforth ye know him, and have seen him.

8 Philip saith unto him, Lord, shew us the Father, and it sufficeth us.

John 20:24–29

24 But Thomas, one of the twelve, called Didymus, was not with them when Jesus came.

25 The other disciples therefore said unto him, We have seen the Lord. But he said unto them, Except I shall see in his hands the print of the nails, and put my finger into the print of the nails, and thrust my hand into his side, I will not believe.

26 And after eight days again his disciples were within, and Thomas with them: then came Jesus, the doors being shut, and stood in the midst, and said, Peace be unto you.

27 Then saith he to Thomas, Reach hither thy finger, and behold my hands; and reach hither thy hand, and thrust it into my side: and be not faithless, but believing.

28 And Thomas answered and said unto him, My Lord and my God.

29 Jesus saith unto him, Thomas, because thou hast seen me, thou hast believed: blessed are they that have not seen, and yet have believed.

John 21:1–2

1 After these things Jesus shewed himself again to the disciples at the sea of Tiberias; and on this wise shewed he himself.

2 There were together Simon Peter, and Thomas called Didymus, and Nathanael of Cana in Galilee, and the sons of Zebedee, and two other of his disciples.

Key Text

Then saith [Jesus] to Thomas, Reach hither thy finger, and behold my hands; and reach hither thy hand, and thrust it into my side: and be not faithless, but believing. **—John 20:27**

The Testimony of
Faithful Witnesses

Unit 3: Faithful Witnesses Spread the Good News

Lessons 9–13

Lesson Aims

After participating in this lesson, each learner will be able to:

1. Identify Thomas's development as an observer of Jesus' life and ministry.

2. Explain why the Gospel of John might emphasize Thomas's refusal to believe without seeing Jesus for himself.

3. Make a plan to share their doubts with fellow believers who can provide encouragement in faith.

Lesson Outline

Introduction
- A. From Doubt to Faith
- B. Lesson Context

I. Physical Death (John 11:14–16)
- A. Bound to See Lazarus (vv. 14–15)
- B. Bold Suggestion (v. 16)

II. Heavenly Realities (John 14:5–8)
- A. Confused Questioner (v. 5)
  - *Confident Navigation*
- B. Way to the Father (vv. 6–7)
- C. Imprudent Request (v. 8)

III. Resurrection Appearances (John 20:24–29)
- A. Thomas's Stipulation (vv. 24–25)
- B. Visit and Invitation (vv. 26–27)
  - *Wide-Eyed Wonder and Evidence*
- C. Belief and Response (vv. 28–29)

IV. At the Sea of Galilee (John 21:1–2)
- A. Important Appearance (v. 1)
- B. Important Audience (v. 2)

Conclusion
- A. Faith Beyond Doubt
- B. Prayer
- C. Thought to Remember

Introduction

A. From Doubt to Faith

"I am an atheist," he said. His wife and children attended our church, but this was his first Sunday. He made it clear he was only there to support his family—he didn't believe in God.

Several months passed, and he reached out again, asking for a meeting. He asked profound and sincere questions about the evidence for Jesus Christ's bodily resurrection. Something was stirring within him. Our discussion was open, honest, and thoughtful. A few weeks later, he chose Jesus as his personal Savior and was baptized.

Skepticism, doubt, and questions characterize some journeys toward faith. Today's lesson highlights one disciple's willingness to ask questions and seek evidence toward sincere belief.

B. Lesson Context

Tradition has labeled Thomas as a pessimist and skeptic. The Gospel of John refers to Thomas as "Didymus" three times (John 11:16; 20:24; 21:2). All these texts are under consideration in today's lesson. Scholars have commented on this designation, which literally means "twin," as meaning "double," like "double-minded." This interpretation has led to the conceptualization of Thomas as a doubter.

The reputation is not entirely fair, however, as it presupposes that Thomas's questions and requests for evidence were extreme or his disbelief was unwarranted. The disciples had no idea that Jesus would return to life. Thomas's desire for proof did not make him a "typical skeptic" because he alone, among the other disciples, had yet to see Jesus.

I. Physical Death
(John 11:14–16)

The setting for our first segment of text is in the vicinity of the village of Bethabara, also known as "Bethany beyond the Jordan" (John 1:28; 10:40). This village is not to be confused with the Bethany that is about two miles east of Jerusalem in Judea. The latter was a frequent stop for Jesus and His disciples (Matthew 26:6; Mark 11:1; 14:3; Luke 19:29;

24:50; John 11:1; 12:1–8). For today's text, however, Jesus heads to the other Bethany, the one on the east side of the Jordan River. This village is where Jesus fled after attempts on His life during the feast of dedication in Jerusalem (10:22, 31–39).

While teaching in or near Bethany beyond the Jordan and establishing many believers (John 10:41–42), Jesus receives word that a friend named Lazarus is ill (11:1–3). Lazarus and his two sisters, Mary and Martha, live in the Bethany near Jerusalem. They have a close relationship with Jesus, hosting Him in their home and learning from Him (Luke 10:38–42). John tells us that Jesus "loved" them (John 11:5).

When Lazarus falls ill, his sisters immediately send word to Jesus (John 11:3). Over the objections of His disciples, Jesus intends to go back to visit them (11:7–9). But He intentionally delays His journey by two days (11:6). During this delay, Lazarus's illness progresses and ultimately leads to his death. Jesus discerns Lazarus's passing and informs His disciples it is time to take a trip to visit their friends (11:7, 11). He uses a figure of speech to describe Lazarus's fate: "Our friend Lazarus sleepeth" (11:11). But the disciples misinterpret this to mean natural sleep (11:12–13). Jesus now corrects the misunderstanding (compare Acts 7:60; 1 Corinthians 11:30; 15:6, 18, 20).

What Do You Think?

How does the setting of a story impact your understanding of the narrative?

Digging Deeper

What tools can you use to increase your awareness of setting (or context) as you study Scripture?

A. Bound to See Lazarus (vv. 14–15)

14. Then said Jesus unto them plainly, Lazarus is dead.

Throughout Jesus' earthly ministry, His disciples have trouble with His use of figurative language (examples: Matthew 13:34; Mark 8:14–21; compare John 16:25–30). In response to the disciples' misunderstanding, Jesus now speaks without figurative language: their friend *Lazarus is dead.* Jesus has divine knowledge of the situation. He demonstrates His omniscience (complete and infinite awareness), which emphasizes His deity. Jesus' deity is a central theme of John's Gospel (compare John 1:47–48; 2:24–25; 4:16–19, 29).

What Do You Think?

What is the definition of "figurative language"?

Digging Deeper

How does the use of figurative language enhance the messages of Matthew 5:13–16; 7:3–5; 10:16; John 10:7–10; and 15:1–4?

15. And I am glad for your sakes that I was not there, to the intent ye may believe; nevertheless let us go unto him.

Jesus begins an explanation for why He has not departed for Bethany sooner. That explanation focuses on the need for the disciples to *believe.* Jesus understands that Lazarus's death will serve a divine purpose. Even to this point in the Gospel accounts, lack of belief lingers among Jesus' followers. This problem must be—and will be—addressed. By waiting until Lazarus has died, Jesus positions Himself to do so.

Jesus uses the word *nevertheless* to transition away from the disciples' concerns and move the conversation forward. He invites His disciples to accompany Him back to Bethany.

What Do You Think?

Have you ever been "glad" something difficult happened for the sake of someone's learning or development?

Digging Deeper

In what ways might you allow the Holy Spirit to readjust your perspective on life's disappointments, difficulties, and challenges?

B. Bold Suggestion (v. 16)

16. Then said Thomas, which is called Didymus, unto his fellowdisciples, Let us also go, that we may die with him.

Typically, Peter is the outspoken disciple (Matthew 16:15–16; Luke 12:41; John 6:68–69; 13:6), but this time it is *Thomas* who speaks up. The verse gives him a second name: *Didymus*, which means "twin" (see Lesson Context). There are four listings of the original 12 apostles in the New Testament (Matthew 10:2–4; Mark 3:16–19; Luke 6:13–16; Acts 1:13). The placing of Thomas in the ordering of the four listings is seventh, eighth, eighth, and sixth, respectively.

The disciples are hesitant to make the trip because the Jews in Judea had already tried to stone Jesus (John 10:31–33; 11:8). Seeing that Jesus is determined to return despite the danger, Thomas makes the bold statement we see here—not to Jesus but to Thomas's *fellow disciples*. Perhaps this emboldens Peter to declare similarly in Matthew 26:33.

II. Heavenly Realities

(John 14:5–8)

We jump to the next time Thomas is featured by name. Jesus is in His final week. On His last observance of the Passover, Jesus washes His disciples' feet (John 13:1–17). He also predicts His betrayal (13:18–30) and Peter's denial (13:31–38). The disciples become distressed and confused (13:22), so Jesus begins to teach again, comforting them (14:1). Jesus says that He is going "to prepare a place" for them (14:2). His words regarding both a destination and a way to get there prompt a question from Thomas (14:4).

A. Confused Questioner (v. 5)

5. Thomas saith unto him, Lord, we know not whither thou goest; and how can we know the way?

The question from *Thomas* asks about both the destination (*whither thou goest)* and the way to get there (*How can we know*?). Thomas is likely thinking of specific, earthly directions—something concrete, like an address. His response reveals desire: Thomas wants to go where Jesus is going, but he doesn't feel like he has enough information. Jesus speaks of a spiritual and heavenly reality, while Thomas contemplates a physical location.

We don't know the tone behind Thomas's reaction, but we know it is honest. Thomas is open with Jesus—he admits, "I don't get it!"—and that opens the door to Jesus' utterance of one of the most well-known passages of Scripture ever spoken, written, and quoted (next verse).

This interaction is not the first time the disciples show their lack of understanding or ask for further clarification, and it won't be the last. They ask Jesus to explain after He tells the parable of the sower (Mark 4:10–13). Another time, they mistake His reference to the leaven of the Pharisees as literal bread (Matthew 16:5–12). Even after His resurrection, the disciples struggle to comprehend. Jesus has to teach them extensively and open their eyes before they recognize Him and can decipher the Scriptures (Luke 24:25–32).

Even Jesus' parents had a hard time comprehending who He is and what He was doing. Recall the story of twelve-year-old Jesus left behind in Jerusalem. After recovering Him in the temple courts, His parents voice their anxiety, and Jesus is incredulous. He asks them, "Wist ye not that I must be about my Father's business?" (Luke 2:49), but they frankly do not understand (2:50).

Confident Navigation

When I was about ten years old, my mom drove me to my grandmother's house for a visit. On the way, I noticed how many turns and stops we had to make to get there. The trip was about 45 minutes long, and to my little mind, it seemed impossible to remember all the directions. How did my mom do it?

Overwhelmed, I suddenly burst into tears. When my mom asked me what was wrong, I said I never wanted to get my driver's license. I confessed that I was afraid I'd never be able to go anywhere without getting hopelessly lost. My mom reassured me that my orientation would come with time and practice, and I am happy to report that I eventually got my license!

Thomas reminds me of ten-year-old me. He asks Jesus how they could possibly know where He was going. Perhaps Thomas felt overwhelmed at the magnitude of it all. Riding along in the car as a passenger is one thing. Taking control as the driver is quite another! How do you handle spiritual navigation and ensure you're following Jesus? —N. M. H.

B. Way to the Father (vv. 6–7)

6a. Jesus saith unto him, I am the way, the truth, and the life.

Regarding Thomas's query about life's destination and how to get there, Jesus begins with the latter: Jesus Himself is *the way*. This is one of seven statements in the Gospel of John that begin "I am the . . ." as self-identifiers for Jesus (the other six are John 6:35; 8:12; 10:7, 11; 11:25; 15:1). Each unveils a unique facet of Jesus' identity as they firmly declare His divinity. The particular "I am the" statement now before us reveals Jesus Himself as the guide and pathway. He is the road that leads to an eternal life that is reconciled with God (compare Romans 5:10–11; 2 Corinthians 5:18–19; Colossians 1:19–22; Ephesians 2:13–16).

6b. No man cometh unto the Father, but by me.

Now Jesus switches from discussing how to get to the destination to specifying it. The destination is nothing less than admittance into the presence of the heavenly *Father*. Before Thomas's query, Jesus spoke of the nature of that presence in terms of the "Father's house" (John 14:2–3). Jesus promises that He will be there with His disciples (14:4).

Jesus is one with the Father, sees Him clearly, and descended from heaven to earth according to His will (John 1:18; 3:13; 10:30). To properly approach the Father is to come by way of Jesus.

What Do You Think?

What does Jesus mean when He calls Himself "the way"? How is He "the life"? "the truth"?

Digging Deeper

How do the seven "I am the . . ." statements of Christ enhance your understanding of Jesus and His role (John 6:35; 8:12; 10:7, 11; 11:25; 14:6; 15:1)?

7. If ye had known me, ye should have known my Father also: and from henceforth ye know him, and have seen him.

There is a unity between the Father and Son that is difficult to put into words. But when a believer knows one, that believer knows something of the other. In fact, knowledge of the Father is conditional on knowing Jesus. This is a challenge to the disciples: Do they really know the Son? The answer to that question comes next.

What Do You Think?

What caused the disciples to miss seeing the Father in Jesus?

Digging Deeper

How does Matthew 25:35–40 deepen your conceptualization of "seeing" God?

C. Imprudent Request (v. 8)

8. Philip saith unto him, Lord, shew us the Father, and it sufficeth us.

This reaction reveals that the disciples continue to struggle to understand Jesus' teaching. *Philip* voices their lack of understanding this time by asking Jesus to *shew* them the Father. His request reveals a continuing misunderstanding regarding the connection between Jesus and the Father.

III. Resurrection Appearances

(John 20:24–29)

Jesus appeared personally and in the flesh to several people on the day of His resurrection (Matthew 28:1–10; John 20:1–23; etc.). Even so, doubts lingered and would continue to linger over the weeks ahead (Matthew 28:17; Luke 24:38). The most articulate of these comes from the apostle Thomas.

A. Thomas's Stipulation (vv. 24–25)

24–25a. But Thomas, one of the twelve, called Didymus, was not with them when Jesus came. The other disciples therefore said unto him, We have seen the Lord.

The phrase *when Jesus came* refers to His appearance in John 20:19–23. It's easy to imagine that the declaration *We have seen the Lord* is the very first thing spoken to Thomas when he rejoins the group.

25b. But he said unto them, Except I shall

Visual for Lesson 9. *Point to the visual and ask, "What doubts or questions of faith do you have? How might other believers encourage you?"*

see in his hands the print of the nails, and put my finger into the print of the nails, and thrust my hand into his side, I will not believe.

This is where the derogatory phrase "doubting Thomas" originates. Eyewitness accounts of his fellow disciples are not good enough for Thomas. He declares his need for physical, tangible evidence (compare John 4:48). Belief in disembodied spirits was common in the ancient world, and Thomas wants firsthand proof that the claim of Jesus' resurrection is more than a ghost story. Only then will Thomas believe that the person the disciples saw is the same Jesus who was crucified, died, was buried, and has risen.

B. Visit and Invitation (vv. 26–27)

26. And after eight days again his disciples were within, and Thomas with them: then came Jesus, the doors being shut, and stood in the midst, and said, Peace be unto you.

Waiting several *days,* Jesus is in no hurry to prove Himself to *Thomas.* We can only imagine the discussions and arguments between Thomas and the other *disciples* during that interim! When the right time does come, the circumstances are almost identical to those of the previous appearance of Jesus (compare John 20:19).

27. Then saith he to Thomas, Reach hither thy finger, and behold my hands; and reach hither thy hand, and thrust it into my side: and be not faithless, but believing.

Jesus, who is very well aware of Thomas's doubt, addresses him directly with the invitation we see here. Worthy of note is the fact that Jesus' invitation exactly mirrors Thomas's stated demand to personally examine Jesus' *hands* and *side* (John 20:25b, above; compare 19:34).

Wide-Eyed Wonder and Evidence

I once heard a child psychologist say that when young children ask *why,* they aren't always looking for a direct answer. Sometimes, they are simply trying to express their wide-eyed wonder. A child might ask, "Why does the moon shine so brightly?" But they may be trying to express something more like, "Wow! What a miraculous thing the moon is! Look how it lights up the night sky!"

A scientific response can diminish the wonder and awe of the moment. A better response might be something like, "I know! Isn't it amazing?"

Thomas often gets a bad rap for disbelieving eyewitness testimony from reliable sources that Jesus rose from the dead. But perhaps he was also expressing wide-eyed wonder and amazement at the miracle. Imagine trying to wrap your mind around the news of someone coming back to life! Here's a good evangelistic tool to use sometime: ask an unbeliever, "What kind of evidence would you need to believe Jesus arose from the dead?" —N. M. H.

C. Belief and Response (vv. 28–29)

28. And Thomas answered and said unto him, My Lord and my God.

John does not specify whether Thomas reaches out and touches Jesus' physical body. Instead, the text suggests that Thomas believes without touching Jesus' side. He responds to Jesus with a personal confession of faith in his *Lord* and *God.*

Thomas thus pulls together everything Jesus taught about Himself in this complete recognition: Jesus embodies the very essence of God the Father, in whom the fullness of the Godhead dwells (John 10:30; Colossians 1:15–19; 2:9; Hebrews 1:3).

29. Jesus saith unto him, Thomas, because thou hast seen me, thou hast believed: blessed are they that have not seen, and yet have believed.

Bible scholars are divided on whether Jesus'

response is a reprimand. On the one hand, those who view it as a rebuke argue that Thomas should have believed on the basis of the eyewitness testimony of the other disciples. On the other hand, the other disciples themselves did not believe until they encountered the risen Christ and saw Him personally (Mark 16:9–11; Luke 24:10–11).

The critical point is that Jesus speaks a message for an audience beyond Thomas—the message reaches toward future generations, toward us today. There is blessing in believing without having firsthand knowledge (compare John 20:31).

IV. At the Sea of Galilee

(John 21:1–2)

In the intervening verses of John 20:30–31, the Gospel writer stresses two things. First, the examples he records are but a sample of "many other signs" that the disciples witnessed from Jesus. Second, the instances John chose are written so that the reader will believe in Jesus. These two verses also serve as a transition into the episode that follows.

A. Important Appearance (v. 1)

1. After these things Jesus shewed himself again to the disciples at the sea of Tiberias; and on this wise shewed he himself.

Here we catch one more glimpse of the risen Christ with His *disciples*. The *sea of Tiberias* is another name for the sea of Galilee (John 6:1; compare Luke 5:1). Jesus' appearance here is in line with Matthew 26:32; 28:7; Mark 14:28; 16:7.

B. Important Audience (v. 2)

2. There were together Simon Peter, and Thomas called Didymus, and Nathanael of Cana in Galilee, and the sons of Zebedee, and two other of his disciples.

Jesus' post-resurrection appearances number about a dozen, depending on how textual overlaps are counted. Collective witness increases the credibility of the testimony (compare 1 Corinthians 15:6). In this particular appearance, John notes the presence of seven disciples, with Thomas named second (compare the four listings of the apostles noted on John 11:16, above). Thomas is poised to observe another miracle (John 21:6) and Peter's restoration (21:15–19).

Conclusion

A. Faith Beyond Doubt

Thomas's doubt mirrors a common human experience: the struggle of faith, which asks us to trust evidence that we ourselves cannot see firsthand. Jesus often taught in parables, His words falling on His hearers' ears like riddles. And His resurrection is a fantastic miracle! Thomas's interactions with Jesus show humans' difficulty with stepping outside the physical world and into a more important spiritual reality. The way toward deep comprehension of Jesus as the Son of God, Messiah, and Lord is challenging. Understanding Jesus as fully God, one with the Father, is difficult too. It takes questioning and wrestling to overcome the doubts and puzzles that inevitably emerge along the journey of faith. We must have the eyes of our understanding enlightened to truly comprehend (Ephesians 1:18). Sometimes that requires honest questions. It always requires engagement with Jesus, with whom the text of Scripture is primarily concerned.

B. Prayer

Heavenly Father, open our eyes to see how we are like Thomas in both our strengths and weaknesses. In Jesus' name we pray. Amen.

C. Thought to Remember

Jesus meets us in our doubts.

How to Say It

Bethabara	*Beth*-**ab**-uh-ruh.
Bethany	*Beth*-uh-nee.
Cana	*Kay*-nuh.
Didymus	*Did*-uh-mus.
Galilee	*Gal*-uh-lee.
omniscience	ahm-*nish*-uns.
Pharisees	*Fair*-ih-seez.
Tiberias	Tie-*beer*-ee-us.
Zebedee	*Zeb*-eh-dee.

Involvement Learning

Enhance your lesson with KJV Bible Student *(from your curriculum supplier) and the reproducible activity page (at www.standardlesson.com or in the back of the* KJV Standard Lesson Commentary Deluxe Edition*).*

Into the Lesson

To open class, ask all participants to think of one true thing about themselves that they are willing to share with the whole group. After each person shares, ask them to "prove it." Require tangible, visible evidence that what they claim is true. (*Hint*: show a photo, ID, scar, etc., but some things might be impossible to prove—and that is alright!)

Option. Follow the instructions on the "Tough Questions (Facilitator Page)" exercise from the activity pages, which you can download.

Lead into Bible study by saying, "We all have doubts and questions—some are inconsequential curiosities, but others have real significance to our faith and worldview. In today's lesson, notice the main character's questions and doubts. Consider the ways you relate to him."

Into the Word

Ask a volunteer to read John 11:14–16 out loud. Divide participants into two groups: **Jesus** and **Disciples**. Instruct both groups to read John 11:1–15. Ask the **Jesus Group** to write down exactly what Jesus said in verses 4, 7, 11, and 14–15. Have them write what He meant beside each statement. Ask the **Disciples Group** to write down exactly what Jesus said in verses 4, 7, 11, and 14–15. Then have them write what Thomas and the other disciples may have *thought* Jesus meant beside each statement. Bring the class back together and invite the groups to share their findings, alternating answers to highlight the differences. Ask: "Why do you think it was so confusing and difficult for Thomas to understand Jesus in this account?" Allow time for voluntary responses.

Ask a volunteer to read John 14:5–8. Divide participants into small groups of four and provide them with blank white copy paper, one full piece of colored construction paper with a ½ inch diameter circle cut out of the middle and labeled "The Way," and pencils. Instruct groups to draw a map on the white copy paper; the map should lead from the current room they are in to anywhere they choose on the surrounding property. Then ask groups to overlay the construction paper on their map, with the hole placed over the current room. Have groups trade their maps with the construction paper in place. Ask groups to follow the other group's map by moving the cover inch by inch along the route until they reach the end destination. Ask groups to discuss: "How did you feel, knowing a path existed but not being able to see it or know where it was leading?"

Ask a volunteer to read John 20:24–29 out loud. Then ask two volunteers to act out the roles of Thomas and Jesus in this scene (all other participants can be the "other disciples"). Ask participants to share what part of this story is most significant to them and why.

Ask a volunteer to read John 21:1–2. Have small groups imagine a conversation between the seven disciples in this scene. Challenge them to write down at least one line that each disciple might have said. Ask: "How is Thomas's presence among this group meaningful to you?"

Alternative. Ask participants to pair up with a partner. Distribute the "Thomas's Journey" exercise from the activity page. Ask pairs to complete the activity as indicated.

Into Life

Distribute index cards and pens. Ask students to divide into pairs. Give them one minute to write down one question or doubt they have in faith. Then say, "Questions and doubts are inevitable from time to time. Jesus is gracious with our needs, and He wants us to trust Him even when we don't understand."

Instruct pairs to work together to make a plan to share their doubts with fellow believers. Ask partners to pray for each other—especially to encourage each other's faith.

August 9
Lesson 10 (KJV)

Stephen, the Unwavering Martyr

Devotional Reading: Luke 23:32–43
Background Scripture: Acts 6–7

Acts 6:7–10

**7 And the word of God increased; and the
number of the disciples multiplied in Jerusa-
lem greatly; and a great company of the priests
were obedient to the faith.
8 And Stephen, full of faith and power, did
great wonders and miracles among the people.
9 Then there arose certain of the synagogue,
which is called the synagogue of the Libertines,
and Cyrenians, and Alexandrians, and of them
of Cilicia and of Asia, disputing with Stephen.
10 And they were not able to resist the wis-
dom and the spirit by which he spake.**

Acts 7:54–60

**54 When they heard these things, they were
cut to the heart, and they gnashed on him with
their teeth.
55 But he, being full of the Holy Ghost,
looked up stedfastly into heaven, and saw the
glory of God, and Jesus standing on the right
hand of God,
56 And said, Behold, I see the heavens
opened, and the Son of man standing on the
right hand of God.
57 Then they cried out with a loud voice,
and stopped their ears, and ran upon him with
one accord,
58 And cast him out of the city, and stoned
him: and the witnesses laid down their clothes
at a young man's feet, whose name was Saul.
59 And they stoned Stephen, calling upon
God, and saying, Lord Jesus, receive my spirit.
60 And he kneeled down, and cried with a
loud voice, Lord, lay not this sin to their charge.
And when he had said this, he fell asleep.**

Key Text

Stephen, full of faith and power, did great wonders and miracles among the people. **—Acts 6:8**

The Testimony of
Faithful Witnesses

Unit 3: Faithful Witnesses Spread the Good News
Lessons 9–13

Lesson Aims

After participating in this lesson, each learner will be able to:

1. Recount the story of Stephen's courageous witness to the good news of Jesus Christ.

2. Describe the parallels that Acts draws between Stephen and Jesus.

3. Write a way that Stephen's courageous witness may inform their own witness to Jesus Christ.

Lesson Outline

Introduction
- A. Handling the Hardships
- B. Lesson Context

I. The Growing Church (Acts 6:7–10)
- A. Disciples and Priests (v. 7)
- B. Power and Wonder (v. 8)
- C. Wisdom and Spirit (vv. 9–10)

II. The Faithful Martyr (Acts 7:54–60)
- A. Furious Reaction (v. 54)
- B. Fervent Realization (vv. 55–56)
  - *The Worst of Times*
- C. Fateful Reaction (vv. 57–60)
  - *Punch Back*

Conclusion
- A. Opposition and Response
- B. Prayer
- C. Thought to Remember

Introduction

A. Handling the Hardships

Max Cleland (1942–2021) led a promising life. In high school, he excelled in sports and received the title of "Most Outstanding Senior." At the age of 24, he volunteered for combat duty in Vietnam, where he served as a captain in the army.

Just one month before returning home, Cleland picked up a grenade that he thought he had dropped accidentally. He was mistaken, and the resulting explosion mangled or altogether severed his right hand, right leg, and left leg. Though not expected to survive, Cleland recovered from his triple amputation, and he recalled the apostle Paul's teaching that hope "maketh not ashamed" (Romans 5:5).

When Cleland returned to civilian life, he entered politics, learned to drive a car specially equipped for him, and traveled extensively to mobilize support for veterans' causes. At age 34 he became the youngest man ever to head the Veterans Administration. Later, he was elected as a US senator from Georgia. Max Cleland summarized his experience: "Life doesn't revolve around an arm and a leg. People look at you the way you look at yourself."

Today's lesson presents a servant of God who faced a catastrophic blow. It was a blow that led directly to his death. The story of God's servants is stained with the blood of prophets and apostles who paid the price for speaking the truth, and today's lesson presents this reality in vivid detail.

B. Lesson Context

The book of Acts begins the story of the earliest church by focusing on its development within Jerusalem. The theme of "witnesses" in Jerusalem, in all Judea and Samaria, and to the ends of the earth (Acts 1:8) is like of a "Table of Contents" for Acts as it sketches the birth of the church. The narrative starts with events on the Day of Pentecost (2:1–41). Predominant in the account is the divine power behind the dynamic Jerusalem fellowship. The church increased in number from only about 120 believers to more than 3,000 in a single day (compare 1:15; 2:41).

The number of believers in Jerusalem continued to increase over the weeks and months after Pentecost (Acts 2:47b; 5:14; 6:1). The expanding number of believers led them to develop habits for their gatherings and expectations for how they would treat each other (2:42–47a; 4:32–35). During that time, almost all followers of Jesus were of Jewish heritage. However, not all had the same cultural upbringing. Some had adopted elements of Greek culture while living in the Greek-speaking (Hellenistic) portions of the Roman Empire (compare 9:29), while others lived in Jewish regions of Palestine. The distinction between Grecian Jews and Hebraic Jews was revealed in a conflict regarding the treatment of widows (6:1).

To resolve conflict, the Twelve selected seven men "full of the Holy Ghost and wisdom" to handle food distribution to the needy. These men included Stephen (Acts 6:3–5).

I. The Growing Church
(Acts 6:7–10)

A. Disciples and Priests (v. 7)

7. And the word of God increased; and the number of the disciples multiplied in Jerusalem greatly; and a great company of the priests were obedient to the faith.

This verse highlights two important aspects of the growth of the first-century church. First, its development is driven by the dramatic spread of *the word of God* (compare Acts 9:31; 12:24; 19:20; 28:31). As the influence of the gospel message increases among people, so does *the number of the disciples.* When the gospel falls on willing hearts, spiritual fruit results, often in abundant measures (see Luke 8:8, 15).

Second, the fact that the church's number *multiplied . . . greatly* implies rapid growth. A comparison of the number of believers in the early chapters of Acts highlights this expansion (Acts 1:15; 2:41; 4:4; see also 2:47; 5:14; 6:1; 16:5).

Counted among these believers are numerous *priests.* These men serve in the temple when their lot is chosen (example: Luke 1:5, 8–10). We may find this surprising since chief priests opposed Jesus and His message in conjunction with both Pharisees (Matthew 21:45; 27:62; John 7:32, 45; 11:47, 57; 18:3) and Sadducees (Acts 4:1–4; 5:17–18, 27–28).

What Do You Think?

What steps can you take to ensure that the Word of God spreads through your family and community?

Digging Deeper

To what extent does the Word of God spread through the Spirit's work, and to what extent does it spread through human effort?

B. Power and Wonder (v. 8)

8. And Stephen, full of faith and power, did great wonders and miracles among the people.

The display of miracles that accredit Jesus of Nazareth (Acts 2:22) and confirm the message of the apostles (2:43; 5:12) now also certify God's approval of the ministry of *Stephen.* These signs confirm the presence of God's grace and the empowerment of His servants (2 Corinthians 12:12).

The book of Acts does not specify the nature of Stephen's miraculous work *among the people.* His calling before this was to be one of seven men to oversee a first-century version of "Meals on Wheels" (see Acts 6:1–4). We presume that Stephen's ministry in that regard did not involve miracles. Therefore, the *great wonders and miracles* he now performs indicate relief from suffering from both physical and spiritual ailments, as has been true of the apostles (compare 3:1–10; 4:30; 5:15–16). Although he is not one of the apostles, Stephen is chosen by God to bear witness to salvation (compare Hebrews 2:3–4). As one who is "*full of faith*

How to Say It

Alexandrians	Al-ex-*an*-dree-unz.
Cyrenians	Sigh-*ree*-nee-unz.
Hellenistic	*Heh*-leh-nihs-tic.
Libertines	*Lib*-er-teens.
Pentecost	*Pent*-ih-kost.
Sadducees	*Sad*-you-seez.
Sanhedrin	*San*-huh-drun or San-*heed*-run.

and of the Holy Ghost" (Acts 6:5), his life demonstrates the spiritual *power* that Jesus promised (1:8).

> **What Do You Think?**
> In what ways can believers develop spiritual power?
>
> **Digging Deeper**
> How can mature believers leverage their spiritual power to encourage the growth of newer believers?

C. Wisdom and Spirit (vv. 9–10)

9. Then there arose certain of the synagogue, which is called the synagogue of the Libertines, and Cyrenians, and Alexandrians, and of them of Cilicia and of Asia, disputing with Stephen.

After the exile of 586 BC, the need for synagogues arose among the Jewish people. By the time of the first century AD, synagogues served as important meeting places for observing religious practices, studying Scripture, gathering on the Sabbath, and discussing Jewish law and tradition (examples: Matthew 4:23; Acts 9:20; 13:14–15; 15:21). Additionally, synagogues were places for financial contribution, elementary education, and hospitality.

More than one *synagogue* may be in view here. Commentators suggest the writer could be considering anywhere from one to five synagogues, although most tend to lean toward one or two. Paul refers to multiple synagogues in Jerusalem (Acts 24:11–12). Therefore, the groups mentioned in this verse may attend different synagogues. Nonetheless, they all had a specific dispute with Stephen.

Libertines are Jews who have been liberated from slavery or who are descendants of those freed; these differ from freeborn citizens who never experienced enslavement. The *Cyrenians* and *Alexandrians* are from what is modern-day North Africa, and *Cilicia* and *Asia* are regions located in what is modern-day Turkey. The mention of these groups heightens anticipation for the movement of the gospel from Jerusalem and its surrounding areas to all nations and peoples (Acts 1:8; 2:5–12).

Acts 6:11–14 indicates that the dispute with Stephen is likely over his interpretation of the Law of Moses and the relevance of the temple. The result is a charge of blasphemy, a charge that Jesus Himself faced (Matthew 26:65; Mark 14:64).

10. And they were not able to resist the wisdom and the spirit by which he spake.

The fact that the synagogue members could not *resist* Stephen does not mean that they agreed with his message; rather, it indicates their inability to refute his teachings. Their powerlessness fulfills Jesus' promise to give His persecuted disciples "a mouth and wisdom, which all your adversaries shall not be able to gainsay nor resist" (Luke 21:15). Such fulfillment suggests that Stephen's wisdom was given to him by Jesus Himself, undoubtedly through His Spirit (compare 12:11–12).

> **What Do You Think?**
> What steps will you take to ensure your speech is filled with wisdom?
>
> **Digging Deeper**
> How do Proverbs 15:1–2; Ephesians 4:29–32; Colossians 4:5–6; and James 1:19; 3:13–18 inform your answer?

II. The Faithful Martyr
(Acts 7:54–60)

The conflict between Stephen and the synagogue members escalates. False accusations lead to Stephen's arrest and trial before the Sanhedrin (Acts 6:11–15). Stephen, speaking in his defense, emphasizes Israel's history of rebellion against God. In that regard, Stephen lodges at least four countercharges: the Jewish leaders (1) are "stiffnecked and uncircumcised in heart and ears" (7:51); (2) resist the Holy Spirit (7:51); (3) have betrayed and murdered the Messiah and His prophets (7:52); and (4) have not obeyed the Law of Moses (7:53).

A. Furious Reaction (v. 54)

54. When they heard these things, they were cut to the heart, and they gnashed on him with their teeth.

The word *they* refers to the members of the Sanhedrin (Acts 6:15), the highest Jewish council in Palestine. It was led by the high priest (5:21, 27; 7:1; 23:2) and was composed of priests, rulers, elders, and teachers of the law, as well as Sadducees and Pharisees (4:5, 23; 5:21, 34; 23:6).

These things include everything that Stephen has spoken in his lengthy speech found in Acts 7:2–53, especially the last three of those verses. His words provoke a sharp reaction from the Sanhedrin. The expression *cut to the heart* conveys their intense anger or rage (compare Acts 5:33). A similar expression also occurs in Acts 2:37, but the Greek wording is different, expressing bewilderment. The phrase *gnashed . . . with their teeth* signifies a corresponding behavior or facial expression. We see increasing hostility on their part as we trace their reactions from Acts 4:1–22 to 5:27–42 to 7:54–58. Their anger escalates as the story unfolds.

B. Fervent Realization (vv. 55–56)

55. But he, being full of the Holy Ghost, looked up stedfastly into heaven, and saw the glory of God, and Jesus standing on the right hand of God.

Stephen, like Moses, is granted the privilege of witnessing God's *glory* (compare Exodus 33:18–23). To be seated at *the right hand* is considered to be in a place of honor (Psalm 110:1 [quoted in Acts 2:34 and Hebrews 1:13]; Matthew 26:64; Luke 22:69; Ephesians 1:20; Colossians 3:1; Hebrews 1:3). But we note that Stephen sees *Jesus standing,* not sitting, at that position. At least three interpretations have been proposed. One theory is that it indicates Jesus' transcendence, meaning that He is supernatural and surpasses creaturely boundaries. A second interpretation is that Jesus is rising from His throne to welcome Stephen into heaven. A third interpretation proposes that it signifies His readiness to judge, either in support of Stephen or against the Sanhedrin—or both (compare Isaiah 3:13). Indeed, this imagery may embrace all three ideas.

56. And said, Behold, I see the heavens opened, and the Son of man standing on the right hand of God.

A vital turning point occurs. On rare occasions, Scripture mentions *the heavens* being *opened* (compare Ezekiel 1:1; Matthew 3:16; Luke 3:21; John 1:51; Acts 10:11; Revelation 4:1). That is no less the case here when we compare the last line of Acts 7:55 (above) with the last line in the verse now before us.

Stephen replaces the name "Jesus" with the designation *the Son of man.* This title was Jesus' favorite self-designation during His earthly ministry. It appears more than 80 times in the Gospels and is associated with Jesus' authority, judgment, and role in salvation (compare Matthew 26:64; Mark 14:62; Luke 12:8; 22:69). This title can be traced to Daniel 7:13–14. Thus Stephen recognizes Jesus as the divine and promised Messiah, something the doubters don't do (compare John 12:34).

Tied to this revelation is the fact that Stephen sees Jesus sharing in God's presence and glory. His acknowledgment of the divinity of Jesus cannot be missed.

Stephen has avoided making direct statements about Christ up to this point. Now Stephen directly associates Christ with God Himself, a confession he knows will not help his case before the Sanhedrin. Jesus was previously convicted of blasphemy by this group for making similar associations with God (Matthew 26:64–65; Luke 22:69–71). One can only admire Stephen's courage in the face of deadly opposition.

What Do You Think?

How does this passage expand your understanding of Jesus' role as an advocate for believers?

Digging Deeper

How does Stephen's vision of Christ's authority and transcendence encourage your faithfulness to Christ?

The Worst of Times

One late autumn day, it felt like everything in my life was going wrong. Our family's plans for the future had crumbled, and we found ourselves searching for jobs. We desperately sought any glimpse of the hope we had lost.

I began taking walks through our neighborhood, praying, crying, and asking God to fix our situation. Over time, those walks became sacred to me. As I walked, I realized I was not alone: God's presence was with me. The more I poured my heart out to Him in prayer, the more I noticed His peace.

I haven't experienced a day like Stephen did in

Acts 7. But when I read his story, I see that God's presence was with him on his worst day—just as God has been with me time and time again through the most challenging seasons of my life.

On your most difficult days, do you experience the comforting and strengthening presence of God's Spirit? If not, why not? —B. R.

C. Fateful Reaction (vv. 57–60)

57–58a. Then they cried out with a loud voice, and stopped their ears, and ran upon him with one accord, And cast him out of the city, and stoned him.

What started as a trial based on false witnesses (Acts 6:13) ends with deadly mob violence. The Jewish leaders sentenced Jesus to death after their perception of blasphemy (Matthew 26:65–66; compare John 10:31–33). Death by stoning is indeed the proper Old Testament punishment for blasphemy (Leviticus 24:10–16). But the members of the Sanhedrin refuse to consider evidence of Jesus' divinity as they cover *their ears.*

Their *loud* voices drown out Stephen's perceived blasphemies (see Acts 6:11). All pretense of due process is out the window as the Jewish leaders act on their belief that Stephen's conviction means he deserves immediate death. We expect mob action from unruly crowds (Ezekiel 16:40; John 10:22–39) but not from the members of the Sanhedrin!

Ironically, Stephen previously accused these leaders of having "uncircumcised" ears, unwilling to hear the truth (Acts 7:51; compare Jeremiah 6:10). Their actions reflect precisely this unwillingness. If they had circumcised ears and hearts (Deuteronomy 10:16; 30:6; Romans 2:29), they would respond with faith and repentance (compare Acts 2:37–41; 4:4).

However, as the Jewish leaders acknowledge in the case of Jesus, Roman law reserved the imposition of capital punishment for itself (John 18:31). Therefore, as the religious leaders rush to execute Stephen, they are simultaneously misapplying the Law of Moses and breaking the Roman legal code.

58b. And the witnesses laid down their clothes at a young man's feet, whose name was Saul.

The *witnesses* are likely the "false witnesses" whose accusations Stephen just addressed (Acts 6:13–14; 7:2–53). Furthermore, their laying *down their clothes* is practical rather than symbolic; it allows them to throw stones more easily and avoid staining their clothes with blood.

The text introduces a new character, a young man named *Saul.* The note that Stephen's executioners place their clothes at Saul's *feet* suggests that he has a position of authority among the Jews (compare Acts 4:35, 37; 5:2). This detail supports the fact that he approves the execution (8:1; 9:1–2; 22:20).

While Stephen's speech likely had little immediate impact on Saul, the arguments about the law and the temple will become foundational to Saul's ministry as he becomes known as Paul (Acts 13:9). He too will be attacked by an angry mob in Jerusalem (21:27) and have to defend himself against charges involving the law and the temple (25:8), not to mention being stoned himself (14:19; compare 2 Corinthians 11:25). Stephen's speech thus will be echoed in ways he does not live to see. Saul's memory of this day will not fade (Acts 22:20).

It is worth noting that there are two references to Saul's age in the New Testament. The designation *young* can indicate an age between 18 and 40, according to the use of that word at that time. At this point, he is young, while in Philemon 9, he is "aged."

59. And they stoned Stephen, calling upon God, and saying, Lord Jesus, receive my spirit.

In prayer, Stephen once again acknowledges Jesus' lordship and divinity. By asking the Lord to *receive my spirit,* Stephen affirms the Christian hope of living with Christ after death. Stephen's prayer also echoes the Lord's final words on the cross: "Father, into thy hands I commend my spirit" (Luke 23:46; compare Psalm 31:5).

60. And he kneeled down, and cried with a loud voice, Lord, lay not this sin to their charge. And when he had said this, he fell asleep.

This element of Stephen's prayer echoes Jesus' prayer on the cross in Luke 23:34 to forgive the executioners. By requesting this, Stephen follows Jesus' teaching to "love your enemies" and "pray for them which despitefully use you" (Luke 6:27–28). In word and deed, Stephen's steadfast witness exemplifies what it means to follow the crucified and risen Messiah (compare 9:23).

The sobering episode concludes as Stephen falls *asleep*—a metaphor for death (compare 1 Thessalonians 4:13–18). Jesus' disciples were often confused by His use of figurative language (examples: Mark 7:17–18; 8:14–21; John 11:11–15; 16:25–30). But there's no mistaking what is happening here.

What Do You Think?

How can we cultivate a heart of forgiveness and love for those who hurt us?

Digging Deeper

What practical steps can you take to show forgiveness to someone who has wronged you, even if they haven't sought reconciliation?

Punch Back

When I was a little girl, my brother and I would play a game during car rides. We'd look for Volkswagen Beetles, or "punch buggies" as we called them. The first person to spot a punch buggy was allowed to punch the other person in the arm. We often added a disclaimer as we punched: "Punch buggy! No punch backs!" As you might imagine, fists frequently flew in the backseat of my parents' vehicle, and revenge hits were part of the game. Pretty soon, we weren't looking for Volkswagens; we were looking for retaliation against each other.

As Stephen faced death, he didn't cry out for revenge against his killers. He didn't call others to "punch back" in revenge. Instead, he followed Jesus' example by asking God to forgive his murderers and offering up his spirit to the Lord.

When was the last time you asked God to forgive your enemies rather than retaliate against them?

—B. R.

Conclusion

A. Opposition and Response

Stephen's suffering was not in vain. The tragedy of his death led to the spread of the gospel (Acts 8:1–8). His Spirit-filled obedience to Christ empowered him to act selflessly in the face of unfair objection. As a result, Stephen is a model of courage in the face of opposition.

Visual for Lesson 10. *Display this visual as you ask the class to list attributes of a faithful witness to Christ Jesus.*

Followers of Jesus can expect opposition—possibly even *bitter* opposition—from others. Stephen faced fierce resistance from many of his fellow Jews. Synagogue members argued with him, false witnesses testified against him, and religious leaders responded with murderous rage. The actions taken against Stephen remind us of Jesus' promises to His disciples: "If [unbelievers] have persecuted me, they will also persecute you" (John 15:20).

When faced with opposition, we can follow Stephen's example and respond with wisdom, love, and a reliance on God's Spirit. God's Spirit and wisdom filled Stephen, which allowed him to present such compelling arguments that no one could effectively counter or refute. And though he rebuked his fellow Jews, he did so out of love and a desire for them to repent and believe in Christ. Indeed, Stephen loved his opponents even to his death, courageously defending the gospel and graciously praying for their forgiveness. The Lord expects nothing less from us today (Luke 6:27–36; 1 Peter 3:15–16).

B. Prayer

Father God, empower us to be courageous witnesses to Your Son in our own settings. Enable us to respond to opposition with as much wisdom, love, and dependence on the Spirit as possible. In Jesus' name we pray. Amen.

C. Thought to Remember

Respond to opposition as Jesus and Stephen did.

Involvement Learning

Enhance your lesson with KJV Bible Student *(from your curriculum supplier) and the reproducible activity page (at www.standardlesson.com or in the back of the* KJV Standard Lesson Commentary Deluxe Edition*).*

Into the Lesson

Ask participants to brainstorm the commitments, responsibilities, and preferences that "fill up" their time, energy, and attention. (Possible examples: God, family, work, church, volunteering, sports, etc.) Write responses on the board.

Alternative. Distribute copies of the "Filled Up" exercise from the activity page, which you can download. Have participants complete it individually in a minute or less before discussing their conclusions.

Lead into Bible study by saying, "Various commitments, responsibilities, and preferences fill our lives. When we encounter difficult circumstances, the priorities that 'fill' us will 'spill out' and become evident to those around us. In today's study, pay attention to how a moment of testing reveals Stephen's priorities."

Into the Word

Prior to class, recruit a volunteer to give a three-minute presentation on Stephen's life and ministry. Encourage the volunteer to read Acts 6:1–8:3 and use online resources for preparation. The presentation should address how Stephen was chosen for ministry, the main points of his speech before the Sanhedrin, and the consequences of his death.

Announce a Bible-marking activity. Provide copies of Acts 6:7–10 and 7:54–60 for those who prefer not to write in their Bibles. Provide handouts (you create) with these instructions:

- Underline any words or phrases that describe Stephen.
- Double underline any words or phrases that describe the actions of Stephen's opposition.
- Draw a circle around any mention of or allusion to God the Father, Jesus, and the Holy Spirit.
- Draw a question mark around any words or phrases you want to study further.

Slowly read the Scripture aloud (or ask volunteers to do so) at least twice and as many as four times. As the Scripture is read, class members should mark their copies in the ways noted.

After the final reading, divide the class into pairs to discuss the following questions: 1–What words or phrases describe Stephen? 2–What words or phrases describe the actions of his opposition? 3–Why do you think they were "not able to resist" his wisdom (Acts 7:10)? 4–What words or phrases describe God the Father, Jesus, and the Holy Spirit? 5–How did those in power respond to the Spirit's work in Stephen? 6–What was the impact of the Spirit's wisdom through Stephen?

Option. Divide participants into three groups and assign each group one of the following Scripture passages: Luke 22:66–70; Luke 23:33–34; and Luke 23:46. Instruct groups to compare their assigned passage to Acts 7:54–60. Ask the following questions for in-group discussion: 1–How are the accounts of Stephen's execution and Jesus' crucifixion similar and different? 2–In what ways did Stephen's understanding of Jesus' suffering help him endure his own suffering?

Alternative. Distribute copies of the "Good News and Bad News" exercise from the activity page. Have participants work in small groups to complete as indicated before discussing responses and conclusions with the whole class.

Into Life

Ask participants to work with a partner to identify aspects of Stephen's example and witness that might strengthen their discipleship to Jesus. Ask, "How can you apply Stephen's example to your life and relationships?" Encourage pairs to brainstorm at least three examples.

Distribute an index card and pen to each participant and ask them to write down how Stephen's courageous witness may inspire their own witness to Jesus Christ in the coming week. After a minute of individual reflection, invite volunteers to share their responses.

August 16
Lesson 11 (KJV)

Saul of Tarsus, the Unlikely Apostle

Devotional Reading: Psalm 86:1–10
Background Scripture: Acts 7:58–8:3; 9:1–31; 22:3–15

Acts 22:3–15

3 I am verily a man which am a Jew, born in Tarsus, a city in Cilicia, yet brought up in this city at the feet of Gamaliel, and taught according to the perfect manner of the law of the fathers, and was zealous toward God, as ye all are this day.

4 And I persecuted this way unto the death, binding and delivering into prisons both men and women.

5 As also the high priest doth bear me witness, and all the estate of the elders: from whom also I received letters unto the brethren, and went to Damascus, to bring them which were there bound unto Jerusalem, for to be punished.

6 And it came to pass, that, as I made my journey, and was come nigh unto Damascus about noon, suddenly there shone from heaven a great light round about me.

7 And I fell unto the ground, and heard a voice saying unto me, Saul, Saul, why persecutest thou me?

8 And I answered, Who art thou, Lord? And he said unto me, I am Jesus of Nazareth, whom thou persecutest.

9 And they that were with me saw indeed the light, and were afraid; but they heard not the voice of him that spake to me.

10 And I said, What shall I do, Lord? And the Lord said unto me, Arise, and go into Damascus; and there it shall be told thee of all things which are appointed for thee to do.

11 And when I could not see for the glory of that light, being led by the hand of them that were with me, I came into Damascus.

12 And one Ananias, a devout man according to the law, having a good report of all the Jews which dwelt there,

13 Came unto me, and stood, and said unto me, Brother Saul, receive thy sight. And the same hour I looked up upon him.

14 And he said, The God of our fathers hath chosen thee, that thou shouldest know his will, and see that Just One, and shouldest hear the voice of his mouth.

15 For thou shalt be his witness unto all men of what thou hast seen and heard.

Key Text

[Ananias] said, The God of our fathers hath chosen thee, that thou shouldest know his will, and see that Just One, and shouldest hear the voice of his mouth. For thou shalt be his witness unto all men of what thou hast seen and heard. —**Acts 22:14–15**

The Testimony of
Faithful Witnesses

Unit 3: Faithful Witnesses Spread the Good News

Lessons 9–13

Lesson Aims

After participating in this lesson, each learner will be able to:

1. Retell Paul's encounter with Jesus and call as Christ's witness.

2. Compare the motivations for Paul's zeal before and after encountering Jesus.

3. Compose his or her own story of meeting Jesus and explain what personal weaknesses God has used for good.

Lesson Outline

Introduction
- A. Fire for Good or Fire for Bad?
- B. Lesson Context

I. Recounting the Past (Acts 22:3–5)
- A. Studied the Law (v. 3)
- B. Persecuted Followers (vv. 4–5)

II. Encountering the Lord (Acts 22:6–11)
- A. Questions and Revelation (vv. 6–10a)
- B. Reply and Command (vv. 10b–11)
  - *Tactical Flashlight*

III. Commissioned for the Future (Acts 22:12–15)
- A. Renewed Sight (vv. 12–13)
- B. Chosen Witness (vv. 14–15)
  - *Unlikely Witness*

Conclusion
- A. Opened Eyes Open Other Eyes
- B. Prayer
- C. Thought to Remember

Introduction

A. Fire for Good or Fire for Bad?

Early in 2024, my small town in the Texas Panhandle was among those affected by a series of wildfires that devastated over 1.2 million acres of land. This was not the first time our town had suffered severe damage from a wildfire. Thankfully, there were no fatalities, but the damage was substantial.

We know all too well the destructive capabilities of fire! It's not surprising, then, that fire is prime imagery for anger, wrath, and destruction. Even so, we continue to use fire in various ways—for warmth, cooking, incineration, and even for controlling other fires.

Our relationship with fire is complicated. We acknowledge it can be both helpful and harmful. So it is with the fiery disposition of *zeal*. It can ignite a passion for good or unleash a destructive force. Ultimately, it all depends on how and for what purpose zeal is used.

B. Lesson Context

In about AD 58, at the end of his third missionary journey, Paul returned to Jerusalem for the final time (Acts 21:17). The centerpiece of that third missionary trip was his lengthy ministry in Ephesus (19:1, 8–10; 20:31), a stay marked by no little controversy. His forebodings and those of others did not indicate that his visit to Jerusalem would be any less controversial—quite the opposite, in fact (20:17–38; 21:4, 10–14). But Paul made the trip anyway.

Upon his arrival, Paul met with leaders of the Jerusalem church and reported on his ministry (Acts 21:17–19). Those leaders also warned Paul of the danger his presence posed (21:20–24). When that danger materialized, Paul was arrested on a false charge of defiling the temple (21:27). Had it not been for the presence of Roman troops to restore order, Paul probably would have been killed right then and there (21:30–36). After being rescued, Paul then surprisingly asked to address the mob that had just tried to kill him. The Roman commander gave permission (21:40–22:2), and that's where our lesson text opens.

I. Recounting the Past

(Acts 22:3–5)

A. Studied the Law (v. 3)

3a. I am verily a man which am a Jew, born in Tarsus, a city in Cilicia, yet brought up in this city at the feet of Gamaliel.

Paul's defense of his ministry includes an account of his own incredible transformation. Details of that experience occur three times in the book of Acts: here, in Acts 9:1–19, and in Acts 26:12–23.

He begins by describing his upbringing as a Diaspora *Jew.* The Greek word *diaspora* means "dispersed" or "scattered," as it is found in John 7:35; James 1:1; and 1 Peter 1:1 (compare Deuteronomy 4:27). Having been born in a Roman province allowed Paul to gain Roman citizenship (compare Acts 22:27–28). *Tarsus,* the capital of *Cilicia,* located in present-day Turkey, is about 360 miles north of Jerusalem. First-century Tarsus was a major trading center that also became the site of many cults. The city was thoroughly Greco-Roman, presenting numerous pressures for someone born a Jew. But Paul strongly implies that he had not been assimilated into that pagan environment, given that he had been *brought up in* Jerusalem.

Paul continues to present his credentials to establish his background as a faithful Jew. A posture of sitting *at the feet* of a teacher was common for Jewish disciples (example: Luke 10:39). In that light, one could hardly do better than having studied at the feet *of Gamaliel.* This man's wisdom and high regard among the people is seen in Acts 5:34–39.

> **What Do You Think?**
> How does your background or life experience shape how you approach your faith today?
>
> **Digging Deeper**
> How has God used these experiences to prepare you for specific opportunities in your faith journey?

3b. And taught according to the perfect manner of the law of the fathers, and was zealous toward God, as ye all are this day.

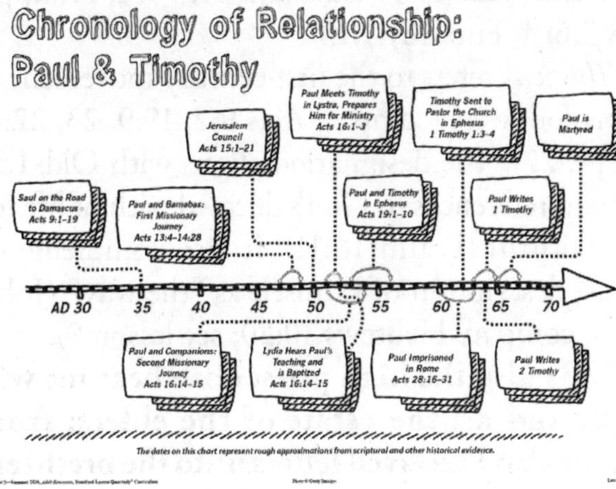

Visual for Lessons 11 & 13. *Display this visual as you review the ministries of Paul and Timothy in the first-century church.*

The rare phrase, *the law of the fathers,* is used instead of the more common phrase, "the Law of Moses" (compare Acts 28:23). This phrasing seems intended to establish common ground with the crowd of Jews.

The word *zealous* conveys an image of a fiery and passionate commitment to a cause. Such a disposition could be understood positively (example: John 2:17) or negatively (example: Galatians 4:17). The ancient world tended to associate the word with qualities worthy of emulation. Intertestamental Judaism associated the term with various religious heroes (examples: see the nonbiblical 1 Maccabees 2:23–27, 50–58; the latter section includes a reference to the zeal of Phinehas in Numbers 25:5–13). As such, the term suggests a willingness to resort to violence to defend religious traditions, the holiness of God's name, or both. Paul's attitude toward the Scriptures and their application resembles what he says in Galatians 1:14 and Philippians 3:5–6.

B. Persecuted Followers (vv. 4–5)

4. And I persecuted this way unto the death, binding and delivering into prisons both men and women.

Paul's address now recalls his participation in the stoning of Stephen (Acts 7:58–8:3; see lesson 10). That event marked the beginning of Paul's persecution of the church (8:1). His zeal in doing so is further noted in Acts 9:1–2, 14, 21; 26:10–11;

1 Corinthians 15:9; Galatians 1:13–14; Philippians 3:6; 1 Timothy 1:13).

This way refers to the first-century movement of Jesus-followers (compare Acts 9:2; 19:9, 23; 22:4; 24:14, 22). The designation aligns with Old Testament references to God's decreed path of life for the faithful (Psalm 16:11). It also complements Jesus' description of Himself as "the way" (John 14:6; compare Hebrews 10:20; see lesson 9).

5. As also the high priest doth bear me witness, and all the estate of the elders: from whom also I received letters unto the brethren, and went to Damascus, to bring them which were there bound unto Jerusalem, for to be punished.

Since Paul once persecuted members of "The Way," the obvious question arises: Why is he now one of its most prominent proclaimers? He presents himself in terms that establish a common ground with an audience who wants to kill him, so what has changed? Paul answers by recalling the story first narrated in Acts 9.

Previously, Paul (as Saul) operated with the support of *the high priest*—most likely Caiaphas, who held that position until AD 36. Saul intended to carry out his persecutions against the Jewish followers of Jesus in Damascus (compare Acts 9:1–2). The fact that *Damascus* is over 130 miles away from *Jerusalem* highlights Saul's fanaticism at the time. Luke, the author of the book of Acts, does not specify how the gospel first came to Damascus. But a general clue is found in Acts 2:5, which notes that Jews from "every nation under heaven" gathered for the day of Pentecost. Another clue is in Acts 11:19, which states that after the persecution described in Acts 8, believers scattered "as far as Phenice." That region adjoins Syria, wherein the city of Damascus is located.

How to Say It

Ananias	An-uh-*nye*-us.
Aramaic	*Air*-uh-**may**-ik.
Caiaphas	*Kay*-uh-fus or *Kye*-uh-fus.
Cilicia	Sih-*lish*-i-uh.
Diaspora	Dee-*as*-puh-ruh.
Ephesus	*Ef*-uh-sus.
Gamaliel	Guh-*may*-lih-ul or Guh-*may*-lee-al.
Maccabees	*Mack*-uh-bees.
Nazareth	*Naz*-uh-reth.
Phinehas	*Fin*-ee-us.
Tarsus	*Tar*-sus.
theophany	the-*ah*-fuh-nee.

II. Encountering the Lord
(Acts 22:6–11)

A. Questions and Revelation (vv. 6–10a)

6. And it came to pass, that, as I made my journey, and was come nigh unto Damascus about noon, suddenly there shone from heaven a great light round about me.

The only notable addition of detail here compared to Acts 9:3 is that Paul specifies that this happened *about noon* (compare Acts 26:13). This detail accentuates how brilliant the *light* must have been to be so perceptible at the brightest time of day.

7–8. And I fell unto the ground, and heard a voice saying unto me, Saul, Saul, why persecutest thou me? And I answered, Who art thou, Lord? And he said unto me, I am Jesus of Nazareth, whom thou persecutest.

The opening statement *Saul, Saul, why persecutes thou me* of the *voice,* as presented here and in Acts 9:4–5, baffled Saul. Having been overwhelmed by the light to the point that he found himself on *the ground*, all he could do was sputter out the question, *Who art thou, Lord?* We should not think that Saul's use of the word *Lord* necessarily means that he recognized the voice as that of God. The underlying Greek is also used in contexts where it means "sir" (example: Matthew 27:63).

Saul's confusion likely deepened when the voice identified itself as *Jesus of Nazareth.* There is no record of Saul's ever having met Jesus prior to this encounter. As Saul's self-assured confidence in his zealous conduct began to melt away, the implication became clear: to persecute Christians is, in essence, to persecute Jesus Himself. This stresses Jesus' identification with them.

This moment thus began a radical reshaping of everything Saul believed about God, who was at the center of his worldview. This reshaping is reflected in texts such as 1 Corinthians 8:6, where Paul reworks traditional statements of faith, like those found in Deuteronomy 6:4, to include Jesus as both Lord and God. Ultimately, this encounter will also radically reshape how Saul lives, as he will transform from being a persecutor of the church into a chief proclaimer of its gospel in service to this Lord (1 Corinthians 15:9; Galatians 1:13–16, 23; 1 Timothy 1:13). Saul's transformation began with his interaction on the road, but he would need a lengthy period of growth (Galatians 1:17–18).

9–10a. And they that were with me saw indeed the light, and were afraid; but they heard not the voice of him that spake to me. And I said, What shall I do, Lord?

We need to keep in mind who Paul is addressing: a hostile crowd who wants him dead (Acts 21:40)! In response, he tailors his address to emphasize the Lord's personal revelation to him and his obedient submission to the Lord's will (compare Galatians 1:11–12).

What we see here in Acts 22:9 is similar to what we read in Acts 9:7, but with two notable variations. Acts 9:7 states that Saul's traveling companions (1) saw nobody, although they (2) heard the voice. Yet here in Acts 22:9, Paul notes that the companions (1) *saw indeed the light*, but they (2) did not hear *the voice.*

The first difference could simply mean that although able to perceive the light, the companions could not see the person at the center of it. That is hardly surprising if the light was so bright as to be distinguishable from the sun at noon (see commentary on Acts 22:6, above).

The other difference may be explainable in several ways. One way is by examining the differing meanings of the verb translated *heard* as contexts change. In some contexts, it simply means "to be aware of by means of the ear" (example: Mark 6:20); in other contexts, the verb takes the more specific meaning of "comprehended" or "understood" (example: 8:18).

The second way is by examining the word translated *voice* in Acts 9:7. It could have the more general meaning of "sound" (example: 1 Corinthians 14:7); if that idea applies here, it suggests that the companions heard an unidentifiable sound rather than comprehensible voice. Third, and less likely, is the possibility that they perceived someone addressing Saul in a language they could not understand. Acts 26:14 says it was Aramaic (compare Acts 21:40–22:1).

What Do You Think?

Are you in a season of asking God, "What shall I do, Lord"? Why, or why not?

Digging Deeper

What steps will you take to be better attentive to God's call on your life?

B. Reply and Command (vv. 10b–11)

10b–11. And the Lord said unto me, Arise, and go into Damascus; and there it shall be told thee of all things which are appointed for thee to do. And when I could not see for the glory of that light, being led by the hand of them that were with me, I came into Damascus.

The first part of this text reflects Jesus' words in Acts 9:6 and 26:16, but with a subtle twist. Acts 9:6 states what Saul "must do," while the passage before us states what Saul was *appointed . . . to do.* That same chapter elaborates on his appointment: he is to witness to God's "name before the Gentiles, and kings, and the children of Israel" (Acts 9:15).

Perhaps Paul opted not to speak of his mission to Gentiles because of the anti-Gentile sentiments present in his hostile audience (Acts 21:27–29; compare 21:19). This seems particularly likely given the crowd's reaction a few verses later (22:21–22).

What Do You Think?

Have you experienced moments where you felt spiritually "blind" before understanding the truth? Explain.

Digging Deeper

How has God revealed Himself to you in ways that changed your perspective or direction?

Tactical Flashlight

I was in the market for a nonlethal self-defense

tool and decided to purchase pepper spray. However, I soon encountered some issues. As I came to find out, pepper spray is considered a "weapon" in certain settings, which means it's prohibited in some places. Additionally, the canisters can lose pressure over time, and I didn't want to do periodic test firings.

But then, I came across a self-defense expert on YouTube who suggested a solution that aligned better with my needs: a tactical flashlight. Such a flashlight can emit a powerful beam of light, temporarily blinding and disorienting an attacker. I bought one with a strobe-light feature for increased effect.

Having tried it on myself, I can attest to its extreme brightness. Even so, I know just enough about "lumens" and "lux" to realize that the sun at noon is much brighter—but how much less so than that of the light that blinded Saul, knocking him to the ground! But that's what it took for Jesus to get his attention. How much does it take for Jesus to get yours? —R. L. N.

III. Commissioned for the Future

(Acts 22:12–15)

A. Renewed Sight (vv. 12–13)

12. And one Ananias, a devout man according to the law, having a good report of all the Jews which dwelt there.

Acts 9:10–17 provides a more detailed account of the actions and attitude of *Ananias.* He is designated as "a disciple," marking him as a follower of Jesus. It's important to note that this *Ananias* should not be confused with men of the same name mentioned in Acts 5:1–11; 23:1–5; or 24:1. To describe him as *a devout man* who has *a good report of all the Jews* suggests that Paul aims to reassure the crowd that a Jew who is above reproach could testify truthfully about Paul's claims.

13. Came unto me, and stood, and said unto me, Brother Saul, receive thy sight. And the same hour I looked up upon him.

The content of this verse is a condensed version of Acts 9:17–18. Here, as in 9:17, Ananias reveals a willingness to refer to *Saul* as *brother* because of the Lord's revelation to Ananias. This is despite Ananias's initial consternation about Saul as a persecutor of Christians.

> **What Do You Think?**
> Who has been an "Ananias" in your life—someone you respect who God has used to guide or encourage your faith?
>
> **Digging Deeper**
> How can you be that person for someone else?

B. Chosen Witness (vv. 14–15)

14. And he said, The God of our fathers hath chosen thee, that thou shouldest know his will, and see that Just One, and shouldest hear the voice of his mouth.

This is not precisely paralleled in Acts 9 since that account does not feature as much dialogue between Ananias and Saul. But it does correspond with what the Lord declares in Acts 9:15. While Luke, the author of Acts, might have wanted to cut down on repetition in chapter 9, Paul needs to include this dialogue from Ananias because his testimony supports Paul's claims.

A particularly significant aspect of Ananias's dialogue that makes this point is referring to God as the *God of our fathers.* This phrase, or a form of it, appears elsewhere in the book of Acts (Acts 3:13; 5:30; 7:32; 24:14). Its formulation has significant parallels in the Old Testament (examples: Deuteronomy 26:7; 1 Chronicles 12:17; 29:18). Ananias gives a power promise of God's fidelity as he connects Old Testament statements with the revelation of God in Christ Jesus. When Saul hears Ananias speak of *that Just One,* Saul may recall that Stephen spoke of "the Just One" (Jesus) in Acts 7:52 (compare 3:14).

This title, *Just One,* appears only twice in the New Testament, both in Acts (here and in Acts 7:52; compare 3:14). This designation highlights Jesus' innocence and divine vindication. But it also signals His fulfillment of prophetic hopes about God's "righteous and just" one (the Hebrew and Greek terms can be translated either way).

Acts 3:13–14 shows a connection to Isaiah

53:11 by referring to Jesus as God's servant, making this description resonate with the idea of God's righteous and just servant. It is also possible that the portrayal evokes broader hopes of God's chosen ruler—a just one sent to Jerusalem (Jeremiah 23:5–6; 33:15; Zechariah 9:9).

Unlikely Witness

One of the most memorable books I read as a teenager was *The Cross and the Switchblade.* It tells the story of Nicky Cruz, a notorious gang leader in New York City. His life seemed destined for crime, violence, and destruction. However, an encounter with evangelist David Wilkerson led to a profound transformation: Cruz surrendered his life to Christ. This dramatic change ignited a passion for sharing the gospel, and Cruz became an influential evangelist who continues to reach the very gangs with which he once identified.

What grips me most about this story is how unlikely it was for Cruz to become an evangelist. But his is not the only such account. The apostle Peter, impulsive and impetuous, denied Jesus three times, yet was appointed as a leader of the first-century church. The apostle Paul, a persecutor of Christians, became one of their greatest advocates. These two examples demonstrate God's ability to work through imperfect people, using their unique experiences to advance His kingdom.

Few people today, if any, will experience a "selection process" as Paul did. Most of the time, God will wait patiently for a volunteer—perhaps finding none (compare Ezekiel 22:30). When the need is obvious, will you be the one? —N. V.

15. For thou shalt be his witness unto all men of what thou hast seen and heard.

The commission Paul receives to be Jesus' *witness unto all men* is a mark of his becoming a disciple of Jesus. But more specifically, in the context of Acts, it also marks him as participating in the commission bestowed on the apostles (Acts 1:8, 22; 2:32; 13:31). This is further stressed by reference to what he has *seen and heard.* That phrase conveys the personal experience of the speaker (compare Luke 7:22; Acts 4:20; 1 John 1:1, 3). For the Lord's purposes in making Paul an apostle to the nations, he needed Paul to be a witness of the risen Jesus. And so Paul experienced Christ firsthand when God interrupted his trip to Damascus.

What Do You Think?

What does it mean to be a witness for God in your own context?

Digging Deeper

How can your personal experiences, the things you have "seen and heard," be a powerful tool for evangelism?

Conclusion

A. Opened Eyes Can Open Other Eyes

It is vital to remember that whenever we read accounts of God's appearing to people, such stories are never the end goal in and of themselves. Such an appearance (called a *theophany*) happens in order to certify something or someone as being of God.

Today, we have the completed witness of the New Testament to guide us. We don't need a theophany, like the one Paul received, to motivate us toward our duty to witness—the New Testament itself is intended to encourage us! God calls His people to align their lives with His path revealed through His Word. Through this alignment, God's Spirit transforms our lives to serve God. As a result, we become agents of the gospel in the world.

Paul's encounter with the risen Jesus was the first step in incorporating him into Christ's body—the church. Our individual stories are part of this larger narrative. Like Paul, who began his extensive work after this encounter, part of glorifying God is edifying others. Let us reflect on our personal life stories in light of what God has done for us so that we may edify others and glorify Him.

B. Prayer

God of our ancestors in the faith, help us meld our stories into Yours! Guide and empower us to be witnesses so that others may know Your salvation. In Jesus' name we pray. Amen.

C. Thought to Remember

Let God use you for His purposes.

Involvement Learning

Enhance your lesson with KJV Bible Student *(from your curriculum supplier) and the reproducible activity page (at www.standardlesson.com or in the back of the* KJV Standard Lesson Commentary Deluxe Edition*).*

Into the Lesson

Ask participants to write down three factual statements about themselves: one strength; one weakness; and one neutral, uncontrollable factor, such as their place of birth or family background. Instruct participants to "introduce" themselves to the class or a partner by reading their three statements.

After everyone has introduced themselves, invite each participant to reflect on how God can use both our strengths and weaknesses for His glory. After one minute of silent reflection, ask if any volunteers would like to share their responses.

Lead into Bible study by saying, "It may be easier for us to understand how God might use our strengths, but what about our weaknesses or the factors we have no control over? Today's study will 'introduce' us to Paul and his mission for God."

Into the Word

Divide participants into two groups: **Synagogue Leaders** and **Church Leaders**. Create two handouts with the headers *Pros* and *Cons* for two columns. Distribute one handout to each group. Instruct each group to read Acts 22:3–5 and write down the pros and cons of Paul's qualifications for ministry within their assigned religious group. Direct the groups to use this information to determine whether Paul would have been a suitable candidate for leadership in their group. After calling time, ask a volunteer from each group to share their findings and explain their conclusions.

Alternative. Distribute copies of the "Saul's Resume" exercise from the activity page, which you can download. Have learners work in pairs to complete as indicated. After calling time, ask volunteers to share their responses.

Ask for six volunteers, assigning each to one of the following roles: Saul, Jesus, Companion 1, Companion 2, Cornelius, and Narrator. Have the volunteers reenact the speeches and events from Acts 22:6–15 while the rest of the class observes. After the performance, ask the class, "What is the most frightening aspect of these scenes, and what is the most amazing? Why?"

Announce a Bible-marking activity. Provide copies of Acts 9:10–19 and Acts 22:12–15 for those who do not want to write in their Bibles. Distribute handouts (you create) with these instructions:

1–Underline words or phrases that appear in both passages.
2–Draw brackets around words or phrases that appear in only one of the passages.
3–Draw a star around the details that you believe are most important.

After completing the activity, ask, "How do you think Ananias felt about what the Lord asked him to do? Why?" Allow time small group discussion.

Option. Invite volunteers to list people from recent history with a reputation among Christ-followers comparable to Saul. Ask, "How would you feel if God gave you the same message for them that He gave to Ananias? How would you respond?"

Into Life

Summarize the study by saying, "Paul shares his story of transformation by detailing his life before meeting Christ, his experience with Christ on the road, and how that interaction changed his life. Every believer has a story of meeting Jesus!"

Distribute a sheet of paper and a pen to each participant. Invite them to write down a brief version of their own story of meeting Jesus and how God used personal weaknesses for good. Allow time for participants to share their testimony in small groups if they choose to do so.

Alternative. Distribute copies of the "Tell Your Story" exercise from the activity page. Have learners complete the exercise as a take-home activity in the upcoming week.

Timothy, a Leader with a Legacy

Devotional Reading: Matthew 12:46–50
Background Scripture: Acts 16:1–3; Philippians 2:19–22;
2 Timothy 1:1–6; 3:14–16

2 Timothy 1:1–6

**1 Paul, an apostle of Jesus Christ by the will
of God, according to the promise of life which
is in Christ Jesus,
2 To Timothy, my dearly beloved son:
Grace, mercy, and peace, from God the Father
and Christ Jesus our Lord.
3 I thank God, whom I serve from my
forefathers with pure conscience, that with-
out ceasing I have remembrance of thee in my
prayers night and day;
4 Greatly desiring to see thee, being mind-
ful of thy tears, that I may be filled with joy;
5 When I call to remembrance the
unfeigned faith that is in thee, which dwelt
first in thy grandmother Lois, and thy mother
Eunice; and I am persuaded that in thee also.
6 Wherefore I put thee in remembrance that
thou stir up the gift of God, which is in thee by
the putting on of my hands.**

2 Timothy 3:14–16

**14 But continue thou in the things which
thou hast learned and hast been assured of,
knowing of whom thou hast learned them;
15 And that from a child thou hast known
the holy scriptures, which are able to make thee
wise unto salvation through faith which is in
Christ Jesus.
16 All scripture is given by inspiration of
God, and is profitable for doctrine, for reproof,
for correction, for instruction in righteousness.**

Key Text

When I call to remembrance the unfeigned faith that is in thee, which dwelt first in thy grandmother Lois, and thy mother Eunice; and I am persuaded that in thee also. **—2 Timothy 1:5**

The Testimony of

Faithful Witnesses

Unit 3: Faithful Witnesses Spread the Good News

Lessons 9–13

Lesson Aims

After participating in this lesson, each learner will be able to:

1. Identify the parts of Timothy's upbringing that contributed to his identity as a faithful witness.

2. Explain the wisdom that comes from the study of God's Word.

3. List practices that might nurture children into becoming faithful witnesses.

Lesson Outline

Introduction

A. Running Partner for Life

B. Lesson Context: Paul

C. Lesson Context: Timothy

I. Sincere Legacy (2 Timothy 1:1–6)

A. From Father to Son (vv. 1–2)

Father in the Faith

B. Foundation of Faith (vv. 3–5)

C. The Gift of God (v. 6)

No Time "Before Christ"

II. Continued Legacy (2 Timothy 3:14–16)

A. Persist in Learning (v. 14)

B. Know the Scriptures (vv. 15–16)

Conclusion

A. Imitation and Encouragement

B. Prayer

C. Thought to Remember

Introduction

A. Running Partner for Life

The individualism of modern culture takes many forms. Recently, I noticed individualistic tendencies in physical fitness. If we eat a balanced diet, it is because we choose one *ourselves*. If we work out each day, it is because we set *ourselves* a routine. In contrast, my fitness breakthrough came when I invited others to join me.

It took three years, but eventually, I lost 60 pounds. I had to commit to personal change: healthy eating, visiting the gym daily, and running. However, I'm sure I wouldn't have followed through if I had made those changes alone. I needed the support of the people closest to me, especially my wife. She prepared healthy meals for the family, came with me to the gym, and joined me on my runs. Somehow, she anticipated trouble and hang-ups that were positioned to frustrate my fitness goals. When I was tempted to throw in the towel, her kindness and companionship encouraged me to persist in the habits that honored my commitments.

B. Lesson Context: Paul

The persecutor-turned-apostle Paul is responsible for writing a large percentage of the New Testament epistles. He wrote letters to churches and individuals. "Writing" is a flexible term for an era without mail service, widespread literacy, or inexpensive paper. Several of his letters list coauthors: Sosthenes (1 Corinthians 1:1); Timothy or Timotheus (2 Corinthians 1:1; Philippians 1:1; Colossians 1:1; Philemon 1:1); and Silvanus together with Timotheus (1 Thessalonians 1:1; 2 Thessalonians 1:1). Paul also employed the help of specialized scribes, perhaps relying heavily upon them when he was confined in Rome. The writing secretary (called an *amanuensis* in Latin) sometimes carried the letter to its destination, delivering and interpreting the contents. For example, see the commendation of Tychicus in Ephesians 6:21 and Colossians 4:7.

As far as we know, Paul had no children and never married. He had a sister and nephew (Acts 23:16), so he was an uncle. Scripture gives us little information about Paul's parents, but we know he received high-level religious education, learned tent-making as a trade, and was a Roman citizen. We know he studied under the famous rabbi, Gamaliel, in Jerusalem (Acts 22:3). Paul's relationship with Gamaliel as a spiritual father may have influenced his decision to consider Timothy as a son in the faith (1 Timothy 1:2).

Since Paul's production of letters involved Timothy to a large degree and he thought of Timothy like a son, it is fitting that Paul would write to him when they were apart. Even as Paul endured imprisonment in Rome and his day of martyrdom drew near (around AD 67), he continued planning correspondences. Paul wrote two letters to Timothy while the younger man served as a pastor in Ephesus. Through them, he offered guidance, reassurance, and encouragement. Eventually, Paul requested that Timothy visit him in Rome and "bring . . . the books [and] especially the parchments" (2 Timothy 4:9, 13). In some ways, 2 Timothy reads like a last will and testament, sent from a spiritual father to a spiritual son (4:6; compare Philippians 2:22). As any father would, Paul wished to see Timothy again before he died.

C. Lesson Context: Timothy

Though Timothy is often perceived as a youth, he was approximately 40 years old when he received Paul's second letter. Paul first met Timothy while traveling through Lystra (Acts 16:1–3). According to Acts 16:1, Timothy's mother was Jewish, but his father was Greek. Strict Jews considered such a relationship dangerous and sometimes even sinful (compare Nehemiah 13:23–27; Ezra 9:1–10:44). Greek culture placed fathers as the head of the household (*paterfamilias*), and therefore, the one responsible for decisions regarding matters of religion. Timothy's Greek paternity is evident in his lack of circumcision, which, as a Jew, should have occurred on the eighth day of his life (Acts 16:3; Leviticus 12:3). However, Timothy possessed some education in Jewish faith by way of his mother and grandmother (2 Timothy 1:5). Much of Timothy's further ministry education and training came from the time he spent with Paul while they served as missionaries planting churches across Macedonia.

How to Say It

amanuensis	uh-man-yew-*en*-sis.
Ephesus	*Ef*-uh-sus.
Gamaliel	Guh-*may*-lih-ul or Guh-*may*-lee-al.
Habakkuk	Huh-*back*-kuk.
Lystra	*Liss*-truh.
Macedonia	Mass-eh-*doe*-nee-uh.
paterfamilias	pah-ter-fah-*mil*-ee-us
presbytery	*prez*-buh-ter-ee.
Septuagint	Sep-*too*-ih-jent.
Sosthenes	*Soss*-thuh-neez.
Tychicus	*Tick*-ih-cuss.

I. Sincere Legacy
(2 Timothy 1:1–6)

A. From Father to Son (vv. 1–2)

1. Paul, an apostle of Jesus Christ by the will of God, according to the promise of life which is in Christ Jesus.

Like other ancient letters, 2 Timothy begins by sharing information that modern letter recipients would find on an envelope. *Paul* identifies himself as the sender and *an apostle of Jesus Christ.* The title "apostle" is significant for Paul because he was not present with Jesus during Jesus' earthly ministry. Nonetheless, *God* is the one who commissions Paul by His *will.* Paul reminds the letter's recipient that in *Christ Jesus* we find *life.* Jesus came "that [we] might have life, and . . . more abundantly" (John 10:10)—it is a *promise.*

2. To Timothy, my dearly beloved son: Grace, mercy, and peace, from God the Father and Christ Jesus our Lord.

Paul identifies *Timothy* as the letter's recipient. He describes Timothy in affectionate and familial terms (compare Titus 1:4). Paul considers Timothy not only a son but one dear to his heart—he is highly cherished.

Grace and *peace* are traditional greetings found in many of Paul's letters. In contrast, the standard salutation in nonreligious Greek writing of the time was a wish for good health. Paul asks instead for marks of spiritual health: God's unearned favor (*grace*) and an anticipation of wholeness in God's restorative work (*peace*). Paul also adds the term *mercy,* which indicates a desire for God's compassionate treatment. As a father in the faith, Paul desires the fullness of favor, compassion, and wholeness for his son.

Father in the Faith

Joe grew up in a single-parent household and wished for a father. He loved his mother and admired her grit, but he spent long hours alone after school and on weekends while she worked two jobs. When Joe was young, he stayed in the house with the doors locked. As he grew older, Joe went home with friends for dinner and to do homework. Participation in other households provided the chance to observe how different families interacted. He witnessed the ways other parents demonstrated love for their children. Joe paid careful attention to the dads.

Joe was in middle school when a friend invited him to church. There, he met a youth pastor with whom he formed a bond. Quickly, Joe became a regular part of this church community. He was baptized and became a true son in the faith to this pastor. Their friendship continues to this day.

Scripture says little about Timothy's biological father, but we know he had a strong spiritual father in Paul. Who are your mentors, guides, and spiritual parents in the faith? —L. M. W.

B. Foundation of Faith (vv. 3–5)

3. I thank God, whom I serve from my forefathers with pure conscience, that without ceasing I have remembrance of thee in my prayers night and day.

This verse begins a sentence in Greek that stretches to the end of verse 5. It is customary in ancient letters to include a note of thanksgiving. Paul offers his gratitude to *God* and then connects his mention of God to the legacy of Jewish and Israelite ancestors (*my forefathers*). In other letters, Paul defends the continuity between his faith and the devotion of Jewish predecessors: those "of faith" are "children of Abraham" (Galatians 3:7–9). Here, he makes the connection more personal—he continues to serve the same God as his Jewish forebears. By reiterating his spiritual heritage, Paul emphasizes the importance of faith that is passed down from one generation to the next.

Paul also introduces the topic of *remembrance* as he describes the consistent prayers he offers for Timothy. He is reflecting upon their relationship from the vantage point of many years of fruitful association. Paul's son in the faith comes to mind throughout the *night and day.* Such frequent prayers indicate deep and enduring love. They model a vital facet of spiritual mentorship: prayers of intercession.

> **What Do You Think?**
> Who are your spiritual ancestors?
> **Digging Deeper**
> In what ways are you supporting the faith of future generations?

4. Greatly desiring to see thee, being mindful of thy tears, that I may be filled with joy.

Paul wants to *see* Timothy in person. There is no substitute for face-to-face interactions with our loved ones! In other epistles, Paul also expresses a longing to see his ministry partners (Romans 1:11). Typically, he intends to do the traveling (15:23; 1 Thessalonians 3:10–11), but in this case, Paul must rely on Timothy to come to him (see Lesson Context: Paul).

The phrase *being mindful* is translated elsewhere as a form of "remember" (Matthew 5:23; 26:75; Luke 23:42; 24:8; Acts 11:16). Paul may recall a previous moment of connection or refer to a message he received from Timothy. He may be acknowledging Timothy's difficulties in opposition to false teachers and the backsliding of close companions (1 Timothy 1:3–7, 18–19).

Paul indicates that the resolution of his wish (and perhaps Timothy's sorrow) shall come at their next meeting. Even without the physical attainment of Paul's desire, his words speak *joy* and encouragement into a season of grief.

5. When I call to remembrance the unfeigned faith that is in thee, which dwelt first in thy grandmother Lois, and thy mother Eunice; and I am persuaded that in thee also.

Visual for Lesson 12. *Display the visual in a prominent place. Point to the visual and ask the class to spend one minute contemplating the question.*

This verse ends the lengthy sentence that began in verse 3. Paul now purposefully remembers Timothy's *unfeigned faith*. The adjective translated as "unfeigned" means "without acting" or "without putting on a show." Paul knows that Timothy's faith is genuine, giving him confidence in his protégé. Moreover, Paul reminds Timothy that he has a legacy of faith from his *grandmother Lois* and his *mother Eunice*.

There is little information about Lois and Eunice in Scripture. Therefore, there are at least two ways of interpreting Paul's statement. First, Lois and Eunice were Jewish followers of Christ, making Timothy a third-generation Christian. Acts 16:1 calls Timothy's mother "faithful" (translated as "and believed"), which could mean that she received the good news of Jesus before Paul arrived in Lystra. Second, since Paul is drawing a parallel to himself—as he connects his faith to the worship of his Jewish ancestors (verse 3 above)—it is also possible that Paul is describing the continuity between Timothy's obedient Jewish training and his later reception of the gospel. In a broad sense, Paul credits Timothy's faith to his Jewish mother and grandmother, who taught him the truths of God from the Old Testament. It may not have been easy for Lois and Eunice to teach Timothy about God since Timothy's father was Greek (Acts 16:1). Timothy's mixed heritage (the son of a Jewish woman and a Greek man) makes him a living parable of Christ's reconciliation, which brings Jews and Gentiles together as one people (see Ephesians 2:13–18).

Paul is impressed with Timothy's faith—he was from their first meeting (Acts 16:1–3). He knows Timothy has not abandoned his devotion to God or renounced the truths he learned in childhood. Paul encourages Timothy to remember that his legacy comes from God.

What Do You Think?

Who do you know who has "unfeigned faith"?

Digging Deeper

What habits or rhythms of remembrance do you use to keep such examples of faith in the forefront of your mind?

C. The Gift of God (v. 6)

6. Wherefore I put thee in remembrance that thou stir up the gift of God, which is in thee by the putting on of my hands.

Paul changes the subject, now encouraging Timothy toward action. He asks Timothy not to let his gift drift into stagnancy. The Greek verb translated *stir up* can be used to describe nursing a flame—one nearly extinguished or burning low. Consider Newton's First Law of Motion or Inertia: "An object in motion stays in motion." The converse is also true—it takes energy and force to initiate motion in resting objects. Paul knows it is important for Timothy to keep his spiritual fervor animated. The spread of the gospel message needs ministers who remain active, alert, and passionate about the work of God in their lives.

Timothy's *gift* is not formally stated but may refer to his leadership, teaching, or shepherding abilities. Later in the letter, Paul also mentions this gift (1 Timothy 4:14). There, Paul calls it "the gift . . . which was given thee by prophecy, with the laying on of the hands of the presbytery." In both places, the *putting on of . . . hands* is significant. The purposeful gesture could refer to the transference of a miraculous gift of the Holy Spirit, like those listed in 1 Corinthians 12:7–10 (healing, performing miracles, prophesying, etc.). However, it certainly refers to Timothy's ministerial commission. By placing their hands upon Timothy, church leaders granted him authority, charged him with the responsibility of ministry leadership, and affirmed his call.

What Do You Think?

In what ways can you encourage others to keep their spiritual fire aflame?

Digging Deeper

What are you doing to "stir up" your faith, ministry gifts, and commitment to God's calling?

No Time "Before Christ"

I was preparing the testimony for my baptism, and I struggled with the question, "Where does my story begin?" My pastor encouraged me to discuss my "BC life" (as in, "before Christ"). I knew what he meant and was happy to tell of God's work in my life. However, the idea bothered me because I knew that God was faithful to me *long* before I was ready to accept Christ. I kept thinking, "I don't think there was a time before Christ." You see, friends prayed, teachers planted seeds of wisdom, and God pursued me with sign after sign of His love.

None of us have ever lived in a "BC world." Jesus was with the Father from the beginning, and Christ rescued us, even while we remained enemies of God (Romans 5:10). Have you thanked God for His faithfulness to you even before you called yourself a believer? Can you identify how God prepared you to hear and respond to the good news of Jesus? —J. D.

II. Continued Legacy

(2 Timothy 3:14–16)

A. Persist in Learning (v. 14)

14. But continue thou in the things which thou hast learned and hast been assured of, knowing of whom thou hast learned them.

Paul encourages Timothy to persist. It is one thing to learn something, and it is another to be entirely confident (*assured*) of its truth. The verb translated *been assured of* is from the same root as the word for "faith." The things Timothy knows fill him with faith. Remembering and trusting in his education will allow confidence and steadfastness to remain in motion. Just before this verse, Paul reminds Timothy that he is also full of endurance and tenacity (2 Timothy 3:10–13). Now he reminds Timothy that his teachers are trustworthy, and that Timothy knows the integrity of his mentor.

B. Know the Scriptures (vv. 15–16)

15. And that from a child thou hast known the holy scriptures, which are able to make thee wise unto salvation through faith which is in Christ Jesus.

Paul returns to the idea that Timothy learned the Scriptures and truths of God from his mother and grandmother (2 Timothy 1:5). What Paul calls *holy scriptures* cannot refer to a complete Bible as modern Christians understand it, since Timothy's childhood came before most of the New Testament was written. Paul is referring to the Old Testament, particularly the Greek translation of the Old Testament called the Septuagint, which Paul frequently quotes in his letters.

Paul gives a theological reason for Scripture as the basis for *faith*: Scripture's contents make a person *wise* and lead toward *salvation*. Salvation comes to fruition through the Messiah, who is *Christ Jesus*. Paul encourages Timothy to remember the incredible tool that he has in his ministry toolbox: long-term knowledge of God's Word.

What Do You Think?

What is your history with Scripture? How do you stand firm on the things you know? How does Scripture increase wisdom?

Digging Deeper

What study tools do you use to thoroughly learn the holy Scriptures?

16. All scripture is given by inspiration of God, and is profitable for doctrine, for reproof, for correction, for instruction in righteousness.

Paul still has the Old Testament in mind as

he speaks of *all scripture*. Paul was masterful at demonstrating the truth of the gospel from texts like Habakkuk 2:4, "The just shall live by faith" (quoted in Romans 1:17; Galatians 3:11). Now we may extend the same principles to the New Testament, including the letters of Paul! Second Peter 3:15–16 describes Paul's letters as containing wisdom, as with "other scriptures."

Paul names two essential truths that apply to Scripture: it is *inspire[ed]* and *profitable*. First, the message is from *God*. The single word translated *inspiration of God* is also translated as "God-breathed" and is a rare compound word. It is possibly original to Paul. This type of original language use is like Shakespeare and other gifted writers who adaptively invent language to communicate new ideas. Paul uses this word to describe the God-givenness of Scripture. Timothy can trust the Scriptures because God is the life force behind them. As 2 Peter 1:20–21 explains, "No prophecy of the scripture is of any private interpretation. For the prophecy came not in old time by the will of man: but holy men of God spake as they were moved by the Holy Ghost." God's Word is entirely true because God cannot lie (Numbers 23:19; Titus 1:2; Hebrews 6:18), but God works through human agency, using human writers.

Second, Paul affirms Scripture's utility. It is helpful for teaching reliable *doctrine* about God and our proper response to Him. Scripture serves as *reproof* by identifying wrong and sinful behavior, giving *correction*, and describing the right way to live. Scripture demonstrates how to live in holiness according to the standard set forth by God. By knowing God's instructions, Paul recognizes that Timothy will "understand righteousness, and judgment, and equity; yea, every good path" (Proverbs 2:9).

Conclusion

A. Imitation and Encouragement

Timothy had a surrogate parent and mentor in Paul. Paul lived a life worthy of imitation and spent significant time reaching out to his son in the faith to encourage and support him. Through Paul's writings, we learn essential truths about Timothy that help us identify him as a faithful witness of Christ.

Timothy's rich heritage of faith was passed to him by his mother, grandmother, and spiritual father. Strong parental influence in faith is an incredible blessing. May we all find the mentors we need for steady growth in discipleship, and may we, in turn, develop into devoted mentors ourselves! Timothy's example shows us that spiritual heritage comes from various places. If you lack spiritual support from your family of origin or extended family, don't dismiss the power of relationships built out of a church family.

God gave Timothy a gift, a church leadership position, and beloved relationships. He had a spark implanted in him that remained burning. Timothy had endurance, a long memory, diligent trust in God, and supportive, helpful companions on the journey. He didn't succumb to discouragement in the face of hardship and opposition. However, Timothy's success didn't come through individualistic means. He submitted to relationships that supported him through tough times.

What Do You Think?

Do you think discipleship and ministry are designed to be done alone? How do Mark 6:7; Acts 13:2–3; and Hebrews 10:24–25 influence your answer?

Digging Deeper

In what specific ways are you leaning on the community of faith?

B. Prayer

Father God, we are grateful for our spiritual fathers and mothers. Develop us into godly mentors and leaders as well. Help us to faithfully encourage our fellow believers when they face discouragement and persecution. In Jesus' name we pray. Amen.

C. Thought to Remember

Remember your faith heritage
and trust Scripture's instruction.

Involvement Learning

Enhance your lesson with KJV Bible Student *(from your curriculum supplier) and the reproducible activity page (at www.standardlesson.com or in the back of the* KJV Standard Lesson Commentary Deluxe Edition*).*

Into the Lesson

Before class begins, write, "Mentors help form our faith" on the board. As class starts, hand an index card and pen to each student. Ask students to take one minute to reflect on the mentors and family members who have deeply formed their faith. Ask them to write as many names as desired on their card. Then give the class two minutes to consider a strong belief those mentors were a part of forming. Ask students to flip over their index cards and write that belief on the back. (*Examples*: God loves me; God is trustworthy; the Holy Spirit uses Scripture powerfully; and Scripture holds the words of life.) Lead a discussion allowing students to share about their mentors and how wisdom and encouragement have formed or strengthened them.

Option. Ask the class to think of a song or a hymn that expresses the importance of encouragement and love in the body of Christ. (*Examples*: "They Will Know We Are Christians by Our Love" or "O Church Arise.")

Lead into Bible study by saying, "Our lesson today revolves around Timothy and the spiritual mentorship he received from his grandmother Lois, mother Eunice, and the apostle Paul."

Into the Word

Divide the class into four groups: **Faith**, **Family**, **Grandparents**, and **Encouragers**. Distribute a piece of paper to each group. Direct groups to read 2 Timothy 1:1–6 and complete the assigned task.

Faith Group: Read the Scripture text and list every word or phrase about passing along the faith. Make notes beside these words or phrases about lessons learned.

Family Group: Read the Scripture text and write down ideas about how families may pass on faith. From your experiences and knowledge, list additional tips or principles for bringing up children to know and serve the Lord.

Grandparents Group: *If there are grandparents present in the class, you may wish to create a special group with this challenge.* Read the Scripture text and write down ideas about how grandparents may play a significant role in passing faith to grandchildren. From your experiences and observations, list additional ideas or tips in helping grandchildren discover the Lord.

Encouragers Group: Make two columns on your sheet of paper with the headings *Encouraging Children* and *Encouraging Young Adults*. Read the Scripture text and write down ideas about how your congregation may encourage its younger people.

Call groups back together. Ask for a volunteer from each group to share their ideas with the class.

Ask a volunteer to read 2 Timothy 3:14–16 out loud. Compile a list on the board of things Paul wants Timothy to know about Scripture. Read the passage a second time if needed.

Option. Distribute copies of the "Letter to a Mentor" exercise from the activity page, which you can download. Instruct students to complete it as indicated.

Into Life

Divide the class into groups of two or three. Ask groups to brainstorm one or two things they think would encourage new believers or children in their faith. Ask groups to be specific about practices that might nurture faithful witness in the young. Then lead a discussion based on each group's brainstorming. Write their answers on the board under the original heading ("Mentors help form our faith").

Option. Distribute copies of the "Letter to a Mentee" exercise from the activity page. Instruct students to complete it as indicated.

Lead the class in prayer for young believers and children. Ask students to spend one minute asking God to bring a particular person to mind who they feel called to support in life and faith. Allow time for "popcorn" prayers for these believers.

August 30
Lesson 13 (KJV)

Lydia, the Generous Hostess

Devotional Reading: James 2:14–26
Background Scripture: Acts 16:11–40

Acts 16:11–15, 40

**11 Therefore loosing from Troas, we came
with a straight course to Samothracia, and the
next day to Neapolis;**
**12 And from thence to Philippi, which is
the chief city of that part of Macedonia, and
a colony: and we were in that city abiding certain days.**
**13 And on the sabbath we went out of the
city by a river side, where prayer was wont to
be made; and we sat down, and spake unto the
women which resorted thither.**
**14 And a certain woman named Lydia, a
seller of purple, of the city of Thyatira, which
worshipped God, heard us: whose heart the
Lord opened, that she attended unto the things
which were spoken of Paul.**
**15 And when she was baptized, and her
household, she besought us, saying, If ye have
judged me to be faithful to the Lord, come
into my house, and abide there. And she constrained us.**

**40 And they went out of the prison, and
entered into the house of Lydia: and when they
had seen the brethren, they comforted them,
and departed.**

Key Text

When [Lydia] was baptized, and her household, she besought us, saying, If ye have judged me to be faithful to the Lord, come into my house, and abide there. And she constrained us. —**Acts 16:15**

The Testimony of

Faithful Witnesses

Unit 3: Faithful Witnesses Spread the Good News

Lessons 9–13

Lesson Aims

After participating in this lesson, each learner will be able to:

1. Summarize the circumstances that God used to bring the good news of Jesus to Lydia's household.

2. Explain why acts of hospitality were vital for Christians of the first century.

3. Make a plan to practice hospitality as a characteristic of his or her own faithful witness.

Lesson Outline

Introduction

A. I Was a Stranger

B. Lesson Context

I. Encouraging Encounters (Acts 16:11–15)

A. Traveling from Troas (vv. 11–12)

B. Encountering Lydia (vv. 13–14)

C. Believing and Baptizing (v. 15)

Breaking Barriers with Hospitality

II. Heartfelt Hospitality (Acts 16:40)

A. Out of Prison (v. 40a)

B. Place of Refuge (v. 40b)

A Stranger's Kindness

Conclusion

A. Practicing Hospitality

B. Prayer

C. Thought to Remember

Introduction

A. I Was a Stranger

After college, I accepted an internship on the other side of the country. For the first time, I was far away from family, friends, and everything familiar. The roads were confusing, the air smelled different, and the local accents took some time to decode. I loved my internship but often felt alone in this unfamiliar place.

I tried to find new friends at church, but the hospitality felt quite cold. While some people greeted me at the door with smiles and goodie bags, no one tried to learn my name or where I was from. Even after attending services for a few weeks, no one seemed to recognize me.

However, an older couple from work showed me generous hospitality that changed everything. They took time to listen to me, invited me into their home for meals, and even took me to the doctor's office when I was sick. When I felt unsafe in my housing situation, they offered me a place to stay. Their kindness and generosity made all the difference. I was a stranger, but they showed me hospitality (compare Hebrews 13:2).

The Bible teaches us to show hospitality to others (Romans 12:13; Hebrews 13:2; 1 Peter 4:9; 3 John 8; etc.). Jesus Himself teaches that when believers extend hospitality to "the least of these my brethren," it is regarded as being done unto the Lord Himself (Matthew 25:34–40). Today's study provides a first-century example of hospitality toward a stranger. Through this example, we will see how Christian love is embodied.

B. Lesson Context

Beginning in Acts 13:1, the book of Acts focuses on the missionary travels of the apostle Paul. The church in Antioch commissioned Paul and Barnabas to carry the gospel beyond that Syrian city to the regions of Cyprus (a large island), Pisidia, Pamphylia, and Galatia. We often refer to this as Paul's first missionary journey (Acts 13:1–14:28).

On the next missionary journey (Acts 15:36–18:22), Paul and Silas visited the previous locations but also pushed farther west toward Roman Asia. This expedition was almost blown apart at the outset when Paul and Barnabas had a tense disagreement over the advisability of taking along John Mark, a relative of Barnabas (Colossians 4:10). Therefore, they divided into two teams: Barnabas and John Mark returned to the island of Cyprus (Acts 15:39), the home territory of Barnabas (4:36), while Paul recruited Silas, a respected church leader (15:22), to accompany him (15:40–41).

Paul then traveled to Lystra, where he met with Timothy and invited him to join the missionary journey (Acts 16:1–5). Paul and his companions then traveled through the regions of Phrygia and Galatia. They reached the port city of Troas, located at the northern end of the Aegean Sea, where Paul received a vision of an unknown man from Macedonia who invited the apostle to come to that region (16:8–10). It is at this point in Paul's second missionary journey that we arrive at today's lesson. The year is around AD 50, and it has been some 15 years since Paul's encounter with the resurrected Christ (see lesson 11).

I. Encouraging Encounters

(Acts 16:11–15)

A. Travels from Troas (vv. 11–12)

11. Therefore loosing from Troas, we came with a straight course to Samothracia, and the next day to Neapolis.

Having received the vision of a man from Macedonia in the verse just before this one, Paul sets out *from Troas* across the Aegean Sea with Silas and Timothy (see Lesson Context). The first-person plural pronoun *we* suggests that Luke, the author of the book of Acts, accompanies them.

Samothracia (also spelled "Samothrace") is a small island-city off the eastern coast of Macedonia. It is about 50 miles northwest of Troas. The prevailing winds in the northern part of the Aegean Sea are from the northeast, so the ship makes good time to *Neapolis*, about 70 miles from Samothrace. Neapolis serves as the port city for Philippi, which is about 10 miles inland (contrast the five days a journey in the opposite direction takes in Acts 20:6).

12. And from thence to Philippi, which is the chief city of that part of Macedonia, and a colony: and we were in that city abiding certain days.

Philippi is a city with a rich history. Named after Philip II, the city came under Roman control in 168 BC. Philippi is located on a major Roman highway, resulting in significant trade traffic across the region. Therefore, it is an important Roman commercial and administrative center in the heart of the Greco-Roman world. Philippi is populated with retired Roman soldiers and not many Jews.

The ministry of Paul and his companions lasts a period of *certain days,* which may mean a stretch as short as a week.

> **What Do You Think?**
> How can you help your church enhance ministry to believers whose occupations require travel?
>
> **Digging Deeper**
> In what ways can you partner with congregations in other towns to achieve this goal?

B. Encountering Lydia (vv. 13–14)

13. And on the sabbath we went out of the city by a river side, where prayer was wont to be made; and we sat down, and spake unto the women which resorted thither.

Paul's usual pattern is first to go to the local synagogue when beginning a ministry in a new city (see Acts 13:14; 14:1; 18:4). In Philippi, however, the procedure is different. Given Philippi's history as a Roman colony, it is possible that not enough Jews live there to call for a synagogue. By Jewish tradition, it takes at least 10 Jewish men to constitute a proper synagogue.

First-century Jewish religious practices seem to necessitate running water for ritual cleansing practices. Therefore, if no synagogue was present in Philippi, then a location *by the river* would be ideal for Jews to gather for *prayer* and worship. The *river* in question may be the Gangites River, about a mile from town.

In first-century Macedonia, *women* experience more independence than they do in other ancient Greco-Roman contexts. In Philippi, in particular,

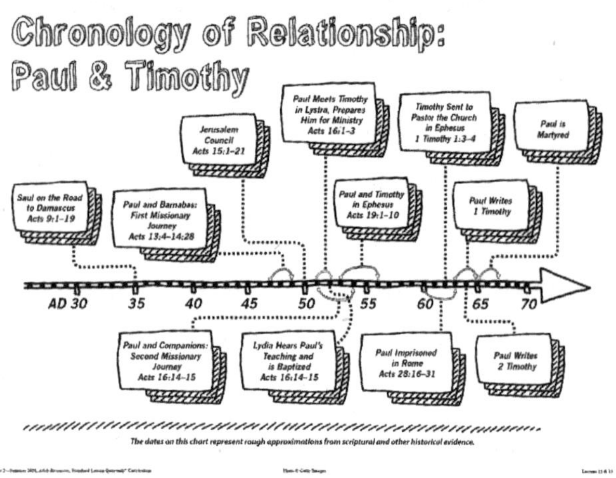

Visual for Lessons 11 & 13. *Display this visual as you review the ministries of Paul and Timothy in the first-century church.*

women held leadership roles in various places for pagan and cultic worship, especially in the temple of Artemis located there.

Most women in this era were expected to follow the religious practices of their husbands. Roman men, however, often complained of the influence of foreign (non-Greco-Roman) religions on their wives. Historians of the period report that a significant number of Gentile women converted to Judaism or were drawn to worship alongside Jewish women. Therefore, it is not surprising that Paul would interact with both Jewish and Gentile women. Furthermore, women played significant roles in the growth of the first-century church (examples: Acts 18:2; Philippians 4:3). At this riverside, Paul meets a woman who would become a key member of the forthcoming church in Philippi.

14a. And a certain woman named Lydia, a seller of purple, of the city of Thyatira.

The name *Lydia* is notable because it is also the name of a district in the Roman province of Asia Minor. Some commentators suggest that this *certain woman* may have been formerly enslaved, as it was common for enslaved individuals to be named after their homeland.

Lydia's hometown, *Thyatira*, is the capital of the district of Lydia and is located on the other side of the Aegean Sea, about 100 miles southeast of Troas (compare Revelation 2:18–29). The city is known for producing dyed textiles, with *purple* being especially prominent. The process of creating purple dye in the first century was unpleasant and often smelly, as it involved extraction from the murex snail. Consequently, purple cloth was typically the most expensive textile, reserved for the wealthy and often worn by royalty. As a *seller* or trader of this dye, Lydia is likely a woman of significant financial means.

14b. Which worshipped God, heard us: whose heart the Lord opened, that she attended unto the things which were spoken of Paul.

The description of Lydia as someone who worships *God* has three possible interpretations: (1) she is Jewish, (2) she is a convert to Judaism, or (3) she is a God-fearing Gentile, similar to Cornelius (see Acts 10:2). The third option is the most likely. The Greek word translated *worshipped* is the same term used to refer to the Gentile converts who follow God (Acts 13:43; 17:17).

Despite her independence and wealth, Lydia's *heart* is ready for the message of Christ. After hearing Paul's teaching, she does not spend the upcoming week reflecting on the message. Instead, as *Paul* speaks the word of God, her heart is *opened* by the *Lord*, perhaps indicating that He removes any misconceptions that may prevent her from accepting a crucified Messiah. This event echoes the events described in the conclusion of Luke's Gospel. During a post-resurrection appearance to His disciples, Jesus "opened . . . their understanding that they might understand the scriptures" (Luke 24:45).

> **What Do You Think?**
> Have you ever had a moment when you felt God opening your heart to something new? How did you respond?
> **Digging Deeper**
> What steps can you take to be better attentive to the Spirit's leading?

C. Believing and Baptizing (v. 15)

15a. And when she was baptized, and her household.

Lydia's decision of faith is followed by her baptism. The text gives the impression that this happens quickly, possibly on the same day.

Throughout the book of Acts, faith and baptism are often mentioned together. For example, the Samaritans who listened to Philip's preaching believed and were baptized (Acts 8:12). The Ethiopian eunuch, after hearing Phillip's proclamation of the gospel, immediately expressed his desire to be baptized (8:35–38). Likewise, the Philippian jailer and his family were baptized (16:31–33). The Corinthians who listened to Paul's preaching also believed and were baptized (18:8). Lydia's conversion follows the same pattern.

This is the first mention in the book of Acts of a *household* receiving baptism. The second instance occurs shortly thereafter (Acts 16:33; see also 1 Corinthians 1:16). The text does not provide details about the composition of Lydia's household. Since her household follows her lead in baptism, she may be a widow, thereby the head of the household with authority over those in it.

15b. She besought us, saying, If ye have judged me to be faithful to the Lord, come into my house, and abide there. And she constrained us.

Lydia is no longer merely one who "worshipped God" (Acts 16:14, above). She experiences a shift in identity that leads her to be *faithful to the Lord.* This change leads her to make a proposal that must not be overlooked. The book of Acts often describes the heart of the person after baptism. In the case of the Ethiopian, he left rejoicing (Acts 8:39). The Philippian jailer is filled with joy but also brings the missionaries into his house and prepares a meal for them (16:34). In this case, part of Lydia's response after her baptism is her insistence that Paul and his companions come lodge at her *house*—a response full of generosity and hospitality.

Such an invitation may be a dangerous arrangement for Lydia. There is potential resistance from her surrounding community that may be opposed to the gospel—like the mob in Ephesus (Acts 19:28). Lydia can invite the missionaries to stay in her home. But she cannot guarantee what the reaction of the neighbors will be. Her invitation, more than just an inconvenience to her busy schedule, is an act of courage.

Additionally, accepting her invitation would be courageous for Paul and his companions. Although Lydia had been worshiping and praying with Jews in Philippi, she is likely not Jewish. Consequently, it is unlikely that her household adheres to Jewish purity laws. Paul's acceptance of her invitation to hospitality implies that he, a Jew, agrees to stay in the home of a Gentile. Such an occurrence is not new by this point in the first-century church (compare Acts 10:9–48). Even so, the decision to stay in the house of a Gentile would have caught the attention of any other Jews in Macedonia.

Acts of hospitality played a vital role in ancient cultures, especially in Jewish culture. These acts included welcoming and caring for travelers, out-of-town visitors, and even strangers, as Genesis 18:1–8 demonstrates. In a time without hotel chains as we know them, the offering of generous hospitality provided a safe place for an individual to rest, have a meal, and care for their animals if they had any. In some areas of the ancient world that are characterized by harsh climates and limited access to water, providing hospitality could mean the difference between life and death for a traveler.

What Do You Think?

How can you be more intentional about welcoming and serving others, both in your church and in your neighborhood?

Digging Deeper

What barriers prevent you from doing so, and how will you address these issues?

Breaking Barriers with Hospitality

I sat in the sweltering heat and humidity of Colombo, the largest city in Sri Lanka. From my observations, a social hierarchy among its residents was evident. Certain areas of the city seemed affluent, while others appeared dilapidated and deprived of wealth. On this particular afternoon, I had the privilege of meeting a local church and governmental leader for lunch.

Halfway through the meal, there was a knock on the door. My new friend excused himself, walked to the front door, and opened it without hesitation. Within seconds, seven men in orange jumpsuits surrounded him. These men were responsible for cleaning the city streets and were regarded as part of the lowest social class. With a warm smile, the leader greeted each man by name and invited them into the house. I later learned that this was a common occurrence; in fact, as many as 25 of these men shared a Christmas meal in that house.

His habits of hospitality moved me. He served people whom society had deemed "less than." In doing so, he demonstrated the radical nature of Christian hospitality—one that transcends social boundaries (see Luke 14:12–14).

Lydia's display of hospitality to Paul was equally radical. Would she lose influence in her community by inviting Jewish men to stay in her home? What would it look like for you to show radical hospitality to those groups that your community has deemed "less than"? —N. V.

III. Heartfelt Hospitality

(Acts 16:40)

A. Out of Prison (v. 40a)

40a. And they went out of the prison.

A dangerous situation resulted in Paul and Silas facing time in *prison*. While still in Philippi, Paul encountered an enslaved woman who possessed a spirit of fortune-telling. She followed Paul and his companions around town, proclaiming their movements and intentions (Acts 16:16–17). Annoyed by her presence and actions, Paul eventually cast out the spirit from her (16:18). This act angered her owners, who were upset about the loss of income caused by the removal of the spirit. They mobilize the townspeople and the authorities against Paul and Silas (16:19–20). Consequently, the two were beaten and thrown into jail (16:22–24).

That night, Paul and his companions experience a miraculous release when an earthquake breaks their chains (Acts 16:26). Rather than retaliate against the jailer, they convert him and his household to faith in Christ (16:28–32). The following morning, after Paul proclaims his Roman citizenship, the authorities escort him from the prison and request that he and his companions leave Philippi (16:35–39).

The shift in narrative from first-person "us" (Acts 16:15b, above) to the third-person *they* indicates that Luke is likely no longer with Paul at this point in the journey.

B. Place of Refuge (v. 40b)

40b. And entered into the house of Lydia: and when they had seen the brethren, they comforted them, and departed.

Before departing from Philippi, Paul and Silas feel compelled to stop again at *the house of Lydia* to rest and recover after being released from prison. Their upcoming travels will lead them to Amphipolis, Apollonia, Thessalonica, Berea, Athens, and Corinth (Acts 17–18). Thus the gospel will spread despite (or because of) persecution.

Once again, Lydia's hospitality takes center stage. This stop also gives Paul and Silas a chance to see and comfort *the brethren* of Christ-followers. For these meetings to occur, a suitable location is needed, and Lydia's home serves this purpose. Lydia's house is not only open to the missionaries but also welcomes other members of the first-century church in Philippi, suggesting that her home is quite spacious by the standards of that era. Later, perhaps Paul's letter to the Philippians would be

How to Say It

Aegean	A-*jee*-un.
Amphipolis	Am-*fip*-o-liss.
Antioch	*An*-tee-ock.
Ephesus	*Ef*-uh-sus.
Galatia	Guh-*lay*-shuh.
Lydia	*Lid*-ee-uh.
Lystra	*Liss*-truh.
Macedonia	Mass-eh-*doe*-nee-uh.
Neapolis	Nee-*ap*-o-lis.
Pamphylia	Pam-*fill*-ee-uh.
Philippi	Fih-*lip*-pie or *Fil*-ih-pie.
Phrygia	*Frij*-e-uh.
Samothracia	Sam-o-*thray*-shuh.
Syrian	*Sear*-ee-un.
Thessalonica	*Thess*-uh-lo-***nye***-kuh (*th* as in *thin*).
Thyatira	*Thy*-uh-***tie***-ruh (*th* as in *thin*).
Troas	*Tro*-az.

read aloud in her house. Despite the potential risk from pagan neighbors, Lydia shows hospitality to those who travel to preach the gospel of Christ.

> **What Do You Think?**
> Who in your life encouraged you in your faith after you faced a trial? What actions did they take?
> **Digging Deeper**
> How can you be that person for someone else?

A Stranger's Kindness

Growing up in South Africa, my family enjoyed many outdoor adventures. One memorable experience came when my father took my brothers and me on a hike along the rocks and cliffs near Kini Bay, a small beach near the city of Gqeberha.

We set off barefoot and without mobile phones, expecting a scenic five-kilometer loop—approximately three miles of hiking. As the sun began to set and evening approached, rain showers appeared, and my brothers and I started to wonder whether our father really did know the way home. "It's just beyond that corner!" he would say. However, each time we looked ahead, we realized another stretch of cliffs lay before us.

With sore feet and tired legs, we finally reached a small village well after dark. We knocked on several doors, hoping someone would answer and allow us to borrow their phone to call our mother. Most doors remained closed, and one even slammed in our faces. Eventually, a kind lady took pity on a father and his three young, rain-drenched, shoeless children on her doorstep. She welcomed us into her home and helped us call for help.

There's something about showing hospitality that reminds me that we are all made in God's image and that we are all sometimes in need of compassion. The Lord has welcomed us into His home and calls us to practice hospitality with others—even strangers. How will you show hospitality to strangers in the upcoming week? You never know who you might be serving (see Hebrews 13:2). —N. V.

Conclusion

A. Practicing Hospitality

Acts of hospitality serve as a faithful witness to the life-changing effect of the gospel. Hospitality is essentially "love in action." When we show hospitality, we demonstrate our love for God and others.

Lydia exemplified this by providing a welcoming space for people to gather, share meals, engage in fellowship and prayer, and encounter Christ. Imagine Paul's experience in Philippi without Lydia's hospitality; he would have lacked a base for his ministry and somewhere to return to after being released from prison.

In today's world, hospitality doesn't have to mean opening your home to missionaries, though that is one way to express it. It can involve sharing a meal with new members of your church community, providing space for prayer and fellowship, or simply being attentive to the needs of your neighbors.

Hospitality should never be used as an opportunity to show off; rather, it should be an expression of love that comes from experiencing the ultimate expression of love: salvation through faith in Christ Jesus. Lydia encountered this transforming love and, in turn, used her hospitality to change the lives of others. How will you use your hospitality to make a difference in the lives of those around you?

> **What Do You Think?**
> How has this lesson changed your perspective on hospitality?
> **Digging Deeper**
> How is hospitality an act of serving Christ Himself (see Matthew 25:34–40)?

B. Prayer

Heavenly Father, thank You for Lydia's example of faithfulness and hospitality. We ask that Your Spirit transform our hearts so that we may be hospitable people. Strengthen us to be willing to open our hearts and homes to welcome others, even strangers. In Jesus' name we pray. Amen.

C. Thought to Remember

God grows the church through our hospitality.

Involvement Learning

Enhance your lesson with KJV Bible Student *(from your curriculum supplier) and the reproducible activity page (at www.standardlesson.com or in the back of the* KJV Standard Lesson Commentary Deluxe Edition*).*

Into the Lesson

Prepare 11 index cards with the following sets of letters front and back, respectively: *H* and *E*; *O* and *V*; *S* and *A*; *P* and *N*; *I* and *G*; *T* and *E*; *A* and *L*; *L* and *I*; *I* and *S*; *T* and *M*; *Y* and an exclamation point. Display the cards so that the word *hospitality* is spelled. (One way to display the cards would be to attach them to the wall with reusable adhesive.)

Say, "Our study today is a lesson about Christian hospitality. Related to hospitality is another Christian responsibility. Behind each of these cards is another letter. Try to guess the letters that will reveal the second Christian responsibility we will examine in today's lesson. As you correctly guess a letter, I will turn over the corresponding card." Allow students to suggest letters until someone correctly identifies the word *evangelism*.

Then lead into Bible study by saying, "Lydia's hospitality resulted from Paul's evangelism. In turn, that hospitality provided an excellent opportunity for more evangelism."

Into the Word

Present the following quiz and direct students to answer each question with a verse number from today's text in Acts 16:11–15, 40. (Verse references to answers are given in parentheses.)

___1. What was Lydia's source of livelihood? *(v. 14a)*
___2. What city was Lydia from? *(v. 14a)*
___3. Who comforted whom when Paul and Silas were finally released from imprisonment? *(v. 40b)*
___4. Where did people assemble for prayer in Philippi? *(v. 13)*
___5. What did Lydia and others in her household do when they accepted Jesus? *(v. 15)*
___6. What kind of sailing weather did Paul encounter from Troas to Neapolis? *(v. 11)*
___7. After Neapolis, where did Paul travel? *(v. 12)*

Recruit a volunteer to act out the following monologue as Lydia. Be sure to give her a copy of the monologue in time for preparation.

"When Paul and Silas were arrested, the news came back to me immediately. Philippi is not the kind of city where such an event escapes notice. Those rascals using that poor girl with a demon's voice would not lose their profit quietly, you understand. Paul and Silas were my honored houseguests. I first thought, *Lydia, you must rush down to the jail and see what you can do.* But family and household members warned me, saying, 'Lydia, to do so is dangerous. You must not go!' All we could do was pray and wait to see the outcome.

"My mind returned to that Saturday evening by the river. Devoted women from all over Philippi were there to pray and worship, for we had no synagogue hall. When strangers arrived, we were leery, but Paul's words clearly were from God.

"We were in the right place. When Paul pictured the death and resurrection of Christ, his instruction to be baptized brought no objections.

"I was exultant. Everything seemed so new. My house is large, but it had the lonely emptiness of business. So I invited Paul and his company to stay with us. What a blessed time we had!"

Option. Distribute copies of the "Finding the Way" exercise from the activity page, which you can download. Have learners complete it as a take-home activity.

Into Life

Lead into the activity by saying, "Lydia demonstrated hospitality as a characteristic of her faithful witness to the transforming power of the gospel. The New Testament encourages us to follow her example and extend hospitality to others." Lead a brainstorming session with the class about how believers can show hospitality as a characteristic of their faithful witness. Write responses on the board. Then ask participants to work with a partner to select one of the listed ways and make a plan to practice it in the upcoming week.

Alternative. Distribute copies of the "Planning Hospitality" exercise from the activity page. Have participants complete it individually in a minute or less before discussing conclusions with a partner.